Strategic Marketing Management

Text and Cases

S.L. Gupta

ATLANTIC
PUBLISHERS & DISTRIBUTORS (P) LTD

Published by

ATLANTIC

PUBLISHERS & DISTRIBUTORS (P) LTD

7/22, Ansari Road, Darya Ganj,
New Delhi-110002
Phones : +91-11-23273880, 23275880, 23280451
Fax : +91-11-23285873
Web : www.atlanticbooks.com
E-mail : info@atlanticbooks.com

Branch Office
5, Nallathambi Street, Wallajah Road,
Chennai-600002
Phones : +91-44-64611085, 32413319
E-mail : chennai@atlanticbooks.com

ISBN 978-81-269-1255-1

Printed in India at Nice Printing Press, A-33/3A, Site-IV, Industrial Area, Sahibabad, Ghaziabad, U.P.

PREFACE

Marketing's new "dominant logic" compels organisations of all hues to collaborate with, and learn from, customers as co-creators of value. Such an imperative challenges the established marketing practices in many profit-driven organisations, but vindicates the long-standing efforts of arts and heritage organisations to cast their customers as active participants in transformational experiences, rather than passive consumers of predetermined products.

The book, *Strategic Marketing Management : Text and Cases,* has systems-based managerial approach. It aims to integrate the vital interests of consumers, marketing managers and society at large.

The concept of marketing has undergone tremendous changes in the emerging economic, technological, social and political scenario. In a fast changing environment, marketing management has to meet the challenge of managing the change, achieving progress and prosperity through marketing innovations. Hence, integrated marketing planning and strategic brilliance will be the keys to the survival of free enterprise system.

The consumers, competition, society and government will require the ultimate in strategic marketing to produce profits sufficient for survival after offering reasonable satisfaction to all the interested parties. The essence of bonafide customer orientation in the marketing concept is based on three fundamental ideas: (i) consumer satisfaction with socio-environment justification for survival of a business enterprise; (ii) profits are a major incentive; and (iii) the profitable satisfaction of customers' wants requires an integration of all business activities. This can be accomplished through customer-oriented plans and strategies.

Marketing managers are bound to be more and more customer oriented. Profits rather than sales volume will be given top consideration. However, profits will be earned as a reward for serving the customers' wants. Above all, marketing managers have to work in coordination with the managers of other functional departments in order to realise total corporate objectives as depicted in the company's master plan and strategy.

The book comprehensively deals with various aspects of strategic marketing management and shall ably serve the needs of students of MBA, PGDBM, M.Com., B.Com. and BBA.

S.L. Gupta

CONTENTS

UNDERSTANDING STRATEGIC MARKETING

1

DEFINITION

In order to bring out clearly the meaning of the term 'Strategic Marketing' we have to analyze two or more definitions.

1. "Strategic Marketing is a total system of business activities designed to plan, price promote and distribute want satisfying goods and services to present and potential customers."

   W.J. Stanton

2. "Strategic Marketing is the business process by which products are matched with markets and through which transfers of ownership are effected."

   E.W. Cundiff

3. "Strategic Marketing consists of the performance of business activities that direct the flow of goods and services from producers or suppliers to consumers or endusers."

   American Marketing Association

4. "Strategic Marketing management is the analysis, planning, implementation and control of programmes designed to bring about desired exchanges with target audiences for the purpose of mutual or personal gain. It relies heavily on the adaptation and coordination of product, price, promotion and place for achieving effective response."

   Philip Kotler

The above definitions give the meaning of Strategic Marketing vividly. According to the modern concept, Strategic Marketing is 'consumer oriented'. It is the consumer who is instrumental in giving meaning to the modern concept of Strategic Marketing. The whole function of Strategic Marketing like production, financing, storing, grading, selling, etc. depends upon the needs of customers.

Strategic Marketing is the basic reason for the existence of a business organisation. In the age of fast changes, marketing is the springboard of all business activities. It works as the guide for all business/non-business organisations. It is a powerful mechanism, which alone can satisfy the needs and wants of consumers at the place and price they desire. The success of a business depends largely on the effectiveness with which its marketing strategies are formulated and implemented. Marketing is said to be the eyes and ears of a business organisation because it keeps the business in close contact with its economic, political, social and technological environment and informs it of events that can influence its activities as per requirements of the market. Strategic Marketing helps in having a good range of products in constant demand and suggests to the management the scope for improving and developing new products to satisfy the changing customer needs. Therefore, we can say strategic marketing satisfies our needs by providing form utility, person utility, exchange utility, place utility and time utility.

Marketing Concept

The marketing concept states that in order for a business to make a profit they must satisfy customers' needs and wants.

Market

- A market is all potential customers who share common needs and wants, and who have the ability and willingness to buy the product.

Mass Marketing

- Mass marketing is the process of using one marketing plan to reach all markets.

Target Marketing

- Target marketing is focusing all marketing decisions on a very specific group of people who you want to reach.

Marketing Mix

- The marketing mix comprises strategies that businesses must make to meet their target market.
- The marketing mix is also known as the four P's of marketing. Marketing strategies are based on these four elements:
  - Product
  - Place
  - Price
  - Promotion.

FUNCTIONS OF STRATEGIC MARKETING

Goods are produced in one place and consumers are spread all over the country and at time abroad. Goods are to be taken the place of their production to the place where it is demanded. When the goods pass from the producers to consumers, they require some preparation and have to pass through many operations and many hands. All these activities and operations are usually termed as Strategic Marketing functions. Strategic Marketing functions could be classified as under.

A. *Functions of exchange* which includes:
   1. Buying and Assembling, and
   2. Selling.

B. *Function of physical supply* which includes:
   1. Transportation, and
   2. Storage and warehousing.

C. *Facilitating functions* which includes:

1. Financing,
2. Pricing,
3. Risk-taking,
4. Standardisation and grading,
5. Market information research (market research), and
6. Advertising and sales promotion.

A brief study of these functions could be made as follows:

A. Functions of Exchange

1. **Buying and Assembling.** Buying is the first step in the process of Strategic Marketing. The purchasing manager has to take a number of decisions regarding what to buy. Again he has to decide as to when to buy, how much to buy, where to buy and how to negotiate price and terms. Manufacturers buy raw materials for converting them into final products. Wholesalers and retailers buy goods for the purpose of re-sale.

Assembling begins after the goods have been purchased. Assembling refers to the bringing together a variety of goods of different quantities or of a large quantities of similar items. In case of retailers assembling is done by buying different items, in different quantities from different sources.

2. **Selling.** Selling is a very important Strategic Marketing function. It is the actual point where transfer of ownership occurs. In the present day of globalisation the seller has to face a number of problems such as advertising, facing competition, creating demand for new products conducting Strategic Marketing research, etc.

B. Functions of Physical Supply

The transfer of goods from the producer to consumer takes place with the help of transportation and storage.

1. **Transportation.** Modern production is characterised by large-scale production and the consumers are spread all over the world. Therefore, transportation is an essential Strategic Marketing activity. Transportation is the movement of goods from the point or production to the point of consumption. Land, Water and Air are the principal means of transport for transporting goods from one place to another.

2. **Storage and Warehousing.** One of the characteristics of modern production is production in anticipation of demand. Therefore, goods are to be stored for sometime at the production centres and also at the distribution point. All the middlemen engaged in Strategic Marketing should do the storage work to hold sufficient stock to meet the anticipated demand and to ensure smooth supply of goods. Storage is also essential for products with uneven demand period and with seasonal demand.

C. Facilitating Functions

1. **Financing.** Finance is the life, blood of business. Money is required at every stage in the process of Strategic Marketing. Without enough finance even the very existence of business concern shall be affected.

Fixed capital and working capital are necessary for a Strategic Marketing concern. The main sources of finance are owned capital, bank credit and trade credit. Owned capital is usually invested by the trader himself or in the case of joint stock companies, it is raised by the issue of shares. Bank credit and trade credit form the bulk of working capital.

2. **Pricing.** Pricing refers to the determination of the price of products. It is a very important function of Strategic Marketing. It is an important decision to be taken by the businessman. There are many methods of pricing like adding a certain amount of profit to cost of production.

3. **Risk-taking.** Risk is a danger of loss, arising out of unforeseen circumstances in the future. Risks are involved at almost all stages in the process of Strategic Marketing. Risks may occur due to changes in demand and supply conditions, loss in storage and transports and other natural hazards. The successful businessman is the one who takes the calculated risk. By carefully anticipating the risk that may arise in future he can avoid or at least minimise the risk.

4. **Standardisation and Grading.** Standardisation is the process of establishing standards for products. A standard is a measure which is generally recognised as having a fixed value. Standards are determined on the basis of colour, shape, appearance, etc.

Grading is part of standardisation. Grading is the division of products into classes made up of units possessing similar characteristics of size and quality.

5. **Market Information Research (Market Research).** In order to make rational decisions, the Strategic Marketing executives must be informed about the market for the firm's product. Information about the attitude of the customers is also necessary. In order to facilitate this, information should be collected, analysed and interpreted. Success in Strategic Marketing to a large extent depends on the volume of information the management has.

APPROACHES TO THE STUDY OF STRATEGIC MARKETING

Strategic Marketing could be studied from different angles or approaches. The different approaches to the study of Strategic Marketing are:

1. **Product or Commodity Approach.** It is an approach on the study of Strategic Marketing on commodity wise basis. In other words, the study relates to the flow of commodity and its movements from the original producer up to the ultimate consumer. The subject-matter under this study is commodity. When we study Strategic Marketing on this basis, we must analyse the sources and conditions of supply, nature and extend of demand, mode of transportation, storage, etc. For example, take rice. Under this approach one has to study the source of rice, location, people involved in buying and selling, means of transportation, problems of selling the products, pricing, storage, packing, etc. Thus, we get a full picture of Strategic Marketing from the original producer to ultimate consumer. The method of study is repeated for each item.
2. **Institutional Approach.** In the institutional approach Strategic Marketing is studied by making a study on the institutions engaged in Strategic Marketing. The institutions engaged in Strategic Marketing are middlemen, importers, exporters, agencies, warehousing, etc. This approach is also known as middleman approach. The activities of each institutions form a part of Strategic Marketing and collectively complete Strategic Marketing function. This system pays attention to the problems and functions

of Strategic Marketing institutions, transporting, banks and other financial institutions, warehousing, advertising, insurance, etc.

3. **Functional Approach.** The functional approach gives importance to various functions of Strategic Marketing. In this approach, Strategic Marketing is split into many functions like buying, selling, pricing, standardisation, storage, advertising, packing, etc. This may be studies one after another. In this approach, Strategic Marketing is regarded as "business of buying and selling and including those business activities involved is the flow of goods and services between producers and customers".
4. **Management Approach.** This is a scientific approach. This approach concentrates upon the activities or Strategic Marketing functions and focuses on the role of decision-making at the level of firm. This approach is mainly concerned with how managers handle specific problems and situations. It aims through evaluation of current Strategic Marketing practices. Generally there are two factors controllables and uncontrollables. Controllables include price, advertisement, etc. Uncontrollables are economic, political, etc. These changes cannot be controlled by any firm. The uncontrollable limit the Strategic Marketing opportunities. Therefore, managerial approach is concerned with the study of uncontrollables and then taking decisions for controllable within the scope set by uncontrollables.
5. **Systems Approach.** The systems approach can be defined as "a set of objects together with the relationship among them and their attributes". This system examines Strategic Marketing linkage inside as well as outside the firm. Inside the firm there is a combination of business activity, engineering, production, Strategic Marketing, price, etc. On the basis of feedback proper control is exercised to modify or alter the production process so that the desired output can be produced. Here the aim is to secure profit through consumer satisfaction.
6. **Societal Approach.** This approach is a recent introduction. The Strategic Marketing process is regarded as a means by which society meets its own consumption needs. This system gives no importance as to how the business meets the consumer's needs. Therefore attention is paid to ecological factors and Strategic Marketing divisions and the impact on the society's wellbeing.
7. **Economic Approach.** This approach deals only with the problems of supply, demand and price. These are important from economic point of view, but fails to give a clear idea of Strategic Marketing.
8. **Legal Approach.** Legal approach emphasises only one aspect, i.e. transfer of ownership to buyer. This aspect deals with the regulatory aspect of Strategic Marketing. In India the Strategic Marketing activities are largely controlled by Sale of Goods Act, Carriers Act, etc. This study concentrates only on legal aspects, leaving aside other important aspects. This approach does not give a full idea of Strategic Marketing.

Innovations in Modern Strategic Marketing

1. **Social Strategic Marketing.** The application of Strategic Marketing principles and techniques to social situations is called social Strategic Marketing. The elements of social Strategic Marketing are satisfaction of human needs extension of ideas on

Strategic Marketing to social fields. (Strategic Marketing techniques can help in attaining social desirable goals like population control.)

2. **De-Strategic Marketing.** De-Strategic Marketing deals with discouraging customers in general or a certain class of customers in particular, or either on a temporary or on a permanent basis, e.g. De-Strategic Marketing is employed by the government of India in the use of petroleum products.
3. **Re-Strategic Marketing.** Re-Strategic Marketing is the finding or creating new uses for an existing product, e.g., baking soda now finds uses as cleaning and deodorizing agent, etc. Thus re-Strategic Marketing is a method by which new types of satisfaction are created for old products.
4. **Over-Strategic Marketing.** Over Strategic Marketing is the stirring by a firm to generate increased sales while neglecting quality control, production efficiency, etc.
5. **Conversional Strategic Marketing.** Negative demand exists when a major part of the market dislikes the product. Sometimes consumer even pays a price in order to avoid it. This is an unfavourable condition. People may have a negative desire to travel in bus or airways. Here the Strategic Marketing management must prepare a plan to convert the negative demand into a positive one. This is referred to as conversional Strategic Marketing.
6. **Stimulational Strategic Marketing.** As far as certain products or services are concerned people are indifferent towards them. Thus there is a stage of no demand, i.e. people have no interest in getting the products. This may also be because they are not found in the market or people are unaware of the product because of lack of publicity by the firm. The Strategic Marketing management has to stimulate the situation, which is a difficult task, by trying to convert demand from no demand to positive demand. This task is referred to as stimulational Strategic Marketing.
7. **Developmental Strategic Marketing.** Many consumers may share a strong desire for something that cannot be satisfied by the existing products or services, e.g. bike riders had a latent desire to have self-starter in the bike instead of kick-starter. Developmental Strategic Marketing is used to convert the latent demand into actual demand.

RE-STRATEGIC MARKETING

Certain firms may find a falling tendency of the demand for the products or service. This situation is known as faltering demand. It refers to a situation in which demand is less than the target, e.g. a politician may find a decline in the number of his followers. The remedy for faltering demand is Re-Strategic Marketing.

Synchro Strategic Marketing

In certain organisations, seasonal demand causes the problems of idle capacity or over-worked capacity, e.g. water pumps are in great demand in summer and no demand in rainy season. This type, irregular demand may be converted into regular demand and the process taken by the management is known as Synchro Strategic Marketing.

1. **Modern Strategic Marketing is Consumer-oriented.** Modern Strategic Marketing recognises consumer's supremacy in Strategic Marketing. The managerial attention is

focused on the market and the consumer. The Strategic Marketing activity is consumer becomes the 'pivot' around whom all business is developed. Creation of satisfied consumers is the main goal of modern Strategic Marketing. Profit can be earned only by serving the consumer's need.

2. **Modern Strategic Marketing Begins and Ends with the Consumers.** The producers of the last century had little care for the consumers. Now the production is carried on in large quantity. The manufacturer produces more than what the society needs. Strategic Marketing has developed from national to international. Competition is the order of the day. Businessmen have started realising it. Earning profit is possible only through the customer's satisfaction. To satisfy a customer, his needs are to be known. Under consumer, oriented Strategic Marketing it becomes essential to know what the customer needs. This is possible only when information is collected from the customers. Thus, we can say modern Strategic Marketing begins and ends with the customers.
3. **Modern Strategic Marketing Proceeds and Succeeds Production**. In the past there was less competition and as such sales were easily made. But the present situation is very much changed. The consumer looks for the usefulness and acceptability of a product. As such it has become essential to find out the needs and desires of customers through Strategic Marketing research. The information from the market or the consumer will decide the future of the product. Thus, product planning and development is undertaken before the actual production. After the actual sale, after-sales service has become very essential. These enable the marketer to face the customer who is the king.
4. **Modern Strategic Marketing is the Guiding Element in Business**. At present competition is more acute because many entrepreneurs provide similar commodities large numbers. The ability of the marketer depends on the ability of finding a customer and to satisfy him. Businessmen have to understand the economic development of a country and must aim to raise the standard of living of the people. Welfare of the people is the aim of Strategic Marketing and thereby the aim of business.

IMPORTANCE OF STRATEGIC MARKETING

Strategic Marketing is a potential force that commands high significance for the society as a whole. The main object of production, nowadays, is distribution of goods and service through Strategic Marketing and to make as much profit as possible. According to Philip Kotler, "Strategic Marketing is analysing, organising, planning and controlling of the firm's customer —impinging resources, policies, activities with a view to satisfying the needs and wants of chosen customer groups at a profit". Wiliam J. Santon mentions, "Strategic Marketing is a total system of interacting business activities designed to plan, price, promote and distribute wants—satisfying products and services to present and potential customers". The president cannot plan, the production manager cannot manage, the purchasing agent cannot purchase, the chief financial officer cannot budget and the engineer and designer cannot design until the basic Strategic Marketing determination have been made. Yet another writer has remarked that "nothing happens in our economy until somebody sells something". We can discuss the importance of Strategic Marketing under following heads:

(A) Importance of Strategic Marketing to Society

1. *Delivery of Standard of Living.* The main object of Strategic Marketing is to provide goods and services to the people in the society according to their needs and taste at reasonable price. It is to satisfy the wants of people by the discovery of needs of the society, produces goods and services accordingly, creates demand for these goods, encourage people to use them and thus improves the standard of living of the people. It is why Paul Mazur has said, "Strategic Marketing is the delivery of Standard of Living to Society." Thus, Strategic Marketing creates, maintains and increases the demand of new and existing products and thus raises the standard of living of the people.
2. *Provides Employment.* According to an estimate, 40 per cent of the labour force in developed economies (USA, Japan, Germany, etc.) is engaged in different Strategic Marketing processes such as Strategic Marketing research work, wholesale and retail business, transport, communications, storing, warehousing and publicity work, etc. In underdeveloped economies like India, there is a great scope for increasing opportunities for employment by developing Strategic Marketing processes.
3. *Decrease in Distribution Cost.* Strategic Marketing aims at reducing the cost of distribution as far as possible so that the commodities might be within the reach of maximum number of consumers. It increases the level of consumption in the society. Reduction in the cost of distribution directly affects the price of the commodity and it will also be reduced. As a result, the product can now be purchased by customers which were unable to purchase it due to high prices. Even if, we assume that the price is not reduced, it will increase the profits of the producer, which will filter down to the shareholders, and debenture-holders. A part of the profit may also be utilised for further research work. Thus indirectly the society is benefited in the long run.
4. *Increase in National Income.* Sound Strategic Marketing system is associated with creation of increased demand for goods and services. An increased demand stimulates production activity in the country which in its turn increases the national income which is in the interest of the whole economy.
5. *Protection against Business Slump.* Trade cycles cause fluctuations in prices. Sometimes there is a period of depression followed by a period of boom. A period of depression and low prices is very harmful to the economy. With the decrease in demand many small units stop production leading to wide spread unemployment and a charm of other evils. A sound Strategic Marketing system can give protection against business slump by discovering new markets, reducing cost of distribution, making it customer-oriented, diversifying and improving the product, suggesting alternative uses.

(B) Importance of Strategic Marketing to the Firm. Strategic Marketing plays an important role for the well-being of a firm. This is evident from the following words of Peter F. Drucker, "Strategic Marketing is the distinguishing and the unique function of the business." The importance of Strategic Marketing to a business firm may be summarised under following heads:

1. *Helpful in Business Planning and Decision Making.* Strategic Marketing is helpful not only to plan the production but it is helpful also in business planning and taking various decisions regarding the business. In today's economy, production is planned according to the sales forecasts and not according to the production capacity of the firm. A firm will produce what it can sell or as much quantity as it can sell and not what and how much it can produce. Thus, Strategic Marketing decisions affect the business decisions. All other activities such as planning, production, purchase, finance or design revolve around the Strategic Marketing decisions.
2. *Helpful in Increasing Profits.* Every business is carried on with the profit motive. Strategic Marketing helps in increasing the business profits by reducing the selling cost on the one hand and by increasing the demand of the product through advertising and sales promotion activities on the other hand.
3. *Helpful in Communication between Firm and Society.* Business collects various information regarding consumers' behaviour and changes therein from time to time through Strategic Marketing. Strategic Marketing also provides information to the firm of the competitors, price policies, production policies, advertising and sales promotion policies or making necessary adjustments therein accordingly. Moreover, Strategic Marketing provides extensive information of the product regarding its quality, price, utility and place of availability to the society. Thus, society comes to know about the new products.

(C) Importance of Strategic Marketing in Underdeveloped or Developing Economy. Strategic Marketing has a special significance in underdeveloped or developing economies. A rapid development of the economy is possible only by adopting the modern methods of Strategic Marketing. Strategic Marketing in underdeveloped economies is still in its infancy. Industrialisation and organisation go hand in hand with application of modern refinements in the field of Strategic Marketing. An effective Strategic Marketing system alone can bring the fruits of production to the people. India provides the best example in this connection. One of he causes for recession is actually the result of recollecting the development of Strategic Marketing. Strategic Marketing is the most important 'multiplier' and an effective engine of development. It mobilises latent economic energy and thus is the creator of small business. It is the developer of standard for product and services as well as conduct, integrity and reliability. Besides, economic integration is made possible through proper distribution of products. Thus, the concept of Strategic Marketing in underdeveloped economies has to go a long way to catch up with the requirements of rapid industrial growth.

(D) Importance of Strategic Marketing in Developed Economy. In rich economies or the economies of abundance the way of life itself connotes a certain degree of development in Strategic Marketing. In such countries the volume of production with all its up-to-date technology is generally more than the demand. In order to maintain the level of production it is absolutely necessary that the produced amount is disposed of readily in the country itself or abroad on the basis of on-price competition. This is possible only by a very sound and advanced Strategic Marketing system because of still competition in the market.

(E) **Importance of Strategic Marketing in a Seller's or Buyer's Market.** A seller's market is one in which the demand for goods and services exceeds the supply. In such a situation there is tendency of growing monopolies. On the other hand, buyer's market's is one in which the supply of goods exceeds the demand. Every firm is eager to sell its goods but only that firm succeeds which adopts the scientific ways of Strategic Marketing of goods which means adopting the designs and quality of goods in accordance with the changing tastes and likings of the common consumers. Thus, the importance of Strategic Marketing in both a seller's or a buyer's market is great indeed.

Thus, Strategic Marketing is a potential force that commands high significance. Briefly, any increase in efficiency of Strategic Marketing results in a lower cost of distribution. Lower prices to consumers mean a real increase in the national income. Low prices are a boon to the entire population. Strategic Marketing process brings new varieties of useful and quality goods to consumers. This helps to improve the standard of living. Strategic Marketing provides wide employment opportunities. It is Strategic Marketing which has counted yesterday's luxuries to today's necessaries. It converts latent demand into effective demand.

Building Customer Satisfaction, Value, and Retention

What is a Customer?

- A Customer is the most important person ever in this office...in person or by mail.
- A Customer is not dependent on us...we are dependent on him.
- A Customer is a person who brings us his wants. It is our job to handle them profitably to him and to ourselves.
- A Customer is not an interruption of our work...he is the purpose of it. We are not doing a favour by serving him...he is doing us a favour by giving us the opportunity to do so.
- A Customer is not someone to argue or match wits with. Nobody ever won an argument with a Customer.

Determinants of Customer Delivered Value

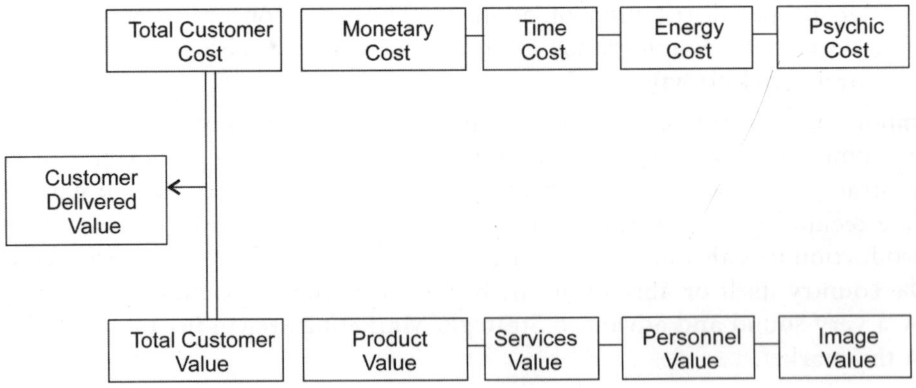

Delivering Customer Value and Satisfaction

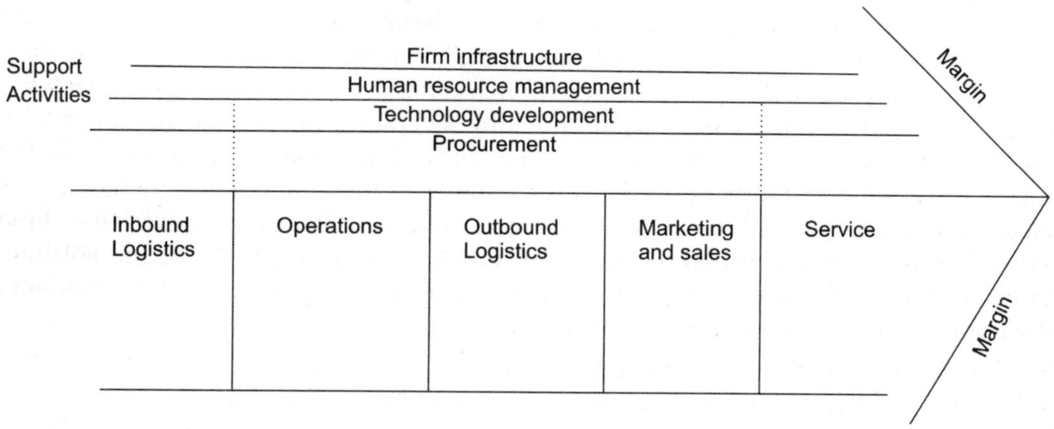

Primary Activities

The Customer—Development Process

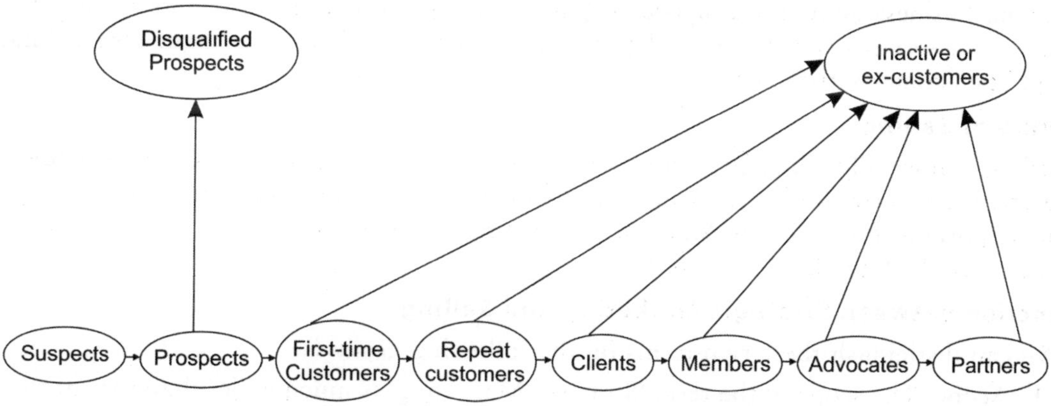

IMPORTANCE OF STRATEGIC MARKETING IN INDIA

Indian economy is a developing economy. Economic environment in India has changed and has been acquiring greater dynamism and robustness. The functions of Strategic Marketing has also undergone tremendous changes. The country has acquired a solid industrial base. Now the concept of Strategic Marketing has undergone a revolutionary change. Strategic Marketing Managers have come to know the importance of consumer-oriented Strategic Marketing to grow. For them, Strategic Marketing means creation of demand and creation of consumers. In other words, it means creation of demand through the satisfaction of customers' wants and thus creation and delivery of standard of living of the people.

India has acquired a solid industrial base. The infrastructure required for further advancement of industry is right now being developed. The 'opening up of the economy' in the 1990s as a sequel to the new economic policies and liberalisation measures has given a new impetus to the process. With the new programmes, the economic and industrial environment of India is moving further towards the forces of market place and away from controls and regulations. There is a remarkable expansion and diversification in the manufacture and Strategic Marketing of consumer goods. A number of multinationals have entered the Indian consumer market and posed a threat to the very existence of Indian industries. Indian industries are facing stiff competition with them. They are now using new Strategic Marketing techniques to survive. The Indian industries are prepared to review their Strategic Marketing policies like production and sales policies, price policies, and other related policies and programmes to commensurate them with those of their foreign counterparts.

Thus, in the light of the above discussion, the Strategic Marketing function in India has acquired a new dimension. It has become more important in the changing environment of India's economy.

Meaning of Strategic Marketing

Strategic Marketing occupies the first place in all business activities. According to modern Strategic Marketing concept, Strategic Marketing starts with the product-idea and ends with customer-satisfaction. According to William Stanton, "Strategic Marketing is a total system of interacting business activities designed to plan, price, promote and distribute want satisfying products and services to present and potential customers." Thus, the main idea behind the concept is customer-satisfaction.

Meaning of Selling

Selling is normally concerned with the transfer of goods and services to the consumers or prospective consumers for the exchange of money. It serves mainly the seller's interest. It is one of the important functions of Strategic Marketing. Selling includes all activities regarding passing of finished goods to the buyers.

Distinction between Strategic Marketing and Selling

We can distinguish these two terms on the following grounds:

1. **Scope.** The scope of the term 'Strategic Marketing' is much wider than that of the term 'selling'. Strategic Marketing includes all activities starting with the idea of producing a product to satisfy the needs of the customers and ending with the satisfaction of customer even after the product is sold. Thus, it involves planning, producing, selling and serving the customers. Changes in product-line, quality, shape and design, price, channels of distribution, etc. are all made on the basis of information picked up from the market through constant and systematic research. On the other hand, selling refers to the functions and activities undertaken to secure the sale or distribution of the quality and design of the products already manufactured by the firm. It involves efforts to sell what has already been produced without taking the trouble of adapting production to consumer needs and preferences.
2. **Object of Profit Earning.** The object of Strategic Marketing is to earn profits through satisfaction of customer needs while, on the other hand, selling concentrates on sale

volume and makes efforts to earn and maximise to profits by selling more quantity of products. Thus, profitability of a Strategic Marketing the oriented firm depends very much on the quality of products as required by customers and their satisfaction while the profitability of a selling-oriented firm is concerned with the sale volume.

3. **Relation.** Strategic Marketing is related to customer satisfaction and therefore includes pre-production and post-sale activities. Selling is concerned only with the physical transfer of goods from one person to another and includes activities relating to transfer of goods. Selling is not concerned with the satisfaction of customers' needs and pre-production and post-sale activities.
4. **Orientation.** Strategic Marketing is consumer oriented and more attention is paid on consumer's needs. It calls upon the corporation to choose products, prices, and methods of distribution and promotion that would meet the needs of the customers. Selling is basically production-oriented and concentrates much on production and distribution of goods. It persuades the customers what is already has or can offer readily.
5. **Solution of Problems.** Solving the Strategic Marketing problems is the main concern of the producers or businessmen while selling problems are solved by other channels of distribution like retailer, wholesaler, etc.
6. **Emphasis.** Strategic Marketing emphasises on innovation in every sphere. It provides better values to customers by adapting the most innovative technology. Whereas in selling, emphasis is on staying with the existing technology and reducing the cost of production with a view to maximise profits.

THE CONCEPT OF STRATEGIC MARKETING AT DIFFERENT STAGES OF ECONOMIC DEVELOPMENT

Economic life has evolved through different stages of economic development. Chronologically, it is different to state how long one stage lasted. For convenience, economic history can be divided into eight stages. The concept of Strategic Marketing in each stage was different depending on the character of the economy.

1. **The Stage of Economic Self-efficiency.** In this earliest stage of economic development, there were small family units carrying out all the work to satisfy all their wants for food, clothing and shelter. There was no exchange at all. It was a stage of self-sufficiency devoid of a concept of Strategic Marketing. There was nothing to market.
2. **The Stage of Primitive Communism.** In this stage, the land was owned in common and the fruits of the labour were shared in common. The Eshimo hunter had no personal right to his catch; it had to be divided among the inhabitants of the whole village. The tools and provisions were the common property of all. There was no need of exchange in this type of society. The absence of exchange removes the basis for a concept of Strategic Marketing.
3. **The Stage of Simple Barter.** Soon it was realised that some people are able to turn out certain goods quickly than others. The led to economic specialisation. Gradually not only individuals and families but the whole tribes and communities turned to specialisation for its beneficial effects on human productivity. The family or tribe

engaged in a particular trade and entered into bartering relationship with others for the goods it did not produce or possess. Those who were in possession of surpluses bartered their goods with those who did not produce or possess the same goods. The agriculturist bartered the corn, cotton, etc. produced by him for the leather, hand tools, utensils and furniture produced by the craftsman. It involved some search and negotiations. Thus, personal selling practices originated at the time of barter.

4. **The Stage of Local Markets.** Barter system encouraged the emergence of local markets. Such markets were at first temporary affairs such as trade fairs taking place only on certain days of the week or at time of festivals. They were also based on barter system. But soon, they took on more permanent shape with stalls, shops and bazars. The rise of these local markets led to specialisation for the first time of certain persons in Strategic Marketing as opposed to production. The appearance of specialisation in selling expanded the concept of Strategic Marketing. Strategic Marketing then was the process of exchange of economic goods and the set up of specialised institutions that facilitated the exchange.
5. **The Stage of Money Economy.** Simple barter system was an advance over economic self-sufficiency but it was wrought with certain difficulties. The economic goods offered for exchange were not always on equal value, double coincidence, difficulties of storage and carrying goods from place to place in search of parties, etc. The solution came through the development of a common medium of exchange which was known as 'money'. Money took several forms. Several articles were used as medium of exchange such as fish, hooks, shells, pearls, beads, sheep, cows, slaves, etc. But ultimately they were given up in favour of metallic coins. The advent of a common circulating medium quickened the pace of trade and provided an even more durable base for the operation of local markets. At this stage, there was no far reaching or fundamental change in production and distribution of goods. The only change was the replacement of barter system with the money system. Now the pricing became the mechanism of exchange process.
6. **The Stage of Early Capitalism.** There were persons who were successful at accumulation by dint of their talent or force. They began to exchange goods and services that they had in surplus for the labour. There arose a property class and a labour class. The early capitalists organised workers into productive units and sought markets to trade their output. Of course, there was no brand, grading, packaging or advertising at that time. A merchant class arose who facilitated the distribution of goods in large towns. Peddlers and hawkers also carried goods from door to door. Early capitalism operated in an economy of scarcity. There was no serious effort to study the needs of consumers. The concept of Strategic Marketing under early capitalism was that of the business activities specially involved in searching for customers or markets and moving goods from producer to consumers for the purpose of the seller's gain. At this stage, it was seller's market.
7. **The Stage of Mass Production.** The industrial revolution, invention of machines, improvement in means of transportation and communication, growth of industrial towns, etc. pushed the growth of large-scale enterprises. Profession of management

developed that increasingly understood how to organise men, machines, material and money to maximise the profitable return on the invested resources. The producers sought means of increasing the stability of demand for their products. Out of this search various modern Strategic Marketing practices originated, i.e. branding and packaging, advertising, agency system, sale promotion, etc. These Strategic Marketing activities became increasingly popular. Thus, in an economy of mass production, Strategic Marketing becomes the name for a whole variety of business activities undertaken by sellers to improve and stimulate the new flow of goods and services form producers to consumers.

8. **The Stage of Competition.** The mass production and mass distribution brought by the industrial revolution soon led to the stage of competition. The ever increasing number and size of the producing firms concentrated the phenomenon of competition. Earlier, the emphasis of the producing firm was disposal or distribution of their products, but now competition became the main issue. Now, the main thrust of the producing firms was to ensure that their products were preferred by customers to those of their competitors.
9. **The Stage of the Affluent Society.** In highly developed economies producers and sellers of goods and services have to probe deep into the question of what people want rather than what they need and adjust their productive capacity and productions to meet these interpreted wants. Emphasis has to be laid on Strategic Marketing research before decisions on product and product lines are ever made. Salesmen are increasingly used to provide feedback on evolving customer wants. Advertising is used to inform buyers of new goods designed to meet new wants in the market place. Various Strategic Marketing tools are used to give consumer-oriented decisions to their business.

It was all because of the abundant choices were made available to the consumers. The industrial firms realised that it was not enough to make one-time sale of their products, they had to ensure repeated visits by the customers who had purchased their products once. They began to offer quality goods at reasonable prices due to competition. They had also to ensure that customer's complaints were attended to promptly. After-sale service was provided and that meant the emergence of Strategic Marketing.

Thus, in an affluent society the concept of Strategic Marketing becomes increasingly that of interpreting consumer desires and creating the goods that will satisfy their desires. The affluent society is a society composed of huge organisations not only business organisations but also military, governmental social and political organisations competing for recognition and acceptance in the public mind.

DIFFERENT CONCEPTS OF STRATEGIC MARKETING

Strategic Marketing occupies an important position in the organisation of a business unit but Strategic Marketing has been defined by different people in different ways. Different definitions represent different views and none have a quality of universal acceptability. Different concepts have been developed so far by the different authorities of management and we are discussing those alternative concepts one by one in the following lines:

1. **Distribution of Goods and Services Concept.** It represents traditional concept of Strategic

Marketing. According to this concept, Strategic Marketing is an economic activity that facilitates the flow of goods and services from producer to consumer. F.E. Clark has defined the Strategic Marketing as "Strategic Marketing consists of those efforts which affect transfers in ownership of goods and care for their physical distribution." The another definition under this category is that of American Strategic Marketing Association that says, "Strategic Marketing is the performance of business activities that direct the flow of goods and services from producer to consumer or user."

According to this concept Strategic Marketing includes all activities relating to transfer of ownership in goods and services to the actual consumer, form their point of origin or production. It has no concern with the present production activity or after sale activity. According to this view, Strategic Marketing begins when production process is complete and ends when goods are sold. The producing firms, under this concept, are more concerned with maximising their profits by making maximum sales.

The definition represents a narrow view of Strategic Marketing that insists much on the flow of goods and services and leaves the other important managerial aspects of Strategic Marketing untouched.

2. **Delivery of Standard of Living Concept.** This concept is originated by Paul Mazur. According to him, "Strategic Marketing is the delivery of standard of living to society." Professor McNair made an important amendment in the definition of Paul Mazur. He added that "Strategic Marketing is the creation and delivery of a standard of living to the society." According to this concept, Strategic Marketing includes all those activities that create and give a better standard of living to the society. In this way, it may be said to be a consumer-oriented concept and is much nearer to the modern concept of Strategic Marketing. Producer tries to know the customers' needs and plans his production accordingly and directs the flow of goods and services to them. He tries to lower down the cost of production by making necessary changes in channels of distribution and taking up of sales promotion activities. In this way, customers get quality goods at cheaper rates and thus better standard of living is delivered to the society.
3. **Creation of Utility Concept.** Bichard Buskirk has resented an idea that Strategic Marketing is an activity that creates form, place, time, and ownership utility. According to him, "Strategic Marketing is an integrated system of action of that creates value in goods through the creation of form, place, time, and ownership utility." This means: (i) Product planning and development activities create form utility; (ii) Flow of goods through different distribution channels from producers to consumers from the place of abundant to the place of scarcity or where they are needed creates place utility; (iii) After production, goods are stored by the manufacturer, wholesalers or retailers till such time the demand of the product is created and such goods are made available to customer at the time when they are needed or demanded. Thus, creating time utility for them; (iv) Goods may be lying in a reliable state with the producer or the manufacturer or their agents while some other person need them. In such cases, possession of goods to the person who needs it. Strategic Marketing, therefore, consists in moving goods from the manufacturers, in a form in which it is required at a time when they required,

to the place where they are to be used and for those who are to use them for various purposes. Thus, under this concept Strategic Marketing creates different types of utilities in goods and make them valuable.

4. **Generation of Revenue Concept.** This concept presents that the main object of any business firm should be to generate revenue or income. The income can be generated only by selling the products. The product should be sold out at a price which allows a reasonable profit to the firm after meeting out the cost and all other reasonable expenses. Strategic Marketing should stress on increasing the selling price. Richard Buskirk has explained the concept as "It is Strategic Marketing responsibility to generate revenue at a cost which will allow a reasonable profit to be realised from operations. Thus, Strategic Marketing consists of all activities which are performed with a view to allow the firm to earn a reasonable profit."

5. **Social System Concept of Strategic Marketing.** This concept was introduced by William J. Stanton. According to him, in this concept just like social system, Strategic Marketing is not only one activity, it is a sum of several business activities and, rather interaction of many activities. In the words of William J. Stanton, "Strategic Marketing is a total system of interacting business activities designed to plan, price, promote, and distribute want satisfying products and services to present and potential customers." Thus, under this concept the entire system of business action is market oriented or customer oriented.

6. **Concept of Customers Satisfaction—Modern Concept.** The modern concept of Strategic Marketing emphasises on the complete satisfaction of customer's needs. This concept is also known as Strategic Marketing Concept. This concept integrates Strategic Marketing function with the other functions of the management with this realisation that business is basically a Strategic Marketing organisation. It is based on two fundamental concepts: (i) that the company policies and operations should be customer-oriented; and (ii) that the goal of the firm should be profitable sales. The philosophy behind this concept is the satisfaction of customer's wants. According to Peter F. Drucker, "The purpose of a business is to create a customer". Creation of customer means the identification of consumer needs and organising the business to meet these needs. Firm makes the sincere efforts, to find out the needs of the members of the community and tries to provide the maximum measure of satisfaction to them.

From this point of view, it appears that everything a firm does is Strategic Marketing. However, it is convenient to separate Strategic Marketing as a distinct activity. The Strategic Marketing thus includes:

(i) Identification and assessment of markets and sales forecasting.

(ii) Formulation of Strategic Marketing policy to cater to the target market.

(iii) The planning and operation of the Strategic Marketing organisation to achieve the desire level of sales and to deal with customers.

(iv) Organisation and conduct of sales promotion through salesmanship, advertising and other media.

(v) Costing and budgeting of Strategic Marketing efforts.

(vi) Review of the Strategic Marketing efforts and to assess whether the desired level of consumer satisfaction is being achieved or not.

STRATEGIC MARKETING MANAGEMENT IN ACTION

Strategic Marketing management involves several activities, including environmental scanning, market opportunity analysis, Strategic Marketing strategy programming and implementation and control. This entire book is devoted to discussing these subjects, shown in Fig. 1.1, which presents an overview of the basic components of Strategic Marketing management and their interrelationships. The organisation's mission provides the priorities for scanning the broader environment and identifying and analysing market opportunities. Understanding the changing Strategic Marketing environment and the organisation's markets, in turn, provides a basis for developing effective Strategic Marketing Strategies. Then, specific target markets are defined, Strategic Marketing objectives delineated for each target market, and the numerous Strategic Marketing programme decisions made (prices, advertising, distribution, etc.). Together, these activities make up a Strategic Marketing Strategy, which is then implemented and controlled. Implementation is often the most difficult stage. It is important to realise that Strategic Marketing management usually involves this sequential

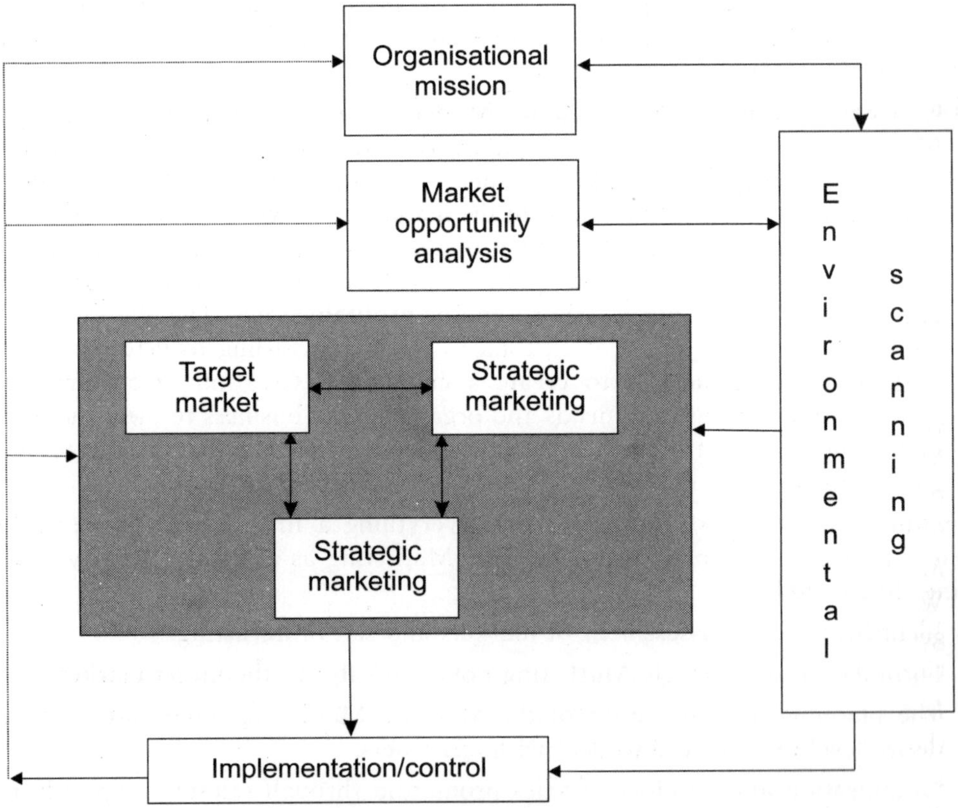

Fig. 1.1: Strategic Marketing Management in Action

process. Implementation occurs only after programming decisions are made; programming decisions are based on target market decisions and realistic objectives; target market decisions and realistic objectives hinge on in-depth market opportunity analyses; all of these stages benefit from keeping a ken eye on the shifting environment; and, together, these stages make a major contribution toward achieving the corporate mission.

Environmental Scanning

Environmental scanning helps identify market opportunities and threats and provides guidelines for the design of Strategic Marketing strategy. Environmental analysis concentrates on the macro-environment—the economic, governmental, technological, social, and natural environments.

The environment can create opportunities for some companies and threats for others, as seen in the $3 billion market for automated building heating and air conditioning controls. Technological change meant a shift from electromechanical to electronic controls in the middle to late 1960s. Then, in the 1970s, global governmental forces contributed to the acceleration of energy prices, making it more economical for building owners to install systems that reduced utility bills.

Market Opportunity Analysis

A product-market is comprised of individual and institutional endusers (ultimate consumers) who are able and willing to purchase a particular product or service.

Market opportunity analysis can be used to investigate a potential market opportunity or better understand a market already served. A precise description of the size and characteristics of a target market can show how a firm's Strategic Marketing approach can be improved.

Wendy's international entered a mature and competitive fast-food market in the 1970s. Firms such as Wendy's need three kinds of information about their market:

- *Market definition and customer profiles* provide market descriptions used by Strategic Marketing management in evaluating market opportunities and designing Strategic Marketing programme to serve target markets. For example, Wendy's end users (consumers of its services) represent a key population group: young adults over 25 years of age. This group had not received emphasis in the Strategic Marketing efforts of McDonald's or Burger King. Customer profiles also include information on buyer perceptions, attitudes, shopping patterns, and so forth. Adopting a customer viewpoint of the marketplace is an essential basis for developing realistic strategies.
- *Market size estimation* builds on a clear definition of an organisation's target market. Wendy's had to estimate how many prospective customers existed in various geographic markets, what share of each market it could capture, what the average rupee purchase would be, and what the repeat purchase rate would be.
- *Industry and competitor analysis* identifies probable trends and operating practices in the industry of which the firm is a part as well as the strengths and weaknesses of each key competitor. For Wendy's, the industry includes all national and regional fast-food chains. Industry analysis includes an investigation of how an industry is reaching its markets through its channels of distribution (e.g. manufacturer-wholesaler-retailer-

consumer). Competitor analysis concentrates on the key firms with which a company competes. Thus, McDonald's and Burger King represent competing firms, whereas Taco Bell is probably not a key competitor for the Wendy's target market.

Knowledge of markets and competitors is essential in designing and managing Strategic Marketing strategy.

Strategic Marketing Strategy

Strategic Marketing cannot fulfil its managerial (or social) role unless customer needs and wants are understood and satisfied. The development of an overall Strategic Marketing Strategy helps ensure that mutually beneficial exchanges occur (part of the definition of Strategic Marketing). It is oriented toward the long run, comprised of fundamental decisions (not day-to-day adjustments), and developed with an eye to competition as well as markets. Developing Strategic Marketing Strategy includes deciding which customers to target and how to position products (and the organisation) relative to competitors in the minds of existing and potential customers.

Developing Strategic Marketing programmes involve identifying alternative combinations of Strategic Marketing variables (for example, higher-quality, higher-priced ham-burgers) and then judging how well these combinations match the market opportunity. The core of such matching is forecasting potential customer response to the mix of Strategic Marketing variables. Then, the programme with the greatest potential is implemented.

Let us consider the luxury car market. The guidelines and policies that constitute a strategy for the luxury car market must be oriented towards creating the highest quality image possible. They include:

- A high, narrow pricing range that conveys an image of price exclusiveness.
- New models that offer high technical quality, few repairs, and excellent warranty coverage.
- Advertising media and messages that impart an exclusive, high-quality image.

These illustrative guidelines and policies (Strategic Marketing Strategy) narrow the range of Strategic Marketing actions that are appropriate given the overall Strategic Marketing objectives (e.g. quality image). Basically, a Strategic Marketing strategy outlines how Strategic Marketing objectives will be achieved.

Target Market Selection

A target market may consist of all end-users or one or more sub-groups in a product-market. Making decisions about target markets is one of management's most important tasks. Wendy's decision to go after a sub-group of the population, young adults, with a particular service offering was a target market decision.

Strategic decision involving target markets include:

- *Deciding whether to go after an entire product-market by using a mass-Strategic Marketing approach or to concentrate Strategic Marketing strategy on only a portion of the market.* The highly successful B. Dalton Bookseller subsidiary of Dayton-Hudson Corporation typically stocks 25,000 books per store and serves the mass-market. Yet its president says, we think there is a new level of the market out there, made up in part of people intimidated by a full selection bookstore.

- *Determining when to modify an existing target market strategy.* The top management of Sherwin-Williams decided to shift from the firm's traditional orientation as a paint store for contractors and to appeal instead to consumers. A completely re-designed Strategic Marketing approach was implemented with home decorating centres that offer paints, floor and wall coverings, and related products.
- *Deciding to stop serving a particular target market.* Increasingly, managements are confronted by the question of whether to withdraw from a market. Maturing products, slow growth rates, competition, and environmental changes gradually alter the attractiveness of target markets.

Target market selection is guided by an organisation's mission and objectives, so target market decisions must be properly positioned within this larger context and their strategic implications assessed. Once selected, the target market provides the focus for setting Strategic Marketing objectives and designing the Strategic Marketing programme.

Strategic Marketing Objectives

Strategic Marketing objectives should be consistent with corporate objectives and should be stated for each target market in terms of sales, market share, profit contribution, and other qualitative aims, such as strengthening a brand image. Objectives are sometimes divided into two groups—market *performance* objectives and market *support* objectives. The former are specific outcomes such as sales and profits. The latter pertain to tasks that precede the final performance outcome and may include building customer awareness, engaging in educational efforts, and creating a brand image.

Objectives help shape the Strategic Marketing mix for each target market. A firm seeking to increase sales in a target market by 6 per cent for the coming year would probably make only limited changes in the existing Strategic Marketing programme. Alternatively, striving for a substantial sales increase, say 20 per cent, could require major change in the composition of the Strategic Marketing programme, including increases in the Strategic Marketing budget for elements of the programme (e.g. size of the sales force).

Objectives must, at least to some degree, be measurable; otherwise, identifying progress towards their achievement is impossible. In Strategic Marketing, measurability is no easy order. A support objective could include changing a brand image in the minds of potential customers—and progress toward that objective could be measured by surveying customer perceptions. This is often done. Objectives should be worded very carefully, with the intention of developing measurable and attainable standards. The following Strategic Marketing performance and support objectives were used in a personal computer education business:

- To increase awareness of our services to at least 70 per cent of our targeted customers.
- To develop over the next year three new class offerings, with high-quality instructors, to serve the personal computer users.
- To develop a targeted, systematic, and coordinated advertising programme.

Strategic Marketing Programme

A firm's Strategic Marketing must consist of an integrated strategy aimed at providing customer's satisfaction. To develop such a strategy, a firm uses demand-influencing variables that together constitute the Strategic Marketing mix. The Strategic Marketing mix, like a puzzle, has numerous pieces that must be appropriately combined for a successful end result. It includes the product (or service) offered by the firm, the distribution channels it uses (wholesalers, distributors, retailers) to make the product available to customers, the price it charges for the product, and promotion (advertising, personal selling, sales promotion and publicity). Other terms often used to describe the components of the Strategic Marketing mix are the Strategic Marketing programme, the Strategic Marketing offer, and the 4-Ps (product, place, price and promotion). These variables must be consistent with one another, and ideally, they complement one another for a synergistic result. Building a quality, prestige product and combining it with inconsistent mix ingredients such as heavy price discounting would yield a poorly integrated, internally inconsistent Strategic Marketing programme. The mix ingredients would conflict with one another in the minds of customers.

Table 1.1: Strategic Marketing Mix Variables

Product	Distribution	Price	Promotion
Features	Types of channels middlemen	List price	Promotion blend Advertising Media
Quality	Store/distributor location	Credit terms	Copy Timing
Packaging	Storage	Discounts	Personal selling Selection and training
Branding Services	Transportation and logistics	Allowances	Motivation Allocation
Guarantees Assortment	Service levels	Flexibility	Sales promotion Publicity

QUESTIONS FOR DISCUSSION

1. Discuss the core concept of Strategic Marketing. How does Strategic Marketing differ from selling? Is there any role of Strategic Marketing for products where demand is in excess of supply?
2. "Marketers can create needs." Do you agree? Give reasons to support your answer.
3. What do you mean by Strategic Marketing? What are the various prerequisites of Strategic Marketing activities? "Strategic Marketing consists of the performance of business activities that direct the flow of goods and services from producers to consumers." Explain this statement in the light of importance of Strategic Marketing.
4. "The present-day Strategic Marketing is consumer-oriented." Explain its objectives.
5. Strategic Marketing begins before production of goods and continues even after the sale has been made. But selling is concerned with transfer of ownership of goods already produced. Explain.
6. What are the important functions to be performed in the process of Strategic Marketing? Discuss them briefly.
7. What is the role of Strategic Marketing in business scenario? Elaborate.
8. State the nature of Strategic Marketing. How does Strategic Marketing satisfy the wants of people?

9. Explain the scope of Strategic Marketing and also elaborate on Strategic Marketing as a career.
10. Briefly explain the internal and external factors influencing Strategic Marketing.
11. Explain the relevance of Strategic Marketing in a developing economy.
12. Differentiate between mass Strategic Marketing and target Strategic Marketing.
13. "Strategic Marketing is the performance of business activities that direct the flow of goods and services from producer to consumer or users." Explain.

CASE STUDY 1.1
LAUNCHING STRATEGY OF DENTA

Denta, a toothpaste was test marketed by ABC and Co., in Delhi in early '98. The brand was similar to Colgate in taste and packaging. The media advertising stressed/highlighted the herbal properties of Denta, which were akin to Promise. Two-three months after the Delhi launch a tracking study revealed that Denta had achieved a 12 per cent trial rate and a 1 per cent repeat purchase rate. The results were not as per the expectations of the company as they had targeted a market share of 10 per cent. After due analysis, it was revealed that while the initial trial and repeat rate was satisfactory for the product category, yet it was felt that media advertising has not been able *to* induce enough people to try the product. It was, therefore, felt that if the trial rate could be increased to 40 per cent and the repeat purchase to 25 per cent, the brand could achieve its targeted market share of 10 per cent dependence purely on advertising was ruled out being very expensive.

QUESTIONS FOR DISCUSSION

1. What are the keys issues in the present case?
2. Suggest alternatives available to ABC and Co., and the most preferred alternative that you would pursue as the Brand Manager for Denta. Rationalise your stand.

CASE STUDY 1.2
SOYABEAN MILK AS AN ALTERNATIVE

Dr. S. Chakrabarty was domiciled in Los Angeless, U.S.A. for the last eight years. After getting his Masters in Food Technology from the University of California, he had obtained a Ph.D. in the same subject specialising in 'high protein products'. After completing his education, he joined a company, HyPro Inc., where he was a Director of R&D. The company had developed different types of high protein product which were marketed through a large number of departmental stores throughout the U.S.A. The company enjoyed a good reputation.

Dr. Chakrabarty was seriously thinking of returning to India and settling down in his hometown of Bangalore. He was also toying with the idea for last two or three years to set up a plant to produce high protein products in India. During his earlier visits, after talking to different people, he had noticed the availability of Soyabeans in abundance. He had carried out several experiments in his laboratory and has developed what he called as "Soyabean Milk". He felt that for a poor country like India with the majority of the children being undernourished, this would be an ideal product.

Soyabean Milk would have some percentage of normal milk, water and different other raw materials added to give it a high protein value. It will be pasteurised, so refrigeration would not be essential and will have almost the same or even better life than average milk. Soyabean Milk would cost about 15 per cent more than the regular milk, which he felt, was justified due to its high protein values. To obtain the same proteins, other substitutes or medicines, he felt would be ten times more costlier.

As he was 15,000 miles away from his potential market, he first wanted ascertain the feasibility of this project. He had several questions to which he wanted to answers. Some of these were:

(i) Whether the tradition-bound Indian population would accept a new concept like Soyabean Milk?

(ii) In which town should he set up his plant? And of what capacity?

(iii) In which form should he introduce this Soyabean Milk? As a substitute to normal milk or by adding different flavours, as a competitive product to the already existing soft drinks market?

(iv) What sort of distribution arrangement should he have?

Technically he was confident about the production of this Soyabean Milk. Marketing-wise and commercially whether such a project will be viable or not was his main doubt. His friends had informed him that recently two companies have already introduced Soyabean Milk in India which was, however, very costly in the market. This did not worry him much as he felt that his product would be superior and what with such a large population in India, even a dozen competitors should do reasonably good business.

(AIMA, Dec. 1997 & IP, MBA, 2001)

QUESTIONS FOR DISCUSSION

1. What type of information should Dr. Chakrabarty collect to decide on the setting up of this project?
2. What strategy would you recommend for marketing of Soyabean Milk in India for him?

CASE STUDY 1.3
XYZ PAPER COMPANY

The XYZ Paper Company, a West-Indian paper mill, had been known for many years as a leading producer of craft papers, used in making various kinds of bags such as grocery and shopping bags. The mill was non-integrated, meaning that the pulp and the papermaking were separate operations, not linked in one continuous process. Rival Southern Mills, has an important competitive advantage because of newer and faster equipment, lower taxes, cheaper labour and greater efficiency because of integrated pulp-paper operations, had seriously infringed in XYZ's market position. A number of different changes were made by the XYZ management in an attempt to regain sales. Coloured papers were introduced, lighter-weight papers were developed and a larger proportion of output was allocated to high-grade speciality papers. When the new kinds of papers failed to bring a substantial increase in sales, the management finally concluded that a major new product would have to be added.

It had been observed that the use of plastic-coated papers for which the company produced the base stock, had expanded considerably in both the industrial (e.g. food packaging) and consumer (e.g. paper picnic plates) areas. Statistics confirmed the accuracy of observations: use of plastic-coated papers had increased tremendously in the most recent five-year period. Convinced that this was an attractive new area for expansion, the XYZ Company purchased the most modern coating equipment available. Recalling the advantage enjoyed by some southern mills because of their larger, faster equipment, XYZ Company purchased a high-speed coater, which, at the time of installation, was one of the largest in the industry. Crews from the paper machines were trained to operate the coating machine, but they experienced considerable difficulty in getting it to perform properly.

The sales force, at its annual sales meeting, was told about the installation of the new machine, and the technical research director described what grades of papers could be coated on the machine, and some of the important uses of the various grades. The sales manager delivered an inspired talk to the sales force on the growth potential of plastic paper; then he distributed price sheets. Shortly afterwards, advertisements were run in the trade press, announcing the new operations and the new programme was put into effect.

The sales response to XYZ's new programme was poor. The coating machine was in use for only about 10 hours-a-week, although, fixed charges on the machine amounted to Rs. 50 per hour on a 24 hours-a-day, 5 day-a-week basis. There seemed to be two chief reasons for the disappointing results. First, the sales force had difficulty in selling the product. Potential buyers asked many technical questions that the salesmen were unable to answer. For example, one prospect wanted to know the temperature at which the plastic would be formed on the paper. To provide technical information, two men from the technical department were designated to help the salesmen on important or difficult calls. The second chief reason for disappointing results was that when orders were received, the coating machine operators had difficulty in meeting the product specifications, which resulted in a high quantity of scrap and many delays in delivery. To combat the situation, the technical director of the company was asked to take charge of the equipment temporarily and regular test runs were made at times when orders were not being filled to augment the training of operating crews. The management felt that these changes would help the situation.

Although, somewhat helpful, these changes did not materially improve the situation. Several months later, two salesmen were hired to handle plastic-coated paper on a full-time basis in the principal markets, which centred around two metropolitan cities. These important markets had not been adequately covered because the regular salesmen were kept busy with their usual accounts in these markets, and also, it seemed, that they were less enthusiastic about the coating phase of the business.

A short time later, management concluded that a re-organisation of the coating operations was necessary. The company president decided to put a general manager in charge of all operations, to avoid divided responsibility and buck-passing. Since the technical director had been put in charge of coating production temporarily (replacing the general production manager), it meant that the same group was responsible for making the product and for judging whether it met quality standards. The sales manager criticised this arrangement, saying that quality control was a major problem in satisfying customers. He also criticised the company for failing to develop specific grades of coated papers for particular product applications. In response, the product development manager explained that the technical department was often unable to formulate the grades of paper the sales manager proposed. Even when the technicians were successful in using pilot equipment in the laboratory, he said, there were numerous delays before the product could actually be made on the high-speed coater.

The president thought the new general manager of coating operations should have a sales background, primarily. Since the organisation appeared qualified, the assistant general sales manager from one of the larger plastic coating firms was hired as general manager of coating operations. After working a few weeks for XYZ the new manager was asked to study the specific markets within the general coated papers field to determine which grades the company was best equipped to make and which were the most attractive from the standpoint of sales potential.

When the market study was completed, the management realised that the company was in an unfavourable position to effectively compete in any of the markets that had originally appeared attractive. In the high-profit-margin speciality papers, XYZ was outclassed by the superior technical skill and specially designed equipment of the custom coaters. Speciality papers usually were produced in short-runs, which would negate the tremendous speed of the XYZ coater. Moreover, the 'Down-time' that would be needed between each run to ready the machine for the next job was economically unsound.

(AIMA, June 1994)

QUESTIONS FOR DISCUSSION

1. What do you think of the company's strategy? Was the expansion programme soundly conceived?
2. What was the reason that the company continued to make mistakes?

CASE STUDY 1.4
FLUID CONTROL DEVICE LIMITED

Fluid Control Device Ltd. is celebrating its Golden Jubilee Year in 1998. Fifty years ago, when the company was started in 1948 for manufacturing pumps, it was considered a pioneering venture. It concentrated on consolidating its business till 1968. In 1968 out of the total pump market of Rs. 24 crore, it alone produced pumps worth Rs. 8 crore. However, today in 1998 out of total pump market of Rs. 120 crore, the company's share is only Rs. 16 crore. This shows that demand has grown much faster and that Fluid Control has missed the bus. Moreover, users carry an image about the company as a producer of agricultural pumps, simple in construction made out of cast iron which three hundred other units can also produce in the country. Though Fluid's R&D dep. has developed alloy steel pumps for industrial applications but company's share of the industrial pumps market is very small.

On the export front too the situation is not at all encouraging as the company has paid little or no attention to the export sector.

This is reflected in reduced profitability for the company and cash balance. In 1968 on a turnover of Rs. 8 crore fluid control had a gross profit of Rs. 1.5 crore while in 1998 the gross profit is only Rs. 60 lakhs on a turnover of Rs. 16 crore. If this trend continues the company will face losses in the coming year. Fluid control has already started facing the problem of working capital and payment to its creditors is also being delayed.

The company still has excellent resources, which include perhaps the best manufacturing and testing set up, wide distribution network and trained manpower. Moreover, with 50 years standing it has generated lot of goodwill in the market. Based on the above credentials a complete turnaround may be possible if appropriate strategies are worked out and implemented at all levels.

(MBA, June 1998)

QUESTIONS FOR DISCUSSION

1. Which do you think could be the areas, viz. R&D, production, finance, marketing, exports where the company could be failing?
2. If you are appointed as an advisor to Fluid Control Device Ltd. what comprehensive strategy would you recommend to its Board of Directors?

CASE STUDY 1.5
SONY CORPORATION

Never has Sony, that exceptionally innovative of Japanese companies, been in greater need of money-spinning new products.

Worldwide recession and cutthroat competition in its prime TV and video recorder markets have depressed its sates and slashed its earnings.

If it had not been for the continued success of its four-year-old "Walkman" cassette player, Sony's profits plunge in the first half of 1983 would have been steeper than the ignominious 66 per cent revealed in the summer.

Recovery to its customary "star" states clearly requires a whole raft of new successes. Yet, several of the company's innovative projects are not doing well. Its much-hyped "Mavica" camera is in the technical doldrums, and a number of office products are taking off disappointingly slowly.

Enter Mr. Yasuo Kuroki, industrial designer. While Sony's development engineers were doing their bit over the last few years, by perfecting the technological wizardry of compact digital discs, video cameras, and floppy disk systems, Mr. Kuroli's 130 strong design was injecting a rather different approach—what he calls "software thinking"—in order to come up with adventurous ideas about future social behaviour, and some appropriate new products.

Two Winners

Over the last three years, Mr. Kuroki has spawned two winners: The opulent "Profeel" component TV, in which the screen, receiver, tuner and speakers are spilt up from each other and the flat screen "Watchman portable".

The latter will prove the prime competitor with the "pocket" TV, which will be launched next week by Britain's Sinclair Research.

Since the launch of the "Watchman" in Japan early last year, Mr. Kuroki's team has gone on to design a tiny security camera that sees in the dark.

So, with several of the still-secret products in the pipeline, Sony's designers are fast becoming a rich fountain of innovation for the company to set alongside its traditional sources: The technology-driven work of its various development laboratories, and the fabled marketing flair of the company's cofounder and chairman, Mr. Akio Morita.

To Judge from some of Mr. Morita's public utterances, one might think he still saw design in conventional terms, as merely styling plus a bit of ergonomics. But he usually corrects himself with alacrity, emphasizing that Mr. Kuroki's group is now also responsible for developing entire product concepts.

Away from the glare of international publicity, he has given his designers an unusually high status. Mr. Kuroki is now the only department head reporting directly to Mr. Morita's deputy, Mr. Norio Ohga, who holds the title of president; the other report to the next level down.

Perhaps more significant in a culture where direct reporting lines are less significant than in the West, Mr. Kuroki also claims to be the only one who receives monthly visits from a delegation consisting of Mr. Morita, Mr. Ohga and rest of the company's top half-dozen executives.

With assiduous regularity, they troop down to Mr. Kuroki's office to inspect the designer's latest ideas.

Though some of Mr. Kuroki's projects—notably the Profeel—have had to be fought through against the opposition of other departments, especially production, his designers now have the clout to discuss, and if necessary argue, on a fairy equal basis with Sony's engineers.

In other Japanese consumer electronics companies, "design tends to be very heavily dominated by the technical division", claims Mr. Kuroki.

So it was at Sony until five years ago. In 1978 the company's designers were all still very much "part of the factory", as Mr. Kuroki puts it.

They worked under the thumb of engineers, salesman and short-term minded product planners.

But in June of that year Mr. Morita created a central design department, something Sony had not had since the 1960s, when it was very much smaller and less divisionalised.

More Staff

To head it, Mr. Morita drafted Mr. Yasuo Kuroki in from the top of the company's domestic advertising department. The majority of the designers retained their location in the divisions, but all became part of the new central department.

In the wake of the centralization, the overall complement of design staff was increased by a good half, to more than 100; the current total is 130, of whom 70 are design professionals, 20 of them working with Mr. Kuroki in Sony's Tokyo headquarters.

In a truly inscrutable Japanese style, Mr. Kuroki says there was "no specific reason" for this centralization: "Mr. Morita simply said 'Try it'."

Part of his motivation does indeed seem to have been the time-honoured Western principle that management structures ossify if they remain settled for too long.

But there were also more substantial reasons for elevating the influence and status of designers by pulling them together under a senior executive.

Most immediate and down-to-earth was the need to cope with the growing convergence of the previously distinct worlds of audio and video.

Before 1978 there was virtually no cross-fertilisation between designers in different parts of the company. They hardly ever had meetings and "there was very little mutual criticism", as Mr. Kuroki puts it.

Now there is intense interaction, with there tiers of formal weekly meetings involving the entire staff, and all sorts of informal communication as well.

More conceptually, Mr. Mortia was beginning to be aware of the need for Sony to develop a greater depth of understanding of social attitudes and behaviour, in order to develop the "software" aspects of its products.

Mr. Kuroki's use of the term has little to do with the narrow world of computer software. Instead, borrowing his terminology form J.K. Galbraith (one of the way Western influences on him and Mr. Mortia), he explains that "up to now Japan has only produced products, paying little attention to considerations of culture and lifestyle. We must change."

Sony's "feel" for how to mould the consumer has always been a key factor in its commercial success, form the transistor radio in the 1950s, through small black and white TVs in the 1960s, to VCRs and the Walkman in the 1970s, and now in the 1980 to Mr. Kuroki's two very different sort of TVs, the Profeel and the Watchman.

This knack will take on even greater competitive significance in the future.

It was to underline top management's changing view of design that the English little to Mr. Kuroki's department was changed, within six months of its creation in 1978, from "design division".

The utterly confusing replacement, "pp Centre", does not, as many outsiders have assumed, refer to "product planning"—within Sony this would be far too restrictive.

Investing

Instead, says Mr. Kuroki with vague sweep of his hand, it means "product presentation proposal, promotion—all those!".

Though Mr. Kuroki is not a believer in the common Western practice of creating multi-department "project teams" to surmount all the inter-departmental hurdles which tend to bedevil the development process, he does admit that even as entrepreneurial—yet consensus-minded a company as Sony is not free of such barriers.

So he is thinking of investing a small group of product "merchandisers" to track project right through from early planning into production, marketing and on into re-design.

Mr. Kuroki and his team scored an essential success by getting their product into the market first. Not only is Sony now further than competitor Sinclair down the so-called "experience curve" of low-cost, mass manufacture, but it has been able, as so often in its history, to create an innovative aura for a Sony product so that it can command a premium price.

QUESTIONS FOR DISCUSSION

1. Which elements of the 7-s framework can you identify in the case's description of event of Sony? Illustrate each element you recognise with quoted material from the case.
2. Are the 7-s' in harmony with each other? Suggest strategies by which this harmony can be maintained.

CASE STUDY 1.6
CUSTOMER COMFORTS LIMITED

'A glorious morning!' muttered Ms. Shakti Rohilla to herself as she arranged her agenda for the day. Ms. Rohilla was the newly appointed marketing manager of Customer Comforts Limited (CCL)—a Rs. 20 crore company in Bombay. First on her engagements for the day, she had a meeting with her Director (marketing) early in the morning. This meeting was to evaluate the initial thoughts of Ms. Rohilla on how to plan marketing efforts for 'waterbeds'—a major product developed recently by CCL.

Customer Comforts Limited (CCL) was set up about a quarter of century ago in New Delhi by Harjinder Singh to create and market a variety of inflatable products. The organisation manufactured rafts, boats life-jackets and collapsible containers for bulk storage purpose. It had acquired both quality image and customer satisfaction. Over the years, the only change that Mr. Singh had allowed in company philosophy was to innovate and add more vigorously to the consumer products in the inflatable category to meet new customer desires.

The waterbed was a major offering in the series by CCL in the middle of 1991 to Indian markets. The product had already been accepted to a large extent abroad and it was hoped that Indian consumers too will accept it.

The Waterbeds

Waterbeds are made of PVC with mattresses full of water. This water needs to be changed once in six months. In winter, if customers desired, the water could be heated to a require temperature.

Among the major benefits of waterbeds over the conventional beds and mattresses whether made of jutes, cotton, or foam, was that a waterbed applied equal pressure on every point in the body. This ensured its users a healthy and comfortable night's sleep. Ms. Rohilla believed that this benefit will be its chief attraction and needed to communicate this.

Further, the PVC used in marketing waterbeds was of high quality. They are sturdy enough as the in-house research and limited field experiments proved to withstand children romping on them. One could even stub a cigarette without springing a leak. Ms. Rohilla knew that this would be a major hurdle to cross as it would take some communication to convince customers. However, she felt confident that the benefit would reach customers.

The Marketing Effort

Ms. Rohilla was to design a comprehensive market plan for the waterbed. Before it, however, she consulted her Director (marketing) with her initial thoughts. The Director seemed to agree but asked her to marshall them in writing and discuss the same again that afternoon.

As she began, as if on cue, her study-room clock chimed. "Oh, nine-thirty! time to get ready for the office" said Ms. Rohilla and spurted out of her study.

(AIMA, June 1997)

QUESTIONS FOR DISCUSSION

1. How do you critically evaluate the opportunity as seen by CCL?
2. How do you prepare a plan for marketing waterbeds?

CASE STUDY 1.7
JOHNSON AND JOHNSON NEW LIFELINE FOR STRATEGY AND SUCCESS

It's all in the mind. Of the consumer who feels the need and of the marketer who taps into that need to come up with a product to satisfy it. It took strong competition through the early 90s to beat this realisation into Johnson and Johnson India.

J&J was lacklustre: corporate image, led by babycare products, was stable; product launches were few and far between. Till dramatically, Procter and Gamble grabbed J&J's leadership in the female sanitary protection category.

"Clearly, we had to start changing the formula and reinventing," says Shripad Nadkarni, vice president marketing. "It wasn't that competition did well, but that we did badly." J&J wasn't listening to consumers, you see. "We needed to get obsessed with consumer focus, on delivering value to them, which would take care of the competition." That's what J&J did, starting 1997. And now, "there's a new certainty about the company".

Raj Gupta, senior associate director, Lintas, expands, "The huge change in J&J today is in recognising the consumer need, gaining insight, and then manufacturing the product. The second big change is that it's far more entrepreneurial today. There is just a three-month lead-time from ideation to production. J&J's brand authority no longer comes from its technology, or know being a global brand. Insight, specially emotional, is a far superior platform. A competitor may better you on a functional insight, but with an intangible, emotional one he doesn't know what he's fighting."

Looking, at last, in the right direction, seems to have paid off. J&J has won back the volume crown from Procter and Gamble in the sanpro market. Its latest moving annual total volume share stands at 51 per cent against P and G's 38.6, though P and G is at 49 per cent of value share to J&J's 43.1 (ORG-MARG figures).

J&J's has also launched a slew of path breaking products over the last two years. Some of these have created new categories altogether. In doing so, its price platform has undergone a shift. Earlier, it sported a premium image. Post revamp, though, "while we are still premium with babycare, where costs are high, we use pricing as a tool to get to the mass market," says Nadkarni. "We're no longer looking at niches, but a value to consumer."

It's value to customer that saw the launch of Stayfree Secure, the Rs. 20 a pack sanitary napkin brand, in October 1997. "It made money for us." In fact, Nadkarni admits that Secure was the turning point in the mindset of the company. "We felt that if we can win against P and G, then we can win against anyone." Secure has picked up 20 per cent volume share of the sanpro market by now.

"Secure is a typically Indian product, and epitomises J&J today," says Gupta. "It was launched for the homemade napkin user who was conscious of the price and the family's prestige. So J&J turned the product proposition around from 'dry feel for me' to 'family prestige at stake'. That's what consumer insight is about."

From the sanpro success, the refocus has flowed on like a welcome flu bug to J&J's other products. The company feels it's a good development. "Focusing on the consumer is no longer just the concern of the marketing department, but of the company as a whole now," concludes Nadkarni.

(*Source:* Brand-equity, Sabiha Hussian)

QUESTIONS FOR DISCUSSION

1. "Marketers no more concentrate on selling the products but focus on value to the consumer." Elaborate.
2. What are the key issues in present one?

CASE STUDY 1.8
AMUL.COM

One day, e-Commerce may even become its bread-and-butter. The Gujarat Cooperative Milk Marketing Federation (GCMMF)—the marketing arm of the National Dairy Development Board—is the first food-products marketing organisation in the country to be e-Commerce enabled. Not only can customers buy products on amul.com the website also succeeds in productively using the Net to promote an endearing Indian brand. And the state-level apex body of milk cooperative in Gujarat—which markets fresh milk, dairy products, edible oils, and ice cream—has beaten transnational food companies to occupy the delicious first-mover position.

Cool as cheese? Cooperative affirms B.M. Vyas, the 49 years old Managing Director of GCMMF. "We are not a food company," he smiles. "We are an infotech company in the foods business." That infotech—and the Net—is underlying the new thinking at GCMMF is apparent from its early bird entry into the Net, in March, 1996. "Mass communication and transparency of operations are key factors in our kind of business." Say Vyas, "and the Net provides the perfect synergy to our business."

Indiaworld Communication Rajesh Jain, who is now better known as the man who sold a clutch of portals of Satyam online last year, agrees. In March 1996, GCMMF approached him to design the Amul Website. Avers Jain, 33: "GCMMF wanted a 6 month contract. This was unusual. "Used to selling Net-space for a week or a month at the maximum, Jain was impressed by GCMMF's long-term view. Says Jain: "We finalised the rates in less than 3 hours, and the Amul topical appeared the next day, just in time for the cricket World Cup semi-final, on the 'IndiaWorld' homepage."

Amui's e-gains

The Pay-offs

A database of 50,000 customer profiles, with buying-patterns and preferences.

Direct feedback from customers and other partners.

Expanded reach among customers not normally accessible.

The Constraints

Optimal delivery mechanism not yet in place for perishable product.

Difficult-to-e-tail limited range of products internal operations not yet Net-enabled.

"The decision to outsource the Website was deliberate," says R.S. Sodhi, 40, Head (Marketing) GCMMF. It was after all a specialised job for which the company did not have in-house skills. "And what is noteworthy is that the page has continuously evolved," he adds.

A Serving of Nostalgia

Taking Amul Topicals—Sylvester da Cunha's long running advertising campaign, featuring the Amul Moppet in a host of topical situations—global was the *raison d'être* of the Amul Website. To start with, GCMMF's goal was modest: reach out to Non-Resident Indians (NRIs). The pitch: nostalgia. Remember, Amul Topicals had been around since 1967. The hoarding were retrieved from the archives and placed on the Net.

Within hours, e-mail started pouring in form NRIs, who had suddenly discovered their roots. And, soon enough, the billboards were being updated every week at amul.com. Like most corporate Websites, amul.com outlines the story of the cooperative effort, gives a profile of the markets and products, and traces the history of the brand. **Spreading Into e-Commerce.** Realising that the site needed a bit more to draw in viewers, amul.com has introduced recipes of Indian dishers an a regular basis. Subsequently, interactivity was slowly built into the site. In August 1998, viewers of Amul *Surabhi*—the long-running weekly programme on Indian art and culture on Doordarshan—were asked to respond to posers at the end of the programme by e-mail. The winner got Amul gift hampers. The site draws up to 3,500 responses via e-mail per episode. And then, in keeping with its focus on cricket, the Amul Cricket Rankings were instituted. Here too, updated posers have been feeding a cricket-crazy audience.

Meanwhile, GCMMF was laying the foundation for e-Commerce. The first development—a comprehensive TQM programme—was initiated around the time amul.com was set up. Three years down the line, the movement—which was conducted in collaboration with Eicher Consultancy—had cascaded down to wholesales, who had been organised into specific Quality Circles. Which worked in tandem with the company's sales force. The domino effect had delivered a structure that had put the customer—both internal and external—of the core of all activities of GCMMF.

Then, in January 1998, the company put into place on Information Systems Technology Plan, whose aim was to make GCMMF a wired organisation that delivers real-time data online. At that stage, a tie-up with the National Informatics Centre was already in place, with a V-Sat connecting 12 member-dairies and 7 zonal offices in Gujarat to GCMMF's headquarters at Anand. The purpose of the 1st Plan was to align more closely, the needs of the business with Infotech, says S. Hegde, 37, GCMMFs head of Infotech. This was done in 3 ways:

Identification of critical business processes-being the marketing arm of NDBB, dispatch and logistics were, clearly, the core processes for the company.

Training workforce in handling real-time on line date.

Finally, apart from designing the hardware platform (a 256-MB Sun Enterprise Server) and the software applications (a customised enterprise-wide Integrated Application System, designed by TCS, with an Oracle Developer 200 front-end platform and sun Solaris & Novell Intranet/ Window NT at the back-end), GCMMF established security protocols and firewalls for the intranet. The latter linked all administrative and manufacturing units, as well as depots.

A Click of India. GCMMF was now ready to move into B2C e-Commerce. The first opportunity came in November, 1998, when it launched select Amul products in the US, in partnership with a US firm, Kanan Dairy Products Inc., NRIs in the US could now visit kanandairy.com to buy select products, like ghee, processed cheddar cheese, and dessert. And then, in June 1999, GCMMF launched a cyber-store for Indian Customers. Explains Vyas: "This was not only a logical extension of our success in the US market, but a logical step for word in our journey in cyberspace." Customers in 75 Indian cities can order the complete range of Amul products online. They have to pay cash on delivery, and have to order a minimum of Rs. 200 worth of products, which takes a couple of days to be delivered.

GCMMF says the e-Commerce component has been a grand success. Avers Jayen Mehta, 30, Marketing Manager, GCMMF: "We now have a database of 50,000 customers with profiles of their buying patterns and preferences. We can reach them for our new product launches even as we get direct feedback from them. The one-to-one communication has an emotive appeal at both ends, which enables us to develop relationship marketing.

And what of the existing distribution chain? To start with the retailer—there are about 5,00,000 of them all over the country—will not drive the e-Commerce initiative. In fact, the number of retail outlets is expected to double to 1 million by 2005. Traditional marketing channels are not going to die in a hurry. But it is the wholesaler who will drive the e-Commerce segment. The reason: all cyber-store orders will be executed by the Net savvy wholesale dealer. The incentive for the wholesaler to execute cyber-sales is that the retailer would normally be entitled to. It does pay to keep all channels happy. Of course, there are issues GCMMF has to tackle. For instance, it is yet to move into online supply and demand-chain management. But, within a year, it foresees dramatic improvements in cash flows, thanks to Net-based financial transactions. As of today, each wholesale distributor sends financial instruments through courier, and it takes nearly a fortnight for sale proceeds to be credited. "Net banking will reduce it to a single day," claims Sodhi.

Then, the delivery mechanism—currently courier—has to improve as the product is, after all, perishable. The company is yet to use the Net to know which SKU is moving faster in the market and, therefore, needs faster replenishment and which SKU is stagnating and, hence, needs to be taken off the shelves. When the company is fully into e-chain management, the information gap will be reduced form 6 weeks to 1 day. "It will enable us to decide quickly on a product mix that would ensure continuous growth for the company and faster movement of tonnage," says Sodhi. Clearly, for Amul, it is just the beginning of a long and finger-licking journey on the Net.

QUESTIONS FOR DISCUSSION

1. Do you think it was a wise decision for Amul to make a foray into e-Commerce? Conduct a SWOT analysis to illustrate your answer.

2. What strategies have been used to drive traffic to the site and to build the online brand?

(AIMA, 2002)

CASE STUDY 1.9
MERCEDES-BENZ USA: CUSTOMER SATISFACTION THROUGH VALUE

In the fall of 1998, Chrysler and Mercedes-Benz merged. Forming Daimler-Chrysler AG. Daimler-Chrysler is the world's third largest car maker in sales and world's fifth largest car maker in the number of cars sold, Daimler-Benz, best known for making luxury sedans, also makes commercial vehicles, sport utility vehicles, and aerospace products. Today Mercedes-Benz USA is a wholly owned subsidiary of Daimler-Chrysler.

Mercedes-Benz cars, which are manufactured in Germany, were first sold in the United States in the 1950s. Mercedes-Benz's strategy in the United States has always been to market premium automobiles. During the 1970s and 1980s, Mercedes-Benz engineers built the best cars they could. They set a premium price tag in the products and for years that was how prices of cars in the United States were established.

When Japanese automobiles Lexus and Infiniti were introduced into the US market, Mercedes-Benz found itself facing increased competition. Lexus and Infiniti, along with a resurgent BMW, elected to compete with Mercedes-Benz by offering comparable quality, at lower prices. These marketing strategies had an impact on Mercedes-Benz business. To combat the increased competition, dealers in the United States became focussed on marketing efforts that would maximize customer satisfaction.

Mercedes-Benz's US strategy for customer satisfaction is based on what it calls a Customer Value Triad. The Customer Value Triad consists of: (1) perceived goods quality; (2) service quality; and (3) value-based prices.

QUESTIONS FOR DISCUSSION

1. Based on the information provided in the case, evaluate Mercedes-Benz's internal strengths and weaknesses and external opportunities and threats (SWOT analysis} when the Lexus and Infiniti automobiles were introduced.
2. What role customer expectations have in a customer's satisfaction with a Mercedes-Benz automobile? How might a company like Mercedes-Benz plan each element of the Customer Value Triad, so that each would help the company to exceed customer expectation?
3. What is the relationship between price and value in the purchase of Mercedes-Benz?

(AIMA, 2001)

CASE STUDY 1.10
AUTOMATIC CITATION ISSURANCE SYSTEM (AUTOCITE)

Etec was founded by an inventor and a former police officer. The company markets AutoCite, which is short for Automatic Citation Issurance System. Using this along with computer and printing device, a police officer can write and record traffic violations much more efficiently. Today AutoCite is used by police departments in more than 350 cities and college campuses. However, Etec sold only three units in its first two years of operation.

AutoCite is durable and works in all types of weather. A police officer who gives multiple tickets in a given location does not have to reprogramme location information into the AutoCite. This allows the officer to produce more tickets in a given time period.

QUESTIONS FOR DISCUSSION

1. How important are customer services and customer training for a period such as AutoCite?
2. In what stage of the product life cycle is AutoCite?
3. Products in the electronics industry often become obsolete because of new technology? How should AutoCite's marketing strategy deal with the issue of obsolescence?

(AIMA, 2001)

MARKETING ENVIRONMENT FOR STRATEGIST

2

The Strategic Marketing Environment is more important to management today than ever before. This is both because the *rate* of environmental change has increased and because there are more *types* of important environmental changes.

First, consider the rate of environmental change. It should be remembered that all of the development experienced by humankind has occurred within a mere moment of history. If we were to equate the earth's history to the distance around the world, the last 50 years, the period of most rapid development, would equal only one foot. Yet an unprecedented acceleration in environmental change occurred during that brief period and people today are experiencing a unique chapter in human history.

In addition, new *types* of environmental change have come to the forefront. Economic factors go core of business activity, and historically they have always been important to Strategic Marketing Management. Until around 1900, such factors effectively represented the firm's entire macro-environment. At the turn of the century, however, governmental and legal forces became more significant, as evidenced by anti-trust legislation. The significance of government has grown greatly over the past few decades. Even the recent deregulation of selected industries has meant turbulent times for the companies involved.

Characteristics of the Strategic Marketing Environment

The environment of anything is as large or small, and as simple or complex, as one's definition of it. Changing consumer incomes, technological innovation, changing government agencies, and shifting consumer values are examples of the strategic marketing environment. This environment includes those things that are external, largely uncontrollable, changing, constraining, and potentially relevant. The Strategic Marketing environment includes non-Strategic Marketing departments within the firm, as well as markets, competitors, and the macro-environment.

Marketers are primarily adapters. They adapt their products, prices, promotion, and distribution to fit the marketplace, as was true for the auto industry during the energy crisis. Certain environmental forces are partially controllable, but most are largely uncontrollable. Some *changes* in environmental factors, such as shifting population characteristics, represent a key source of uncertainty. Other changes constrain management to the extent of defining a straight and narrow path for it. The Flammable Fabrics Act, for example, imposes constraints on the product decisions of apparel marketers. The Strategic Marketing environment must be *potentially relevant* to Strategic Marketing decision-making in the organisation. The potentially relevant environment for an electronic calculator firm is very different from that for a soap producer.

Perhaps the most important aspect of the intra-organisation environment is the internal corporate culture, or "the collection of beliefs, expectations, and values shared by the corporation members and transmitted from one generation of employees to another". Leading companies seem to exhibit a relatively open, creative, and adaptive corporate culture. A more entrepreneurial corporate culture, popularised by the best seller. *In Search of Excellence*, has been fostered by such companies as General Electric. Achieving such a culture is a delicate and difficult task. AT&T Information Systems, in contrast, shuffled an innovative vice president for Strategic Marketing into a staff position, despite the VP's impressive sales and profit record. His 'style' was apparently too radical for the entrenched culture.

NEED FOR ENVIRONMENTAL ANALYSIS

Environmental analysis attempts to give an extensive insight as to the current market conditions as well as of impact of external factors that are uncontrollable by the marketers. These variables play an important role in convincing potential customers regarding changes in market trends, market conditions, etc.

In analysing the environment, Johnson and Scholes suggested five stages of environmental analysis which are as given below:

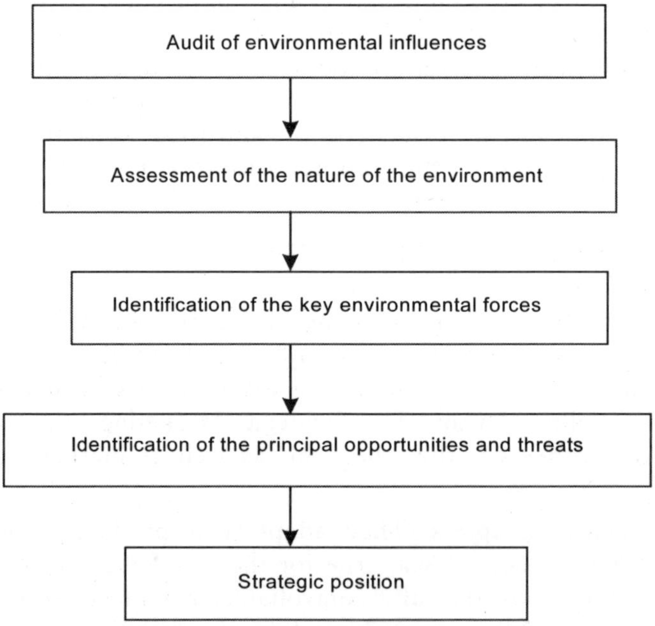

Fig. 2.1: Five Stages of Environmental Analysis

Source: Adapted from Johnson and Scholes (1988), p. 54.

After environmental analysis, the marketer has to handle the different environmental conditions. For doing so, Johnson and Scholes suggested the following model:

Table 2.1: Model for Handling Environmental Conditions

	Conditions		
	Simple/Static	Dynamic	Complex
Aims	To achieve through historical understanding of the environment.	To understand the future rather than simply relying on past experiences.	The reduction of complexity. Greater structural understanding.
Methods	Analysis of past influences and their effect on organisational performance. Identification of key forces. Analysis of existing relationships.	Manager's sensitivity to change. Scenario planning. Contingency planning. Sensitivity planning.	Specialist attention to elements of complexity. Model building.
Dangers	The sudden emergence of unpredicted change. Mechanistic organisational structures. Lack of skills. Focus on existing relationships. Lack of willingness to accept that conditions are changing. Stereotypes responses.	Management myopia. Mechanistic organisational structures. Lack of skills. Inappropriate forecasting. Failure to recognise significant new players.	Unsuitable organisational structure of control systems. Innapropriate reactions. Inappropriate focuses. Overreaction.

Source: Adapted from Johnson and Scholes (1988), *op. cit.*

NATURE OF THE STRATEGIC MARKETING ENVIRONMENT

The Strategic Marketing environment has been defined in a variety of ways. According to Philip Kotler, the company's Strategic Marketing environment is made up of the sectors and forces outside the firm's Strategic Marketing function which infringe upon the ability of Strategic Marketing management to develop and maintain a successful relationship with the firm's target audience. Within the environment there are two distinct components; the micro-environment and the macro-environment. This is explained in the Fig. 2.2 following.

Fundamental Shift in Indian Marketing

1. Rapid growth of services Industries,
2. Emergence of organised Retailing,
3. Potential growth in rural India,
4. Rise of Demanding new products/services Consumers,
5. India getting globally integrated, and
6. Technology advancements.

Types of Strategic Marketing Environment

Strategic Marketing environment may broadly be classified into: (1) Economic environment, (2) Demographic environment, (3) Socio-cultural environment, (4) Technological environment, (5) Political environment, and (6) Legal environment.

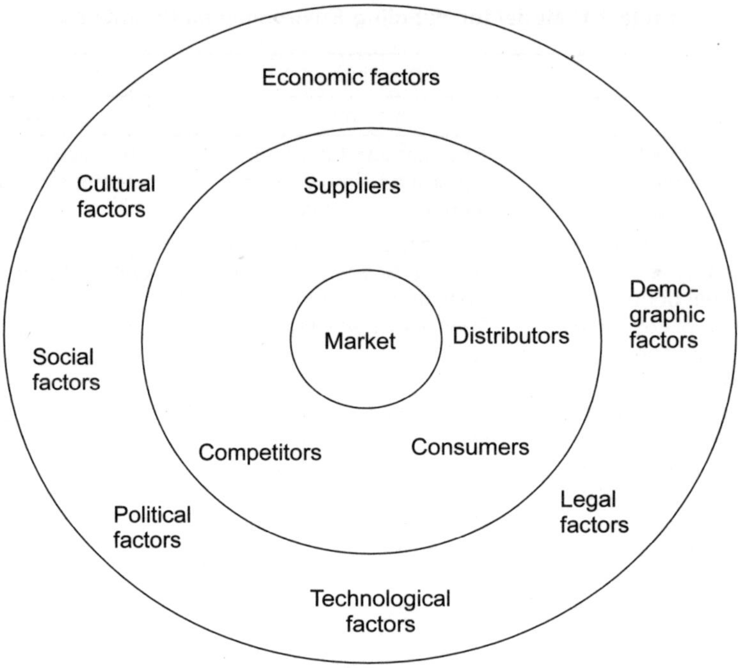

Fig. 2.2

1. Economic environment

Economic environment is the most significant component of the Strategic Marketing environment. It affects the survival of a business organisation as well as its success. The economic environmental forces can be studied into three broad categories: (a) General economic conditions, (b) Industrial conditions, and (c) State of supply of resources for production.

(a) **General Economic Conditions.** General economic conditions in a country are influenced by various factors. The following factors are important:

(i) Agricultural trends,
(ii) Industrial output trends,
(iii) Per capita income trends,
(iv) Pattern of income distribution,
(v) Pattern of savings and expenditures,
(vi) Price levels,
(vii) Employment trends,
(viii) Impact of government policies, and
(ix) Economic systems.

(b) **Industrial Conditions.** Economic environment of a country is influenced by the prevalent industrial conditions as well as industrial policies of a country. A marketer needs to pay attention to the following aspects of the industrial conditions:

(i) Market growth of the industry,
(ii) Demand patterns of the industry, and
(iii) Its stage in product life cycle.

(c) **State of Supply of Resources for Production.** Supply of resources required for production determines inputs which are available for production. These are the most important resources required for production:
(i) Land,
(ii) Labour,
(iii) Capital,
(iv) Machinery and equipment, and
(v) Managers.

The above stated environmental forces determine the economic environment of a country. The statement (Table 2.2) provides various statistical indicators of a country's economic goals.

To sum up, economic environment describes the overall economic situation in a country and helps in analysing GNP per capita, rate of economic growth, inflation rate, interest rates, unemployment problems, etc. Therefore, it is necessary to examine carefully the economic environment of the country.

2. Demographic environment

Demographic environment explains the pattern and changes in the society based on age, sex, educational background, marital status, family size, family life style, religion, nationality, etc.

Demographic environment is useful for Strategic Marketing decisions, market segmentation and formulation of Strategic Marketing strategies. A knowledge of the demographic environment is very important to a marketer for performance of his functions. People constitute the market and market depends on customers. Demography provides quantitative as well as qualitative aspects of population. It is also helpful in behavioural analysis of population.

Table 2.2: Statistical Indicators of Economic Goals

	Economic Goal	Statistical Indicator
1.	High level of aggregate output and income	GNP, GDP
2.	Rapid growth of income	Average annual rates of growth of GNP, GDP
3.	Greater equality in income distribution	Gini coefficient
4.	More productive employment	Distribution of labour force by industrial and occupational classification and income
5.	Lower international dependence	Foreign trade and international payments proportions in total output
6.	Price stability	Price indexes
7.	Greater regional balance	Gross regional product per capita

Source: Adapted from David P. Loucks, "Planning for Multiple Goals" in C. Blitzer, P. Clark and L. Taylor (eds.) *Economywide Models and Development Planning* (OUP, London, 1975), p. 214.

3. Socio-cultural environment

The social environment of a nation determines the value system of the society which 'in turn' affects the Strategic Marketing of products. Social factors are caste, customs, conventions, cultural heritage and respect for seniority, etc. For example, the nature of goods and services in demand depends upon people's attitudes, customs, social values, etc. In India, social environment is continuously changing.

One of the most profound social changes in recent years is the large number of women entering the job market. It affected the hiring and compensation policies and resource capabilities of firms employing them. They have also created or greatly expanded the demand for a wide range of products and services necessitated by their absence from the home. There is a lot of change in quality of lifestyles and people are willing to have many durable consumer goods like T.V., fridge and washing machines even when they cannot afford them because of their availability on hire-purchase or installment basis. One more change in social environment is the shift in national age distribution. Changing social values and increased acceptance of improved birth control methods have resulted in a rise in the mean age of various countries. To sum up, we can say that social environment has the following dimensions:

— Changes in people's lifestyles,

— Concerns for social problems, and

— Growth of consumerism.

Culture influences every aspect of Strategic Marketing. Strategic Marketing decisions are based on recognition of needs and wants of the customer, a function of customer perceptions. These help in understanding of lifestyles and behaviour patterns as they have grown in the society's culture in which the individual has been groomed. Thus a person's perspective is generated, groomed and conditioned by culture.

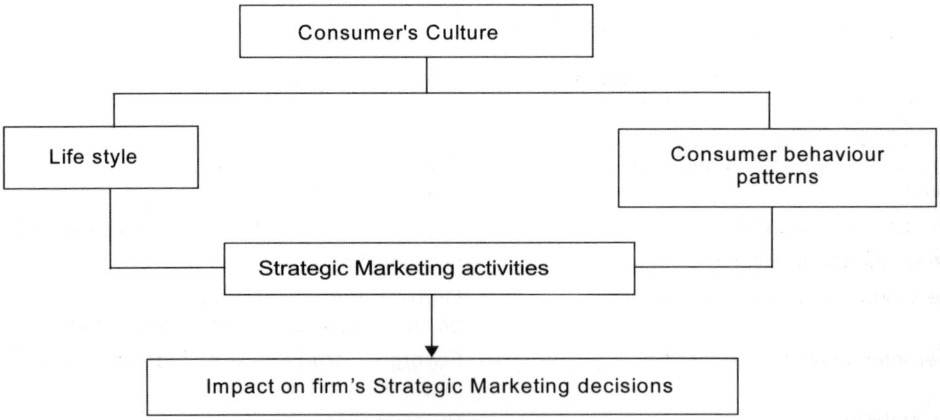

Fig. 2.3: Impact of Culture on Strategic Marketing Decisions

4. Technological environment

Technological environment provides both opportunities and threats, and its impact is direct as well as indirect. Kotler suggests that the aspects to which a Strategic Marketing planner should pay attention include:

— High expenditure on research and development,

— Concentration on product improvement and development,

— Unlimited innovations in technology,

— Accelerating pace of technological change, and

— Greater emphasis upon the regulation of technological change.

Advances in technology are difficult to predict. However, the marketer should consider potential, technological developments determined from resources committed by major industries or the government. Being in a market that is rapidly changing due to technological development, will require the marketer to make careful short-term Strategic Marketing decisions as well as being prepared with contingency plans given any new technological developments that may affect product or services.

Technological environment in India is guided by technology policy which is framed by the Government of India and is updated from time to time. We should understand the salient features of technology policy as detailed below:

The new economic and technology policy comprises the various policy measures and changes introduced since July 1991. The objective of these measures it to improve the overall technology and economic system. The new policy provides for imports of technology and facilitates substantial exports. It requires upgradation of technology and facilitates substantial exports. It requires upgradation of technology through domestic R&D efforts for improvement of overall quality. In the new policy, the following items are discussed broadly:

— Selecting the few areas where we would concentrate on research in terms of breakthrough.

— In other areas, we need more open systems to assimilate the great advances being made.

— Technology is genuinely an area of planning initiatives and India cannot afford to neglect this aspect.

From the above discussion, it can be concluded that it is possible for India to catch up with other developed countries only by technological advancements.

5. Political environment

Strategic Marketing decisions are strongly affected by development in the political environment. A marketer has to operate his business in a given political environment and his operations are affected in greater or less degree by government programmes at different levels. Changes in political climate lead to changes in government policies. Political changes may take the following forms:

(1) Stable governments leading to very few policy changes,

(2) Frequent changes in government leading to frequent changes in policies, and

(3) Cyclical changes.

Political factors play a major role in shaping the environment in which business organisations operate. Thus a business organisation has to attempt to study and analyse political environment. Such a study and analysis help in estimating risks, opportunities and threats involved, and then adjusting their decisions and operations to anticipated changes.

To conclude, the various political factors that a marketer should consider are:

(a) Role of private sector in the economy;

(b) Government procedures and changes in government policy;

(c) Type of government and stability in government;

(d) Role of small-scale industry in the economy; and

(e) Role of service sector in the economy.

6. Legal environment

Strategic Marketing decisions are strongly affected by laws pertaining to competition, price setting, distribution arrangements, advertising, etc. It is necessary for a marketer to understand the legal environment of the country and the jurisdiction of its courts. The following laws affecting business in India are important:

1. Indian Contract Act, 1872
2. Factories Act, 1948
3. Minimum Wages Act, 1948
4. Essential Commodities Act, 1955
5. Securities Contract Regulation Act, 1956 (Now replaced by SEBI Act)
6. The Companies Act, 1956
7. Trade and Merchandise Marks Act, 1958
8. Monopolies and Restrictive Trade Practices Act, 1969
9. The Water (Prevention and Control of Pollution) Act, 1974
10. The Air (Prevention and Control of Pollution) Act, 1981
11. Sick Industrial Companies (Special Provisions) Act, 1985
12. Environment Protection Act, 1986
13. Consumer Protection Act, 1986
14. Securities and Exchange Board of India (SEBI) Act, 1992
15. Taxation Laws (covering Corporate Tax, Indirect Taxes like Excise, Customs, Sales Tax and Wealth Tax).

SWOT Analysis

- Strengths
- Weaknesses
- Opportunities
- Threats

The purpose of SWOT analysis

- It is an easy-to-use tool for developing an overview of a company's strategic situation.
  - It forms a basis for matching your company's strategy to its situation.

SWOT is the starting point

- It provides an overview of the strategic situation.
- It provides the "raw material" to do more extensive internal and external analysis.

Opportunities

- An OPPORTUNITY is a chance for firm growth or progress due to a favourable juncture of circumstances in the business environment.
- Possible Opportunities:
  - Emerging customer needs
  - Quality Improvements
  - Expanding global markets
  - Vertical Integration.

Components of the General Environment

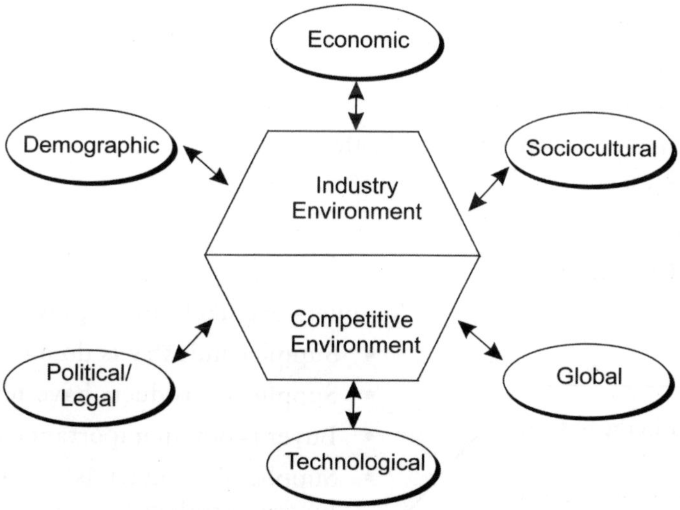

Threats

- A THREAT is a factor in your company's external environment that poses a danger to its well-being.
- Possible Threats:
  - New entry by competitors
  - Changing demographics/shifting demand
  - Emergence of cheaper technologies
  - Regulatory requirements.

Opportunities and Threats form a basis of EXTERNAL analysis

- By examining opportunities, you can discover untapped markets, and new products or technologies, or identify potential avenues for diversification.
- By examining threats, you can identify unfavourable market shifts or changes in technology, and create a defensive posture aimed at preserving your competitive position.

The purpose of five-forces analysis

- The five forces are environmental forces that impact on a company's ability to compete in a given market.
- The purpose of five-forces analysis is to diagnose the principal competitive pressures in a market and assess how strong and important each one is.

PORTER'S FIVE FORCES MODEL OF COMPETITION

Threat of New Entrants

- Economies of Scale
- Product Differentiation
- Capital Requirements
- Switching Costs
- Access to Distribution Channels
- Cost Disadvantages Independent of Scale
- Government Policy
- *Expected Retaliation*

Bargaining Power of Suppliers

Suppliers exert power in the industry by:

- Threatening to raise prices or to reduce quality

  Powerful suppliers can squeeze industry profitability if firms are unable to recover cost increases

Suppliers are likely to be powerful if:

- Supplier industry is dominated by a few firms
- Suppliers' products have few substitutes
- Buyer is not an important customer to supplier
- Suppliers' product is an important input to buyers' product
- Suppliers' products are differentiated
- Suppliers' products have high switching costs
- Supplier poses credible threat of forward integration

Bargaining Power of Buyers

Buyer groups are likely to be powerful if:

- Buyers are concentrated or purchases are large relative to seller's sales
- Purchase accounts for a significant fraction of supplier's sales
- Products are undifferentiated
- Buyers face few switching costs
- Buyers' industry earns low profits
- Buyer presents a credible threat of backward integration
- Product unimportant to quality
- Buyer has full information

Buyers complete with the supplying industry by:

- Bargaining down prices
  - Forcing higher quality
    - Playing firms off of each other

Threat of Substitute Products

Products with similar *function* limit the prices firms can charge

Keys to evaluate substitute products:

Products with improving price/performance tradeoffs relative to present industry products

Example:

- Electronic security systems in place of security guards
- Fax machines in place of overnight mail delivery

Porter's Five Forces Model of Competition

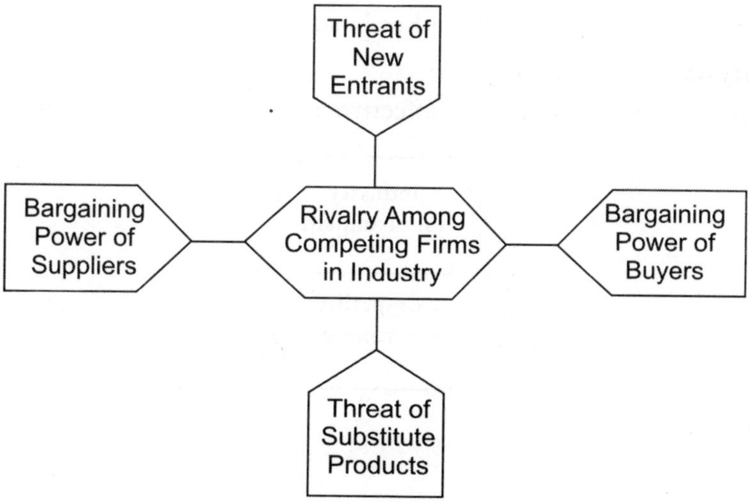

Rivalry Among Existing Competitors

Intense rivalry often plays out in the following ways:

- Jockeying for strategic position
- Using price competition
- Staging advertising battles
- Increasing consumer warranties or service
- Making new product introductions.

Occurs when a firm is pressured or sees an opportunity

- Price competition often leaves the entire industry worse off
- Advertising battles may increase total industry demand, but may be costly to smaller competitors.

Cutthroat competition is more likely to occur when:

- Numerous or equally balanced competitors
- Slow growth industry
- High fixes costs
- High storage costs
- Lack of differentiation or switching costs
- Capacity added in large increments
- Diverse competitors
- High strategic stakes
- High exit barriers.

The Five Forces are Unique to Your Industry

- Five-Forces Analysis is a framework for analyzing a particular industry.
- Yet, the five forces affect all the other businesses in that industry.

Competitor Analysis

The follow-up to Industry Analysis is effective analysis of a firm's *Competitors*

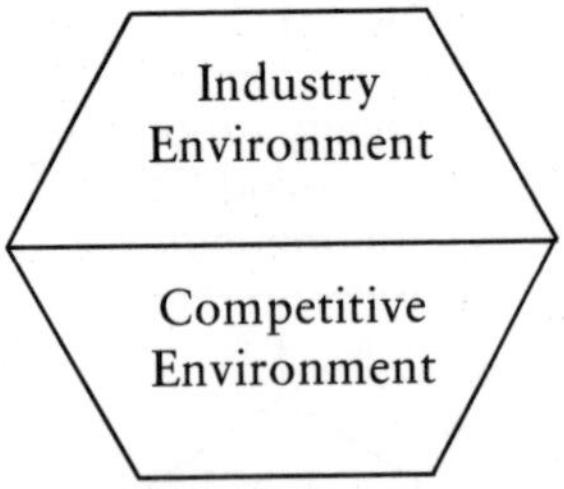

Assumptions

What assumptions do our competitors hold about the future of industry and themselves?

Current Strategy

Does our current strategy support changes in the competitive environment?

Future Objectives

How do our goals compare to our competitors' goals?

Capabilities

How do our capabilities compare to our competitors?

Response

- What will our competitors do in the future?
- Where do we have a competitive advantage?
- How will this change our relationship with our competition?

Future Objectives

- How do our goals compare to our competitors' goals?
- Where will emphasis be placed in the future?
- What is the attitude toward risk?

What Drives the competitor?

Current Strategy

- How are we currently competing?
- Does this strategy support changes in the competitive structure?

What is the competitor doing?
What can be competitor do?

Assumptions

- Do we assume the future will be volatile?
- What assumptions do our competitors hold about the industry and themselves?
- Are we assuming stable competitive conditions?

What does the competitor believe about itself and the industry?

Capabilities

- What are my competitors' strengths and weaknesses?
- How do our capabilities compare to our competitors?

What are the competitor's capabilities?

QUESTIONS FOR DISCUSSION

1. What are the factors that influence the Strategic Marketing environment of an organisation?
2. Explain in brief the various types of Strategic Marketing environment. Give the salient features of each.
3. "The Indian market is gradually becoming consumer-oriented." Discuss the statement with reference to consumerism.
4. What is consumerism? What are the various rights of consumers? Discuss the causes of the growth of consumer movement in India.
5. Explain the meaning of consumerism. How would you evolve Strategic Marketing strategies to meet consumerism?
6. Do you agree that "Consumer and the business environment are mutually inclusive; one cannot exist without the other? Explain with suitable examples.
7. What is "PEST (political, economic, social and technological) method of environmental scanning? Explain the utility of product life cycle concept for technological environmental scanning.
8. What can be the possible ramifications of a change in government's fiscal and economic policies on the Strategic Marketing environment? Support your answer with reference to India.
9. "Marketer has to be more aware of changes in the external environment than any other department in the organisation." Do you agree? Elucidate.

CASE STUDY 2.1
USING THE WEB FOR ELECTRONIC COMMERCE

After deciding that its extranet and private World Wide Web site for large corporate customers was a success, $6.7 billion Office Depot, Inc., launched a public version that targets small and at-home businesses.

The new Web site ties a Web browser application with the Company's inventory and ordering systems and conducts real time warehouse checks to ensure stock is available nearby. The site, at www.officedepot.com. also verifies addresses and credit cards on the fly.

"What they've created seems to be a highly integrated website, leveraging their sales delivery systems," said Gregory Wester, research director at The Yankee Group, in Boston.

Office Depot, in Delray Beach, Florida, won't disclose how much it is spending on its new Internet storefront. But savings could be substantial if customers move online: Processing an electronic order costs about 10 per cent of the cost of a telephone order, said Paul Gaffney, senior vice-president of systems development.

The new website is taking advantage of tens of millions of dollars the company have invested in its computing and telecommunications systems, he said. "It's an incremental investment", Gaffney said. Issues of how to integrate a web interface with back-end systems were hashed out a year and a half ago when the private website was launched.

The site is using Microsoft Internet Information Server and Commerce Server software on a 12-processor IBM AS/400 messaging and ordering system and an IBM mainframe center for delivery data. The company uses its own trucks and drivers for nationwide shipping.

Office Depot outsourced the design of the site to Studio Verso, in San Francisco, after determining it didn't have the expertise to do the work in-house. Studio Verso developed the look, selected art elements and fonts, and determined web-specific issues such as how much information to put on one page and how to make it easy for customers to find what they want.

The website allows users to find specific products by keyword or numbers as well as by browsing the catalogue. It uses characters from the popular Dilbert comic strip to keep surfers interested. Office Depot tested initial concepts with focus groups, said Beth Van Story, vice-president of Office Depot Online, in San Francisco.

Although it may seem late to establish a consumer website for business machines and office supplies, Wester said he believes Office Depot's marketing muscle carries enough weight to make up for the timing. Office Depot said it is first in the fragmented office supply market, with about a 4 per cent share. "There's no such thing as being late when you're carrying a big brand name." Wester said.

QUESTIONS FOR DISCUSSION

1. What business benefits does Office Depot hope to gain with their new Web site?
2. Was their delayed entry into public electronic commerce a good business decision? Why or why not?
3. Visit the office depot. Com Web site. Did Studio Verso and Office Depot do a good job of Web site development? Why or Why not?

Source: Adapted from Sharon Machlis, "Office Store Site Goes Public." Computer World. January 26, 1998, pp. 47-48. Copyright 1998 by Computer World Inc., Framigham, MA 01701, Reprinted from computer World.

CASE STUDY 2.2
USING THE INTERNET AS A VIRTUAL PRIVATE NETWORK

Sandal, shoe, and bootmaker Deckers Outdoor Corporation recently switched to an Internet Networking technology called virtual private network to interconnect their global company.

Virtual private networks (VPNs) use the power of the Internet instead of using private telecommunications lines or other network links. A virtual private network is a secure and encrypted connection between two points across the Internet. It transfers information by encrypting and encapsulating telecommunications traffic in to packets and sending the packets over the Internet. Most VPNs are built and run by Internet service providers. Companies that go with a VPNs from an Internet service provider essentially outsource their networks to a save money on having to acquire and manage their own wide area network equipment and bandwidth requirements.

Deckers is a $100 million company whose 20 person office in Hoek Van Holland, the Netherlands, collaborates on products development with its staff in Goleta, California. The

VPN costs roughly $31,000 to implement and saves Deckers $10,000 per month compared with leasing their previous high-speed network connections.

"We needed a network that would serve as the foundation for our international expansion," says Steve Miley, MIS director at Deckers. "It will be critical...because our offices will use it to make sure projects are done on time."

Employees at the two sites use the VPN to update the status of product development projects through Lotus Notes groupware databases. The VPN supports Note's ability to replicate databases of projects information at each work site, which is crucial to groupware support of project team collaboration.

VPN performance "is slow but workable for interactive Notes database access", Miley says. And as the quality of Internet service improves, VPN performance can only improve, he adds.

Security, a reported shortcoming of virtual networks, is improved with Net Fortress software from Fortress Technologies. It automatically changes encryption keys every 24 hours. "We feel very secure with their products on our network," he says.

Offices for production management in Hong Kong, Mexico, and Macao will be added to the VPN this year. Miley says. Those sites currently use expensive international telephone calls to access servers in Goleta. Desktop video conferencing over the VPN, to cut international travel costs, is also planned.

Deckers doesn't mind being among the first to implement a virtual private network. "VPNs are here to stay," Miley says. And we are on the leading edge, not the bleeding edge.

QUESTIONS FOR DISCUSSION

1. What are the business benefits of Decker's switch to a virtual private network?
2. What can be done to overcome several limitation of virtual private networks?
3. Does it make business sense for any company to use the Internet as their private telecommunications network? Why or Why not.

Source: Adapted from Bob Wallance, "Onsite: Remote Users to Make Gains with New Network." Computer World February 2, 1988, p. 28. Copyright 1988 by Computer World Inc., Framigham, MA 01701, Reprinted from Computer World.

CASE STUDY 2.3
DOW CHEMICAL CO. (AD)

Dow Chemical Company is one of the larger chemical companies in the United States, making a diversified line of organic and inorganic chemicals, plastics, by-products, and metals. Research has played a vital role in the company's growth. Recently, Dow's research laboratories developed a new product in the antifreeze line—Dowtherm 209. Much research was devoted to the technical phase, involving various experiments concerned with the quality of the components in the new product.

The antifreeze commonly used now is ethylene glycol. If it leaks into the crankcase oil, it forms a thick pasty sludge that can produce baring damage, cylinder scoring, or a dozen other costly and time-consuming troubles for both the operator and owner heavy-duty equipment.

Dowtherm 209 has been proven in the laboratory to prevent seizing of rod and main bearings, pistons, rights, and piston pins, which are common with glycol leakage. The new product will not remain in the engine oil and will cut down on the sludge residue. At first, Dow thought it had two attractive markets for the product: (1) the manufacturers of heavy-duty equipment, and (2) the users of heavy-duty equipment. Dow salesmen have made numerous calls and so far neither type of customer has been found to be very interested. The manufacturers are reluctant to show interest in the product until it has been proven in actual use. The buyers for construction companies and other firms using heavy-duty equipment have also been hesitant. Some felt the price was far too high for the advantage offered. Others didn't understand what was wrong with the present antifreeze and dismissed the idea of paying extra for 'just another' antifreeze.

The price Dowtherm 209 is $7.98 per gallon, which is more than twice the price of regular antifreeze. The higher price is a result of higher costs in producing the product and an investment for making a better type of antifreeze.

QUESTIONS FOR DISCUSSION

1. Explain what has happened so far.
2. What would you do if you were responsible for this product?

CASE STUDY 2.4
MARKETING ACROSS BOUNDARIES

F. Rozen, President of the Best Frozen Foods Company, was reviewing the latest sales figure for his company. He noticed that the greatest profit margins came from sales in the military commissary system in Europe. The commissaries are essentially no frill American type supermarkets that sell grocery products that Americans want and need. The commissary system encompasses food stores run by Americans Army to serve military soldiers assigned to Europe. Most of the commissaries and the personnel are located in Germany. Only military and American civilians connected with U.S. government and their dependents can shop at these stores.

F. Rozen called his vice-president, N.E.W. Market, into his office and said "Our frozen foods are making profits in the German commissaries, especially without giant-size meals. As in America, our frozen corn is the best seller. Family meals with corn as a vegetable are outselling meals that have vegetables other than corn. Sales of frozen of corn have exceeded our highest expectations. I remember that when I was with the American Army in Germany, you could not get frozen food. This will make a great market for us to expand our frozen food line. Since then our warehouse and transportation network have been established and the additional distribution costs are negligible.

Whenever expanding our market area, we have used a massive television campaign, going with a successful theme "Better than Fresh". Since the German population drinks a lot of beer, let us use local actors drinking a cold beer while eating a meal. I want you to go to Germany, get the shelf space, arrange the television advertising, promotion, and everything else involved in introducing the frozen food line in Germany. The food will be shipped next week and will be available for shipment to the stores in three months.

"In the U.S., refrigerators are large and have very large freezing compartments. Many Americans even own separate freezes. The typical German refrigerator is smaller and there is little room for frozen food. Germans are not used to frozen foods and even drink their beer warm. You have to request for ice in the restaurant. There are many food stands in front of grocery stores that sell sausages and french fries. Grocery stores sell plenty of fresh meat, fish, cheese, etc. There is plenty of help in the shops who give out samples and conduct demonstration. But there is little refrigerator or freezer space.

"I showed the package to potential customers. We had forgotten to print instructions in German. Most packaging is printed in four or five languages, including German, English, French and Spanish. People said they could not follow the English instruction on our package. They were also not sure how large a pound or ounce was."

"Their product also noted some advertising problems. A major problem exists with television advertising. The only advertising occurs between 6.30 and 7.00 p.m. There is an all advertising show that is one of the most popular shows: but to get space you have to bid for it at least 18 months in advance. There is no guarantee when the commercial will be shown. Comparative advertising is banned. The food industry will not let us use the theme better than fresh. This is considered derogatory to the fresh food industry.

"I cannot find shelf space for our product. Stores do not have freezer space, nor do they want an untried product. Please advise what action should I take. What should I do with the product which is arriving?"

QUESTIONS FOR DISCUSSION

1. Summarise the problems involved in marketing frozen foods in Germany.
2. What should F. Rozen advise N.E.W. Market to do?
3. Should the product be introduced? What suggestions would you have if the product is introduced?

STRATEGIC MARKETING MIX

3

The basic task of the strategic marketing manager is the successful management of the Strategic Marketing mix. Success means that the customer is satisfied and that the organisation's resources are effectively deployed to that end.

Strategic marketing mix is the set of controllable variables and their levels that the firm uses to influence its target market. McCarthy popularised a four-factor classification of these tools called the four Ps: product, price, place and promotion.

Product	—	What decisions relate to product or service range.
Price	—	What price should be set for each product/service.
Place	—	Identification and selection of channels for distribution and deciding what levels of service are appropriate thus defining the logistics involved.
Promotion	—	How to communicate with the target market and persuade the people concerned to buy.

The concept of the strategic marketing mix is a schematic plan to guide analysis of Strategic Marketing problems through utilisation of:

(a) A list of important forces emanating from the market which bear upon the strategic marketing operations of the enterprise; and

(b) A list of elements (procedures and policies) of strategic marketing programmes.

MARKETING SITUATION ANALYSIS

A marketing situation analysis helps management design a new strategy or change the existing strategy. The strategy is being implemented, a marketing situation analysis is conducted on a regular basis to guide strategy changes.

A market situation analysis involves three activities: Market Analysis, Analyzing Competition, and Segmenting markets.

Market Analysis involves analyzing product-markets and forecasting how they will change in the future. Through market analysis, companies try to describe buyers, understand their preferences for product, and estimate the size and rate of growth of the market. It also involves finding what companies and products are competing in the market.

- Analysing Competition involves the evaluation of competitor's strategies, strengths, limitation and plans. It is also important to identify existing as well as potential competitors. An industry may consist of several players, but only a few will be the competitors for an organization competitor analysis includes evaluating each of the key competitor.
- Segmenting Markets involves looking at the nature and extent of diversity of the buyer's needs and wants in a market and then focusing the organization's business

capabilities on the requirements of one or more groups of buyers. The primary objective behind segmenting markets is to examine the differences in needs and wants and then choosing a segment that is very profitable to the organization.

The 4 Ps of Strategic Marketing

Product Mix

- Quality, Technology
- Packaging
- Labeling
- Branding
- Trade mark
- Merchandising
- Size, design, colour and features
- Services
- Warranty
- Product line and range

Price Mix

- Pricing policies
- Credit terms
- Cost and profit
- Allowance and discounts
- Competition
- Terms of delivery

Place Mix

- Distribution channels
- Transportation
- Warehousing and storage
- Inventory level
- Positioning

UNDERSTANDING STRATEGIC MARKETING MIX

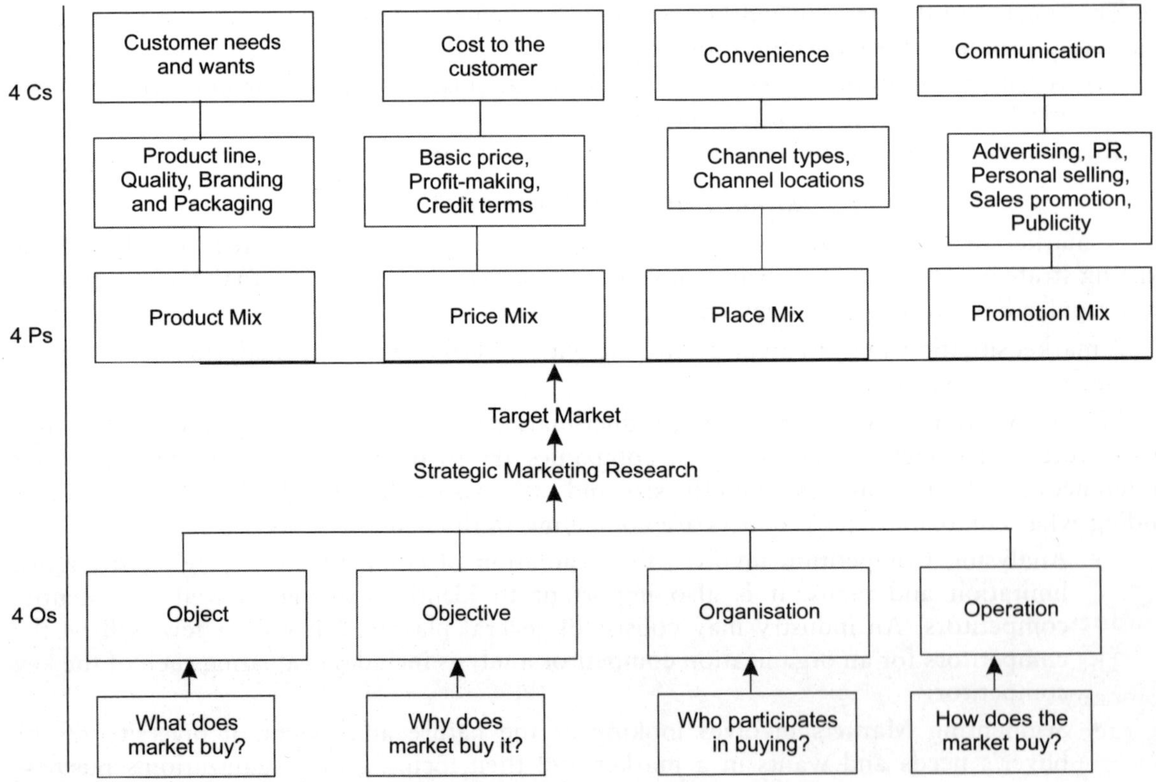

Promotion Mix

- Advertising
- Sales promotion
- Personal selling
- Public relations
- Publicity
- Direct responses.

The 4 Ps of Strategic Marketing Mix Operate Within a Business Environment

1. Strategic Marketing mix
2. Micro environment
3. Macro environment
4. Physical environment.

PRODUCT

A product has both tangible and intangible components. Customers view products as 'bundles of satisfaction' rather than just physical things.

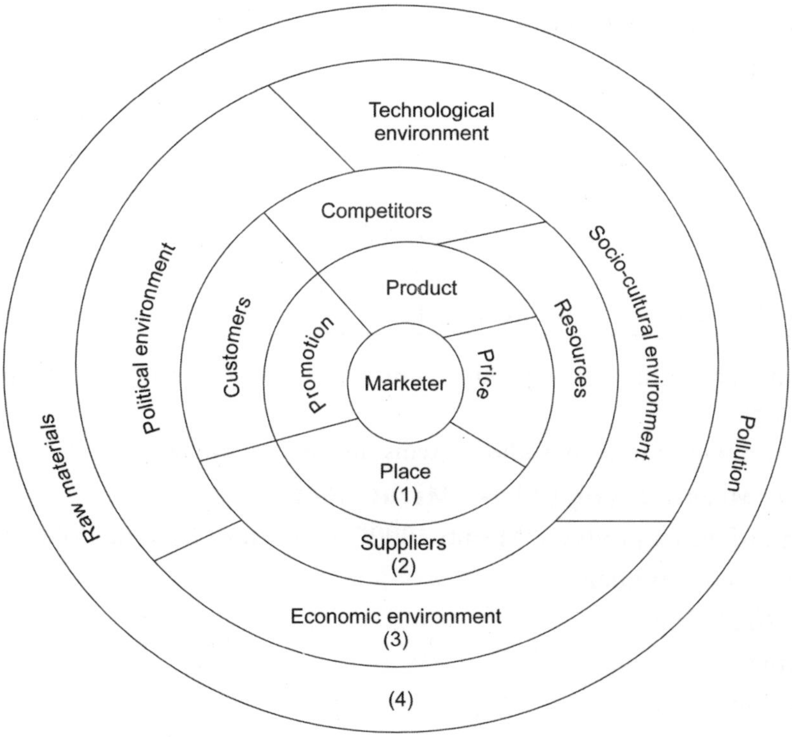

Product Mix

The word 'product mix' is used to describe the assortment of different product types that a company produces and markets. The product line is the number of brands or related products in each product type. Proctor and Gamble, for example, have four major product lines: detergents, toothpastes, soaps and deodorants. For each line, there are a number of brands

(DAZ, Ariel, etc.) and the number of different brands represents the length of product line and the number of different lines represents the width of the product mix.

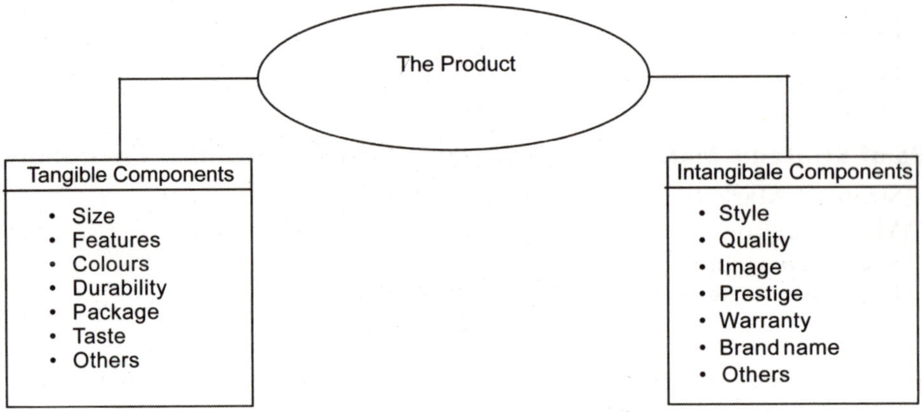

Examples of Product Line and range

- Bajaj Auto Ltd.

	Product line	Product range
1.	Scooters	Bajaj Super, Bajaj Cub, Chetak, Chetak Electronic, Priya, Bajaj Super FE
2.	Motorcycles	Kawasaki Bajaj-KB 100
3.	Mopeds	M-80, Sunny 50 cc
4.	Three Wheelers	Various models

- Hindustan Lever Ltd. has a product line consisting of vanaspati, soaps, detergents, cosmetics, etc.
- Philips has a wide range in audio systems and home appliances.

Another Example: Maruti Udyog Ltd. — 'Maruti 1000'

Maruti Udyog Ltd. has a product "Maruti 1000" designed to have the following attributes:

- Powerful air-conditioning
- Superior Road Grip
- Added Safety
- Safer Driving
- Luxurious Interiors
- Eco-friendly.

Dimensions

– Length	4,075 mm
– Width	1,575 mm

– Height	1,395 mm
– Wheelbase	2,365 mm
– Tread (Front)	1,365 mm
– Tread (Rear)	1,340 mm
– Turning Radius	4.8 mm
– bnGround Clearance	180 mm
– Seating Capacity	5 persons
Weight	
– Unladen Weight	825 kgs.
– Laden Weight	1,240 kgs.
Engine	
– Type	4 stroke cycle, Water cooled SOHC
– Number of cylinders	4 cylinders
– Piston displacement	970 cc
– Maximum output	46 hp @ 5,500 rpm
– Maximum torque	7.2 kgm. @ 3,500 rpm
Power Transmission	
– Transmission Type	5 Forward, all synchromesh 1 reverse
Chassis	
– Steering	Rack and pinion
– Suspension (Front)	Macpherson strut and coil spring
– Suspension (Rear)	– do –
– Breaks (Front)	Booster assisted disc
– Brakes (Rear)	Booster assisted drum
– Type size	155/80 R 13
Capacity	
– Fuel tank	40 litres
– Body Colours	
– Lonion Blue**	
– Golden Beige**	
– Henna Green**	
– Wine Red*	
– Pearl Black*	
– Milky White	

**Metallic colours

*Mica colours

Price Mix

Price is an important consideration in buying decisions. Price also denotes quality in the consumers' mind—a psychological factor. For some products, when many identical brands are competing with each other for consumer preference, the price may be an important influencing factor. Price consumer preference, the price may be an important influencing factor. Price is the basic vehicle for telling the consumer about the value and associated conditions of a particular product.

Price is an important element of strategic marketing mix. It may be defined as the value of product attributes expressed in monetary terms, which a consumer pays or is expected to pay in exchange. Pricing is a strategic marketing function, which has an important role to play in strategic marketing decisions. Pricing influences the profit level, the operational level, etc. The following determines the price of a product:

- Pricing objectives
- Demand for a product or service
- Competition
- Profitability
- Distribution channels.

Prices and Positioning of Kwality Wall's Ice creams

Price Range (Rs.)	Brands	Product Form	Target Segment
60 to 100	Dairy Classic	Take Home	The Indian woman
20	Cornetto	Novelty	Young adults and teenagers
16 to 19	Feast, Dairy Classic Cassatta	Novelty	Young adults and teenagers
11 to 15	Maha Choco Bar, Dairy Classic Range	Mainly Cups	Adults
7 to 10	Split	Stick	Children
4 to 6	Hattrik, Fruitline	Stick	Children
2.50	Solo	Stick	Children

Place Mix

The marketer has the responsibility of making his product available near the place of consumption so that the consumers can easily buy it. If the brand preferred by the consumer is not easily available at a convenient location, he may buy some other brand. Thus a marketer has to ensure that his product is available to the target consumers wherever required. There are two major areas in place mix: (1) strategic marketing channels, and (2) Physical distribution (Logistics Management).

It is true that channel decisions affect other strategic marketing mix elements, and involve a relatively long-term commitment of resources. It may take a marketer years to build up relations with the intermediaries and sometimes these are contractual. As we know, intermediaries are independent organisations and, therefore, their needs must be taken into account while evaluating various channel alternatives. In fact, the success of a company's Strategic Marketing effort depends to a large extent on the soundness of its distribution network. Physical distribution involves transportation, warehousing, material handling, and bulk packaging among others. Some of these activities will also be performed by the intermediaries and a great deal of coordination is required between the various links in the channel in order to get the optimum results. For many years, physical distribution was a neglected area of strategic marketing management, but now companies have become generally conscious of its importance in the overall strategic marketing strategy.

Promotion Mix

Strategic marketing promotion is a management process through which an organisation develops, presents, and evaluates a series of messages to an identified audience. So, effective promotion depends on:

- The nature of communication
- The target audience
- The environment in which it is received
- The receivers' perception of the source as, e.g. friends, reference, groups, etc.
- The medium used to transmit the message.

A System of Promotion Mix

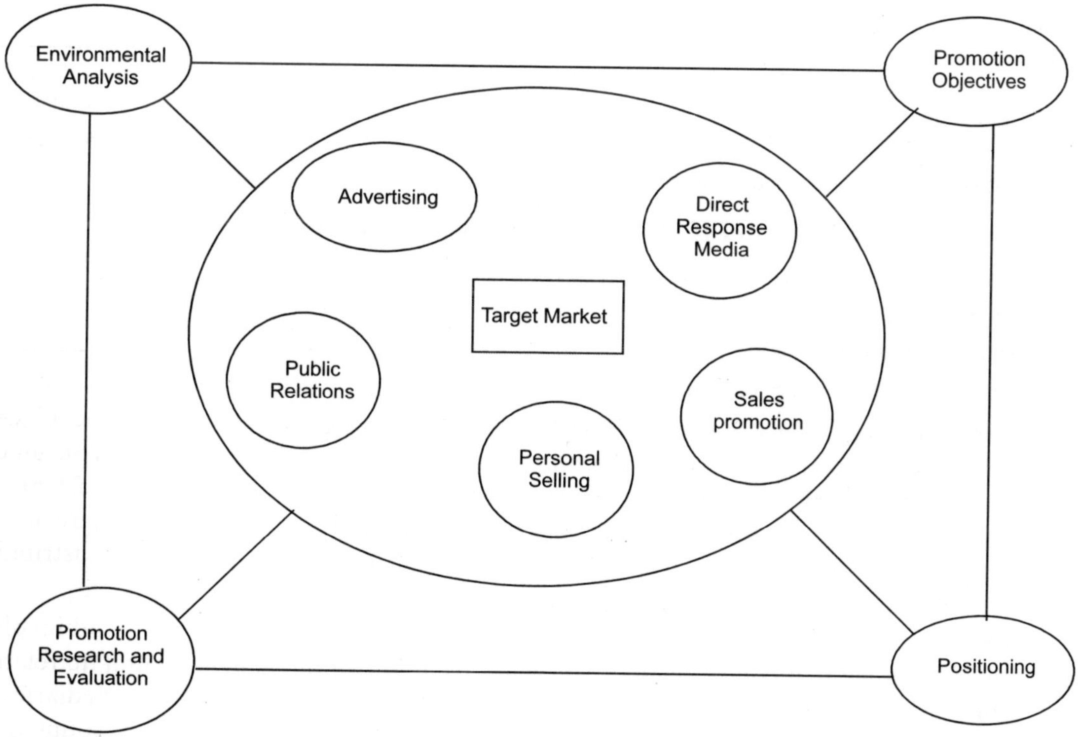

A summary of the key characteristics of the tools of strategic marketing communication is indicated in the following table:

	Advertising	Sales Promotion	Public Relations	Personal Selling	Direct Response Media
Communications:					
Ability to deliver a personal message	Low	Low	Low	High	High
Ability to reach a large audience	High	Medium	Medium	Low	Medium
Level of interaction	Low	Low	Low	High	High
Credibility given by target audience	Low	Medium	High	Medium	Medium
Costs:					
Absolute Costs	High	Medium	High	High	Medium
Cost per contract	Low	Medium	Low	High	High
Wastage	High	Medium	High	Low	Low
Size of investment	High	Medium	Low	High	Medium
Control:					
Ability to target particular audience	Medium	High	Low	Medium	High
Management's ability to adjust the deployment of the tools as circumstances change	Medium	High	Low	Medium	High

Source: Strategic Marketing Communications Framework, Theories and Applications by Chris Fill.

FACTORS AFFECTING THE STRATEGIC MARKETING MIX

There are innumerable factors that influence the strategic marketing mix. These factors can be divided into two categories:

(a) Market Factors; and

(b) Strategic Marketing Factors

(a) **Market Factors.** Market factors affecting the strategic marketing mix are such factors which relate to the market and over which company has no control. But they affect the strategic marketing activities of the company. Such factors are:

1. Consumer Behaviour. Consumer behaviour (needs, will and preferences of the consumers) affect the demand of the products. A strategic marketing manager must study the needs, wills and the preferences of the customers and also analyse their effects on the demand of the product. Consumers' needs, will and preferences are also affected by the change in income, fashion, social status, etc. and the manager should also study these factors also.
2. Competition. Before deciding upon the strategic marketing mix, the strategic marketing manager should also study the competitive conditions in the market. For this purpose,

he should take into account basis of competition, the number of competitors' viewpoint towards the consumers, quality and characteristics of the product.

3. Government Control. Government in India and in other countries also, control the various activities of the strategic marketing. In India the government intervention as regards the price, quality, distribution system, and packing of the products is too much. So, a Strategic Marketing manager should think over the various government controls on the various strategic marketing activities regarding the products of the company in preparing the strategic marketing mix.

(b) **Strategic Marketing Factors.** The strategic marketing manager should also consider the strategic marketing factor before preparing the strategic marketing mix. Strategic marketing factors are such factors over which the company has complete control and make them fit according to the requirements of the market. These factors include: (i) Product Planning; (ii) Brand Policy; (iii) Packaging Policy; (iv) Distribution Channels; (v) Personal Selling; (vi) Advertisement Policy. The description of these factors are as follows:

(1) Product Planning. The product of the company must have the quality of satisfying the needs of the customers and it should plan and develop its products accordingly. Product planning is the "act of making out and supervising the search, screening, development and commercialisation of new products, modification of existing lines and the discontinuance of marginal or unprofitable items" so that the product quality may be improved to suit the customer's needs.

(2) Brand Policy. It includes decisions regards trade marks and brand name because it influences the sale volume of the product of the company. The strategic marketing manager may go for the alternative policies regarding brands. He may decide one brand name for the different products of the company or different brands may be used for different qualities of the same product. He may also decide that the product should be sold without any brand name.

(3) Packaging Policy. Packaging also has an important effect on sales. The strategic marketing manager is to decide whether product should be sold loose or in packs. If he decides to sell the product in packs, the size and quality and get-up of packing should be considered very carefully because sometimes customers prefer the product only because of its attractive packing. It also serves three main purposes: (i) Protection of merchandise; (ii) Enhancement of the product value; and (iii) Advertising the product. It improves the total profits of the company by increasing total demand due to improved product image.

(4) Distribution Channels. There are three main channels of distribution: (i) from the manufacturer to the wholesaler, then to the retailers and finally to the customers; (ii) from the producer to the retailers and then to the final consumers, thus avoiding the wholesaler; and (iii) from the producer to consumers directly. The strategic marketing manager is to take the decision regarding appropriate channel of distribution for his products taking into account the nature of the product, nature of the distributors, their needs, their attitudes towards the product and their attitude towards the product and their morale. The strategic marketing manager may opt one type of distribution channel for all the products or different channels for different products.

(5) Personal Selling. In many respects, salesmen are the simplest heroes of strategic marketing. It is his skill with the help of which he matches the customers' needs with the company's products in effecting ownership transfer or making sales. Personal selling involves social behaviour. The strategic marketing manager is to decide whether to promote the sales through personal selling. It involves decisions regarding recruitment, training and the organisation of salesmen.

(6) Advertisement Policy. Advertisement has its own role to play in the strategic marketing. It is used not only to stimulate the demand of the product but for many other purposes, i.e., to maintain the demand of the existing products.

ASSEMBLING THE STRATEGIC MARKETING MIX—THE MAIN TASK IN STRATEGIC MARKETING

Since strategic marketing is essentially an interaction between the strategic marketing mix and the environmental variables, and, since the latter are non-controllable, strategic marketing becomes synonymous with assembling and managing the strategic marketing mix. Of course, while assembling the strategic marketing mix, the strategic marketing manager will take due note of the environmental variables. Not only will he take due note of them, he will also ensure that his strategic marketing mix suits the environmental variables. And, it is this factor that renders the task much more complex.

It is by assembling and operating its strategic marketing mix that a firm executes its strategic marketing strategy. Assembling the strategic marketing mix involves a number of decisions relating to each of the strategic marketing mix elements, product, price, channel and promotion. Decisions are also required on the linkages among the elements. And all these decisions form an integral part of the strategic marketing strategy.

- What is the best combination of the four Ps in a given situation?
- Which line of products, or which individual products, should be offered to an identified target market?
- What should be the price structure?
- Which channel has to be selected?
- What is the right promotion strategy?
- How should the total strategic marketing effort and resources of the firm be apportioned among the four Ps?
- How to balance the impact of an increase or decrease in the allocations to a particular element on the other elements?

In the chapter on Strategic Marketing Planning and Strategic Marketing Strategy, we shall be discussing this subject in detail.

Selecting an Optimum Combination is the Name of the Game

We have seen that it is possible to combine the four Ps in countless ways. And, these combinations vary from one another, in the impact on the market and on costs. The name of the game is to select a combination, which will have the desired impact on the market and will also be cost-effective. The task is basically one of giving correct weightage to the different elements of the mix and ensuring that al the elements are integrated. In fact, the effectiveness of any strategic marketing programme depends directly on the extent to which the Strategic Marketing mix is able to harmonise and synthesise the different elements into a unified entity.

Strategic Marketing Mix has to be Juggled Constantly

Assembling the strategic marketing mix is a continuous task and not a one-shot assignment. No strategic marketing manager can assume that his job is over once the strategic marketing mix is assembled. The mix will require periodical changes and, in some cases, constant changes. In fact, there is no such thing as a for-ever-valid strategic marketing mix. The strategic marketing manager has to carefully monitor the conditions and keep juggling the mix.

Change in Environmental Variables

In the first place, the environmental variables are constantly in a flux. This reality compels the strategic marketing manager to keep juggling the strategic marketing mix. Without doing so, he will not be in a position to respond properly to the changes. Let us, for instance, take competition, which is one major environmental variable. The competitors in any given industry will be making their tactical manoeuvres in the market all the time. They will introduce a new product, or initiate an aggressive promotion campaign, or announce a price reduction. The competing strategic marketing manager has to meet all these manoeuvres and take care of the competitive position of his firm/brand in the market. The only way he can achieve this is by juggling the strategic marketing mix. Similar is the case with other major environmental variables like economic conditions, government policies and climatic conditions. All of them keep changing and the strategic marketing manager has to keep adjusting the strategic marketing mix accordingly.

Change in Customer Preference

In many businesses, the customer is, perhaps, the most fluctuating of all the environmental variables. Often, customer's tastes and preferences change very fast; today, he may want a cheaper version of the product; tomorrow he may be bothered more about quality or after-sales service. Brand loyalty also changes; customer's purchasing power too changes over time. The strategic marketing manager is vitally concerned with these changes relating to the customer. Through customer analysis and market research, he has to gather the relevant information about the customer and the changes taking place in his needs, tastes and preferences and respond to them through appropriate modification of the strategic marketing mix.

Changes Within the Firm

There is yet another reason why the strategic marketing mix needs to be juggled frequently. Besides the changes in the external environment, changes taking place within the firm too, necessitate modifications in the strategic marketing mix. For example, changes in the corporate/competitive strategy of the firm, changes in the product lines of the firm, changes in the organisation or resource level of the firm, will all lead to changes in the strategic marketing mix for a given product/brand.

QUESTIONS FOR DISCUSSION

1. What is meant by the term Strategic Marketing Mix?
2. What are the various elements of Strategic Marketing Mix? Discuss.
3. What is relationship between Strategic Marketing Mix and Strategic Marketing Strategy?
4. Explain the relevance of place in Strategic Marketing Mix.
5. What is meant by Strategic Marketing Mix? How does Strategic Marketing Mix influence the organisation's growth?

MARKET SEGMENTATION FOR STRATEGIST

4

INTRODUCTION

The concept of market segment is based on the fact that the markets of commodities are not homogeneous but they are heterogeneous. Market represents a group of customers having common characteristics but two customers are never common in their nature, habits, hobbies, income and purchasing techniques. They differ in their behaviour and buying decisions. On the basis of these characteristics, customers having similar qualities are grouped in segments. The characteristics of customers of one segment differ with those of other segments. In this way market segmentation refers to the various segments of the market based on the common characteristics of the customers.

Definitions of Market Segmentation

Market segmentation has been defined by various authors as follows:

> "Whenever, a market for a product or service consists of two or more buyers, the market is capable of being segmented, that is divided into meaningful buyer groups. The purpose of segmentation is to determine differences among buyers which may be consequential in choosing away them or marketing to them."
>
> *Philip Kotler*

> "Market segmentation consists of taking the total heterogeneous market for a product and dividing it into several sub-markets or segments, each of which tends to be homogeneous in full significant aspects."
>
> *William J. Stanton*

> "The purpose of market segmentation is to determine the differences among purchasers which may effect the choice of market area of marketing methods. The market is divided into sectors or segments in such a way that the purchasers in each segment while not being exactly identical are of a similar nature and are influenced by similar buying motives."
>
> *Esmond Pearce*

> "Market segments are grouping of consumers according to such characteristics as income, age, degree of urbanisation, race, or either classification, geographic location or education."
>
> *Cundiff and Still*

> ".... Grouping of buyers or segmenting the market is described as market segmentation."
>
> *R.S. Davar*

In the modern marketing concept all marketing activities have to revolve around the consumers. Effective marketing requires a clear picture of the consumer characteristics that can be described as the customer profile. Thus, marketing segmentation means dividing the customers of a product into several homogeneous groups having common characteristics, such as income, sex, age, profession, etc. The main aim of market segmentation is to prepare separate programmes or strategies to all segments so that maximum satisfaction to consumers of different segments may be provided.

Objects of Market Segmentation

The customers of a product are in quite a large number and scattered and all have different characteristics. No two buyers have similar characteristics. This difference affects the demand of a product to a great extent. A successful marketer is one who understands and considers these differences of the customers of his product. For making his product more popular and for providing maximum possible satisfaction to maximum possible customers, he groups the customers on some common basis of similarity of characteristics.

Thus, the main object of segmentation of market is to identify the differences and provide maximum satisfaction to customers. In the words of Philip Kotler, "The purpose of market segmentation is to determine difference among the buyers which may be consequential in choosing among them or marketing to them."

The producer can frame his marketing policies and strategies on the basis of these differences.

Importance of Market Segmentation

The market segmentation affords the following advantages to the seller or producer:

1. **Adjustment of Product and Marketing Appeals.** Market segmentation presents an opportunity to understand the nature of the market. The seller can adjust his thrust to attract the maximum number of customers by various publicity media and appeals. More resources may be allocated to market segments where sales opportunities are better.
2. **Better Position to Spot Marketing Opportunities.** The producer can make a fair estimate of the volume of his sale and the possibilities of furthering his sales. In the regions where response of the customers is poor the strategy of approach can be readjusted accordingly to push the sales on the basis of marketing research. On the basis of research, habits, tastes, hobbies and nature of consumers of different markets can be understood deeply to harness marketing opportunities.
3. **Allocation of Marketing Budget.** It is on the basis of market segmentation that marketing budget is adjusted for a particular region or locality. In the place where the sales opportunities are limited, it is no use allocating a huge budget there.
4. **Making the Competition Effectively.** It helps the producer to face the competition of his rivals effectively. The producer can adopt different policies, programmes and strategies for different markets taking into account the rivals strategies, policies and programmes.
5. **Effective Marketing Programme.** It also helps the producer to adopt an effective

marketing programme and serve the consumer better at comparatively low cost. Different marketing programmes can be attached for different segments.

6. **Evaluation of Marketing Activities.** Thus market segmentation helps the manufacturer to find out and compare the marketing potentialities of the products. It helps to adjust production and using his resources in the most profitable manner. As soon as the product becomes obsolete, the product line could be diversified or discontinued.
7. **Increase in Sales Volume.** By segmenting, the market, the producer can increase his sales volume. As we know, each segment has different demand pattern and the producer satisfies the demand of each segment, by improving his product. The total sales volume for the enterprise increases. It is based on the fact that multiple demand curves in a market are better than a single demand curve.

Thus, we can conclude that market segmentation helps the producer to increase his sales volume. Customer is also benefitted by the market segmentation as the producer produces and supplies the goods which serve their interest and satisfy their needs and wants.

Bases for Market Segmentation

There may be several criteria or bases for market segmentation. The bases may differ from product to product because the sensitivity of customers differ. For example, the bases for consumer goods may be age, sex, education, income, etc. whereas for capital or industrial goods it may be nature and size of the business, location, purchasing procedure, etc. **Gundiff and Still** has mentioned the following criteria for market segmentation:

Bases for Consumer Product	Bases for Industrial Product
1. Income of the consumer	1. Kinds of business
2. Age of the consumer	2. Usual purchasing procedure
3. Sex of the consumer	3. Size of user
4. Degree of urbanisation of the consumer	4. Geographical markets segmentation
5. Geographical market segmentation	
6. Educational attainment of the consumer	
7. Religion of the consumer	

1. Bases for Consumer Products

The various criteria for segmenting the consumer product markets may be grouped in the following four categories:

(i) Socio-economic Factors,

(ii) Geographical Factors,

(iii) Personality Factors, and

(iv) Consumer Behaviour Factors.

(i) **Socio-economic Factors.** It is the most common way of segmenting the markets on he basis of socio-economic characteristics of the consumers dispersed over a geographical segments. Such factors are:

(a) *Age.* Age is one of the most important factor for segmenting the market. The producer should know for what age group his product would be most suited so that he can plan his pricing policy, advertisement policy, marketing policy, and strategy accordingly. For example, some breakfast products are aimed to suit the tastes of children while some others are attractive to consumers within a broader range of ages. Similarly cloth market or garment market may be segmented on this basis of age as children, young, adults and old. Different types of tooth brushes are produced for customers of different age groups.

(b) *Sex.* Markets may also be divided on the basis of sex, i.e. ladies and gents. Some products are exclusively produced for women while some others are for men. For example, lipstick is meant for women and on the other hand shaving cream is only for men. As because the attitude, needs, mental and physical attributes and motivational factors are different in men and women, therefore, advertisement strategy may differ for both types of products. Manly desires, personality, sense of family security and social prestige are some of the factors which are given top priority in an advertisement for a product meant exclusively for men. On the other hand, beauty and purchasing ability are some factors for advertising a product meant for women.

(c) *Income.* The producer should also bear in mind while preparing his marketing policy, the income of the prospective buyers of his product. This factor also affects the advertising and distribution policy, i.e. media of advertisement, and pricing policy. Consumers' needs, behaviour, habits, preferences, persuasion, etc. differ in different income groups. For example, people in high income group prefer quality of goods, design, fashion-oriented products, etc. hence they can be motivated on these factors. People in low income group attracts towards low priced goods. Different models of television sets are introduced to meet the needs of buyers of different income groups. Similarly certain items like Refrigerators, new VCD/DVD are produced only for high income group people.

(d) *Educational Level.* The consumers can be divided on the basis of educational levels such as educated, semi-educated and uneducated and the marketing activities and strategies are ascertained accordingly. For example, a book market may be segmented on the basis in Primary, Junior High School, High School, Intermediate and Degree books markets. Advertising policy may be chosen accordingly. Products used by uneducated or low-educated people, may be advertised through Radio and Television, Cinema whereas the advertisement for educated people may be given in newspapers, journals and magazines, etc.

(e) *Race and Religion.* India has the co-existence of many religions, communities, castes and sub-castes and the market may also be segmented on the basis because their feelings, life styles, and attitudes differ depending on their origin and communal associations. Brands, design, language on packing and packing decisions may differ for a product meant for different religions. For example, utensils or book market may be divided on the basis of religion.

(f) *Size of Family.* Market may also be segmented on the basis of size of family. Refrigerators and cookers are produced in different sizes to suit the needs of families cf different sizes.

(g) *Business or Profession.* It is also an important criterion to segment the market. On the basis market may be divided in businessmen, professionals and employed persons.

Professionals may further be sub-divided into Doctors, Lawyers, etc. Employed persons may be classified as Clerks, Officers, Teachers, Executives, Judges and Army personnel. The needs, attitudes and preferences differ in all these customers.

(ii) **Geographical Factors.** The second most popular criteria for segmenting the market may be the geographical segmentation of the whole operational area. The markets are divided on the basis of geographical factors, such as area, climate and the density of population. According to area states may be taken the basis for segmentation. Each State may be recognised a separate market. The area may further be segmented in rural, town and urban areas or where market is international the division may be national or international market. On the basis of climate, markets may be hill areas and plain areas. Such type of segmentation is best where the customers are stretched over a vast area and the production is done on large scale. The producer may design his marketing strategies taking the characteristics of the individual markets into consideration.

(iii) **Psychographic or Personality Factors.** Personality, thinking, etc. are not the same in all the consumers. Some customers are crazy for noval design or products of new fashion that may increase their prestige in the society. The motto of some other customers is simple-living and high-thinking and they never aspire for showy-items. For example, Congress workers wear *khadi* irrespective of their income-level or social status.

(iv) **Consumer Behaviour Factors.** Consumer behaviour may also form the basis of market segmentation. Consumer behaviour divides the markets on three bases: (i) Usage-rate; (ii) Buyer Motives; and (iii) Brand loyalty. Customers may be grouped according to their *usage habits*, i.e. non-users, light-users, medium-users and heavy-users, etc. Non-users may also be divided in expected and unexpected users. In *Buyers' motives* we may include factors like economic quality of goods, reliability, and prestige in society, etc. Several groups may be formed on these bases and market may be segmented accordingly. Customers may also be grouped to their *loyalty to a particular brand.* If, suppose, four brands of a commodity are in the market customers may be grouped in four classes on the basis of their preference of a particular brand.

2. Bases for Industrial Product

The industrial market is nearly as large as the consumer market. The industrial market, like the consumer market, is also made up of different market segments. This market segmentation is as appropriate for industrial products as for consumer products. Many different bases are used for segmenting the industrial market, the four most important and most used bases are: (i) Kind of business or activity; (ii) Usual purchasing procedure; (iii) Geographical location of the users; and (iv) The size of user.

(i) **Kind of Business or Activity.** Market segmentation by kind of business is generally used where the industrial house produces several products or services. For example, insurance company's market may be segmented in fire, marine, general and life insurance business. A separate division may be formed for each segment representing a specific kind of activity. This may again be broken down in procurement division and lending division.

(ii) **Usual Purchasing Procedure.** Industrial buyers are generally more systematic buyers than ultimate consumers. But among industrial users there is much variation in the amount of consideration given to buying different items. The decision to buy a major installation, requires extensive market and other technical investigations plus the approval of several high executives and technical experts in the industrial user's organisation. But the same firm may purchase some routine articles like stationery or pens, etc. through ordinary suppliers and agents. The industrial marketers must apply different selling tactics and strategies to each of these buying situations.

(iii) **Geographical Location of the User.** Factors like variation in geographical climate and historical traditions cause considerable variation in the way industrial marketing is conducted in different areas. The topography of an area affects the transportation cost. Variation in climate affects the needs the industrial users for building materials, and heating and cooling equipments. Geographical segmentation may also exist because some kinds of business and service organisations seem to settle in particular areas.

(iv) **The Size of User.** Sizes of industrial purchases vary according to the size of industrial user. The market according to size may be divided in large buyers and small buyers. Since it is generally more economical to sell in large lots than small, the industrial markets quote lower rates to buyers of large quantities. This is often the main reason why marketer use different methods for reaching industrial users who vary greatly in size.

Thus, there are several bases on which market for consumer and industrial products may be segmented.

MARKET SEGMENTATION

- Market segmentation is a way of analyzing a market by specific characteristics in order to create a target market. Once that market is clearly identified, a business can customize its product offer. The market is segmented by the following characteristics:
  - Demographics
  - Psychographics
  - Geographics
  - Product Benefits

Demographics

- Demographics refers to statistics that describe a population in terms of personal characteristics.
  - Age
  - Income
- Disposable income is the money left after taking out taxes.
- Discretionary income is the money left after paying for basic living necessities such as food, shelter, and clothing.
  - Ethnic Background
  - Gender
  - Education
  - Occupation

Psychographics

- Psychographics involves studies of consumers based on social and psychological characteristics. These characteristics could include
  - Attitudes
  - Values
  - Feelings

Geographics

- Geographics refers to segmentation of the market based on where people live.
- To segment a market geographically, you can refer to local, regional, national, or even global markets.

Product Benefits

- Segmenting a market by product benefits involves studying consumers' needs and wants and then marketing your product to the specific market who will be using your product.

MARKET AGGREGATION

Buyer's behaviour is never the same and the market could be segmented on the basis of buyers' characteristics. The producer must understand the behaviour of his customers and adopt different strategies according to the needs and characteristics of his customers, so that physical and human resources of the enterprise may be fully exploited and marketing objectives may be fully met. There are three types of marketing strategies viz. (i) Undifferentiated or market aggregation strategy; (ii) Market segmentation or differentiated marketing strategy; and (iii) Concentrated marketing strategy.

(i) **Market Aggregation or Undifferentiated Marketing Strategy.** Market aggregation is just the opposite of segmentation. Aggregation implies the policy of limping together into one mass of all the markets for the product. Production-oriented firms usually adopt the method of aggregation instead of segmentation. Under this concept management having only one product considers the entire buyers as one group. Market aggregation enables an organisation to maximise its economies of scale of production, pricing, physical distribution and promotion. However, the applicability of this concept in consumer-oriented market is doubtful. The total market concept as envisaged by market aggregation may not be realistic in the present-day marketing when consumers fall under heterogeneous groups.

When the economies of organisations do not permit the division of market into segments, they conceive the total market concept. In the case of fully standardised product and where substitutes are not available, differentiation need not to be undertaken. Under such circumstances firms may adopt mass-advertising and other mass methods in marketing.

Advantages. A firm adopting this strategy (i) can produce and sell its product on large-scale and can get large scale economies; (ii) the firm can make use of standardisation specialisation and division of labour; and (iii) the firm can utilise its resources to the maximum.

Disadvantages. The drawbacks of this strategy are: (i) This is a product-oriented (and not a customer-oriented) strategy; (ii) The effectiveness of the strategy is doubtful in consumer-oriented market; and (iii) This strategy is successful only in short run.

(ii) **Market Segmentation or Differentiated Marketing Strategy.** Under this strategy, the firm groups the buyers on the basis of their common needs and desires. It differentiates one group from the other on the basis of their needs, region, characteristics, personality or behaviour. In other words, the classification of markets based on consumers' characteristics is called market segmentation. Market segmentation is "the process of taking the total heterogeneous markets for a product and dividing it into several sub-markets or segments each of which tends to be homogeneous in all significant." For instance, instead of mentioning a single market for shoes, it may be segmented and differentiated into several sub-markets, e.g. shoes for executives, doctors, students, etc. or on the basis of sex, i.e. shoes for children, ladies and gents, and so on. Geographical segmentation on the very similar lines is also possible for certain other products.

Under this concept, a firm decides to operate in several or all segments of the market and designs separate product-marketing programmes. This also helps developing intimacy between the producer and the consumer. Most firms nowadays prefer to have a strategy of differentiated marketing because consumers' demand is diversified. It provides an opportunity to the consumers to select his or her choice. Each kind of product offers a basis for segmentation. As the differentiated marketing is sales-oriented, it is a costly affair for the organisation.

Advantages of Differentiated Marketing Strategy. The differentiated marketing strategy offers the following advantages: (i) It is a consumer-oriented market. Stress is laid on the needs of different types of consumers; (ii) It attracts a large number of customers from all corners; and (iii) It increases sales and profits of the enterprise.

Disadvantages of Differentiated Marketing Strategy. Its drawbacks are: (i) Different types of products are to be produced for different segments of the market to satisfy the needs of the customers; (ii) It requires intensive marketing research; (iii) Different marketing programmes and strategies are required for different segments of the market; and (iv) It increases the overall cost of the product because it increases the cost of research, product planning and development, physical distribution, advertising and sales promotion substantially.

This strategy is useful for firms producing different products on large-scale basis.

(iii) **Concentrated Marketing Strategy.** Both the concepts of undifferentiated marketing and differentiated marketing imply the approach of total market. Another option is to have concentrated efforts in a few markets capable of opportunities. Instead of spreading itself in many parts of the market it concentrates its forces to gain a good market position in a few areas. When new products are introduced, this method is adopted. Another feature of this method is that the advantage of one segment is never offset by the other because firm's efforts are concentrated only in one segment of the market.

Advantages. It offers the following advantages: (i) It concentrates its efforts in certain markets to gain good position; (ii) It provides best possible satisfaction of customers of selected segments; (iii) It makes full exploitation of resources; and (iv) It reduces cost of production and administration substantially.

Disadvantages. The disadvantages of this strategy are: (i) It is risky because if a wrong segment is selected, the very existence of the firm is endangered; and (ii) It increases the possibilities of competition.

The three kinds of segmentation could be illustrated as follows:

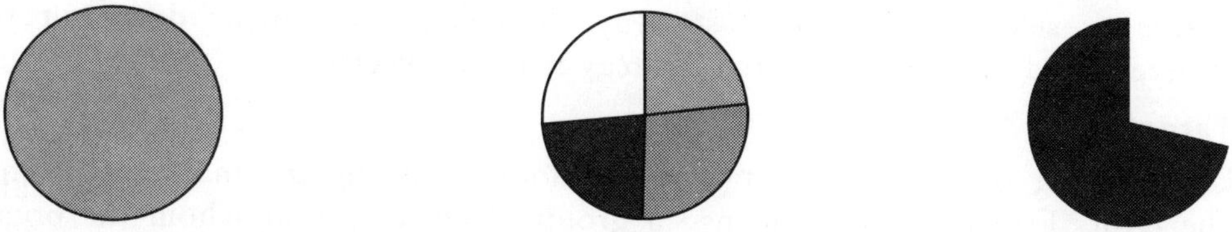

UNDIFFERENTATED MARKETING DIFFERENTATED MARKETING CONCENTRATED MARKETING

Source: Philip Kotler, *Marketing Management*.

Elements of Market Segmentation

An important question for the organisation is how should a policy be purposefully adopted in segmenting the markets. This question arises because of the alternative strategies available for a manufacturer. The basic elements that influence in deciding the principle of segmentation are:

1. **Company Resources.** Market segmentation involves heavy expenditure in implementing it. It is not a mere blueprint in paper. Unless the company has got enough resources, market segmentation cannot be undertaken at all.
2. **Product Characteristics.** Most products are heterogeneous in character but some other products show homogeneity. In the case of former type, market differentiated strategy is adopted but in the latter case the necessity of segmentation is disputed. Salt, kerosene, etc. come under this group of articles and in their case undifferentiated marketing is to be selected.
3. **Position of the Products in the Product Life Cycle.** The various stages of a product cycle, viz., introduction, growth, maturity, saturation and decline have to be taken into consideration. In the first and last stages market segmentation is meaningless and therefore undifferentiated marketing strategy should be selected. During the introduction stage the necessary data cannot be collected and at this stage also undifferentiated strategy would be better. If the product is at the stage of growth or development, concentrated marketing strategy should be selected. Differentiated strategy would be in the interest of the company at the stages of maturity and saturation. At the stage of obsolescence, it would be better to discontinue the product.
4. **Homogeneous Nature of Market.** When the market is of a homogeneous nature there is not much use of segmentation. Proper segmentation of market is required only when the customer preferences vary from group to group.
5. **Competitive Marketing Strategies.** Sometimes it becomes quite necessary to fall in line with the competitors' activity of market segmentation. Similar arrangements by competitors have to be made to meet the competition effectively. Experience shows

that it is difficult for an organisation to be successful through undifferentiated marketing when competitors are practising active segmentation.

6. **Government Policy.** Government policy also affects the decision of adopting marketing strategy. When government interferes, it is better to adopt the strategy which suits Government orders. For example, if Government orders to produce Janata cloth, it is better to select concentrated strategy. In case, government does not interfere, differentiated or undifferentiated strategy may be selected.

Market Targeting

Market targeting is a process of taking decisions regarding the market segments to be served. The term 'Target Market' means "a group of customers at whom the organisation specifically intends to aim its marketing effort". On the other hand, the term 'Marketing Target' is one in which the seller distinguishes the major market segments, targets one or more of these segments and develops products and marketing programmes tailored to each selected segments.

Market targeting consists of two steps namely:

1. Evaluating the market segments, and
2. Selecting the market segments.

1. **Evaluating the Market Segments.** In evaluating the different market segments the firm must look at three factors, namely:
   a. Segment size and growth,
   b. Segment structural attractiveness, and
   c. Company objectives and resources.

   (a) ***Segment Size and Growth.*** While selecting the segment the firm should see whether the potential segment has the right size and growth characteristics. Right size is a relative term. Large firms prefer segments with large sales volumes. Small firms, on the other hand, prefer small segments. As far as growth is concerned it is desired by all firms because it facilitates growing sales and profits.

   (b) ***Segment Structural Attractiveness.*** One segment must have profit attractiveness. According to **Porter**, there are five forces that determine the long-run profit attractiveness of a market or segment. They are:
   1. Industry competitors,
   2. Potential entrants,
   3. Substitutes,
   4. Buyers, and
   5. Suppliers.

The threats that are posed by these forces are as follows:

(i) Threat of intense segment rivalry,
(ii) Threat of new entrants,
(iii) Threat of substitute products,

(iv) Threat of growing bargaining power of buyers, and

(v) Threat of growing bargaining power of suppliers.

c. ***Company Objectives and Resources.*** The third factor to be considered by a company in the evaluation of market segment is its own objectives and resources. At this stage, company should see whether the company possesses the requisite skills and resources to succeed in that segment.

2. **Selecting the Market Segments.** Having evaluated the market segments, the company should now decide how many segments to serve. Following are the patterns of market selection:

   a. ***Single Segment Concentration.*** Under this pattern, the company selects one of the various segments and concentrates thereon. It has its own merits and demerits.

   b. ***Selective Specialisation.*** Under this pattern, the firm selects a number of appropriate and attractive segments. This is called multi segment strategy and has merit of diversification of firm's risk. If this strategy is adopted, even if one segment becomes attractive the firm can contribute to earn money in other segments.

   c. ***Product Specialisation.*** In product specialisation, the firm concentrates on the production of a certain product and sells it to several segments. This strategy enables the firm to build up a strong reputation in the specific product area.

   d. ***Market Specialisation.*** In this pattern, the firm concentrates on satisfying the needs of a particular group of customers, e.g. children.

   e. ***Full Market Coverage.*** In this case, the firm tries to serve all customer groups with all products that they might need. This is possible only in case of large firms.

Market Positioning

Once the marketer has decided as to which segments of the market a company will enter, then it must decide as to what positions it likes to occupy in these segments.

A product's position is the way the product is defined by consumers on important attributes. It is the place the product occupies in consumers' minds relative to competing products, e.g. Lux is positioned as beauty soap.

There are several positioning strategies. They are:

1. **Positioning on Product Attributes.** The marketer can position his product on specific product attributes. For example, BPL features technical and performance attributes.
2. **Positioning on Benefits.** Products can be positioned on the needs they fill or benefits they offer, e.g. Colgate reduces cavities.
3. **Positioning According to Usage Occasions.** Another way of positioning the products is as per their usage occasions, that is, products can be positioned for specific usage occasions.
4. Another approach is to ***position the products for certain class*** of users. Certain cine films are released as adult films, as films for children, etc.
5. **Positioning Away from Competitors.** A product may also be positioned away from competitors. 7-up became the number three soft drink when it was positioned as the un-cola, the fresh alternative to Coke and Pepsi.

QUESTIONS FOR DISCUSSION

1. What is the object of market segmentation? What are the bases of market segmentation?
2. What is meant by marketing segmentation? What will be the suitable base for the marketing of Televisions?
3. What are the elements that influence in deciding the principles of segmentation?
4. Write a short note on Product Differentiation and Product Positioning.
5. Write a short note on marketing strategy for industrial products.
6. Discuss major market segmentation variables for the toothpaste market highlighting benefit segments.
7. "Market targeting follows market segmentation." Discuss.
8. "Successful segmentation is pre-requisite to profitability." What are the different approaches used to identify and measure differences between market segments. Illustrate with examples.

CASE STUDY 4.1

MARKETING TO COLLEGE STUDENTS

The college market is an important one for many companies. About thirteen million U.S. College students spend about $20 million annually on discretionary purchases (approximately $ 30 per month per student) based on a recent study sponsored by the National Association of College Stores. One-fifth of college students have $250 or more to spend each month. Table 4.1 shows how college students spend their money. Another survey of college students examined their leisure-time activities. The highlights of this study are shown in Table 4.2.

Table 4.1: How College Students Spend Their Money (as a percentage of discretionary income)

Expenditure Category	Per cent of Discretionary Income
Clothing	14.6
Groceries and toiletries	14.3
Auto care	10.0
Restaurants	8.4
Bars and clubs	7.3
Gifts	6.3
Travel to visit family	4.6
Movies	4.0
Travel for vocation	2.7
Concerts/theatre	2.5
Attending sporting events	2.2
Magazines/newspapers	1.9
Participation in sports	1.9
Cameras and equipment	1.2

Total does not equal 100 per cent because not every college student purchases items from each category

Source: National Association of College Stores, Reprinted by permission.

Table 4.2: How College Students Spend Their Free Time (Mean hours per week)

Activity	Hours per week
Listening to FM radio	13.0
Listening to records, tapes and CDs	9.0
Watching television	7.2
Watching opted videotapes	4.8
Participating in sports	4.6
Going to fast-food restaurants	4.3
Reading newspapers	4.2
Shopping	3.6
Reading magazines	3.1
Going to the movies	3.1
Working on a hobby	3.0
Attending sports events	2.2
Playing musical instruments	1.5
Going to concerts	1.2
Using PCs at home	1.2

Source: National Association of College Stores, Reprinted by permission.

Although the number of 18-24 years old in the U.S. population is expected to decline over the next several years, college enrolment should remain strong. A higher proportion of young adults in this age group will go to college, and more older adults and other non-traditional students will be attending college.

Many firms have found that appealing to the college market is not a simple task. Colllege students are somewhat of a paradox—students are "easy to find but hard to reach", e.g., many college students may not be reached through traditional advertising media because they live on a unique time schedule and have little spare time. As indicated in Table 4.2, the typical college student spends just over 7 hours per week watching T.V.

One promotion executive recommends that firms seeking this market utilise on-campus advertising promotions (such as contests), magazines targeted specifically to college students, and sports sponsorships. Words-of-mouth communication among students and displays in college stores also represent unique opportunity due to the homogeneous nature of the college market: "the firm is guaranteed that walk-in traffic is the audience it wants to reach."

QUESTIONS FOR DISCUSSION

1. How could a firm use a differentiated marketing approach to appeal to college student?
2. Evaluate the college market from the perspective of the requirements for successful segmentation.

CASE STUDY 4.2

SEGMENT TO SELL

India's diversity could provide plenty of opportunities should marketing strategies be designed and executed well. Unfortunately several companies have failed to grasp the nuances of Indian consumer behaviour and hence, their products bombed in the marketplace.

Segmentation is a powerful tool through which markets can be handled and brands built. Two case studies illustrate how poor segmentation has led to miscalculation. Result: Companies entering India have either failed or taken a lot of time to succeed.

First, cars. Lack of proper segmentation of the automobile market resulted in most cars being launched in the mid-size segment. Soon, the mid-size segment was choked with cars like Daewoo's Cielo, Opel's Astra and Ford's Escort among others. The mid-size segment is a niche market, but there were few takers here. Today, most of these companies are unable to achieve even 25 to 30 per cent of their target and have landed up with heavy inventory. Now they are forced to offer deep discount and resort to desperate sales.

Had proper segmentation been done, the focus would have been on small-size cars that are mostly affordable and comprise the largest and the fastest growing segment. This has been proved by the success of Maruti 800 and Zen. It took a lot of time for people to realise the segmentation folly. So car manufacturers by excess capacity and may ultimately lead to price wars.

Had proper segmentation been adopted, there would have been another brand to challenge the Maruti 800 and Zen monopoly long ago and that brand would have gained good sales and market share.

There are certain brands of cars, which are doing well. Take the Zen, for example. Its better aesthetics, more leg space than the Maruti 800 and better technology inputs, make it popular. This car is ideal for a distinct segment.

The positioning of the Zen has been directed towards a segment defined by the parameter of usage. Segmentation for usage is a powerful weapon in the marketing armoury. Customers desirous of upgrading themselves from a Maruti 800 or those who desire a mix of aesthetics and manoeuvrability for regular usage, find the Zen an extremely lucrative option. Result: at a time when the car industry is facing rough weather, the Zen seems to have done better, primarily because it is segmented by usage—kids can be dropped at schools, it is decent enough to be driven to office or can even be used to comfortably drive down to an informal party.

Many a times, companies can track usage patterns and segment the market by usage and gain.

Let us take another case study of a recently-launched beverage which has also pegged usage as the criterion for segmenting its market and achieved considerable trials and healthy repeat purchases. Fosters beer has recently been launched in pint-sized bottled alongside the usual larger pack size. The shape and size of the bottle is targeted toward young, trendy, light-users who consider drinking beer as a part of their lifestyle. San Miguel and Ice have also been launched in the same size.

In my opinion this particular pack size, which is handy, shapely and international in its look, gained huge ground among light-users. In terms of segmentation, the usage pattern goes alongside a sport like bowling or as a quick accompaniment drink or even as a trendy teenage drink where holding the Fosters bottle transports young customers to a different world of lifestyle and minority. There is, of course, multiple usage, which takes place and the fact that it is a low cash-ring product. The size also helps.

Since the segment defined by usage is the light, young, trendy user who apes the West, a certain usage chunk of the young women segment also falls in the consumption segment.

In both the cases of cars as well as the newly-launched beers, focusing and selecting specific usage criteria for segmenting the market helps increase trials and market share.

Segmentation by usage could be on the basis of light or heavy consumption, regular or occasional consumption, home-out-of-home consumption as well as the method and style of usage.

As the market becomes more competitive, whether in cars or in beer, a clear segmentation strategy would help launch, increase or even retain market shares and profitability. It product is not segmented specifically and is aimed at everyone, then it is most probably aimed at on one. This could be the beginning of the end of any brand.

QUESTIONS FOR DISCUSSION

1. What criteria have been used in segmentation of the market?
2. "Market segments are essential to reach target markets." Comment on this statement in context of above case.

CASE STUDY 4.3

A CASE OF SEGMENTATION: LACOSTE

"Lacoste does not use price as an excluding factor." That is, the target wearer is described in psychographic, not demographic, terms. It is a brand for the arrived, for the early adopter "who runs a successful business, is respected in his field, has two children and no plans of having any more" according to SLA. The consumer "works harder and plays hard", and appreciated the value of finer, non-fashion-led leisure wear. Teeny-boppers are *persona non grata*. Puneet Malhotra, an employee of Junach Pvt. Ltd. (an SLA franchisee which runs seven outlets), says that most customers are "30 plus".

Lacoste's perceived value stays high because its wearers form a club of like-minded folk, snooty to the extent that all club member are. As the brand's wearers are walking-talking advertisements on the desired social circuitry, the prospective buyer charmed by the kind of people he see wearing the crocodile.

The quintessential Lacoste wearer is a mobile phone-equipped, leisure-loving globetrotting yuppie in his 30s or 40s, bent on staying fit, and a keen golfer or weekend tennis buff, he's a great spender of self-earned money, casual at the right times, global in his thinking and with little time for woolly "intellectuals" who refuse to admit that clothes are a personality statement or think that getting mournful about Indian poverty is achieving more than what he does with his time (adding to GDP growth).

Of course, the audience is only a subset of India's wealthy. Casualness and leisure are not well-in-graned concepts here, shown by the weak response to Club Med's activity packed foreign holidays, "People come with an 'I am sorry' look when forwarding their leave application," says Kochar, lamenting the stigma attached to splurging. Thanks to the Gandhi-Nehru legacy, "the belief is, if he's so rich he must have had a hand in some scam. We are not comfortable with wealth, with success".

Change has begun. Back in 1993, Lacoste came with the understanding that there were about half-a-million potential buyers. In four years, the tribe is said to have doubled. "Of these, about a lakh are buying Lacoste," believes Kochar. He predicts that the group should swell by half in the next five years. By then, much of the current segment of 20s, in fashionable professions, with good degrees from premier institutes, "in the words of Darlie O. Koshy, professor and chairman, apparel marketing and merchandising. National Institutes of Fashion Technology (NIFT). "Their purchasing power is rising, aspirations are high and they can afford to buy on impulse as they pay by plastic."

QUESTION FOR DISCUSSION

1. Discuss Lactose approach for segmentation of their market.

CASE STUDY 4.4

HAPPY HOLIDAY RESORTS LIMITED

The time-sharing concept of enjoying life long holidays year after year for only a reasonable one-time investment in holidays for the future at today's low price is still a relatively new one. The concept is based on the premise that since most people visited tourist spots annually, their requirements as far as holiday resorts were concerned, could be met by periodical week long ownership on an annually recurring basis, with similar week long slots being sold to others.

When this concept was introduced in India way back in 1985, it drew a lot of flak because of several reasons. First, people were not very well aware of the concept although it was very popular abroad.

People did not want to be committed to going every year at a particular fixed period for 99 years. People did not always get a resort at a place of their proximity preference and this meant a large amount of time and money in travelling to far off resorts. As a result, several companies, which had entered this business had to close down their operations. The concept itself was left with a stigma attached to it.

Happy Holiday Resorts was started in 1990 as a private limited company based at Chennai. It contacted customers door-to-door explaining to them about the time-share concept and extending additional facilities like ticketing, pick up and drop facilities, getting or renting your time-share, easy installment payments, off season discounts and most of all, honouring its commitments.

The company hired about 50 bungalows in Kodai and Ooty initially. But within the next 4 years, it had six resorts fully operational. It has plans to come up with 25 resorts by the year 2000. It has an impressive 22,000 strong customer base with a 45 per cent of the market under its hold.

The awareness and acceptance of the time-share concept has led to a number of companies entering this business, offering holidays at exotic places on competitive rates. The time-share concept has entered the growth phase of its life cycle and it is imperative for Happy Holiday Resorts to identify segments on new bases so that it can concentrate its efforts on them and maintain its lead.

QUESTIONS FOR DISCUSSION

1. Which approach to segmenting should Happy Holiday Resorts adopt and why?
2. What are the statistical techniques that you would apply to the approach that you suggest.

CASE STUDY 4.5

THE WAR OF COLOURS

In September '95, when the $1.8 billion international cosmetics giant Revlon International began operations in India, every market watcher felt their entry spelt danger for local numero uno Lakme. Not only was Revlon a formidable force in colour cosmetics worldwide, every consumer research showed that the Indian woman caved for foreign labels. So if Modi Revlon—the 76:24 joint venture company—could get its price-value equation right the opportunity was enormous, in all, the market signals were right for Revlon on quickly ramp up to its desired slot of being the number one player in cosmetics in India.

But two and a half years later, the picture isn't exactly as pretty. Although Revlon has sneaked up behind Lakme in the colours business, it is still way behind its original targets. By the end of financial year 1997-98, the joint venture company had targeted to reach the Rs. 100 crore sales figure. Instead, in the first year, 1995-96, the JV reached a turnover of Rs. 20 crore, but in 1996-97, it felt to Rs. 19 crore. Profits too, are now expected only after the fourth year.

Right now, the company is rolling back its ambitious plans by withdrawing from as many as 100 towns and focusing instead on the top 100 towns. Besides, in deferences to its heady ambitions, apart from colour, Revlon had spread its product portfolio to skincare products, haircare, eyecare and perfumes, none of which paid off.

Today, the watchword is caution. But has the realisation come wee bit late?

That's because while Revlon coped with its initial hiccups, rivals have braced themselves with new warpaint. And much of the battle in colour cosmetics—Revlon's international strength—is now being fought on affordability. Besides, the small premium market will soon see the entry of genuinely premium brands from the world market. So will Revlon climb down from its premium perch in India.

Image Above All Else

Ask any marketer about purchase determinants in colour cosmetics and invariably, shades and price are mentioned together. Colours is Revlon's international strength; so is price. "It is a mass market brand abroad," agrees Pradeep Pant director, sales and marketing, Modi Revlon.

But when Revlon started out, its first set of "soft targets" clearly included those who had interacted with the brand on trips abroad. And as it typically happens with foreign brands in India, these consumers would rather prefer to pick it from abroad. So apart from the grey market, Modi's team had to first gun for this clientele. "We had to beat that old feeling among Indians that whatever sells here in inferior to the company's products sold abroad," explains Pant.

An exhaustive study was conducted to understand pricing for the Indian market and the product portfolio. Work began early in 1993, involving market research agencies, to gather market data and test products imported from abroad. It took into account three things.

- Revlon's international strengths of colours;
- The level of local awareness of Revlon products; and
- Local opportunities.

Revlon came out in tests as a well-recognised brand, Surprisingly, so did Flex, its sub-brand of shampoos, which is not very big internationally. And courtesy the grey market, even Carlie perfume scored well. That got the Revlon team quite excited. So they also hunted for market-specific opportunities, as in fairness creams. Since Revlon sells these in some countries, it did have the technical expertise. The positioning of Revlon was decided: the international colour and beauty authority.

The launch hamper comprised two ranges of lipsticks and nail enamels—Super Lustrous, at Rs. 99 a stick, and Out-rageous, at Rs. 250 a stick. Flex shampoo was available for Rs. 39 (100 ml), slightly expensive than Ultra Doux's equivolume offering. It was not possible to price colours below that. A Revlon lipstick that retails in India for Rs. 99, says pant, would be available in the US for about Rs. 240.

At that time, Lakme Ultra was the most premium brand below that price band. Revlon was double its price. Before Revlon's entry, the colours market was divided into three clear segments-budget (or popular), mass and premium. And before Lakme even sniffed the entry of foreign players, the market could be divided into only popular and discount brands. That was till Lakme introduced Orchids, a premium range, in 1994. Under it, a lipstick could be had for Rs. 195 and a bottle of nail enamel for Rs. 165.

It was a huge jump for a brand like Lakme, whose other sub-brand Ultra sold colours close to the Rs. 50 price point. Orchids was meant to keep competition at bay in the premium segment, as well as to lend a premium image to Lakme as such. It didn't work. The premium end grew in bare single digits while the budget segment showed growth rates of 30 per cent. Because by 1994, excise duties had plummeted to 40 per cent from 70 per cent. Newer customers were coming in, and obviously at the lower end.

No wonder Orchids did not sprout. The ladder was too steep. So Lakme turned to tap the lower segment where Tips and Toes was making a dent. It had priced its products slightly below the Rs. 50 price point. More importantly, it was cleverly targeted to a younger, fun-loving teenager, as against Lakme's sophisticated, memsahib image. It was clever because teenagers were beginning to cast their influence on the colours market.

Elle 18 did the trick. It was an upgradation vehicle for users of unorganised sector brands to move to a high-pitch brand from a known company. This included a lot of teenagers. The ladder of upgradation was about Rs. 3-4 more. For the class of upgrades, anything beyond that would not have succeeded, remembers an ex-Lakme person who was part of the team that conceived Elle 18 Ultra, nearly Rs. 20 higher, continued to cater to the affluent woman. So when Revlon entered the scene a few months later, it hoped to spur graduations from Ultra into a newly-created upper mass segment.

A Ladder Too Steep

As soon as Lakme, which had been monitoring the Revlon launch closely, noticed Revlon settling down to a price point of Rs. 100 and below, it reached quickly by dropping price on Orchids. Today, Orchids is believed to be retailing its colours at close to Rs. 100. But given that the difference between Ultra and Revlon was almost 100 per cent, the upgradation prices was understandably slow.

Revlon would have known this. And it must be said that it did initiate a lot many efforts to smoothen and accelerate this upgradation. The first was to keep strict check on quality, it meant a large import content, as high as 70-80 per cent. The company hired sub-contractors—five in all, as of now—who were "educated", informs Pant, by a Revlon team from New York. They were later evaluated on product samples. Samples are sent abroad for regular tests even now. Till date, a Revlon International executive sits as director, quality control, in the Indian venture's Delhi office.

Like its products, the company also attended to the quality of people. Pant himself served in Yves Saint Laurent earlier. There were the US executives for technical inputs; some came from Lakme. With domestic market insights, they helped build an enviable distribution chain: 22C and FAs and 100 distributors reaching out to 15,000 'doors' (industry parlance for retail outlets) in 100 towns.

Newly half of all 15,000 doors are in the four metros plus Bangalore. The company has tried to match rivals on margins by extending mark-up of 12 per cent, 5-8 per cent and 2-3 per cent respectively to the retailer, distributor and C and FAs. Since 1996 however, Tips and Toes, which has begun to move up the price ladder, has edged up the margins in its distribution chain.

New Colours in the Market

Revlon's entry squrred competition to upgrade. Soon after Revlon entered, 'Tips and Toes' marketer, Paramount Costmetics, hired ace make-up artist, Mickey Contractor to develop shades as well as endorse the brand. Ads turned cosmopolitan. Against Revlon's 30-plus shades each in lipsticks and nail enamels, Tips and Toes extended to some 80-odd shades. Late last year, it launched a credible upgradation vehicle of its own—Duo Tone.

With two shades in one stick, Duo Tone was priced at a convenient Rs. 52. It comes in 16 combinations. On the day of the launch, it is said, 50,000 units were booked in two hours, courtesy four samples, Rajesh Mehta, marketing manager, Paramount, says the price is now being hiked to Rs. 60. Besides, the Rs. 27.5 crore increase in its market share to 15 per cent in lipsticks and 18 per cent in nail enamel.

Revlon, on its own, notched up a size of nearly Rs. 9 crore in lipsticks and Rs. 6 crore in nail enamels. Elle 18 too, if Lakme's claims are to be believed, has growth to as big as Revlon—at 18 per cent of the colours market. Says a market observer. "The experimental teeny generation is responsible for this. While all companies kept on talking about targets as the urban woman, most forgot to attend to the teenager". Elle 18 offered them a short, shared ladder.

Since colour cosmetics are perceived as a "frivolous product" (compared to serious treatment products for skin-care or hair-care), in the words of the head of an international cosmetics company, teenagers are more likely to try out something new here, and keep returning for more. Revlon's pricing did not permit them to Elle 18's or Duo Tone's did. The marred, relatively older woman could afford it. But here, loyalty levels are high, believes Tagore Berry of Enhance (on the Tips and Toes account). "She may buy one Rs. 100 lipstick, but if she does not find it good after trial, then the high price will continue to haunt her whenever she open her drawer," reasons he adding, "That is why reasonably—priced lipsticks do well."

It was no secret. "Worldwide dressing tables have lots of mass-market shades, and few premium labels," affirms a senior marketing manager of a rival cosmetics company. No wonder then that Revlon's premium positioning made sustaining business in a place like Parwanoo (in Himachal Pradesh) inviable. Today, Revlon has withdrawn from 100 odd towns beginning April 1996, to concentrate on the core100 towns.

Besides, it is warning to the customer through beauty advisor-addisted (BAA) doors. Of the 100 that it runs now, most are in metros. Young—looking BAs work for Revlon on a contract basis, earning a salary of Rs. 4,000 a month. Additionally, they are incentivised on sales. Their single biggest contribution to the company, besides sales, is the feedback on choices and fashion. For the company, it helps in colour predictions.

What decides their sustenance is the considerable investment that the company is making in merchandising material placed at all BAA doors. Together with BA's salaries, it turns out to been investment of Rs. 10,000-25,000 (depending on size) in opening a counter. The returns are not divulged. Industry watchers say that Revlon keeps a sales target of eight times the cost incurred on such a door internationally (in countries where it runs BAAs), while that attained in India is three. That is, sales of around Rs. 40,000 per outlet.

The Nub of the Matter

Despite all its efforts, the key questions before the Modi-Revlon team is when should it dismantle its premium positioning? So far, Revlon has chosen not to tinker with its prices, despite the fact it acts as a barrier to upgrades. But the fragmented selling environment in the country does little to support that premium image.

Source: Iqbal Singh in Business Standard.

QUESTIONS FOR DISCUSSION

1. Discuss the marketing strategy adopted by Revlon's competition.
2. Explain the factors which are influencing in purchase decisions in colours business.

CASE STUDY 4.6

SUCCESS STORY OF NIPPO

Navin Mehta, a fresh Chemical Engineer, developed a new detergent during his M. Tech. Course. Upon passing out he invested a small capital to start manufacturing and selling the detergent under the brand name 'Nippo'. Coming from a middle class family himself Mehta decided to price his detergent much lower than the other detergents available in the market at that time. His pricing strategy, paid right dividends and 'Nippo' became an instant success. Using his newly acquired financial strength Navin developed a premium quality bathing soap with a unique colour and perfume combination. Although the cost price of this soap was itself high, Navin again priced it substantially lower to comparable products in the market by maintaining a low profit margin.

(AIMA, June 1996)

QUESTIONS FOR DISCUSSION

1. Suggest an appropriate marketing plan to Navin Mehta.
2. Do you feel Navin has committed a pricing this time? Give reasons for your answer.

CASE STUDY 4.7

SEGMENT TO SELL

India's diversity could provide plenty of opportunities should marketing strategies be designed and executed well. Unfortunately, several companies have failed to grasp the nuances of Indian consumer behaviour and hence, their products bombed in the marketplace.

Segmentation is a powerful tool through which markets can be handled and brands built. Two case studies illustrate how poor segmentation has led to miscalculation. Result: Companies entering India have either failed or taken a lot of time to succeed.

First, cars. Lack of proper segmentation of the automobile market resulted in most cars being launched in the mid-size segment. Soon, the mid-size segment was choked with cars like Daewod's Cielo, Opel's Astra and Ford's Escort among others. The mid-size segment is a niche market, but there were few takers here. Today, most of these companies are unable to achieve even 25 to 30 per cent of their target and have landed up with heavy inventory. Now they are forced to offer deep discounts and resort to desperate sales.

Had proper segmentation been done, the focus would have been on small-size cars that are mostly affordable and comprise the largest and the fastest growing segment. This has been proved by the success of Maruti 800 and Zen. It look a lot of time for people to realise the segmentation folly. So car manufacturers are now making a beeline for the small car segment, which again is threatened by excess capacity and may ultimately lead to price wars.

Had proper segmentation been adopted, there would have been another brand to challenge the Maruti 800 and Zen monopoly long ago and that brand would have gained good sales and market share.

There are certain brands of cars, which are doing well. Take the Zen, for example. Its better aesthetics, more leg space than the Maruti 800 and better take technology inputs, make it popular. This car is ideal for a distinct segment.

The positioning of the Zen has been directed towards a segment defined by the parameter of usage. Segmentation for usage is a powerful weapon in the marketing armoury. Customers desirous of upgrading themselves from a Maruti 800 or those who desire a mix of aesthetics and manoeuvrability for regular usage, find the Zen an extremely lucrative option. Result: at a time when the car industry is facing rough weather, the Zen an extremely lucrative option seems to have done better, primarily because it is segmented by usage-kids can be dropped at schools, it is decent enough to be driven to office or can even be used to comfortably drive down to an informal party.

Many times, companies can track usage patterns and segment the market by usage and gain.

Let us take another case study of a recently-launched beverage which has also pegged usage as the criteria for segmenting its market and achieved considerable trails and healthy repeat purchases. Fosters beer has recently been launched in pint-sized bottled alongside the usual larger pack size. The shape and size of the bottle is targeted towards young, trendy, light-users who consider drinking beer as a part of their lifestyle. San Migial and Ice have also been launched in the same size.

In my opinion this particular pack size, which is handy, shapely and international in its look, gained huge ground among light-users. In terms of segmentation, the usage pattern goes alongside a sport like bowling or as a quick accompaniment drink or even as a trendy teenage drink where holding the fosters bottle transports young customers to a different world of lifestyle and minority. There is, of course, multiple usage which takes place and the fact that it is a low cash-ring product. The size also helps.

Since the segment defined by usage is the light, young, trendy user who apes the West, a certain chunk of the young women segment also fall in the consumption segment.

In both the cases of cars as well as the newly-launched beers, focussing and selecting specific usage criteria for segmenting the market helps increase trials and market share.

Segmentation by usage could be on the basis of light or heavy consumption, regular or occasional consumption, home-out-of-home consumption as well as the method and style of usage.

As the market becomes more competitive, whether in cars or in beer, a clear segmentation strategy would help launch, increase or even retain market shares and profitability. If a product is not segmented specifically and is aimed at everyone, then it is most probably aimed at no one. This could be the beginning of the end of any brand.

QUESTIONS OF DISCUSSION

1. What criteria has been used in segmentation of the market?
2. "Market segments are essential to reach target markets." Comment on this statement in context of above case.

DEMAND MEASUREMENT AND SALES FORECASTING

5

All business firms like to know the current as well as the likely demand for their products. Demand forecasting and sales forecasting are important for any marketing planning and control as they serve as the basis for comparison over a period of time. Forecasting helps in identifying and solving marketing and sales problems.

MARKET POTENTIAL

Forecasting exercise involves an understanding of market potential. Consider the example of purchase of a newspaper. To estimate the market potential for newspapers in India, we have to know the number of householders, libraries and other establishments. If we want to know about the market potential of the household sector only, we can assume that each household is subscribing a newspaper each. Thus we can say that the market potential for newspapers is equal to the number of households in the country. Again, if we assume that six people constitute a household, we have about 145 million households. Ideally, this is the household market for newspapers. But then, we know that 25 per cent of Indian population is below the poverty line and hence will not be able to buy newspapers. Besides, almost 40 per cent of Indians fall under the low-income group and given the prices of newspapers, they too may not be able to afford one. So, one is left with only 35 per cent of the total population which is the real market that needs to be targeted.

"Market potential is the limit approached by the market demand as industry's marketing expenditures approach infinity, for a given environment."

In other words, market potential refers to the upper limit of market demand. It is important for us to understand that there are three key terms involved in defining the market potential. These are:

(a) Market demand,
(b) Market expenditure by the industry, and
(c) Defined market environment.

MARKET DEMAND

Market demand is always defined with reference to a price and a time period. It is meaningless to specify demand without reference to price and time period. The statement that demand for cars is 1,00,000 is meaningless. The price at which these cars are demanded is to be mentioned, as with change in price, the quantity demanded may also change, depending upon the time period under consideration. Demand for a commodity may be defined as the, "quantity of a commodity that will be bought at a particular price and during a given period or point of time."

Market demand means the demand of all the consumers in the market for a commodity at a particular price. Market demand schedule shows the total demand of all the consumers in the market at various prices.

MARKET FORECAST

Market forecast refer to the estimates of future sales of a company's products in the market. The following diagram explains the concept of market demand and basic kinds of market measurement:

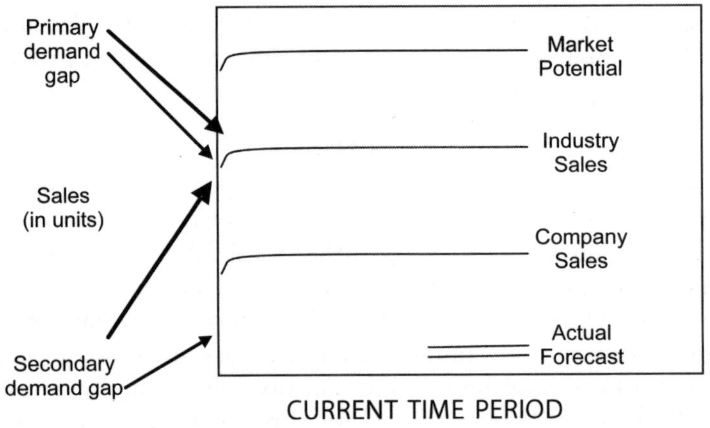

Source: Guitinan, Joseph P. and Paul, Gordon W., *Marketing Management*, McGraw Hill, 1994, p. 107.

Sales Forecasting

Accurate sales forecasting is essential for a firm to enable it to produce the required quantities at the right time and arrange well in advance for the various factors of production, viz., buildings, equipment, machine accessories, raw materials, labour, etc. Some firms may as a policy produce to order but, generally, firms produce in anticipation of future demand. Sales forecasting helps a firm to assess the probable demand for its products and plan its production accordingly. In can also help management in reducing its dependence on chance.

Sales forecasting is also helpful in better planning and allocation of various resources. Planning is always based on certain assumptions about the future course of events. In a world of uncertainty, future conditions can never be predicted perfectly. Yet, the marketer or the administrator must plan and take decisions using whatever, in his judgment, constitutes the best estimate about future developments. Sales forecasting is very popular in industrially advanced countries where demand conditions are always more uncertain than the supply conditions. In developing countries, however, instead of demand, supply is often the limiting factor. High prices and black-markets point to supply bottlenecks.

Sales Budget

A Sales Budget is a programme designed for a stipulated time frame that highlights the selling expenses and the anticipated sales—quantitatively and in value terms. This helps in making an objective estimate of net profit on the selling operations. In real sense, it is a statement aimed at comparing the revenue, net profits, sales volume and the selling expenses relating to a product or entire business.

Since the volume of sales and selling expenses have their bearing on personal selling strategy, it becomes important to consider rather seriously the two key issues, viz.

(a) The quality of sales force, and

(b) The size of the sales force.

The sales volume for the period of question is estimated by using the sales forecast. The sales volume derived at through sales forecast is classified to highlight the quantities of products that are to be sold, sales personnel who would handle their sales and the respective sales districts, the prospective buyers, and the quantities to be sold during different time periods during the plan periods.

After arriving at such a wide based classification, the likely selling expenses that would be incurred in the implementation of the year-round sales programme are then estimated.

The first point in designing a sales budget is the anticipated sales volume. The top sales executives would be involved to the extent of their participation in the sales forecast.

Demand Estimation And Measurement

An accurate estimate of the demand or the response of demand to change in price or other explanatory variables is very difficult. Further, the cost of statistical analysis required for this purpose may exceed the benefits, particularly, when uncertainty is great or when the volume of work involved is too small to provide a reasonable return on the research expenditure. That is why, business firms have to rely on subjective estimates of experienced managers for an effective analysis of a wide range of business problems relating to pricing and marketing. Such empirical estimates and their interpretations are useful for control and management of external factors. For this purpose, surveys and statistical techniques can be used.

1. Surveys

Consumers buy some minimum quantities of various commodities, irrespective of prices. These are minimum requirements to keep the consumers alive. The supernumerary income (income left after the minimum quantities are covered) is allocated among the different commodities on the basis of prices. Consumer surveys deal with intentions of the consumers. They help in demand estimation. However, the likely demand revealed by these surveys may not coincide with the actual demand. Alternatively, experimental surveys or controlled experiments can be used to estimate the effect of demand determinants under management control. But, care should be taken to reduce the influence of unimportant variables to a minimum.

2. Statistical techniques

Statistical techniques combined with the controlled experiments provide reliable estimate of the demand function. Since, trend analysis variable postulating time series of a single independent variable generally ignores the important determinants of demand such as prices, more sophisticated techniques are used. That is why, economists normally use regression techniques to isolate and measure the fluctuations in demand occurring in response to main demand determinants like price and disposable income. This technique involves four steps:

(a) **Identification of Casual Variables.** Casual variables should be chosen with utmost care for estimating the demand function. Non-inclusion of important variables (determinants) as well as inclusion of irrelevant variables jeopardizes the accuracy of estimates. Further, the units of measurements for different variables have to be carefully specified.

(b) **Collection of Historical Data.** Data is the raw material for estimation. If the data on relevant variable are inaccurate, estimated function will be unreliable. The estimation could be based on either time series or cross-section data or both, depending upon the data availability and problem in hand. While the former refers to observations on a variable of a given population over time, the latter pertains to observations on a variable at a point of time across different populations. Another important thing is the sample size for data. The greater the sample size, the more reliable are the estimates. The size of the sample should be greater than the numbers of demand determinants to use the regression method of estimation. If the data on an important variable are not available, proxy or dummy variables could be used. Researchers often use time variable as a proxy for consumers' tastes and preferences.

(c) **Choice of an Appropriate Functional Form.** This stage relates to choice of an appropriate form of the function. The functional form could be linear, quadratic, cubic, double log, semi-log or reciprocal on the basis of experiment with theoretically plausible forms. The form actually chosen by the researcher should be ideal on both theoretical and empirical grounds. For this, the researcher will have to estimate the function in a few alternative forms. Thereafter, with the aid of some statistical tests and a prior knowledge of some of the signs and magnitudes of the coefficients, the most appropriate form can be chosen. The linear and double-log forms and some of the most popular functional forms.

(d) **Estimation of Function.** The last step is economic estimation of the function. The most popular method available for this purpose is the least-squares method of estimation, which is based on unconstrained optimization technique. In this method, estimates of parameters are obtained in such a manner that the sum of the squares of the errors between the actual values of the dependent variable and its estimated value is minimized with respect to each of the parameters under estimation. This method can also be used for estimating equations with more than one cause variable, called as multiple regression equation.

Analysis of Estimated Demand Functions

Estimated demand function has an edge over the theoretical demand function. It not only explains the factors influencing the market as well as the direction of their effects (like the theoretical demand function), but also the magnitudes of such effects. Thus, the managers and decision-makers prefer the estimated demand function to its theoretical counterpart.

Statistically estimated empirical demand functions give us information on elasticities. Such information is very useful for corporate planning and business policy decisions. The specific values of elasticities can be used to analyse the effect (magnitude as well as direction) of market forces on demand, as explained in this chapter under 'Demand Forecasting'. Further, the estimated demand function can be used to derive the equations of the demand and Engel Curves for given values of other variables by substituting the values of all variables other than the own price or income (as the case may be) in the estimated demand function. This can then be used to derive equation for average revenue (AR), total revenue (TR) and marginal revenue (MR) curves. Furthermore, the estimated demand function can be used to provide policy guidelines. Finally, the estimated demand function can be used for forecasting demand by setting the values of casual (independent) variables in the forecast period.

DEMAND FORECASTING

Good strategic planning rests on the foundation of good forecasting. Unlike back casting (backward projection of data), it is forward projection of data. It is an essential tool in developing new products, scheduling production, determining necessary inventory levels and creating a distribution system. Its essence is estimating future events according to the past patterns and applying judgement to those projections. In other words, forecasting is an attempt to foresee the future by examining the past. Business firms can estimate and minimise the future risk and uncertainty through forecasting and forward planning. Without forecasting, forward planning will be directionless and meaningless. These *ex-ente forecasts* are often made for a number of periods in future. The forecasts for past and present periods, which are carried out to test the credibility of the forecasting models, are called *ex-post* forecasts.

Forecasts are not to be confused with guesses. Guesses are estimates of future events, but they are not necessarily unbiased or objectively calculated. Through intuition, some self-styled prophets envision devastating earthquakes in Southern California or the imminent demise of human through the nuclear war or global plague. But, generally these are not forecasts; since, most are based on neither systematic nor objective measurement of facts. They are opinions. In contrast, good forecasts are built by applying sound scientific procedures, so as to minimise the error of estimation.

Virtually all types of national and international organisations—Government, social and business engage in some type of sales forecasting. The goal, of course, is to improve management's ability to plan and control operations. Churches try to predict future revenues from members' contributions to develop reasonable budgets. School administrators use enrolment forecasts to determine faculty sizes, supplies and classroom requirements. Similarly, commercial firms also forecast sales in one way or another. They are integral part of corporate planning and decision-making. Sales forecasting is a crucial activity for planning, survival and growth of a corporate unit.

As production takes time (called gestation period), business firms would like to know the likely sales for a product at a future date to plan and execute its production properly. It assumes greater relevance, where demand conditions are more uncertain than supply conditions. Sales forecasting is an attempt to estimate the future level of demand on the basis of past as well as present knowledge and experience to avoid both under production and over production. It may be based on estimates of demand potential of the entire industry. The demand forecasting serves as the reference point for all marketing control efforts. It is indispensable in modern business.

Most estimates generated in high-quality sales forecasting are derived objectively and systematically rather than subjectively with guesses and hunches. An analyst carefully selects a forecasting tool, like an equation, and then applies it to quantitative data.

Sales forecasts may be passive or active. The former predict the future demand by extrapolating the demands of the previous years in the absence of any action by the firm. Here, the things are assumed to continue the way they have been in the past. These forecasts are used only to assess the impact of new policies on the market. While, the latter estimate the future scenario inclusive of own future actions and strategies of the firm itself. These forecasts are more meaningful, as they take into account the likely changes in the relevant variable in estimating future demand. Here, the firm manipulates the demand by changing price, product quality, promotion effort, etc.

Sales forecast methods vary according to whether they apply to a large aggregate, such as the whole economy (macro forecasts), or to a component of this aggregate, such as an industry or a company (micro forecasts). A frequent practice is to translate forecasts of overall levels into industry forecasts by trade associations and to use these, in turn, to generate company forecasts. However, small firms cannot afford these sophisticated techniques.

Macro forecasts are based on national income, production, general price level, etc. These forecasts help the Government in implementing price control policy, export-import policy, etc. Management should consider the macro forecasts while taking decision. Macro parameters like levels of GNP, rate of interest; savings, investment, taxation, Government expenditure, unemployment, prices, income and population are few macro variables of concern. Which aggregate measures are important and what impact they have depends on the particular company and situation. To illustrate, movie attendance tends to increase during recessions, whereas the demand for housing tends to decrease. Further, rise in national income, per capita income, investment, population and Government expenditure raise sales. While rise in savings and taxation contract demand.

Demand forecasting is very popular in developed countries, where demand conditions are relatively more uncertain. In India also, economic liberalisation and consequent rising competition during recent years have increased the importance of demand forecasting. That is why, the National Council of Applied Economic Research (NCAER) prepares macro demand forecasts for a number of products. These forecasts help in forecasting industry demand, company demand and market segment demand.

Characteristics of Good Sales Forecasting Methods

The following eight major characteristics can be identified with forecasting methods (techniques):

1. Time horizon

The length of time over which a decision is being made has a bearing on the appropriate technique to use. The probability of forecasting error generally decreases with increase in the length of the time horizon. Long periods, such as more than a year, are difficult to model in a way that these are based on extrapolation of history. Sales forecasts for consumer durables and plant replacements are generally on long-term time horizon. Whereas, sales forecasts for consumer goods are bound to be of shorter time horizon. Generally speaking, qualitative forecasting procedures are better suited for forecasting long periods into the future. On the other hand, quantitative techniques are more accurate in the short run, such as within a year or less.

2. Level of detail

The level of detail needed should match the focus of the decision-making unit in the forecast. For example, production planning must make its decision at the individual product level, whereas the corporate planning department is likely to be happy with aggregate sales forecasts by product categories. The more items that forecasts are required for, the greater is the need to use straightforward models that require little time to implement.

3. Stability

Forecasting in situations that are relatively stable over time requires less attention than those that are in constant flux. In stable situations, the existing pattern is assumed to continue in the future and past patterns can be easily extrapolated in future. On the other hand, unstable and uncertain situations require more attention by management and a greater total forecasting effort, particularly, for latest information.

4. Pattern of data

Data required to use the underlying relationships should be available on timely basis. Each forecasting method is based on an underlying assumption about the data. As different forecasting methods vary in their ability to identify different patterns, it is useful to make the pattern in the data with the method that suits it the most. To judge whether the model fits the data being forecast, it is imperative to know the assumptions behind the model selected.

Many data are available within the firm. Some appear in records and reports such as annual statements, shipping documents, invoices, employment records and production reports. The organisation might have a management information system (MIS) responsible for gathering and pre-processing relevant data. Other information is often collected from sources outside the firm, including publications by Government (like, Central Statistical Organisation), universities, foundations, trade associations and professional research firms. Government sources are particularly valuable, since federal agencies acquire a huge quantity and variety of data and publish the results in an easily available and inexpensive form.

Analysts must strive to ensure that data obtained from others are accurate, precise and relevant; otherwise sales forecasts will be in error. They should be especially careful to determine that adequate diligence and care were exercised by the source. They may have to examine the definitions of variables used by others. Because these may not agree with there own. Further, analysts should try to uncover evidence of purposeful distortion of the data by others in the light of their own special interests. For example, a trade association or special-cause group might overstate some data to support its position on some matter.

5. Type of model

Other assumptions are also made in each forecasting technique that must fit the situation under consideration. To illustrate, regression (one type of technique) assumes causality by one or more independent variables. This causal it must be realistic (not just mathematically convenient), for the model to be used. Management usually need not be expert in the mathematical details of each method, but they should know the assumptions of any model and whether these fit a particular situation. The technique used should be easily comprehended by the management to give quick meaningful results.

6. Cost

Several costs are associated with adopting forecasting procedure within an organisation like managerial development, storage, operation and opportunity (in terms of other techniques that might have been applied). Naturally, the variation in costs affects the selection of the forecasting method. There is a need for an economic consideration of balancing the benefits against the extra cost of providing the improved forecasting.

7. Accuracy

It is measured by the degree of deviations between past forecasts and current actual performance or present forecasts and future performance. If the likely state comes close to the actual state, it means that the forecast is dependable. The level of accuracy required has a bearing on the model to be selected. A tolerable error might be 10 per cent in some instances, whereas a five per cent error spells disaster in others. Of course, the greater the required accuracy, the greater the cost of generating a forecast. The forecaster has to make a trade-off between the accuracy required and the cost to achieve that accuracy through cost-revenue analysis.

8. Ease of application

Models must be chosen within the abilities of the users to understand them and within the time allowed for using them. This will enable management to properly interpret the results. Simplicity of handling the method matters in the selection of the method.

Steps in Sales Forecasting

Sales forecasting is a scientific exercise. It has to go through a number of steps. At each step, critical considerations are required to be made. The following steps are necessary for sales forecasting. These steps present a systematic way of initiating, designing and implementing a forecasting system.

1. Identification of objective

To begin with, the economist should be clear about the uses of forecast data and how it is related to forward planning by the firm. Depending upon its use, the economist has to choose the type of forecasts—short-run or long-run, active or passive, conditional or non-conditional, etc.

2. Nature of product and market

The important consideration is the nature of product or service for which we are attempting a sales forecast. We have to examine carefully whether the product is consumer or producer good, perishable or durable good. While analyzing the sales for finished goods, sales for corresponding raw materials and intermediate goods should also be analysed. The elasticity of sales for intermediate goods depends on their relative importance in the price of the final product. Further advertising and price-cutting is more important for final goods than intermediate goods. Time factor is a crucial determinant in sales forecasting. Perishable commodities such as fresh vegetables and fruits can be sold over a limited period of time. If there are storage facilities, consumers can adjust sales according to price, income and availability. Here, sales forecasting can avoid the waste. Furthermore, the forecasting of sales must consider the stage, where the product belongs, i.e. introduction (slow rise in sales), growth (rapid rise in sales with acceptance of the product), maturity and saturation (maximum sales), obsolescence and decline (sales taper off with introduction of substitute products). Finally, the nature of competition in the market (perfect or imperfect) should not be overlooked.

3. Determinants of demand

Depending on the nature of product and nature of forecasts, different determinants will assume different degree of importance in different demand functions. In addition, it is important to consider socio-psychological determinants; specially demographic, sociological and psychological factor affecting the demand.

4. Analysis of factors

In an analysis of statistical demand function, it is customary to classify the explanatory factors into (i) trend factors; (ii) cyclical factors; (iii) seasonal factors; and (iv) random factors. An analyse is of factors is specially important depending upon whether it is the aggregate demand in the economy or the industry's demand or the company's demand or the consumer's demand, which is being predicted.

5. Choice of method

This is a very important step. The economist has to choose a particular technique from among various techniques of demand forecasting, depending upon the nature of the product. Then, data is collected to make the forecast. In some cases, it may be possible to use more than one method. However, the choice of method should be logical and appropriate, as accuracy, to a great extent, depends on this choice. The choice itself depends on a number of factors—the degree of accuracy required, reference period of the forecast, complexity of the relationship postulated in the demand function, available time for forecasting exercise, availability of data, size of cost budget for the forecast, etc.

6. Testing accuracy

There are various methods for testing statistical accuracy in a given forecast. Some of them are simple and inexpensive; others are quite complex and difficult. This testing is needed to avoid/reduce the margin of forecasting error and thereby to improve the decision-making. The 'absolute level of forecasting error' is equal to the difference between the actual value and the forecast value. Graphically, it is measured by the vertical distance between the forecast value curve and the 45° line (showing perfect accuracy due to coincidence of forecast value and realised value) for a particular period. If forecasts are made for more than one year, then average absolute level of error is found out by taking the arithmetic mean of the absolute values of forecasting errors of different periods. However, Percentage Absolute Error (PAE) test is better, which is mathematically shown as:

$$PAE = \frac{Y_t \hat{Y}_t}{Y_t} \times 100$$

Y_t is forecasted (estimated) value.

Y_t is realised (actual or true) value.

Significance, Role and Objectives of Demand Forecasting

Significance of demand forecasting in the context of business policy decisions can hardly be over-emphasised. There is no choice between forecasting and non-forecasting, as changes are natural in the present dynamic world. The demand forecasts of particular products provide a guideline for demand forecasts for related industries. For example, the demand forecast for cotton textiles may provide an idea of the likely sales for the textile machinery industry, dyestuff industry as also for readymade garments industry. At the macro-level, demand forecasts may also help the government in determining whether imports are necessary to meet any possible deficit in the domestic supply, or in devising appropriate export promotion policies, if there is a surplus.

The need of forecasting differs according to the times span of forecasting. When the fluctuations in demand are more, relatively shorter period should be chosen.

Need or Objectives of Short-term Forecasting

Short-term forecasting may cover a period of three months, six months to one year, depending upon the nature of business. It is generally concerned with forecasting products. Short-term forecasting is useful in the following ways:

(a) **Appropriate Production Scheduling.** The firm can avoid the problem of over-production and the problem of short supply by estimating seasonal variation in demand. For this purpose, production schedules have to be geared to expected demand.

(b) **Suitable Purchase Policy.** Demand forecasting helps the firm in reducing costs of purchasing raw materials and controlling inventory by determining its future resource requirement.

(c) **Appropriate Price Policy.** Appropriate price policy can be determined depending upon the anticipation of market demand conditions. It can also avoid an increase in price, when the market conditions are expected to be weak and a reduction in price, when the market is going to be strong.

(d) **Setting Realistic Sales Targets for Salesmen.** If targets are set too high, they will discourage salesmen, who fail to achieve them. If targets are set at unrealistically low level, the targets will be achieved easily and hence incentives given by management will prove to be meaningless.

(e) **Forecasting Financial Requirements.** Cash requirements depend on demand level and production operations. Moreover, it takes time to arrange for funds on reasonable terms. Demand forecasts will, therefore, enable arrangement of sufficient funds on reasonable terms well in advance for production, advertisement, etc.

Need or Objectives of Long-term Forecasting

Long-term forecasting covers a period of five, ten or twenty years. It provides information for major strategic decisions. Introduction of new products, invariably, involves a long-term forecast. In this case, researcher has to consider long-term changes in population, tastes and preferences of the buyers, technology, product life-cycle, etc. Following are the important uses of long-term forecasting,

(a) **Business Planning.** Starting of a new unit or expansion of an existing unit of production requires an analysis of the long-term demand potential of the products in question. A multi-product firm must ascertain not only the total sales situation, but also the demand and its distribution over various products. If a company has better knowledge than its rivals of the growth trends of the aggregate demand and its distribution over various products, its competitive position would be much better.

(b) **Financial Planning.** Planning for raising funds requires considerable advance notice. Long-term demand forecasts are quite essential to assess long-term financial requirements for purchasing machines, raw materials, research and development programmes, etc.

(c) **Planning Manpower Requirements.** Training and personnel development are long-term propositions, taking considerable time to complete. They can be started well in advance only on the basis of estimates of manpower requirements assessed according to long-term demand forecasts.

METHODS OR TECHNIQUES OF SALES FORECASTING

The importance of selecting the right sales forecasting method cannot be overstated. However, the choice is complicated, because each situation might require a different method. Management should be aware of the factors favouring one method over another in a given sales-forecasting situation. In some cases, managers are interested in the total sales for a product or service. In other circumstances, the projection may focus on the firm's probable market share. Forecasts can also provide information on the product mix. Major decisions in large business houses are generally based on forecasts of some type. In some cases, the forecast may be little more than an intuitive assessment of value judgement of the future by those involved in the decision. Thus, no forecasting method is suitable for all circumstances. Selection of a forecast has to be appropriate to the situation, i.e. objective, urgency, data availability, nature of the product, time horizon, cost the firm can afford and accuracy level required. Further, various forecasts have to be linked properly for correct decision making. It is always prudent to use more than one forecast for cross-checking and for improving the credence of forecast. Various forecasting method are shown in Chart 5.1. None of these methods is perfect. These methods can be used to derive macro as well as micro forecasts. When requisite data or firm forecasts are not available, the firm's sales can be forecasted by multiplying the forecasted firm's share in industry sales (through some statistical method like trend method to the past data of variable) and forecasted industry's sales of the product. Similarly, likely regional sales can derived from the aggregate sales in the industry as a whole. The following are important methods of forecasting.

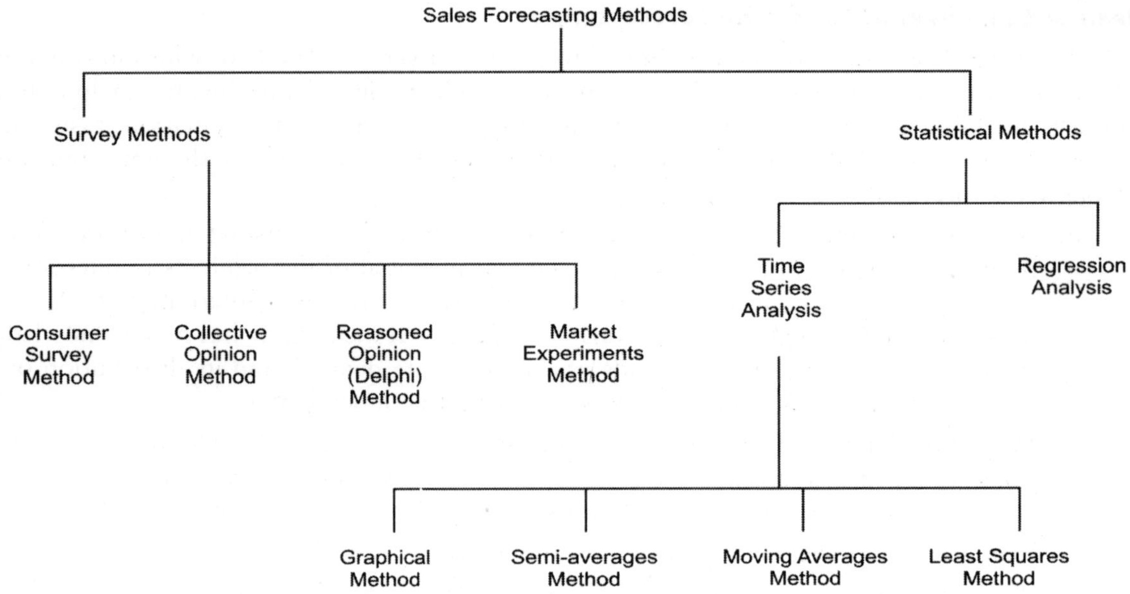

Chart 5.1

Survey Methods

Under this approach surveys are conducted about the intentions of consumers (individuals, firms or industries), option in experts or of markets. Under census survey, all consumers/ experts/markets are surveyed. When sample surveys, a selected sub-set of them are surveyed and through study, inferences whole population are drawn. These methods are usually suitable for short-term forecasts due nature of consumers' intentions. New products sales forecast also makes use of survey approach, as data availability problem is overcome through surveys of consumers. Few important survey methods are discussed here.

1. Consumer survey method

Surveys of managerial plans can be one of the important methods of forecasting. The rationale for conducting such surveys is that plans generally form the basis for future actions. By using this method, a firm can ask consumers, what and how much they are planning to buy at various prices of the product for the forthcoming time period, usually a year. If the product happens to be a consumer good, the consumers are firms or industries using that product. The survey may involve a complete enumeration of all consumers of the given product, whose demand is to be forecasted. If there are 'n' consumers in all, each demand D_i then the total demand forecast will be

$$\frac{\Sigma D_i}{i = 1}$$

This type of complete enumeration or census method is time consuming, tedious and cumbersome, particularly, for a product having vast market. So, a relatively cost-effective, less tedious, less time-consuming sample or survey method may be used. The forecaster selects a few consuming units out of the relevant population and then collects data on the likely demands for the product. If the probable demand of the selected consumers is D_i, then the total demand forecast for the commodity will be estimated

where D_i is the number of consumers in group. Here, a care needs to be taken that forecaster's bias does not creep into the sampling procedure. Further, the consumers may be uncertain about the quantity they intend to purchase from a particular firm.

Merits

(a) It is a simple method, as it is not based on past historical record.

(b) It is a direct method of assessing information from the primary sources.

(c) It saves time and cost by conducting survey on a representative sample through issue of questionnaires or otherwise depending upon the complexities of the problem.

(d) It does not introduce any bias or value judgement, particularly, 'census method', where the data is simply recorded and aggregated.

Demerits

(a) There may be personal bias of the consumers in answering the questions of questionnaire.

(b) It becomes difficult for a firm to ascertain the number of consumers that intend to buy from that firm. These methods only give information about demand for a product of the industry. Survey method may not be directly useful for estimating demand for a particular firm. Tools like Markov chain-process has to be employed to find the firm's share in the total estimated demand for the product market.

(c) Utility of these estimates is limited to a period of about one year.

(d) There may be sampling error, if the sample is not properly chosen.

2. Collective opinion method

Under this method (also called sales-force polling), salesmen or experts are required to estimate expected future demand of the product in their respective territories and sections. The rationale of this method is that salesmen, being the closest to the customers, are likely to have the most intimate feel of the market, i.e. customer reaction to the products of the firm and their sales trends. The estimates of individual salesmen are averaged or consolidated to find out the total estimated sales, and then reviewed by the top executives to eliminate the bias of optimism on the part of some salesmen and pessimism on the part of others. These revised estimates are further examined in the light of factors like proposed changes in selling prices, product designs and advertisement programmes, expected changes in competition, changes in secular forces like purchasing power, income distribution, employment, population, etc. The final sales forecast would emerge after these factors have been taken into account. This method is known as the 'collective opinion method', as it takes advantage of collective wisdom of salesmen, departmental heads like production manager, sales manager, marketing manager, managerial economist, etc. and the top executives.

Merits

(a) The method is simple and does not involve the use of statistical techniques.

(b) The forecasts are based on first-hand knowledge of salesmen and others directly connected with sales.

(c) The method may prove quite useful in forecasting sales of new products. Of course, here salesmen will have to depend more on their judgement than in the case of existing products.

Demerits

(a) It is almost completely subjective, as personal opinions can possibly influence the forecast. Salesmen may even understate the forecast, if their sales quotas are to be based on it.

(b) The usefulness of this method is restricted to short-term forecasting, i.e., for a period of about one year. These forecasts may not be useful for long-term production planning.

(c) Salesmen may be unaware of the broader economic changes likely to have an impact on the future demand.

3. Reasoned opinion (Delphi) method

A variant of opinion poll and survey method is Delphi method, developed by Rand Corporation of South America in late 1940s for predicting technical changes. This method was earlier followed by Greeks. It consists of an attempt to arrive at a consensus in an uncertain area by questioning a group of experts, until the responses appear to converge along a single line or the issues causing disagreement clearly defined. The researcher or coordinator provides each expert with the previous responses including the reasons thereof. He may also bridge the gap between opinions of experts by arranging more meetings and bringing them together. He can also temper the 'interval forecast' (i.e. the lower and upper limits within which the demand forecast to be) to needed 'point forecast' through his conceived overall assessment and judgement. Thus, like collective opinion method, Delphi method also uses opinion of the experts to come to a logical conclusion regarding future demand. However, in this method, the group of experts employed should not be directly involved with that particular firm or industry.

Merits

(a) It facilitates the maintenance of anonymity of the respondent's identity throughout the discussion.

(b) This method renders it possible to pose the problem to the expert at one time and have their response. The experts can even revise their responses.

(c) This technique saves time and other resources in approaching a large number of experts for views.

Demerits

(a) Since, it is a tedious method, the panelists must be rich in their expertise, possess wide knowledge, experience of the subject along with an aptitude and earnest disposition towards the participants.

(b) The Delphi method presupposes that its conductors are objective in their job, possess ample abilities to conceptualise the problems for discussion, generate considerable thinking, stimulate dialogue among panelists and make inferential analysis of the multitudinal view of the participants. However, this may not happen.

4. Market experiments method

This method is very popular in developed countries, but relatively new and less tried in India. Under this method, the main determinants of the demand of a product like price, advertising, product design, packaging, quality, etc., are identified. These factors are then varied separately over different markets or over different time periods, holding other factors constant. The effect of the experiment on consumer behaviour is studied under actual or controlled market conditions, which is used for overall forecasting purpose. Here, the market divisions must be homogeneous with regard to income, population, caste, religion, sex, age, tastes, preferences, etc. For example, controlled experiment was performed by the Parker Pen Company in USA to gauge the effect of the price rise on the demand for Quink Ink. In controlled experiments, token money may be provided to the consumers and they may be asked to shop around in a simulated market. This method is called as simulation method or laboratory experiment technique.

Merits

(a) This carefully carried out exercise can help the researcher to come out with a demand function, indicating quantities that the consumers would be ready to take off from the market at various prices, levels of incomes, etc.

(b) This method can be used to check the results of demand forecasting obtained from other methods.

Demerits

(a) These experiments are expensive and time-consuming. A large number of buyers can never be involved in these experiments.

(b) Potential buyers may treat these experiments as a game and may not behave in a natural manner.

(c) There methods are risky as they might send wrong signals to the consumers, dealers and competitors, which may lead to unfavourable situation for the concerned firm.

(d) The conclusions and inferences derived from the experiments in some section of the market cannot be applied to the whole market.

(e) It is difficult to satisfy the condition of homogeneity.

Statistical Methods

These methods make use of historical data (time series or cross-section) as a basis for extrapolating quantitative relationships to arrive at the future demand patterns and trends. The data may also be analysed through econometric models. These are useful for long-term forecasting and for old products for larger levels of aggregations. They are based on scientific ways of estimation, which are logical, unbiased and proved to be useful. However, the biggest disadvantage is that it is difficult to apply these methods. One needs a competent person to handle, interpret and manipulate the data for statistical purposes. Further, these methods cannot be used for forecasting the demand for new products and products, which have short existence due to data problem. Furthermore, past may not be repeated in future. Statistical methods are broadly classified under the following two categories:

1. Time Series analysis

It is an arrangement of statistical data in a chronological order, i.e. in accordance with its time of occurrence. It reflects the dynamic pace of steady movements of a phenomenon over a period of time. Most of the variables in business, economics and commerce, may be a series related to price, production, consumption, national income, foreign trade, foreign exchange reserves, investment, sales, projects, dividends, etc. are all time series data spread over long period of time. The data may be presented in the form of a table or a graph. Here, the time series data on the variable under forecast are used to fit a trend line or a curve graphically. Trend line can be worked out by fitting a trend equation to time series data through least squares method or some other estimation method.

Time series analysis can be used for demand forecasting by first evaluating, extracting and interpreting its various components so as to make it understandable and explainable. These four *components* are described below:

(a) **Trend.** It shows the underlying, long-term tendency of the data, which may be the result of basic developments in population, capital, technology, etc. Any event of future period can be forecasted using trend line.

(b) **Seasonal Variation.** These are short-term cyclic fluctuations in the data about the trend, which is measured in an interval in a year. If the average monthly sales of a product for a particular month are 10 per cent above the trend line, a seasonal adjustment factor of 1.10 can be applied to the trend projection to forecast sales in that month. However, here, the word 'season' can have different meanings. It may be related to weather, holidays, customs, festivals, fashions, etc. Here, a series fluctuates according to seasons of the year. Daily 'seasons' over a weekly cycle for sales in a supermarket, monthly 'seasons' over an yearly cycle for purchases of a company and quarterly 'seasons' over an yearly cycle for sales of electricity in the domestic sector are some examples. There is some regularity with regard to their occurrence.

(c) **Cyclical Variation.** It can be thought of as underlying economic cause outside the scope of immediate environment. Here, the length of the cycle is generally longer than one year. Study of these variations is essential for predicting the turning points in business cycles. Cyclical variations are affected by swings in general economic activity, wherein recovery and boom are followed by recession and depression and *vice versa.* Capital goods industry shows such pattern of business cycles of constant amplitude and periodicity. Though, the trend and the seasonal factors can be forecasted, the prediction of cycles is difficult, as they do not always repeat at constant intervals of time.

(d) **Residual Variation.** These include other factors not explained by *(a)*, *(b)* and *(c)* above. These are disturbances due to unforeseen future events such as weather conditions, illness, strikes, lockouts, riots, fires, wars, transport breakdowns and so on. The evaluation of these components is not usually required in examinations, but its interpretation should be known. They create disturbances, which are erratic in nature. Their operation and effects are not orderly.

Depending on the nature, complexity and extent of the analysis required, there are various types of models that can be used to describe time series data. However, the additive and multiplicative models are the simplest standard time series models, which assume that the effects of component factors are independent of each other.

The components that go to make up each value of a time series are described below:

Time series additive model

$$Y = t + s + c + r$$

Time series multiplicative model

$$Y = t \times s \times c \times r$$

Where Y is given time series value.

t is the trend component.

c is the cyclical component.

s is the seasonal component.

r is the residual component.

In other words, given a set of time series data, every single given (Y) value can be expressed as the sum or product of four components. Decomposition of these components is necessary for understanding the nature of business fluctuations. It is important to note that the trend component will be the same, no matter which of the two models are used. In other words, given a set of data to which both models are being applied, both trend values would be identical, whereas the respective seasonal and residual components would be quite different.

The demand can be forecasted through identification of trends and estimation of extraneous factors. The trend can be projected into the future using the following methods:

A. Graphical Method

This method gives the basic tendency of a series to grow, decline or remain steady over a period of time. This method is useful in forecasting India's population, demand for cement, textiles, steel paper, etc., where the future is not too much different from the average of the past. The period of time in the trend analysis is always a long time period. The concept of trend does not include short-time oscillations and fluctuations.

Trend can be both linear and non-linear. If the time series values are plotted on a graph, one can pass a straight line depicting the trend such that most of the values will fall on or near the line. This line may be drawn up to the present period or the period for which the data is available. It can then be extrapolated for the forecast period. Fig. 5.1 *(a)* shows that there is an upward linear trend, while Fig. 5.1 *(b)* shows that there is a downward linear trend. We observe that the straight trend line has been fitted around the fluctuations. The actual movement of the data is shown by the dotted curve.

If the values of the variables are such that they cluster around a non-linear path, we get a curvilinear or non-linear trend. Non-linear trend can be either quadratic or cubic. Fig. 5.2 *(a)* and Fig. 5.2 *(b)* show a quadratic trend. Fig. 5.2 *(a)* represents an inverse parabola with a maximum point. Fig. 5.2 *(b)* also shows a parabola, but, with a minimum point. This is called a straight parabola. Fig. 5.2 *(c)* and Fig. 5.2 *(d)* represent a cubic trend.

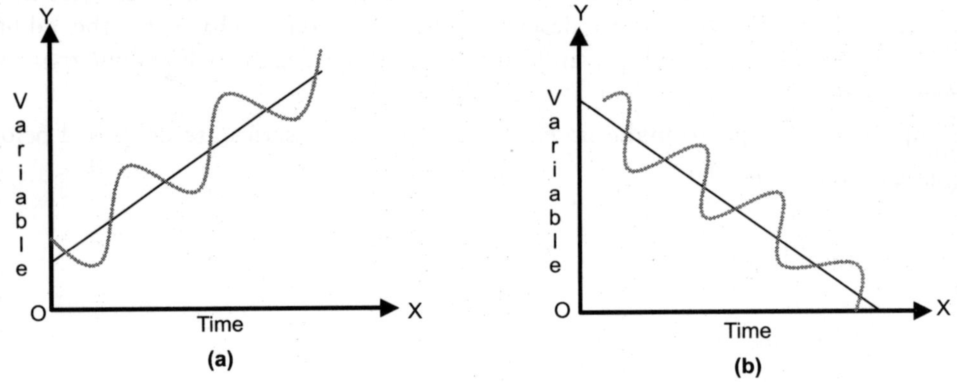

Fig. 5.1

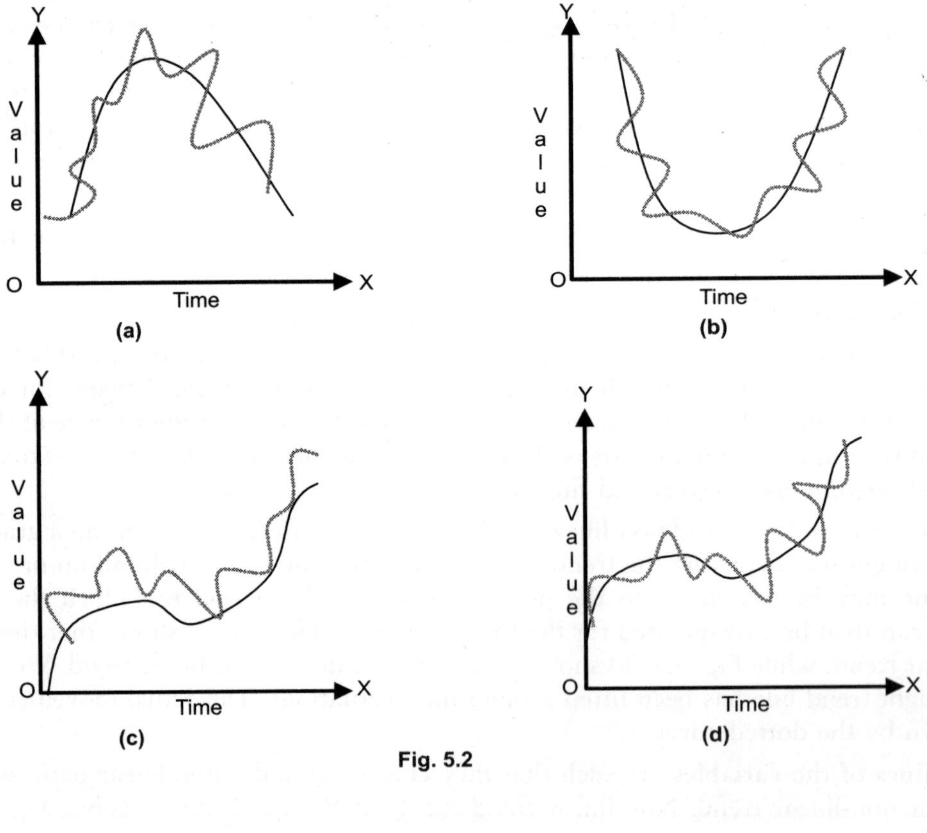

Fig. 5.2

Study of trend enables the managers and firms to forecast their business in the long-run and to plan future operations without formal knowledge of economic theory and the market. It only needs the time series data. For example, we get a negative linear trend of demand for a particular commodity. The managers know that unless something fundamental changes, the production of this commodity will have to be reduced in a phased manner. Accordingly, inventory and investment have to be planned.

Although trends are for long-run use, we can find out the fluctuations and oscillations in the trend values by breaking down the trend into small intervals. For example, in Fig. 5.3, there are certain times intervals, when the values plotted are not strictly on the trend. These are the time periods, when there was fluctuation in the value of the variable.

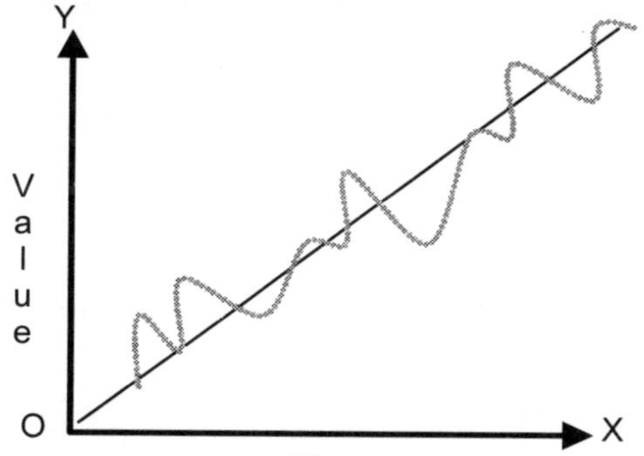

Fig. 5.3

B. Semi-averages Method

According to this method, the data is divided into two parts, preferably with the same number of years. The averages of the first and second parts are calculated separately. These averages are called semi-averages. Semi-averages are plotted as points against middle point of the respective time periods covered by each part. The line joining these points gives the straight-line trend fitting the given data. In case of odd number of years, the two equal parts are obtained by omitting the values for the middle period. For example, for the data of 9 years from 1994 to 2002, the two parts will be the data for years 1994 to 1997 and 1999 to 2002; the value for 1998 will be omitted. Let us take an example to see how this method is used to fit a trend line, which is further used for forecasting. This is a more accurate method than the graphical trend method.

Example 5.1. Apply the method of semi-averages for determining trend of the following data and estimate the value for 2004 A.D.

Years	Sales in ('00)
1997	20
1998	24
1999	22
2000	30
2001	28
2002	32

Solution:

Year	Sales ('00)	3 Yearly Semi-totals	Semi-average
1997	20		
1998	24	66	66/3=22
1999	22		
2000	30		
2001	28	90	90/3=30
2002	32		

22 will now be plotted against the mid year of the first part, i.e. 1998 and likewise 30 will be plotted against the mid-year of the second part, i.e. 2001. Joining the two points, we obtain the trend line as shown in Fig. 5.4.

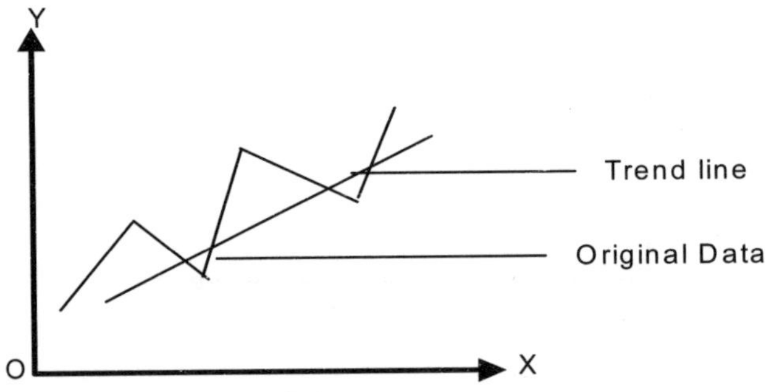

Fig. 5.4

From the trend line, we find that between 1998 and 2001, the sales have increased from 2,200 units to 3,000 units. This implies that annually there is an increment of (800/3) 267 units approximately. Applying this value, we get the value of sales in the year 2004 A.D. as 3,800 units.

Now, suppose the actual sales value in 2004 A.D. is found to be 3,600 units. This value differs from the value obtained from the semi-averages method because of the assumption of a linear trend. This difference may be on account of the seasonal or other fluctuations.

C. Moving Averages Method

When time series analysis does not reveal a significant trend of any kind, the moving averages method may be used to smoothen the series. This is a very simple and flexible method of measuring trend. It consists of obtaining a series of moving averages of successive overlapping groups of the time series. The averaging process smoothens out fluctuations as well as the ups and downs in the given data. The moving average is characterised by a constant known as the period of extent of the moving average. Thus, the moving averages of period *'m'* is a series of successive averages of *'m'* overlapping values at a time, starting with 1st , 2nd, 3rd value and so on,

Example 5.2: Find the trend in the demand in rupees for a particular product in Delhi by the method of moving averages:

Years	Demand (in Rs. '00)
1983	40
1984	42
1985	40
1986	44
1987	49
1988	46
1989	42
1990	44
1991	44
1992	50
1993	42
1994	48
1995	46
1996	52
1997	58
1998	56
1999	51
2000	57
2001	54
2002	63

Solution: The appropriate period for the moving average is the period of cyclical variation. The given data does not reveal any regular cycle. But, if we examine the data, we have the peaks at the following points.

Year	1981		1984		1989		1991		1994		1997		1999
Peak value	42		49		50		48		58		57		63
Period		3		5		2		3		3		2	

Data exhibits 6 cycles, but, with varying periods. The appropriate period of the moving averages is given by the average values of these periods, i.e. (3+5+2+3+3+2)/6 = 18/6 = 3. Hence, we will apply a three-yearly moving average.

Year	Demand (in Rs. '000)	3 Yearly Moving Total	3 Yearly Moving Average
1	2	3	4
1983	40	–	–
1984	42	122	40.67
1985	40	126	42.00
1986	44	133	44.33

Contd...

1	2	3	4
1987	49	139	46.33
1988	46	137	45.67
1989	42	132	44.00
1990	44	130	43.33
1991	44	138	46.00
1992	50	136	45.33
1993	42	140	46.67
1994	48	136	45.33
1995	46	146	48.67
1996	52	156	52.00
1997	58	166	55.33
1998	56	165	55.00
1999	51	164	54.67
2000	57	162	54.00
2001	54	174	58.00
2002	63	–	–

We can roughly say that the demand for this product on an average touches its peak after 3 years.

D. Least Squares Method

The principle of least squares provides us an analytical tool to obtain an objective fit to the trend of the given time series. Most of the data relating to economic and business time series confirm to definite laws of growth or decay. Thus, in such situations, trend fitting will be most reliable way of forecasting. Here, the assumption is that past rate of change for the given variable would continue in the future. Least squares can fit both linear and non-linear trends. However, trend projection breaks down, when a turning point occurs.

Fitting Linear Trend. There will be constant absolute amount of change every period. The typical linear trend will be given by trend equation Y = a + bt.

Here, 'Y' is variable, say demand, 'a' is constant and 'b' is coefficient of the trend variable 't'. If we can find the value of 'a' and 'b', we can get the relation of 'Y' to time.

For any given time, the estimated value of 'Y' is Y_e. Hence, the estimation error $E=Y-Y_e$. There may be positive or negative error. Hence in the actual data, certain points will lie above the trend line and some points will lie below it. The principle of least squares tells us that the sum of the squares of the error should be minimum. In other words, ΣE^2 should be minimised. This will be so if

$$\frac{\partial\left(\Sigma E^2\right)}{\partial a}=0 \quad \Rightarrow \quad \frac{\partial\left[\Sigma\left(Y - Y_e\right)^2\right]}{\partial a}=0$$

$$\frac{\partial\left(\Sigma E^2\right)}{\partial b} = 0 \Rightarrow \frac{\partial\left[\Sigma\left(Y - Y_e\right)^2\right]}{\partial b} = 0$$

$$\frac{\partial\left(\Sigma E^2\right)}{\partial a} = 0 \quad \Rightarrow \sim 2\Sigma t\left(Y - a - bt\right) = 0$$

$$\frac{\partial\left(\Sigma E^2\right)}{\partial b} = 0 \quad \Rightarrow \sim 2\Sigma t\left(Y - a - bt\right) = 0$$

On implification, we get

$\Sigma Y - na + b\Sigma t$

$\Sigma ty = a\Sigma t + b\Sigma t^2$

There are called the least square equations. Solving these two equations, we get the values of 'a' and 'b' and hence the trend line.

Example 5.3. Following is the sales (in Rs. Lakh) data of hand pumps. Find out what can be the likely value of sales in the year 2003 A.D.:

Year	Sales (in Rs. Lakh)
1996	80
1997	90
1998	92
1999	83
2000	94
2001	99
2002	92

Solution: Let us fit a straight line trend Y = a + bt

Year	Sales (in Rs. Lakh)	T = year-1996	t^2	ΣtY
1996	80	-3	9	-240
1997	90	-2	4	-180
1998	92	-1	1	-92
1999	83	0	0	0
2000	94	1	1	94
2001	99	2	4	98
2002	92	3	9	276
	$\Sigma Y = 630$	$\Sigma t = 0$	$\Sigma t^2 = 28$	$\Sigma tY = 56$

From the above calculations, we get

$$a = \frac{\Sigma Y}{n} = \frac{630}{7} = 90$$

$$b = \frac{\Sigma tY}{\Sigma t^2} = \frac{56}{28} = 2$$

Hence, the trend line for the sales of hand pumps is Y = 90 + 2t

If, t = 4 (i.e. year 2003 A.D.), Y = 90 + 2 (4) = Rs. 98 lakh

The trend values for other years are given in the following table:

Year	Sales (in Rs. Lakh)
1996	84
1997	86
1998	88
1999	90
2000	92
2001	94
2002	96

The method of least squares is the most popular and one of most accurate methods of demand forecasting, particularly, for long-run demand projections, because of its simplicity and inexpensiveness. One can predict the demand for any period or sub-period in future. However, it cannot satisfactorily explain market fluctuations of trade cycles.

Fitting Non-linear Trend. Demand or sales having a linear function in time, is an over simplistic assumption. The demand function can be a parabola, exponential logarithmic curve, etc. Least squares method can be used to fit such cases of non-linear trends too. Suppose, a new product is launched in the market. The market itself is not matured. We may expect that in the initial phase, the demand will grow at a slow rate followed by a fast rate till it reaches a saturation point. We will get somewhat like the curve shown in Fig. 5.5. We have to fit a logarithmic trend here, which is very common in industrial growth.

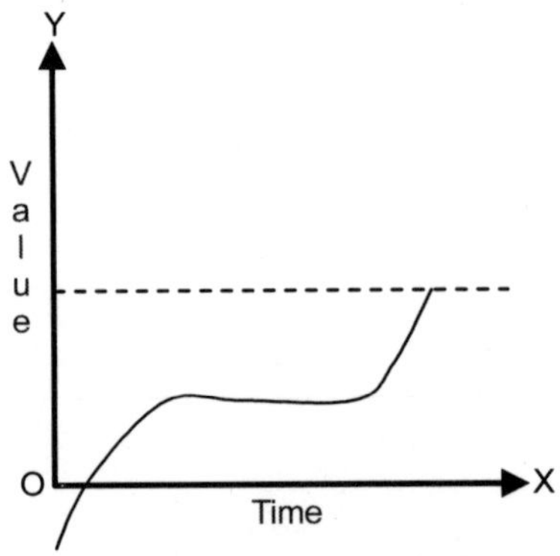

Fig. 5.5: Non-Linear Trend

Example 5.4. Computer industry has registered an exponential growth in the country. Data is given for this industry for 5 years, from 1997-2001. Find out the demand for the year 2005.

Year	Sales (Rs. lakh)
1997	1.6
1998	4.5
1999	13.8
2000	402.0
2001	125.0

Solution: Data on sales shows that there is an exponential growth. So, we have the following model.

$Y = ab^t$

$\Rightarrow$ $\log Y = \log a + t \log b$

Or, $Y = A + Bt$

where $Y = \log Y$, $A = \log a$, and $B = \log b$

The least square equations will be

$\Sigma y = nA + B\Sigma_t$

$\Sigma ty = A\Sigma_t + B\Sigma_t^{\,2}$

Computation of exponential trend is shown in the following table:

t	Y	Y=log Y	yt	t^2
1	1.6	0.2041	0.2041	1
2	4.5	0.6532	1.3064	4
3	13.8	1.1399	3.4197	9
4	40.2	1.6042	6.4168	16
5	125.0	2.0969	10.4845	25
$\Sigma t = 15$		$\Sigma t = 5.6983$	$\Sigma ty = 21.8315$	$\Sigma t^2 = 55$

Substituting the aggregate values in the above two least square equations, we get

$5.6983 = 5A + 15B$

$21.8315 = 15A + 55B$

On solving these two simultaneous equations, we have

$A = \log a = -0.2814$ and $B = \log b = 0.4737$

Therefore,

$a = \text{Antilog } A = \text{Antilog } (-0.2814) = \text{Antilog } (-1.7186) = 0.5231$

$b = \text{Antilog } B = \text{Antilog } (0.4737) = 2.977$

ÞY = ab^t

ÞY = $(0.5231)(2.977)^t$

For year 2005, t = 9

ÞY = $(0.5231)(2.977)^9$

=Rs. 9,607.142 lakhs

Thus, the demand for year 2005 is predicted as Rs. 9,607.142 lakhs.

2. Regression analysis

Regression analysis is perhaps the most popular method of forecasting among the economists. It is a mathematical analysis of the average relation between two or more variables in terms of the original units of the data. Here, the data analysis should be based on the logic of economic theory. Further, explanatory variable whose value is influenced or is to be predicted is called the regressed or dependent variable. While the variable, which influences the dependent or predicted value, is called the regress or predictor or explanatory variable.

When the regression analysis is confined to the study of two variables, it is called simple regression. But, quite often the studied regressed variable depends on multiple factors simultaneously. In that case, we have to study the effect of more than one predictor on the value of the predicted variable. It is called multiple regression. The general form of multiple regression is $Y = f(x_1, x_2, x_{3,}...............)$.

We have already studied the simple regression under the method of least squares, where we have seen how time can affect the demand or sale of a commodity. Multiple regressions are a more realistic and accurate way of predicting the future demand. Demand for money (M_t) in an economy as a function of national income, rate of interest and time is a common example. We can write

$$M_t = a(Y_t)^{b_1}(r_t)^{b_2}(t)^{b_3}$$

Where,

M_t is stock of money in time period 't'

Y_t is national income in time period 't'

r_t is rate of interest in time period 't'

This is an exponential function in which 'a' is constant and b_1, b_2 and b_3 are the respective coefficients. Here, the dependent variable M_t is to be predicted and Y_t, r_t and 't' are independent variables.

Now, take a completely different kind of demand, i.e., demand for roses during the festival and marriage seasons. It will depend on price of roses, price of other flowers and family's disposable income. Empirical study shows that the demand for roses during the peak season grows exponentially.

$$D_R = a(P_R)-b_1(P_{OF})^{b2}(I)b_3$$

$$\log D_R = \log a - b_1 \log P_R + b_2 \log P_{OF} + b_3 \log I$$

Here, D_R is demand for roses, P_R is price of roses, P_{OF} is price of other flowers and 'I' is family's disposable income. Further, 'a' is a constant, while $-b_1$ tells us that if P_R increases by 1% D_R will decrease by b_1%. Similarly, 1% increase in P_{OF} and 'I' will increase D_R by b_2% and b_3% respectively. $-b_1$ (own price elasticity), b_2 (cross price elasticity) and b_3 (income elasticity) are called partial regression coefficients, which measure the responsiveness of the regressed variable on the regresses.

The method of solving multiple regression analysis is similar to the simple regression analysis, i.e. solving the least square equations for the values of the parameters.

Merits

(a) This method is prescriptive as well as descriptive. Besides generating demand forecast, it explains why the demand is, what it is. Thus, technique has both explanatory and predictive value.

(b) It is objective method using time series as well as cross-section data.

Demerits

(a) If some explanatory variables are not realistically chosen, they tend to be misleading.

(b) Forecast will be wrong to the extent future relationship deviated from the past average experience.

(c) Regression results will be biased in case of auto-correlation, i.e. when for one year, demand is highly correlated with the demand of preceding years.

QUESTIONS FOR DISCUSSION

1. Discuss the method of estimating the future demand. Write brief note on analysis of estimated demand function.
2. What is sales forecasting? Discuss the various steps involved in sales forecasting.
3. What is the need for sales forecasting? Discuss its importance in product planning.
4. "After all in the final analysis, the best forecasting method is obviously the one which yields the highest percentage of correct predictions." Suggest factors, which should be considered in choosing a forecasting technique.
5. Explain the various methods of demand forecasting. Point out their merits and demerits.
6. How is demand for durable and perishable goods forecasted?
7. "Forecasting is like trying to drive a car blind fold and following directions given by a person who is looking out of the back window". Comment.
8. Which forecasting technique would you use to forecast demand for *(i)* steel, *(ii)* car, and *(iii)* cement?
9. ABC Ltd. wants to set up a new plant for producing automotive batteries. However, it wants to assess the market before deciding on the production. You are approached by ABC Ltd. to advise on the existence of a market before deciding on the venture. Explain fully the various steps you would follow in estimating the demand for automotive batteries. Under what conditions would you recommend starting of the new venture?
10. A district manager proposes that his division develops its own State-level input/output model for use in forecasting. Is this a good idea? Why or why not.
11. How is demand for new products forecasted? A business firm surveys its customers to generate information about the demand for a proposed new product.

CASE STUDY 5.1

ABC COMPANY—SALES POLICIES

ABC Company was a producer of several kinds of industrial equipment listed in Exhibit 1. It developed from the efforts in the late 1940s of a gifted engineer and inventor, Srirang Pandey, who patented several of his ideas for variations on standard products. He founded and was active in the firm for more than 26 years until his death.

Pandey had been very interested in the selling activity of his company and had a strong sense of professionalism that he used in personally selecting people for his sales force. He managed the sales force until it grew to a size of three men, at which time he secured the services of Hiren Shah as Sates Manager.

Before Shah's arrival and for several years thereafter, Pandey told the salesman expressly the names of firms he wanted them to call on. The founder was actually interested in the reputation of his young company. His concern for reputation included product characteristics as promised, delivery on time (critical to customers for these goods), and ethical, highly reserved business conduct by the salesmen. However, his concern for reputation was not restricted to these factors. Pandey also wanted to have customers who enjoyed the finest reputations. For example, he told his salesmen never to solicit the orders of a small firm known by the name of Rohan and Lovely, for he considered the owners to be social climbers without proper backgrounds. In addition, he did not like an advertisement of theirs he once saw in a weekly business newspaper. He also instructed his salesmen not to call on Kapoor Glow Ltd. because it had been turned down for a loan at the bank that Pandey used. This was despite the fact that Kapoor Glow Ltd. had found credit at another bank.

Not all the instructions were negative, however, Pandey had the salesmen, all of whom were engineers, visit Camden Mills, Stone and Kruger, and South Indian Metals time after time even though all three were committed to other sellers and other product designs. He wanted ABC Company to be a name that such firms knew and respected. He also cultivated several large national companies, such as Combustion Engineering, Indian Machine and Foundary, Westinghouse, and Melpar.

After Pandey's death, Shah continued these policies for the better part of a year. At that point Jeven Vats, the new president hired from the outside, had a long talk with the sales manager and explained that he thought some changes were desirable. The firm should try to maximise sales and abandon all the 'notions and pretentions' as he termed them. The salesmen should be put on a combination of salary plus commission. The two other executives in the company, the finance man and the production man, spoke up with thorough endorsements of such changes. The existing policy was straight salary.

With some misgivings, Shah devised a new compensation structure for his four salesman. Under this plan he estimated that a salesman would earn about 80 per cent of his compensation through salary and about 20 per cent through commission. The plan was announced on August 1 and the men were told it would go into effect in thirty days. Sales in August slumped about 17 per cent from the same month one year earlier and 14 per cent from the same month two years earlier.

After one month of use, the sales manager conducted a preliminary inquiry into the results of the new compensation policy. The results appeared to be that the easier to sell items in the product line were moving well, those of average difficulty to sell were moving adequately, and the one item that was rather difficult to sell (the dryer) was moving very poorly. Exhibit 1 gives the comparison of September to the last month under the old policy (July) and to September one year before. Shah presented his analysis to Vats but cautioned him about premature inferences from these data. The sales manager said that he would repeat his comparison after another month. In the meanwhile, the president told the sales manager to urge the salesmen to solicit orders for dryers.

Exhibit 1: ABC Company Sales by Product Selected Months

Product	September (Rs.)	July (Rs.)	September last year (Rs.)	September two years before (Rs.)
Dryers	2,10,000	3,45,000	3,50,000	3,22,000
Sprayers	77,000	75,000	80,000	78,000
Planers	41,000	43,000	40,000	39,000
Power saws	32,000	30,000	30,000	31,000
Drills	42,000	41,000	40,000	39,000
Sanders	95,000	73,000	72,000	70,000
Metal buffers	75,000	49,000	50,000	48,000

QUESTIONS FOR DISCUSSION

1. Do you think, as a promoter, Pandey was right in promoting the kind of sales policies he did? Justify your comment.
2. Evaluate the compensation package in light of the facts given in the case. What are the suggestions that you would have for an ideal compensation plan in this case?

CASE STUDY 5.2

INDIRA PHARMACEUTICALS—SALES AND PROMOTION STRATEGIES

Indira Pharmaceuticals was established in 1985 to manufacture, distribute and market pharmaceutical drugs. It was purely an Indian company and had to face tough competition from multinational companies during the initial years. The company survived mainly on institutional buying, i.e. various government and charitable hospitals and in the last decade with the help of effective market strategics, has set up a place for itself, amongst the leading pharmaceutical companies in the country.

In 2004, the managing director of the company stressed the need for diversification and addition of new products to its existing product range. Looking at the success of the Threptin brand of high protein biscuits, he floated the idea of manufacturing and marketing the biscuits rich in protein, minerals and vitamins. His advisers suggested that since most of the people in the country were suffering from protein deficiency, such products enriched with protein, would be desirable, and should be a big success, specially in view of its competitors brand. The marketing research department of the company also gave the green signal to the project after conducting a brief survey.

The company promoted its biscuits with the Triple Plus Protein brand name. It was supplied in a 400 gm. packet consisting of 60 biscuits at the price of Rs. 75. The product was heavily advertised in the newspapers, health magazines, radio and television. The target audience was middle class, who it was believed suffered most from protein deficiency and can afford triple plus protein biscuits. The ordinary biscuits were available in the market at the rate of Rs. 30 to Rs. 40 per kg. The thrust of triple plus biscuits in the promotion campaign was that these biscuits contain three times more protein and have additional mineral and vitamin value.

The company has 50 stockists covering the entire country and has a sales force of about 150 medical representatives, for promoting its products, through doctor and registered medical practitioners. The medical representatives of the company had very good rapport with government and charitable hospitals. To promote the triple plus brand of biscuits its medical representatives gave discount coupons to the doctors for passing over to their patients to buying their biscuits.

The buyer was entitled to Rs. 5 discount per packet of 400 gm. The scheme continued for about six months.

Despite heavy advertisement and canvassing by its medical representatives, the product was unable to attract customers. It was observed that the launching of this product has not affected the market position of Threptin biscuits at all which was being sold at Rs. 90 for a pack of 275 gm. Rather, it was observed that the sale of Threptin biscuits have increased marginally consequent to the advertisement campaign by the Indira Pharmaceuticals. The company could achieve only 25% of its sales target in the first year and it remained almost static for the next year.

QUESTIONS FOR DISCUSSION

1. How do you account the failure of the company to achieve its sales target?
2. Critically evaluate the advertising and sales promotion strategy.
3. Suggest a suitable promotion plan which can increase the sales of the company.
4. Do you think that change in the channels of distribution can improve the sales of this product? If yes, please elaborate.

CASE STUDY 5.3

COOL-HEADS—RE-DESIGNING SALES STRATEGIES

Cool-Heads was established in 1985 to manufacture, distribute and market pharmaceutical soft drinks. It was purely an Indian company and had to face tough competition from multi-national companies during the initial years. The company in the last decade with the help of effective market strategies has set up a place for itself, amongst the leading pharmaceutical companies in the country.

In 1995, the Managing Director of the company stressed the need for diversification and addition of new products to its existing product range. He floated the idea of manufacturing and marketing coffee with milk, cocoa and sugar. His advisers suggested that such products enriched with cocoa, would be desirable, and should be a big success, specially in view of its competitors' brand. The marketing research department of the company also gave the green signal to the project after conducting a brief survey.

The company promoted its coffee with Choco-Coffee as the brand name. It was supplied in a 400 grams packet at the price of Rs. 75. The product was heavily advertised in the newspapers, health magazines, radio and television. The target audience was middle class, who it was believed could afford Choco-Coffee. Ordinary coffee was available in the market at the rate of Rs. 30 to Rs. 40 per kg. The thrust of Choco-Coffee in the promotion campaign was that this contained cocoa, milk and sugar.

The company has 50 stockists covering all of the country and has a sales force of about 150 representatives, for promoting its products, through supermarkets and shops. The representatives of the company had very good rapport with supermarket and shops. To promote the coffee its representatives gave discount coupons to the stockists for passing over to their customers to induce them to buy their coffee. The buyer was entitled to Rs. 5 discount per packet of 400 grams. The scheme continued for about 6 months.

Despite heavy advertisement and canvassing by its representatives, the product was unable to attract customers. It was observed that launching of this product has not affected the market position of other branded coffee at all which was being sold at Rs. 90 for a pack of 275 grams. Rather, it was observed that the sales of the other brands of coffee increased marginally, consequent to the advertisement campaign by the Cool-Heads. The company could achieve only 25% of its sales target in the first year and it remained almost static for the next year.

(AIMA, Dec. 98)

QUESTIONS FOR DISCUSSION

1. What do you think are the reasons for the failure of the company to achieve its target?
2. Suggest a sales promotion plan for increasing the sales volume of the company.
3. Can a change in the distribution channel bring improvements in the sale of the product?

CASE STUDY 5.4

PERFORMANCE APPRAISAL OF SALES FORCE

A company sells a large number of products, which are accessories for a certain class of machine. For India, it has nine salesmen, each of whom is responsible for sales in a separate territory.

Estimates of total market potential are Rs. 12 crore and Rs. 14.2 crore for the year ended 31st March 1997 and 1998 respectively. Data for two individual salesmen and for the company as a whole are:

Territory area ('000 sq. km.)	10.4	21.9	328.8
No. of machines (lacs)	16.5	8.3	128.0
Potential number of accounts	699	423	5965

Year ended 31.03.1997	Amal	Bimal	
Sales (Rs. '000s)	1940	2020	24220
Customer (number of accounts)	412	323	3318
Gross Margin (Rs. '000s)	680	780	8520
Call made	1410	1163	10901

Territory

Territories 1 2 1 and 2			Total India (including)
Year ended 31.03.1998			
Sales (Rs. '000s)	2240	2460	29200
Customer (number of accounts)	398	364	3271
Gross Margin (Rs. '000s)	780	940	9960
Calls made	1450	1220	11030
Salary (Rs. '000s)	142	120	1216
Commission (Rs. '000s)	34	37	432
Total Remuneration (Rs. '000s)	176	157	1648
Expenses (Rs. '000s)	39	64	561

You are required to calculate:

(a) For the average of all the nine salesmen and for any one salesman Amal and Bimal for the year ended 31st March 1998.

(i) Sales potential;

(ii) Sales Penetration percentage;

(iii) Sales potential per account;

(iv) Any seven relevant indices that would help to assess the performance of Salesmen under the following heading:

- customers;
- gross margin;
- calls made;
- remuneration;
- expenses.

At least one index should be calculated for each heading.

(b) To assess the performance of Bimal for the year ended 31st March 1998 based on a combination of the data in (a) above, plus any other data, that you may consider relevant.

(ICWA, Final 1998)

CASE STUDY 5.5

RAJ TYRES LIMITED—PERFORMANCE EVALUATION OF SALES FORCE

Raj Tyres is a company involved in the import and marketing of car tyres manufactured in the Far East. Raj Tyres established the business in 1998 when a friend living in Singapore told him of the supply of tyres from that area which substantially undercut European prices. Although Far Eastern tyres were not as long lasting as European they were produced to a high standard which meant that problems like weak spots, cracks and leaks were no more serious than with European tyres.

Raj Tyres believed that a viable target market existed for the sale of these tyres in India. He was of the opinion that a substantial number of people were interested primarily in the purchase price of tyres. This price-sensitive target market could roughly be described as the mid-lower income, working-class family man who owned a second-hand car which was over three years old.

He decided to buy a consignment of tyres and visited tyre centers to sell them. Initially business was slow but gradually, as distributors began to believe in the quality of the tyres, sales grew.

By 1999 Raj Tyres had taken on the role of General Manager and had recruited five sales people to handle the sales function. A brief personal profile produced by MacLaren of each of his salespersons is given below.

Profiles of Raj Tyres Salesmen

Raj Mani

Joined the company in 1995. Has an M.B.A. (Marketing) and previously worked as an insurance salesman for three years. Aged 27. Handles the South area. Gregarious and extrovert.

Raj Lata

Joined the company in 1996. No formal qualifications but sound track record as a car salesman and, later, as a toy salesman. Aged 35. Handles the North area. Appears to be hardworking but lacks initiative.

Raj Laxmi

Joined the company in 1996. Has an M.B.A. (Marketing). Was a technical representative for an engineering firm. Aged 28. Handles the East area. Appears to enjoy his work but lacks the necessary 'push' to be really successful in selling.

Rajan

Joined the company in 1997. Has a degree in industrial management? Previous experience includes selling bathroom suits and textiles fabrics. Aged 29. Covers the Western area. Appears to lack enthusiasm but sales record is about average.

Raj Kumar

Joined the company in 1997. Has a degree in business studies? Only previous experience was as a marketing assistant during the industrial training period of his degree. Aged 25. Handles the Central area. Keen but still very raw.

Sales Force Data

Raj Tyres decided that the time had come to look in detail at the sales records of his men. His plan was to complete a series of statistics, which would be useful in evaluating their performance. Basic data for the year 1997/98 relevant to each man is contained below.

	Sales (Rs. 000s)	Gross Profits (1997/98)	Live accounts	Call made	Number of different customers called upon
Raj Mani	298	101	222	1,472	441
Raj Lata	589	191	333	1,463	432
Raj Laxmi	391	121	235	1,321	402
Rajan	440	132	181	1,152	211
Raj Kumar	240	65	296	1,396	421

Market Data

From trade sources, and from knowledge of the working boundaries each man operated in, MacLaren was able to produce estimates of the number of potential accounts and territory potential for each area.

	No. of potential accounts	Territory potential (Rs. 000's)
Raj Mani (South)	503	34,620
Raj Lata (North)	524	36,360
Raj Laxmi (East)	711	62,100
Rajan (Western)	483	43,800
Raj Kumar (Central)	462	38,620

QUESTIONS FOR DISCUSSION

1. Evaluate the performance of each Raj Tyres salesperson.
2. What further information is needed to produce a more complete appraisal?
3. What action would you take?

CASE STUDY 5.6

SOFTEK LIMITED—TRAINING METHODOLOGY FOR SALES EXECUTIVES

Company Preview

Softek was founded in 1979. At that time, the nascent software industry in India was concentrating on software development for mainframes and propriety systems. Softek's founders visualised the emerging dominant role of microprocessor-based systems in the corporate world. In keeping with this vision, Softek developed and launched a range of operating systems, compilers, databases, word-processors, data entry packages, utilities and multilingual interfaces for these systems.

Not content with being a pioneer system and application developer in India, Softek developed customised solutions for clients in manufacturing, banking, financial and hospitality industry.

For its clients Softek has become synonymous with *quality, expertise* and *dependability.*

Softek has developed the parallel Fortran for the first indigenously developed super computer in India. Softek is the only company in the country to have developed Devnagiri word-processor, database and COBOL compiler. Softek products are available from all the leading hardware and software vendors in the country.

Most of the products of Softek are available on DOS, LAN platforms. Softek's products are also available on HP-9000, DRS-6000, RS-6000, ORG Sypermax, Magnum, Unipower, ECIL Oscar, etc.

SALES FORCE TRAINING IN SOFTEK LIMITED

The company conducts two types of training programmes:

1. Induction training programme,
2. Continuous training programme.

Induction Training

Recruits: Training is meant for newly recruited sales trainees from various MBA institutes.

Purpose: Most of the new recruits do not generally have any work experience and if they do have experience then it may not be in the IT industry.

Since the company is into development and marketing of software products, the marketing and sales strategies of these products are very unique and hence it is necessary for the company to undergo detailed detailed Induction Training.

Location: The training is given at the head office of the company at G.K.-II, New-Delhi. The development centre is also in Delhi and training includes visit to the development centre as well.

Duration: 7 days in-house training and 15 days on-job-training.

Who Conducts Training?

Training is conducted by various officers at different stages of training.

- Customer-support managers,
- Product managers of different products,
- Accounts manager.

The training is divided in three stages:

Introductory stage

The introductory stage involves combined training to the summer trainees as well as new recruits. This stage is for two days.

Company Preview: The initial training opens with a detailed description of Company's Portfolio. This includes all the relevant information about the company, like when was it started, about promoters, etc. This stage also includes a brief introduction of the company's product range.

Product Details: The range of products is listed out and then each product is taken one by one and discussed in detail.

- The upgradation of the older versions to newer ones.

- The platform on which package works.
- The front-end tool and the back-end tool used.
- Whether the product is available on LAN or standalone.
- Main features of the product.
- Price ranges of the various products.
- The major competitors of each product and a brief comparison of their features against company's products.
- Main users, companies, of the product.

The flagship product is then taken up in great detail. For instance, this year the product was WinCA and Nostradamus—a product which was to be test marketed.

While discussing the features of the product same features/functions are demonstrated on the monitor for better understanding.

This session is taken up by the Customer-support Manager and Regional Sales Manager.

During the initial phase, a session is also taken up by the Accounts Manager. He gives a detailed knowledge about:

- How to receive an order requisition form, the formalities to undergo in it?
- How to fill in challans etc.?
- How to fill in expense reimbursement forms along with the last date of submission every month?

In the last session of the total initial phase the trainees are sent to the development centre so as to get acquainted with the procedures and the infrastructure facilities. Also, since the HR department is situated there itself, they are told about incentive schemes etc.

Intermediate phase

In the intermediate phase the entire newly recruited team is divided on the basis of the specific product that they have to market. Thereby, they are given a very detailed demonstration of the product by the Product Manager. Each feature is taken up in great detail and discussed vis-a-vis the features in the major competitors products.

- The market share and awareness of the product is highlighted.
- Various methods to approach a client are demonstrated.

Final phase

During this phase recruits are allocated computers to work on and understand the package to which they are assigned.

Presentation: After having ample exposure of the product each one of the recruits is supposed to give a presentation in the presence of the Regional Sales Manager and Regional Marketing Manager. This is basically to test the grasp of the individual and to see how much he/she has been able to assimilate.

On-the-job training

After the 7 day classroom training, the recruits are given a 15 day on-the-job training.

- In the first week the trainees accompany senior marketing executives to whom they would be reporting in the future and watch while the boss gives the demonstration of the package to the prospective buyer, explaining the features in detail.
- During the next week recruits make sales calls, while their boss accompanies them on the calls. Once the trainee attains confidence in giving demonstrations, he is allowed to make calls independently.

Continuous Training

Senior marketing executives and experienced sales personnel are given training time and again to keep them abreast of the market scenario. Various data collected from market research executives and summer trainees are tabled before them along with the interpretation of data. Open discussions are held and various marketing strategies vis-a-vis competitors are discussed. Most of the times these sessions are presided by the GM. Even mock sessions are held for all the sales personnel during which all the management personnel drill sales personnel on various issues regarding sales.

QUESTIONS FOR DISCUSSION

1. Evaluate Softek's training methodology and suggest any modifications which you feel can improve the performance of sales executives.
2. What is the relevance of continuous training. Design the contents of a continuous training programme for Software sales executive.

CASE STUDY 5.7

LAKSHMI FERTILISER LIMITED—SALESMAN'S DILEMMA

Employed in Lakshmi Fertilisers Company, Ramu is the Sales Officer-in-Charge of its Product Distribution Depot at Dharmapuri.

The Regional Manager of Lakshmi Fertilisers Co. is Mr. Venu, who is the immediate boss in whom Ramu has full faith and devoted loyalty.

M/s. Venkateswara & Sons is in the speculation business and are also a wholesale dealer of Fertilisers in Dharmapuri area. Also, they have long standing business dealings with Lakshmi Fertiliser Co., receiving regular supplies at Dharmapuri Dept. In early September 1977 two wagon loads of urea arrived at Dharmapuri Station and Ramu had no storage facilities to stock the goods. He therefore contacted M/s. Venkateswara & Sons to clear the wagons costing Rs. 68,000 but they expressed helplessness due to shortage of money for cash payment but were prepared to lift the material, if the payment was deferred till Oct. '77. Only the Regional Manager at Coimbatore had the powers to allow such a deal. Therefore, Ramu attempted to contact Venu whose phone was found out of order. The reason was threatening rains.

In view of the circumstances, Ramu issued wagons on credit to M/s. Venkateswara & Sons who went completely bankrupt in February 1978.

An enquiry into the non-payment was made by Marketing Manager, Madras and as a result Ramu has been suspended and is threatened dismissal by the Marketing Manager for incurring heavy loss to the company.

QUESTIONS FOR DISCUSSION

1. Was justice done to Ram? If not, why?
2. If you were the marketing manager, what would you do?

CONSUMER BEHAVIOUR

6

INTRODUCTION

Understanding the consumer behaviour of the target market is the essential task of marketing managers. Consumers differ fundamentally in income, education level, taste and age. In the past marketers had close and direct contact with the consumers which enabled them to understand consumers. But the growth in the size of the firms and markets has made it impossible on the part of the marketers to have such a close contact. This necessitated the present-day marketing managers to conduct consumer research to have an idea about behaviour of consumers.

Meaning of Consumer Behaviour

According to Boone and Kurtz, "Consumer behaviour is the outcome of both individual and environmental influences." To be specific, consumer behaviour refers to the act of consuming a good or service.

Consumer is the king around whom the entire system of marketing revolves. If anybody makes out the marketing programme ignoring the consumer preferences, he cannot probably achieve his ultimate objective. Therefore, marketer must know more and more about the consumers so that the products can be produced in such a fashion to give satisfaction to them.

Major Factors Affecting Consumer Behaviour

A buyer purchase decision is influenced by three major factors which are detailed below:

1. Cultural Factors. Culture decides a person's wants and behaviour. It refers to the set of learned beliefs, attitudes, values, customs, habits, etc. and determines the human wants and behaviour. Culture is active and keep on changing. Actually much of human behaviour is determined by culture. For each culture a separate marketing strategy can be developed. Based on culture, market can also be segmented. This is because patterns of behaviour would vary between different cultures like India, America, Saudi Arabia, etc.

2. Social Factors. Social factors include, reference group, family and social class.

a. ***Reference Group.*** Reference groups refer to all the groups that have an influence whether direct or indirect on the person's behaviour. The following are the various groups which have influence over a person's behaviour:

(i) Membership Groups. Membership groups refer to those groups to which the person belongs and interacts. These groups have a direct influence on its member's behaviour.

(ii) *Primary Groups.* Primary groups include groups of friends, family members, neighbours, co-staff, etc. Here there is a continuous interaction.

(iii) *Secondary Groups.* Here there is only a less continuous interaction and includes religions groups, professional groups, etc.

(iv) *Aspiration Groups.* These are the groups to which a person would like to become its members. People are also influenced by such groups.

(v) *Dissociative Groups.* These are the groups where an individual reflects values.

b. ***Family.*** The family is considered as the most important consumer buying organisation in the society. So it has to be researched extensively. Markets should study the role and relative influence of the husband, wife and children in the purchase of products or services. For products like grocery articles, provision, etc., the housewife is the deciding authority. In case of purchases which involve heavy amount, the decision is normally made by both the husband and wife.

c. ***Social Class.*** Consumer behaviour is determined by social class to which they belong or by which they are attracted, etc. There are three different social classes in our country. They are the upper class, middle class and lower class. All these three social classes will differ in their buying behaviour.

3. Personal Factor. A buyers behaviour is also influenced by personal factors which normally include age, occupation, income, life-style, etc.

a. ***Age.*** People buy different products at their different life stages. Their tastes, preferences, etc. also change with change in life stages.

b. ***Occupation.*** A person's buyer behaviour is also influenced by his occupation. For certain occupations, the purchase of certain types of product is necessary. For example, a sales representative will buy fancy dress, shoes, suit, etc. to win the attention of the people.

c. ***Income.*** Income level of the people is another factor which can exert influence in shaping the consumption pattern. Income is the main source of purchasing power.

d. ***Life Style.*** The term lifestyle refers to the person pattern of living in the world. People belong to the same social class, occupation may lead quiet different lifestyles. Therefore, marketer should find out the relationship between his products and various lifestyles.

e. ***Psychological Factors.*** A person's buyer behaviour is also influenced by the following psychological factors:

(i) *Motivation.* Motive is an inner urge that moves a person to some action. People buy goods as a result of certain mental as well as economical forces that create a desire of buying such goods.

(ii) *Perception.* Perception actually shapes human behaviour. If expressed in a different manner, perception gives the path to be taken by the behaviour.

(iii) *Learning.* People learn when they act. Learning may be defined as all the changes in an individual behaviour arising from the past experience. Buying decisions are affected critically by the learning experience of buyers.

(iv) *Attitudes.* An attitude is a state of mind or feeling. It may be described as a person emotional feeling, action, tendency towards some idea or objects. People have attitude towards each and everything i.e. cloth, food, dress, religion, etc. If a person has an attitude towards product it is difficult to change his attitudes because a person attitude settles into a consistent pattern.

Meaning of Buying Motives

We purchase goods, due to certain motives. Motives refer to thought, urge, motion drive, etc. which make a buyer to react in the form of decision. Any urge which makes a person to take purchase decision is called as buying motive. Motive is an inner urge which moves one into action. It is not mere desire to buy. The term 'buying motive' may refer to the feelings, thoughts, emotion and instinct which arise in a customer a desire to purchase and possess something.

The forces that are motivating an individual to buy be broadly classified into two, namely, external forces and internal forces.

External Forces. External forces include nationality, religion, education, occupation, income, social status, area of residence, culture of the society in which the customer moves.

Internal Forces. Internal forces are those forces which have an origin in minds of the people. These forces may be of physical and psychological nature. Internal forces which motivate the buying behaviour may be classified into two group:

(i) Rational motives, and

(ii) Irrational motives.

Rational motives include dependability in quality, durability, happiness, efficiency in operation and use, economy in use, enhancement of earnings and productivity of property.

Irrational motives include pride and ambition, security, personal comfort, security from danger, comfort and obtaining greater leisure, cleanliness and emotional appetite.

Important Buying Motives

The following are some of the important buying motives:

1. ***Comfort and Convenience.*** Comfort and convenience motive is an important factor in purchasing luxury articles, labour saving devices and convenience at work, at home, and in recreation. Human beings always would like to do things in an easy way and in comfort.
2. ***Gain and Economy Motive.*** Some people desire to earn and save money. Making a profit or saving is a human desire. This desire induce to purchase goods at lower prices to and have monetary gains. Every consumer desires his money's worth.
3. ***Compliments.*** Persons' desires are to be complimented. He wants to be recognised as an important person by others. He likes to be in a higher position where he can command others. To ensure these things we may buy certain products.
4. ***Fashion.*** Everybody wants to be a fashionable man. According to the change in fashion, the buying motives also changes. Marketer can utilise this motive of the consumer very well and should produce goods accordingly do suit the change in fashion.

5. ***Variety.*** Everybody wants to be admired by others. They like to be important in the society, among friends, etc. So they spend more money, time and effort on their personal appearances. Hence variety can be used by the marketer to design their products.
6. ***Sex and Romance.*** This motive occurs in both the young and the old. Sex is a motive in the sale of articles like cosmetics, fancy clothes, etc. For example, men use cars, etc. to attract women. Hence the sex motive is a powerful motive which marketer can make use to achieve his marketing objective.
7. ***To Live Longer.*** To live longer is a desire of all people. They purchase products with this motive. For example, certain products like refined oil which have no cholesterol in it are purchased by people.
8. ***Curiosity.*** If any product is newly introduced into the market at the first instance, people may have curiosity to know about its usage, etc. This may also be one of the buying motives.
9. ***Freedom from Fear and Danger.*** Everybody will do anything to assure guarantee to his safety. Fear can market almost anything. In order to get relief from fear and danger, people will buy anything at the cost of any amount.
10. ***To Get Love of Others.*** Consumer is a social animal. So the motive of affection and attachment for others in greater is case of human beings, e.g., mother, children, etc. Such attachment forces members to purchase goods, e.g., mother purchases toys for kids.

Types of Buying Behaviour

There is a lot of difference between the purchase of a new car and a toothpaste. Therefore, based on the degree of buyers' involvement and the degree of difference among brands, buying behaviour can be classified into four types:

1. Complex buying behaviour,
2. Dissonance reducing buying behaviour,
3. Habitual buying behaviour, and
4. Variety seeking buying behaviour.

LEVELS OF CONSUMER DECISIONS

As a buyer or consumer you are all the time making decisions such as what product to buy (a book or a shirt as a birthday present for your friend), which brand (Lux, Liril, Hamam, Rexona or Breaze toilet soap) from where (Super Bazar, nearby corner shop, chemist), etc. Table 6.1 presents a summary of the different levels of purchase-related decisions most commonly encountered by consumers. The table highlights the broad range of choices the consumers have to select from when making a decision, starting from the generic product category level to the brand level and retail outlet level.

Table 6.1: Levels of Purchase-related Consumer Decisions for Personal Transport

Levels of Decision Generic Product Category Level	Alternative Power Driven Two Wheel or Four Wheel Vehicle	
	Scooter	Car
	Motorcycle	Jeep
	Moped	
Brand Level	**Scooter**	***Car***
	Bajaj	Ambassador
	Lohia	Premier Padmini
	Kinetic	Contessa
		Maruti Car
		Maruti Van
	Motorcycle	
	TVS	
	Yamaha	
	Ind-Suzuki	
	Hero Honda	
	Moped	***Jeep***
	Luna	Maruti Gypsy
	Kinetic	Mahindra
	TVS	
Retail Level	***Types of retail Outlet***	
	(i) Company showroom	
	(ii) Exclusive brand dealer outlet	
	(iii) Multi-brand dealer outlet	
	(iv) Dealer outlet with own servicing facility	
	(v) Dealer outlet closest to home	
	(vi) Dealer outlet recommended by friend	

Process of Decision-Making

The most basic and important requirement for the marketer is to understand how consumers make choices. Ajzen and Fishbeing have attempted to explain human choice behaviour in their theory of reasoned action which states that:

"Generally speaking—human beings are usually quite rational and make systematic use of information available to them. People consider the implications of their actions before they decide to engage or not to engage in a given behaviour."

Thus, decision-making is a rational and conscious process in which the consumer evaluates each of the available alternatives to select the best amongst them. Each decision you make involves an elaborate mental thought process, a degree of active reasoning, though on the surface it may not always seem to be so. This may be because over a period of time you have taken certain decisions so many times that they now seem to be made almost automatically but that is not true at all. Even your daily decision of buying a loaf of bread involves the element of active reasoning as buying a new sofa set for your drawing room. However, in the former case, the extent and intensity of active reasoning may be much less as compared to the latter case.

In the case of bread, the only decision variables may be which brand, quantity and retail outlet. But in case of buying a sofa set the decision variables are far more in number. These may be:

- readymade or made to order
- from a furniture shop or to be built at home
- type of material for frame: Wood, Steel, Aluminium
- type of material for cushion: Cloth, Rexine, Leather
- design: with or without arm-rests, height, depth of seat, seating capacity, loose or fixed cushion.

Thus, depending on the type of decision being made, the degree and strength of active reasoning will vary.

There are three factors which influence the degree of active reasoning that is undertaken by the consumer in his process of decision-making. These are:

(i) Involvement,

(ii) Alternative differentiation, and

(iii) Time pressure.

(i) ***Involvement.*** When a product is perceived to be of great personal importance to the customer, such as personal clothing, or its purchase involves a great deal of money or risk such as jewellery, car, house, company shares, the level of involvement in making the decision is likely to be very high. The consumer is likely to spend a great deal of time before arriving at the final decision. In contrast, when buying items which do not reflect much on the consumer's personality or their purchase involves small amount of money or the risk associated with them is not high, the degree of involvement of the consumer is likely to be low. Products such as shoes, polish, toilet soap, toothpaste, biscuits, etc. would fill in this category.

(ii) ***Alternative Differentiation.*** When the consumer perceives that the various alternatives which are available are very different from one another in terms of their features and benefits offered, he is likely to spend more time in gathering information about and evaluating these different features. On the other hand, in case of products which are not very different from one another either in terms of their features or benefits offered, the consumer is bound to perceive them as being almost the same and buy the first available product/brand which satisfies his minimum expectation. He will not like to spend much time in evaluating the various alternatives. The various brands of washing powder available in the market today are an excellent example of low level of differentiation with the consumer perceiving the different brands to be offering almost identical benefits. All the brands, such as Nirma, Vimal, Vijay, etc. look similar with identical packing and carry almost the same price tag.

Till a few years ago, the two-wheel scooter market in India was highly undifferentiated with Vespa and Lambretta offering almost identical scooter to the consumers in terms of basic features. But today the same market is highly differentiated. The consumer has a wide range of brands to choose from such Kinetic-Honda, Lohia, Bajaj, etc. each offering a variety of shapes, horse power and many other innovative features to choose from. A potential consumer of scooter would have to spend considerable time in evaluating each brand before he is in a position to make his decision.

(iii) ***Time Pressure.*** When you are under pressure to make a decision quickly, you cannot afford to spend a long time finding out about the various products or brands. You would probably buy whatever is readily available. While travelling in your car to a hill station your car tyre bursts and you need to buy a new one. At that time you would buy the brand that is available at whatever price without giving it too much thought. But under a different situation, when you need to buy new tyres, you would certainly like to find the features of nylon and radial tyres and evaluate various brands e.g. Modi, MRF, Dunlop and Apollo, etc. on their individual advantages and disadvantages.

Stages in the Buyer Decision Process

Even buying decision involves an element of active reasoning. The manner in which this active reasoning manifests itself is illustrated in Figure 6.1. In making a purchase decision, the consumer goes through the five stages of:

(i) problem recognition,

(ii) pre-purchase information search,

(iii) evaluation of alternatives,

(iv) purchase decision, and

(v) post-purchase behaviour.

However, in case of routine purchases, the consumer may skip the second and third stages and straight away go to the stage of purchase decision. But in case of purchase decision involving extensive problem-solving, the consumer is likely to go through all the five stages in the specified sequence.

The important point to note is that the buying process starts much before the actual purchase and has implications even after the purchase has been made. This should give ideas to the marketer as to how he has to start designing his marketing strategy in order to achieve his specified marketing objectives.

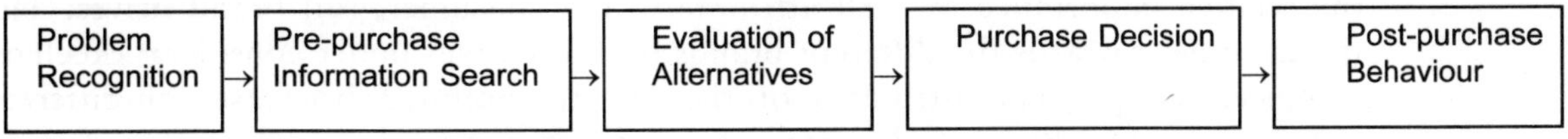

Fig. 6.1: Stages in Buyer Decision Process

Let us understand the stages in decision-making process with the help of Mr. Rao's specific decision to purchase a briefcase:

(i) ***Problem Recognition.*** The buying process starts with the buyer recognising a need or problem. Mr. Rao feels very uncomfortable carrying his papers, files and lunch packet in his hand or in a plastic bag to his work place. Sometimes, the papers and files even fall from his hand and get soiled. Mr. Rao feels the need for a suitable receptacle to carry papers to and fro from his office and has identified a briefcase as the solution to his problem.

(ii) ***Pre-purchase Information Search.*** In response to the stimuli provided by the need for a briefcase, Mr. Rao starts searching for information on the kinds of briefcases available in the market. Search can be of two types: internal and external. *Internal search* refers to recalling relevant information stored in the memory. For instance, Mr. Rao may recall having seen the different kinds of briefcases used by his colleagues. Or he may recall having seen some advertisements for briefcases on the television or in some magazines and newspapers. *External search* refers to the deliberate and voluntary seeking of new information regarding the product/brand under consideration. Mr. Rao can seek information from the following three sources:

- **Personal sources** – family, friends, colleagues, neighbours.
- **Commercial sources** – advertisements, retailers, salesmen.
- **Public sources** – seeing others, consumer information centres.

By tapping all these sources of information, Mr. Rao is able to identify the different types of briefcase on the basis of material, branded *versus* unbranded, high-medium-low priced. A wide variety of materials are used for making briefcases ranging from the best leather to rexine to plastic. There are branded briefcases available and Mr. Rao can choose from the well known VIP, Safari and Aristocrat and some less known local brands, or he can choose to buy an unbranded briefcase. The price ranges from Rs. 125 to Rs. 1,200. Also, there are a number of other features which can influence the choice, such as type of lock, and number of partitions and pockets for keeping different documents.

By the end of this stage, Mr. Rao has gathered enough information about different kinds of briefcases available and has narrowed down his alternatives to moulded plastic, branded briefcase. Within this broad range there are various brands and price ranges to make the final choice from.

(iii) ***Evaluation of Alternatives.*** Mr. Rao will make his final decision using certain evaluative criteria. The most commonly used criteria are: (i) product attribute; (ii) the relative importance of each attribute to the consumer; (iii) brand image; and (iv) attitudes towards the different brands or alternatives under considerations. For instance, the product attributes of the (plastic branded briefcase) alternatives identified by Mr. Rao attaches maximum importance to the product attributes of light weight and spaciousness as compared to other attributes. He already has some kind of attitude towards the various brands developed in the stage of information search which will affect his final decision.

This stage of the buying-decision process gives the marketer a chance to modify his product offering in keeping with the relative importance attached to each attribute by various consumer segments, altering beliefs and attitudes about his own brand, and calling attention to neglected product attributes.

(iv) ***Purchase Decision.*** In the evaluation stage, Mr. Rao has ranked the various brands in terms of his first, second and third preferences. In short, he has made up his mind about which brand he wants to buy. However, Mr. Rao may finally end up buying a brand which is not his most preferred. This may happen because attitudes of others and situational factors.

For instance, when Mr. Rao goes to the shop to make his purchase, the shopkeeper's negative remarks about his (Mr. Roa's) most preferred brand may make him change his mind. Also, it is possible that Mr. Rao's preferred brand is not available, or there is a very attractive price discount on the brand ranked third by him which eventually makes him change his mind.

(v) ***Post-purchase Behaviour.*** After purchasing the briefcase, if Mr. Rao find that its performance or utility matches up to his expectation, Mr. Rao will feel satisfied with his purchase. The satisfaction will reinforce Mr. Rao's perceived favourable image of the brand, which is likely to be extended to the entire range of products manufactured by the company. Also, Mr. Rao is likely to strongly recommend the brand when his friends ask his advice for buying a new briefcase. A satisfied customer is thus a very powerful source of influence for potential customers.

However, if Mr. Rao feels that the briefcase which he has purchased is not up to his expectation, then he is likely to feel dissatisfied. The gap between expected (or perceived) and the actual performances causes discomfort or dissonance to the buyer. As a result of this, Mr. Rao may decide to stop buying other products sold by the same company and also warn his friends about the poor utility of his briefcase. To reduce his own state of discomfort or dissonance arising from the feeling that he has not made the right choice, Mr. Rao can: (i) re-evaluate the unchosen brands and downgrade their desirability by identifying some negative features; and (ii) search for information to confirm his choice.

TYPES OF MODEL

Market researcher traditionally used economic models to predict the consumer behaviour. The concept of price, income, etc. and their relation to buying behaviour to predict the outcome. But, in reality it was found, socio-psychological factors go to a great extent in forming a buying behaviour. As a result marketer started using psychological models to predict the buying behaviour. Whether pure economic models were used or pure psychological models were used, the researchers were using Monadic models, i.e. using only one discipline of study. Real buying behaviour is affected and influenced by economics, sociology, psychological, environmental and various other factors simultaneously. Thus the eclectic models or the multivariable models which take into account all these influences simultaneously are much more comprehensive and relevant, although checking the validity of these models becomes relatively difficult.

Monadic Models of Consumer Behaviour

Elasticity Model

This is a pure economic, more precisely, micro-economic model. The model says as the price increases, other things remaining constant (*ceteris paribus*), demand of the commodity will go down. By how much it will go down will depend on the nature of the commodity. For example, in case of diamond which is a non-essential luxury commodity, even if price goes up slightly, demand will fall by much large margin. Diamond is, therefore, known as highly price elastic, while a commodity like petrol may not be very cheap, but life comes to a standstill without it. If price of petrol increases, people cannot reduce the consumption, and, in general, decrease in quantity is much less than the increase in price. All such commodity is called price inelastic (this sets a relation between the change in consumer income and change in the quantity demanded).

Response Hierarchy Model

The model attempts to predict the sequence of mental stages that the consumer passes through on the way to purchase. Like elasticity model, which was purely economics, this model is purely psychological. There are three mental stages, namely, cognitive, affective and behavioural. Cognitive stage deals with creation of knowledge or awareness in the mind of the consumer. The next stage is concerned with developing an attitude or change in attitude towards the specific product. The attitude formation finally brings us to the behaviour formation, the buying behaviour. One of the most popular response hierarchy models is the AIDA Model. AIDA stand for attention, interest, desire and action, depicting the sequence of mental stages that the consumer passes through before the action of buying.

Stage	AIDA Model
↓	Attention
Cognitive	↓
↓	Interest
Affective	↓
↓	Desire
Behaviour	↓
	Action

Fig. 6.2: Response Hierarchy Model

The Black Box Model

Black Box model is also called stimulus response model. Consumer's mind and thought processing is treated like a "black box" which cannot be opened to find out how it is working. The model highlights the input stimulus like a promotional advertisement and resultant output, the purchase behaviour, as shown in Fig. 6.3.

Black Box model although does not go on to describe as how purchase behaviour is formed, but mentions personality, motivation, attitude and learning process as the factors standing in between input stimulus and output behaviour. Later on market researchers have developed the model into complex multivariable model.

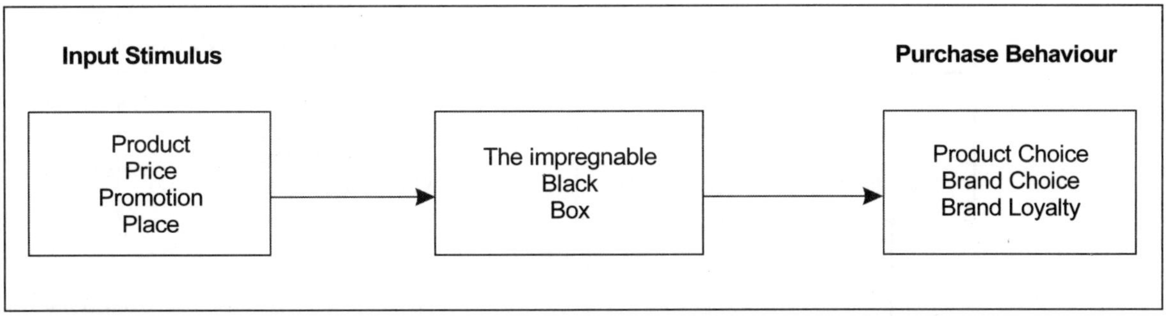

Fig. 6.3: The Black Box Model

As mentioned earlier, monadic theories fail to explain the complex, multifaceted buying behaviour, as a consumer is a mixture of rational (highlighted by economic price elasticity model) and emotional and cognitive (highlighted by psychological model) buyer. May prices of certain products go up and knowingly the consumer continues to buy it due to brand loyality (a learning experience), or has a strong preference for a particular product, buying of a CRY (Child Relief and You) card as it has a social benefit (an attitude formation), at other times the rational behaviour becomes prominent. If there is a persistent increase in LPG and kerosene prices, which is happening in a phased manner due to liberalisation process, consumers will find other means of cooking, like solar cookers or electric ovens. As a result demand for LPG and kerosene will come down.

Eclectic or Multivariable Models of Consumer Behaviour

More comprehensive and relevant models formalising the multiple influences on the purchase decision are the multivariable models. Consumer is taken as a problem solver, the problem is "to buy or not to buy". The consumer receives information from various sources, which is processed in the central processing unit (the mind), influenced by external environment, like economic, social, cultural and psychological. Some of the wellknown multivariable models are:

The model explains the buyer decision process using six sets of *variables* as can be seen in Fig. 6.4. These sets of variables are:

(a) ***Input Variables.*** These include information inputs about the alternative services or products available including rational and emotional elements. For example, the customer wants to possess a Standard Chartered gold card, he will seek information regarding the facilities of such a card, the interest charged and will also be affected by the promotional ad of Standard Chartered gold card.

(b) ***Behavioural Determinants.*** These variables are the pre-existing elements in consumer's mind and existing predisposition of the consumer influence by his culture, family and other such factors. Behavioural determinants do not play an overt role, nevertheless, play a significant role in buying decisions. While buying a Standard Chartered gold card, if the potential buyer considers possessing a credit card as status symbol, or he is frequent buyer of expensive item, these will bear a positive impact on his decision of owning the card.

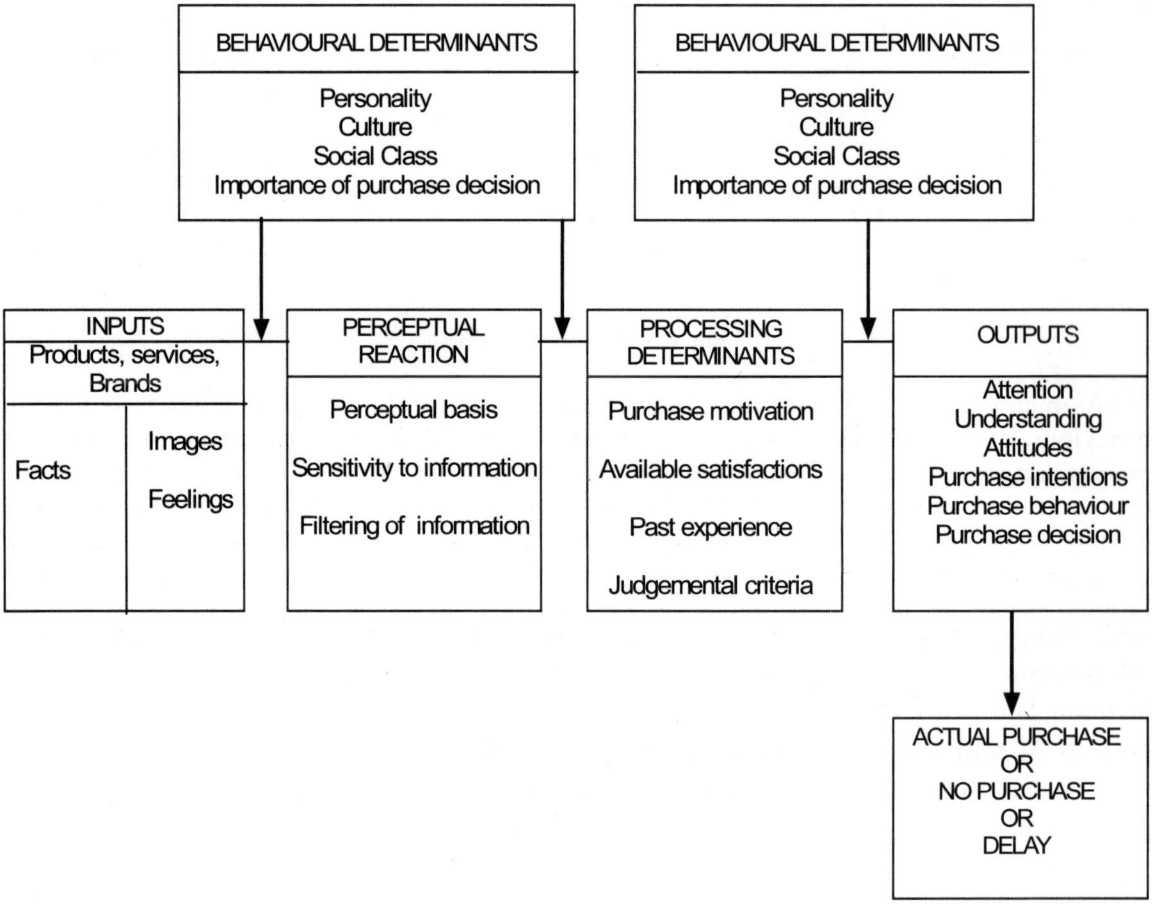

Fig. 6.4: The Howard-Seth Model

Source: Adapted from J. Howard and N. Sheth: Theory of Buyer Behaviour.

(c) ***Perceptual Reaction.*** Information from inputs are not accepted at their face value by the consumer but are processed in the minds of the consumers and then interpreted. For example, a person who is serious about possessing a gold card will compare the advantages and disadvantages with other similar credit card, he will seek information actively. He will go out of the way to get information try to assimilate as far as possible and filter all the information he thinks is important, but passively may be on the TV set and will not be sensitive to the information and hence won't filter much of it for processing purpose.

(d) ***Processing Determinants.*** These are the factors affecting as to how the gathered information is evaluated. Factors affecting are, motivating and the past relevant experiences (the learning process). Learning process will include experience about the product and also on post-purchase services. Consumer will apply some judgemental criteria to evaluate the alternatives. This subjectivity element is crucial

in the whole process. Result of market and marketing research can be useful to identify and assess the subjectivity element in the consumer buying process.

(e) ***Inhibitors.*** These are the external constraints, inhibiting the actual or potential purchase behaviour. For possessing the gold card, the inhibitors can be:

(i) Rates of interest charged,

(ii) Income of the persons,

(iii) Relative price of other equivalent credit cards,

(iv) Any formality that has to be fulfilled, for example one has to submit his income statement, his permanent income tax account number (PAN), etc.

(f) ***Output Variable.*** The outcome of the process of interacting elements may results in the purchase decision, not-to-purchase decision, or post-dated purchase.

Howard-Sheth model has a number of distinct features like—it highlights the role of consumer satisfaction, which consumers seek in relation to the purchase of goods and services. Along with this model also highlights the need to clearly understand the motivational force, which guides the purchase behaviour. Models bring out that the buying process is an end product of the objective (rational) as well as subjective (emotional) element.

Selected Characteristics of Major Indian Social Classes

1. Upper Uppers
2. Lower Uppers
3. Upper Middles
4. Middle Class
5. Working Class
6. Upper Lowers
7. Lower Lowers

Analyzing Consumer Markets and Buyer Behaviour

1. Personal Factors
   - Age and Stage in the Life Cycle
   - Occupation and Economic Circumstances
   - Life Style
2. Psychographics
   - Actualizers
   - Fulfillers
   - Achievers
   - Experiencers
   - Believers
   - Strivers
   - Makers
   - Strugglers

3. Psychological Factors
   - Motivation
   - Perception
   - Beliefs and Attitudes

   The consumer Buying Decision Process
   - Buying Roles
   - Buying Behaviour

QUESTIONS FOR DISCUSSION

1. Distinguish between consumer behaviour and consumption behaviour.
2. Name the sociological determinants of buyer behaviour.
3. Discuss the buying motives.
4. How far groups influence consumer decisions?
5. Explain the various factors, which affect the consumer buying behaviour.
6. Discuss the various stages in the buying process.
7. Explain the various theories of buying behaviour. What is their importance in marketing?
8. Discuss the role of psychological factors in taking a purchasing decision by an individual.
9. How can the study of consumer behaviour assist marketers in segmenting markets and positioning products?
10. What is consumer behaviour? What is the importance of studying consumer behaviour?
11. What are the reasons responsible for developing the field of consumer behaviour?
12. Discuss how and why is the field of consumer behaviour is developed.
13. How does the study of economic theory, psychology, sociology and anthropology help in understanding the buyer behaviour?

CASE STUDY 6.1

XYZ PHOTOCOPIER COMPANY—HANDLING CUSTOMER CONCERN

You have an appointment to see Mr. Bhatnagar, Sales Office Manager of ABC Corporation with regard to the purchase of and XYZ Photocopier. You are bristling with anticipation as you know that the present contract that the ABC Corporation has with Clearprint, you closest competitor, is about to expire. You have not met Mr. Bhatnagar before.

As you enter Bhatnagar's office you notice that he appears to be little under pressure. After introducing yourself, you say "I would like to talk with you about how we can improve the efficiency of your photocopier operation. I think that you use Clearprint photocopier at the moment. What kind of documents do you photocopy in the Sales Office?"

The discussion continues, with you attempting to assess Bhatnagar's office requirements regarding photocopying facilities and his attitude towards the Clearprint machine.

One need is the ability of the photocopier to copy two sides of the document automatically since some of the documents, which are photocopied are quite lengthy.

Another requirement is for the photocopy itself to be of highest quality since it is usual for photocopies of standards letters to be sent to clients. The Clearprint photocopier does not have a double-sided photocopying facility, and the quality, while passable is not totally satisfactory. Further, there are sometimes delays in repairing the machine when it breaks down, although generally, it is quite reliable. At the end of discussion, you summarise the points that have been raised: staff time is being spent disproportionately, the quality of the copies is not totally satisfactory; and repairs are not carried out promptly. Mr. Bhatnagar agrees that this is a fair summary.

QUESTIONS FOR DISCUSSION

1. During the sales interview the following objections were raised. How would you deal with each of them?

Objection 1

I am sorry, I have an urgent meeting in 10 minutes time. Can we make it quick?

Objection 2

We have not had any major objections with Clearprint so far.

Objection 3

Doesn't your firm have a bad reputation?

Objection 4

Aren't your prices and service charges much higher than Clearprint?

Objection 5

How do I know your services will be any better than Clearprint?

Objection 6

My staff have got used to using this Clearprint. I have to spend time showing them how to use your machine.

Objection 7

Let me think about it. The Clearprint is coming next week. I would like to discuss the point you have raised with him.

CASE STUDY 6.2

INDIAN CYCLES LIMITED

Introduction

Indian Cycles Limited is in the business of manufacturing cycles and light mopeds for the last twenty years. The company is the undisputed market leader in the Rs. 600 crore market of cycles and has retained this position for the last ten years. The reasons behind this extraordinary achievement are many. For instance the company has an excellent dealer network of 2,500 dealers across the country and offers the highest margins to them. Another reason is the ability of the management to innovate and bring new products before any other competitor does.

Around the late 1980s, the company anticipated some changes in the consumers' needs and the influx of multinational as well as the impact of these factors would have on the Indian economy. 'Fitness' and 'exercise' were beginning to mark their presence in the minds of consumers and an up-market section of people was getting more aware of physical fitness. This was evident from a sudden flooding of the markets with health foods, new gyms and body-care parlours and new products, such as low-calorie oils and snacks, etc. there was also the realisation that irregular working hours and lack of open spaces have limited the outdoor activities of people and they were ready for an alternative.

The Product

At this time, the company felt the potential of health equipment sector and launched two products namely, 'power-kit' and 'Exerflo'. Powerkit is a stationary exercise cycle with special features, such as a speedometre to show speed of cycling and a stopwatch built in the front panel. The 16.5 kg. machine was based on stimulated cycling action and offered varied features —four different colours to choose from, adjustable heights and handles and cushioned paddles and handles. The second product, Exerflo is an exercise bike, which offered simulated rowing action to exercise the upper body as well, along with the cycling action (meant for lower body exercise), the product offered features, such as speedometre, adjustable height and a manual chart which showed preferred exercise routine for different age groups and other fitness related information.

The Market

Indian Cycles estimated the market for these equipments at 15,000 units per month with 70 per cent demand coming from cities such as Delhi, Mumbai, Chandigarh, Bangalore and Calcutta.

The main competition was from two other cycle manufacturers offering exercise cycles with routine features. The competitor products were priced at almost the same level of Power-kit and were sold through dealers.

The market was, however, very small and grew at a slow pace. Hence, most of the companies stayed away from the market and no new player entered the market till the early 1990s.

The Strategy

The company decided to storm the market with its aggressive marketing and promotion. The first step was a four-month long awareness drive to create an interest among customers and cash the changing attitude towards exercise. The event was planned in a systematic way with advertisements appearing in local print media in five cities. It was followed by product display at around twenty centres in central locations. The two products were displayed at dealer's shops and leaflets were distributed in households.

Another strategy opted for by the company to promote its long-term interest was to promote health and fitness awareness. The company organised fitness camps at strategic locations in all five cities where the benefit of the product and its features were explained. Live demonstrations and product displays along with small videos of fitness and exercise were shown at these stalls on regular intervals. These small camps were mobile, placed on a big van and covered popular places in cities. The whole exercise was carried on for almost four months at an estimated budget of Rs. 70 lakh.

Table 6.2: The Advertising Expenditure of the Event

The medium	Amount spent (in lakhs)
Local newspaper	34
Magazines	5
Leaflets	1
The stalls	30

The company followed this campaign with a second stage of promotion—now only the print media was used and five leading newspapers were selected to come out with detailed advertisements, which were based on main themes such as:

(i) Promoting Power kit and Exerflo as unisex exercising equipments to combat the misconception that exercise equipments are for women only.

(ii) Promote Exerflo as a complete head-to-toe body exercise equipment.

(iii) Create awareness about body weight—maintaining correct height to weight ratio.

(iv) Promote health benefits of staying fit, etc.

Staying on Top

In the last five years, many new companies have launched products in different health equipment categories. Home based gyms, all-in-one small gyms, and other products have entered the market. The major competitor, Majesty, has also launched a product similar to Exerflo with fanfare.

To combat the competition, Exerflo is targeted at segments of various age-groups, such as for businessmen and working executives, for teenagers and the young and for housewives through specially created advertisements in different mediums.

Despite all competition, the company claims to have almost 35 per cent of the market share in health equipment sector.

QUESTIONS FOR DISCUSSION

1. What is the concept of buying motive? What motives can different consumers of this product have?
2. Discuss the role of reference groups in consumer decision market.
3. What are the different mediums Indian cycle manufactures can use to target the market of:
   - Housewives
   - Businessmen.

CASE STUDY 6.3

F.M.C.G. ONGOING WAR

The major players involved in the ongoing war of the detergent industry are Hindustan Lever Ltd., Proctor & Gamble and Nirma. Over the years, there has been a continuous tussile between HLL and P&G for the top slot and the top position has frequently changed hands with Nirma staying on the top of consumer rankings for lower end of the market segment. Of late, there has been a full-fledged action by Nirma to jump into the premium section.

Today, Nirma is a professionally managed entity with substantially decentralised management with the sole aim of providing the best value for the consumers' money Nirma is fastly changing its image, among the customers as a synonym for quality by developing a phosphate free, environment friendly detergent. According to Karsanbhai Patel, the doyen of Rs. 1,000 crore Nirma empire, "Nirma is not merely a brand or a product; it is a dynamic phenomenon, a revolution, a philosophy."

The Nirma management is aspiring to acquire an up-market image for the company. Nirma has chosen to use its product portfolio to enhance the company's image. Accordingly, in January 1996, it introduced mid-priced version of its flagship economy detergent brand Nirma, called Super Nirma detergent powder (Rs. 38.30 per kg.). Besides scaling the portfolio upwards, Nirma is also widening it. The image revamp started one and half years ago when Nirma commissioned its advertising agency, FCB-ULKA to gauge, how the consumers perceived the company. Much to their consternation, research revealed that Nirma was perceived merely as a manufacturer of low cost products. Unfortunately for the company, consumer perceptions were still found to be heavily influenced by the coup Nirma pulled off in the detergent market more than a decade ago. Then the company had humbled the likes of HLL was selling at Rs. 13 per kg., Nirma challenged it with an economy detergent priced at Rs. 3.50 per kg.

Although research indicated that consumers were ready to use any product offered under the Nirma brand name, they were unaware of the fact that Nirma was the No. 1 detergent brand in India. Clearly the Unique Selling Proposition (USP) of low price began to affect the corporate image of the company. "Nirma's strong presence in the lower end of the market went against the company's image."

Due to the low price of its product, the common perception of the company was highly distorted. Most people are still unaware that the company has a sales turnover of Rs. 1,000 crore. Ironically enough, despite graduation to the premium segment, price continues to be the primary weapon in the company's arsenal.

Advertising has been an important ingredient of the Operation Face Lift at Nirma. Just before it started rolling out products in the premium segment in late 1996, Nirma ran a corporate campaign beginning September to ease the perception bottleneck. The campaign comprised a three ad series in print and a 40 second TVC. The ad objective was encapsulated in a tagline—Better products, Better value, Better limit. The campaign hammered the fact that Nirma was Rs. 1,000 crore company with one of the ad copies reading: when you are a Rs. 1,000 crore company, you have to earn the trust of 250 million people. The company spent Rs. 27 crore in 1997 on promoting the new products and its new image.

Nirma, which has taken the multinational consumer product giant HLL headlong in the detergent market by its unique value for money proposition, became the undisputed leader in the detergent market with a share of over 43 per cent in the early nineties. But lately Nirma seems to be trapped in its own brand image.

Unlike most of the other FMCG companies, Nirma has not created any new brand. Rather it has launched new products like soaps, shampoos and toothpaste under the same umbrella brand. Though Nirma has saved the cost of new brand launch and promotion, this has resulted in a wrong consumer perception. To an average consumer, Nirma still means a cheap detergent and they don't associate it to any premium product. But Nirma is trying to change the perception.

Now the efforts are directed to overtake HLL and P&G. Given Nirma's past records it is expected to give HLL and P&G a tough competition in the future.

The brand war has gained momentum of late with most of the companies furiously introducing new brands, most of them higher on the technology for money scale, and spending a steep Rs. 10,106 on an average for advertising each brand. In 1996, detergent makers effectively cannibalised their own old products. Thus despite growing by 90 per cent, the 25 new brands forced down sales of earlier brands by 3 per cent.

In 1990, long after the Nirma phenomenon had finished being envied in marketing circles, few could foresee the technology wave that was headed towards Indian shores. That year, the market was placed at 1.3 million tonnes, growing at 5 per cent a year. Rural penetration was the main game, and all action was at the lower end. At the top end, Hindustan Lever's Surf and Rin ruled unchallenged, though Godrej was a key player in the West.

The early stages of liberalisation brought a player that shook Lever like none other could: P&G. It was more than a mere ripple in the pond. In 1992, P&G launched Ariel, a compact detergent that forced Lever-flushed with technology inputs from its Anglo-Dutch parent—to respond with Surf Ultra. The two brands fought for the urbane housewife's attention, even as Henkel, a German company, came in with Henko and other brands.

Since then, the action has been riveting, with both the main players pressing their R&D to develop economy. The challenger moved swiftly, entering segments that had been Lever's playing field for years. Perhaps P&G's biggest move came in 1994 when it launched Ariel Super Soaker, a high-tech product developed to upgrade Nirma users at the low end. Today, this product's success is unparalleled. Lever's innovations have been no less, and Nirma is rushing to move upscale too. Henkel has not got very far.

The market's value has steeply gone up, the excise duties are down. Urban opportunity may have expanding distribution too, still very much on the agenda of all detergent players. Lever is issuing VSAT communications to keep its complex logistical operations in order. Efficiency levels are higher than ever before.

The detergents market currently stands at 2.2 million tonnes; valued at Rs. 4,500 crores. The premium segment accounts for almost 8 per cent of the value. India is the world's second largest market for detergents, the USA being the largest, consuming some 3 million tonnes. But the breadth of products available here is far more impressive. Demographic and psychographic heterogeneity makes it all the more challenging to listen to consumers. And that, in today's market, is a strategic necessity, not a cute saying to frame up on the wall.

QUESTIONS FOR DISCUSSION

1. Do you think the consumer perception of Nirma as a manufacturer of low-cost products can be changed by introducing premium product under a new name? Suggest a suitable brand name.
2. Has Nirma become a victim of the coup it started against the multinational giants more than a decade ago.
3. What should Nirma do to change consumers' perception about it of being a brand for the low end of the market?
4. The ongoing war among the FMCG giants has placed the consumer in an enviable position with each one of the FMCG giants vying and wooing the consumer for his attention. Suggest some promotional measures that can be used by these leading players to give them the winner's edge.

CASE STUDY 6.4

IMPULSE SHOPPING

"The sweater was following me" the 38-year-old man said. "I had gone on to a different part of the store, but it pulled me back to the men's dept., where I finally bought it."

That might be an extreme example, but similar feelings are common among people who engage in impulse buying, says an assistant professor of marketing. Nine out of ten people have succumbed to the urge to make an unplanned purchase, and most regret it later, says Mr. Aggarwal who recently surveyed more than 500 people to find out how they feel when that happens and how they resist the urge.

Many said, the sudden urge to buy is exciting, thrilling, stimulating—almost like falling in love. "The impulse can be so strong" that it even produces physical symptoms such as goose bumps, hot flashes and tingling sensations", said Mr. Aggarwal adding that "at the same time, the impulse also triggers feelings of guilt, distress, helplessness, and even panic". "This ambivalence emphasises the psychological complexity. Much marketing research has treated it simply as unplanned purchasing, but it is not just that. Essentially, impulse buying is an irrational process in which the urge to gratify an impulse triumphs over the rational parts of the mind," he said and it can be a powerful force.

According to Mr. Aggarwal, most of the people he interviewed for the survey said that they felt hypnotised or mesmerised during an impulse buying episode. "They said they would find objects of their desire. They talked about candy bars calling out to them, about shoes staring at them. This way of thinking allowed them to transfer some of their guilt on to the product itself," he informed.

Resistance often is not easy, and people use a wide variety of strategies to maintain, or regain self-control, the survey showed. More than 70 per cent of the respondents said they tried to conduct an emergency cost-benefit analysis on the spot, asking themselves questions such as these: Do I really want it? Can I afford it? Would I get my money's worth or would I use the product once and forget it?

Several other techniques were also reported by the respondents:

(1) Distancing themselves in time or space by trying to wait for the urge to go away or by leaving the store or the department.

(2) Substituting a small purchase for a larger, more costly or flattering one.

(3) Imposing rationing devices such as leaving credit cards at home and carrying a limited amount of cash.

(4) Inviting others to shop with them knowing that they are more likely to succumb to the impulse buying urge when they are alone.

However, according to Mr. Aggarwal, the survey shows that such strategies frequently fail. "At their strongest, impulses to consume are impossible to resist. And recent marketing innovations such as 24 hours retailing. Instant credit and telemarketing make the urge to buy even easier to gratify, without even setting foot in a shopping centre," he remarked.

According to him, more than 80 per cent of the respondents said they had suffered negative consequences in the wake of impulse buying episodes. These included financial difficulties, disappointment with the product and the disapproval of other people.

Talking on its psychological impact, Mr. Aggarwal intones, "some people suffer a tremendous amount of guilt just for having the impulse, irrespective of whether they give into it or not". "On the other hand", he added, "some people said that impulse buying elevates their mood and boost their energy. For them, giving in to the urge is a highly satisfying experience—a way to fill the emptiness of their lives, either literally or figuratively."

QUESTIONS FOR DISCUSSION

1. What are the consumerism issues that exist for impulse shopping?
2. What are the suggestions to improve over the impulse shopping?
3. Discuss the problem of impulse buying.

CASE STUDY 6.5

FLYWAY SUCCESS: FEDERAL EXPRESS

Frederick W. Smith had transportation coursing through his veins. But the fact that he drew his ancestry from a line of transportation entrepreneurs, including a riverboat pilot and a founder of an interstate bus service, had little to do with it. As a little boy, Mississippi-born Smith has a passion for planes and learnt to fly at the age of 15, a talent that eventually saw him make it as a US Marine pilot. But numerous combat missions in Vietnam didn't really make him the quintessential battle-hardened war veteran. Quite the opposite, the agony of war stirred in him a craving for more productive and enriching pursuits. So with Nam behind him, Smith acquired Arkansas Aviation, a firm which dealt in corporate jets, in 1969.

But Smith wasn't happy just selling aircrafts. He yearned to do something more radical, something world-challenging. He scouted around a bit, before stumbling upon an idea that had first occurred to him as a student at Yale. Smith has then submitted a paper on the logistical challenges faced by firms in the information technology industry. In the paper, he had reasoned that no company could afford to maintain a full inventory of spare parts for computers and other data processing machines. And as the dependence on computers increased, the need for quick replacements of faulty parts would put immense pressure on suppliers. He had concluded that a system that moved parts overnight, door-to-door supply would have to be devised to save time.

There! Smith realised that this was the business opportunity he had been waiting for. He would start the world's first airline dedicated exclusively to meet the requirements of companies desperately in need of parts. It would work, simply because the air-cargo services on offer were non-starters to begin with. After all, the consignments were shipped in the bellies of passenger planes, and as most planes scheduled their flights during the day to suit travellers, next-day delivery was rarely possible. And servicing areas outside the limits of large cities posed their own problems. Smith's logic was simple. His company would streamline operations using the husband-spoke distribution pattern, where all packages arrived at a central point for sorting, were loaded into planes, and then flown to their destinations.

In 1971, Smith incorporated Federal Express with headquarters in Little Rock, Arkansas, but he still needed financial backing for his enterprise. Many investors he solicited saw no future in his project. Some doubted the viability of an overnight delivery service. Smith eventually hired two firms to study his plan and research the potential customer base. Their findings sent Smith into raptures—each projected annual business in the US in excess of $1 billion. Smith promptly tossed in $4 million and persuaded investors to add another $80 million to the kitty. Next, he began recruiting staff, a motley crew that included many former members of the military.

In 1972, federal Express bought its first fleet of 33 Dassault Falcons. Each Falcon had a capacity of 6,500 pounds, and could cover a range of 1,400 to 1,800 miles. Meanwhile, FedEx was negotiating with the airport authorities at Little Rock about setting up its home basis there. The city's central location suited FedEx's operation structure all right. But dim-sighted officials were apprehensive about backing this embryonic venture for they would lose precious dollars if the airline failed.

Just as it appeared that the airlines troubles had begun even before the first cargo flight had been undertaken, the solution presented itself to FedEx in the form of the airport authorities of Memphis, Tennessee. The airport here had some old hangers available, which it put at FedEx's disposal. The idea the officials at Memphis had was to leverage the spillover from FedEx operations to bring new jobs to the city, keep the airport busy at night, and make the city a shipping centre. FedEx fell for the offer, and in March 1973, moved its Airlines Operations Department to Memphis. The rest of the company soon followed suit.

On a March night in 1973, FedEx kicked off the express delivery concept. Twelve cities in the East and Midwest were the markets. The Falcons waited dutifully for the packages to arrive. By dawn the next day, a total of seven packages had been received by the system fewer than the number of planes owned by FedEx!

The company realised that 12 cities were not sufficient to make a deal or it. FedEx also redefined its service commitment. Priority One, meaning door-to-door delivery by noon the next business day, and Economy Air, that of providing door-to-door on the second business day. The company reactivated its system April 17, 1973. The network had been expanded to include 25 cities (and a radius of 25 miles around them). By the next morning, 186 packages had arrived at FedEx.

All in a Day's Work

If the FedEx experience is anything to go by, cargo freighting doesn't always need to be a hackneyed job of shuttling around dull documents and the like. For example, in 1994, Peregrine Fund hired FedEx to transport 12 of the world's last 76 California condors for relocation! Another of FedEx's unique shipments involved transporting thousands of copies of the Koran on CD-ROMS, bound for Spain. These high-tech texts worth several thousand dollars were gifts from the Saudi Arabian King and his ambassador to Spain. More recently, FedEx worked on Motorola's satellite communications project. Iridium, ferrying the 72 satellites from the US to the launch site in China and Russia.

The first year had FedEx tripling its workforce to 1,100. Package volume first crossed the 1,000 per night threshold, then pushed the 1,500 per night mark. But teething problems were far from over, as financial stability eluded the company. Though already the most heavily financed entrant in US transportation history, more money needed to be pumped into expand the network of cities, increase employee strength, and maintain the planes. In November 1973, another $52 million was fed into FedEx by investors. In February 1975, FedEx finally emerged from the red by inking a profit of $20,000, erasing a two-year run of average monthly losses of more than $1 million.

All through the lean years, FedEx unflinchingly stood by its 'People-Service-Profit' motto. Employee satisfaction was accorded the highest status. Smith believed that treating employee well would engender the highest levels of service, and with service a given profits would naturally flow.

Target: The Fed

When Fred Smith decided on air-cargo service as his chosen sphere of business, he determined that the new enterprise should be called Federal Express. His reasoning was well thought out. To begin with the name had that true-blue, 'stars-and-stripes' American flavour that would appeal to his clientele. Secondly, the name suggested that it was not a regional player. But, maybe, what ultimately inspired Smith to settle for this name was the regular inflow of business he hoped to garner from the Federal Reserve Bank. In 1994 Federal Express launched FedEx as the official brand name of the company, with the slogan 'The World On Time'.

In 1975, FedEx engineered a coup of sort when it reached out directly to potential customers through mass-media advertising. The trend among cargo carriers had been to advertise in professional or trade journals. FedEx, in an effort to take the decision-making into front offices, spend $350,000 on publicity in consumer magazines and, more radically, on television, "America, you've got a new airline," was the FedEx line. America responded heartily. By the end of 1975, daily package volume rose to 13,500, and revenues touched $60 million. The figures for 1976 were even better. The service received 19,000 packages daily to deliver to 75 cities, and garnered $96 million in turnover. Predictably, business Cassandras warned of the inevitable tailspin.

In the meantime, FedEx realised that its market expansion plans and future growth potential was being hampered by the limited load capacity available in its fleet of falcons. The company petitioned the Civil Aeronautics Board (CAB) to allow it to acquire five larger-capacity aircraft with payload of up to 15,000 pounds. The CAB dismissed the request on the ground of an existing law that forbade air-taxi services from operating plane with capacities greater than 75,00 pounds. However this rule had been enacted for passenger aircraft and freight carriers. FedEx lobbied long and hard to get the law amended. The company based its argument on the issue of deregulation, and how its made greater economic sense to fly one large plane between two cities than many smaller ones. The clincher was the fact that regulation cost every family in the US a sum of $250 a year, because of the indirect payment towards the industry's inventory maintenance and excess equipment. In November 1977, President Jimmy Carter finally gave his nod to rescinding the law.

I-Tech Strategy

As early as 1972, FedEx had its first computer, a Burroughs 1,700, installed in its office. Six years down the line, with the daily volumes barely measuring 40,000 packages, two large IBM mainframes running at a fraction of their capacity occupied space at FedEx. Such is the emphasis the company has laid on information technology. The ethos at FedEx has been one of stretching the limits of technology to serve customers better. The Digitally Assisted Dispatch System (DADS) introduced in 1980 is a good example. It involves the digital transmission of data to in-vehicle terminals, thereby guiding couriers to their next pickup. Other technological firsts include arming couriers with bar-code scanners to track package status in transit, Zap Mail, the FedEx Power Ship automated shipping capability, and the FedEx Inter Net Ship that allows customers to process packages on the Internet.

FedEx immediately purchased seven Boeing 727s for $26 million, each with a capacity of 40,000 pounds—seven times the load of a Falcon Operations commenced in January 1978 and the company's shares began being publicly traded on the New York Stock Exchange the same year. In 1983, it became the first US Company to achieve revenues of $1 million in 10 years without relying on acquisitions or mergers.

The next year, FedEx launched its international operation in Europe and the Asia Pacific on following the acquisition of Gelco Express International. December 22, 1986, was a red-letter day for FedEx—the company freighted over one million packages!

Today, the FedEx network links 210 countries across the world has a 1,40,000 plus strength on its muster-roll, and delivers more than three million shipments each business day. As Fred Smith's vision of delivering the world moves closer to realisation, the company is charting a new course for its future—where it creates 'connectivity' for people on an ever—expanding horizon—Marketing hyermtroia?

QUESTIONS FOR DISCUSSION

1. What strategies were adopted by Federal Express to maintain service commitments and delivery?
2. How could Federal Express directly reach its potential customer? Explain.

3. How successful if Federal Express international operations and how they could show their presence globally?
4. Describe the distribution strategy of Federal Express.

CASE STUDY 6.6

LAXMI MILLS

Rajan Kohali along with his brothers, started making and selling edible oils way back in 1910. In 1930, Rajan along with his sons, stated Laxmi Mills with factories operating in Bombay and Hyderabad. The change was not only in name but also in a major technological difference. The Laxmi Mills was subjected to a new process: refining. The mill had to get people to accept a "tasteless" cooking medium because that is what the oil became after refining. However, Rajan had all that taken care of. By generating an export market, he covered the risk of being left with excess stocks while he experimented with excess stocks while he experimented with the Indian market. At that time, there was a sufficient number of Europeans in India to form the base of his local market.

Rajan had chosen, groundnut oil for the following reasons:

(i) It was very commonly used in Indian families and the potential customer base was wide.

(ii) Groundnut was grown widely.

(iii) The oilseeds yielded a good quantity of oil.

The oil was sold in 15 and 50 kg barrels to cater to both the nuclear and joint family needs.

Rajan sold the concept of refined oil as one that is pure as it undergoes a thorough cleaning process retaining the flavour of the foodstuff itself. The concept being new, the buyers had to be convinced that it was not harmful.

The company enjoyed 80 per cent of the market share till 1970. Other companies saw the growing potential and entered the market. To remain in the market as a leader the Laxmi Mills changed the pack size to one, two, five, ten, fifteen and twenty-five kg. However, competition became fairly intense in 1980. A number of big players entered the market. In 1980, Maruti Oil Mills launched refined Kardai Oil which help to lower cholesterol levels, the primary cause of heart attacks.

Mumbai Oil Mills exploited this to the hilt. Doctors also started prescribing Kardai Oil. Any person with a heart problem was immediately prescribed to change his cooking medium to Kardai Oil.

Consumer queries started coming into Laxmi Mills. People wanted to know if was safe to use refined groundnut oil. The market share dropped sharply to 65 per cent.

(MBA, June 1997)

QUESTIONS FOR DISCUSSION

1. How would you advice the company to clear its reputation and re-establish its credibility?

2. What according to you, should the Laxmi Mills have done immediately after sensing the change?

CASE STUDY 6.7

THE STORY OF MACNINE SHOES

Walking down the streets of Delhi's Connaught Place, Capital's business heart, Mike Steve, 50 years old CEO of Macnine Shoes (India), was looking at the feet of the busy office goers. The CEO purposely walked to his office near Super Bazar from the Palika car parking to have a first hand feeling of the market response to the Macnine shoes, and in general the foot-wear habit of urban Indians. Macnine shoes brought an image of simple no fuss yet elegant office-going shoes. The shoes, known for its comfort and reasonable prices shared a good market share in face of competition from Windsor, Red Tape, Lee Cooper, Woodland, etc. But as the days passed Mike's trained eyes could see the changing scenario. Office goers no longer seemed to be preferring "no fuss" shoes. There was a distinct preference for heavy looking chunky shoes. People's perception about office-going shoes was changing from regular 6 hole laced shoes to these heavy looking shoes. As a result, Macnine shoes' market share decreased by 10 per cent between 1998 and 1999.

Disturbed by the fact, Mr. Steve called a meeting of the departmental heads and after five-hour long meeting it was accepted, Indian consumers had undergone a sea change in their attitudes and perceptions about the products. Office was no long seen as a boring workplace where a "no nonsense" rather "stiff upper lip" attitude has to be maintained. Office was seen as more a part of regular life and a relaxed "as you want to be" (of course within limits) attitude. Keeping pace with the time, Macnine shoes also should shed its "traditional" image. More importantly, consumers are going more and more for branded shoes, rather than mass production shoes that will be available at the retail shops. The departmental heads agreed that there is a definite price-quality perception in the minds of the consumers. Consumers perceive high price as a certificate of high quality that will be associated with the branded products. Based on the price-quality perception, Macnine shoes were decided to be positioned in the market. Dramatically changing from the basic principle of quality and affordability targeting the growing middle class, the company saw a better prospect in developing a high necessity but it was a part of life style marketing where shoes were seen as fashion accessories.

Macnine shoes which for over two decades was known for making popular affordable shoes, took a one eighty degree turn and developed dedicated showrooms with premium shoes and other accessories like T-shirts, bags, socks, etc. But, the results were quite contrary to what was expected, the decrease in market share continued despite these efforts. The reason seems quite simple, or decades consumer has known the shoe to be in the affordable range. With this sudden change, the loyal buyers felt betrayed and turned away towards other local brands. The main selling point of the company was missing the consumer no longer felt the urge to come to buy Macnine shoes. The fact was the brands who started as selling premium shoes were perceived to be in a category of catering the upper category of consumers with extremely focused range of shoes which borne a premium price. Talk of Red Tape, talk of Lee Cooper, the image that comes to the consumer's mind is of premium shoes with all its associated characteristics. While past experience brings in the minds of the consumer an "affordability" image of Macnine shoes. When the company drastically wanted to change the image, they could not fit into consumer perception of a premium shoe, while high price deterred people who wanted affordability foremost. Macnine lost on both the grounds.

QUESTIONS FOR DISCUSSION

1. How will you apply Gestalt Theory to explain the above case?
2. Suggest some ways of changing consumer perception of Macnine Shoes.
3. Explain the role of "role and status" for Macnine shoes.

CASE STUDY 6.8

WHAT MOTIVATES MEN AND WOMEN TO BUY?

If you have to buy a product for your family, generally who takes the initiative? This is a fundamental query by the marketers. A product, which is used by the whole family, more often than not it is the women folk who take active interest in buying it. What motivates a woman to buy a product, which is to be used by everyone in the family? Motivational research, as carried out by a consultancy in Mumbai, specializing in sales and marketing, reveals that women are psychologically more attuned to the process of shopping. The consultancy reveals that a woman buyer will take time, evaluate more, be more value conscious and less brand conscious while buying a product. So it is always not that women are "emotional buyers". Men, on the other hand, have natural inclination towards buying image enhancing "object of power" products. Woman is the principal buyer not because the number of working women is on rise. Even in the families where the man is the bread earner, woman is the principal buyer, and for day to day use product, the marketer has to motivate the woman. A woman loves to get an image of a "cognitive buyer". Many companies have realized this much earlier. Take, for example, Hindustan Lever Ltd., a known name in manufacturing of detergents and soaps. Way back in 1950's and 60's, their advertisement for the detergents showed the head of the family, the bread earner as the buyer, but during 1970's with the study of the buying pattern, the company realized that showing a woman as taking the decision of buying, motivates the principal buyers. Further, rather than a docile image, what motivates these buyers, is an intelligent consumer who, by her conscious decision, buys a product. An image like this became an instant hit with the buyers and the image of "Lalitaji" a middle aged mother of a boy, taking a prudent decision on buying Surf, helped the company in a big way.

Motivational research further proves that what motivates a man into buying is the shape, structure and technicality of the product. So if the aim is to target the male buyers who are less frequent buyers but involves larger sum of money, the marketer will have to emphasise on the shape and structure of the product, with definite and detailed information. A man wants to see himself as "time pressed, valued oriented" shopper, who also values the brand name more than the women.

QUESTIONS FOR DISCUSSION

1. Discuss all the factors that have gone into developing the image of an "intelligent woman" buyer. Discuss what is the motivational process if you want to promote your product through such an advertisement.

2. Colgate Palmolive, another known brand in manufacturing of soaps and detergents, may develop a campaign based on "negative" motive. Discuss how their advertisement should be like. Can you also think of developing an ad campaign based on emotional motive for such products? Discuss.

CASE STUDY 6.9

CROSS-CULTURAL EFFECT ON THE INDIAN FOOD HABITS

As the newly acquired Modern Foods was a new feather added to HLL's cap, developing this public sector plant into HLL's mainstream was not an easy job. To begin with, HLL management had a stiff battle with its opponents like Britannia, Nestle, etc. After Modern Foods was acquired, the challenge was to integrate it to HLL's philosophy, buying dying brands, consolidate it and slowly penetrate into the market and then steadily increase the market share. HLL has done this with Tata's TOMCO and Lake, Ravi Ghai's Kwality and many others. In 1993, when HLL acquired TOMCO, Hamam was a dying brand. Today, it has a market share of 4.2 per cent. When HLL took over Kwality in mid 1990's, its market share was 52 per cent. By 1999, Kwality Walls' market share was over 60 per cent. Keeping with parent Unilevers portfolio, HLL wants to keep half its turnover from food industry. Whether it is Annapurna brand or newly acquired Modern Foods, there has to be brand extension. The new management found that the strong point of loss making Modern Food was its R&D Department. In a country where significant population is vegetarian and where religious reasons make non-vegetarian people also consume vegetarian food during occasions like Ram Navami, to develop "Market share increasing" strategies for a bakery will require studying carefully the ingredients used in the food. Here Modern Food scores high points. The Company has the recipe of developing egg-less cakes and they taste as good as the "with egg" cakes by leading name in the cake manufacturing—Britannia. That is what the new MD of Modern Food Industries, Peter Selvarajan feels.

To have mass attraction and dealing in "volumes" has been HLL's categories in every segment of consumer products. While this strategy is easier soaps and detergent segments, food is a different ball game. The kitchen cabinet is infested with many causalities. Even if you are a known name in the business, world wide, if you cannot adopt the eating habits of the particular region, you may meet with failures, and will not be able to expand. For example, American Food giant Heinz Foods, way back in 1994, acquired the consumer product division of Glaxo. Seven years down the line, Heinz is still selling for what Glaxo had become a household name, namely, Farex, Complan, Glucon D. Being immensely successful in USA, Heinz India still has to make one of its own products popular to Indian pallet. Till now very few MNCs have been successful to make the foreign recipe successful in India. Take the case of another Michigan based food giant Kellogg's. Worldwide Kellogg's breakfast cereal are famous, but is exactly not a successful case to be studied by the students of Indian marketing and consumer behaviour. Another MNC, Best Foods, have made roads into Indian household through Captain Cook salt and acquiring the age old Taria Dalal brand. The market is so risky as it is inherently related to cultural issues, HLL has to be very cautious with churning out modern menu for the Indian palate. Unlike other success stories in soaps and detergents, food items, in order to be mass marketed, certain issues pertaining to consumer food habits if overlooked, can earn losses for the company.

MARKETING RESEARCH

7

INTRODUCTION

In the past marketing and sales people just went out, met people and tried to sell them 'something. But now the problem of distribution has become very complex. Consumer orientation became the philosophy of business and markets are expanded and widened to an international level. Expansion of market, necessitated collection of information about competition, consumers and their behaviour, etc. In all these cases producers required information like who are the customers and where do they live? What are the products needed by the consumers? Why do they insist on a particular product? When do they want the product? How big is the market? Where are the products to be made available? For answering these questions the manufacturers require plenty of knowledge about customers, their behaviour, their beliefs and their reactions to marketing effort. This required collection, analysis and interpretation of proper, relevant and timely information that flow between the consumer and the firm. This is the role of recently added marketing function, i.e. marketing research. This function is capable of creating confidence in the minds of producers to meet any changed situation.

Definition of Marketing Research

The American Marketing Association (AMA) has defined marketing research as "the systematic gathering, recording and analysis of data about problems relating to the marketing of goods and services. Richard D. Crisp defines marketing research as "the systematic, objective and exhaustive research for and study of the facts relevant to every problem in the field of marketing".

As per the above definitions, marketing research is the scientific method of collection, analysis and interpretation of data for helping marketing manager in making wise decisions in the field of marketing. It includes other research, etc. It is also concerned with channels of distribution, pricing, decision of the product, etc. It studies people as buyers, sellers and consumers, their attitude, preference, purchasing power, etc.

Though there is a difference in the meaning of the two terms marketing research and market research, they are used interchangeably by some people. Market research is only part of marketing research and only a few aspects of marketing. According to Philip Kotler the term market research is accurate for describing research into the market, its size, geographical distribution of income, and so on. Market here is used to mean potential buyers. Marketing research has a wider meaning. It studies product planning, product development, sales promotion, distribution strategies, consumption, buyer behaviour, etc.

Objectives or Aims of Marketing Research

The aims or objectives of marketing research can be illustrated as follows:

1. To define the probable market for a particular product and to find out general market conditions and tendencies.
2. To assess competitive strength and policies.
3. To estimate potential buying power.
4. To find out a distribution method best suited for the product.
5. To assess the probable volume of further sales.
6. To know consumers' acceptance.

Thus marketing research is the vehicle by which information is obtained about present and potential customers, their reactions to present and prospective marketing mixes.

Importance of Marketing Research

Marketing research helps the management in making better marketing decisions, increasing efficiency and reducing the costs of marketing. As an important tool of decision-making, it helps management in minimising the mistakes in marketing decisions.

Marketing research provides information about market conditions, consumer demands and changes in the pattern of demand. This will predict the potential demand for the products thereby facilitating planned production. Marketing research tells the management where the company stands in the ocean of market.

Only marketing research can provide first hand knowledge about consumers and changes in the pattern of demand. Present marketing requires numerous middlemen between producer and consumer. Each middleman erects a sort of wall which blocks the backward flow of communication regarding consumer needs and dealer needs to the manufacturer. There is no direct communication between producer and consumer. The consumer-oriented marketing greatly requires marketing research to ensure maximum consumer satisfaction and to develop appropriate marketing strategies to meet competition.

Elements of Marketing Research

1. **Market research.** It covers aspects regarding size and nature of market, including export markets, dividing the customers in terms of age, sex, etc.
2. **Sales research.** It relates to the problem of regional variations in sales territories, measurement of effectiveness of salesman, evaluation of sales methods, etc.
3. **Product research.** It relates to the analysis of the strength and weakness of the existing product, product testing, problems relating to diversification, simplification, etc.
4. **Packaging research.** In essence it is a part of product research. But recent developments in packing and its contribution to advertising has led to occupy an independent position. To know its impact and its response in the market has become an independent research field.
5. **Advertising research.** It undertakes a study relating to the preparation of advertisement copy, the media to be used and the measurement of advertising effectiveness.

6. **Business economics research.** Problems relating to input and output analysis, forecasting price and profit analysis and preparation of break even charts are the main fields in this research.
7. **Export marketing research.** This research is intended to study the export potentials of the product.
8. **Media research.** It is the evaluation of various media of advertisement to ensure the most effective and economical advertisement campaigns.

Classification of Marketing Research

1. **Adhoc research.** This refers to situations where the identification of research problems lead to a specific information requirement, e.g. if one particular brand or firms product fails in the market, specific study will have to be made.
2. **Continuous research.** In this case market research is conducted on an almost, permanent basis to collect information about marketplace, product performance, etc. Consumer goods falling under the category of shopping goods need such continuous information.
3. **Exploratory research.** It is a pilot testing before a fullfledged research is undertaken. Such a research would reveal the areas in which research should concentrate finally.
4. **Conclusive research.** It is the final research which is both expensive and time consuming. It would be based on a defined and scientific procedure. For long-term decisions, this form of research is preferred.

Steps in Marketing Research

Mere collection of information does not complete marketing research. The information must be collected and processed in a scientific manner to make it more useful and meaningful.

1. **Problem formation.** The precise definition of the problem helps in determining the techniques to be used, the extent of information to be collected, etc. In simple terms, one should be clear in his mind as to what is exactly required.
2. **Decision or fact-gathering procedure.** The second step is to find out the best procedure for getting information. The procedure requires the following steps.
   (a) Establishing the facts available at present and additional facts required.
   (b) Determining the reliable data.
   (c) Setting an information for the collection of additional information required.
3. **Data collection.** When the available data are insufficient, fresh data have to be collected. Usually survey techniques are used to gather information. A sample survey would be quite sufficient. A sample is a small group taken from the total group. The total may be a city, a nation or the world.
4. **Data evaluation.** Locating the source and collecting the information is only a part of the job. The collected data can't be simply accepted because they might contain unnecessary facts. From the same set of facts several conclusions will be drawn.
5. **Interpreting data.** Correct interpretation of the data makes the research meaningful and purposeful. It is at this level that unorganised and unscientific research fails. Technical

competence and intimate knowledge of the problem are the prerequisites of correct interpretation.

6. **Report preparation.** The final step in market research is summarising the result of the research and making a report. The findings and recommendations are put in such a manner that the recipients of a report can understand them effectively.

Sources of Marketing Research

The sources of marketing research can be classified into:

(a) Primary data, and

(b) Secondary data.

Primary Data

Primary data are collected from first hand sources for a specific purpose. They specifically collected for a problem and that too originally by the researcher. The primary data can be gathered from customers, middlemen, salesmen, competitors and other information sources. There are three important methods for collecting primary data:

1. Survey Method

This is the usual method of generating primary data. There are two types of survey method —sampling survey and census survey. In sampling survey data is collected by interviewing a limited number of people selected from a bigger group. In the census method the marketer surveys the entire market. Data under the survey method can be collected in the following ways:

(a) Personal interview method,

(b) Mail survey by questionnaire, and

(c) Telephone survey method.

(a) **Personal Interview Method.** Under this method people contribute the data directly to the researcher. This is a good method of collecting data because the researcher can alter questions to suit the needs of particular situation. Flexibility is the most important characteristic feature of this method. Personal interviews can be held with or without a questionnaire.

(b) **Mail Survey by questionnaire.** Under this method questionnaires are sent to potential respondents by post for securing fast hand information. The respondents acre asked to return them within a particular period of time after filling the questionnaire. Mail questionnaire is an effective and cheap method of conducting surveys. This method is followed by leading business firms. It gives the personal opinion of consumers directly. A manufacturer, retailer or other dealer can achieve the maximum benefit when this method is used for securing necessary information. This method is applied to get information from people who are neither personally available nor available on telephone.

(c) **Telephone Survey Method.** In urban areas it has became a practice to interview respondents through telephone. In this method instead of meeting the respondents personally and asking questions, they can be interviewed over telephone. We can have a large number of interviews over a shorter period. Telephone survey can be quick and less costly. This method is very easy to administer.

Secondary Data

Data collected from published records are known as secondary data. Secondary data can be adopted where great accuracy is not needed. The data might be absolute, inaccurate, incomplete and unreliable. The user must satisfy himself that the data available are suitable for the purpose of his enquiry.

Sources of Secondary Data. There are several sources from which secondary data are available. They are:

(1) **The company's own office.** The marketing researcher's company may be a source of secondary data, e.g. data collected for some other purpose may be available from the company's offices.

(2) **Libraries.** Some business firms have developed good library facilities of their own. Where such company library is available it will be a source of information. Data are available from public library also.

(3) **General publications.** Some publishers conduct detailed studies of the subject in which the readers are interested and publish the report in their publications, e.g. *Economic Times, The Hindu,* etc.

(4) **Government.** Government publications and records sometimes become available source of information for marketing research.

(5) **Research organisations.** There are some independent non-profit making research organisations which provide valuable marketing information, e.g. the Indian Management Association, Delhi.

(6) **Commercial Organisations.** Many marketing research and consultant organisations and advertising agencies conduct research on a variety of problems. Many of their studies are meant for their clients.

(7) **Other Firms.** Reports of study conducted by other business firms on similar problems are good source of secondary data.

Advantages of Marketing Research

(a) Marketing research helps the manufacturer to adjust his production according to the conditions of demand.

(b) It helps the manufacturer to secure economies in the distribution of his products.

(c) Marketing research makes the marketing of goods economical by eliminating wastages.

(d) It helps the manufacturers and traders to find out the best way of approaching the potential buyers.

(e) It helps the manufacturer to find out defects in the existing products and to take the required corrective steps to improve the products.

(f) Marketing research helps the manufacturer to ascertain the reactions, attitudes, preferences, buying motives, etc. of customers.

(g) It helps the manufacturer in finding out the effectiveness of the existing channels of distribution and in finding out the best way of distributing goods to the ultimate consumers. It helps in finding out new uses for the existing products.

(h) Marketing research guides the manufacturer in planning his advertising and sales efforts.

(i) Marketing research is helpful in assessing the effectiveness of advertisement.

(j) Marketing research minimises the risk of uncertainties and helps in taking in sound decisions.

(k) It reveals the causes of consumer resistance.

(l) Marketing research reveals the nature of demand for the product, i.e. it indicates whether the nature of demand for this product is seasonal or constant.

(m) Marketing research is helpful is evaluating selling methods.

It is helpful in evaluating the relative efficiency of the various advertisement media.

Limitations of Marketing Research

(a) Marketing research is a time-consuming process. It takes a very long time.

(b) Marketing research is highly expensive. It involves considerable amount of expenditure.

(c) A good marketing research requires highly qualified and skilled personnel. And every firm may not have them.

(d) The data provided by marketing research may not be exact.

(e) The result of marketing research is intangible.

QUESTIONS FOR DISCUSSION

1. Define marketing research?
2. Explain the objectives of marketing research.
3. Describe the process of marketing research.
4. What are the elements of marketing research? What are its objectives?
5. What are the advantages and disadvantages of marketing research?
6. What is meant by marketing research?
7. Explain in detail the different methods of marketing research.

CASE STUDY 7.1

RESEARCH ON THE YOUNG INDIAN'S MIND

Young Indians surely knows their minds. Recently, the music channel MTV commissioned a study with the primary objective of mapping values, attitudes, lifestyles, music and music-related preferences. The quantitative study conducted by the Indian Market Research Bureau (IMRB) covered 2,745 respondents in Mumbai, Delhi, Chennai, Bangalore, Kanpur and

Lucknow between ages of 15 and 34 years. Using a random sampling methodology, they covered respondents from A, B and C households classified according to their socio-economic standing with cable and satellite availability and the ability to view any of the available music channels.

Although there has not been much change in the understanding of the young Indian on the basis of the research conducted last year, there has been a certain firming up of values, says Sudhanshu Sarronwala, senior vice-president, marketing, research and communications at MTV, "The young India is more clear about what defines him then he was a year ago. Even if he is saying essentially the same things, he or she is more convinced about them now."

THE SHOPPING SPREE

Young Indians consider it important to be seen as the best buyers, are keen to wear what suits them irrespective of whether it is in vogue or not. They subscribe to the proposition that Indians should buy Indian products. Take a look at some of the propositions.

People recognize that I buy only the best: Young respondents overwhelmingly respond in favour of being seen as the best buyers. Around 64.4 per cent of the respondents are bullish on the idea. To what may seem as a surprise to some, more class C respondents subscribe to the proposition than class B and class A respondents Chennai with 78 per cent is the strongest votary of all the six metros. Around 65 per cent of women subscribe to the "Buy the Best" belief as opposed to 61 per cent of them.

I always seek the advice of friends regarding brands and products: Around 52.19 per cent of respondents look to friends for advice on brand buying. Around 55 per cent men and 49 per cent women subscribe to the proposition. Class C respondents come out more strongly in favour of the proposition than class A and B respondents. Youngsters in Mumbai display the most independent disposition.

I wear what suits me, irrespective of whether its fashionable or not: Around 69.44 per cent are in favour of the proposition. Interestingly, Chennai often perceived as being conservative and traditional comes out strongly in favour of fashion over comfort. Class A respondents display a more individualistic streak than their B and C counterparts.

Indians should always buy Indian products: Around 52.16 per cent of the respondents agree to the proposition especially in Kanpur and Lucknow. Class C respondents agree to the proposition more vehemently than class A and B respondents. The relatively more mellow 25-34 years old set subscribe to the same more strongly than the 15-24 years olds.

THE BIG ISSUES

Life should not be taken too seriously: Around 57.66 per cent of the respondents say yes. A sluggish economy and political undertainly not withstanding, young Indians believe in having fun. Here, Chennai continues to dominate the stereotype, rooting most strongly for the proposition. There are very few *no* differences across categories.

One should rebel if someone is being unreasonable: This proposition is supported by 57.46 per cent. Mumbai displays the highest levels of expediency. Kanpur and Lucknow are high on the inclination to rebel against the injustice factor. Class A and B respondents muster a bigger fighting spirit than claps C respondents.

Job security is more important than money: Not money, nor adventure, it is security and stability that young Indians look for in their jobs more than anything else. Chennai displays a stronger materialistic streak than all other metros, rather surprising given its otherwise high agreement on all issues deemed safe. More female respondents than male and class A and B respondents than C agreed with the proposition.

RIDDING ON RELATIONSHIP

Pre-marital sex is a way of life: It is a far from being a way of life for young Indians in the nineties. Living in is not yet acceptable and "we will marry out of our own choice" is the chorus. Of all the respondents, only 29.33 per cent agree with the proposition. Mumbai, is most responsive to the idea. Confirming widely held perceptions, more class A respondents than class B and C are positively disposed towards the proposition. More male respondents than female respondents are open to the idea with 32 per cent of males and around 22 per cent of females agreeing with the proposition.

Couples should live together before marriage: Only 31.35 per cent of the respondents are in favour of the proposition. More class C and B respondents are in favour of the proposition. Kanpur and Lucknow, in a not so regular display of openness, subscribe more strongly than the rest of the metros. Around 35 per cent of makes and 28 per cent of female respondents agree.

ON PARENTS AND FRIENDS

Young Indians are comfortable viewing parents not only as providers, guides, philosophers but also as friends and would obey their parents even if it hurt them. More female respondents than male respondents maintain a friendly equation with their parents. Mumbaites are relatively the most muted in their support of the proposition that "parents are friends" and so are class A respondents.

Friends are the center of all my activities: More than half the respondents (53.07 per cent) root in favour of the proposition. The pub capital of the country, Bangalore, with its high number of college campuses roots most strongly for the idea. Understandably, more 15-24 year old than 25-34 year old view life as being friend-centric. More class C respondents than class A and B subscribe to the idea.

I try to obey my elders even if it hurts: Of the respondents, 65.63 per cent agree with the proposition. Mumbai, stays true to its individualistic and self-indulgent streak by scoring the lowest amongst the metros. Bangalore with nearly 80 per cent scores the highest. The class breaks display hardly any differences, dispelling populations of class A youngsters being more spoilt and rebellious than their class B and C counterparts.

It's okay to take parental help to make it in life: People in Mumbai are the most reluctant in this regard. Often viewed as being individualistic and self-sufficient, they score the lowest among all metros confirming popular perceptions. More class C respondents than class A and B and more 15-24 year olds than 24-34 year olds agree with the proposition. Overall, young Indians are very comfortable viewing parents as providers.

THE SONG AND DANCE TRIP

When it come to entertainment, youngsters are extremely bullish on television, and construct their ideal music channel around a music mix, 72.25 per cent are in favour of Hindi film/Hindi pop and regional language music. Hindi film music, both old and new reigns supreme appealing to all age groups and class groups. Delhities are more bullish on Hindi pop. Regional language music finds greatest favour down south, more in Chennai than Bangalore. International music and India pop are patronised more by the 15-24 year old segment than the older lot. The 25-34 year old prefer Hindi film music and regional music.

Television is the ultimate entertainment: More than half (55.22 per cent) of the respondents agree with the proposition. Given the multiplicity of entertainment sources, Mumbai is the least bullish, while Chennai, Kanpur and Lucknow display the greatest enthusiasm, class C respondents root more strongly for the proposition than class A and B respondents, access to the entertainment opportunities in all probability being the deciding factor. Teenagers and young Indians patronise music channels more than the 25-34 year olds. As expected, class A respondents are less enthusiastic than class B and C respondents.

QUESTIONS FOR DISCUSSION

1. What type of research study is this?
2. What are the limitations of this study?
3. Which sampling technique is used and why?

CASE STUDY 7.2

REVIVAL OF THREE STAR HOTEL

A three-star hotel located in Delhi has been experiencing a decline in its occupancy during the past one year. The management has recently reviewed the problem and is seriously considering attracting business executives as also to provide adequate facilities for holding business conferences, workshops, etc.

Since this would involve some renovation of the existing building in addition to new furniture and equipment, the management realises it must be cautious in undertaking such an expenditure.

Since its inception several years ago, the hotel has been maintaining a complete record of its guests. When a person visits the hotel for the first time, details such as his name, age, sex, permanent address, purpose of visit and duration of stay along with dates are entered on a card. All subsequent visits along with the duration of stay are dated and recorded on the same card.

The guest file has expanded tremendously and contains over 8,000 cards. The management wants to make use of this readily available information along with any additional information necessary in this regard.

Assuming that the management has entrusted you with this job, answer the following questions:

(a) Specify the statistical universe implicit in the management's choice of the sample.

(b) If a sample is to be drawn from the guest file, describe the procedure you would adopt in each of the following sample designs:

   (i) Simple random sampling,

   (ii) Systematic random sampling,

(iii) Stratified random sampling,

(iv) Cluster sampling.

(c) Which one of these sample designs would you select and why?

(d) Specify the nature of data that you would collect from the sample respondents.

(AIMA, Dec. 1996)

CASE STUDY 7.3

INDIAN CHEMICAL AND PHARMACEUTICAL LIMITED

The Indian Chemical and Pharmaceutical Ltd. (IPCL) produces highly ethical products sold throughout the country on the recommendation of doctors. IPCL is now planning to enter the household insecticides market. They have the technical know how to manufacture and the infrastructure to market the insecticides. Its sales force of 250 sales representatives is supported by 20 sales offices located in all major cities. The sales forces contacted all important doctors and chemists and made a direct distribution of company products to retail outlets.

The marketing research department was given the job of making a quick study and providing suitable information so as to facilitate the company taking a decision about entering the household insecticides market.

QUESTIONS FOR DISCUSSION

1. Outline the information requirements of the company for its new product planning and suggest a suitable investigation process.
2. Draw a suitable time frame, plan the manpower requirement and draw budget estimates for carrying out such a study.
3. Suggest a suitable format of the final report to be submitted to the Managing Director.

CASE STUDY 7.4

FRANK CORPORATION LIMITED

In a large organisation, viz., Frank Corporation Ltd. there have been an increasing number of strikes in the recent past. You are requested to determine the factors responsible for the increasing number of strikes in Frank Corp. You have to work out the following:

(a) Broad and specific objectives.

(b) Information that will be required to meet the objectives.

(c) Methodology and sampling procedure to be followed.

(d) A suitable questionnaire for the respondents.

(e) The first five and last five lines of your report must be written as formally presented to Frank Corporation.

(AIMA, June 1997)

CASE STUDY 7.5

L'OREAL COMES OUT OF ITS NICHE

Just when most of the new multinational cosmetic players are taking *a* hard look at Iheir Indian business, the $12 billion French company, L'Oreal, is slowly and steadily making a splash. If there is any serious competitor to the established Lakme-Lever it is L'Oreal industry watchers say.

Already, while most of the players have been reworking their India strategy, L'Oreal with an estimated turnover of Rs. 12 crore has been working to script. A script, which has seen it gradually unfurl a portfolio in the various categories of the Rs. 1,300 crore Indian cosmetics market. From shampoos to skin care to hair colour, it has now taken competition head on with the Maybelline range of coloured cosmetics.

L'Oreal's India strategy is simple identify the gaps and plug them. Instead of launching a clutch of products at the same time, it has gone in for a slow and steady, well-paced portfolio expansion. After establishing equity with premium products, it is now attacking me mass markets. Says Geoff Skingsley, Managing Director Indelor, the fully-owned subsidiary of the L'Oreal group. "Our strategy is largely product feature-driven. We are trying to introduce new products and categories that are already existing in other markets."

In a way, L'Oreal used niche products to test the market before plunging headlong with mass based brands. Like after the high priced skin care and hair care brands, the newly launched Maybelline colour cosmetics is dearly competitively pitched. And this has got competition worried, "After Hindustan Lever, L'Oreal has the largest portfolio of brands which is making us very alert to market demands," says a Lakme Manager.

Worldwide, the L'Oreal group has over 900 brands in cosmetics alone. In fact, last year cosmetics with brands in hair care, skin care, make-up, sun care, toiletries and perfumes accounted for 81.3 per cent of the total turnover. This was followed by producers in pharma 17 per cent, dermatology 1.1 per cent and others (0.6 per cent).

In India, too, cosmetics and toiletries has been their mainstay, This when competitors are reshuffling portfolios or abandoning the market. A few months ago, the $3.5 billion Benckiser pulled out of India after slogging it out for four years. Recently, Modi Revlon deserted the skin care segment and is reworking its marketing strategy to focus on colour cosmetics. It is also developing the beauty parlour channel. Delhi-based Qriflame and Avon's direct marketing strategy has not made much of a dent with the consumer. Most of these players have realised the need for differentiated products at different price points to survive in the extremely fragmented Indian market.

And L'Oreal hasn't been in a great hurry. It has entered India with two of its mainline umbrella brands—Laboratories Garnier and L'Oreal Paris. Lancome, another umbrella brand is being imported and retails at some of the up markets stores in Mumbai and Delhi. But the launch pad was Garnier's Ultra Doux shampoo in 1991.

Today, the brand has only a one per cent share in the Rs. 350 crore shampoo category. This was followed by the Garnier's Synergic skin care range and the Excellence hair colour.

Says Binita Kripalani, marketing director, Indelor, "We decided to get into skin care first because hair colour is very difficult to manufacture and we would have had to import the product which was not allowed." The foray into skin care helped build the distribution channels and establish the L'Oreal name. Apart from one or two basic moisturisers and a face wash, the Synergie range consisted of differentiated products like anti-wrinkle cream/day cream and night wear cream.

By staying clear of the extremely competitive basic category, L'Oreal evolved-product focus helped it gain a toehold in the Rs. 650 crore skin care segment. It did so by launching only non-basic, special-benefit offerings. It concentrated on building entirely new categories according to the needs that were tapped by continuous research. Says Skingsley, "The degree of persuasiveness required to build new categories based on entirely new products is immense."

Although Synergie has been able to garner only three per cent of the Rs. 650 crore skin care market, certain products in the line like the wrinkle-free formulation is used by around one-third of the two million targeted users. Says Skingsley, "According to the needs tapped we have launched a select portfolio of products and our effort is to create product feature-led categories."

There was a distinct need for an age-controlling product among the 30-plus consumers in the 12-15 million urban educated women segment. In this Rs. 165 crore niche segment, Lakme is the market leader with a 32 per cent share. It is followed by Synergie at 28 per cent and Pond's at 22 per cent.

Last year L'Oreal made a foray into the Rs. 38 crore hair colour category. Internationally, hair care accounts for 52 per cent of the entire L'Oreal portfolio. The Indian hair dye market was largely dominated by Godrej, which had 86 per cent market share and JK Helene Curtis's Trutone, besides a range of herbal dye from the unorganised sector. Hair dye was perceived as an undesirable but necessary product with no aspirational or pleasurable associations.

The L'Oreal strategy for hair colour was similar. Says Kripalani, "Our objective was to change the existing perceptions about hair colour and to, expand the segment in India. Earlier hair colour addressed only those who were greying but we wanted to expand the user-base to those who used colour for style." Which meant appealing to entirely new users.

To make this happen, booklets and leaflets were given to retailers and around 50 sales persons spent time educating the retailers about the products and destroying existing myths about hair colour. Excellence Cream and Castings is now available in around 4,000 retail outlets. Currently the hair colour products have achieved around 11 per cent penetration in the category, even as Godrej dominates the market with a share of 86 per cent.

Realising the opticism over such products and the lack of awareness and research on the category, L'Oreal decided to tap the influencers. Last year, it set up the salon division and launched L'Oreal Professional. World over, the Professional Division was introduced to rope in the beauty parlours and hairdressers. This was not in keeping with their international trend of taking the professional route before the consumer. Says Tarun Mehra, Marketing Manager, L'Oreal Professional, "Beauty parlours and hair-dressers are more in touch with our target customer and to provide exclusivity of product portfolio we decided to launch separate brands under the professional division. These products—Majirel, Diacolour and Osmose came under the hair colour, hair care, perm and cutting categories."

Research conducted by the company revealed that there was a serious need for technical training. So, L'Oreal decided to cultivate this very important channel through which they could tap the beauty needs of their target segment. So far, L'Oreal has around 1,500 hairdressers which stock its products—Majirel, Diacolour (non-ammonia which it launched recently), Perm and hair care and Osmose conditioner. Osmose was launched when customers using L'Oreal products expressed the need for a hair care shampoo or conditioner.

Having established a presence, L'Oreal has now positioned Maybelline as a technologically superior product in the Rs. 400 crore colour cosmetics market. Says Kingsley, "Quality aspirations of Indian consumers are the same. The three sub areas of differentiation are price value perceptions, choice and the retail experience". Adds Sunita Bagard, group product manager for Maybelline, "The price premium is very reasonable given the value provided by each of the products in the basket." In fact, it is the cheapest of all the new foreign brands and is today, in the Rs. 400 crore colour cosmetic market, Lakme, along with its sub-brands Elle 18 and Orchids has a 52 per cent share. It is followed by Tips and Toes at seven per cent and Revlon at three per cent. In the next three years, L'Oreal wants to be the number one or two player in each of its product categories. And it knows that taking on Lakme Lever is not going to be cakewalk.

QUESTIONS FOR DISCUSSION

1. What research design has been adopted for this study?
2. Prepare a sample questionnaire which might be used to collect data for this study?

CASE STUDY 7.6

CREATING DATA BANK FOR MANAGEMENT STUDENTS

You are retained by an organisation to find out how MBA students from Delhi/nearby town institutes are absorbed into employment circles soon after completing their studies. No information is available at present. The placement officers of these institutes have limited information concerning their own students. The organisation would like to know the nature of organisation, the nature of job, salary perks, promotions, relevance of MBA training to the jobs they are engaged in. You are required to work out the following questions:

(a) The objectives of the study.

(b) The methodology to be adopted.

(c) Prepare a questionnaire for conducting the study.

(AIMA, Dec. 1997)

CASE STUDY 7.7

CHILDREN'S MAGAZINE

You are working for a consulting organisation providing consultancy services in the areas of marketing and sales. You had been asked to lead the team assigned to conduct a survey in selected schools regarding the preferences of teenagers regarding the contents of a new children's magazine to be launched by a publishing company. The following data has been collected:

(i) 50 schools (10 each in 5 metro cities—Delhi, Calcutta, Bombay, Chennai and Bangalore) were covered under the survey.

(ii) 8,000 children were given pre-designed questionnaires for the survey.

(iii) The students were asked to give 5 preferred areas that should be covered by the magazine and the preferences as reflected by the survey are:

Sports: 80%, Current affairs: 65%, Nature and Wildlife: 60%, Science: 70%, Cartoons: 80%, Quiz: 60%, Stories and Poems: 75%, Government and Politics: 25%, Hobbies: 45%, Academics: 30%, Career counselling: 48%. Rest of the areas scored less than 10%.

(iv) The most preferred categories (first preference) were Stories and Poems (45%), Cartoons (24%), Sports (16%), Current affairs (10%) and Nature and Wildlife (5%).

(v) To the question "Do you think there is a need for a new magazine?" 46% said "Yes", 20% and 24% said "Don't know" while 10% did not respond to the question.

Now you have been asked to write a report based on the above data and present it to the client organisation. You are required to work out the following:

(i) Explain the steps you would follow to write the report.

(ii) Describe in brief the layout of your report and prepare the table of contents.

(iii) Write in brief the executive summary of the report. For making the summary more realistic you are free to include additional data/feedback (presumably received from the survey) that you think may be relevant and useful.

(iv) Enumerate briefly the factors you will take care of while presenting your report to the technical team of the client organisation.

(AIMA, June 1998)

CASE STUDY 7.8

DAIRY SLIM

Question

You are marketing manager for a company, which specializes in producing dairy products for the 'slimming market'. The results of your latest research have just been published (see below) and you have been asked to:

(a) Write a short formal report to the marketing director giving terms of reference, procedure, findings, conclusions and recommendations. Your recommendations will be used to help identify new products for possible development in the market.

(b) Choose an appropriate method for graphical presentation of each of the categories of research information provided and use it to present this data more effectively.

Market Research Results

This research was carried out from January to June 2003, using in-depth interviews in the respondents' homes, recorded on tape and interpreted by ourselves, 'The XYZ Research Agency', specialists in market research for the food industry.

Sample size: 500

Age range: 15-55

Socio-economic groups
(i) Higher managerial, chief executives, etc.
(ii) Managerial, executives, etc.
(iii) Higher clerical, supervisory, etc.

Location: Metros

Sex: Males and females

Motives for wanting to lose weight	**% of respondent mentioning weight problems**
To feel physically good	68
For health reasons	67
To stay fit	43
Because I want to live longer	25
To stay mentally alert	23
To be more attractive	21
To be more popular	15
Methods for weight control	
Avoid certain foods, eat 'slimming items'	32
Eat and drink less	23
Play sports, keep fit	22
Have certain 'diet days'	7
Take medicines, stimulants	3
Foods which people dislike giving up	
Cakes, pies, bakery products	31
Sweets, sugar	23
Beer, alcoholic beverages	17
Meat, sausages, etc.	15
Chocolate	13
Cream	9
Fruit juices	9
Potatoes	9
Pasta	9

In general, the comments also revealed that dieting means a loss of pleasure at mealtimes, causes problems when one can't eat the same as the rest of the family and also one is regarded as being 'ill' when dieting.

CASE STUDY 7.9

SHRI RAM CONSULTANTS

Shri Ram Consultants have been appointed by a leading group in hotel industry to prepare a feasibility report for opening a five-star hotel in Pune. The group had been the most successful one in the industry and had always kept its eyes open for new opportunities.

In view of the very fast industrial growth in the city of Pune, the city had attracted the attention of the group. Pune, apart from being a modern city, has the added advantage of pleasant weather and several places of tourist attraction in the neighbourhood. Moreover, the closeness to Mumbai, a city of international stature, made it very easily accessible to international tourists.

For Shri Ram Consultants this was the first time that an assignment concerning the hotel industry had been received. They, however, soon realised that the assignment was not as simple as it appeared to be in the first place. The feasibility of such a hotel would depend essentially on two factors. Businessmen visiting the city for work would constitute one segment of the market, while tourists would constitute the other. Further, the tourists could be Indians or foreigners. The success of such a hotel would also depend upon the relative attraction of other tourist centres in the vicinity.

Further, it was necessary to estimate fluctuations in demand for hotel accommodation so that attractive discounts could be offered during the off-season for business conferences, executive development programmes, etc.

The consultants realised that they would have to undertake a market research on a national scale to assess the tourist potential of the city. They would also have to survey the foreign tourists to estimate one of the most important segments of the market.

The consultants wondered whether such a survey will have to extend over a period of one full year to completely take into account the seasonal variations in tourists traffic. They were also undecided about the manner in which the survey should be conducted. The company also feared that in the absence of an accurate definition of the problem, they may land up surveying the compete tourist market in India rather than studying the feasibility of a hotel in Pune. They had heard that ITBC had appointed lady interviewers at several major airports for conducting such surveys and wondered if such a methodology could be of use to them.

The problem appeared well defined and they were concerned as the preliminary report explaining methodology of the research and the questionnaires to be used had to be submitted to the client along with the estimate of expenses within one month.

QUESTIONS FOR DISCUSSION

1. How would you define the problem of assessing the feasibility of the hotel so as to help design the survey?

2. How would you plan a survey for actually collecting information on expected demand for hotel space? How would you estimate the cost of such a survey?

CASE STUDY 7.10

ANAND NISHIKAWA COMPANY LIMITED

The rubber industry in India has both been dominated by branded as well as unbranded rubber (generally more dominant in the unbranded category). Consumption of rubber has been in the form of solid rubber as well as in the form of rubber profiles made up of solid, sponge and flocked rubber. Generally, the rubber sold in the Indian market in the form of natural rubber has been in the price range of Rs. 13 to Rs. 22 per kg. These qualities are sold from Delhi to other parts of the country with sales amounting from hundreds of kgs to a few hundred tons per month. In contrast, rubber profiles are also sold lengthwise, i.e. in rupees per metre. Such rubber are being used in metal frames, windows, etc. and also along with fabricated parts sent from Delhi to U.P., Punjab, Vijayawada, Rajasthan, etc. The other application of such rubber and rubber profiles include shipping containers, building profiles, bus/truck body buildings, solar panel equipments, control panels, air-conditioning units, helmets, etc. There have been numerous players in the market with major unbranded players thriving in this highly price sensitive market.

Anand Nishikawa Co. Ltd. was started by Iqbal Singh Anand with very limited capital resource. It's plant was set up in Rudrapur near Nainital district in Uttrakhand. The company was a pioneer in introducing synthetic EPDM rubber profile (Ethylene Propylene Diene Monomer, as it is chemically known) with manufacturing capability brought from Lescuyer, France in an effort to convert customers from natural rubber products to synthetic rubber (EPDM) product users. The company also collaborated with Nishikawa Rubber Co. and Sumitomo Corporation of Japan for upgrading technology and extendings its product range.

The advantages of synthetic rubber profiles is numerous. Some important one's are:

- The life of EPDM rubber is much more than that of natural rubber.
- The finish of EPDM rubber is much better than natural rubber.
- Most importantly, the length of profile per kg for the same profile is approximately 45 per cent longer in EPDM than natural rubber. This reduces cost/metre for EPDM substantially (for varieties sold in metres than in kgs).
- In addition to the above, the EPDM rubber is weather resistant, ozone resistant, heat resistant, acid and alkali resistant, has colour stability and does not crack as we see in natural rubber which contains more clay content.

Anand Nishikawa Company would like to conduct a marketing research study to evaluate the synthetic rubber product opportunities that the rubber markets would offer. The present market offers a potential of Rs. 1300 million in the organised sector with an annual market industry growth of 15 per cent. However, the potential threat to the company is offered by unbranded players in the market selling rubber at low prices and being localised (in and around Delhi) with quick delivery schedules. The branded category also witnesses key players such as ASP, NER, Gold Seal, WADCO and others (including local players) having significant market share of 17, 11, 12, 12, and 40 per cent respectively.

QUESTIONS FOR DISCUSSION

1. What marketing information could help ANCO decide whether the consumer would be ready to use the new product?
2. Should only a few cases be studied or a large sample be surveyed?
3. What action plan could ANCO adopt after the result of the research? Give alternate action plans.

CASE STUDY 7.11

ALFA POWER

With the onset of the summer, demand for the petrol/kerosene operated domestic generators and battery operated inverters increases. The total market for portable generators and inverters is estimated to be around Rs. 150 crore for North India which is badly affected because of the massive power cuts. There are 2 leading manufacturers of petrol/kerosene operated portable generators. Both along with a few other manufacturers have 80 per cent of the market. The remaining market is captured by large number of small-scale inverter manufacturers. The inverter uses 1 or 2 batteries and has a back-up time of 3 to 6 hours whereas generator sets can operate interrupted for a longer period. The voltage obtained from a portable generator set is consistent whereas in the case of inverters, the voltage reduces drastically after the back-up time. The batteries, which are used in the inverters are automatically charged but have a life of 2/3 years. No other maintenance is required for the inverters, but in the case of portable generators, proper service is recommended every 6 months. Some drawbacks to portable generators is that they make lot of noise, vibrations and emit lot of smoke while in operation. Besides, the users will have to stock kerosene/petrol/diesel in the house for the operation of the set. This has become a problem especially in small flats, with working parents and small children (Recently in an incident it is alleged that two children of the family died because of the smoke emitted by the portable generator set).

M/s Alfa Power is a professionally managed concern. The chief executive of the concern, Kapoor after completing his electronic engineering has opted for self-employment instead of a wage employment. He set up a unit for manufacturing electronic power generators in 1995 and within a period of one year other products such as CVTs and online UPS systems were added. All the products with state-of-art technology proved highly reliable and user-friendly. The foremost aim of the concern is to produce high quality products for total customer satisfaction. The products of the concern were being used as OEM's for various concerns.

Looking at the vast opportunities available for the inverter market, Kapoor decided to engage a marketing agency to carry out a market survey for its product, which may be used for domestic/shops/establishments as a substitute for portable generator sets. The cost in the case of a portable generator was in the range of Rs. 15,000 to 30,000 (fuel extra). In case of inverters, the range was Rs. 7,000 to 19,000 (the cost of battery varies between Rs. 3,000 to 5,000 depending upon the brand).

QUESTIONS FOR DISCUSSION

1. Draw up suitable terms of reference highlighting the aims and objectives of the study for the market survey agency which Kapoor is proposing to hire.
2. What are the salient features which Kapoor should look for when selecting the marketing agency?
3. What changes will Kapoor have to bring about in his marketing department?

STRATEGIC PRODUCT PLANNING—AN INTRODUCTION

8

INTRODUCTION

Planning is deciding in the present what to do in the future. Thus, product planning means deciding about the product what it should be in future in terms of product items, product lines, modification of present items, addition or deletion of products, etc. According to W.J. Santon, "Product planning embraces all activities which enable producers and middlemen to determine what should constitute a Company's line of products." Again Johnson defines product planning as "Product planning determines the characteristics of product best meeting the consumer's numerous desires, characteristics that add stability, to products and incorporates these characteristics into the finished product."

Kari H. Tietji defines product planning "as the act of making out and supervising the search, screening, development and commercialisation of new products; the modification of existing lines, and discontinuance of marginal or unprofitable items."

Thus product planning signifies three important considerations:

(i) Development and introduction of new products.

(ii) Modification of existing lines as may be needed in terms of changing consumer needs and preferences.

(iii) Discontinuance or elimination of marginal or unprofitable products.

The idea for new or modified products is secured from external sources like competitors, distribution channels, and ultimate consumers. Product ideas require preliminary screening and evaluation. Market research helps in such fields.

Market-Oriented Strategic Planning for Products

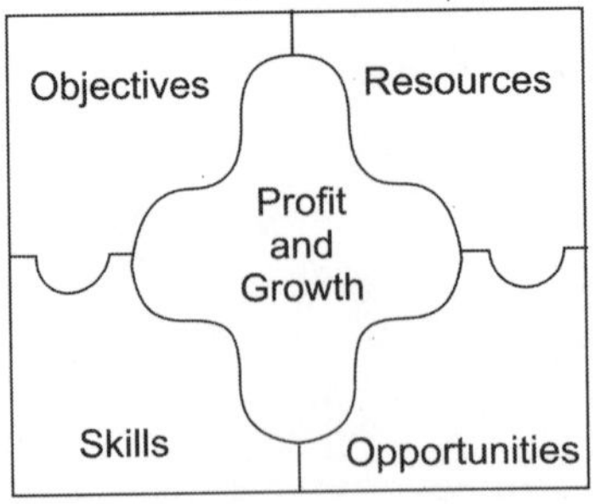

Corporate Headquarters Planning for Products

- Define the corporate mission
- Establish strategic business units (SBUs)
- Assign resources to SBUs
- Plan new business, downsize older businesses

Strategic Planning, Implementation, and Control Process for Products

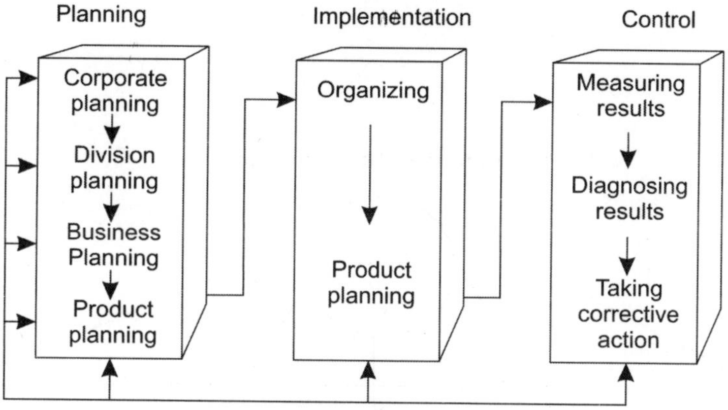

The Strategic Planning Gap

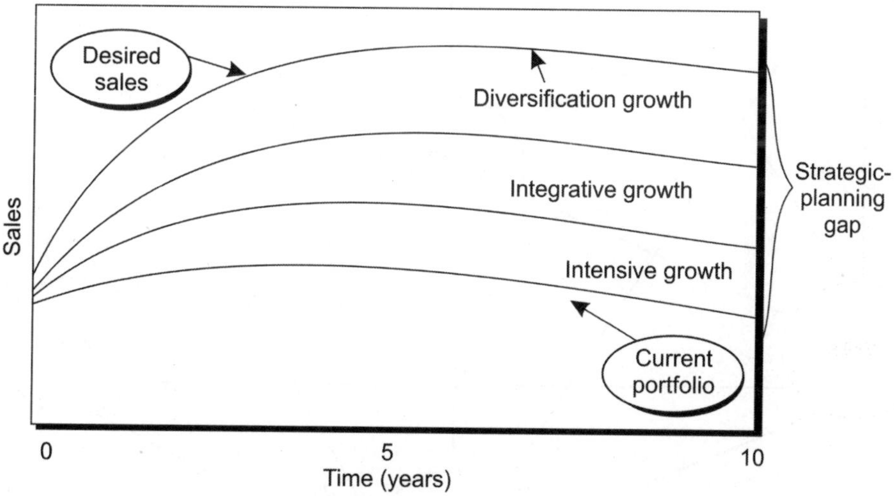

Three Intensive Growth Strategies: Ansoff's Product/Market Expansion Grid

	Existing Products	New Products
Existing markets	1. Market penetration	3. Product development
New markets	2. Market development	4. Diversification

Opportunity Matrix

Attractiveness	Success Probability: High	Opportunities: Low
High	1	2
Low	3	4

The McKinsey 7-S Framework

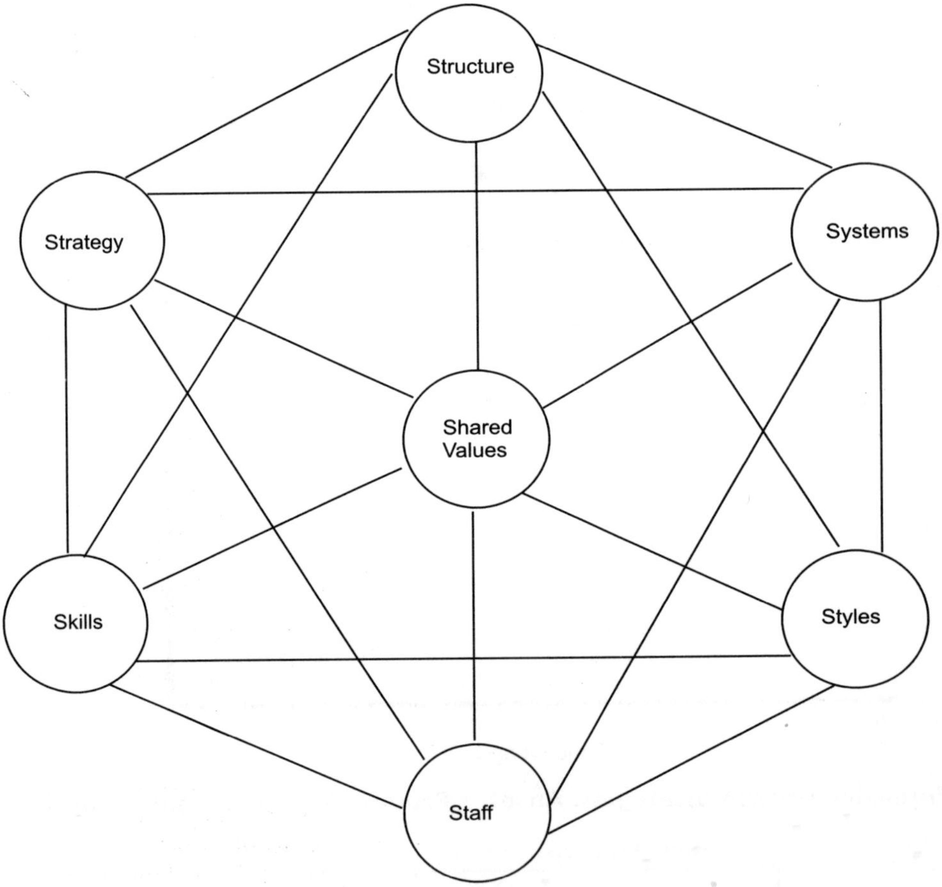

The Value-Delivery Process

(a) Traditional physical process sequence

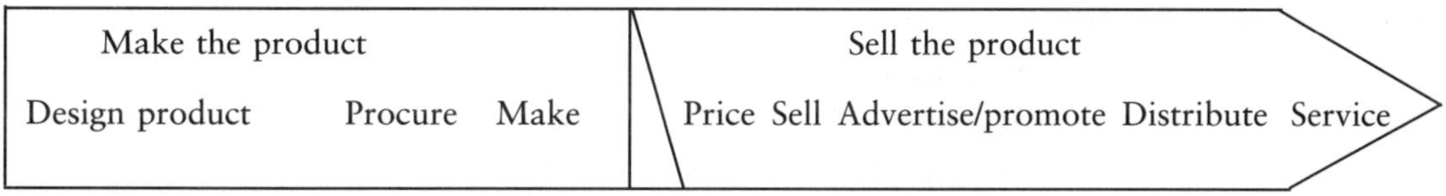

(b) Value creation & delivery sequence

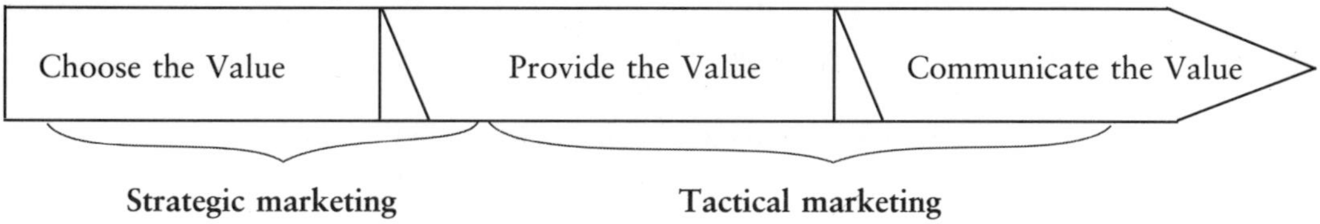

The Marketing Plan

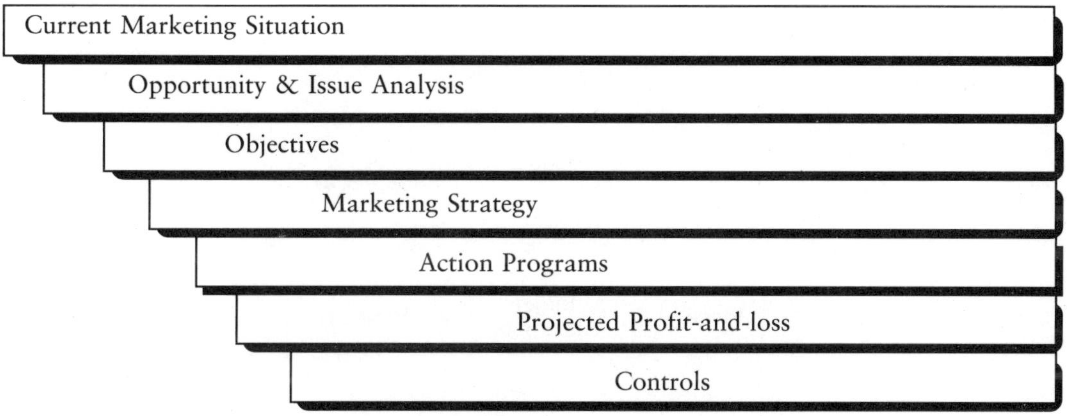

The Concept of Strategic Business Unit (SBU)

HMT: HMT is a 50-year-old public sector undertaking, with 16 production units, 24 divisions, 35,000 employees and a large basket of products, which include machine tools, flexible manufacturing systems and factory automation, tractors, printing machines, moulding machines, dairy machinery, bearings, lamps and lamp making machines and a wide range of watches: mechanical, quartz analogue and digital watches.

In it obvious that these products are meant for diverse purpose, and diverse markets/ consumers. They have to be handled separately for strategic planning treatment, and subsequently, marketed and evaluated separately. It does not mean that every single item has to be taken care of separately. It is possible to group some of them, as they are related in their basic function and the markets they serve. For example, the above-mentioned products of HMT can be grouped into five groups:

(i) Machine tools,
(ii) Consumer products,
(iii) Tractors,

(iv) Engineering components and industrial machinery,
(v) Technology and information systems.

Importance of Planning

The importance of planning can best be understood with reference to the oft-quoted poem:

For want of a nail, the shoe was lost,
For want of a shoe, the horse was lost,
For want of a horse, the rider was lost,
For want of a rider, the battle was lost,
For want of a battle, the kingdom was lost,
And all for want of a horse-shoe nail.

Factors Influencing Company Marketing Strategy

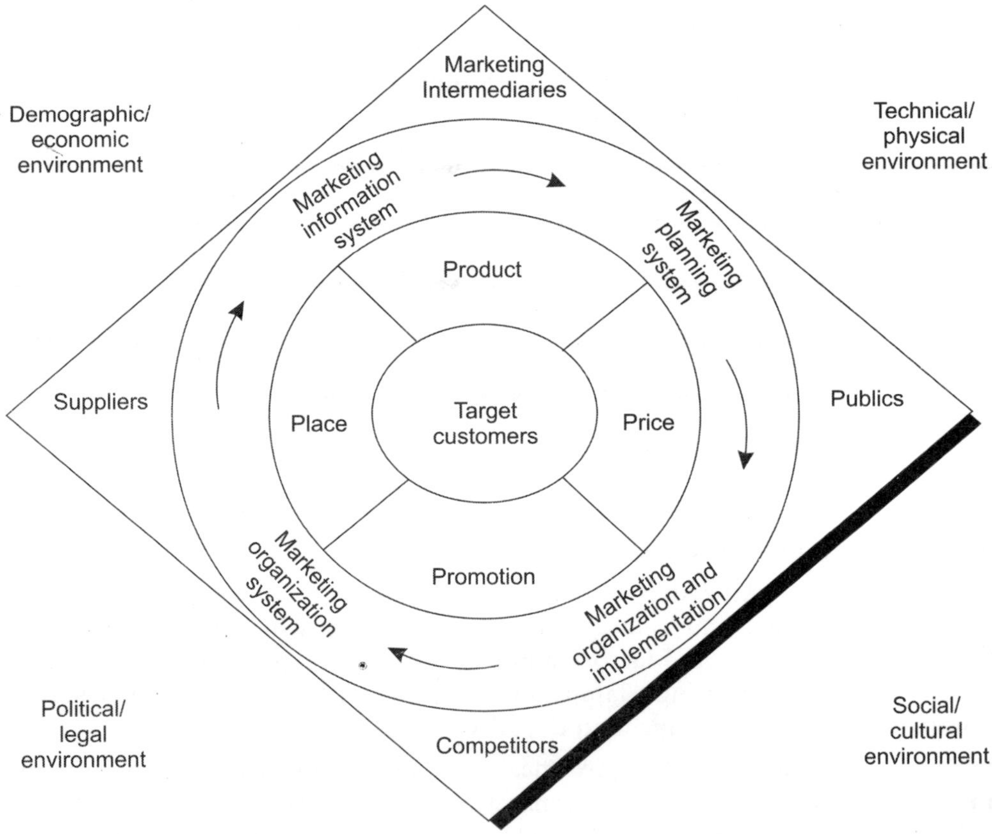

Elements of Product Planning

The various definitions of product planning given above bring out the following essential elements of product planning:

1. **Research before Production.** Before taking a decision to produce a new item, market research should be carried out extensively with a view to know the needs, wants, tastes, habits, preferences, attitudes, etc. of the consumers. The company must know before

hand what should be produced and for whom? It should decide the characteristics of the product, e.g. size, colour, quality, design, brand, packing, price, etc. that can meet the requirements of the people. Such type of research provides the base for product planning.

2. **Possibility of Production.** What production method would be followed and is it practicable to develop a product exactly what the consumer wants? This possibility should also be examined before taking a decision of producing a new product.
3. **Modification in Existing Lines.** The existing production lines should also be diagnosed whether they can be improved to meet the new requirements of the consumer or a new product is to be developed. If it is possible to modify the existing line, then, to what extent?
4. **Elimination of the Product.** Product planning involves the decision regarding the elimination of the unprofitable product (which has reached final stage of its life-cycle) or product lines so that the resources may be used to some other product profitably.
5. **Improvement in the Product.** Product planning includes decisions regarding the improvement of the existing product in terms of quality, packing, etc. taking in view the competitors' strategies in the market.
6. **Price Determination.** Determining the price of the product is the main element of the planning. Would the prices be fixed on the basis of the prices fixed by the competitors for their products or on the basis of the prices fixed by the competitors for their products or on the basis of its cost of production or on the basis of the forces of its demand and supply in the market? This is an important decision by the management concerning product planning.
7. **Commercialisation of the Product.** Product planning includes product commercialisation and sale of the product which can earn a good profit to the company on the one hand and may satisfy the needs of the consumer on the other hand. It also involves attractive introduction of the product in the market.
8. **Coordination.** Product planning also attempts to coordinate the various products and their efforts so that the company can maintain or rather improve its competitive position. It can be done by taking timely decisions for marketing conditions from time to time.

Thus, it is clear from the study of various elements of product planning that every decision from the start of an idea of producing a product to its elimination from the product of the company forms the part of the product planning.

Importance of Product Planning

Why product planning is a very pertinent question because there are firms having no concern with the product planning are successful in marketing their products while some others fail in their marketing activities inspite of planning. But it is not because the planning is made or not. It may be because of the defective planning. Product planning is necessary due to the following facts:

Product planning involves decisions regarding the product at different stages of its life-cycle from time to time. Why to produce a particular product; What to be produced When and How to be produce; Why not a particular product be improved or abolished from the product line? are certain questions which require adequate attention of the management. Any decision regarding the production, modification and elimination of a product may affect the Strategic Marketing policies, programmes, procedures and product and strategies. If decision is taken without proper consideration or planning, it may ruin the firm because other programmes, policies, etc. are the outcome of the product plans. So product planning is the starting point of all marketing programmes.

Lack of product planning implies managerial bankruptcy in the organisation and amounts to leaving the enterprise to trust its own luck. Strategic Marketing activities revolve around the product planning. All elements of marketing programme of a business unit, i.e. price policies, distribution channels, advertising policies and programmes, sales promotion and personal selling, etc. are affected by the decisions concerning product planning.

It is the main philosophy of the modern marketing management. What the customer needs, should be the main consideration in the product planning and it should be the main consideration in product planning and it should decide how the product must contain those qualities which can satisfy those needs. Production is made accordingly. It is not the company to decide what to sell. Company can sell which is required by the customers otherwise life-cycle of the product would be very short and company may lose its existence even. Thus product would be very short and company may lose its existence even. Thus, product planning determines how to satisfy the consumers' needs.

Profit is the main concern of the business. No businessman would be ready to do anything without profit motive. Customers' needs must be satisfied on the one hand and reasonable and sufficient profits must be earned by the firm on the other hand. Product planning is one of the ways to coordinate the customers' satisfaction and the profitability. For this purpose, the firm should carry out different types of surveys to know the changing habits, needs, latest fashion and the status of the customers and should modify its product accordingly. It will ensure profitability and consumer satisfaction both at the same time.

The firm knows the life cycle concept of a product. It can very well predict its profits during various stages of life cycle but only through product planning. It can decide what new product should be developed or eliminated to maintain the profits of the firm even in declining or obsolescence stage.

Product planning is necessary to face the competition in the marketing. The success of marketing efforts depends very much upon the extent to which product of the enterprise is able to face the competition. Decisions regarding modification or improvement in the product are taken with a view to keep the competitive forces out of the market or to have an edge over competitors' products.

Thus, product planning is an important tool in the hands of Strategic Marketing management to make the product and the marketing programmes successful if product planning is lacking, it will certainly affect the marketing activities and will ruin the business completely. It is a foundation on which the whole structure of marketing programme stands.

Layers of Product

The product has got different layer like onion and each of the layers contributes to the total product image. According to Kotler product has five layers which must be distinguished.

These layers are:

(i) Core product
(ii) Basic product
(iii) Expected product
(iv) Augmented product
(v) Potential product

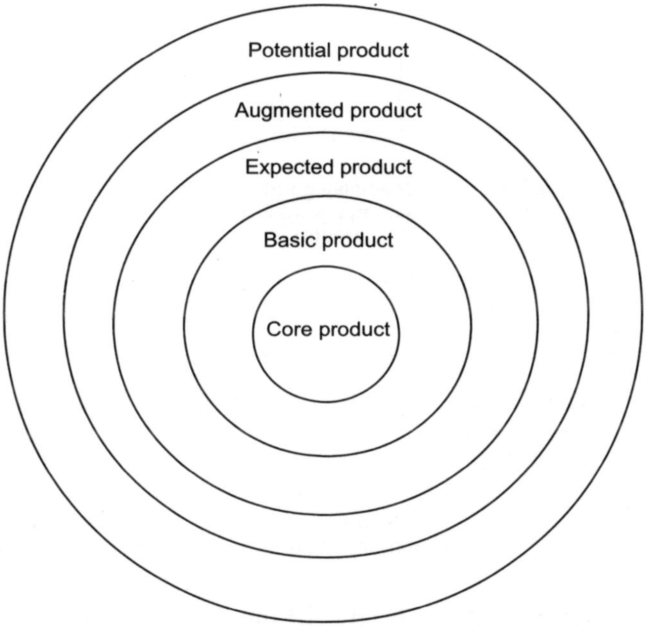

Fig. 8.1

Essential Features of Products and Services

- Customer satisfaction
- Business need satisfaction
- Value for money
- Associated attributes
- Tangible attributes
- Intangible attributes

The Chart 8.1 given below shows classification of goods and services.

Chart 8.1: Classification of Goods and Services

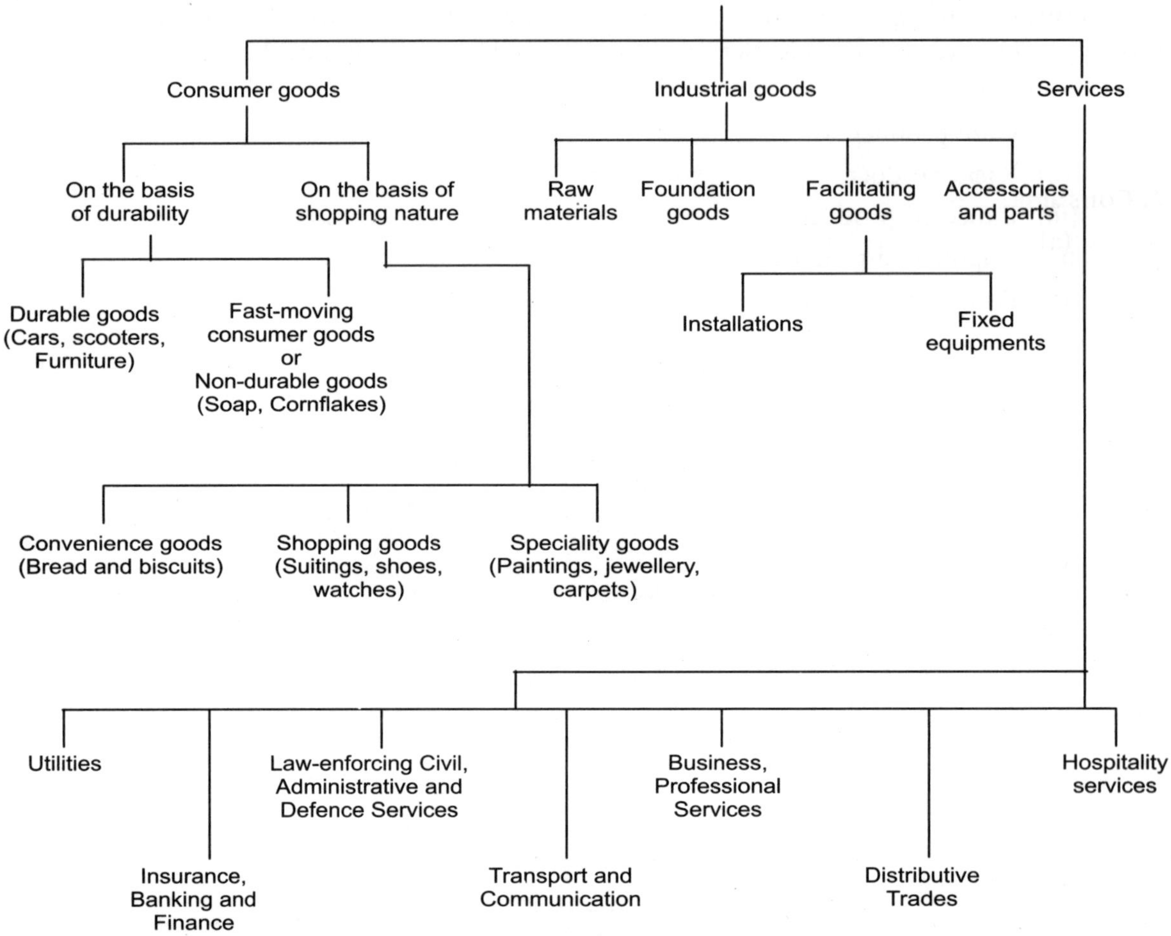

The future of the product manager is bright. In the decade of the 2000, he or she should have more authority and responsibility than ever before. The greatest expansion of responsibility will occur in long-range planning, achieving profit objectives, and general product decisions.

PRODUCT CLASSIFICATIONS

Marketers have traditionally classified products on the basis of three characteristics: durability, tangibility and use. The Chart 8.2 shows the product classification:

Chart 8.2: Product Classification

(1) Durability and Tangibility
- (a) Non-durable goods
- (b) Durable goods
- (c) Services

(2) Consumer goods
- (a) Convenience goods
- (b) Shopping goods
- (c) Specialty goods
- (d) Unsought goods

(3) Industrial goods
- (a) Material & parts
- (b) Capital items
- (c) Supplies and business services

1. Durability and Tangibility

(a) *Non-durable goods.* Non-durable goods are tangible goods normally consumed in one or a few uses. For example, soap, salt and biscuits.

(b) *Durable goods.* Durable goods are tangible goods that can normally be used for many years. For example, colour TV, refrigerators, washing machines and vacuum cleaners.

(c) *Services.* Services rate intangible, inseparable, variable and perishable products. For example, airline and banking services.

2. Consumer Goods

(a) *Convenience goods.* These are goods that the customer usually purchases frequently, immediately and with a minimum of effort. Examples include soaps and newspapers.

Convenience goods can be further classified into three categories:

(i) *Stable goods.* Consumer purchases on regular basis.

(ii) *Impulse goods.* Consumer purchases without any planning or search effort.

(iii) *Emergency goods.* Consumer purchases on urgent need.

(b) *Shopping goods.* These are goods that the customer, in the process of selection and purchase characteristically compares on such bases as suitability and quality. For example, Furniture, Electrical Appliances, etc.

(c) *Special goods.* These are goods with unique characteristics or brand identification for which a sufficient number of buyers are willing to make a special purchasing effort. For example, cars.

(d) *Unsought goods.* These are goods the consumer does not know about or does not normally think of buying. The classic examples of known but unsought goods are life insurance.

3. Industrial Goods

(a) *Materials and Parts.* These are goods that enter the manufacturer's product completely. They fall into two classes: raw materials and manufactured materials and parts.

(b) *Capital Items.* These are long-lasting goods that facilitate developing or managing the finished product. They include two groups: installations and equipment.

(c) *Supplies and Business Services.* These are short-listing goods and services that facilitate developing or managing the finished product.

PRODUCT MIX DECISIONS

Most companies—whether large or small, whether in manufacturing, or retailing—generally handle a multitude of products and product varieties. In course of time, the companies may expand new lines or contract the old lines, after the existing product or develop new uses for the existing products. These activities involve managerial strategies and policy making with respect to the company's line of products and services.

The proliferation of products within the company means that product policy decisions are made at three different levels of product aggregation, viz., product item, product lines and product mix:

(i) It is a specific version of a product that has a separate designation in the seller's list. For example, Hindustan Motors' Ambassador Mark II is a product item.

(ii) A group of products that are closely related either because they satisfy a class of need, or used together, are sold to the same customer group, are marketed through the same types of outlets, or fall within given price ranges or that are considered a unit because of marketing, technical, or end-use considerations. In other words, a broad group of products, which are meant for essentially similar uses and possess reasonably similar physical characteristics, constitute product line. For example, Kodak Camera, or wearing apparel is a product line; or non-food product line for babies include baby clothes, nursery equipment, vaporizers, and toiletries.

(iii) Products offered for sale by a firm or a business unit. In other words, product mix is the full list of all products offered for sale by a company. For example, Kodak's cameras, photographic supplies, chemicals, plastics and fibres are its product mix; or Tata's hair oil, cosmetics, locomotives, textiles, iron and steel goods, mercedes trucks, etc. are product mix.

Organisational Goals and Product Mix

The efficient fulfilment of the marketer's goal to supply goods and services to consumer for satisfaction of their needs can be possible if due attention is given to three issues which govern the product mix—sales growth, sales stability and profits.

Sales growth can be achieved either by increasing its share in existing markets or by finding new markets. Four ways can be adopted by which product mix can be adjusted to achieve goals. These are: (i) *Market penetration*, under which market share is increased by expanding sales of present products in existing uses; (ii) *Market development* under which markets are expanded by creating new uses of present products; (iii) *Product development* where market share is increased by developing new products to satisfy existing needs; and (iv) *Diversification*, whereby market is expanded by developing new products to satisfy new consumer needs.

Sales stability allows for more efficient planning in all phases of production and distribution. It is also desirable to maintain a proper balance in total sales and product mix so that a product losing marketing may be counteracted by another selling high.

Profits are determined by the components of the product mix. Some items are usually more profitable than others. Low profit items may be performing a valuable part in helping to sell company's more profitable product; and they may also prove as insurance against an unforeseen failure in profitable products.

Structure of Product Mix

The structure of product mix has dimensions of both 'width' and 'depth'.

By 'width of the product mix' is meant the number of different product lines found within the company. In other words, breadth is measured by the number of product lines carried. For example, Bajaj Electricals produces bulbs, fluorescent lights, mixies and grinders, toasters, scooters, pressure cookers and a host of other electrical appliances.

Product mix items = 12

Number of lines = 4

Average depth = 3

The 'depth of the product mix' refers to the average number of items offered by the company within each product line. In other words, the depth is measured by assortment of sizes, colours, models, prices and quality offered within each product line.

The 'consistency of product mix' refers to how closely related the various product lines are in terms of consumer behaviour, production requirements, 'distribution channels' or in some other way. For example, the products produced by the General Electric Company have an overall consistency in that most products involve electricity is one way or the other.

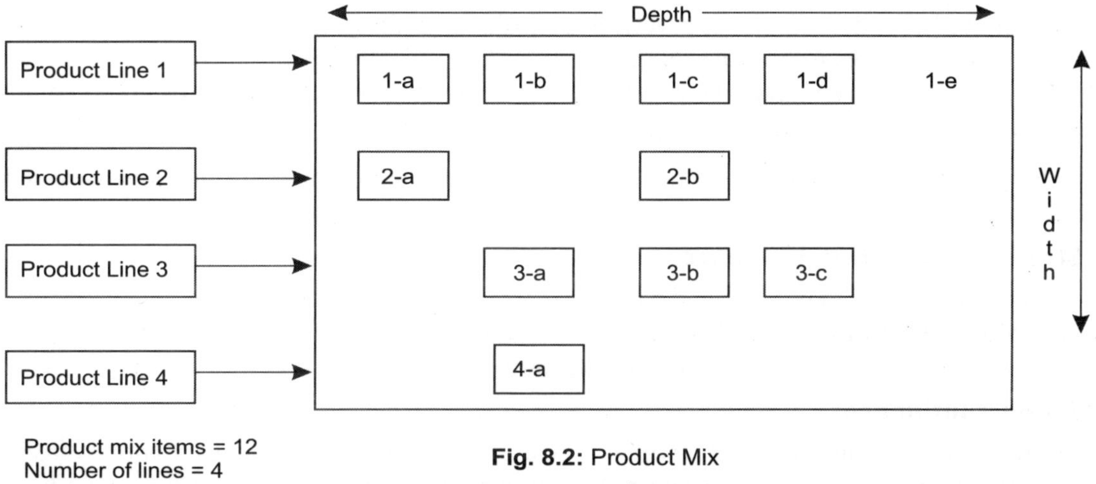

Fig. 8.2: Product Mix

observes, "All three dimensions of product mix have a market rationale. Through increasing the width of the product mix, the company hopes to capitalise on its good reputation and skills in present markets. Through increasing depth of its product mix, the company hopes to entice the patronage of buyers of widely differing tastes and needs. Through increasing the consistency of its product mix, the company hopes to acquire an unparalleled reputation in a particular area of endeavour."

The dimensions of the product mix and the ways in which they relate to each other are important for marketing management. Changing the *product item* involves the issues whether to modify, or add or drop product items. Changing the *width of the product mix* involves altering policy at the product-line level, whether to deepen or shorten an existing product line. Changing the product mix involves the issues what markets the marketer should enter or leave; and how to handle communications for the various product lines or items.

PRODUCT LINE DECISION STRATEGIES

Taking of decisions about change in product line depends upon a number of factors, such as the preferences of consumers, the tactics of competitors, the firms cost structures and the spill over of demand from one product to another, etc.

1. Changes in Market Demand

Changes in market demand may be due to changes in the component of population served. If there is an increase in the number of births the business would like to increase new lines of baby products, such as baby food, baby shoes, perambulators, toys, etc. with other lines.

Increase in the purchasing power of the consumers also leads to the improvement in the quality of the product as also the dropping out of the line certain low-price, low-quality goods.

Change in the consumer behaviour, through changes in his motivation, attitudes, preferences and buying habits may also encourage the marketing executive to expand or contract his product mix. To satisfy the more varying needs, he may add many new lines; such as the departmental stores do by adding to the general merchandise, the light reading material, health and beauty aids, ready-to wear apparels, household requisites, indoor games, sports materials, etc. Sometimes changes in product mix are also made to suit the requirements of the middlemen who would like to have varied line of products for reasons of competition, cost and promotion.

2. Competitive Action and Reaction

The firm may differentiate its product line to meet price competitions, and save it from unduly low profits.

3. Strategic Marketing Influences

New product line may be added for two reasons. *First*, to increase sales by exploiting new market or expanding the present ones; and *second*, to use the firm's capacity more efficiently by a better use of its resources of salesmen, warehouses or branch offices.

4. Product Influences

A firm may change its product mix to use its manufacturing capacity more effectively, thereby reducing its net production cost. New line may be added when its production has been discontinued by another firm. To make a better use of the by-products or waste products new lines may be added.

5. Financial Influences

The firm may add or drop out product line as per its financial resources. The product mix may be expanded to increase a firm's profitable sales volume; or a product line may be dropped to meet depression in the market.

PRODUCT LINE STRATEGIES

A company has several strategies at its disposal, with respect to the width, depth and consistency of its product mix. Most of these strategies involve a change in the product mix. Major product line strategies are:

1. Expansion of product mix;
2. Contraction of product mix;

3. Alteration of existing product;
4. Development of new uses for existing product;
5. Trading-up and trading-down; and
6. Product differentiation and market segmentation.

Expansion of the line may be a valid decision if it is in an area in which consumers traditionally enjoy a wide variety of brands to choose from and are accustomed to switching from one to another; or if the competitors lack a comparable product or if competitors have already expanded into this area themselves. However, the main limitation in expansion is the availability of sufficiently finance, time and equipment.

Expansion in the present product mix may be done by increasing the number of lines and/or the depth within a line. Such new lines may be related or unrelated to the present products. For example, the large provision stores may add drugs, cosmetics and house wares (width) while at the same time increasing their assortments of dry fruits, baby foods, detergents (depth), etc.

This is rather more difficult, because much money has already been invested; and therefore, as fast as possible, products are allowed to linger on for long until they become a loss. When contraction is decided upon, various alternatives are available to the marketers. The product may be consolidated with several others in the line so that fewer styles, sizes, or added benefits are offered. Or, the position can be simplified within a line. If even then a product fails, the company may stop it altogether.

Sometimes experience may show that improving an existing product may be more profitable and less risky than developing and launching a new product. Alterations may be made either in the designs, size, colour, texture, or flavour, or packaging, or in the use of raw materials or in the advertising appeal, or a quality may be changed. This strategy is to be followed regardless of the width and depth of the product mix.

The company may find out new uses for the existing product as when *Sway of Surf* may be used not only for washing clothes but also for cleaning the floor, utensils and glass product.

It involves an expansion of the product lines as well as the promotional strategies.

(i) *Trading-up* refers to the adding of a higher priced prestige product to the existing lines with the intention of increasing sales of the existing low-priced product. Under trading-up, the seller continues to depend upon the older, low-priced product for the major portion of the sales. Ultimately he may shift the promotional emphasis to the new product so that larger share of sales may go to the new products.

(ii) *Trading-down* refers to the adding of the low-priced items to its line of prestige product, with the expectation that the people who cannot buy the original product may buy these new ones because these carry some of the status of the higher-priced

goods. An instance on the point is that of Allwyn Company, which attempted to broaden its market for Allwyn Refrigerators by introducing five sizes in an attempt to compete at all price levels. Wills cigarettes also traded down by bringing out the lower priced Wills-Flake cigarette pack.

But this type of trading-up and trading-down is harmful because, the consumer may be confused about the new product, and the sale in the new line is also adversely affected as it is done at the expense of the older product. This situation may be avoided by using differentiating brands, channels of distribution, promotional programmes, or product design.

These strategies are often employed by the firms who wish to engage in no-price competition in markets characterised by imperfect or monopolistic competition. Since these strategies require large financial involvement in promotional efforts they are usually known as both promotional and product planning strategies.

(i) *Product Differentiation.* Product Differentiation involves "developing and promoting an awareness of difference between the advertiser's product and the products of the competitors". The strategy when used enables a company to remove itself from price competition so that it may compete on the non-price basis, viz., that its product is different from and better than, competitive models. This differentiation is done either in quality, design, brand or packaging. Where reasonably standardized products are sold, such as soaps, cigarettes, gasoline, etc. to a broad horizontal market which is fairly homogeneous in its wants, this strategy is mostly used.

(ii) *Market Segmentation.* Under market segmentation strategy, the seller knows that the total market is made of many smaller homogeneous units, each of its units has different wants, motivations, etc. To meet these different demands, different products are developed, i.e. products are tailor-made to suit these requirements. This strategy attempts to penetrate a limited market in depth, whereas the product differentiation seeks breadth in a more generalized market. Smith observes, "The differentiator seeks to secure a layer of the market cake, whereas one who employs market segmentation strives to secure one or more wedge-shaped pieces."

PRODUCT MIX FOR SERVICE PRODUCTS

Product mix consists of all the different product lines a company offers. The product mix of a large bank might easily include more than 100 different, bank-related services. This is usually described in terms of three dimensions:

- Width of the product mix
- Depth of the product mix
- Consistency of the product.

Width of the Product Mix

Width of the product mix is number of different product lines a company is offering. The product width could be narrow or wide. As an example, Project Management Institute of India only offers course on Project Management whereas Indian Institute of Technology, New De[illegible] offers courses on engineering, management, research and pure sciences. In the first case the product line is narrow whereas wide in the second. A wide mix encourages one-stop shopping as firms are able to diversify products or services appeal to different consumer needs. It also needs investments in resources and expertise in different product categories. Firms choose of offer wide or narrow product or service lines on the basis of organisational objectives and capabilities and market expectations.

Depth of the Product Mix

Depth of the product mix (Product Line Depth) is the number of product items within each product line. As an example Institute of Business Technology is offering product lines of engineering, management, research and pure sciences under each product items satisfying the need of several consumer segments for the same product. Some typical examples of product width and depth are illustrated in Fig. 8.3.

Width →

Depth ↓

Checking	Savings	CDS	Loans	Fee Based
(Basic checking &	Pass Book	Short-term	Installment	Discount Brokerage
Regular checking	Saving	Long-term	loans fixed	Safe deposits
Interest Checking	- Recurring	rate Installment	Traveller cheques	
	saving	low	Annuities	
	valuable	valuable		
			rate unsecured	
			Revolving	
			Credit Cards	

Example: Wide width

Speciality Services (National Heart Institute) Narrow Width

Width →

Depth ↓

Services related
to heart only

- Engography
- Ballooing
- By-Pass Surgery

Example: Narrow width

Fig. 8.3: Width and Depth of Product Line (Typical examples)

As the firms grow, if find that its expertise in a particular type of product or service can be exploited with little risk by expanding on the number of variations of that product. It is also usually able to broaden its customer base by offering more type of services. This causes higher cost of inventory, product or service alternations and processing of orders. In wide mix environment it becomes difficult for a consumer to differentiate two different products or service offerings, for example, it becomes difficult for a student to decide whether to select marketing or finance stream.

Consistency in Product Mix

Consistency in product mix is the relationship amongst product lines in terms of their sharing the end use, distribution outlets, consumer group(s), and price range. Generally a consistent mix is easily manageable compared to inconsistent one. In the consistent mix environment the firms concentrate on marketing and service delivery expertise, create a strong image and generate solid interpersonal relationships. Excessive consistency in product mix, however, may lead to limited product or service product assortments.

As Strategic Marketing manager you will not concentrate on marketing just one service but range of services. The following issues find great relevance in deciding the market offering:

1. What should be length and width of the range of services?
2. In which manner they supplement and support each other?
3. How will they create competitive edge to outsmart competition?

The above issues should be evaluated keeping in view the service product objectives and policies to be established. It will enable marketers to decide:

- How many products line a firm should market? (Width)
- How many items there should be in any product line? (Depth)

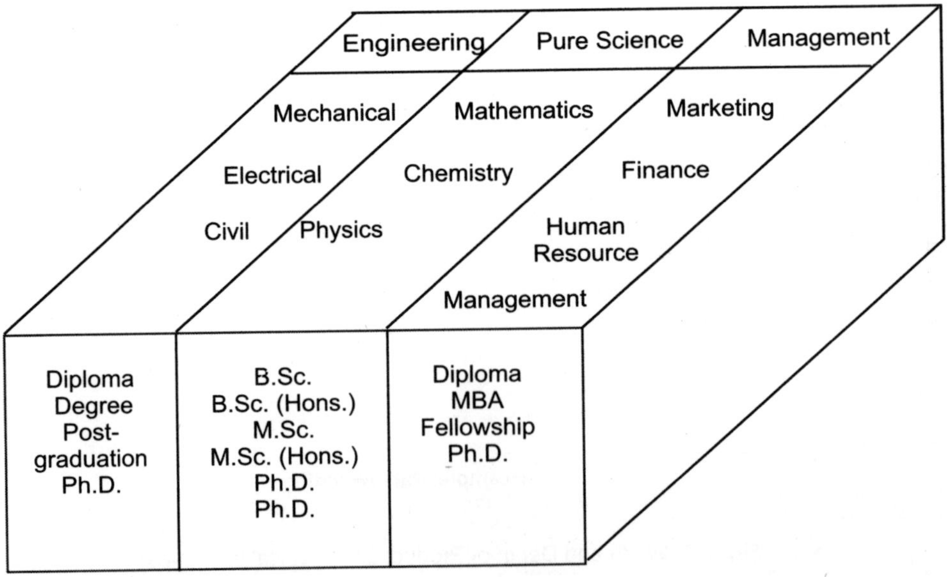

Fig. 8.4: Concept of Width, Depth and Range of Service Product

Strategic Marketing managers must offer services to specific target segments which has a specific need for the services.

For example:

The MBA in marketing would succeed only if students seeking admission to this course perceive a definite advantage in terms of value for the money and time.

So it becomes necessary to decide how different products fit into the overall range of the firm's products offered to the marketplace.

For example:

A tour operator has to decide whether to include five star or three star hotels in the range of offerings or it should operate to traditional or newly emerging destinations. The range of offers and how each product fit into the product mix, therefore, are important considerations.

A customer may buy a particular product because it is from the same company that supplies a range of other products to the customer. Often the customer will be able to negotiate a favourable deal across the whole range.

QUESTIONS FOR DISCUSSION

1. Write an essay on product policy for any marketing organisation.
2. Why are the objectives and strategies considered as the pillars for the success of any product? Discuss with examples.
3. Critically examine the factors that influence the product mix strategies.
4. "The elements of product policy are difficult to determine." Comment.
5. What is meant by product modification, product elimination and product line modification? What are the various strategies used for product line modification? Elaborate.
6. What is meant by product line expansion? Are product line expansion and diversification synonyms? What are the reasons of going in for diversification? Explain with the help of examples.
7. What is meant by product differentiation? Compare the advantages of product differentiation and market segmentation.
8. What is meant by standardisation of products? What are the advantages of standardisation of products?

STRATEGIC BRANDING DECISIONS

9

INTRODUCTION

Many consumer products, besides their basic features, need attractive packaging and a 'brand name'. A brand is a symbol or a mark that helps a customer in instant recall, differentiating it thereby from the competing products of a similar nature. According to the American Marketing Association, "A brand name is a part of a brand consisting of a word, letter, group of words or letters to identify the goods or services of a seller or a group of sellers and to differentiate them from those of the competitors." David Ogilvy defined a brand as 'the consumer's idea of a product'. A brand distinguishes a product or service from similar offerings on the basis of unique features perceived by the consumers. The best examples of brand names are: Lux, Liril, Rexona, Evita, Protex, Hamam, and Le Sansi in case of toilet soaps; Surf, Ariel and Nirma in case of detergents and Nivea, Fem, Oil of Oley, Charmis and Vaseline in case of vanishing creams.

A *brand mark* is a symbol or a design used for the purpose of identification. For example, Air India's Maharaja.

The legal version of a brand mark is the 'trade mark', e.g. Ashok Masale and good Health Atta.

A brand is given legal protection from being used by others because it is capable of exclusive approbation.

SELECTING A BRAND NAME

In selecting a brand name, the following aspects are taken into consideration:

1. A brand name should reflect directly or indirectly some aspects of the product, like benefits and functions. For example, Ezee implies that is easy to use; Good Knight, a mosquito repellent, suggests that one can have a good sleep at night with it; and Puma conjures up the celebrated speed of a 'cheetah'.
2. It should be distinctive, e.g. a name like "Chancellor" for a cigarette portrays status, power and an opulent life-style.
3. It should be easy to pronounce and remember. Some of the classic examples are: Vimal, Taj, Onida, Bajaj, MRF, Fem, Lux, Thums Up, 100 Per Cent, Bush, Garden and Rin.
4. It should be legally protected.

Brand Equity. The overall strength of a brand in the marketplace and its value to the company that owns it; increasingly, companies are trying to assign financial value to brand equity.

Brand Loyalty. The level of commitment that customers feel toward a given brand, as represented by their continuing purchase of that brand.

Advantages and Disadvantages of Branding

Advantages to Buyers

1. A brand name denotes uniform quality. With it, the consumer has the assurance of quality when he buys the products having a particular brand name.
2. Brand names make shopping easier. The customer has to spend less time and energy in buying, as brand names make product identification easier. Moreover, the customer has just to go to the market and buy the products of the brands he prefers without wasting time.
3. Competition among brands can and does, in due course of time, lead to quality improvement.
4. Purchasing a socially visible brand gives immense psychological satisfaction to the buyer.

Disadvantages to Buyers

1. The product price tends to go up.
2. Manufacturers, taking advantage of the popularity of their brand names, may reduce the quality gradually.
3. Branding creates confusion. Consumers are not able to decide which brand is the best in quality, because all the brands claim to be the best ever in quality.

Advantages to Manufacturer

1. Branding is a means of product identification.
2. In a highly competitive market, brand names can carve out niches for themselves through product differentiation.
3. If brand loyalty can be developed through successful promotion, the sellers will be able to exert quasi-monopolistic power.
4. Branding gives greater bargaining power to the manufacturer with the dealers. This is because there is already a 'pull' in favour of the product; there may be no need for a great 'push' by the retailers.
5. Brand makes 'recall' easier. The stronger the brand, the stronger its recall among the people.

A brand plays an important role in improving and maintaining product quality. In fact a brand is a seal of consistency and reliability of quality. Brand also helps in better dissemination of product knowledge which can contribute to scientific and rational decision-making. For example, the very word 'Tata' denotes an image of a robust responsiveness and indigenous product. 'Lifebuoy' denotes a health soap. 'Dove' is recognized as a moisturising soap. Some brands become so popular that they become generic name for the product as, for example, 'Dalda' for vanaspati.

Brands are even more important in the case of durable consumer goods and industrial products which require before and after-sales service and which have potential resale value.

Branded products are sold at a higher price than unbranded ones. 'Captain Cook' atta costs more than the wheat flour sold by the neighborhood grocer. 'Tanishq' jewellery from Tatas costs 20 per cent more than comparable piece sold by an ordinary jeweller.

Alexander L. Biel advances some arguments for elevating strong brands to the sacred category:

1. Strong brands enjoy higher loyalty than their weaker counterparts.
2. Strong brands offer a platform for brand extension that simply is not available to weaker brands.
3. Strong brands have more leverage with trade.
4. Strong brands are allowed to make a mistake and are given a second chance.
5. Strong brands have a very long life.

According to a survey by *A* and *M* magazine, the top 10 Indian brands are Vicks, Colgate, Dettol, Rin, Close up, Ponds, Bata, Iodex, Doordarshan and Horlicks. Except Doordarshan, all brands are owned by MNCs. The top ten brands owned by wholly Indian companies are Doordarshan, Nirma, VIP luggage, Dalda, Tata, HMT, Usha, SBI, Godrej and Dabur.

Brands–Valuable Tradable Assets

Brands provide a strong competitive advantage to the companies owning them and hence they are increasingly becoming important tradable assets. In 1993, Coca-Cola paid about Rs. 175 crore to buy Thums-Up, Limca, Citra and Gold Spot brands. In 1994, Godrej Soaps paid Rs. 12 crore to acquire the Rs. 67 crore Translectra (maker of Goodknight mosquito repellent). In 1995, SmithKline Beecham paid Rs. 42 crore to acquire the Crocin Brand from Duphar Interfan. In 1997, Knoll Pharma sold Coldarin and Burnol for Rs. 34 crore. Ranbaxy paid Rs. 80 crore to Gufic Labs for Mox, Zole Excel and Suprimox. In 1997, Hindustan Lever paid Rs. 110 crore for lakme's basket of brands and only Rs. 29 crore for Lakme's two plants. In 1999 Marico Industries bought Parachute and Suffola brands from Bombay Oil Industries for Rs. 30 crores. The Gramophone Company of India acquired Sangeetha, a leading audio producer of classical and devotional songs in the South. Acquiring a brand is a better, superior option over purchasing the entire operations of the company owing them for 3 reasons: (1) The buyer buys only the brand name (and may be associated technology). The brand name could be used to sell anything which comes under the established brand personality. For example, the Burnol brand name could be used to sell an antiseptic like Dettol; (2) Buying a brand provides a readymade market. Apparently, Ranbaxy bought Mox because its brand in the same family, Amoxycillin was not doing too well; and (3) Buying a brand saves lot of brand building time and cost. Drug companies are known to recoup the cost of acquiring a brand in less than four years.

Extent of Brand Loyalty

An experimental study on the 'Impact of Price, Brand on Consumer's Choice' showed that *(a)* the name of a well-known brand does induce the consumer to be favourably disposed towards that brand in terms of quality and price perception, *(b)* the consumers also seem to be willing to pay a higher price for the well-known brand, and *(c)* a marketer does have considerably flexibility in pricing his product provided he can create a psychological image about quality. This perhaps explains why many foreign-controlled companies have been buying out the output of Indian companies in products like car batteries, tonics and menthol lozenges, razor blades, cables, etc., and marketing them as their own products and making huge profits thereby.

Many large houses are purchasing products manufactured by small-scale industries and are marketing their products under their own brand names. This has given a boost to many small industries. NELCO, a Tata Company, purchases its calculators from small units, and then advertises, markets and distributes them under its own brand name.

Empirical evidence in other countries shows that there is not much scientific evidence in other countries shows that there is not much scientific and strong brand loyalty. More often, there is a marginal preference for one brand within a range of acceptable brands. In India, however, brand loyalty has been found to be high. The Indian consumer legitimately expects that his favourite brand will keep pace with the latest developments. However, there is no doubt in the fact that as between well-known brands, price elasticity may be very high and choices can fluctuate by a slight reduction in price. Brand loyalty depends upon the nature of the product as well. While there is a strong brand loyalty in products like headache pills and pressure cookers, there is less brand loyalty in products like washing powders, light bulbs and toothpastes. In textiles, brand image is more effective in urban areas than in rural areas. In such cases, price cutting may give one manufacturer an edge over the other.

Despite the obvious value of a brand, brand loyalty levels are falling and price is becoming the more salient feature of a product. Customers cannot be expected to be loyal to a particular brand for long. The reason lies in proliferation of brands which has made the differences marginal for products in similar categories. With the emergence of a buyers' market, companies will have to find ways to be innovative in building and sustaining brands. Akai has swept the colour TV market at one time dominated by Videocon, BPL and Onida, because there was not much difference at the physical level and the price offered by Akai was very attractive for the customers. However, the point to be stressed is that while initially a product may be bought on the basis of its brand image, in the long run the product must perform up to the buyers' expectations.

Mascot as Brands

Amul introduced a little girl to project its butter as "utterly butterly delicious". After a gap of 40 years, Amul has created a new character—Amul cheese boy to give a new identity to the brand. Cheese boy will feature on cheese packs.

Essential Elements of Business Portfolio Analysis for Brand Analysis

B.P.A. increases Employee Productivity and Profits.

B.P.A. must prioritize customers and it's efforts based on corporate objectives.

B.P.A. must help to build a performance culture.

B.P.A. provides a competitive advantage.

B.P.A. makes fact-based decision using metrics.

B.P.A. Strategy Model

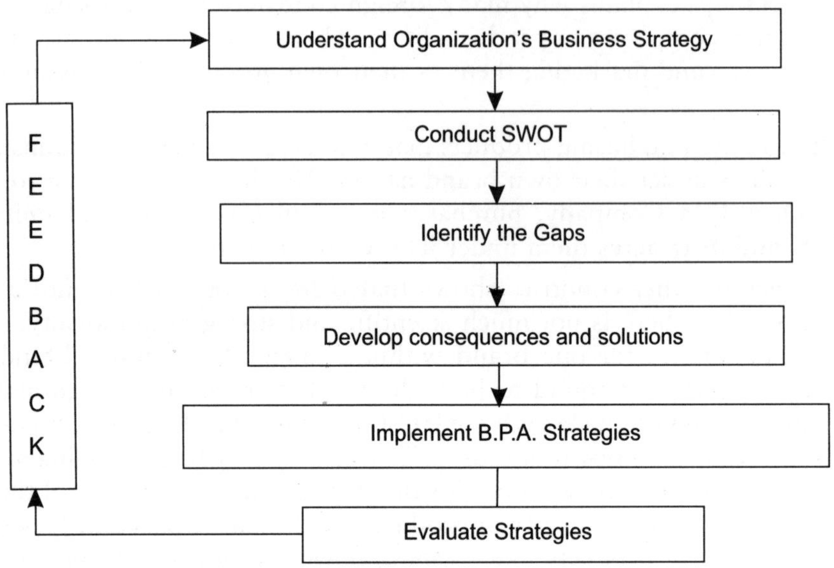

Business Portfolio Mind Map

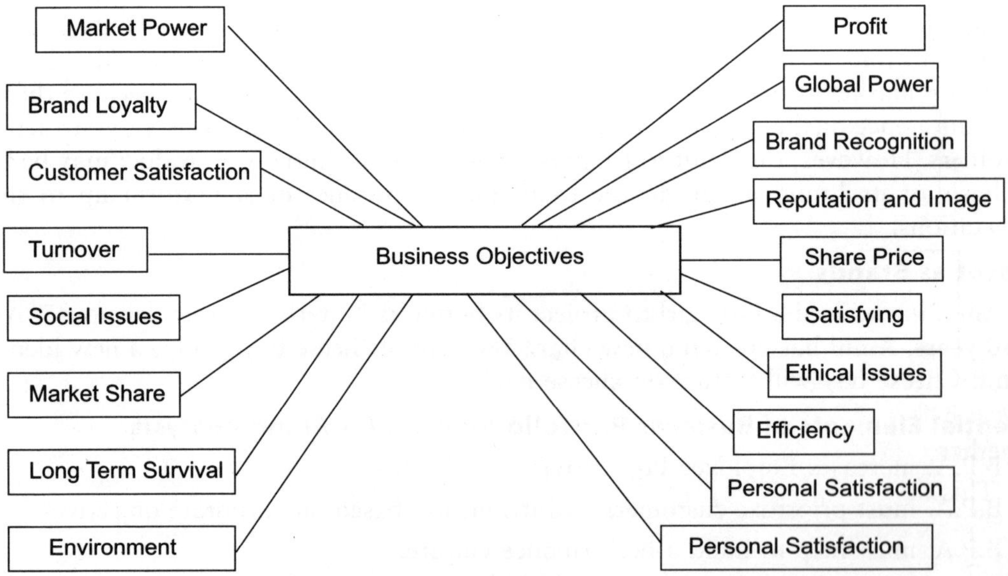

BRANDING DECISIONS

Philip Kotler has listed various questions to be considered for making brand decisions, especially for consumer products:

1. Should product be branded at all?
2. Who should sponsor the product?
3. What quality should be built into the brand?
4. Should the product be individually branded or family branded?
5. Should two or more products be developed in the same product category?
6. Should the established brand be given a new meaning?

An Overview of Brand Decision

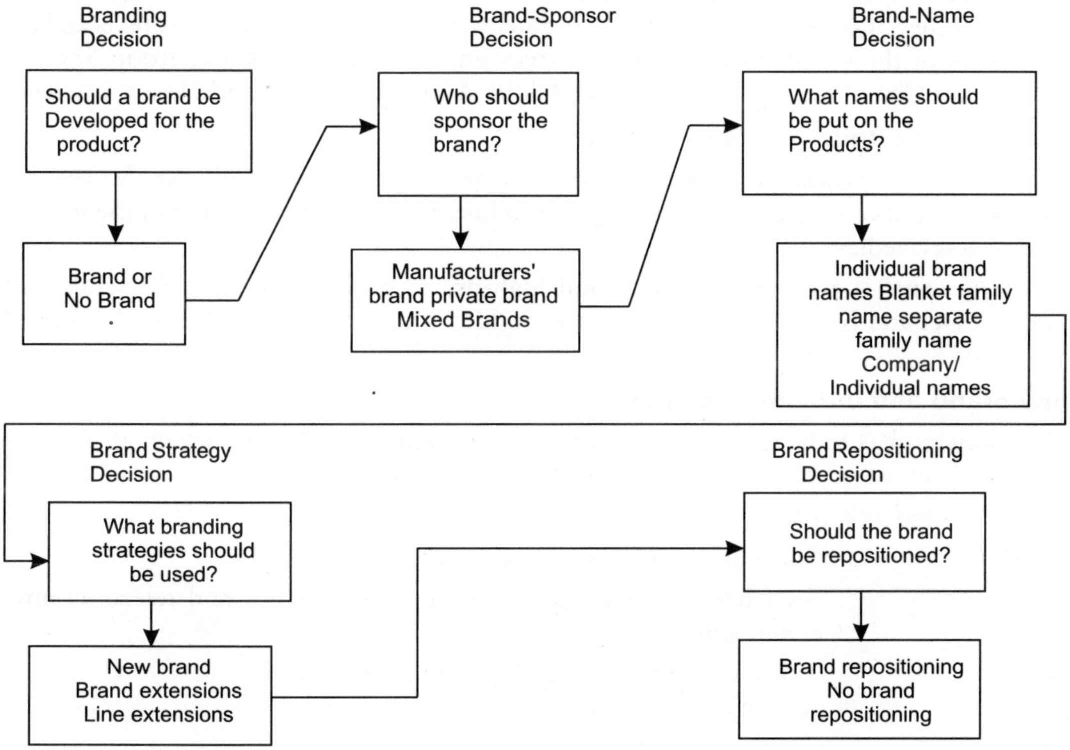

Source: Kotler, *Marketing Management*, 1994, p. 447

Whether to Brand or Not?

This depends on the following factors:

1. Nature of the product,
2. Type of the outlet assigned for the product,
3. Perceived advantages of branding, and
4. Estimated cost of developing the brand.

Historically, it has been found that brand development is closely correlated with increase in disposable income, sophistication of distribution system and increasing size of the national market. These trends are manifest in India also at the moment.

Example: A few years back, nobody could have thought of selling branded rice or refined flour in India. But several firms in the recent past have been successful even in such product categories. These are: Shakti Bhog Atta, Atithi Bhog Atta, and Lal Quila Rice.

National Brand or Private Brand

This decision is more relevant in developed countries where department stores dominate the retail distribution system. This is, however, largely a hypothetical question in India. Only Super Bazars have started marketing a few products, which are specially packed and sold under their names. Some recent examples are Nanz Super Market and Mera Bazar. However, if outlets of Super Bazar, Mother Dairy and National Consumers Co-operative Federation increase in sufficient number, it is possible that private brands will become a reality in future. Some popular brand names in the product-categories of Sarees and car accessories are: Roop Sarees, Ram Chand Kishan Chand Sarees, Kala Niketan, Globe Auto Accessories and Desert Coolers.

Attributes to be Built into the Product

This is a very crucial decision. The matrix of such attributes will decide, the product positioning. A marketer has the option to position his product at any segment of the market-top, bottom or intermediate.

Example: Surf is a premium-quality and high-priced product. At the other end, Nirma is low-priced: Det and Key are somewhere at the middle in quality: Titan is high-priced and HMT is low-priced.

Family Brand and Individual Brand

The decision has to be taken whether to adopt a family brand under which all the products of a company come or an individual brand for each product.

Family brand examples:

Kissan	-	Squashes, sauce, jams and ketch-up
L&T	-	Switches, control gears, change-over switches and telecommunication equipments.
Vimal	-	Fabrics – Suitings, shirtings and accessories
Maggi	-	Noodles and sauce
Tata	-	Steel, oil watches, salt, tea, machinery
Bata	-	Shoes and socks
Godrej	-	Soap, refrigerator, almirah, hair dye and cosmetic
Ponds	-	cold cream, soap and talcum powder.

Advantages of a family brand

1. A family brand reduces the cost of product launching.
2. It reduces the ongoing promotional expenditure.
3. If a brand is successful, it would be able to sell the entire product-line.

4. It is very cost-effective.
5. If one product under a family brand does exceptionally well, there is a strong possibility of a positive fallout for other products under the same brand.

Disadvantages of a family brand

1. A family brand is not justified, if the products offered are of uneven quality.
2. It will not be a good strategy if the markets are dissimilar in terms of consumer profile.
3. A family brand does not recognise that each product can be given a specific identity by a suitable brand, which can go a long way in making it a fabulous success in its own right.

Individual Brands: Individual brands are those where each product has a unique brand name.

Examples:

HLL	–	Rexona, Lux, Lifebuoy, Pears, Close-up toothpaste and Surf.
Godrej	–	Evita, Key, Vigil, Ganga, Crowning Glory and Cinthol.

Advantages:
1. If there is a product failure, it will not affect the whole range of products.
2. It stands on its feet for its reputation.

Disadvantages: Individual brand is costly.

Multibrand Decision

It is a strategy where a seller develops two or more brands in the same product category. Some examples are:

I.T.C.	–	Wills and Gold Flake in cigarettes.
Godrej	–	Cinthol, Marvel, Evita, Ganga, Vigil and Crowning Glory in toilet soaps.
Bata	–	Ambassador and North Star in men's wear.

Advantages:

1. Multibrands create excitement and develop efficiency within the manufacturer's organisation.
2. They mean more shelf-space for the manufacturers.
3. They catch 'brand-switchers'—consumers who switch over from one brand to the other.

Building a Brand

Building a strong brand involves efforts to make the product occupy a prominent place in the perceptive mind of the targeted customer. What is intended is that the brand being built up edges out the competing brand images. The distinctiveness could be derived from just about anything. Coca-Cola has a distinctive shape of the bottle, colour and script of the can, besides the youthful messages. ITC'S super-refined groundnut oil Crystal had to be 'so clear, so pure' that it had to be practically invisible, The product has to be packaged with a clear brand image.

Both Amul and Britannia have launched sliced cheese but they projected it differently. The smartest thing that Britannia did was to position its cheese as a milk product. Each slice is worth a glass of milk, says its advertisement.

The value of an establishment brand is in part due to the realisation that it is more difficult to build brands today than a decade ago. The cost of advertising and distribution is much higher now. "It takes in the order of $1 billion of advertising to build a significant share of mind with consumers across North America, Asia and Europe."

As the consumers and markets change, so too the brand image. The *Dove* beauty bar was introduced with an accent on a softer skin because it contained "one quarter cleansing cream". When sales of cleansing cream products declined, *Dove* was promoted as "one quarter moisturizing cream". The brand zoomed past its competitors.

Branding Strategy

This is a powerful strategy which is directly related to product strategy. A brand is used to identify an offering and set it apart from competing offerings.

Brand plays an important role in marketing strategies. We can say that a product is something that is made in factory but a brand is something that is bought by a customer. A product can be copied, but a successful brand is unique and achieves its own brand personality.

Brand personality creates a goodwill for the product in the market as reflected in its wide acceptance and leads to customer satisfaction. It is the discriminator in the market place. For example, Surf, Dalda and Colgate are not just products of daily use; they have resplendent personalities in the consumer's mind.

Brand Piracy

One persistent problem that well-known brands face in domestic market as well as foreign markets is counterfeiting. Consider, for example, Nirma is sold as Nirmla, Fair and Lovely is sold as Friends and Lovely. There are three forms of piracy: Imitation, faking and preemption. Imitation amounts simply to copying an established brand. For example, a manufacturer in Hong Kong may produce cheap jeans and put on the Raymonds label for sale as a genuine Raymonds product. Faking refers to identifying the fraudulent product with a symbol, logo or brand name that is very similar to the famous brand. For example, in rural markets of our country, Cadbury's brands are sold as Chaudary brands. Piracy through preemption of brand names is very popular in various countries. It is feasible in those countries where the law permits wholesale registration of brand names. In such countries, a person may register in his or her name a large number of well-known brand names and then get benefit of their registration in a country's market.

Apart from this, well-known brand names are very often used by manufacturers of entirely unrelated products, e.g. Lux *banians* and underwear and Sony cockroach trap.

Brand Development

A marketer has to develop a brand strategy over time and to overcome environmental conditions. It shows the need for brand development through the following principles identified by Davidson:

- Understand your brands;
- Determine how all your brand names fit;
- Decide which brand names can be stretched and how far;
- Know when to develop new brand names;
- Consider licensing your brand name;
- Have a five-year brand development plan.

Brand stretching and market attractiveness are two major factors, which help in brand development as shown below in the Fig. 9.1.

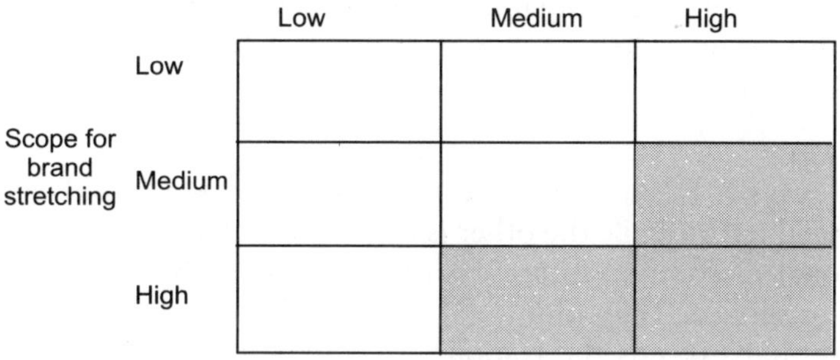

Fig. 9.1: Market Attractiveness

The aim should, therefore, be to operate only in the three cells in the bottom right-hand corner in the above figure.

Brand Extension

A successful brand is like a powerhouse light which has a strong reputation in the market. Brand extension is a useful strategy which creates a lot of goodwill in the market. For example, Nirma Washing Powder to Nirma Soap, Dettol Antiseptic to Dettol Soap. The reason for the success of this strategy is reduction of launching media cost. With increasingly competitive markets and escalating media costs, it makes sound financial and marketing sense to spin out the inner force of a respected brand for new incarnations. A marketer should undertake the following criteria for a brand extension decision.

(i) **The 'Fit'.** The extended brand must fit the new category. Management judgement should be supplemented by the study of consumer perceptions.

(ii) **The value perception.** It must be consistent with all the categories where the brand is extended. For example, the essential value of North Star is exclusiveness, and consistent quality. All North Star extensions represent this.

(iii) **Competitive edge.** The brand name should have some in-built advantage that gives it competitive strength against established brands in the new categories. We would like to discuss one latest example of brand extension. Strategic shift is also taking place at the Rs. 1,350 crore Karsenbhai Patel promoted Nirma. In what is the first evidence of a brand extension from the acknowledged umbrella-branding strategiest, the detergent manufacturer introduced a new soap brand, Nirma Lime, in Gujarat and Maharashtra. Nirma Lime targets the popular segment of Rs. 2,000 crore toilet soaps market.

Brand Rejuvenation

Brand rejuvenation is an integral part of product management. It keeps adding value to an existing brand through improving the product quality, and its overall attributes and appeal. It is considered to refocus the attention of consumers on the ongoing brand. It helps overcome the consumer's boredom in seeing the same product on the shelves year after year. Titan and Hindustan Lever are examples of companies which believe in giving their products importance through brands rejuvenation. They have a strong R&D base and are constantly striving to improve their existing brands.

Brand Equity

According to Alexander L. Biel, brand equity consists of two linked elements—one element is expressed in financial terms while the other is described in terms of consumer response. Brand equity is the additional discounted future cash flow achieved by associating a brand with the underlying product or service. That additional future cash flow is driven by a buyer response to the branded offering that exceeds the response that would be achieved by that same offering without brand identity.

In the words of David Aaker, "Brand Equity is the set of assets (and liabilities) inked to a brand's name and symbol that adds to (or substracts from) the value provided by a product or service to a firm and/or that firm's customers."

The components of brand equity are shown in the Fig. 9.2 below:

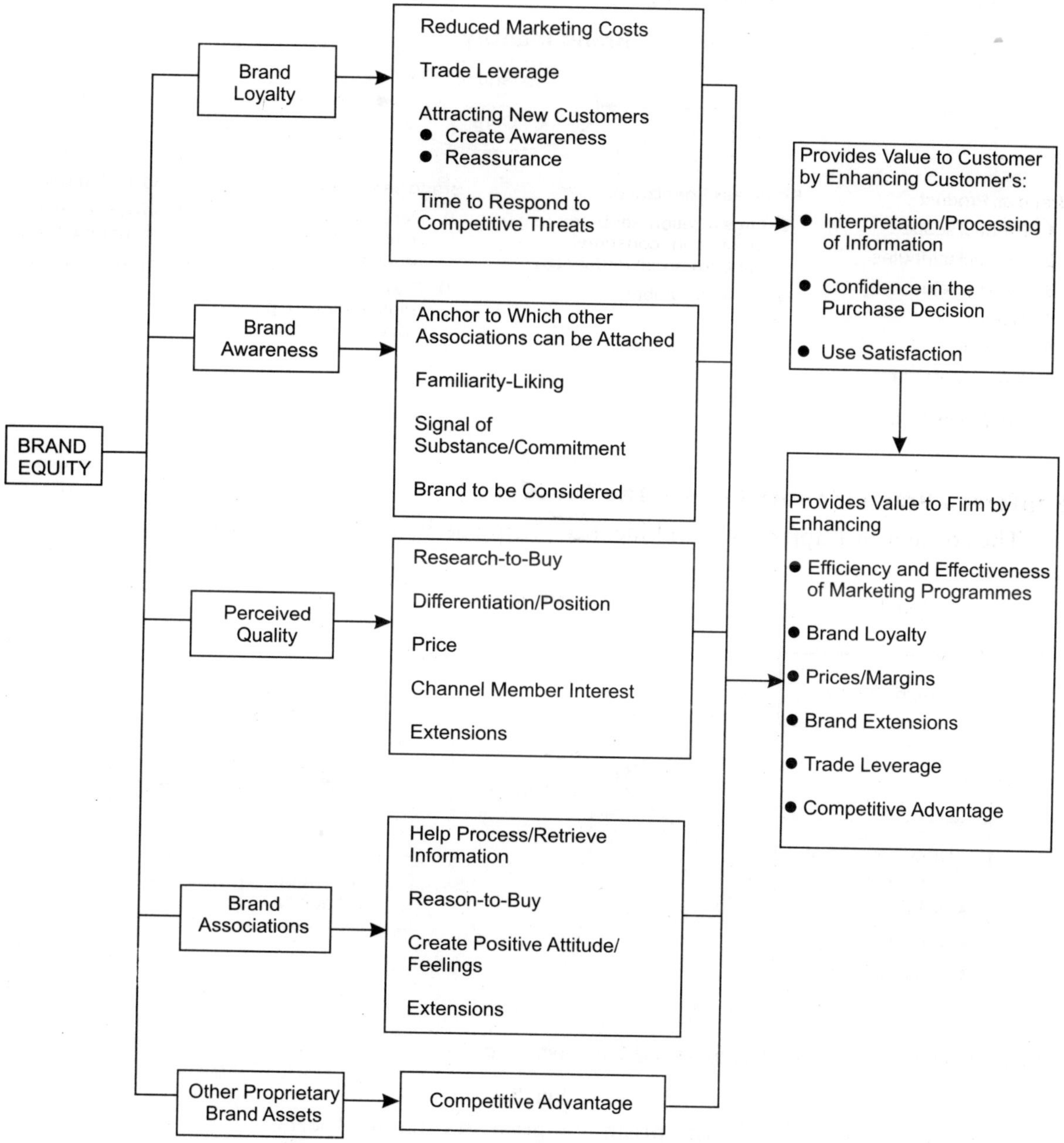

Fig. 9.2

Source: David Aaker, 'Building Strong Brands', The Free Press, New York, 1996, p. 9.

As shown in the figure above, the *perceived quality* of a product or service and the *brand associations* drive the brand identity.

The brand identity-What does it comprise?

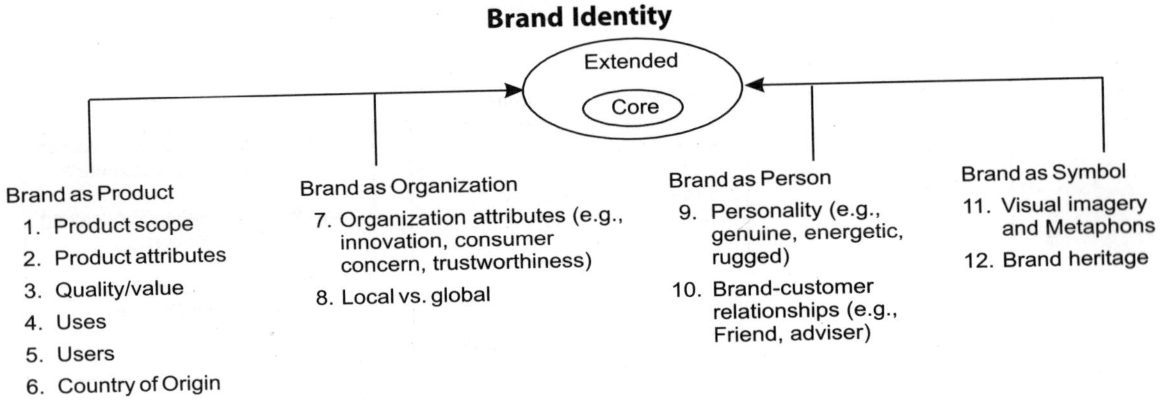

Source: David Aaker, *ibid.*, 79.

Fig. 9.3

Kapferer's Brand Identity Prism—The Concept

The concept of Kapferer's brand identity prism has been illustrated below:

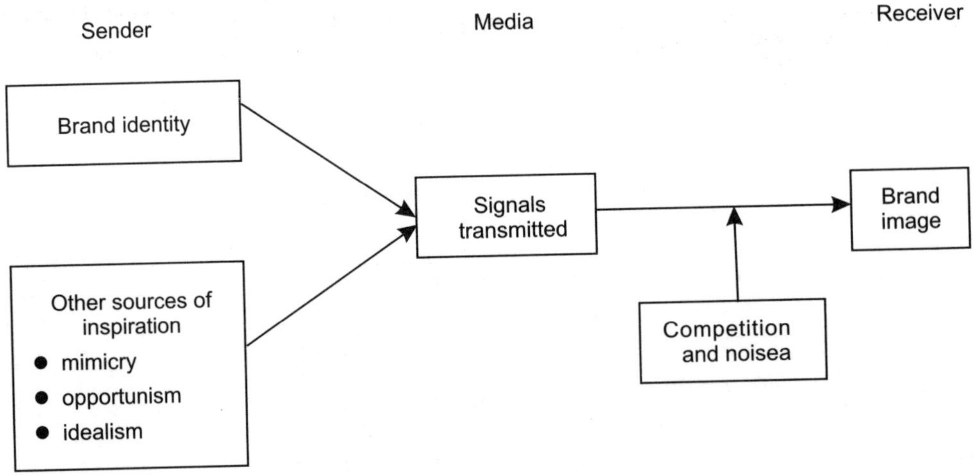

Source: Kapferer, Kan-Noel, *Strategic Brand Management*, p. 95.

Fig. 9.4

The Kapferer's brand identity prism comprises six major aspects:

1. Physique, 2. Personality, 3. Culture, 4. Relationship, 5. Reflection, and 6. Self-image.

These aspects which drive the brand identity are explained below:

- **Physique.** The term 'physique' refers to a combination of independent characteristics, which may be either prominent, i.e. springing readily to the mind when the brand is mentioned, or dormant.
- **Personality.** If we identify the brand with a person, we form a picture of that person by the way in which he speaks and communicates. In this regard, the marketing communications and promotion of brand play a very important role.
- **Culture.** This implies a system of values, a source inspiration and *brand energy*. The cultural facet relates to the basic principles governing the brand in its outward signs, i.e. products and communication. It is a link between brand and the product.
- **Relationship.** A brand is a relationship. It often provides the opportunity for an intangible exchange between persons. It is something which permeates both products and the customer appeal, even though no personal presence may be evident.
- **Reflection.** A brand reflects a customer's image. It is the image of the brand offered to the brand's potential purchasers or users. It is a type of identification.
- **Self-image.** If reflection is the target's outward mirror, self-image is the target's own internal mirror. Through our attitude towards certain brands, we develop a certain type of inner relationship with ourselves.

The Brand Identity rism demonstrates that these facets form a structured whole. The content of one facet echoes that of another. The prism structure is derived from one basic concept—that the *brand has a voice*.

A brand does not function unless it communicates. It would decline in strength if allowed to remain silent and unused for too long. The Brand Identity Prism allows us to examine the brand in detail in order to detect its strengths and weaknesses. It incorporates a vertical division.

The three facets—*physique, relationship and reflection*—are the social facets, which give the brand its outward expression. These three are the *visible facets* of the brand. *Personality, culture and self-image* are those facets that are incorporated into the brand itself, within its spirit.

QUESTIONS FOR DISCUSSION

1. What is branding? Why should a marketer brand his products?
2. What is meant by brand? What are the various branding decisions which must be kept in mind before branding any product?
3. Define brand name. How should brand name be decided for any product?
4. Is brand name and trade-mark synonyms? What are the important decisions to be adopted for brand marks?
5. What are the advantages and disadvantages of branding a product?
6. What are the benefits and limitations of branding a product?
7. What is meant by branding? What are the difficulties faced by marketers in branding their products?

STRATEGIC MANAGING NEW PRODUCT DEVELOPMENT

10

INTRODUCTION

New product planning has been defined by the American Marketing Association as "the act of making out and supervising the search, screening, development and commercialisation of new products; the modification of existing lines; and the discontinuance of marginal or unprofitable items". Simply stated, product planning decides the nature and other related aspects of the articles produced and sold. Product development is more limited term but includes the technical activities of product research, engineering and design. Product planning and development is the result of the coordinated efforts of large number of specialists—engineers, scientists, marketers, etc. Product planning is usually described 'Merchandising' and it covers both the proper balance between the old and the new products.

New product planning is a very long and complex process and it deals with changes in:

1. The kinds of goods or services offered by a marketer for various segments.
2. The number or kinds of products, or different lines, the company offers in various segments.
3. The width of product line offered.
4. The quality levels or levels acceptable to various classes of consumers in various target markets.
5. The degree of distinctiveness.
6. Increased societal and governmental constraints.
7. The growing shortage of new product ideas in certain areas.
8. Shorter time spans between the emergence of the idea and the physical launch of the products.
9. The costliness of the new product development process.

The following decisions are important in new product planning:

1. Improving the existing product lines and services
2. Weeding out unprofitable items in the product line (simplification),
3. Expansion of the current product line (diversification),
4. New product development for the present customers, and
5. New product development for new customers (diversified products).

Steps in New Product Development

The following are the usual steps involved in the planning of new products:

1. Idea generation,
2. Screening the ideas,
3. Business analysis,
4. Developing the product, and
5. Testing the product and commercialisation of the product.

1. Idea generation

The first stage of the new product's evolution begins with an idea for the product. Hence this stage is also termed as 'Idea Generation'. Ideas may originate from the following sources:

Sales personnel
Marketing personnel
Research and development
Top management executives
Production department
Customer service decision
Employee suggestion system
Customer
Competitive products
Foreign products
Consultants
Advertising agencies
Researchers
Distribution channels
Public unsolicited ideas.

New product ideas can be generated both directly and indirectly. Both approaches can be undertaken simultaneously and can vary from highly structured, and loosely structured to unstructured procedures.

Direct methods rely heavily upon the creativity of individuals as well as groups and the consumer survey data for technique, e.g., forced relationship, transfer analysis, brainstorming, motivation research, multi-dimensional scaling, etc.

Indirect methods refer to the 'synthetic' methods, methods that are used for other purposes but, with little ingenuity, they can be employed just as well in exploration, for example, quadrant analysis and magnitude estimation have been used in product testing.

2. Screening the ideas

At this stage, the ideas collected are scrutinized to eliminate those inconsistent with the product policies and objectives of the firm. Some ideas may already be protected by patents and some others may not be fit for consideration because of the non-availability of raw materials for production. Thus most of the ideas screened need not essentially be good. They may be further subjected to a more detailed examination. The main intention of this phase is only to eliminate unsuitable ideas as quickly as possible. The procedure adopted includes:

Screening criteria are established as evaluative standards in new product development. They make arbitrary decisions less likely. They provide a unity of purpose they provide a perspective for new product planners.

Screening criteria usually concern themselves with three factors-markets, products and finances. More frequently used market-criteria are market size, market growth, market positioning, distribution features, etc. the following sets of "must have" and 'would like' criteria have been suggested for the planners of new products.

'MUST HAVE' criteria

- Fill a perceived need with a sufficiently defined group of heavy users for the product.
- Have unique product characteristics that offer distinctive benefits to the user.
- Be saleable in large, expanding territories.

'WOULD LIKE' criteria

- Be compatible with and able to carry the company's brand name.
- Provide the basis for a continuing business.
- Lend itself to mass media advertising.

3. Business analysis

Business analysis is only a continuation of the evaluative process that began when the new-product idea was first generated. Once the product concept is developed, business analysis can evaluate the business attractiveness of the proposal.

The purpose of business analysis is to serve as a basis for a decision as to whether the corporate resources should be committed to the development of new product.

As per Sachs and Benson, the decisions of business analysis hinge on the following considerations: demand, profitability, and return on investment. Will market demand be sufficient to meet the company's profit goals? And, how much investment will be necessary?

4. Developing the product

During this stage, the 'idea-on-the-paper' is turned into a 'product-on-hand'. In other words, the idea is converted into a product that is producible and demonstrable. This stage is also termed as 'Technical Development'. It is during this period that all developments of the product, from idea to final physical form, take place.

The final decision whether a product should be developed on a commercial scale or not is decided at this stage because the time-lag required to attain this stage is a long one and it is possible that some adverse developments might have taken place during this period. Once the management decides to go ahead with the product idea, the following activities are undertaken:

(a) Establishing development projects for each product,

(b) Building the product with the changed specifications, if necessary, and

(c) Completing laboratory evaluation and sending the product for testing and then launching.

5. Testing the product

It is at the stage of testing that one could testify the accuracy of the information on the basis of which various stages were completed. These commercial experiments are necessary to verify earlier business judgements. Thus, the object of this stage is basically to assess whether the product meets the technical and commercial objectives at various levels in order to ascertain the product acceptability. There are three types of tests usually conducted:

(a) Concept testing,

(b) Product testing, and

(c) Test marketing.

Concept Testing

This is concerned with measuring customer reactions to the idea or concept of a product. In fact, it is a kind of research in which the product idea is screened before any money, time or labour are committed to making the prototype products. The idea of a product with as many details as possible is made known to the customers either verbally or through the use of suitable blueprints. The response of the customers is checked and only if it is found encouraging, then the development of product prototype is taken up. For instance, when the rest of the world had largely gone in for synthetic detergent in the powder form, it was decided by the Hindustan Lever Limited to test a detergent bar as a concept, because in India most people do not use washing machines or even buckets and are accustomed to using a bar to rub on the fabric.

Concept testing can tell whether the product is likely to be a success or not. To achieve better results, however, the product concept should include the finished product itself with all details, viz., packaging, price range, the brand name, etc. On the basis of these details, interviews are conducted to collect the opinion of the would be purchasers.

The major advantage of concept testing is that the management could form early judgements on the likelihood of the market success of the new ideas. The other objectives of concept testing could be:

(a) To evaluate the relative merits of several new product proposals,

(b) To determine whether the product idea is to be abandoned or modified,

(c) To determine the size of the potential market, and

(d) To guide the management to adopt suitable marketing policies in advance.

Concept testing has the following limitations or drawbacks: It entails some risk of disclosing the company plans to competitors. There is a time-lag in obtaining and assessing the results. Respondents may overstate their interest and encourage unsound development. The validity of any measure of potential market size obtained through early stage concept testing may often be dubious. Findings may also be misleading if the test is not carried out properly.

Product Testing

Once the concept test of the product is successful, the next step is to put the real product into a few selected markets. This test will prove whether the product performs as expected or whether it lives up to the promise of the concept. Such a test enables the management to pick out the likes and dislikes of the consumers towards the product. It also gives an opportunity to the buyers to compare the product with the competitive products.

The objectives of product testing are:

(a) To assess proper product performance,

(b) To minimize the risks attached to full-scale launching of a new product,

(c) To identify the most productive market segments, and

(d) To collect necessary data about the responsiveness of the customers.

However, this is not a foolproof system for predicting the future. It cannot help to forecast the market size, sales volume, brand share, repeat buying, etc. Correct pricing can also not be assessed.

Test Strategic Marketing

Even the most favourable results form the two tests mentioned above are not a conclusive evidence for the success of a new product. For instance, even where the product is seen to possess a high quality, market failure is still a possibility if other important factors in the Strategic Marketing mix show weakness. It is, therefore, logical to examine how the company's total marketing mix may be tested by conducting test marketing. Under test marketing, the product is introduced in selected areas often at different prices in different areas. These tests would provide the management an idea of the amount and elasticity of the demand for the product, the competition it is likely to face, and the expected sales volume and profits it might yield at different prices. Experience shows that the chances of a new product being successful are 'significantly greater' if it is first put into a controlled test market where it is exposed to realistic competitive conditions.

The ***objectives*** of test marketing are:

(a) To evaluate a complete marketing plan including advertising, distribution, sales, pricing, etc.,

(b) To determine the promotional media mix, channels, etc., and

(c) To forecast the likely sales volume.

Though test marketing has definite advantages, there are some limitations as well:

(a) Competitors' response and their defensive action may not allow test marketing to provide a conclusive result.

(b) Test marketing is a costly affair.

(c) It is a time-consuming method. Many firms avoid test marketing since they wish to be 'the first in the market'.

Though test marketing is not a perfect simulation of full-scale production and distribution, yet it may provide very useful information for better planning of the full-scale effort. It also permits initial pricing mistakes to be made on a small rather than on a large scale. "Test marketing does not eliminate risks, it only improves knowledge, and reduces chances of expensive mistakes." Therefore, most firms do resort to test marketing. For example, Liril Soap, introduced by Hindustan Lever Limited, was originally tested in two towns (Hyderabad and Lucknow). These towns were selected because of their different characteristics, which make them representative of a large spectrum of towns in India. The product was distributed in all normal outlets in the whole town and supported by advertising to inform the customers. The results of the test enabled the company to make several improvements which were successfully incorporated before the product was nationally extended.

To make test marketing more fruitful, a 'post-launching' survey should be conducted. The survey will reveal whether the earlier satisfaction continues to be derived, whether people like the product and make re-purchase, whether the advertising is appealing, etc. on the basis of the findings, changes will have to be incorporated before the product is finally launched in the market.

The following procedures may be adopted for test marketing:

1. For determining the number of cities, the two factors, which must be considered, are:
   (i) Representativeness, and
   (ii) The cost of marketing.
2. For selection of cities, they must essentially possess the following characteristics:
   (i) Average competition,
   (ii) Presence for chain and departmental stores,
   (iii) Existence of various types of basic industries, and
   (iv) Optimum size of population.
3. The duration of testing. It depends upon the following factors:
   (i) Average purchase period,
   (ii) The competitive situation, and
   (iii) Cost of testing.
4. Collection of necessary information. It is important to collect the necessary information with respect to the nature of the product, the nature of customers, channels of distribution, buyers' behaviour, etc.
5. Launching of the new product.

COMMERCIALISATION

In this stage, the product is submitted to the market, and thus commences its life-cycle. Commercialisation is also the phase where Strategic Marketing is most active in connection with the new product. This stage is considered to be a critical one for any anew product and should, therefore, be handled carefully. For instance, it should be checked whether advertising and personal selling have been done effectively and whether proper outlets have been arranged for the distribution. Despite the care with which the previous development stages have been planned, unforeseen events can impair commercialization seriously. The following activities are usually undertaken during this stage:

(1) Completing final plans for production and marketing,

(2) Initiating coordinated production and selling programmes, and

(3) Checking results at regular intervals.

It should be remembered that new products should be launched in the market only stage by stage. In other words, introduction may be restricted to a few regions in the first instance. This is to avoid short supply of the product due to initial gaps in production and distribution. It is not prudent to extend a product nationally and then not be able to meet demand or to come across some unexpected deficiency. 'Gold Café' was heavily advertised nationally in 1987 but it was not available at retail stores.

All the stages explained above stress the fact that the development of a new product must pass through certain logical stages. Innovation is necessarily an orderly and predictable process and could be performed only in a sequence. For example, commercialisation cannot precede the development stage of a product.

Factors Determining the Scope of Product–Line

The extent to which a company can add new products is not unlimited. Very often, the scope for having new products is in some way related to the existing conditions of the firm. The goods may be:

(1) Cost related goods,

(2) Demand related goods,

(3) Commodities related in advertisement and distribution,

(4) Research related goods, and

(5) Common raw materials.

(1) **Cost Related Goods.** A company may decide to add a product, which may be the result of a common production process. For example, a company, which strikes oil, may decide to produce petrol or mobile oil, kerosene, gas, wax, etc. A company producing sugar may decide to produce molasses.

(2) **Demand Related Goods.** A firm may decide to add a product, which is jointly demanded. For example, manufactures of Sulekha Ink have gone in for production of other related items of stationery like sealing wax. Food Specialities Ltd. added Maggi to their various food products. Weston Electronics, manufacturers of tape recorder and television sets, have diversified into consumer electronics like video cassette recorders, colour TV sets, two-in-ones, calculators, video games, audio duplicating machines, video tapes and cassettes. They plan to enter into medical electronics (e.g. blood pressure instruments).

Sometimes, a firm having earned reputation for its products may like to add to its product-line in the hope that people will continue to patronise its goods because of the reputation established by it. For example, Hindustan Lever Ltd., manufacturers of Dalda, went into production of dehydrated vegetables, pure ghee and mustard oil in the hope that consumers who are after quality will purchase ghee, oil and other products manufactured by them.

Sometimes, manufacturers of quality products may add to their product-line to utilise raw materials found sub-standard for their quality product. While the quality product is sold under the company's brand name to attract quality customers, the inferior product may be sold under a different brand name without emphasising the name of the manufacturers. Production of different brands of goods by the same manufacturer may be the result of a number of factors: (i) Merger or amalgamation of firms producing the same goods but under different brand names—the different brand names may be retained to retain customer loyalty, (ii) Known consumer preferences for different varieties—here the firm may like to cater to the requirements of most of the customers by producing different varieties according to the demand of the consumers. (iii) The keenness of the firm to cater to the requirements of customers who are choosy and want wide variety of goods to select from. Some brand variety may appeal to one class the other variety to some others. Advertisement efforts may also be geared accordingly to appeal to different types of customers. (iv) To retain dealer loyalty, a firm may produce goods of different brands, though more or less of the same quality one brand being sold through exclusive dealers and the other one being sold to all other dealers. Bata produces two types of goods: one under the brand name of Bata to be sold exclusively at Bata shops, the other BSC (standing for Bata Shoe Company) for distribution through other dealers.

(3) **Commodities Related in Advertising and Distribution.** Frequently, firm may find it advantageous to handle multiple products because they are related in advertising or distribution. For example, a number of travel goods can be conveniently advertised together, say, holdalls, suitcases, etc. Likewise, one salesman can conveniently sell tea, coffee, Bournvita, etc.

(4) **Research Related Goods.** Common research facilities may enable a company to produce an additional product or commodity.

(5) **Common Raw Materials.** Companies often decide to add products using the same raw material or its by-products. Sometimes the basic source of raw material may be controlled by the companies and this also helps in the addition of a particular product.

Need for Market Research for Product Addition

If decisions regarding product addition are taken without adequate planning, i.e. without adequate forecasting and market research, the added product may turn out to be a money loser rather than a money-spinner. It may be useful to cite here the example of the introduction of HIMA brand of packaged convenience foods by Hindustan Lever Ltd. The products failed because of lack of demand forecasting and market research. The launch of these Indian consumers. The Indian consumer, particularly the Indian housewife, perceived very little need for such convenience because of the following factors:

(i) General preference for fresh foods in India,

(ii) Easy availability of fresh foods in India unlike the west,

(iii) High retail prices due to *(a)* avoidable packaging, and *(b)* lack of economies of scale,

(iv) Widely spread out market segments posing distribution problems, and

(v) Diversified food tastes in India.

It may be noted that other companies in packaged foods industry like Kissan and Dipy's have a small but established market constituting bulk sale to hotels, restaurants and canteens. There is not much demand for their products in the household sector due to high prices.

Very often, a company may introduce a new, improved product to justify a higher price tag. Very often this is done by changing its composition. However, it should be done after thorough research through personal discussion with the consumers. If a change is made without thorough research a lot of unnecessary and avoidable expenditure would have to be incurred. Recently Nestle changed the composition of its Maggi Noodles. Children who are the core customers for the product did not like the taste of the improved noodles. Nestle had to return to the original composition and is now spending a lot on advertising to emphasise that everything is as before:

सब कुछ पहले जैसा

Something similar was done by Coca Cola in America in 1985 by introducing New Coke. Americans did not like the taste of the new coke. As a result the company had to revert to its original composition.

Marketers would be well advised to take a more active role in finding out what their customers want. Every time they talk to their customers, they would be more knowledgeable and get away smarter.

Improve, Buy or Drop a Product

If a product is not showing profitable performance, the company may consider one of the alternatives, viz., improve, buy or drop product.

Improve

If the firm continues to make the product, it may be required to make improvement in its production or distribution so as to yield adequate return. Improvement may mean redesigning the product or producing it at a lower cost. Product has become apparently obsolete or out of fashion. Indian companies need to continuously upgrade their products and technology to withstand the pace of change in their business environment and to meet the challenges thrown up the emergence of a buyers' market. Product improvement is very important in durable goods, for example, automobiles, refrigerators, etc. This explains the development of a camera with a built-in coupled exposure meter which proved to be a more saleable product than a camera with a conventional exposure meter fitted to the outside case.

Adapt

Multinationals operating in India have found it necessary to adapt the product to Indian tastes or to Indian psyche. McDonald has introduced McAloo tikki burger and vegetable nuggets. During Navratras, they serve only vegetable stuff. The Pilsbury chakki-fresh atta proposition illustrates the desi bug that has bitten the big white man on the prowl in Indian markets. They have realised that not only have the products to be tailor made for local requirements with modifications that may be necessary, but the entire tone and tenor of the marketing mix seeks a distinct Indian identity. Harish Bijoor columnist has termed it as 'Desi customisation'.

Buy

A decision to buy the product rather than improve it, may be appropriate where the ailing product makes positive strategic or merchandising contribution. Buying the product is possible only if the supplying firm can provide the product in sufficient volume and at sufficiently low costs.

In general, buying instead of making and improving gives a firm certain flexibility, i.e. it can shop around and buy from the most economical source. It can also change its quality standards, if necessary. Further, buying gives the company the advantages of the supplying firm's specification and large-scale production.

For the buying firm, however, this decision may have the following *consequences*:

(1) It makes the firm dependent upon others, which may be a disadvantage if the supply of the product is not assured and continuous.

(2) If the supplying firm is part of an oligopolistic industry, its pricing practices may be erratic enough to complicate profit, cost and sales planning by the buying company.

Drop

A planned and systematic product elimination programme may contribute substantially to the firm's profitability and future growth. Profits can be enhanced by eliminating certain costs associated with products in the later stages of their life as well as by increasing the productivity of the resources released the older products.

Very often product elimination is avoided out of sentiment and blinkers are developed in connection with products, which have been in the company's line of products for a large number of years. However, deletion of products is as important a consideration as introduction of new products. A sick product generally loses its market appeal. It requires a disproportionately larger amount of executive time merely to prop up the marginal product. Further, continuation of sick products would affect a company's profitability. Also such product may even spoil the company's reputation if they are unsuitable to the consumers. Besides, capital is tied up in such a sick product which could be released for more profitable products. Finally, if resources are scarce, the company can ill-afford sick products in the product-mix. A systematic approach is, therefore, required for considering the question of elimination of marginal or unprofitable products. It is also essential to first assign definite responsibility for selecting products which are to be considered for elimination. The next step would be to collect the necessary information and analyse it so that a final decision can be taken regarding elimination.

There are certain *indicators* which suggest a careful analysis to determine whether or not to eliminate a particular product. These include the following:

(1) Reduction in product effectiveness;

(2) Emergence of a superior substitute product;

(3) Use of disproportionate executive time;

(4) Declining sales trend;

(5) Decreasing price; and

(6) Downward profit trend.

These indicators can help management to identify products, which should be considered for deletion. An analysis may, however, result in a decision not to eliminate but may suggest further improvements in the products.

Let us now consider these indicators in some detail. Over a period of time, certain products lose their effectiveness for providing the benefits for which they were produced originally. This particularly happens in the case of pharmaceutical products and certain drugs may have to be eliminated or substituted by other drugs. Where a substitute product emerges which is a considerable improvement on the old product, management must consider this seriously even though the substitute product had been introduced by a competitor. A study of the executive time devoted to various products in the product-mix can highlight the product taking excessive time which may be due to the product being sick. However, this must be distinguished from the growing pains of a new product. A declining sales trend over a reasonably long-time period would require a careful analysis of the product concerned. Similarly, decreasing price trend might indicate that obsolescence state cannot be warded off much further.

A downward profit trend is a powerful indicator. The company may even work out a practical minimum profit standard for each of its products. However, all products need not show a profit as at times a product is included to provide a 'full line' for the customers. If the dropping of such a product forces the customer to purchase from another supplier products which constitute a profitable group of the company, then elimination may not be justified. Again the declining trend in profits can be arrested by other tactics such as analyzing possible reductions in production costs, the use of more effective marketing and even by increasing the marketing expense provided the increased sale and profitability are greater than the extra marketing expense involved. The decision to drop the product entirely is warranted if its long-run net profit is below what would be attained from an alternative product using the same resources. In the long run, there may be new products which would produce a greater contribution to overheads than the old product.

The Electronics Corporation of India Ltd. decided to suspend production of certain microwave equipment on the ground of unremunerative price, low demand, obsolete technology and stiff competition from small-scale units. The Gramophone Company decided to phase out gradually the manufacture of consumer electronic products like stereos and record players as a part of readjustment and realignment of operations. ICI in the UK decided to close two uneconomic plants and withdraw several unprofitable products in its synthetic fibres division to reduce losses.

STRATEGIES FOR MARKET LEADERS

Market Leader: In the majority of industries there is one firm, which is generally recognized to be the leader. It typically has the largest market share, and by virtue of its pricing, advertising intensity, distribution coverage, technological advance, and rate of new product introductions, it determines the nature, pace and bases of competition. It is this dominance which typically provides the benchmark for other companies in the industry.

In doing this, there are three major areas to which the marketing strategist needs to pay attention:

1. How best to expand the total market;
2. How to protect the organization's current share of the market;
3. How to increase market share.

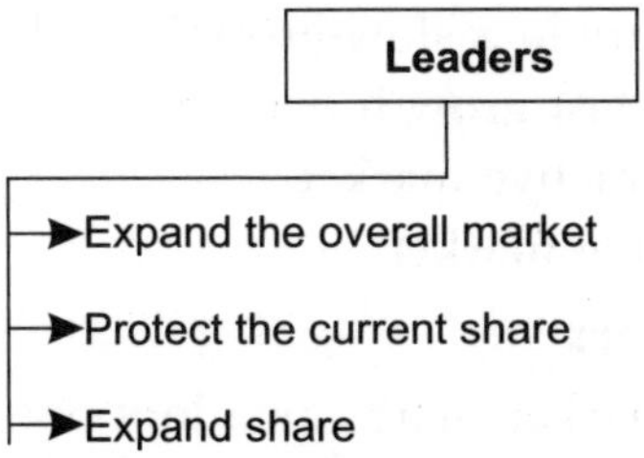

MARKET LEADERSHIP

Expansion of the Overall Market

- Targeting groups which currently are non-users
- Identifying new uses for the product/service
- Increasing usage rates

Guarding the Existing Market Share

- **Position defence:** This strategy involves pouring maximum firm's resources into its current successful brands. To overcome a position defence an attacker therefore typically adopts an indirect approach rather than the head-on attack that the defender expects. For example, HLL increased its ad-spend on Clinic and Sunsilk shampoos and gave heavy promotions through price reduction.
- **Mobile defence:** This strategy involves the leader's broadening and expanding its territories into new market areas by diversifying. The leader takes innovation works in both these directions, e.g. a five-star hotel can become foreign exchange dealer. Diversification into related areas is used in mobile defence.
- Strong market positioning.
- The development and refinement of meaningful competitive advantage(s).
- Continuous product and process innovation.
- Heavy advertising.
- Strong customer relations.
- Strong distribution relations.

Expansion of the Current Market Share

- Heavy advertising.
- Improved distribution.
- Price incentives.
- New product development.
- Mergers.
- Takeovers.
- Geographic expansion.
- Distributor expansion.

Strategic Market Plans for Leaders

- Protect high-share position in a mature market.

- Invest to grow market share in a slow-growth market.
- Protect market share in a fast-growth market.
- Harvest share in an unattractive market.
- Enter an attractive emerging market.

Market Challengers and Followers

Firms with a slightly smaller market share can adopt one of two stances. They may choose to adopt an aggressive stance and attack other firms, including the market leader, in an attempt to gain share and perhaps dominance (market challengers), or they may adopt a less aggressive stance in order to maintain the status quo (market followers).

Market Nichers

Virtually every industry has a series of small firms which survive, and indeed often prosper, by choosing to specialize in parts of the market which are too limited in size and potential to be of real interest to larger firms; a case in point would be Morgan specializing in traditional sports cars. By concentrating their efforts in this way, market nichers are able to build up specialist market knowledge and avoid expensive head-on fights with larger companies.

Strategies for Market Followers

1. Following closely with as similar as a marketing mix and market segmentation combination as possible;
2. Following at a distance so that although there are obvious similarities, there are also area of differentiation between the two;
3. Following selectively both in product and market terms so that the likelihood of direct competition is minimized.

Strategies for Market Nichers

1. Specializing geographically;
2. Specializing by the type of end user;
3. Specializing by product or product line;
4. Specializing on a quality/price spectrum;
5. Specializing by service;
6. Specializing by size of customer;
7. Specializing by product feature.

QUESTIONS FOR DISCUSSION

1. Define product planning. How is it different from product development?
2. Distinguish between the terms concept: 'testing', 'product testing' and 'test marketing'.
3. Describe the important criteria used to screen new product ideas.
4. What are the steps involved in new product launch. Discuss with the help of a suitable example.
5. How would you select the right target market for your new product?

STRATEGIC MANAGING PRODUCT LIFE CYCLE

11

INTRODUCTION

Product Life Cycle (PLC) theory was one of the first analytical attempts to determine marketing strategies. The product life cycle concept describes the stages in the sales history of a product. The basic features of this theory are:

- A product has a limited life.
- Product sales generally follow an 'S' curve until sales eventually start declining.

The product life cycle is marked by 4 different stages:

A — Introduction

B — Growth

C — Maturity

D — Decline

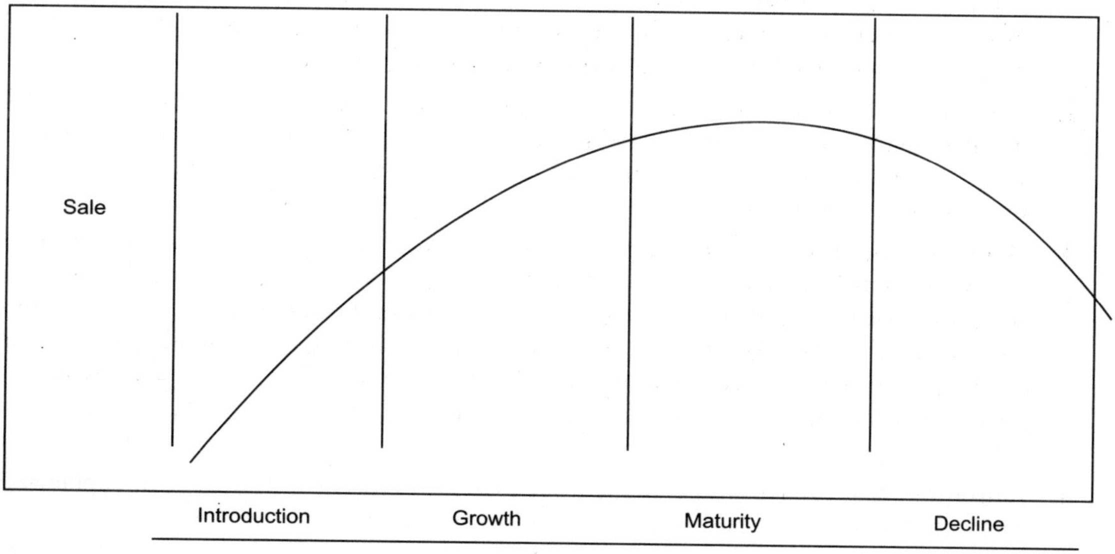

Fig. 11.1: Product Life Cycle

Each stage of the Product Life Cycle represents different marketing challenges and opportunities. Also, in actual practice, all products may not pass through all stages. Therefore, each stage requires a different marketing strategy. Product life cycle concept is remarkably enduring mainly because of the intuitive logical richness if derives from diffusion theory of innovations, and theory of monopolistic competition. Diffusion theory of innovations explains the process of new product adoption over period of time. Monopolistic competition theory elaborates the behaviour of firms over the productivity life cycle. Monopolistic competition theory explains the variations in the number of firms in different stages of productivity life cycle.

Product Life Cycle Stages

Many products generally have a characteristic known as 'perishable distinctiveness'. This means that a product which is distinct when new, degenerates over the years into a common commodity. The process by which the distinctiveness gradually disappears as the product merges with other competitive products has been rightly termed by Joel Dean as "the cycle of competitive degeneration". The cycle begins with the invention of a new product, and is often followed by patent protection, and further development to make it saleable. This is usually followed by a rapid expansion in its sales as the product gains market acceptance. Then competitors enter the field with imitation and rival products and the distinctiveness of the new product starts diminishing. The speed of degeneration differs from product to product. While some products fail immediately on birth or a little later, others may live long enough. BPL's picture in picture TC was eliminated at the introduction stage itself. The innovation of a new product and its degeneration into a common product is termed as the life cycle of a product.

There are five distinct stages in the life cycle of a product as shown below:

1. **Introduction.** Research or engineering skill leads to product development. The product is put on the market: awareness and acceptance are minimal. There are high promotional costs. Sometimes a product may generate a new demand, for example, Maggi. Volume of sales is low and there may be heavy losses.
2. **Growth.** The product begins to make rapid sales gains because of the cumulative effects of introductory promotion, distribution, and word-of-mouth influence. High and sharply rising profits may be witnessed. But to sustain growth, consumer satisfaction must be ensure at this stage.
3. **Maturity.** Sales growth continues, but at a diminishing rate, because of the declining number of potential customers who remain unaware of the product or who have taken no action. Also, the last of the unsuccessful competing brands will probably withdraw from the market. For this reason, sales are likely to continue to rise while the customers for the withdrawn brands are mopped up by the survivors. There is no improvement in the product but changes in selling effort are common. Profit margins slip despite using sales.
4. **Saturation.** Sales reach and remain on a plateau marked by the level of replacement demand. There is little additional demand to be stimulated.
5. **Decline.** Sales begin to diminish absolutely as the customers begin to tire of the product and the product is gradually edged out by better products of substitutes, for example, dial telephones and petrol jeeps.

There are several reasons why the life cycle of a product tends to be short: (a) continuous research for product development; (b) simultaneous attempts by several companies in the same direction; and (c) tendency of a new idea to attract competitors. Improvements offered by one company are likely to be met and, if possible, exceeded by competitors in a relatively short period. If competitor hits upon a real improvement (perhaps based on an entirely new technology) and he markets it well, both sales and profits for the original product innovator may decline drastically.

It may be noted that products may begin a new cycle or revert to an early stage as a result of (a) the discovery of new uses; (b) the appearance of new users; and (c) introduction of new features.

As the distinctiveness of the product fades, the pricing discretion enjoyed by their producers gradually declines. This is what happened in the case of many products like ball-point pens, transistors, radios, etc. Throughout the cycle, changes take place in price and promotional elasticity of demand as also in the production and distribution costs of the product. Pricing policy, therefore, must be adjusted over the various phases of the cycle.

The following table 11.1 shows the Product Life Cycle and its different stages and the various characteristics which they reflect in the varying stages:

Table 11.1

PLC Elements	Introduction	Growth	Maturity	Decline
Characteristics				
Sales	Low	Fast growth	Slow growth	Declining
Profits	Negligible	Peak level	Declining	Low
Cash inflow	Negative	Moderate	High	Low
Competitors	Few	Growing	Many	Declining
Customers	Innovative	Mass market	Mass market	Laggards

Source: Peter Doyle, "The Realities of the Product Life Cycle", *Quarterly Review Marketing*, Summer 1976.

Strategic Considerations in the PLC Concept

Competition

At the introductory stage, competition is given no importance. At the growth stage, it is given a little importance while at the maturity stage, there are many rivals in the market. Slowly, however, the number of competitors or rivals gets reduced with the declining stage.

Overall strategic focus

At the first stage, emphasis is laid on market establishment. At the growth stage, market penetration and persuasion of mass market are emphasised. Creation of brand loyalty and brand preferences is focused at the maturity stage. At the decline stage, the strategy aims at overall preparation for renewal.

Profit

At the introductory stage, profits are negligible but at the growth stage, they reach the peak levels as a result of growing demand. At the maturity stage, they decline due to the increasing competition. At the last stage, the declining volume pushes costs up and eliminates profits.

Distribution strategies

At the introductory stage, distribution is selective. However, at the growth and maturity stages, it is intensive. At the decline stage, it becomes selective and hence low-end strategies are used.

Advertising strategies

At the introduction stage, advertising strategies aim at the needs of early adopters; at the growth stage, an attempt is made to make the mass market aware of brand benefits. At maturity stage, advertising is used as a vehicle for differentiating among otherwise similar brands. At the last stage, however it emphasises, on low price of the product and minimum advertising expenditure.

MARKETING STRATEGIES IN PLC

Product life cycle concentrate only on the life cycle of a product beginning with its introduction into the market to the post-marketing phase. However, a series of processes are to be undertaken by the management even prior to the introduction of a product in the market. These processes include exploration, screening, analysis, development, testing, etc. The concept of product life cycle may be used as a managerial tool.

Marketing strategies, however, have to be changed with changes in the phase of the life cycle of a product. An understanding of the cycle is helpful to the managers for a rational understanding of the future sales activities as also planning of marketing strategies. Hence, PLC is synonymous with the pattern of demand for a product over time.

The length of time that a product spends at any one stage varies from product to product. A product might not pass through every stage in the cycle. Some products, for instance, might not get pass the introductory stage, while others might not get pass the growth or even the maturity stage. There might be still other products that might pass through the introduction to maturity stages but might take longer period to reach the saturation stage and hence might take a longer period to reach the decline in an amazingly short period. In certain cases, there might even be a repositioning of a product, which might trigger off a new growth cycle. Repositioning involves changing basically the image.

Table 11.2: PLC: Marketing Implications and Strategies

Effects and Responses	Introduction	Growth	Maturity	Decline
Characteristics of the stage				
Consumers	Innovators	Early adopters	Middle Majority	Laggards
Competitors	Few, hence less important	Growing in numbers, and followers	Stable, intense competition	Declining, shakeout
Sales	Low sales	Sales will be growing rapidly	Stagnating sales	Declining sales
Costs	High cost per consumer	Cost starts declining	Low cost due to higher volume	Low cost per consumer

Marketing Objectives				
	Establishment in the market: Creating product awareness and trial	Market penetration: Increasing market share	Defined the market shares, brands	Cost cutting, Milking the products
Marketing Strategies				
Product	Basic product offering	Augmenting products	Diversification of brands and models	Divesting weak products
Distribution	Building distribution selectively	Intensive distribution	Retention of higher shelf space	Unprofitable ones are phased out
Price	High, cost plus to recover the cost of introduction	Price to penetrate the market	What consumers can bear and best competitors are offering	Low price
Advertising	Building awareness especially targeted innovators and distribution channels	Mass communication	Stress on brand differences	Reduced just to retain loyal consumers
Sales Promotion	High to increase trials	Moderate	High to build loyal consumers	Low

Source: Kotler P., *Marketing Management*, Wind Y.J., *Product Policy.*

STRATEGIES FOR LIFE CYCLE STAGES

Introduction

This stage starts when the product is launched. The characteristics of this stage are:

- Sales are low.
- High distribution and promotion expenses.
- Profits are negative or low.
- Since it is too early for refinements, basic versions of the product are sold.
- Focus of marketing is on those buyers who are the readiest to buy.
- Better quality/features and superior performance of the basic product helps.

Based on these characteristics, a company may use an appropriate marketing strategy commensurate with the company objectives and resources.

Introduction Strategies

At this stage, since the product is new, all competitors will be focussing on building the distribution network and product awareness. The success in the market would revolve around pricing and promotions. The options could be as follows:

(a) **High Price-Low Promotion Spending.** This strategy will yield high profit per unit and also keep the marketing costs down. It is likely to succeed when:

- Competition is limited.
- Market size is limited.
- Product awareness already exists.
- Customers are willing to pay a high price.

(b) **Low Price-Heavy Promotion Spending.** This will help in concerning a bigger market share and faster market penetration. The conditions under which it is likely to succeed are:

- Large market.
- Price sensitive buyers.
- Product unawareness.
- Strong competition.
- Economy of sale in production-low unit manufacturing costs (Hyundai's **SONATA** is a new entrant in India).

Growth Stage

This stage is most rewarding if the introduced product has been considered to be satisfactory by the market. *Characteristics* of this stage are:

- Sales climb rapidly.
- Market increase in profits.
- Increase in competition.
- New market segments are opened.

Growth Strategies

As the sales and profit rapidly as compared to the introduction stage, companies use varying strategies in the growth stage. Some typical strategies are:

- Lured by high sales and the correspondingly high profits, competition enters the market. Therefore, *improving and/or adding features* will expand the market for a company.
- Because of the high volume of business and increase in competition, price should not be raised. On the other hand, strategic *lowering of prices* should be resorted to attract more buyers.
- *Increased* emphasis on *promotions* will play a very important role in educating the market as well as in meeting the challenges of the competition.
- *Distribution* channel would need to be *strengthened* and new channels opened to handle additional volumes and new markets.
- In advertising, some emphasis would shift from product awareness to **product conviction.**
- **General strategy** would be prepared and face a **trade off** between high profits and high market share. As mentioned above, increased investment on product improvement, promotion and distribution may lower the current profits but the company can make it up in the next stage.

  (**TROPICANA** Orange Juice and Hyundai's **ACCENT** are growing rapidly.)

Maturity Stage

In this stage, though the sales growth slows down, the stage in itself continues for a long period. Therefore, it poses a strong challenge to marketing managers.

The characters of this stage are:

- *Slowdown* in sales growth
- Increased *capacities* (Inventories)
- Competition brings the *prices down*
- *Profits drop.*

Maturity Strategies

Because of the intense competition and falling profits, not all companies can survive this stage. Thus, a number of proactive steps are needed to stay profitable. Some of the strategies are:

(a) Market Modification

In order to increase the consumption, the companies look for:

- New *Users*
- New Market *Segments*
- Increased *usage* among present customers.

(PEPSI is bombarding India with "Yeh Dil Maange More".)

(b) Production Modification

In order to increase consumption and to attract more users, a company may attempt *product* characteristic *improvements* such as:

- Quality
- Features
- Styles

(**Maruti** introducing MPFI for "800", Esteem gets Power Steering.)

(c) Marketing Mix

Value-for-money concepts, Contests, Prizes, etc. (Frequent Flier Programme of Jet Airways).

Decline Stage

There are sayings like "Nothing lasts forever" or "All good things must come to an end". The sale of any product eventually dips. They may plunge to zero or continue at a very low level for some years. This indicates the stage of decline.

The ***characteristics*** of this stage are:

- Declining sales
- Very low or no profits
- Reduced competition due to low volumes and margins
- Few customers (Laggards).

Strategies for 'Decline' Stage

A company may have a number of products introduced simultaneously but the extent of decline may not be the same for all products. Companies should therefore identify and pay more attention to **aging products** because the strategy for each product would depend upon its **health.**

The health can be gauged by reviewing the sales, market shares and extent of profits. Based on these observations, a company can follow the following strategies:

(i) **Maintain.** Hoping that with passage of time, the competition will drop out and the product will continue to sell a company may decide to continue with the product.

(Modi Xerox, Global and Network dropped the **FAX** machines but **Panasonic** didn't. They continue to sell in India.)

(ii) **Harvest.** This strategy is aimed at reducing the costs (Production, maintenance, advertising, sales force, etc.) and hoping that the product sales will be profitable for some time to come.

(**Hindustan Motors** continue to produce **Ambassador**.)

(iii) **Drop.** This is the end of the line for a particular product. However, it may be sold other company if there is a corporate buyer.

(**Carona** dropped **Puma** shoes.)

QUESTIONS FOR DISCUSSION

1. What are the reasons for Hyundai's success? What is the product life cycle stage of SANTRO in your opinion?
2. Name the 3 best product life cycle strategiest in India.
3. Name some products that have stayed in the maturity stage for a long time.
4. Briefly describe each of the four distinct stages of the product life cycle by taking an example each from consumer and industrial products you are familiar with.
5. "Marketers should view product life cycle as an indication of opportunities to a firm." Discuss in the light of product planning and business strategy of the firm.

CASE STUDY 11.1

ROTOMATIC ELECTRONICS

Rotomatic Electronics was small company with product lines in accessories for medium to large computers. The company specialised in the manufacture and sale of magnetic disc drives. The product being a complex one required extensive electric controls. As the product required high quality control, it has a high unit cost and was manufactured to meet customer satisfaction.

Rotomatic's business in the computer industry was highly competitive. Many larger companies manufactured their own magnetic disc drives and there were also quite a large number of small manufactures who had entered the field recently. Rotomatic's disc drives offered large capacity and high speed and could interface with any existing computers. The company could expand its operations due to attractive features and flexibility.

However, as the company was not occupying leadership position in the market, had to constantly come up with innovations to increase sales. In order to attain more corporate ability the management decided to diversify into new product areas. They asked the R&D department to design the single board efficient computer. As a result of six months hard work, the R&D department gave the prototype.

QUESTIONS FOR DISCUSSION

1. What are the issue in the present case?
2. You are requested to suggest alternatives to reach the customers. Also suggest the ways and means of positioning the new product in a highly competitive market.

CASE STUDY 11.2

A COMPARATIVE BRANDING STRATEGY

A. THE PEPSI CO.

Pepsi Co. Inc. was founded in the year 1965. Major products of the new company are Pepsi Cola, Diet Pepsi and Mountain Dew. Pepsi entered the Indian market in 1992 and now is the market leader with a market share of 27 per cent in the cola segment. Pepsi is in between the two of its closed competitors as far as marketing strategies are concerned. Pepsi is an international drink with Indian imagery in its communication. Traditional focus of Pepsi has been on the early teenager with a gender skew more to the females. Pepsi is by far the more aggressive player in the market with its continuous advertising. Event marketing, targeting the new generation and eye-catching merchandising. It is got its selling strategy well mapped out.

The company has always been innovating its ad campaigns which has helped the company to get top of the mind recall. From "The choice of the new generation to the Freedom" campaign, the company has been able to Indianise the brand. With the help of promotional schemes, Pepsi has managed to keep the brand alive and has not let it become old. During 1996, the total ad spend by the company was Rs. 6.98 crores only on television. Pepsi spent Rs. 8 crores for its advertising programme in the run-up to and during the cricket world cup.

On 2 April 1996, Pepsi announced that the second most popular drink in the world would henceforth come in Blue packaging. Pepsi had spent $500 million to relaunch its products. But the results of this exercise are still awaited, and it is expected they would not be as good as expected by the company.

According to the President of Pepsi Co., much of the ammunition that the two companies lob at each other in the cola was its "damn stuff" and the CEO Coca-Cola claiming that "the cola war is over", but the cola war continues.

B. THE COCA-COLA COMPANY

The product that has given the world its best known taste was born in Atlanta. Georgia on 8th May 1886. Coca plant and Kola nut being the main ingredients of the drink. Initially the drink was positioned as a medicine to cure headache and depression.

Coca-Cola's success came from advertising, which made it an emblem of good things in America. The theme of all the ads for the drink have remained more or less constant since the early days, that is, "Drink Coca-Cola, Delicious and Refreshing" to "Always the Real Thing". Coca-Cola is now available in 198 countries which is more than the UN membership, the turnover of the company being $18 billion which is less than Pepsi Co's turnover. The reason being that Pepsi Co. has diversified into fast food and snacks business as well, but Coca-Cola is much more focused on its core area of business. The market value of the company is 8 times greater than that of Pepsi.

After leaving India in the year 1977, Coca-Cola relaunched its drink in the subcontinent in 1993 by taking over the Rs. 150 crores Parle Company. The company took over all the brands of Parle including Thums-Up.

Coca-Cola has been a subdued player with sub-standard marketing and expenditure being another hurdle. There has been a drop in sales of all the brands of the Coca-Cola Company. This could be because of Coca-Cola's neglect of its Indian brands especially Thums-Up which was the strongest player in the Indian market. Out of the total expenditure of Rs. 27 crores, 81 per cent was spent on Coca-Cola and only 9 per cent was spent on Thums-Up. Now Coca-Cola has earmarked Rs. 40 crores to promote its products.

The move by the company to acquire an equity stake in its 53 bottlers has backfired, with the bottles retaliating strongly. The company is channelising $700 million in expanding bottling capacities to create an integrated bottling system.

Coca-Cola was the first in the country to launch cans, plastic cap leak proof bottles and also full-length delivery crates.

Coca-Cola has also diffused its strategy between its own and the acquired brands. All the bottles of Coke are franchisees as compared to Pepsi's, whose half the bottlers are self-owned.

Coca-Cola was airing Creative Artists agency ads till 1995, which were looked on with interest by the young urban consumer but the older lot seemed dazed. In February 1995, the advertising changed with Sushmita Sen as the model. And at the end of it no one seemed to be sure of what Coke really wanted to say to do. It has not said anything about being the real thing that is the positioning it wants to adopt, whereas the competitors like Pepsi are very clear about their positioning as the choice of the new generation.

Coke has been an erratic markcter, the print campaigns are more often than product launch announcements and promises, and when they happen, are too poorly publicised.

Today the company is in a peculiar situation with competing brands in its portfolio. The company has now decided that applying international strategies will not work here: one has to localise its venture like Pepsi has done. The company must beef up the existing brands or do away with them. Coke has been the longest surviving sponsor of the Olympics.

QUESTIONS FOR DISCUSSION

1. How should Coke position itself to take on Pepsi in this Battle of the Giants?
2. How would you differentiate Coke's promotional strategy from that of Pepsi?
3. List the attributes that you consider relevant to this product class. Even though most attributes in the products are the same, suggest an attribute that can be considered a USP or can be used to differentiate among the brands.

CASE STUDY 11.3

MDH-THE SPICE OF LIFE

Introduction. India is recognised all over the World as the 'SPICE KING', a land with innumerable food tastes and an exotic range of food preparations. The blend of various spices has been a traditional secret transferred from generation to generation.

Mahashian Di Hatti (MDH) began in the year 1999, with a humble beginning as a spice manufacturer and trader. Through these glorious eight decades, MDH has witnessed a growth, which is both phenomenal and remarkable. MDH has not only pioneered the marketing of powdered spices in handy attractive consumer packs, but has also established itself as the leader in its own right as a trust-worthy processor of pure and high quality mixed blended spices and condiments.

Keeping in pace with the modern times, MDH has constantly been updating and modernising its units, by evolving blended spices, condiments and powders for preparation of popular and exclusive dishes which India is famous for.

MDH stands a class apart, being India's leading manufacturer of blended spices, through fully automated plants located at New Delhi, Haryana and Rajasthan. MDH has always believed that quality comes first before anything else. MDH spices are unique. MDH maintains its consistency in procurement and blending of spices. The blends are processed from the very best and fresh spices, which are ensured by a series of sampling, quality tests and controls at its highly equipped research and development centres.

Because of commitment to quality, MDH has the distinction of being co-opted as a member of various committees of Bureau of Indian Standards, which is a nodal agency responsible for formulating specifications and approval for Indian spices and their blends within and outside India.

The demand for MDH spices is increasing rapidly in the Export horizon. Apart from the million of Indian families abroad even foreigners, who are always health conscious, have reposed their faith in MDH spices. Thus its Export performance has risen tremendously.

The philosophy of Mahashay Dharampalji, founder and establisher of MDH—"Give to the World the best you can, and the best will automatically come back to you," has virtually been a proverbial come true by the fact that today MDH is a name that stands synonymous, not only for quality spices but also for its vast contribution towards the welfare of society and upliftment of the needy, by way of establishing educational institutes, hospitals and trusts. MDH today stands as a name in every household, trusted and realished all over the World by millions.

Historical Background. The force that has been moving the wheels of MDH was created on 27th of March, 1919 at Sialkot, by 'Mahashay Dharampalji' popularly known as Shahji.

As a young aspiring man, Mahashay Dharampalji began his career, working in a cloth shop. The next was at hardware shop, and lastly at a rice mill where he gained knowledge of procurement and sorting. A visit with his father, Mahashay Chunnilal, to Kashmir added on to his quest for business and trade.

Mahashay Dharampalji's venture as a grocery shop along with his elder brother Mahashay Dharamvir was unsuccessful. His father's masala shop, which his uncle and elder brother used to run, was also not to Mahashay Dharampalji level of interest and he thus went over to his father's godown where spices (masala) were sorted and ground. At the godown, Mahashay Dharampalji was vested with in-depth knowledge about procurement, sorting and grinding of various spices. He took special interest in grinding Haldi and Mirch Power.

Innovation had always been the key line of Mahashay Dharampalji, who made small packets of MDH Henna (Mehandi) powder by the name of 'Rang Rangoli' and sold them on wheel-carts in the streets and lanes of Sialkot. The response was excellent and the next product to be introduced was 'Deggi Mirch'. Mahashian Di Hatti became a family name in those days.

Mahashay Dharampalji soon joined the political world. During pre-Independence days, he was arrested and sent to prison for his contribution towards India's Independence. He was soon released and on August 15, 1947 when India was declared Independent, the entire family of MDH shifted over to India. Starting with a meagre Rs. 1,500 in those days, Mahashay Dharampalji bought a 'Tonga', and put it to use for carrying passengers for 2 annas (12 paise) each.

With the savings, he bought a shop at Karol Bagh, Ajmal Khan Road, measuring 14′ × 9′ × 8′ and started Mahashian Di Hatti again.

FAMILIARITY WITH BRAND

MDH	=	90%
EVEREST	=	6%
NANZ	=	4%
BADSHAH	=	20%

PRODUCT DEVELOPMENT STRATEGY

The main attention is on quality improvement.

SEGMENTATION. Segmentation on the basic of habit of consumers.

Example: Eastern people prefer Mirch in food.
Rajasthani people also prefer Mirch in their food.
Southern population prefers Kali Mirch Sambar Masala.
Foreigners prefer Chicken Masala.

DISTRIBUTION — No direct marketing.

DISTRIBUTION CHANNEL — Super Stockist
↓
Distributors
↓
(Ready Stock) — Retail outlets
↓
Consumers

PRICING: High price strategy with high quality product. There is no difference in price level for Urban and Rural people. Price is same for both.

Export: U.S.A., U.K., Germany, Canada, etc.

BRANDS: More than 70 brands.

OTHER PRODUCTS: Agarbatti, Hawan Samagri (used in Pooja).

PRODUCT DIMENSION:

1. Products are designed to meet consumer needs.
2. Are different from those of the competitors.
3. Are market leaders.
4. Offer good value for money.

MARKETING DIMENSIONS:
1. Successful product launches.
2. Brand extension
3. Good relations with retailers/consumers.
4. Extensive and attractive advertisements.

PACKAGING: Pouch, Attractive Box/Packet, Polythene packing for Agarbattis

PRODUCT PROFILE: Most demanded products in the market.

1.	MDH Chilli Powder (Deggi)	=	Rs. 86 (per packet)
2.	MDH Chilli Powder (Kashmiri)	=	Rs. 18 (per packet)
3.	MDH Kitchen King	=	Rs. 115 (per packet)
4.	MDH Pavbhaji Masala	=	Rs. 23 (per packet)
5.	MDH Kali Mirch Powder	=	Rs. 52 (per packet)
6.	MDH White Pepper Powder	=	Rs. 75 (per packet)
7.	MDH Dhania Powder	=	Rs. 54 (per packet)
8.	MDH Haldi Powder	=	Rs. 39 (per packet)
9.	MDH Hawan Samagri	=	Rs. 14 (per packet) & Rs. 32 (per packet)
10.	MDH Chandan Agarbatti	=	Rs. 10 (per packet)

QUESTIONS FOR DISCUSSION

1. What are the main factors associated with the tremendous success of MDH (Pvt.) Ltd.?
2. If you are the marketing manager, how would you introduce a new product?
3. MDH has same price level for Urban and Rural population. Is it harmful for the market extension of MDH (Pvt.) Ltd.?

CASE STUDY 11.4

HERO HONDA MOTORS LIMITED

vs.

ESCORTS YAMAHA LIMITED

The major cycle segment is currently dominated by Hero Honda, which is the number one selling brand in this segment with a market share of 43 per cent. Hero Honda was established in Delhi. It was a 26:26 joint venture between Hero group, already into bicycles and mopeds, and Japan's Honda Motor Co. by 1985, the company was selling every third bike in India.

The selling proposition of the bike became its fuel efficiency and the company was able to expand its market dramatically. Technicians at the plant have been adapting Hero Honda CD 100 to Indian roads. The company claimed that the bike can deliver 80 km. To a litre—almost twice what a scooter was known to give. Launch ads flaunted this and Honda's global reputation as a mobike maker. In 1985-86, the ad agency of the company came up with a catchy slogan "Fill it, Shut it, forget it."

The product was sold only through exclusive dealers who got the right to do so after promising to adhere to Hero Honda Motor Ltd's, guidelines. Distribution is a bug area of strength for the company, with the network now expanded to semi-urban and rural areas. Today over 270 of its 430 dealers serve this part of the market.

By this time it had two other competitors—Yamaha RX 100 from Escorts and Kawasaki Bajaj RTZ from Bajaj Auto along with Ind-Suzuki from TVS. Both Yamaha and Kawasaki had two stroke engines, which meant more petrol but performed better in terms of speed, acceleration and were better given to rough handling. A new ad campaign was aired featuring youngsters testifying to CD 100's secondary benefits: low pollution and relatively less maintenance costs, the ad line being: "You have got the good thing going". This effort paid off and Hero Honda retained its number one slot in the year 1988-89 by recording a sales of over 74,000 units in the last three quarters of the financial year. Since the style segment was growing rapidly and the market was evolving to a higher level of sophistication, the company decided to widen its range of offerings. Finally, in 1989, the company introduced Hero Honda Sleek. It was advertised on lifestyle and attempted to talk in the language of youth. "What's life without a little passion?" asked the print ad. Next on the company's agenda was to attack the rural and small town markets. In 1991, Hero Honda CD 100 SS was introduced. Some fundamental design changes were done to make it more suitable for the roads in rural India. The company searched for the possibility of marketing a superior 100-cc four-stroke mobike. As a result Hero Honda Splendor launched in 1994.

With the selling proposition of fuel efficiency deeply sunk in the mind of the target customers, the company is planning to launch another model in the coming year.

Today the company is a Rs. 641 crores company. It has four 100-cc models, styled differentially but all united by the eco-friendliness of the original engine. All these bikes have served the needs of the Indian consumer beautifully so far. The company has invested Rs. 55 crores in its expansion, all from internal accruals and expects to sell one million vehicles by the year 2005.

Escorts Yamaha Motors Limited

Escorts Yamaha Motor Ltd. is a joint venture between Escorts Ltd. and Yamaha Motor Company of Japan. In 1986, the production of Yamaha RX 100 started. The main competitor of the mobike was Hero Honda CD 100 and Kawasaki Bajaj KB 100. Yamaha had a two-stroke engine, which meant that it took more petrol, but performed better on speed, acceleration and was better given for rough handling. RX 100 struck an aggressive power stance and decided to show up the down side of a four-stroke engine by repositioning CD 100 as a delicate machine. The ads talked about "how long will fuel last, think about how long the bike will last". The market was about to bifurcate into economy and power segment. Their ads have used various catchy slogans, viz., "Listen to the heart-beat of Yamaha". 'Born to lead', etc.

Today the market share of Yamaha is 17 per cent, which is only third to Hero Honda's share. The company has commenced production of a new generation of eco-friendly bikes that conform to stringent global emission standards, making them attractive to both the domestic and international markets. These measures were taken due to the imposition of the Government's new laws on emission and two strokes in particular. Yamaha RXG, a 135-cc mobike, was introduced to combat the new emission laws while not losing out on any inherent strong qualities of its predecessor.

Both partners have signed agreement for a Rs. 525 crore expansion plan introducing new vehicles. In the next 2-3 years, the new products offered will include 4-stroke mobike, scooters and mopeds. Escorts expect to produce 7 lakh bike wheelers by the year 2005.

In the years to come, Escorts will have to complete even harder to sustain its current market position as it is now facing a tough competition from Bajaj Auto who have recently launched a 125-cc model. To become a market leader, the company will have to displace TVS Suzuki, which has a 23 per cent market share and them aim at Hero Honda.

All the companies in this sector are gearing up to face the challenge in the years to come. This sector has and will see a lot new players enter the market.

QUESTIONS FOR DISCUSSION

1. Chalk out a growth plan for Bajaj Auto who have decided to expand and capture the market.
2. Suggest newer markets that can be entered into by the players in the motorcycle segment so as to strengthen their foothold in the market.

PACKAGING AND SUPPORT SERVICES

12

INTRODUCTION

Packaging can be defined as an art, science and technology of preparing goods for transport and sale. Packaging as an industry has two sectors—those who make packaging material and those who convert these materials into packages. New packaging materials are fast replacing the old ones. Good packaging covers an idea of the quality of the product; it has a value which is distinct from the value of the product. Attractive packaging is an effective point of purchase (POP), and stimulate as publicity for sales. We can also say that packaging is an important advertising medium, carrying messages from the marketer to the consumer. Packaging as a function has two separate dimensions—the physical aspects related to the science and technology and the behavioural aspect related to the art of product design associated with buyer behaviour and motivational research.

Packaging may be 'primary' which refers to the product's immediate container, such as the can or a box; or secondary, which refers to additional layers of protection that are removed once the product is ready for the such as the tube of toothpaste, which covers in a card board box.

Importance of Packaging

Packaging was considered a production related function and activity. Today, however, marketing significance of packaging is fully changed due to competitive strategies by various companies. New developments in packaging, occurring rapidly and in a seemingly endless flow, required Marketing Manager's constant attention to packaging design. The following points give us idea for significance of packaging in Marketing:

- Information about the product
- Identify brand name
- Protecting the product
- Helping in product handling
- Promoting the product
- Offering customer convenience and satisfaction.

PACKAGING CONCEPT

Packages have now come to be defined as the fifth 'P' of marketing. It gives an enhanced value to the product. These are three levels of material for package:

A – A primary package

B – A secondary package

C – The transportation package

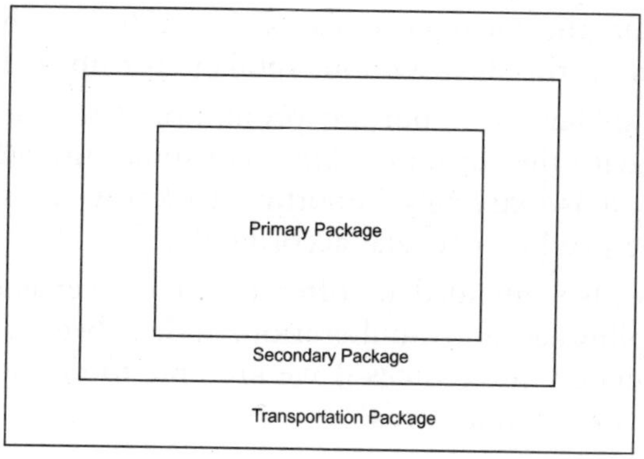

The different levels of packaging, type and importance would vary with the type of product, whether FMCG, durable, industrial and liquid product. It would also vary with the distance over which it has to be transported. Packaging should be regarded as a basic essential requirement for a manufactured product and not arising incidentally in the course of transportation and marketing. All that goes into the quality control of a product during manufacturer will become meaningless unless the package is designed to carry on the good work in the long and unpredictable journey from the factory to the ultimate consumer.

PACKAGING DECISIONS

Packaging is an important tool for 'face-lifting' of a product. Packaging in India is emerging from dark ages. Indian marketers did not first realise its importance. But now they have begun to give it a prime place in their marketing plans. An attractive pack is the most important factor in impulse purchases. The basic functions of a pack are to attract the potential customer's attention, protect the product that is packed and reveal its identity. Packaging is an important tool for two important categories of people—first, end-users of a product; and second, retailers. The following materials are generally used for packaging:

(a) Wood (b) Metals

(c) Plastics (d) Paper

(e) Glass (f) Polyster

Role of Packaging

Packaging is an important element in the formulation of the marketing plan for a product. With the advent of self-service stores and supermarkets, the package of a product has to perform the function of a silent salesman, in addition to its traditional function of protecting the product. When there is no salesman to promote the product in the stores, the package as kept on the shelf must be able to capture the fancy of the buyers. Good packaging may lead to improved consumer acceptance.

Some examples may make the point clear. An Indian blade manufacturer has achieved a breakthrough in export to Australia just by redesigning its packaging to suit the local market for blades. Indian shirts do not sell well in Europe because of the poor quality of their packaging and presentation. Hormel and General Foods of America have adopted packaging processes that pressure, seal and steam the meal in a plastic container so that the food requires no refrigeration and can remain on the shelf without spoilage for up to 18 months.

Thus the product package has an important promotional function. In fact, it established meaningful communication with the consumer. Since consumer preferences and attitudes differ widely in different markets, it is extremely important to know the special attributes of each target market and design the product package accordingly.

Consumer packaging is also intended to offer better convenience to the consumer and protect the product from pilferage and adulteration. It has been estimated that unit value realisation can rise approximately three times if we are able to develop and bring about retail packs for a large number of exportable items.

Role of Packaging

1. It helps increase sales.
2. It adds to the use of a product.
3. It helps promote a product.
4. It contributes to the safety of a product.
5. It helps in storage.
6. It helps in product differentiation.

Earlier, packaging was considered a major expense in marketing. For some toiletries, packaging costs actually exceeded the costs of contents. Today, it is, however, fully recognised that packaging helps in branding and promoting brand loyalty. It also enables the buyers to handle and carry their products with ease. Moreover, packaging may cut marketing costs thus adding to profit.

Packaging Decision

1. ***Packaging design.*** It is not easy to design a package for various items. For example, all shaving creams come in tubes, but different brands of shaving cream have different packaging. Because of the high cost of packaging some companies have resorted to refill packs.
2. ***Colour.*** Colour is an important factor for determining customer acceptance or rejection of a product. The use of right colours in packaging may help marketers reap huge advantage. Packaging colour should be attractive so that it may help promote sales.
3. ***Packaging the Product Line.*** A company must decide whether to develop a family resemblance in the packaging of its several products. Family packaging involves the use of identical packages for all products or the use of packages with some common feature.

Functions of Packaging

Packaging should perform the following basic functions:

1. Protection

The primary function is to protect the products from the environmental and physical hazards to which the product can be exposed to, in transit from the manufacturer's plant to the retailer's shelves and while on display on the shelves.

The following are specific functions, which provides protection to products:

- Pilferage during transit or storage.
- Absorption of moisture.
- Breakage/damage due to rough mechanical or manual handling during transportation.
- Loss of liquid or vapour.

2. Appeal

The importance is substantially due to the changed structure of retail business, especially the emergence of self-service stores. The following characteristics have been identified to help a package perform the self-selling tasks:

- It helps in attract attention.
- It helps in tell the product story.
- It helps in build confidence.
- It helps in look clean and hygienic.

3. Performance

This is the third function of a package. It must be able to perform the task for which it is designed. This aspect becomes crucial in certain types of packaging. For example, Maggi Ketchup which was introduced in the market in 400 grams Bottle, while the industry-wise standard size is 500 grams bottle.

4. Packaging for Convenience

It provides convenience to distribution channel members, such as wholesalers and retailers. The convenience will relate to handling and stocking of packages. It helps in the following ways:

- The package must be convenient to stock.
- The package must be convenient to display.
- The package does not waste shelf-space.

5. Cost-effectiveness

The package finally must be cost-effective. Packaging cost as a percentage of product cost varies dramatically from one industry to another. It is important to appreciate that while analysing packaging costs, it is not enough to consider only the cost of package. The following costs are considered in element of the total costs associated with packaging:

- Handling cost
- Storage cost

- Transport cost
- Insurance cost for the transit period.

Strategies for Packaging

1. **Multiple Packaging Strategy.** For many years these has been a trend toward multiple packaging or the practice of placing several units in one container.
2. **Reuse Packaging Strategy.** It is considered as re-use packaging. The company should design and promote a package that can serve other purposes after the original contents have been consumed. Re-use packaging also should stimulate repeat purchases as the consumer attempts to acquire a watching set of containers.
3. **Changing the Package Strategy.** A firm must take advantage of new materials from time to time. A new package may be used as a major appeal in advertising copy or because the old container may not show up well in advertisements.
4. **Cost-effectiveness Strategy.** Packaging is essential for a product, it should not become an unnecessary evil. It is important to study and compare the costs involved in packaging against benefits generated additionally.

Attributes or Requisites of a Good Package

A well-designed and attractive package is 'shelf-salesman' for the retailer, for the package design itself works as a brand. Package must have informative labeling. The headlines, illustrations, guidelines and selling points on the package must be clear and prominent so that the matter is readable by every shopper at a glance. Visibility of the product in the package must be clear and prominent so that the matter is readable by every shopper at a glance. Visibility of the product in the package helps to sell the product better, Hence, glass, celophane and plastic packages have become very popular these days.

Packages to be effective to are made with great caution and design. It must possess the following qualities:

(i) It must attract attention.
(ii) It must tell the product story—What is it? What size? How much?
(iii) It must build confidence.
(iv) It must look clean and sanitary.
(v) It must be convenient to handle, to carry out of the store and to use.
(vi) It must look like good value.
(vii) It must look like a fast seller.
(viii) It must deserve a preferred display.
(ix) It must minimise the clerk's time.
(x) It must be convenient to stock and display.
(xi) It must prevent spoilage during the selling period.
(xii) It must resist soiling.

Type of Packages

There are four types of packages: (i) a consumer package; (ii) a bulk package; (iii) an industrial package; and (iv) a dual usage package, and are discussed hereunder:

(i) *A consumer package* is one which holds the required volume of a product for ultimate consumption and is within the means of a buying household. In other words, the consumer has the option to purchase the pack size which he considers adequate for the consumption of his family over a length of time and which does not involve extra investment during that period.

(ii) *A bulk package* is its opposite. It is either for the industrial consumer's use, e.g. steel drums for paint; or for loose dispensing, e.g. 4 gallon or 18 litre kerosene can, as sack of rice, etc. The consumer package itself very often requires an outside package in which it is transported and which is sometimes referred to a transit package or an out container.

(iii) *An industrial package* can either describe a bulk package or the package for durable consumer goods. These are the basic package types although many subdivisions can be listed, e.g. strip package, multiple package, etc. which can all be broadly listed under these basic headings.

(iv) *A dual usage package* is one which has a secondary usefulness after its contents have been consumed. Drinking glasses, boxes of jewellery or cigarettes, waste baskets, refrigerator dishes, cloth from flour and feed sacks are the examples.

Evaluating a Package's Effectiveness

The package is the producer's last chance to communicate the product's message to the consumer. After all the advertising and public relations work has been done, the package must frequently stand on its own in face-to-face confrontation with customers in the market place. Positive answers to all the questions below will help to ensure a successful package:

- Does the package tell consumers what they want and need to know?
- Does it instantly identify the type of product the package contains, i.e. does it reflect quality?
- Is the package distinctive?
- Does its size make it compatible with similar products?
- Is it adaptable to other products? Does it suit the product?
- Is it acceptable to the trade? Will it stack?
- Will it last? Is it tamper proof?
- Does it attract attention from a reasonable distance?
- Does it tell the consumer how to use the product or suggest new ways of using it?
- Does it set the consumer's appetite for product?
- Is it easy to open?
- Does it protect the product?
- Is there a prominent spot for the price?
- Are the brand, symbol, and name easy to see?

LABELLING

Labelling means putting identification marks on the package. Label consists of verbal information that accompanies the product. A label identifies: Who made the product? Dates of manufacturer and expiry; the price to be charged; brand name, net quantity of contents (weight, measure, numerical count, etc.). Some labels consist of tags attached to the product or package, as in the case of most clothing or hosiery articles. Others are imprinted on the product itself. Labels are part of the printed material on the package. The label is a strong sales tool and an integral part of the point of purchase advertising.

Although some products may be adequately identified by giving the name of the product and the producer, most require a somewhat more extensive description of their nature and use. For example, processed foods, patent drugs, some cosmetics, textiles, and other goods are required by law to carry a fairly complete idea about their ingredients. Many products also must furnish instructions for their use, as in the case of commercial plant food. Safety warnings are also necessary on labels of all potentially hazardous products or packages. If a substance is poisonous, the label must tell the user what steps to take if any is ingested and must list the antidotes. For example, there is often a warning on medicines "To be used under the direction of a medical practitioner".

New Dimension of Labels

Environmental awareness among the consumers is increasing at a faster rate because of which they prefer environment friendly products. In many countries 'eco-label' is awarded on the basis of a product's environment friendliness. It is hoped that *green marketing* would become a world-wide phenomenon in the 21st century. A label must fulfil all legal requirements. In fact, properly conceived, a good label can be an important sales instrument. Since a label is the nearest source of information on product, for a buyer who otherwise may be ignorant of the product or loyal to a different brand. The consumer can be persuaded to read the label, and he may in fact try the product even if he had no such premeditation. This is especially true of purchases made in super markets and departmental stores, where self-service is the rule.

A good label is one which helps a potential buyer to make his decision by providing relevant and correct information. Apart from the information which must be statutorily given, the label should provide:

(i) Picture of the product accurate as to size, colour and appearance.

(ii) Description of raw products used along with methods of processing.

(iii) Directions for use, including cautions against misuse.

(iv) Brand names.

(v) Dates of manufacture and expiry.

(vi) Statutory warning, if any.

(vii) Contra-indications and adverse effects, if any.

QUESTIONS FOR DISCUSSION

1. "Packaging is considered as the 5th P of Marketing Mix." What are its implications on the PLC? Discuss.

2. Discuss the importance of packaging as a tool for product differentiation and market cultivation.
3. Packaging has been criticises as being expensive, giving no additional value and often deceptive. How would you justify marketers use of packaging?
4. What is packaging concept? Explain various packaging decisions in brief.
5. What are the functions of packaging? Explain various packaging strategies.

STRATEGIC PRICING DECISIONS

13

INTRODUCTION

Price is the only element in the marketing mix of a firm that generates revenue. All else generate only cost. Price and sales volume together decide the revenue of any business. As sales volume in itself is dependent to a considerable extent on price, the latter becomes key to the revenue of the business. Price is also the most important determinant of the profitability of the business.

It is competition that contributes the maximum to the importance of pricing. For, if one does not need to meet competition, pricing decision can be handled in a comfortable manner. It is competition again that makes pricing a highly dynamic function.

Pricing acquires its importance on account of yet another factor. It is a highly risky decision area and mistakes in pricing seriously affect the firm, its profits, growth and future.

Price remain vague until all the details about it are spelt out. For instance, it is essential to know whether the price is ex-works, or f.o.b or f.o.r. destination, or at customers' doors. Similarly, it is essential to know whether the price is for cash purchase or credit, or installment purchase; whether it includes or excludes servicing; whether it is applicable for the trade or the consumer; whether it is applicable for a small quantity of purchase, or for a minimum prescribed bulk, and so on.

FACTORS INFLUENCING PRICING

Two sets of factors-internal and external-influence pricing decisions of any enterprise. In each, some factors may be economic and some psychological; again, some may be quantitative and yet others qualitative.

Internal Factors

In pricing a firm has certain objectives. For example, it seeks to recover its costs of manufacturing and marketing through the price. It also wants its pricing decisions to be consistent with its basic philosophy on pricing in case it has such a philosophy. Pricing also has to be consistent with the overall objectives of the firm. The firm may also seek a particular public image through its pricing policies. All these constitute the internal factors that influence pricing. Pricing strategy has also to fit the overall marketing strategy of the firm. In this sense, the firm's marketing strategy is another internal factor that influences pricing.

External Factors

In addition to the internal factors, any business firm has to encounter a set of external factors while formulating its pricing strategy. In the first place, the conditions of the economy have to be reckoned with. Second is the nature of competition. The bargaining power of customers and suppliers are the other important considerations. Sometimes, the government exercises controls over the price of certain products. All these constitute the external factors that influence the pricing decision.

PRICING OBJECTIVES

A business firm will have a number of objectives in the area of pricing. Usually, some of these will be long term while others will be short term. Also some will be primary objectives while others will be secondary. And all theses objectives emanate from the corporate and marketing objectives of the firm.

Profit is one of the major objectives of pricing. Firms usually adopt profit optimisation rather than profit maximisation as the objective, as they consider optimum profit over a long period to be a sounder objective than maximum profits in the shorter term. Obviously, 'optimum' is a relative term here and its definition will vary from firm to firm. The firm must evolve a clear idea of the optimum from its perception of business realities and the objectives and standards it has set for itself.

Different Permutations of Objectives Apply to Different Firms

Obviously, all the objectives of pricing mentioned above may not be relevant to all firms. For example, the last two objectives in the list are relevant only to providers of essential commodities and public utility services; as regards commercial firms, these considerations enter the pricing decisions only a subdued manner, their pricing cannot be principally based on such considerations. The other objectives too apply only selectively, different firms adopting different permutations.

PRICING METHODS/STRATEGIES

By pricing method, or strategy, we mean the route taken by the firm in fixing the price. Evidently, the method/strategy must be appropriate for achieving the desired pricing objectives.

There are several methods of pricing. Each of them may be appropriate for achieving a particular pricing objective, or a particular combinations of pricing objectives. For example, skimming pricing is suited for achieving the objective of short-term profit maximisation.

Broad Categories of Pricing Methods

Under each of the above categories, we can think of many different pricing methods. They will vary from one another in some respects, but as a category they share a common orientation. We will discuss the commonly used pricing methods under each of the categories.

Cost-based pricing

Under the cost-based category, the following approaches/methods are the commonly used ones:

- Mark-up pricing/Cost-plus pricing
- Absorption cost pricing (Full cost pricing)
- Target rate of return pricing
- Marginal Cost pricing.

While these methods vary form one another in some respects, all of them are based on costs.

Mark-up Pricing

Mark-up pricing refers to the pricing method in which the selling price of the product is fixed by adding a margin to its cost price. The mark-ups may vary depending on the nature of the product and the market. Usually, the higher the value of the product (unit cost of the product), the larger is the mark-up and *vice versa*. Again, the slower the turnaround of the product, the larger is the mark-up and *vice versa*.

Mark-up pricing proceeds on the assumption that demand cannot be known accurately, but costs are known. A reasonable mark-up is added to the costs. And the price as well as the mark-up is adjusted by trial and error. The objective is to maximise profits in the short and medium run without sales being scarified due to excessive price. Usually, distributive trade and marketing firms, who do not have any manufacturing of their own, prefer this pricing method.

Absorption Cost Pricing

Absorption cost pricing or full cost pricing rests on the estimated unit cost of the product at the normal level of production and sales. The method used standard costing techniques and works out the variable and fixed costs involved in manufacturing, selling and administering the product. By adding the costs of these three operations, we get the total cost. The selling price of the product is arrived at by adding the required margin towards profit to such total costs. This method is also known as full cost pricing since it envisages the realisation of full costs from each unit sold. The method has some merits and a number of limitations.

Merit and Demerits of Absorption Cost Pricing. The main merit of this method is that as long as the market can absorb the production at the determined price, the firm is assured of its profits without any risks whatsoever. Firms preferring safety in their pricing may follow this method.

On the demerits side, it must be mentioned first that the method does not take cognisance of the demand factors at all; it simply assumes price to be function of cost alone. In a competitive market, where demand for the firm's product at the determined price cannot be taken for granted, this method becomes ineffective. In fact, in a competitive market, if a firm swears by absorption cost pricing, it is most likely to lose a pat of its sales. *Second*, the method relies excessively on standard costing and normal level of production and sales. The calculations are upset if the actual production and sales fall short of the normal (assumed) level. *Third*, often variations occur in the cost of the inputs, between the time when the absorption costs were worked out and the time of actual production/sale of the product. So, frequent updating of the costs becomes necessary in this method, and this may not be practicable in all cases. *Fourth*, absorption cost pricing is not a dynamic method of pricing. In certain situations, it may be advantageous for the firm to compete in the market and attract additional sales at prices that are lower than the absorption cost prices. But when a firm sticks to the policy of absorption of all costs on each unit of sale, it loses the opportunity of trying other pricing alternatives and benefiting from them.

Target Rate of Return Pricing

Target rate of return pricing is similar to absorption cost pricing. In absorption cost pricing after the costs of manufacturing, selling and administration are absorbed on a per unit basis, the firm adds its mark-up towards profits. This mark-up is often decided on an arbitrary basis. Against this, the rate of return pricing uses a rational approach to arrive at the mark-up. It is arrived at in such a way that the return on investment criteria of the firm is met in the process.

Merits and Demerits of Rate of Return Pricing. The rate of return pricing too has its merits and limitations. It amounts to an improvement over absorption costs pricing since it uses a rational basis for arriving at the mark-up. *Second*, since the rate of return on the funds employed is a function of mark-up as well as turnaround of capital employed, rate of return pricing constantly reminds the firm that there are two routes for profits—improvement in the capital turnover and increase in the mark-up. The main limitation of the method is that the rate of return is linked to the level of production and sales assumed. When these levels change, the rate of return also changes.

Marginal Cost Pricing

Marginal cost pricing aims at maximizing the contribution towards fixed costs. Marginal costs include all the direct variable costs of the product. In marginal cost pricing, these direct variable costs are fully realised. In addition, a portion of the fixed costs is also realised. The main difference between absorption cost pricing and marginal cost of pricing is that the latter gives the flexibility not to recover a portion of the fixed costs depending on the market situation. It also gives the flexibility to recover a larger share of the fixed costs from certain customers, or a certain segment of the business and a smaller share from the others.

Merits and Demerits of Marginal Cost Pricing. Marginal cost pricing too has its associated merits and limitations. On the merits sides is that in the first place, unlike the other two cost-based pricing approaches, the marginal cost approach takes into account cost aspects as well as demand aspects, though it is basically a cost-based method. Thus, under competitive market conditions, marginal cost pricing is more useful. Moreover, when a firm has a number of products/product lines, marginal cost pricing is useful. It gives the flexibility for realising fixed costs through difference products/product lines at difference rates depending on market conditions while recovering all the marginal costs (i.e. direct variable costs) directly from the concerned product. The method may be particularly useful in quoting for competitive tenders and in export marketing. On the demerits side, marginal costing makes certain assumptions regarding cost and revenue behaviour, which can turn out to be incorrect in some cases. Moreover, while marginal costing rests on a twofold classification of cost into fixed costs and variable costs, in reality, there can be a third class of costs—the semi-fixed, semi-variable costs, or mixed costs. Marginal costing ignores this reality. As a result, some distortions can enter the picture and affect the validity of the marginal cost pricing. Again marginal cost pricing can be employed only in the short run and under certain specific circumstances. No firm can afford to depend on this method as a sole or permanent method. In fact, in highly capital-intensive industries, selling on marginal cost basis may pose an additional problem, as the difference between the marginal cost price and full cost price will be very large.

Common Merits and Demerits of all Cost-based Methods of Pricing

Cost-based methods as a class have certain merits and demerits. The main merit is that so long as the method works, the firm is assured of the target profit. The risk involved is minimal. The main demerit is that the method assumes a level of demand for the product independent of price. Also, the profit per centage is often arbitrary. There is the chance that a much better opportunity for profits is long by keeping the price too low; there is also the chance that the sales volume is lost because of insistence on a higher level of profit, which the market cannot return.

Break-even Concept

An idea of the break-even concept is essential for correctly understanding most of the cost-based methods of pricing. We shall, therefore, touch upon this concept before proceeding with the discussion on the other methods of pricing.

In any business, costs, volume, price and profits are interrelated. For most products, different demand levels and sales volume may materialise at difference price levels. Also, the different volume levels have different associated cost levels. A particular volume level and its associated cost level generates a particular profit level, the price remaining the same. When we consider different price levels, we have different profit levels, resulting through their associated levels of volume and costs. The firm can accordingly project profits at different price levels and choose the one that is particularly suited to it.

In producing and selling a certain volume of any product, certain fixed costs and certain variable costs are incurred. When the volume is increased or decreased, the variable costs go up or down. The fixed costs usually remain the same. The firm is essentially concerned with the total of the variable and fixed costs incurred for the particular volume. At that volume and at the assumed level of price, a particular level of total revenue is generated.

The break-even exercise is aimed at relating these two entities—the total costs and the total revenues—at different levels of volume and consequently at different levels of prices.

At a level where the total costs exactly equal the total revenues, the breaking even of costs and revenues takes place. The result is zero profit. At a level where the revenues exceed the costs, profits are earned and at the other level, losses are incurred. The number of units that are required to be produced and sold in order to reach a no-loss-no-profit position at the given level of unit price is known as the break-even point. When more units that the break-even level are produced and sold at the given price, the profits go up. And each additional unit made and sold brings in some additional profit. By the same token, each unit made and sold below the break-even point results in a loss. The graph in Fig. 13.1 illustrates the break-even concept.

Many business firms use the break-even concept in their pricing methods. They use the concept not only for price fixation but also for determining levels of production, or levels of utilisation of the production capacity, that is required for achieving the desired levels of profits. The concept is also used in the appraisal of new projects. It is a tool for making cost-volume-profit analysis. The various methods listed under cost-based pricing utilise the break-even idea in one way or the other.

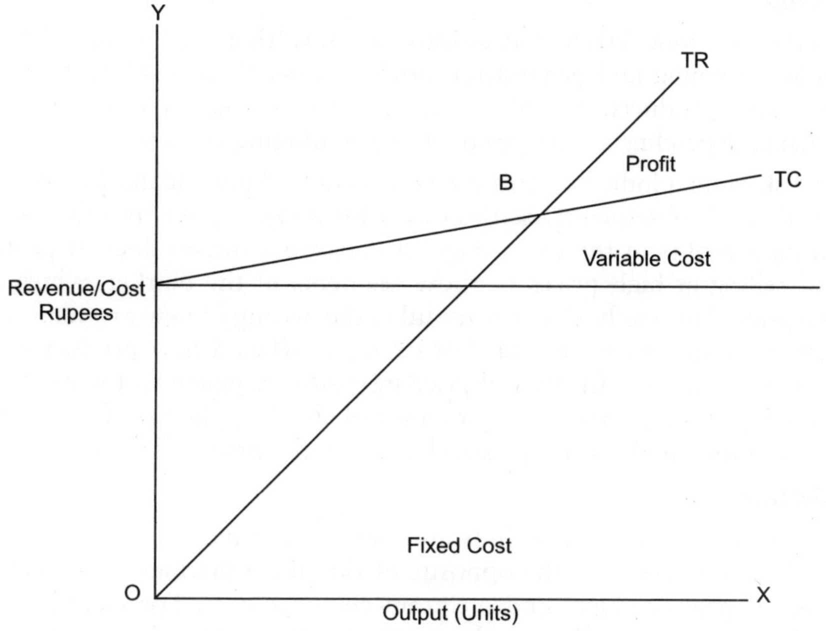

Fig. 13.1: Break-even Concept

TR – Total Revenue

TC – Total Cost

B – Break-even point

Demand/Market-based pricing

The following methods belong to the category of demand/market-based pricing:

- 'What the traffic can bear' pricing
- Skimming pricing
- Penetration pricing.

The basic idea in all the demand-based methods is that sales profits can be independent of costs, but are dependent on the demand and hence, pricing has to relate to demand.

'What the Traffic can Bear' Pricing

As per 'what the traffic can bear' pricing, the seller takes the maximum price that the customers are willing to pay for the product under the given circumstances. In effect, it is a variant of skimming pricing. It is not a sophisticated method and is used more by retail traders that by manufacturing firms. This method brings high profits in the short-term. But in the long run, 'what the traffic can bear' is not a safe concept. Chances of errors in judgement are very high. Also, it involves trial and error. It can be used where monopoly/oligopoly conditions exist and demand is quite inelastic with respect to price. Buyer opposition or consumerism is bound to set in over time when a firm sets its prices on the basis of what the traffic can bear. New competitors will also enter the industry and make the game difficult for the firm.

Skimming Pricing

In the chapter on New Product decisions, we saw that demand/market-related pricing methods, such as skimming and penetration pricing rather than cost-based pricing can be the apt strategy for new products. We also saw that the firm can choose either skimming or penetration pricing, depending on the product and marketing context.

As the word skimming indicates, this method literally skims the market in the first instance through high price and subsequently settles down for a lower price. In other works, it aims at high price and high profits in the early stage of marketing the product. It profitably taps the opportunity for selling at high prices to those segments of the market, which do not bother much about the price. This method is very useful in the pricing of new products, especially those that have a luxury or speciality element. For example, when a new product is a luxury item, enjoying the patronage of an affluent and price-insensitive segment of the market, the firm can opt for the skimming strategy. Skimming pricing will also help the firm feel the market/demand for the product and then make appropriate changes in the pricing decision.

Penetration Pricing

Penetration pricing, as the name indicates, seeks to achieve greater market penetration through relatively low prices. It is the opposite of skimming pricing. This method too is quite useful in pricing of new products under certain circumstances. For example, when the new product is capable of bringing in large volume of sales, but is not a luxury item and there is no affluent/price-insensitive segment backing it, the firm can choose the penetration pricing and make price-insensitive segment backing it, the firm can large-size sales at a reasonable price before competitors enter the market with a similar product. The strategy suits such products and also brings many advantages to the firm. For, here the quantity that can be sold is highly sensitive to the price level even in the introductory stage. Also, soon after introduction, the product may encounter stiff price competition from other brands/substitutes. Penetration pricing in such cases will help the firm have a good coverage of the market and keep competition out for quite some time. Moreover, for such products, large sales may be necessary for break-even in the initial stages and penetration pricing alone can bring in the high volume of sales required for breaking even and making profits.

The Concept of Price Elasticity of Demand

In all demand-based pricing methods, the price elasticity of demand is taken into account directly or indirectly. In fact, whatever be the method of pricing adopted, the firm has to keep in view the price elasticity of demand of the products. We shall, therefore, discuss this concept in some detail.

Price elasticity of demand refers to the relative sensitivity of demand for a product to changes in its price—in other words, how significantly the sales of the product are affected when price is changed. If an increase or decrease in the price of the product results in significant decrease or increase in its offtake, the product is said to be price elastic. Conversely, if the price change does not significantly affect the sales volume, a product is said to be price inelastic. Through the concept of price elasticity of demand we can describe the changes in the buying responses of customers to changes in price of the product. It is usually described as a ratio of the variation in demand to the variation in price.

Price Elasticity of Demand, a Relative Idea

It, however, is to be noted that both the terms—price elastic and price inelastic—are relative and not absolute. Total elasticity and inelasticity of demand is rare. Elasticity is basically a matter of degree. It also depends on the magnitude of the price increase/decrease. If the price variation is small, its effect on elasticity of demand may not be perceptible in the case of several products. Against, this, if the change is big, even the leas elastic products may show some change in demand. The base price from which further increases are made is another factor. The effect of the same amount of price change from two different base prices will be different. Sometimes, with one or two price changes, the elasticity response may not show up; but with the third price variation, demand may tend to change. Yet another point about elasticity is that it may show up differently in the short run and in the long run.

Use of the Elasticity Concept in Pricing Decisions

Despite all these problems, the concept still has a useful application in pricing since the elastic or inelastic position of demand of a product has a lot of bearing on pricing decisions. In the case of products whose demand is highly price elastic, the pricing decision has to be based on how it will affect the demand/sales volume. In the case of products with a low price elasticity of demand, the pricing decision can be made based on other considerations, ignoring the effect on demand due to changes in the price. The concept of price elasticity of demand can also be used to test and assess whether the existing level of price is high or low. If the elasticity ratio is high, the indication is that the existing price level is high and if the ratio is low, i.e. if demand is inelastic, the indication is that the price level is low. However, care should be taken in using the concept of price elasticity while making price changes. The response of the total market or a large part of the customer group must be considered and not just the response of a few individual customers. If the price sensitive segment forms the majority of the total customer group, the elasticity will be naturally significant.

Competition-oriented pricing

In a competitive economy, in most industries, competition-oriented pricing methods are common. The methods in this category rest on the principle of competitive parity in the matter of pricing. Competition-based pricing, or competitive parity pricing, however, does not necessarily mean matching competition in price. Three policy options are available to the firm under this pricing method:

- Premium pricing
- Discount Pricing
- Parity pricing/Going rate pricing.

For all of them, a competitor's price serves as the reference point. Premium pricing means pricing above the level adopted by competitors; discount pricing means pricing below such level; and parity pricing means matching competitors pricing. Where supply is more than adequate to meet demand and the market remains competitive in a stable manner, and where the channel and consumers are well aware of their choices, parity pricing can be the answer. Similarly, when a market leader has established a market price, with the intention of stabilising the price, the smaller firms in the industry may have to go in for parity pricing.

PRICING TO VALUE

Pricing methods based on cost, demand and competition, which we have discussed so far, belong to the conventional/standard category of pricing methods. Value pricing, in contrast, is a modern, innovative and distinctive method of pricing.

Relationship between Price and Value

Let us begin with the relationship between price and value. The price and value have a relationship with each other is obvious. The crux is that price represents the exchange value of a product. In fact, in the nature of things, price revolves totally around value. Of course, price is related to utility as well. But value is the larger concept and contains utility within it. While utility refers to the generic ability of the product to satisfy a need, value is the worth the consumer attaches to it. It represents the quantum of money, which he is willing to part with for owning the product. Pricing methods based on cost, demand and competition, fail to recognise adequately this vital fact. Value pricing avoids this lacuna and fully exploits the natural linkage between price and value.

Essence of Value Pricing

Value pricing rests on the premise that the purpose of pricing is not to recover costs, but to capture the value of the product perceived by the customer.

Analysis will readily show that the following scenarios are possible with the cost-value price chain:

(i) Value > price > costs

(ii) Price > value > costs

(iii) Price > costs > value

(iv) Price = value > costs

Under scenario (i), the marketer recovers his costs through price, but fails to recover the value of his product and thus misses out the profit opportunity. Under scenario (ii), he recovers his costs as well as the value, but errs on the excess side by giving less value to the customer than what is due as per the price. He will lose the loyalty of the customer and the equity of his brand. Under scenario (iii), the value that he passes on to the customer is still lesser and it is doubtful if he will adequately sell his product at all. Here, his cost itself is higher than the value of the product and by maintaining his price above his costs, he makes his value delivery to the customer all the more negative. In scenario (iv), he matches the value and price, and wins customer loyalty; and since the value creates is larger than his costs, he ensure his profits. It is obvious that scenario (iv) has the maximum merit. It guarantees sustained sales and profits to the marketer. It is to be noted that in all the four scenarios, his price covers his costs alright and thus ensures his profitability, but only scenario (iv) is helpful to him in the true sense. The chief merit of value pricing is the recognition that the customer is interested only the value or worth of the product, and not in its costs. Value pricing will win customer loyalty to the marketer. And, as long as the marketer is able to deliver value in excess of his costs, his profits are also ensured.

Product line pricing

When a firm markets a variety of products grouped into suitable product lines, a special possibility in pricing arises. As the products in a given product line are related to each other, sales of one influences that of the others. They also have interrelated costs of manufacturing and distribution. In such a situation, the firm need not necessarily fix optimal price for each product, independent of other products in the line. It can fix the prices of the different products in such a manner that the product line as a whole is priced optimally, resulting an optimal sales of all the products put together and optimum total profits from the line. A set of interrelated prices for the various products in the line will be the outcome of such a policy. The total costs and the total desired profits from the entire product line go into such pricing. A further refinement is that the tentative prices for the various products in the line are worked out and are adjusted later, based on competitors' prices for similar products, and the demand reactions at different prices. Two important aspects, however, should be kept in mind while resorting to product line pricing. *First*, the joint cost and the joint revenue problems can be quite complex and formidable. *Second*, a price change cannot be initiated in respect of any one item in the product line without considering its effect on the line as a whole. No item can be treated as an independent product for pricing. The method is also sometimes referred to as the product line promotion method of pricing.

Tender pricing

Business firms are often required to fix the prices of their products on a tender basis. Tender pricing is of a special type, though it is also a competition-oriented method. It is more applicable to industrial products and products/services purchased/contracted by institutional customers. Such customers usually go by competitive bidding through sealed tenders/quotations. They seek the best (the lowest possible) price consistent with the minimum quality specifications. Obviously, the marketer cannot get his best price from such customers. His objective in tender pricing can only be to get the 'best possible price under the circumstances' and to bag the order.

When he is unable to, or unwilling to, offer his product at the lowest quotation basis, he can still compete in the tender with his other strengths, such as after-sale service, deferred payment terms, etc. The problem faced by any firm in tender pricing is basically one of finding a price that is consistent with costs, profits and other objectives, and also low enough to get the business. A related problem is one of avoiding regrets of having missed a better price and profits due to over anxiety in securing the order and/or wrong estimation of competitors' bids. The marketer has to set his price lower than what his competitors would quote for their products. His actual quotation will depend on his costs and how badly he needs the particular order. He has to thoroughly analyse the tender pricing policy of his competitors and decide his offer. He should also keep alternative offers ready, based on possible changes in the decisions of buyers and competitors.

Affordability-based pricing

The affordability-based method is relevant in respect of essential commodities, which meet the basic needs of all sections of people. The idea here is to set prices in such a way that all sections of the population, are in a position to buy and consume the products to the required extent. The price is set independent of the costs involved; often an element of state subsidy is involved; and the items are often distributed by the public distribution system. This method of pricing is also referred to sometimes as social welfare pricing.

Differentiated pricing

Some firms charge different prices for the same product in different zones/areas of the market. Sometimes, the differentiation in pricing is made on the basis of customer class rather than marketing territory. Sometimes, the differentiation is one the basis of volume of purchase, which is the most commonly used method in this category.

PRICING PROCEDURE

The term pricing procedure refers to the actual process/mechanics of working out the price. The steps involved in the pricing procedure will vary depending on the pricing objectives and pricing methods chosen by the firm. Some of the steps are common for all methods, while some are not relevant for some methods. The general steps involved in pricing procedure are listed in Table 13.2.

Table 13.2: Steps Involved in Pricing Procedure

- Identify the target customer segments and draw up their profiles.
- Decide the market position and price image that the firm desires for the brand.
- Determine the extent of price elasticity of demand of the product, and the extent of price sensitivity of target customer groups.
- Take into account the life-cycle stage of the product.
- Analyse competitor's prices.
- Analyse other environmental factors.
- Choose the pricing method to be adopted, taking all the above factors into account.
- Select the final price.
- Periodically review the pricing method as well as procedure.

TERMS OF SALE

We have said earlier that price remains vague unless all details about the terms of sale are clearly spelt out. Price and terms of sale go as a package. Various possibilities are available in fixing prices and terms of sale. This can be easily understood from a perusal of the expressions relating to price and terms of sale, listed below:

- Ex-works price
- F.O.B. price
- C.I.F. price
- F.O.R./destination price
- 'Delivered at customers' doors anywhere' price
- Ex-warehouse price
- Cash sale price
- Credit sale price
- Installment sale price.

Further, most firms offer a variety of rebates and discounts that form part of the terms of sale. The common types of discounts and rebates are stated below:

- Trade discount
- Discounts related to specific types of channels
- Discounts related to specific classes of customers
- Discounts related to quantity purchased in a year/quarter
- Off season rebates
- Festival rebates
- Special/*ad hoc* rebates to stimulate sales
- Rebates for cash down purchases
- Special price deals/bargains.

Obviously, decisions on price cannot be dissociated from decisions regarding terms of sale and discounts/rebates.

PROACTIVE APPROACH IN PRICING

Some firms have a proactive culture in pricing while others have a reactive or reflexive culture. Firms having a proactive approach to pricing are usually way ahead of those with a reactive/reflexive approach in tapping market opportunities, in retaining the customer under changing market conditions and in optimising profits. While firms with reactive/reflexive approach remain satisfied with certain simple criteria, like covering costs, maintaining a particular market share and matching the competition, the proactive approach goes far beyond these criteria and helps the firm realise the full opportunity that is available in the market. Proactive pricing calls for greater innovativeness and a deeper understanding of the pricing mechanism as also of the market forces.

Proactive pricing is not synonymous with rash pioneering in price fixing. On the other hand, shrewd pioneering is a part of proactive pricing. Again, a proactive pricer need not necessarily be an initiator of price changes. Instead, he may deliberately decide to be a follower in a particular case of price change. Shrewdness is the real touchstone of proactive pricing. It is seen that in many businesses, proactive pricers are constantly out-manoeuvring reflexive pricers. While reflexive pricers quite often lose great sums in the form of foregone profits due to their simplistic approach, proactive pricers seldom lose on this score; nor do they lose the business that is their due, because of overpricing. They reduce prices where it is warranted and realise a better price wherever it is possible to do so. They fully understand the competitive dynamics of pricing in their respective industries. They understand equally well the purchasing approaches of their customers and the pricing approaches of their competitors.

Proactive pricers also try to separate some performance features and service features from the product, and make them available as special features and price them extra. They structure the price intelligently and make them appear competitive. For example, they separate prices of accessories from the prices of the main products, and juggle upward or downward the prices of select accessories and of the main product in such a way that they favourably influence their customers' perception of the price. They also intelligently use other aspects like credit terms, cash discount, volume discount and year-end rebates and structure their prices in such a way to give the best appearance to the customers while realising the best appearance to the customers while realising the best possible prices for their products. Even in communicating the prices to the customers, they are innovative.

Proactive pricers gather all relevant information and use them to their advantage in pricing. For example, they gather information on the value that a given customer places on the product, its performance and the service. They have ready information on their own costs and profit position, and the price reference point in the market for the product. They use all such information in fixing the prices as well as in structuring and communicating the prices.

OTHER RELATED DIMENSIONS

Having discussed in detail the pricing objectives, the pricing methods and the typical steps involved in the pricing process, it will be pertinent now to mention some other related dimensions of pricing decisions.

Price Plays a Communicative Role

Many firms use price as an index of quality, or luxury, or status, or technical excellence of their products. Such products are usually sold on the exclusiveness idea. Firms also use price to communicate that the product is a common man's product. In other words, price also involves psychological factors over and above the economic factors and transmits certain communication clues to the consumers. That is why consumers classify products as 'costly', 'reasonably', and 'cheap'. They process a price in their minds and judge whether it is high, low or reasonable.

In the chapter on Marketing Communications, we shall explain how price communicates something more than price.

Re-sale Price Maintenance

Some firms believe in re-sale price maintenance while others leave it to the trade. Often there are statutory provisions on this. Where the matter is governed by law, the firm has very little freedom. Where there is no such restriction, the firm can have its own policy. Again, some firms follow a policy of protecting the trade from the losses resulting from price reductions, while others leave both the losses and gains arising out of fluctuations in prices to the trade.

Judgement, A Key Factor in Pricing

In making price decisions, judgement is as important as facts and formulae. Analytical and quantitative approach is no doubt a must in handling the pricing issue, but pricing still remains an area where judgement plays a vital role.

Psychological Pricing

Marketers often try to get around consumers' psychological barrier in respect of price through psychological pricing. For example, they put on a price tag of Rs. 295 instead of Rs. 300, or a tag of Rs. 9,990 instead of Rs. 10,000. In the earlier days, in India, this kind of pricing was known as Bata pricing, since Bata used to price most of its footwear in this fashion. Now, producers across product categories are resorting to this practice.

Example of BPL

BPL, for example, has priced its popular model 21 inch colour television set at Rs. 10,990. In this case, based on costs and profit requirements, BPL had to price the set upwards of Rs. 11,000. It has, however, preferred to play on the psychology of the consumers, and fixed it at Rs. 10,990. Although the price fixed is close to Rs. 11,000, the consumer may mentally place it in the price band of Rs. 10,000. At least, that is what BPL hopes.

Example of Godrej

Similarly, Godrej has priced its popular model computer chair at Rs. 1,900 *plus duties and taxes*. In this instance, the seller has actually gone one extra step in psychological pricing. In order to psychologically appeal to the consumers, the company has separated the duties and taxes, and pegged the price at Rs. 1,900. This way, it has made it appear that the price is well below the Rs. 2,000 band. There was no way otherwise that it could have fixed the price tag at Rs. 1,900. It can easily be surmised that based on costs and profits sought, the company would have been required to price the chair around Rs. 2,400 inclusive of taxes and duties. So, it has separated the duties and taxes from the price, and pegged the price at Rs. 1,900.

It can be argued that a reduction of Re. 1 on a price of Rs. 100 will not make much difference to the consumers. The point is that while setting out to buy a product, most consumers draw a price band for it and as far as possible do not want to go beyond it. They often operate in price bands and not at a price point that is predetermined to the last pie. While 99 is the two-digit territory, 100 is the three-digit territory. The consumer is comfortable with the thought that he has stayed within his preferred price band.

Research indicates that consumers do not consider a price too high when it varies within the band that they are looking for, but they react adversely the moment it crosses the band. Any price that suggests a lower price band seems to confer a benefit on the seller, as it plays on the psychology of the buyer. It is a fact that in many cases, a small fractional difference in price does create the impression of a much larger difference.

Another point—psychological again—is that it gives a good feeling to the consumers if they received back some change after a purchase. The strategy makes the product seem more affordable.

The strategy, in fact, provides yet another advantage to the seller. Supposing that based on costs and profit requirements, the product is to be priced at, say, Rs. 9,800, the seller can price it at Rs. 9,900 or even Rs. 9,999, still remaining below the price band preferred by the consumer. This way, he can make an additional profit.

QUESTIONS FOR DISCUSSION

1. Explain the objectives of pricing policy of a business firm.
2. What is meant by pricing? Why is pricing a very important element of marketing mix?
3. What are the determinants of price of a product?
4. What are the factors that affect pricing decisions in a marketing organisation?
5. Why do pricing objectives vary from organisation to organisation? What is the importance of pricing objectives? Discuss.

6. Discuss the basic methods of pricing adopted by Indian industry.
7. What is meant by pricing policy? How can the pricing policy be developed for an organisation?
8. What are various kinds of pricing strategies? Discuss.
9. Write an essay on legal restrictions on fixing a price for a product.
10. What are the factors affecting price-sensitivity?
11. Describe the factors that influence the pricing strategy of a firm.
12. Explain penetration pricing strategy.
13. Explain advantages and disadvantages of 'Marginal Cost Pricing'.
14. "Price is the only element in the marketing mix that produces revenues." Discuss.
15. (a) Explain the various methods of determining prices.
    (b) What are the factors that influence pricing?
16. Define pricing as a function of marketing and discuss its contribution in the success of the marketing strategy of a company.
17. Mention the various methods of pricing a product in terms of objectives and costs.
18. What do you understand by administration of prices? Discuss the various decisions that you take in administrating prices.
19. As the president of a home video recording machine company, you must decide between a penetration or skimming pricing policy. Explain the factors you would consider in making your choice.
20. Describe the methods that firms use to set the prices of their products.

CASE STUDY 13.1

PRICE CUTS AND PREEBIES SPELL SUCCESS FOR AKAI PRICING

Akai Electronic Co. Ltd. of Japan, set up in 1929 to make radio parts, was taken over in 1995 by a Hong Kong-based conglomerate: Semi Tech Global Co. Ltd. (STG 1996-97 turnover: HK $1.2 billion, or Rs. 5,667 crores), which also markets Singer, Sansui and Pfaff. The holding company has a 65 per cent stake in Akai. Since 1992, Akai has been closing plants in Japan and using cheaper bases elsewhere in Asia. In 1995, it acquired Kong Wah Holdings Ltd. claimed to be the largest TV plant in Finland, Malaysia, England and China. It also controls over 18 component plants in southern China. Together the group's companies make over 6 million TV's 2 million VCRs and 1 million audio systems apart from telecom products. The group gets most of its sales from Russia and the ex-Soviet countries, the Indian subcontinent and China. But the brand sells in 47 countries.

The group's success formula has been its judicious eye for cheap inputs, even from non-group manufacturing units. The potential it sees in selling recognised names such as Akai and Sansui in emerging markets. STG plans to emerge as a big player in newer product categories such as—Digital videodisc players-at a later stage. ATV with an internet browser is also coming up.

Akai and Baron

Baron International, which once sold Bush, is owned mainly by the Muchandants (Akai's stake 10 per cent). Around 1991, the company wanted to bring in a foreign brand. Since Korean brands were relatively unknown, it had to be a Japanese brand, felt the family. These could be sold at a premium because of the perceived quality of Japanese products. But most brands had already found Indian partners. Thus the choice was Akai, a brand that Indian had been somewhat familiar with (its music systems and VCRs had been coming form the Gulf).

The tie up took place in April 1994 after 7 months of negotiations. The first contract signed with Akai was totally one-sided: Baron had no exclusive right to the brand name, Akai could walk out of the deal at will and nothing prevented Akai from entering India on its own. Baron pulled it off by promising a market share of 7% by value within 2 years of launch. (This has been exceeded.) Having proved their ability in markets where big Japanese brands have floundered, Baron swung through a more favourable contract with Akai recently. Baron now has exclusive rights to the brand till 2004 in India and AKAI cannot set up any subsidiary here directly or indirectly.

Baron International set up its Akai operation with an investment of just Rs. 25 crores in 1994 (it got a Rs. 52 crores loan from Akai). Sales since 1995-96 were about Rs. 151.8 crores. In the 15 months period from April 1996 to June 1997, the sales rose to Rs. 494.7 crores (Rs. 396 crores p.a.): profit after tax was Rs. 28 crores. Now in the 12 months leading up to July 1998, Akai wants to place 4.5 lakh TVs in consumers' homes in a market estimated at 2.2 million units for this period, a Rs. 1,000 crore target.

The Product

A typical 21″ CTV's marked retail price is Rs. 20,000. The cost break-up is as follows:

Item	Particular	Rupees
1.	Landed cost	7,500
2.	Customs duty (25%)	1,875
3.	Excise and sales tax (from 3% to 17%)	3,000
4.	Dealer margin (5% to 6% on MRP)	1,500 – 2,000
5.	Gross margin	3,000 – 4,000
6.	Net margin	800 – 1,000

Akai meanwhile has been saving money everywhere. Consider its 21″ CTV marketed at Rs. 21,490 before the excise change. The possible costing structure is as follows:

Item	Particular	Rupees
1.	Landed cost	5,460
2.	Customs duty (25%)	1,365
3.	Direct assembling cost	50
4.	Excise (18% on ex-factory tag)	1,200
5.	Sales tax	700
6.	Dealer margin (3% on MRP)	644
7.	Interest costs (sometimes operates on cash and carry)	0 – 100

POSITIONING AND STRATEGY

"Price-Quality Positioning"

The consumer looks at the products in a category at different levels of price offering different standard of quality and decides which price-cum-quality level is most suitable for a given need. The importance of the concept is that the consumer in such a heterogeneous market as ours has different expectations of quality, at different levels of social mobility and offer the opportunity for greater price quality stratification and positioning than in any other Third World country.

What inspires these marketing activities is the belief that in India varying levels of price-quality for products will attract different segments of consumers.

Give quality at the right price and whatever you make will sell on its own.

Akai's goods are routed via Baron's 30 branches (not through a distributor), which saves on cost while allowing flexibility and control). Balance sheet figures show that no item is in stock for more than 5 days. There are only 2,000 dealers (BPL has 7,000) and even at a 3% margin (others offer 5-6%), they cannot do without the bargain buyer. "When Videocon gives a Mercedes benz to its dealers, consumers are paying for it, not the company." Akai's strategy is to target the customer, not the dealer. Thanks to aggressive marketing, BPL, Videocon, Akai, Onida and Samsung appear to be the winners so far in this free-for-all competition. Last year BPL and Videocon led the field with a combined market share of 41 to 45 per cent depending on whether an independent industry or ORG estimates were used. Akai sold a whopping 3,74,000 sets last year. According to Akai, the economics of this business does not work out on a per set basis, but on rising volumes, to take into account not only conversion but also marketing costs.

What do they do with the old sets being exchanged for new ones? Refurnish them and make them available at a bargain to existing B&W TV owners (who numbered 5.6-6 million last year). The consumer now has a choice, which was never there before. Manufacturers are being forced to innovate and bring a home theatre and other world class goods to the middle class drawing room.

Even after counting selling and other expenses, Akai ends up with a good Rs. 10,000 or so to buy gifts. The 14″ CTVs it was giving away free, for instance, were estimated to cost Baron just Rs. 6,500 per set, but the consumers' perceived value was Rs. 10,000 the retail price.

Some competitors feel that Akai juggles its product composition (invoicing speaker as a separate product) to get the better of Indian's excise structure. "Tax planning is not tax evasion", argues Akai. Others wonder if the "cheap kits" are in fact underinvoiced. Some even suspect Akai of using old parts from China where many old for new schemes have taken place, effectively packing CTVs that have been swept out of the market. Akai, however, says these rumours are baseless.

The kits are put together from super cheap components bought from high volume manufacturers in East Asia, where over-capacity has been a problem. Sharp depreciation in several currencies ensure that local components make up just 30 per cent of the value of production. Baron gets its CTVs made by Viacom Electronics, Gujarat unit (unit capacity—half million units, soon to be doubled). Salaries make up just 0.7 per cent of the turnover. No money is spent on R&D.

The Market

Akai is clearly upfront in marketing. It has priced a brand new 21″ CTV set at less than Rs. 10,000 and is offering a 29″ set for the price of a 21″, cornering a large market in the process. Other manufacturers have followed suit. Videocon is now offering a 21″ CTV in exchange for an old one for Rs. 8,990. Sony too has cut its 21″ CTV prices effective from February. Samsung is yet to take a decision. Dealers are skeptical because over the last 10 to 15 years there has never been such a slump and also point out that even with the price cuts, a 21″ Sony is still costlier by Rs. 2,000 than those offered by Samsung. While Sony is down, Akai, Samsung and LG dealers have reported brisk consumer demand.

Meanwhile estimates of CTV sales vary in 1997, ranging from 2-2 million to 2-8 million sets, up from 1-95 million in 1996. According to industry sources, 2-2 million perhaps is closer to reality. On this basis, the industry grew by 13-14 per cent in 1997 over 1996. This year 2.5 million sets are expected to be sold, implying a similar growth of 14 per cent. ORG is reported to have forecast a growth rate of 10.8 per cent this year. These numbers are much lower than the 25 per cent growth expected by the Consumer Electronics and Television Manufacturers' Association. For the 15 month period of 1996-97, Baron in addition to spending Rs. 160 crores on commissions, discounts and rebates, also spent Rs. 35 crores on advertising (Agency—Trikaya Grey). When BPL tried to match an Akai offer in Pune last year by giving Rs. 1,000 off on its 21″ CTV, Akai took 3 days to drop its price by a further Rs. 3,000 (BPL withdrew its scheme).

Earlier, Akai's 21″ CTV made up just a third of all the CTVs sold (20″ and 14″ models were much cheaper). Akai began to target the first timer (who settles for a 20″ or 14″ model) by bundling fridges, scooters and small CTV with its products. The schemes are designed to break inertia and alleviate the guilt in disposing of a durable that works, says Trikaya Grey. The old CTVs were supplied to the rural and semi-urban markets after some retouching (and with the loose guarantee for minor repairs) at prices ranging from Rs. 2,000 to Rs. 4,000 a piece, setting off a wave of upgrades from B&Ws. The typical second-hand buyer is a roadside shop. Akai believes that the TV is a commodity now and runs on volumes. They maintain that they give benefits rather than price-offs and that the price points is set by the market; its deal is in the gift. Akai claims to have expanded the segment from 8,000 units per annum to 800 units per month and now offers a home theatre—a 21″ CTV, a VCD player, a sub-woofer and 5 speakers with 1,000 watt surround sound—at Rs. 26,990.

Akai is positioned as the price player. This is the Wal-Mart logic. Once the buyer is positive that the brand offers the best deal, he goes for it without checking any other and may purchase an Akai once sure that all standard CTVs are on par as far as attributes go. Selling the consumer this idea that CTVs are a commodity however, will take smarter advertising than Akai has had so far.

QUESTIONS FOR DISCUSSION

1. Akai is accused of using sub-standard products in its TV sets: else how can it work on such low margins. Do you agree with this statement? Support your answer with logical reasons.
2. In this price war of colour TVs, which player will be the winner and on what basis?

3. Having had so much success in the past few years, what should be Akai's next move to further secure its position and also to move up the success ladder?
4. Chalk out a future promotional plan for Akai.

CASE STUDY 13.2

VIP STORY

The Indian moulded-luggage market estimated at around Rs. 8,500 million per annum is largely dominated by the small and unorganized-sector units. In terms of volume, only about 15-18 per cent luggage sold every year is accounted for by the organized sector, where Blow last Limited and VIP brand is the market leader. After acquiring the Universal Luggage company (Aristocrat brand) in 1988, Aristocrat ad VIP together now account for a hefty 85 per cent share of the organized market which was till the early 1990s growing at the low rat of 2-3 per cent per annum. The growth rate refused to pick up in spite of VIP's persistent efforts to expand the market by adding several new models to their range at regular intervals.

Way back in 1981, VIP introduced a soft-luggage range, sub-banded as 'Skybag'. It was aimed at the up market frequent travelers. But the product failed to take off because the soft-luggage concept was alien to the Indian consumer. The brand was also let down by imitators. For every piece of genuine Skybag sold, there were 40 fake pieces being sold by the unorganized sector. In 1986, the company launched another premium sub-brand 'Odyssey' made with a new 'vacuum foaming' technology, which gives a pseudo leather finish to the product. In spite of its step price the brand was well received by the market. However, the success of one or two models was just not enough to give the required momentum for growth to a company of VIP's size and stature.

In the meantime, Aristocrat launched a frameless suitcase. The innovation reduced assembly time, and lowered the product weight and material cost resulting in significant reduction in the production cost. It enabled them to sell a 20 inch suitcase for about Rs. 200. Not to be left behind, VIP also launched its own frameless economy model 'International Tourister' aimed at the lower end of the market. But somehow, an up market brand name and the urban appeal of its ads did not match the middle-class consumer profile. The promotional efforts resulted only in further alienating the low-end buyer. The product fell felt and had to be withdrawn.

In 1988, the price war between VIP and Aristocrat ended rather dramatically with the buy-out of Universal Luggage by Blowplast. This was the most significant development on the market place, resulting in Blowplast's virtual monopoly in the moulded-luggage market.

In 1989, another economy range named 'Alfa' was launched at the lower end of the market. It was even cheaper than the International Tourister brand and was basically aimed at competing with the unorganized sector products as a 'loss leader' brand of the firm. Alfa, as expected by the firm, brought large volumes to the company, and in 1994, contributed about half of VIP's Rs. 2,700 million turnover; however, in terms of profits its contribution was very low. Second, the brand name and the features were as usual readily copied by the unorganized sector resulting in several lookalike Alfas. Selling the Alfa was not a problem for VIP; the real problem was to increase the demand for those models, which could bring a higher revenue to the firm.

In 1993, the company reworked their entire marketing strategy. It was at this stage that the firm started looking at the premium segment for growth. The Odyssey range, which was against 2-3 per cent growth rate of the regular and the economy range, showed the way. A detailed study of each premium model was conducted to chalk out the strategy. In the global market soft luggage is the largest selling variety, but in India if failed to take off, probably due to improper positioning and inadequate promotion. The firm realized this mistake and started promoting it vigorously.

The revised focus ad greater stress on premium range yielded good results. The sale of Skybag range increased by 25 per cent in 1994. Under the Odyssey range, new models named 'Lumina' suitcases and 'ZX' briefcase were launched in March 1994. These sub-brands are reported to be growing now at the rate of 30 per cent per annum.

QUESTIONS FOR DISCUSSION

1. Comment on the loss-leader pricing strategy followed by VIP in case of Alfa. Was the strategy in conformity with the company's objectives?
2. Did the company accomplish the marketing objectives by adopting premium pricing strategy for "Odyssey"?

CASE STUDY 13.3

PRICE PLUS

No exchange, No bond, post-dated cheque. Simple redemption. Bonus profit, announced the tag-line of a full ad in one of the capital's leading English language dailies. No, the ad is not there to sell fixed deposit coupons for some non-banking financial company (NBFC) or even the much maligned 'teak bonds' for some obscure plantation company. Instead it spells out in vivid details, now hold your breath, on how good money can be made almost six years down the line by buying an Akai colour television today.

Flip a few pages, and there is yet another one of them, this time form Videocon, which announces it as the "Greatest Money Back Offer". The superlative here, it seems, is only an age-old advertisers tendency to exaggerate.

But get the subtle drift. It is no longer your television against mine. Or even your technology against mine. Or even your brand against mine. But my 'financial offer' against everyone elses! For that is what is what marketing, or whatever we understood of it, in the consumer durable market has been reduced to. Simply, and some would add sadly, an act of 'financial jugglery', re-engineering if you like.

Well, we should have seen it coming. First, it was the bundling. Don't just sell a television set alone-throw in the CD video and audio player, high-wattage speakers and call it a 'home theatre' or something of the sort. Never mind if the consumer is completely flumoxed on the individual value of the respective elements.

Then came bundling by any other name, brand associations. So you had a hotch-potch of refrigerators, washing machines and television brands peddled as the homemaker of sorts. Akai initiated 'exchange mania'—your old television for new-almost became marketing currency with durable marketers across the board.

But what takes the cake, is this latest 'money back' salvo from Akai and Videocon? Amidst all these 'innovative approaches', whatever happened to good old classical marketing and branding?

"To justify the blatant disregard for accepted consumer marketing, these durable marketers are terming it as redefinition in consumer value. In fact, their version of it is essentially a function of just price. They have thrown all concepts of branding to the wind," adds Suhel Seth, Chief Executive Officer, Equus Advertising. Simply put, consumer value cannot be on mere price corollary, it has other elements to it.

"You need to look at this phenomenon from the category's lifecycle—I have seen it happening with all sorts of categories, tyres for instance," opines Vinayak Chatterjee, Chairman, Feedback Ventures Private Ltd.

"Ultimately, two things will happen. One some people may not find it worthwhile to operate in such a market, and then some degree of shakeout may happen. Plus, demand perk up in the future will somewhat restore demand-supply imbalance. And then back to old classical marketing games."

However, there is another school of thought, which is more charitable. "Marketing looks at making sure to create consumers in the short medium and the long run. Akai is doing fine on the short and the medium levels. I think it will be a player in the long run as well," adds Shumu Sen of Quadra Consultants.

Even others agree on the fact that such 'innovative offers' have managed to attract a very basic-need oriented consumer. But what beyond that? "In the long run, brands have to be built," adds Seth. The moot question, however, remains whether or not brands such as Akai are able to brands such as Akai are able to sustain them self sans any 'offer'?

Such offers may bring relevance (price related) and even salience (schemes advertising related) to the brand but what about consumer empathy and esteem, so very essential for the survival of the brand in the long run? "That can only be built working around the entire spectrum of the marketing rainbow, and not just on price," adds Rajeev Karwal, Vice-President, marketing and sales, LG India Electronics Pvt. Ltd.

"My hypothesis is that you can turn a brand into a commodity and sell it on price sensitivity, the way Akai is doing. But over the time the game perforce has to come back to the brand," adds Gautam Bhattacharya, professor of marketing at a New Delhi—based management institute.

"Marketing is about creating consumer empathy with the brand. When the consumer feels that 'this' is may brand," adds Karwal. Where is that quintessential quality of marketing in today'' consumer durable market? Or are we to live forever with the age-old adage, "There's no brand loyalty which two cents off can't overtake."

QUESTIONS FOR DISCUSSION

1. In the era of price war-are marketers formulating their strategies on price or value for money. Comment in light of above case?
2. Is co-branding an alternative to price cutting? Explain.

STRATEGIC CHANNELS OF DISTRIBUTION

14

INTRODUCTION

The origin of the word channel can be traced to a French word 'Canal'. Canal means an artificial pathway used for transportation and irrigation.

In the context of marketing, channel of distribution could be regarded as the way in which the goods flow from the producers to consumers or industrial users. According to Prof. W.J. Stanton, "Channel of distribution is the route taken by the title to the goods as they move from the producer to ultimate consumer or industrial user."

Factors Determining a Suitable Channel of Distribution

The selection of a particular channel of distribution for the selling of a particular product is a highly complex task. The channel selection depends upon the particular market where the company intends to sell its products. An all-inclusive channel for all products and all circumstances is difficult to chalk out. Each producer gives shape to his channel of distribution keeping in mind the characteristics of the customer, the extent of competition faced, etc. The factors which generally influence channel selection could be discussed as follows:

1. Customer characteristics

One of the most important factors which influences the channel selection is the characteristics of the customers. Customer characteristics refer to the number of customers, their scatteredness, regularity of purchase and their reaction to different selling methods. If the number of customers is substantial, a channel with a number of intermediaries is preferred by producers. On the other hand, if the customers are clustered around a particular place, producers will opt for direct selling. If there is greater frequency in the purchase of a product, then a lengthier channel will be necessary.

2. Product characteristics

It is a common knowledge that each product has a number of attributes. Attributes like perishability, bulk, degree of standardisation, service requirements, value, etc. have a definite say in the marketing of a product.

In case of perishable products producers prefer few and controlled levels of distribution. Such products are not amenable for repeated purchases and handling. Similarly shorter channels are preferred for bulky articles due to the difficulty in repeatedly handling the goods. The shortest channel is also used for products whose sale requires technical expertise as well as product with high unit value. On the other hand longer and diversified channel as well as is used for convenience and durable goods.

3. Middlemen characteristics

By middlemen characteristics we assume the following points. At first, the middlemen, who can provide the required marketing function must be given preference. Secondly, the willing accept the policies of the producer and must help him in the implementation of the policies. Depending on how best the middlemen can put in the above functions, the length of the channel of distribution is also determined.

4. Competitive characteristics

The channels used by rivals are closely observed by marketers. Sometimes producers use similar channel used by the rivals, if that is a profitable one. Sometimes to compete effectively competition customary channels will be deliberately avoided and some other channels will be used. For example, if the rival is using a retail store channel, then door-to-door sales can be adopted.

5. Company characteristics

The characteristics of the company also affect the channels of distribution. The size of the company, the product mix, past channel experience and overall marketing policies come under company characteristics. If the size of the company is big it chooses a channel of its own. It can easily enlist the cooperation of middlemen. Secondly, a company with adequate financial resources need not rely too much on the middlemen. It can easily reduce the levels of distribution as against small ones. New companies have got to rely on middlemen due to their inexperience in handling the marketing function. But a shorter channel will be used by a company which wants to control the channel. Therefore quantity choice of marketing services provided by the company can influence the channel choice.

6. Environmental characteristics

No doubt, channel selection is also influenced by environmental factors like economic conditions. During depression producers want the goods to be sold at the cheapest possible price. Hence, they resort to the shortest channels. Therefore commission need not be paid to numerous intermediaries.

7. Distribution policies of the manufacturer

All companies can follow a policy of intensive, selective or exclusive distribution. Depending on the one selected by the company, the channel selected differs. If the policy of the firm is to have an intensive distribution, it will utilize all the available channels. Generally intensive distribution is essential when price is low, buying is often and changes in brand is a common thing. But in case of selective distribution the number of outlets is limited in a given geographical area. This method is particularly useful when special services are needed like TV sets, etc. If the number of middlemen are limited, they will put their whole-hearted support for sales promotion. Exclusive distribution is used when the amount of product service needed by the final consumer is very high. In such a case there will be only one wholesaler or retailer for the entire market. The cheapest advantage of this method is that the manufacturer can have greater control over prices and markets. This method is specially useful in the sale of consumer specialy goods.

Types of Channels of Distribution

Channels of distribution can be broadly classified into two categories. They are:

(a) Direct selling by producers to final consumers, and

(b) Indirect selling or selling through middlemen.

(a) Direct selling or Manufacturer-consumer

Here the producer sells his products directly to the final users without the help of any intermediaries. This is the shortest distribution channel. The following are the methods used by producers under direct channel.

(i) Opening sales counter at manufacturer plant, e.g. Bakery's items, Icecream, etc.

(ii) Door-to-door sales, e.g. ladies garments, utensils, etc.

(iii) Sales by opening own shops, e.g. Raymonds, Bata, etc.

(iv) Sales through mechanical devices, e.g. Newspapers, milk, etc. are sold through mechanical devices.

Usefulness of the Method

(a) This method is specially useful in marketing goods which are highly perishable like vegetables, milk, etc., which should be sold to final consumers immediately.

(b) If the manufacturer has got sound financial standing and has got an efficient managerial personnel to take up the challenges of marketing system.

(c) If the products are such which could be sold through post.

(d) If the product marketed is a new one which requires effective salesmanship for its successful marketing.

(e) This method is very important to market many types of industrial goods as they require servicing by an expert hand for which the producer is the best.

(b) Indirect selling or selling through intermediaries

Under this channel of distribution the manufacturer does not sell the goods directly to the final users. Instead of this he calls in the services of one or more intermediaries. Indirect selling can take any of the following forms:

1. **Manufacturer-Retailer-Consumer Channel.** In this type of channel of distribution goods are directly sold by manufacturers to the retailers. It is the duty of the retailers to sell these goads to the final consumers, as wholesalers have no place in this type of channel of distribution. This channel could be effected through:

(a) The salesmen of the manufacturers visit the retailers and collect the orders and executes them.

(b) The order could be through post or by some other means and executed directly to retailers.

(c) Sales are made at the factory of the producer.

In order to reach the consumers, this is the commonly used method. The manufacturers do away with the services of wholesalers in this method. They are compelled to do so on account of the following reasons:

(a) To speed up distribution of product as the products are perishable either physically or fashion-wise

(b) Sometimes the retailers themselves may be large business organisations who want to deal with the producers directly without any wholesales in between.

(c) Another reason is that the manufacturers are simply closer to the consumers without anybody in between.

2. **Manufacturer-Wholesaler-Retailer-Consumer Channel.** In this type of channel there are two parties in between the producer and the final consumer. They ate wholesalers and retailers. Such a linkage between the first owner and the last owner is also known as P.W.R.C. This is a normal, regular and popular channel option used. This channel is employed in the marketing of drugs, hardware, etc. The services of wholesalers and retailers are generally pressed into for the industries where there are several producers and a large number of consumers who make their purchases small quantities.

3. **Manufacturer-Agent Middlemen-Wholesaler-Retailer-Consumer Channel.** In this channel the producer sells the products to the agent middleman. The Agent middleman in this turn disposes the goods to the wholesaler, the wholesaler selles the goods to the retailers and they sell to the final consumer. The significant aspect of this type of dealing is that the agent middlemen do not assume title to goods. They merely act as facilitating parties in the movement of goods on a commission basis. While marketing the manufactured goods, agent middlemen are used by manufacturers to free themselves from the marketing tasks and also when the manufacturer is unable to have their own sales force.

4. **Manufacturer-Agent Middleman-Retailer-Consumer Channel.** In this type of channel the service of wholesalers are not used by the producers. Therefore wholesaling functions are performed by the agent middlemen.

5. **Manufacturer-Agent Middlemen-Consumer Channel**-The full responsibility of selling the goods is entrusted to the agent middlemen in this channel. The agent middlemen usually take the form of commission agents and brokers. This type of channel is maintained by producers who cannot keep salesmen themselves. This method is applied in the marketing of industrial, agricultural as well as manufactured consumer goods.

Integrated Channels

Integrated channels are networks in which channel components participate in a coordinated manner. Integrated channels may be vertical or horizontal. Vertical distribution channels are professionally managed networks to achieve operating economies and maximum market impact.

Horizontal channel may be defined as an alignment of two or more companies to jointly exploit a marketing opportunity either by themselves by creating a third entity. It is also called as 'symbiotic marketing'.

MIDDLEMEN

According to American Marketing Association (AMA). "Middleman is one who specialises in performing operations or rendering services that are directly involved in the purchase and sale of goods in the process of their flow from producer to final buyer."

Classification of Middlemen

Middlemen are classified into: (1) Functional middlemen (Mercantile agent or agent middlemen); and (2) Merchant middlemen.

Agent middlemen

They are mostly engaged in wholesaling. They assist in negotiating sales or purchases or both on behalf of the seller or buyer. They do not take title to goods which they handle. The important types of agent middlemen are brokers, commission agents, manufacturer agents, resident buyers, auctioneers, etc.

Characteristics of Agent Middlemen

1. They serve mainly the industrial users.
2. They get a certain percentage of commission on the volume of purchase or sales negotiated by them.
3. They take more interest to work for the buyers.

Kinds of Agent Middlemen

1. ***Broker.*** A broker is an agent. He represents the buyer or seller in negotiating purchases or sales. He does not have a physical control over the goods involved. His main function is to bring the buyers and sellers together.

   He is acting as an intermediary. He has limited powers over price and terms of sales. He has no authority to bargain on behalf of his principal. He sells the goods by description or samples. When the broker arranges the sales, the seller sells the goods directly to the buyer and the broker receives the commission from the principal. Brokers are used by producers who sell their products at frequent intervals. Large manufacturers also appoint brokers. The brokers' job is over when the transaction is over. They can be engaged when the producers need their services. Brokers are instrumental in opening new markets.
2. ***Commission Agent.*** Commission agent is an agent, individual, firm or even companies. He negotiates the sale of goods belonging to the principal. He customarily exercises physical control over the sale of goods. Commission agent has the power on prices and terms of sale under the condition that he must obey the instruction of the principal. He may arrange for delivery. Commission agent may extend necessary credit. He may grade and standardise the products. After deduction their fees he may remit the balance amount to the principal.
3. ***Manufacturers Agent.*** Manufacturer agents are employed by the manufacturers to sell their products. The features of manufacturer's agents are:
   (i) They have extended contractual relationship.
   (ii) They handle sales for each of the principals within an exclusive territory.

(iii) They represent manufacturers of non-competing, but related lines of business.

(iv) They possess limited authority with regard prices and terms of sale.

4. ***Selling Agents.*** Selling agent is an independent middleman. He operates on a contractual basis. He negotiates all sales of a merchandize or the entire output of his principal. He has authority over the price, terms and other conditions of sale. He is the sole selling agent for the line he represents.

   Selling agents are in close contact with the buyers. They guide the manufactures on styling, designing and pricing matters. They assist the manufactures in sales promotion and advertising.

5. ***Resident Buyers.*** Resident buyer is an independent agent and he specialises in buying for retailers. He receives compensation or a fee on commission basis. He operates in lines of trade such as furniture, garments, etc. He has helps the retailers to but the product. The resident buyers are simply an independent agent specialised in buying for principals who are retailers.

6. ***Auctioneers.*** They are generally appointed by business firms. The auctioneer receives the goods and invites bids for the goods. The highest bidder gets the goods and the auctioneer collects the amount from them. They collect commission from the sellers for their services.

There are also other types of agents like:

(i) Packing and forwarding agents employed to collect, deliver and forward the goods to proper destination.

(ii) Warehousers who receive the goods from or on behalf of the principal for storing purpose. They receive remuneration for the storage.

(iii) Export and import agents are those agents who serve their principals in their needs of seeking foreign markets or overseas supply.

(iv) Purchasing agents who specialise in locating the sources of supply for buyer of industrial goods.

(v) Factors who are appointed to sell goods.

Merchant middlemen

Merchant middlemen buy and sell goods on their own account and risk. They take the title to goods. They re-sell the goods at a profit. They are divided into two categories: Wholesalers and Retailers.

Wholesaler. Wholesalers occupy an important place in the channels of distribution. They assemble the goods from many of sources, warehouse it and re-arrange the goods for convenient buying by retailers. They help the manufacturers to whom goods cannot be sold directly from the factory.

TYPES OF RETAILERS

Itinerent Retailers

(a) Hawkers and Pedlars
(b) Cheap Jacks
(c) Market Traders
(d) Street Traders.

Fixed Shop Retailers

(a) Street stall holders
(b) Second-hand goods dealers
(c) Speciality goods shop
(d) General shops.

Another way of classifying retailers is classifying retailers into small-scale retailers and large scale retailers.

Small-scale Retailers	Large-scale Retailers
(a) Independent stores	(a) Departmental stores
(b) Automatic vending	(b) Multiple shops
(c) Discount houses	(c) Mail order shops
(d) Syndicate stores	(d) Hire-purchase and installment
	(e) Co-operative stores
	(f) Supermarkets
	(g) Hypermarkets

Itinerent Retailers

Itinerent retailing or house-to-house selling is in vogue from time immemorial. These people are mainly dealers in agricultural products and have no fixed place of business. A brief explanation could be given as follows:

(a) **Hawkers and Pedlars.** These retailers are found in big cities, places of exhibition etc. They either carry the goods on their person or with the help of a handcart. They carry the goods to the door of the customers. The goods handled by these people are with low unit value like pens, toys, etc.

The advantages of such sales are:

1. This method reduces the need for a retail trade operation.
2. The sales could be effected at the will of the salesman.
3. If this method is resorted to there is no question of selling and advertisement expenses.

(b) **Cheap Jacks.** Cheap jack is also a retailer. Though he has a fixed shop, it is not a permanent place of business. He shifts place of business the moment he sees that other localities are more profitable than the present one.

(c) **Market Traders.** These people open their shops on fixed places on market days. They may carry on their business in one locality or on different places on different days when the market is open.

(d) **Street Traders.** Another class of retailers is street traders. They usually deal only in one kind of goods at a time. Such people do business near railway stations, bus stands, foot paths, etc. where people come in large numbers.

Fixed Shop Retailers

With regard to the fixity of the place of operation retailers can be grouped into another class namely fixed shop retailers. They have got a fixed or permanent place of operation. They have got a fixed or permanent place of operation. They are of the following types.

1. **The Street-stall Vendors.** The street stall vendors open theirs shops where there is heavy traffic. There is a permanent stall and they deal in a variety of articles like toys, lungis, etc.
2. **Second Land Goods Dealers.** These retailers deal in second hand articles like books, furniture, etc. The customers are those who are unable to purchase new ones.
3. **Speciality Shops.** These people deals in a particular variety of goods. They may deal exclusively in books, leather, etc.
4. **General Goods Shop.** In these shops a whole line of products demanded by everybody for everyday use are sold. The dealers of this category have got permanent local customers.

Classification of Retailers According to Size of Operation

According to the size of operation retailers are classified into small scale and large scale ones. Small scale retailers are of the following types:

(i) Independent stores,

(ii) Vending machines,

(iii) Discount houses,

(i) **Independent Stores.** Independent stores are small-scale retailer establishments. In these independent stores, the owner himself manages the business. Here the seller has got an intimate contact with the customers. The required stocks for the seller is supplied by the wholesalers.

(ii) **Vending Machines or Automatic Vending.** Automatic vending is also known as automatic selling. It is the process of selling to ultimate consumers through coin operated machines. This business has become so advanced that the machine will give back the balance. The main items dealt with automatic vending machines are cigarettes, soft drinks, chocolates, etc. The goods sold through such machines are to be of small in value, uniform in size and there should be a large turnover.

(iii) **Discount Houses.** Another type of retail business which could be included in small-scale ones is the discount houses. The features of discount houses are:

(a) It is a retailing unit which sells consumer durable items.

(b) The price charged by discount house is relatively low.

(c) The customer services provided by discount houses is very low.

LARGE SCALE RETAILING INSTITUTIONS

Department Stores

The department store is of French origin. They are found in almost all countries. A department store is a huge retail shop, situated at a central place in the city and is divided into a number of small shops each dealing with one or two lines of goods and specialising in those lines. All such departments are under one roof and under one management and control.

The *main features* of a departmental store are:

(a) It is a large retailing organisation offering a number of products.

(b) The department heads are assigned the duty of buying and selling the goods. They also offer credit facility to their customers.

A department store is usually organised on a joint stock company basis. It is controlled by aboard of directors. It is the usual practice to divide department stores into 5 sections, namely: merchandising, staff management, maintenance and service, advertising, accounting and finance section.

Merits of department stores

(a) A department store being a bulk purchaser has the advantage of barge-scale baying.

(b) The department store is situated in the central part in a city. Because of this a department store can service the needs of all people from the city.

(c) Large number of goods are offered by the department stores to customers. Because of this, the customers can have all their purchases from a single place without going from place to place.

Demerits

(a) The price charged by the department store is very high as the cost of running a department is very high.

(b) It is also argued that since department stores are situated in big cities away from residential areas, it cannot service the people very effectively.

(c) Another criticism levelled against department store is that its existence serves only rich customers. The items traded on a department store is usually luxuries and thus are bought only by rich people.

The development and growth of department stores in India is far from satisfactory. The reasons could be many. In India, there is always the shortage of managerial personnel and capital necessary for the running of the department stores. The situation of department stores in the heart of the city makes it inaccessible to a vast majority of people. The high prices charged by department stores scare away customers.

Multiple Shops or Chain Store System

If there is a network of branches situated at different localities in the city or different parts of the country, it is an example of multiple stores or chain store system. According to C.W. Cundiff and R.R. Still "A chain store system is a group of retail shops of essentially and with some degree of centralised control of operations." Chain store system is a via media between large-scale and small-scale organisation. This system tries to eliminate disadvantages of both, retaining the advantages.

Multiple shops made their first appearance is UK. Now they are found in most of the developed countries. Multiple shops are also found in India, examples being Bata Shoe Co., Bombay Dyeing, etc.

Main features of multiple shops

(a) They are a very large retailing organisation.

(b) They specialise in one or limited variety of goods.

(c) The effort of multiple store is to sell articles of everyday use or necessaries of life like dress, footwear, etc.

(d) Though the management and control is centralised, selling activity is completely decentralised and branch shops are similar to other retail shops.

(e) There is no necessity to undertake vigorous advertisement campaign and the sales are made strictly on cash basis.

Advantages of multiple shops

Multiple shops are large-scale retail organisations. As these organisations operate on a large-scale basis, they enjoy all advantages of large-scale organisations.

Secondly, since they are owned by manufacturers, multiple shops eliminate all kinds of middlemen between producer and consumer.

Under this system of retailing there are a number of shops throughout the country. This helps the transfer of goods from one place where they are not needed to places where they are much needed.

There is considerable saving in advertisement costs with regard to multiple shops. Advertisement of one branch is in fact advertisement for all branches.

The sale policy of multiple shops is cash and carry basis. Due to this the loss with regard to collection of debts and bad debts is minimised.

There is flexity in the operation of multiple shops. A branch could be opened easily. Similarly a branch which is not run on profitable lines could be easily closed down.

Demerits of multiple shops

Under multiple shop system, standardised goods are sold. This makes it impossible for them to meet the demands of a particular communit

Multiple shops do not entertain any credit system. Cash and carry system of sale may be burdensome for many customers.

Such shops deal only in few articles. That too in well-known brands. Because of this buyers have only limited choice. They are unable to make all their purchases from a single place.

Another disadvantage associated with multiple shop system is the absence of initiative on the part of salesman. The management of a multiple shop is centralised. The manager of a branch has only limited powers. The branch manager of a shop is merely a head salesman, without any real interest in pushing up sales.

Lastly, in case of multiple shops there is the absence of relation between employers and employees. Similarly any kind of relationship is absent between employees and customers.

Supermarkets

Supermarkets are yet another innovation in the art of retailing. They made their first appearance during 1930, when the great depression took, place.

The supermarket is a large retailing unit mainly selling food items. Such markets need not have shop assistants or salesmen to sell their goods. The customers themselves pick up the goods and therefore super markets are also known as self-service stores.

Features of supermarkets

A supermarket is a large-scale retail business housed in a spacious building.

The goods are traded on a supermarket strictly on cash and carry basis.

A supermarket has got a number of departments each dealing in separate goods under the same roof. The items mainly dealt on a supermarket are dairy products, vegetables, fruits, etc. With an idea to improve profit potentials supermarkets have added non-food items like household utensils, hardware items, etc.

Advantages

(a) Being a large-scale retail organization supermarkets enjoy all the advantages of large-scale organisations.

(b) There is perfect freedom for customers. Buyers are at ease to take sufficient time for selection of goods. There is no unnecessary pressure from salesmen as they are absent.

(c) The prices charged in a supermarket is very low due to the elimination of various organisational and establishment charges.

Mail Order Shops

Sales by mail order method is a system by which products are sold to consumers. The post-office plays a significant role. Customers are approached by sending catalogues, price lists, pamphlets, etc. by post. The mail order system is suitable and profitable, when—

1. The goods are standardised and graded.
2. The goods are known to the customers.
3. The goods can be advertised precisely.
4. Wide publicity is made.
5. The price is low.
6. An improved system of post offices.
7. Merchandising is effective.
8. Goods are non-peristable.

Advantages of mail order system

1. Business can be housed in any place by looking at the economy of rent.

2. Capital requirement is less.
3. The buyer gets home delivery.
4. The market is unlimited.
5. Bad debts can be avoided to a great extent.

Disadvantages

1. Buyers cannot inspect or select the goods.
2. Demonstration is not possible
3. After sale service is not extended.
4. Generally high prices are charged.
5. Honesty of the seller is questionable.
6. Cheating is common.

The success of the mail order business has been due to the following reasons:

1. High literacy and wide circulation of periodicals.
2. Inadequacy and unpreparedness of local retailers.
3. Lower prices.
4. Unconditional guarantee of satisfaction or money refunded.
5. A reputation for truthful advertising.
6. Improvement of post office system.
7. Rapid service in sending out orders.

Hire-purchase and Installment

Hire-purchase trading is a system by which the seller agrees to sell the articles to the buyer on condition that the payment of the article will be made to the seller in a fixed number of installments till the sale price is recovered. If the buyer makes any default in remitting the installments due, the article will be seized by the seller and the amount, paid so far, will be treated as mere hire charges.

Installment

Hire-purchase and installment purchase are similar except for certain legal differences. Under installment system title to the article as well as articles are received by the purchaser. On default of payment the seller cannot seize the article but can approach the court of law.

Consumer Cooperatives

The history of modem Consumer Cooperative Society can be hued back to 1844, when one such was started in England. Today consumer cooperative society can be found anywhere in the world. In India the development of consumer cooperative society is not that encouraging due to the lack of efficient managerial personnel and the requisite funds.

A consumer cooperative store is a retail business owned and operated by the final consumers and distributes goods and services primarily to their members. The aim of consumer cooperative is to supply pure, unadulterated consumer goods like provision, stationery, textile, etc.

Features

A consumer cooperative store is a voluntary association of consumers duly registered under the existing Cooperative Society Act.

The membership of a consumer cooperative store is open to all. All adults irrespective of caste, creed, sex, etc. can become members.

The management of the store is democratic. The members of a consumer cooperative store have equal status with regard to voting rights. Here each member only one vote irrespective of the number of shares held by them.

Another feature of a consumer cooperative store is that goods are generally sold an cash basis.

Merits of consumer cooperative stores

The aim of consumer cooperative store is to supply goods to the members. Since only members are the purchasers cost of operation can be kept down, e.g. advertisement expenditures can be avoided.

The motive of profit is absent with regard to consumer cooperation and, therefore, articles are available at moderate rates.

For the purpose of setting up of the society, it is not necessary that the place has to be a busy one.

Cooperatives usually do not allow any credit and, therefore, no need of debts, the question of bad debts does not arise.

It is said that the spirit of cooperation is enhanced among the people.

Demerits

A serious demerit of a consumer cooperative store is that it does not serve the rich people as the items traded on such a store is mostly demanded by poor people.

Secondly, the belief that consumer cooperatives strengthen the spirit of cooperation is also challenged. Instead of cooperation between members, they usually compete with each other.

Functions of Middlemen

According to Cundiff and R.R. Still, middlemen specialise in performing operations or rendering services which are directly involved in the purchase and sale of goods in the process of their flow from producer to consumer. Producers and consumers owe much to their existence. Producers need not have to undertake the functions of marketing and similarly consumers and industrial users regard middlemen as their contact with producers.

The functions performed by middlemen could be summarised as follows:

First of all, they are the connecting link between the manufacturer and consumer.

Secondly, some of the important marketing functions are performed by middlemen. They are the functions of concentration, equalisation and dispersion of goods.

They add time, place and possession utilities to goods in the right time, at the right place and in the right proportion.

Middlemen are the people who specialise in the marketing functions. As they are specialist in the field of marketing, they can perform the marketing functions economically and effectively.

In some cases middlemen with a sound financial background provide financial assistance to manufacturers.

Another function, breaking the bulk is performed by middlemen. When the goods are sent out of the factory they are in the bulk form. It is the middleman who splits this bulk in convenient quantities and distributes them to consumers.

Lastly, middlemen provide useful service to small-scale producers. They, the small producers are unable to undertake direct marketing due to the lack of finance. Middlemen help such producers in marketing the goods.

Elimination of Middlemen

The channels of distribution perform the function of transferring goods from the place of production to the place of consumption. These functions are performed at a cost and this cost is to be borne by the consumers. Due to the existence of middlemen customers have got to pay a higher price for the product. Therefore, some people are against utilizing the services of middlemen.

Before going into the arguments in favour of eliminating middlemen, one fact has to be borne in mind. The discussion is not an eliminating the functions performed by middleman, but only the elimination of middlemen. The functions performed by middleman have to be performed by someone.

The main arguments in favour of the elimination of middleman are the following:

First, the main criticism is that the middlemen prevent any contact between the producer and the consumer. As the middlemen stand in between the producer and the consumer, the producer does not know the actual needs of the customers and it is never possible for the customers to make the producers aware of their genuine grievances.

Secondly, the existence of middleman can lead to over production and all risks associated with over production.

The reason for such an occurrence is producer's limited knowledge about customer requirements.

Thirdly, it is possible that the middlemen control the entire supply of a commodity. In such a case the middlemen are in a position to charge in proper prices.

Another complaint raised by the producer is that the middlemen are not at all interested in the volume of sales. They are only bothered about their commission.

Due to the defects associated with the functioning of middleman, producers are trying to eliminate middleman and sell the products directly. But still middlemen form a very important place in the marketing of the commodities. The reasons for this are:

(a) To eliminate the retailers from the chain of distribution is highly difficult.

(b) If one decides to eliminate wholesalers, wholesaling functions are to be performed by either manufacturers or retailers. But expecting manufacturers or retailers to perform wholesaling function is too much. Wholesaling is a skilled and specialised job which could effectively handled only by wholesalers.

(c) Even if producers think of direct marketing themselves, only big firms can do this. Small firms are unable to undertake such function due to the cost as well as task is involved. Therefore, middlemen are essential and their services cannot be dispensed with.

QUESTIONS FOR DISCUSSION

1. What is the distinction between physical distribution and channels of distribution?
2. Compare and contrast the term, physical distribution, and, channel of distribution.
3. "It is rightly said that survival of a sales organisation depends upon effective methods of distribution." Comment in the light of the various kinds of channels.
4. What are the various types of channels? Elaborate.
5. What are the various factors which must be considered while making channel selection?
6. What types of alternative distribution channels are available to a manufacturing company? Enumerate the factors determining the channel choices of a company.
7. Explain the major considerations in the selection of a distribution channel for consumer products. Give examples.
8. What is 'Retailing'? briefly describe with examples the most important store types.
9. What are the criteria that can be used for the evaluation of channel members? Illustrate your answer with appropriate examples.
10. What do you understand by distribution channel? A multinational is planning to launch its brand of cosmetics in India. What channels of distribution should it adopt to make an impact in the already crowded market of cosmetics?

STRATEGIC LOGISTICS AND PHYSICAL DISTRIBUTION MANAGEMENT

15

INTRODUCTION

Logistics has always been a central and essential feature of all economic activities. The concept of logistics as an integrative activity in business has developed within the last twenty years. For the clear understanding of logistics system, let us define logistics first. Logistics can be variously defined, but expressed most simply it is:

> "The process of strategically managing the movement and storage of materials, parts and finished inventory from supplier through the firm and on to customers."

Logistics is thus concerned with the management of the physical distribution of material. It begins from sources of supply and ends at the point of consumption. It is, therefore, much wider in its reach than simply a concern with the movement of finished goods—a commonly held view of physical distribution. Logistics deals with all activities that facilitate product flow from the point of raw material acquisition to the point of final consumption as well as the information flow that set the production in motion for the purpose of providing adequate levels of customer service at a reasonable cost. The scope of logistics is twofold: *First*, it is the movement of raw materials to the plant which is called *physical supply* or material management and *second*, it is the flow of finished products from the plant to the customers, called physical distribution.

Therefore, activities of physical distribution can be grouped under two sub-heads:

(a) Primary activities:
- — Transportation
- — Warehousing
- — Order processing
- — Inventory maintenance

(b) Secondary activities:
- — Product packaging
- — Product handling
- — Acquisition
- — Product scheduling
- — Information maintenance

Therefore, we can say that physical distribution is a part of Business Logistics. Physical distribution is thus the process of reaching the product to the customers and it encompasses all the activities in the physical flow of products from producer to customer.

The output of the logistics system is customer service, and how efficiently it is delivered is the standard against which physical distribution systems are measured. The physical distribution system is a semi-structured system. In the Indian context, it may be either open or closed system. To provide the appropriate level of customer service, physical distribution managers must make decisions concerning warehousing, inventory management and control and transportation system.

Here, Kotler's definition, finally, is a definition of market logistics: "Market logistics involve planning, implementing and controlling the physical flow of materials and final (finished) goods from point of origin to the point of use to meet customer requirements at a profit."

Source: Ronald H. Ballou, *Business Logistics Management: Planning and Control.*

THE CONCEPT OF LOGISTICS MANAGEMENT

The logistics concept is based on a total system view of the material and goods flow activity from the source of supply through to the final point of consumption. It recognises the interconnections and interrelationships between the multitude of functions involved in this movement from source to users and in so doing forces management to think in terms of managing the total system rather than just one part of it.

The logistics management task is concerned with the integration and coordination of marketing activities in a way that end markets are served in the most effective way. Although managers have used logistics in the military to fine-tune the process of delivery that is time and location specific, there is a lag in the incorporation of military logistics requirements in the civilian sector. Usually when the term logistics is used, the purpose is to reduce the transportation cost by adding warehousing information system.

THE STRATEGIC IMPORTANCE OF PHYSICAL DISTRIBUTION

Physical distribution doesn't have the prestige of advertising or personal selling, but can be every bit as important. At the most obvious level, you can't satisfy customers unless you can deliver the goods literally. From a strategic perspective, physical distribution is often one of the biggest influences on a company's product and managers responsible for distribution are playing a crucial role in marketing.

PHYSICAL DISTRIBUTION

Physical distribution refers to the movement of goods from producers to customers. It encompasses order processing, inventory management, materials handling, warehousing and transportation. It used to be regarded as a necessary evil, a tactical problem in which managers tried to do everything possible to minimise costs and hassles. However, this perception is changing quickly as organisations realise the strategic importance of physical distribution. In the beverage industry, for example, company leaders such as Henry Schimberg of Juhnston Coca-Cola Bottling Group, recognise that getting the product on store shelves quickly and efficiently is critical to building competitive advantage in the 1990s. To emphasize the importance of distribution he estimated that more than half of all new product failures results not from technology or market factors, but from mistakes in physical distribution.

Physical Distribution in the Marketing Mix

Even if you put together a clever, aggressive marketing strategy, you won't succeed if your firm's distribution system cannot provide the necessary support. Here is a quick look at how physical distribution can affect product design, pricing, and promotional activities.

Product Design

Distribution interacts with product design in three areas: physical product attributes, packaging, and competitive differentiation. Physical product attributes that affect distribution include weight, size, value and risk. For instance, a product such as ready-mix concrete needs specialised delivery equipment (including trucks and pumps) because it is heavy and has a short-life span. On the other hand, you can't spend a lot of money delivering cement because it is a product with low differentiation, and customers frequently look for the lowest price. Concrete suppliers usually specify a minimum order size such as four or eight cubic metres because it is too expensive to deliver smaller amounts.

Product packaging is an area that demands close cooperation between the marketing and shipping departments. Packaging often plays an important role in promotions, but it must not be at the expense of distribution. The packaging design has to provide adequate protection for the product, and it should be compatible with existing delivery systems. For example, the size and shape of a package can affect your ability to fill, stack it, or ship it.

Finally, marketers can use delivery to differentiate their products. The ability to deliver goods quickly or according to a customer-defined schedule is becoming an important means of establishing competitive advantage. Mail-order firms such as Lands' End, for example, use fast, guaranteed delivery to attract last minute Christmas or Deepawali shoppers. In years past, people who normally preferred to buy gifts from Lands' End would switch to retail stores as Christmas or Deepawali approached, out of worry that gifts wouldn't arrive on time. By using an express delivery service sellers maintain their competitive advantage for many more days in the peak-shopping season of the year.

Pricing

Pricing takes into account two sets of variables: market conditions and the cost providing products. To maximize profits, you do everything you can to minimize costs. In many industries, physical distribution is a big part of these costs. Companies that provide hospital supplies, for example, pay an average of 13.1 per cent of their revenues just to get the products to their customers. If a hospital supplier such as Baxter Health Care Corporation wants to lower its prices to gain competitive advantage, one of the first strings it might try to pull is lowering its distribution costs.

Major Costs of Business

1.	Manufacturing Cost	(48%)	:	Form Utility
2.	Marketing Cost	(27%)	:	Possession Utility
3.	Logistics Cost	(21%)	:	Time and Place Utility
4.	Profit	(4%)	:	

Promotion

Promotional programmes affect physical distribution when they create unexpected or irregular demand. Similarly, if a manufacturer runs a trade promotion for its distributor or an incentive contest for its sales force, the company's marketing, manufacturing and distribution staffs need to work together to create adequate product supply during the period of increased demand.

On the other hand, marketers sometimes intentionally limit the physical distribution of products, perhaps to increase the prices they're able to charge or to build mystique or to do both. For example, to create an exclusive image for their products, perfume suppliers are increasingly limiting the availability of their products. When perfumer Nina Ricci introduced its new Nina Scent, it made the product available only at Nordstrom department store chain. Such a move increases the market value of Nina because perfume buyers tend to seek out products that are more difficult to obtain.

OBJECTIVES OF PHYSICAL DISTRIBUTION

Physical distribution has two major goals: decreasing the cost of delivery and increasing customer satisfaction. (The customers of physical distribution include wholesalers, retailers, and final consumers.) Meeting these goals can be a complex problem that involves technological, marketing and administrative decisions. Here is a closer look at the objectives of physical distribution.

Total Cost Goals

Total cost concept refers to the practice of considering all the costs associated with distribution in order to attain the best balance among all the cost factors. A physical distribution system encompasses many cost elements, including transportation, storage, materials handling and the cost of sales lost due to inventory shortages. Often these cost elements are inversely related. For example, you can lower the cost of inventory by increasing your turnover. But it costs money to increase your inventory. These competing cost elements present a balancing challenge for management. The total cost concept of physical distribution refers to the goal of lowering the overall cost of distribution of striking the best balance among all the individual cost elements.

Customer Service Goals

More and more companies are realising that customer service is an integral part of their operations: not a nicety tacked on at the end of the process. Popular books such as *In Search of Excellence*; by Tom Peters and Robert Waterman, highlight the need for a company-wide approach to customer service. One result of this new awareness is increased attention to the role that physical distribution plays in satisfying customers. The customer service goals that are influenced by distribution fall into six categories: time, dependability, communication, convenience, product protection, and accuracy in filling the order.

Time. Reducing the time from ordering to delivery, is an important distribution goal for many companies. In this context, time is defined as lead time, order cycle time, or replenishment time. All of these terms refer to the time a company takes to deliver a product once a customer places an order. Time is the central issue in the cost-*versus*-service balance because decreasing delivery time often increases transportation and storage costs. In time-sensitive situations, however, customers are willing to pay the price for fast service.

Dependability. Dependability has two meanings in physical distribution. *First*, it indicates a supplier's ability to deliver products on schedule. Late deliveries to a manufacturing plant, for example, can shut down production lines and cause severe sales problems. On the other hand, early deliveries might sound like a good idea, but they have the potential to upset a customer's inventory system. *Second*, dependability refers to a supplier's overall consistency. As Robert Wayman of electronics and computer manufacturer Hewlett-Packard notes, "When somebody pays $5,00,000 for a piece computer equipment, they are not tolerant of poor delivery. They want it in a timely, complete fashion." Consequently, Hewlett-Packard has increased its attention to providing dependable delivery.

Communication. Suppliers and customers depend on communication to ensure efficient physical distribution. Communication must occur in three stages: receiving the order, tracking the delivery while it is in transit, and being able to trace3 deliveries that don't arrive on time. As customers increasingly demand fast, error-free shipments, communication will become more important.

Convenience. Suppliers can also gain competitive advantage by making distribution more convenient for their customers. For example, a textile producer makes life easier for one of its major customers by loading its delivery trucks in a particular sequence. Rather than tossing the rolls of cloth into the truck in random order, the producer loads them in the reverse order that the customers needs to unload them. This allows the customer to immediately unload the cloth and take it to the store without reshuffling materials inside its factory.

Product Protection. Safe and sound delivery relies on both adequate packaging and careful handling while in transit. Companies that control the distribution channel all the way to the final customer, have an advantage in this respect because they can directly oversee the handling of goods. However, companies that rely on wholesalers, retailers or transportation companies need to work with these channel members to see that the products are delivered without damage. Some van lines, for example, provide specialised trucks for transporting sensitive, scientific and engineering equipment.

Accuracy. Finally, customers demand that suppliers accurately fill and deliver the orders. This involves delivering the right goods to the right location and making sure that orders are complete. Delivering complete orders can be a challenge for companies with widespread manufacturing facilities. If an order is filled from more than one location, the company should take steps to ensure that shipments are coordinated and that all the pieces arrive simultaneously to minimize disruption at the customer's end.

Cost-Service Trade-offs

As you have probably surmised by now, the two major goals for physical distribution—decreasing cost and increasing customer satisfaction—are often in direct conflict. To achieve the right balance of cost and service, you need to understand the level of service that customers expect and that competitors deliver. Customers don't always define satisfaction in the same terms as suppliers, and various customers have different standards. In some cases, suppliers spend too much money on physical distribution, erroneously thinking they must do so to meet customer expectations. In other cases, companies choose the wrong standard or the wrong level to be considered good service.

High expenditures on distribution are often both warranted and necessary. For example, the distribution industry in Japan gets reviews for its efficiency and high level of service, but is also comparatively expensive. Consumers, however, apparently demand the extra level of service and are willing to pay for it.

Flexibility is an important part of this balancing act. You may want to provide a higher level of service to larger customers than you provide to smaller customers. In certain situations, you will need to exceed normal standards of service ongoing customer relationships.

ROLE OF LOGISTICS IN PRODUCTION AND SALES

- Major Factor performance as profit centre
  - Collection of Customer Information
  - Development of Transportation
  - Shift from Mass Production to Small Production for meeting various Consumer Needs.
- Logistics is the management function that controls all departments, but is not a sub-system that connects every department. The manufacturer can supply or distribute any kind of goods in any place under a good logistics system.

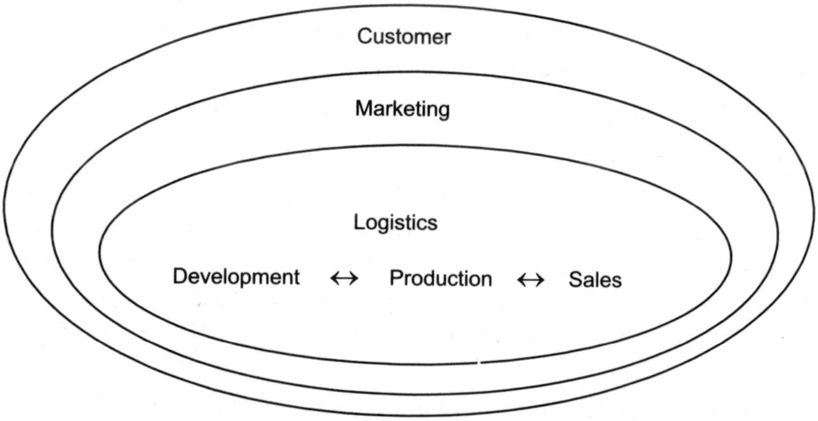

The Increasing Importance of Customer Service in Logistics of Marketing Activity

Marketing Activity	Rank in Order of Importance		
	1964	1975	1984
Pricing	5	1	2
Customer service	4	2	1
Sales personnel management	3	3	5
Product research and development	1	4	3
Market research	2	5	4

Source: Douglas M. Lambert and James R. Stock, *Strategic Logistics Management,* 1993, p. 28.

Types of Logistics

1. Supplier logistics

The key concept is to buy the right things. This clause has two requirements:

(a) To evaluate the quality of the supplier prior to issuing purchase orders.

(b) To clearly describe the products to be ordered in order to make sure that the supplier knows exactly what the firm wants.

For physical distribution management, the product is transportation and delivery services. Product to be purchased from the supplier may include:

1. Transportation services, and
2. Product storage (warehousing) services.

The suppliers should be evaluated regarded their capability to provide required services of acceptable quality level. Questions to be asked include:

(a) Do they have sufficient and reliable equipment?

(b) Do they have enough resources including manpower, storage space, etc.?

(c) Are their resources and equipment well managed?

(d) Do they have the system to allocate their resources?

Orders to be placed to the supplier should be presented with all necessary information, which may include:

1. Desired date, time and routing of the required transportation service.
2. Required storage conditions of the merchandise, etc.

These are essential macro elements for growth of healthy logistics plan.

2. Production/Corporate logistics

To cater to growing market needs, we need to establish a new production system for our logistics as well as production areas to accomplish the true REAL TIME SALES system. For this a new revolutionary production project team is to be formed whose sole purpose is to establish "Production/Sales/Logistics total linkage system" that will eventually eliminate overstock and shortage problems. This kind of a production system is called *Market Linkage Production System (MLPS)*.

If this system is adopted in India, the following results will be achieved:

Current Situation

(a) The time period spend on establishing sales and production plans is too long. The longer it gets, the accuracy of such plans is reduced. In a constantly changing market, it is inevitable to adjust or modify plans.

(b) Too many departments are involved in approving a "production/supply plan". These departments are the sales, the product marketing, the product management and purchasing departments. Such successive operations from one department to another require a long period of time and also there is no consistency in transferring of all information.

(c) There is a low level of utilisation of information systems in formulating all plans. All the necessary data from production and purchase plans are not generated by the information systems but are maintained manually. Real time sale system cannot be achieved under current system due to rapid changes of various production plans within a company as well as other companies such as suppliers or vendors.

Situation After Using MLPS

1. In order to produce and supply the actual market demand, it is very crucial to establish a logistic system closely linked with the market trends. It is imperative to develop the information that will enable the production/supply system to cope with market variations. MLPS consists of "Replenishment Production System". That supports the production and the "Purchase Support System", and aids the ordering of parts and materials as sub-system.
2. All project operations should be executed by the task force team consisting of those who have accumulated much experience from earlier operations. The corporate logistics management department supports directing each phase of operation and developing and designing of the system. The task force team should be led by the Logistics Management Department's Logistics Information System (LIS) team leader and should consist of members from various departments, such as production, logistics, purchasing, corporate logistics management and information systems.

ORGANISATION

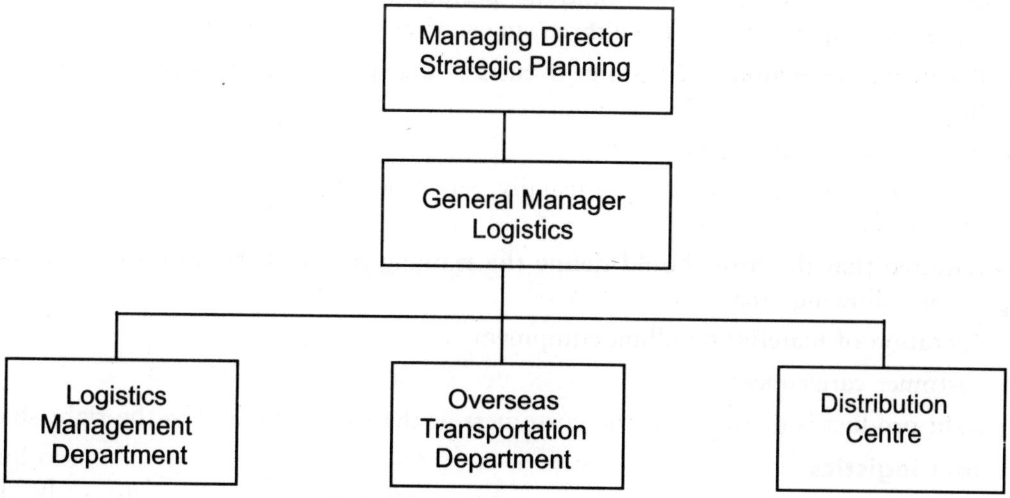

3. All team members should follow their role in executing their top responsibilities.

Now we shall explain certain specific terms under MLPS:

(a) **Replenishment Production System (RPS).** RPS analyses the trends of all outgoing shipments from distribution centres to all dealers and of inventory movements at factory warehouse. It then generates "Actual demand/Marketing information" from which the most suitable production plan by model/line is established. It then creates the optimal production level and decides the production order for days (2 and 3) by everyday simulation process. The production would exist just for a specified number of days. This means that the company possesses production plan in terms of days rather than in terms of months. It also means that the daily market changes are represented on production plans since the system relies on "Actual demand marketing information" instead of on the "more sales plan".

(b) **Purchase Support System (PSS).** PSS makes possible RPS to work successfully and consists of (1) single resource plan, (2) ordering, and (3) payments. Such standard MPLs can re-establish the business process that will cut down the "Total Cycle Time" from customers to vendors. This process will expedite the process responding to the customer needs, prevent shortage problems and reduce the unnecessary cost, which arises from overstock. MLPS has several requirements:

(i) Documented procedures defining the number of processes.

(ii) Use of suitable equipment and working environment.

(iii) Monitoring suitable process parameters.

(iv) Maintenance of equipment.

The firm should establish some procedures or instructions to define the proper manner of handling, transporting, storing and delivering products. Transportation equipment and storage equipment and storage equipment should be periodically serviced to insure the customer functioning. The company should have three stages of inspection, which are:

(1) Receiving, inspection and testing. It ensures that product arrives in company in good shape.

(2) In-process inspection and testing.

(3) Final inspection and testing are usually performed before dispatching the product to the customer.

It is required that the firm should define the training needs of its employees and provide training in the following areas:.

(A) Operation of material handling equipment

(B) Customer care/concern

The right product is delivered to the customers at the right time and in the right shape.

3. Customer logistics

Customer logistic mainly a framework of "7 Rs": "Right quantity of the Right product or service to the Right place in the Right conditions at the Right cost and the Right time with the Right impression."

Intention to achieve on-time delivery and realise customer satisfaction by implementing a swift and flexible Customer Logistic System and utilising it as:

It includes various activities:

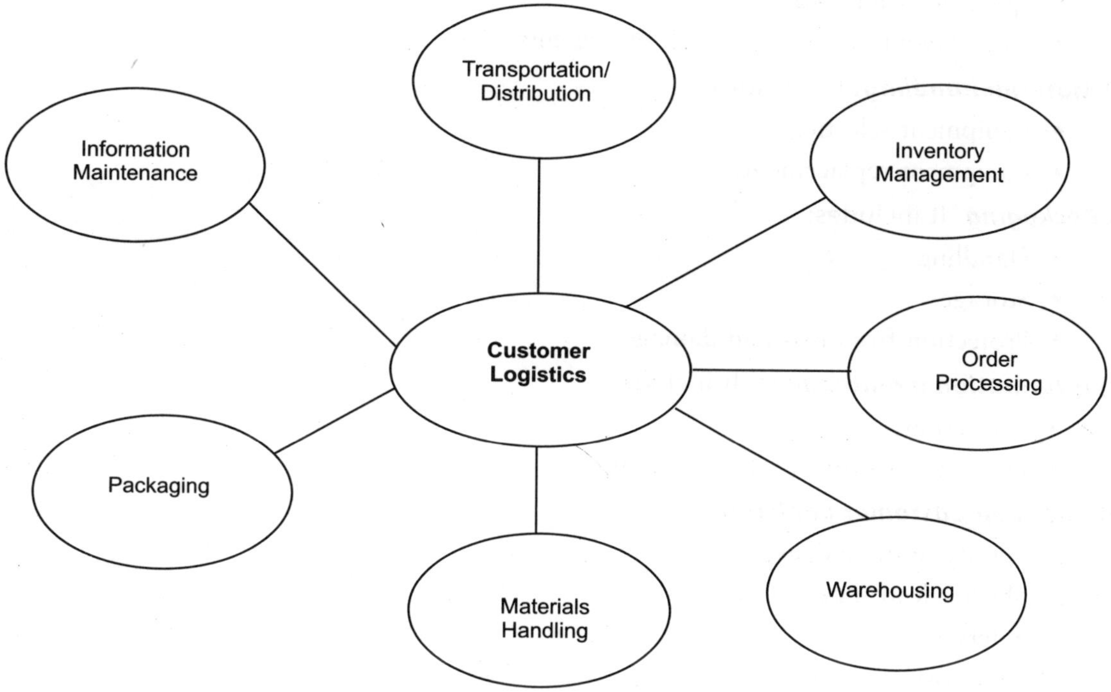

(a) *Transportation.* It includes:

- Decision to be taken regarding the mode of transport
- Service selection
- Freight consolidation
- Carrier routing
- Vehicle scheduling
- Claims processing
- Freight rate and quality of service.

(b) *Inventory management.* It includes:

- Short-term sales forecasting
- Product mix at stocking points
- Number, size and location of stocking points
- Just in time (JIT) or push or pull strategies.

(c) *Order processing.* It includes:

- Order Information transmittal methods
- Ordering intervals.

(d) *Warehousing.* It includes:

- Space determination
- Stock layout and design Stock placements.

(e) *Material handling.* It includes:

- Equipment selection
- Equipment replacement.

(f) *Packaging.* It includes:

- Handling
- Storage
- Protection from loss and damage.

(g) *Information maintenance.* It includes:

- Collection
- Data analysis and control procedure.

(h) *Focus on Customer Logistics*

1. Speedy on-time delivery
2. Shorter lead time
3. Safety
4. Low cost.

FUNCTIONAL AREAS OF PHYSICAL DISTRIBUTION

There are seven important functional areas of physical distribution.

1. Network Design

Manufacturing plants, warehouses, material handling, distribution and after-sales services are typical logistics facilities. Network design is one of the prime responsibilities of physical distribution management. It is essential to determine the number and location of all types of facilities required to perform physical distribution task. The selection of a superior locational network can provide the first step towards competitive advantage. Physical distribution efficiency directly depends on the proper design of network and infrastructure.

2. Information Technology

Two major areas that depend on information are:

- *Sales forecasting.* Sales forecasting is done to estimate the future requirements of physical distribution. It helps inventory management to satisfy anticipated customer requirements.
- *Order management.* Customer's order is very important in physical customers. External customers are those who consume the products or services as also any trading partner who purchases products or services for resale.

Internal customers are organisational units within a company.

The more efficient the design of company's physical distribution system, the more sensitive it is to information accuracy. Incorrect information and delays in order processing can cripple the performance of physical distribution elements.

3. Transportation

It helps in positioning inventory geographically. There are three forms of transport, i.e., private cartage, contract carriage and public carriage.

There are two fundamental factors affecting transportation performance:

- *Cost.* It is the payment for movement between two locations and expenses related to administration and maintaining in-transit inventory. Hence, physical distribution systems should be designed to utilise transportation that minimizes total system cost.
- *Speed.* It is the time required to complete a specific movement. Speed and cost of transportation are related in two ways:
  (i) Faster service with higher rates, and
  (ii) Faster service means shorter time interval.

Therefore, balancing of speed and cost is necessary.

4. Just-in-time (JIT) Transport Management

Just-in-transport management is an increasingly popular method used to manage inventory levels. Manufacturers in a number of industries employ it to help them reduce the amount of production supplies they keep on hand. The following the benefits of implementing JIT concept in transport and inventory management:

Benefits and Justification of JIT Implementation in Transport and Inventory Management

Multitudes of JIT benefits are identified in the early JIT literature. However, some of them seem inappropriate in practical life. Some are elements, which have been advocated as components of the implementation process itself (i.e. some authors say that a variable is a component of the implementation process itself, while some say that it is a result of JIT implementation, e.g., transport improvement or inventory reduction are pre-requisites to JIT implementation or result of implementation). To describe a variable as a component of JIT implementation and then designate it as a benefit utilised in measuring the level of success of JIT implementation is a circular logic. Specifically, if reductions in lead-time, set-up time and lot sizes are seen as a part of the implementation process itself, can these reductions be seen as success factors? Apparently, a more 'cause-and effect-type' relationship is desirable for measuring successful implementation.

Seven results were selected for this study as benefits of JIT implementation:

(a) Downtime reduction

(b) Inventory reduction

(c) Workspace reduction

(d) Increased quality

(e) Increased manpower utilization

(f) Increased equipment utilization

(g) Increased inventory turnover.

Each of these is discussed here:

(a) Downtime reduction

In order to make the lot size cuts proposed by JIT advocates, equipment must be readily available for use. The demise of buffer stock means that product machinery must be capable of running what is needed, when it is needed, if the current demand is to be met. In situations where 'just-in-case' inventory has not been made, unexpected downtime can result in inability to respond to the demand. In addition, the increased use of preventive maintenance in a JIT environment can also result in decreased downtime.

(b) Inventory reduction

In a JIT environment, total inventory level falls. Raw material is reduced by smaller purchased lot sizes and more frequent deliveries. Work-in-process is reduced by the shift to smaller lot sizes, which are, in turn, made possible by shorter set-up times. When the firm produces at a rate demanded in the market, goods are shipped as soon as they are finished. Also there is no need to accumulate finished goods in the warehouse. Even very early JIT literature contains numerous examples, which support the contention that inventory reduction is an indicator of JIT implementation success. These examples display inventory reduction benefits, ranging up to 97 per cent.

(c) Workspace reduction

Less workspace is needed in a JIT environment owing to the smaller lot sizes and reduces inventory levels. This reduction is mostly due to the absence of stored inventory, both between and within work centres. This absence of inventory, in addition to the use of group technology techniques, has allowed some firms to move work centres closer together, freeing space and reducing material handling distances. This results in a neater, more organised facility, which provides for speed identification of bottlenecks and fewer lost parts. Japanese plants are typically one-third the size of US plants providing a comparable output. An average company adopting JIT should be able to reduce workspace by 25 to 50 per cent.

(d) Increased quality

Reduction of 'in-house' lot sizes promotes rapid feedback from downstream work centres when there is a quality problem. This feedback results in a reduction of scrap, rework and ultimately a higher overall level of quality. Further cross training of workers as an element of JIT implementation enables them to assist each other, whenever a quality problem arises. For purposes of this study, increased quality is measured as a decrease in scrap and rework.

(e) Increased manpower utilization

Cross training of employees allows less worker idle time when a machine is not needed for production. Having workers with the ability to move from one work centre to another results in increased manpower utilisation. The number of workers needed, can then be reduced with no consequential drop in output.

(f) Increased equipment utilization

The introduction of total preventive maintenance, the cross training of workers, smaller and more flexible machinery and the use of group technology techniques, combine to increase equipment utilisation.

(g) Increased inventory turnover

Reduction in inventory and lot sizes results in increased inventory turnover. Inventory turnovers at Haworth doubled in one year after implementing JIT, while other examples include threefold, fourfold and even six-fold increase.

Inventory Management

The interest of management in better inventory management is much more than it was few years back. Management knows the need, importance and practicability of scientific inventory management.

The conflicting objectives of inventory control are reflected in the seemingly conflicting demands, which are made on an inventory manager from time to time. For example, stocks are to be kept at a low level but not too low; turnover is to be increased by only at satisfactory profit rate; bulk purchases are to be attempted to obtain better prices but over-buying is to be controlled; special attention is to be given to the disposal of obsolete or near obsolete items but not before the point of obsolescence is identified; and so on.

Selecting Inventory Control Techniques

S. No.	Title	Basis	Main uses
1.	A.B.C. (Always Better Control)	Value of consumption	To control raw material components and work-in-progress inventories in the normal course of business
2.	H.M.L. (High, Medium, Low)	Unit price of material	Mainly to control purchases
3.	X.Y.Z.	Value of items in storage	To review the inventories and their uses at scheduled intervals
4.	V.E.D. (Vital Essential Desirable)	Criticality of component	To determine the stocking levels of spare parts
5.	F.N.S.D. (Fast, Nominal, Slow, Dead, etc.)	Consumption pattern of the component	To control obsolescence
6.	S.D.E. (Scarce, Difficult, Easy to obtain)	Problems faced in procurement	Lead-time analysis and purchasing strategies
7.	G.O.L.F. (Government, Ordinary, Local, Foreign sources)	Source of the material	Procurement strategies
8.	S.O.S. (Seasonal, off-seasonal)	Nature of supplies	Procurement/Holding strategies for seasonal items like agricultural products

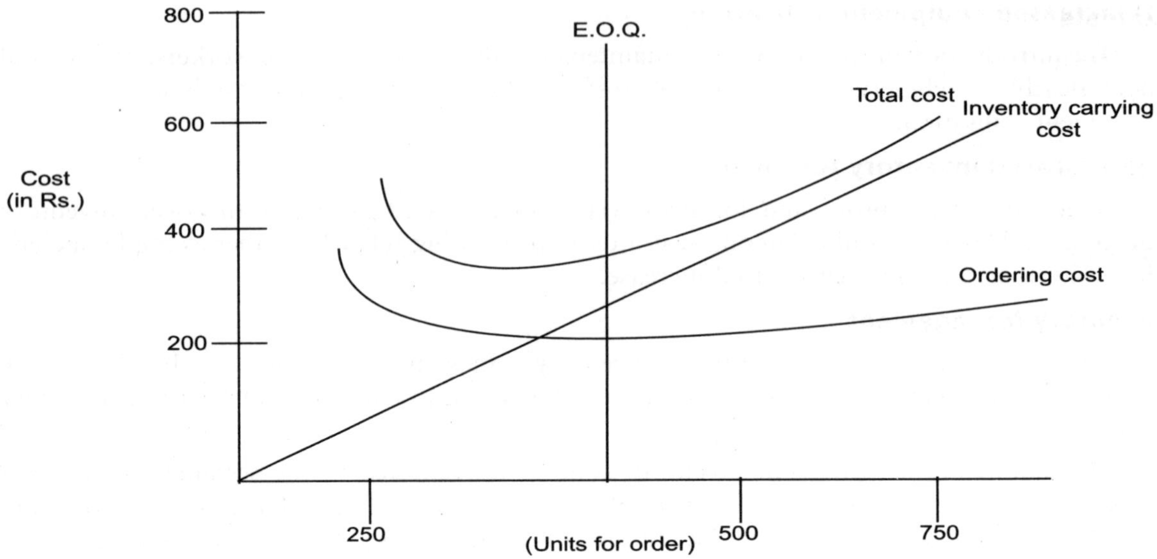

Economic Order Quantity (E.O.Q.)

Economic order quantity is the quantity for which orders are placed when stock reaches the re-order level. E.O.Q. is the quantity, which is most economical to order. In other words, E.O.Q. is that size of the order, which gives maximum economy in purchasing material and ultimately contributes towards maintaining the material at the optimum level and at minimum cost.

With E.O.Q., two types of costs should be taken into account:

(1) **Ordering cost.** This is the cost of placing an order with supplier. Because of so many factors involved, it is quite difficult to quantify this cost.

(2) **Inventory carrying cost.** It includes the following:

   (a) Cost of operating the stores,
   (b) The incidence of insurance costs,
   (c) Interest on capital locked up in store, and
   (d) Deterioration and wastage of material.

Mathematical Formulae

E.O.Q. can also be calculated with the help of a formula as given below:

$$\text{E.O.Q.} = \sqrt{\frac{2.A.B}{CS}}$$

where E.O.Q. = Economic Order Quantity
A = Annual Consumption in Units
B = Cost of placing an order
CS = Storage or carrying cost per unit

Example

The annual demand for a product is 64,000 units. The unit cost is Rs. 6 and inventory – carrying cost is 2.5% per annum. If the cost of one procurement is Rs. 75, determine:

(i) E.O.Q.

(ii) Numbers of orders per year

(iii) Time between two consecutive orders

Solution

$$\text{E.O.Q.} = \sqrt{\frac{2.A.B}{CS}}$$

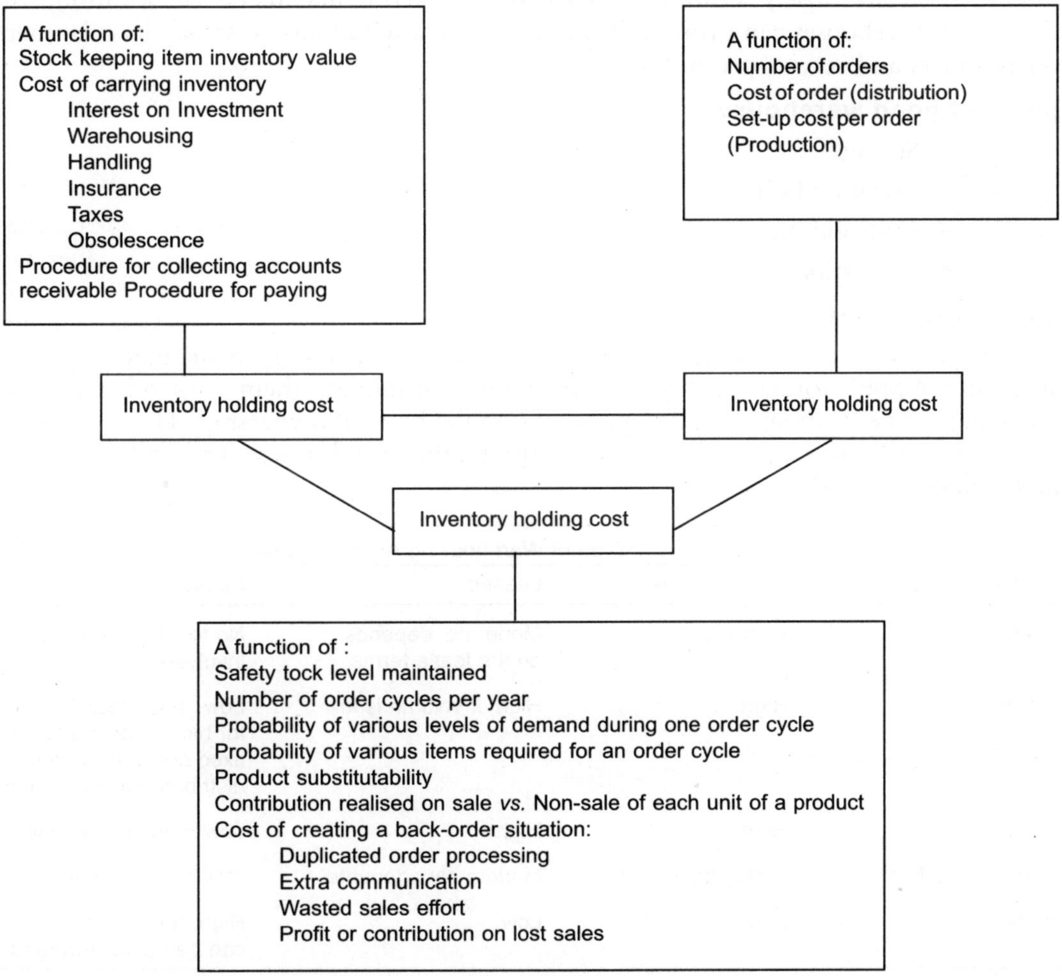

Source: James L. Heskett, Nicholas A. Claskowsky, Jr. and Robert M. Ivie, Business Logistics.

$$= \sqrt{\frac{2 \times 64000 \times 75}{6 \times 2.5\%}} = 8,000 \text{ units}$$

(i) Number of orders per year = 64000/8000 = 8 orders in a year

(ii) Time between two consecutive orders

12 months/8 orders = 1½ months

The above figure shows the trade-off typically found in managing and controlling inventory levels:

5. Warehousing

Warehouses provide a key link in the physical distribution chain, and like other stages of distribution, they are closely scrutinised by today's marketing managers. The location, size and capabilities of warehouses can profoundly affect a company's ability to satisfy its customers and deliver products and service profitability.

Purposes of good warehouse

- Storage
- Breaking bulk
- Consolidation
- Utilisation

Types of warehouses

The basic purpose of warehousing in distribution logistics is to arrange placement of products and supply storage facility to store them, consolidate them with other and similar products and divide them into smaller quantities on the basis of ownership. There are two types of warehouses: (i) private warehouses, and (ii) public warehouses. The following decision variables can be considered:

	Type of Warehousing Arrangements		
Decision Variables	Private Owned	Leased	Public
1. Fixed Investment	Very high	Moderate, depends on the lease terms	No fixed investment is involved
2. Unit cost	High	High, if volume is low	Low, since facilities are on for hire as needed and fixed costs are widely distributed among users
3. Control	High	High	Low managerial control
4. Adequate product line	Highly adequate	Moderately adequate	May not be convenient
5. Flexibility	Low	Low	High; termination of usage can be easily arranged

Fig. 15.1: Decision variables in choosing among types of warehouses

Factors affecting warehousing choice

The warehousing decision is influenced by the difficulty of moving goods directly from the assembly line to buyers or public warehouses. The following factors have to be kept in mind when deciding the location of a warehouse:

- Product type
- Transportation cost
- Markets
- Rent
- Labour supply
- Taxes
- Geography
- Competition

6. Material Handling Equipment

Material handling is such an important activity that it cannot be avoided in the performance of logistics. Material handling activities should be minimized, as it requires a very high capital investment and direct labour cost. The network of facilities forms a structure from which logistical operations are performed within a network design framework as per the requirement of customers.

Transportation is required for materials handling—for efficient loading and unloading. In warehouse operations, materials handling involves products to be received, moved, sorted and assembled to meet requirements of customers and distributors.

Products in the forms of cans, bottles or boxes are combined into larger units to make master cartons because it protects the products during the logistical process.

Materials handling system in logistics is designed under certain guidelines. These are very important to assist management. These are:

1. Equipment for materials handling and storage should be standardised.
2. The system should be designed to provide maximum continuous product flow as per the requirements of the company.
3. Handling equipment should be properly utilised.

Classification of material handling system

Material handling systems in logistics are mainly divided into three categories.

1. **Mechanised System.** These systems utilise a combination of labour and handling equipment to facilities receiving, processing and/or shipping. Labour constitutes a high percentage of overall cost in mechanised handling. Even then, the mechanised-handling systems are very common. They employ a wide range of handling equipments. These are:

   (a) Forklift trucks

   (b) Walkie-rider pallet trucks

   (c) Town lines

(d) Tow tractors with trailors
(e) Electric hoists or cranes
(f) Conveyors.

2. **Semi-automated system.** When selected handling functions are performed using automated equipment and the remaining job is completed on a mechanised basis then the system is said to be semi-automated. It can be called as a mixture of automated and mechanised handling.

The main equipments used in semi-automated system are:

(i) Automated-guided vehicle system (AGVS)
(ii) Sortations
(iii) Robotics

3. **Automated system.** Automated system attempts to minimise labour as much as practicable by substituting capital investment in equipment.

7. Secondary Packaging

Secondary packaging includes handling and storage of finished goods. It also emphasises on protection from loss and damage.

To sum up, physical distribution management is the framework of seven 'Rs'—*right* quantity of the *right* product or service to the *right* place in the *right* conditions at the *right* cost and the *right* time with *right* impression. Excellence in each aspect of functional work is relevant and must be viewed in terms of improving the overall efficiency and effectiveness of integrated physical distribution.

PHYSICAL DISTRIBUTION—TASKS AND APPROACHES

The physical distribution process comprises two interrelated efforts, i.e., goods flow and information flow. Information from and about customers flows through the enterprise in the form of sales activity, forecasts and orders. This information is refined into manufacturing and procurement plans. A value-added inventory flow results in transfer of finished products to customers.

There are three major components of physical distribution operations:

(a) **Physical distribution.** Physical distribution refers to those activities, which are related to providing customer service. It requires performing order receipt and processing, deploying inventories, storage, handling and outbound transportation within a channel of distribution. It coordinates with market planning such as pricing, promotional support, customer service levels, delivery standards, handling returns and lifecycle support. Its main objective is to assist in revenue generation by providing desired customer service levels at the lowest total cost.

(b) **Manufacturing support.** These activities are related to planning scheduling and supporting manufacturing operations. It requires master schedule planning and performing work-in-progress storage, handling, transportation and time phasing of components. It is responsible for storage of inventory at manufacturing site and maximum coordination between manufacturing and physical distribution activities.

(c) **Procurement.** It is related to obtaining products and materials from outside suppliers. It performs resource planning, supply sourcing, negotiation, order placement, inbound transportation, receiving and inspection, storage and handling and quality assurance. It is responsible for coordination with suppliers for better scheduling, supply continuity, hedging and speculation as well as research leading to new sources or programmes. Its main objective is to support manufacturing or resale organisations by providing timely purchase at the lowest total cost.

Inventory flows. It is concerned with the movement and storage of materials and finished products. It starts with the shipment of materials or component parts from a supplier and ends when a manufactured or processed product is delivered to a customer.

The physical distribution process adds value by moving inventory when and where needed. Work-in-process inventory must be moved to support final assembly, thereby gaining value at each step of its transportation into finished inventory.

Information flows. Information integrates these three operating components. These components contain the actual physical distribution work and information facilities, coordination of planning and control of day-to-day operations.

QUESTIONS FOR DISCUSSION

1. How can logistics be used to gain critical customer service advantage? Use examples from the Indian market to illustrate your answer.
2. How does a marketing manager select logistics?
3. Explain the terms distribution channels, physical distribution and logistics and identify how they together relate to distribution strategy.

CASE STUDY 15.1

NATIONAL FERTILIZERS LIMITED: DISTRIBUTION CHALLENGES

The modern concept of marketing is the management orientation holds that the key of organisations is to determine the needs and wants of targets markets and to adopt the organisation to deliver the desired satisfaction more effectively and efficiently than its competitors.

One more step ahead, there is the societal marketing concept, which answer to the dilemmas of marketing concepts like the conflicts between consumer wants, consumer interests and long run societal welfare.

The National Fertilizers Limited (NFL) follows the latter concept. The basic objective of NFL is not only the sale and distribution of fertilizers and other agricultural inputs, but also promoting their use to increase fertilizer use efficiency and to provide complete package of practices. Every fertilizer manufacturer and marketer in the country, thus has both social and economic responsibility not only in popularizing the fertilizer manufactured and marketed by them but also in ensuring their balanced and judicious use by the farmers in obtaining a favourable cost benefit ratio.

The objectives which lay the foundation of marketing philosophy of NFL are as under:

(a) To arrange fertilizers at the right time at the right time at the right place and at the door steps of farmers.

(b) To evolve modern technology for efficient and judicious use of fertilizers.

(c) To educate the farmers to use fertilizers in the most efficient and scientific way for increasing crop production.

(d) To study the demand forecast and provide after-sales service.

As marketing of fertilizers differs from marketing of other consumer items because of basic differences in its use pattern and clientele, fertilizers is neither consumer nor industrial good. The end product of consumer good may be better health, personality, etc., but not better economy. But in case of fertilizers the end product is better economy.

Thus, the factor economy and the market of fertilizers being the rural sector essentially, marketing fertilizers poses a fascinating the exciting challenge to the company. The requires a lot of creativity, imagination, institutional power alertness and firm decisive actions in dealing with rural farmers who provide tremendous range of contradictions and paradoxes, different characteristic life styles, the problem of huge distance due to the highly dispersed, thinly populated farmer community. The pressures of varying religious cultural and social atmosphere also adds to this challenge. So due to the above-mentioned hurdles, group situation in which the communicator finds himself at the time when he is moved to make the desired response.

Marketing Organisation

National Fertilizers Limited concentrates on its target market from its central marketing office, Chandigarh. This office coordinates and controls the marketing activities for all the three plants of NFL, viz., Panipat, Bhatinda and Nangal. The marketing area of NFL comprises of the States of Punjab, Haryana, Rajasthan, Jammu and Kashmir, Himachal Pradesh, Delhi and some districts of Western Uttar Pradesh and the Union Territory of Chandigarh.

The location of regional offices in different states are as under:

Haryana	:	Karnal
Punjab	:	Jalandhar and Bhatinda
Rajasthan	:	Jaipur
Uttar Pradesh	:	Lucknow

The area offices for the state of Jammu and Kashmir are at Jammu and for Himachal Pradesh at Shimla.

A regional marketing manager heads each regional marketing office. The regional marketing manager of each state is assisted by a deputy manager (marketing), deputy manager (finance and accounts), assistant manager (publicity and public relations), statistician and other personnel.

Each are office is headed by areas officer. There are a number of area offices under each regional marketing office. The area office comprises of a number of districts and its area officer gets assistance from area agronomists, junior manager and an accounts assistants.

There are dispatch and coordination cells, one each at Panipat, Nangal and Bhatinda. These are supervised by an assistant manager (D&C) who is responsible for the entire dispatch and coordination with the producing units. There are also invoicing sections one each at Panipat, Nangal and Bhatinda, which look after the entire invoicing of the material dispatched from the unit.

Head Office: NFL has it's corporate office at 20 Community Centre, East of Kailash, New Delhi.

Central Marketing Office: A common marketing office for the plants of NFL (Panipat, Bhatinda and Nangal) is located at Chandigarh.

Fertilizer Distribution

Fertilizers are manufactured in our country by various factories in the private and public sector. So far quite a significant quantum of fertilizer is imported to fill the gap between production and requirement. This requirement is met by imports called Central Fertilizer Pool being imported on Government's account.

As demand for fertilizers is seasonal in nature, fertilizers are sold twice in a year. So to make available the product to the consumers at the peak of the season, a walking distribution system is adopted to catch the opportunity even for the sale of one bag of fertilizer. The philosophy of NFL is to provide the product at the doorstep of the farmer and as such it holds the view that even the slightest demand should not be lost.

As a matter of fact the fertilizers need to be reached to ultimate consumption ends, that is, farmers, at the right time, at the right place at optimum cost through right kinds of modes of distribution. As far as selling and distribution in case of fertilizers is concerned, care must be taken of the following points:

1. Determination of mode of transport (rail or both)
2. Consideration of time factor
3. Elimination of cross movement to reduce cost
4. Use of cheaper modes subject to satisfy and time factor.

Fertilizers are manufactured round the year but its consumption is seasonal in nature. It envisages the managerial skill to maintain an optimum level of inventory and search for potential markets, which can lift fertilizers even in the off season so that inventory carrying certain off season discount/rebates to concerned parties are lifted in off seasons.

Channel of Distribution

Punjab and Haryana are the major markets for NFL's produce out of the total production of fertilizers in NFL plants. The specific quota has been fixed for the distribution of different states and union territories by the Government of India. Quota allotted to different states and union territories is liable to increase or decrease up to some extent depending upon whether or not a state or union territory is able to lift the product in the off season and the demand for the whole allotted quota in the beginning of the season. Therefore, distribution is done accordingly and thus the policy is flexible.

NFL's fertilizers are marketed through a well established two tier marketing organisation. Although the policy of NFL is to promote as much sale through the cooperatives and the other institutional agencies as possible yet the private dealers are key figure in the distribution network. They help NFL in distribution, creating product awareness and developing organisations image, collecting marketing intelligence and providing vital feedback with regard to quality demand and consumer satisfaction.

Distribution channels of their two tier marketing organization is as under:

Apex Bodies

These are the institutional agencies, viz.,

1. Hafed (Haryana)
2. Markfed (Punjab)
3. Agro Industries Corporation of various states
4. Himfed (H.P.)
5. Nafed (New Delhi)
6. Rajasthan State Cooperative Marketing Federation Ltd., Jaipur
7. Mini Banks (Haryana)
8. Focal Institutional Agencies place their order with Central Marketing Office, Chandigarh. It coordinates departmental work and informs dispatch

In order to make sure availability of rail rakes, marketing people hold their meeting with the railway management to have sufficient rakes available at the plant sites. Though the policy of NFL is to promote as much sales through the apex bodies a possible yet the private dealers' network is the kingpin of the distribution strategy of NFL. Approximately 50% of the quota allotted to a state by the central government is distributed through Apex Bodies. Apex Bodies also get different shares of quota from NFL. For example, in the State of the Haryana Hafed distribution 50% and the Haryana State Agro Industries Corporation 7% of the quota allotted to cooperative channels. In Punjab, Markfed gets 50%, and Punjab State Agro Industries Corporation gets 25% which is distributed through focal points (in the interiors of Punjab).

Private Dealers Network

As channelization of fertilizers by the company is through institutional buyers and private dealers, about half of the product is distributed through private dealer channels.

The primary demand projections are made for the districts by the concerned development of fertilizers, keeping in view the potential of the area, prospective of irrigation in the district, further coverage under high yielding variety (HYV), cropping intensity. These sales estimates are prepared for the whole state involving the interaction of agronomists and district managers.

The dealer category is constituted by:

1. Traditional dealers.
2. Small scale traders.
3. Ex-servicemen.
4. Entrepreneurial development scheme.

5. Scheduled and backward classes.
6. M.P.D.C., i.e. multipurpose distribution centre under the central government's scheme for unemployed graduates and for economically weaker sections.
7. Ad-hoc dealers.

Allocation of Quata to Dealers of NFL

In the beginning, NFL quota fixation policy was on the basis of taking overage lifting of fertilizer in the slack period (from March to May) for the seasonal period. If a dealer lifted 100 tonnes each in the three months of the slack period, his quota was determined by taking the simple average of lifting (100+100+100) that is 100 tonnes. To avoid this, he did not lift fertilizers in the month of March and April but in May be lifted 300 tonnes which saved the two months storing charges and making no effect on the determination of quota for the season. Average is still 100 tonnes.

$$\frac{(\text{Zero} + \text{Zero} + 300)}{3} = 100 \text{ tonnes}$$

As a result NFL had to incur the storing charges for the huge stock of fertilizers. The overcome this situation, NFL adopted the policy of taking the weighted average instead of simple average. For example, it a dealer lifted 3x tonnes in March, 2y tonnes in April and 1z tonnes in May, his quota for season was determined by taking weighted average as follows:

$$\frac{3\times = 2y = 1z}{6} = \text{K tonnes}$$

Mode of Distribution of Fertilizers

Major carriers of fertilizers from factory to farm in the country are railways and road transportation. The monthly rake plane from different units is made based on sales estimates for different locations. This is forwarded to the railways for approval. After the necessary moderation and approval, the copies are forwarded to dispatch units as well as to the field staff.

When the rake actually moves from the unit to the concerned destination (called primary movement), a telegraphic message is sent to the field staff. By the time the rake reaches, the entire field force is in a position to assist the concerned officials in handling and disposal of rake. It is on the record that at certain destinations three rakes reached at tone time from different units, but the entire stock was delivered to dealers without any wastage and damage.

Development of NFL Agro Service Centers

NFL has developed a new promotional technology by establishing a chain of Agro Service Centers in different states for opening a direct sales point purpose. The work of these Agro Service Centers is not only to provide fertilizers but also supplies quality seeds for various cereals, pulses and cash crops, pesticides and chemicals needed for plant protection, hiring services, soil testing facilities, etc.

The main objectives of Agro Service Centers are as under:

1. To ensure timely supply of NFL's fertilizers and other fertilizers, seeds, agrochemicals, etc., through Agro Service Centers and sales points.
2. To provide hire services to the weaker section of farmers by a equipping the Agro Service Centers and sales points with dusters, sprayers, seed testing drums, etc.
3. To provide soil and water-testing service to the farmers in the different villages with the objective of efficient use of fertilizers.
4. To educate the farmers and salesmen by arranging the training programme, crop seminars, field days, etc.
5. To create a good impact on the public, government, officers, farmers, etc., through meetings and discussions.
6. To popularize the use of bio-fertilizers by installation of Gobar Gas Plants.
7. To provide free distribution of crop literature.
8. To assist farmers by way of necessary credit for purchasing various agriculture input through commercial banks.
9. To extend all possible help which is conductive to the attainment of the above objective.

Market Control System

Having a rational plan and strategy need not necessarily result in rational implementation of the same. NFL always remains aware of this part. Thus the sales/supply plan is backed up by monthly review and timely removal of bottlenecks that keep on emerging from time to time. Every effort is made to keep the inventory low because inventory is recognised cost, marketing control is a natural sequel to planning and action programme involving continuous monitoring of marketing activities and spotting of trends, problems and opportunities in the market. Marketing control is carried out by:

1. Sales analysis
2. Market share analysis
3. Sales to expense ratio
4. Tracing of cultivators, attitudes/efficiency of service rendered to the company.

These studies are conducted regularly by the market research section to close the gap that has occurred, in targeting fixed and action performance. Regular forms of marketing territory are made by supervisory personnel at various levels for dual functions, controlling and helping to resolve the day to day problems of not only the staff but dealers as well as farmers.

QUESTIONS FOR DISCUSSION

1. Do you think the existing distribution channel is sufficient for NFL? Support your answer.
2. Is NFL covering the whole country market? If yes how? If not why?
3. How can NFL improve its distribution channel for the access of its product in the whole Indian market?

CASE STUDY 15.2

CHANNEL MANAGEMENT AT MAXWELL

The President of Maxwell Corporation is considering whether the company should set up its own distribution system or whether it should outsource the entire distribution and logistics function to a third party service provider. The company has set up a manufacturing plant at Vizag where wide range of orthopaedic equipments, viz., crutches, wheel chairs, walkers, back braces, heating pads, elastic bandages, canes, knee braces, shoulder braces, and so forth are manufactured. Presently, the finished goods warehouse is located at Vizag itself and the products are sent to all major towns in India as a point-to-point dispatch. The company is supplying these equipments directly to retail stores at all these locations. Marketing activity is headed by a General Manager-Marketing based at Vishakapatnam who is supported by a sales team comprising of Sales Officers. The company is not resorting to advertisements and publicity though the products of the company are fairly well known. But, it is felt that all the customers want quick response to their orders as the products are catered to emergency patients. But, these retail outlets carry only very limited inventories. This is due to the fact that most of the products come in a variety of styles, shapes and sizes and the requirement is more customers driven and keeping even a moderate inventory of all types is economically not viable and leads to development of dead stocks in the long run. The company is looking at various options which include:

1. Setting up of hub and spoke type of a distribution network wherein it proposes to set up a stock point or mother warehouse in each zone, viz., East, West, North and South and respective retail outlets which are to be fed from the mother warehouse located in that zone.
2. Setting up of a central warehouse anywhere in Central India and feeding retail outlets from this location.
3. Changing the distribution channel from the present numerous retail outlet systems to a more efficient system.
4. Outsourcing the entire distribution and logistics to a third party wherein the entire activity of transportation and distribution till the ultimate retail outlet will be taken care of by this service provider so that the company can focus more on activities related to marketing and sales.

QUESTIONS FOR DISCUSSION

1. Out of the given options, which should Maxwell Corporation follow for maximum benefit and why?
2. What should be the distribution channel for Maxwell and what advantages would having such a type of a set up have?
3. What type of a marketing and sales set up would you recommend for Maxwell Corporation?

CASE STUDY 15.3

GODREJ—INDIA'S DEPENDABLE DOORKEEPER

The Godrej Empire was founded on padlocks. Ardeshir Godrej, a young lawyer-turned businessman, set up a manufacturing facility for lever-based mechanical padlocks in 1897. Using both indigenous and imported technology, he designed a product which offered resistance to being picked by burglars as its main benefit, and durability as its edge over the crude shed-made options available then.

The first range from the company's stable was the Nav-Tal series, which was available in four sizes and lever variants—85 mm with eight levers, 65 mm with seven levers, 50 mm with six levers and 40 mm with five levers.

The padlocks were made of a combination of metals like zinc, nickel, aluminum, mazak (a zinc-aluminum alloy) and stainless steel, and had a brass cover. The internal components were rust-resistant. Over the years, these were constantly upgraded and made more secure and strong, but Nav-Tal's basic brass design stays unchanged.

The manufacture of safes in 1900 was a logical extension to the lock business, as was the launch of steel cupboards in 1923.

The lock business grew steadily over the years. Although no exact turnover figures are available, the company says that it sold, whatever it produced. However, production capacities were restricted, because lock-making was reserved by the Government for the small-scale sector which spawned hundreds of local levels of lockmakers.

Being among the only national players, 'Godrej, touted as the trusted doorkeeper for your home, was priced at a premium to local makes, though this was from cost-plus calculation, rather than party of any strategy. The consumer was willing to shell out the extra money in return for the brand's guarantee of safety.

With the success of Nav-Tals, Godrej & Boyce (the company which took charge of Godrej's durables business; 1993-94 turnover Rs. 482 crore) decided to make a broader assortment of locking systems. The idea was to offer complete security and thus peace of mind to the consumer. Its Night Latch and Taper resistant front door locking mechanism with a safety catch was introduced in the late 80s, at prices in the range of Rs. 250-305 bracket. The product targeted at the safety conscious was a hand on winner. Other lock designs were also introduced. With its promise of dependability, Godrej remained a market leader. Operating in a seller's market, the company did little to promote the brand. It just didn't need to.

Meanwhile Godrej & Boyce's marketing focus shifted to higher-tech and more profitable areas such as refrigerators and cupboards along with office equipment. Locks got sidelines, and their contribution fell below to under a tenth of the company's turnover.

With Harrison, Link, Tiger and a handful of others as its only branded competitors, the locks unit slid into complacency.

Even when product prices would shoot up as a result of rising inputs costs, sales held firm, claims Godrej, because of the consumer's faith in its uncompromising quality. The company didn't need to invest in the brand. However, what the company had perhaps not realized was that in a low involvement category such as locks, consumer loyalties shift easily. And they did in the '80s, as lower-priced players attacked it with padlock clones that looked as slick as its products. Some were imitations with the stylished Godrej insignia spelt a bit differently. The market crept along at 3-4 per cent a year.

The Break Out

The days of neglect ended in 1991 when Godrej & Boyce streamlined its product portfolio and Godrej Locks became a separate division. Business Data Bureau, a Pune-based market research agency, deputed to study the market in 1992, estimated that the unorganised sector (concentrated in Aligarh (Uttar Pradesh) was selling more than thrice as many locks as the organised sector. Rough estimates value the overall market at around Rs. 400 crore currently.

An eight-lever Nav-Tal is priced at Rs. 247 while a lesser known label sells for only Rs. 100 or so. It realized that in the absence of product innovation, it was getting increasingly difficult to charge a premium for what was becoming too basic a need satisfier-durability. For its traditional padlocks, the company decided to squash costs and reduce the price gap with local makes.

The company claims to have cut down on rejects. It also recycles waste metal among its other efforts in cost-cutting.

According to Godrej, raw material costs had risen by about 50 per cent in 1994. Godrej started Top Brass Manufacturing Ltd., another plant in Goa. Costs are lower here, and the production of the smaller products is being shifted. The company is also considering sub-contracting the work to small-scale lockmakers who could adhere to its quality standards.

Also, the company is actively penetrating the market deeper by way of geographical coverage. It is furiously roping in the exclusive dealers of which there are 550 now—to sell its door-locking systems to builders and architects for installation in new constructions.

Institutions account for 30 per cent of sales, the bulk coming from homes. Advertising handled by Ulka aims to emphasize product quality and reduce the target consumer's price sensitivity. For 1994-95, the budget was nearly doubled to Rs. 1 crore from the previous year's spend.

However, with its lock-making capacity restricted to 7.5 million units a year, the company must rely on high value, top-end products for growth. And while the lower-end of the market has flourished, the top-end has barely moved in terms of either product development or brand competitiveness.

The entry of the UK-based global best seller, Yale (with a plant in Pune) in 1992, has shaken Godrej's innovative faculties out of slumber. Godrej doesn't want to be stuck in the middle with neither the price nor the product advantage.

Currently a series of new designs are being churned out. Some to attract the aesthetically inclined, and others for the buyer seeking technical sophistication. In 1994, the company launched cylindrical padlocks priced between Rs. 300-400 which are sourced from a Delhi-based trader, come in finished, lacquered, powder-coated, and so on. These, it hopes, will spur replacement demand and tackle the faddy-daddy image of the brand.

The just launched Vertibolt lock (for door) price at Rs. 1,500, uses the technical finesse of Swiss lockmaker Kab. It has vertical twin deadbolts (which can't be pried open, claimedly) and the lock is operated with a dimple key (which has dimples in a computer—given random pattern, making it almost impossible to duplicate) from the outside, and with the turn of a knob from the inside.

Electronic and remote-controlled products are now in the pipeline. With these, the locks division hopes to touch a turnover of Rs. 100 crore in the year 1996-97, up from Rs. 55 crore last year.

QUESTIONS FOR DISCUSSION

1. Outline the complete distribution strategy Godrej should adopt with reference to (i) The type of channels used, (ii) Commissions to the channel members, (iii) Type of motivation to be provided, and (iv) Inventory level and cycle period.
2. Suggest a suitable sales-promotion scheme to induce the sales volume and to ensure high visibility to the product in the market.

CASE STUDY 15.4

DAIRY DEVELOPMENT CORPORATION

1. Introduction to the Country

1.1 Nepal is a small land locked kingdom situated between two big countries. India in the South and Republic China in the north. It has a total land area of 1,47,181 sq. kilometers (56,000 sq. miles) and it is 700 miles away from the nearest seaport of Kolkata, India.

1.2 Geographically, Nepal is divided in 3 regions, i.e., Himalayan, region in the north, Hill region in the middle and plain land of Terai region in the south. Similarly, the country is also divided into 5 development regions, 14 zones and 75 districts for administrative purposes. The total population of the country, as estimated in 1991 census, was 18.49 million, with the annual growth rate of 2.1%. The distribution ratio of population is 7.8% in Himalayan region, 45.5% in mid-hills and 46.7% in Terai region while the total land area covered by Himalayan and mid-hill regions is 83% and only 17% of land lies in Terai regional. Hence, Nepal is basically a mountaineous Himalayan country with the world's highest mountain peak Mt. Everest.

1.3 Economically, Nepal falls under the list of least developed countries on the basis of low per capita income of about US $180. Agriculture has still remained the mainstay of Nepalese economy with 80% of the people being dependent on it. The growth of Nepalese economy can be boosted with the optimum utilization of production potentialities in agriculture and agro-based industries. It is necessary to deliver adequate agricultural inputs to rural areas like fertilizers and improved seeds, cattle feeds, etc. and provide marketing facilities to their products like foodgrains, fruits, vegetables, milk and milk products as well as other cash crops plus raw materials for agro-industries.

2. Status of Physical Distribution in Nepal

2.1 To facilitate physical distribution, every country should have the basic infrastructural development of air, road and sea-way transport as well as adequate storage facilities.

For a land-locked nation, predominant with the difficult mountainous topography, the development and extension of transport infrastructure in Nepal has become difficult and high cost-oriented. The total length of road network in Nepal is 11,109 km., out of which only 3,432 km. are black-topped pitch, 2,439 km. are gravelled and 4,238 km. are transportable only in fair whether. In total 15,776 trucks/tankers and 12,505 tractors/trailers are registered for transportation of goods.

The physical distribution of commodities is mainly dependent on porters or on mule back where motorable roads are not developed. This is very time-consuming and costly.

2.2 Air transport is available to 44 districts and 6 other domestic airports are under construction. To facilitate air-transport, the government has recently encouraged the private sector airlines to operate. As a result, a number of private airlines, freight forwarders and transport agencies have come forward in private sector which has facilitated the distribution of goods to some extent. Besides the road and air-transport one ropeway line of 42 km. from Hetauda to Kathmandu and one railway of 52 km. length to Terai region have been operating to carry goods.

2.3 Inadequate storage facilities, difficult transportation all over the country and lack of knowledge towards the modern cost effective marketing management systems and lack of mechanized loading and unloading provisions have been the cause for high cost in physical distribution. The government through its liberal and market oriented economic policy has encouraged the private sector to build up coldstorages, refrigeration plants and to develop the modern system of packaging. As a result, attractive packing materials are coming up in the market and a few storages have been constructed.

2.4 Nevertheless, the private enterprises are unwilling to market the basic need consumer goods to rural remote areas due to high cost involved in physical distribution. The public enterprises in the government sector are supporting the distribution of basic need goods such as fertilizers, foodgrains, salt sugar, fuel, medicines, etc. to such remote mountainous rural places bearing high distribution cost on subsidy. The cost of distribution such products comes up to 25 to 50 per cent depending upon the area and the nature of products.

In consideration of this, the government has announced a policy to emphasize development of transport system and construction of roads and storage with allocation of budget at top priority. It is hoped that this will have a positive effect on the distribution system.

3. Physical Distribution System at Corporate Level

3.1 In Nepal, mild production is an integrated part of traditional production system of the small non-commercial holdings. People in the rural area keep cattle at their households for the consumption of milk for their family and use the manure as fertilizers as well as a source of energy for cooking the meals. In the past, most of these small farmers have been selling their mild to urban areas, directly, by themselves carrying it on bicycles or on their shoulders which is very time consuming, costly and sometimes causes spoilage of milk during transit.

3.2 The dairy development activities in Nepal at an organised level started in 1952 when the government established a small milk processing plant at Banepa near Kathmandu valley under the Department of Agriculture. Later it was converted into Dairy Development Corporation (DDC) in 1969 under the Corporation Act as a public enterprise. At present, this Corporation handles about 80 per cent of the urban market share of mild. The main objectives of the Corporation are to:

- Provide a guaranteed market for rural mild producers with a fair price at their door step.
- Supply pasteurised milk and mild products to urban consumers.
- Develop an organised milk collection system, i.e., bring the rural mild to urban areas.
- Develop an organised marketing and distribution system for pasteurized milk and milk products in urban areas.

3.3 To boost the level of milk production at the rural farm level, commensurate with growing mild demand in the urban areas, the government implemented the ten year dairy development plan in 1991. It assesses the present situation of mild production, marketing systems, the structural development of dairy industries and outlines the appropriate policy and strategies. National Dairy Development Board is also constituted to streamline the dairy development activities in Nepal.

3.4 Distribution system of mild and mild products can be classified into two parts:

(a) Collection of raw milk, i.e. acquisition of raw milk from the rural milk producers; and

(b) Marketing or distribution of pasteurized milk and milk products to ultimate consumers mainly in urban areas.

4. Milk Collection Network and Processing

4.1 The raw milk produced by the rural farmers is carried in small containers and delivered, to the nearest Milk Producers Association (MPA). The MPA/MPCS carries the mild in mild cans through porters, tractors or mini-trucks and through ropeway at some hilly places and delivers the milk to the nearest chilling centre established by DDC. The milk so collected from MPA/MPCS is stored and chilled in the chilling centers to preserve the quality of milk. The chilled milk is again transported to processing plants situated at urban areas through the insulated milk tankers. The collection net work at present is as follows:

MPA/MPCS	Chilling Centers	Collected mil quantity
772	42	44.1 million litres

4.2 The collected milk is pasteurized, standardized and processed for different products. At present 4 milk processing plants in different parts of Nepal and one milk products production and supply scheme are operating to produce and market the pasteurized milk and milk products under DDC.

5. Distribution of Milk and Milk Products

5.1 Pasteurized milk is distributed daily to ultimate consumers directly by the above mentioned four milk supply schemes (processing plants), though their 761 milk selling booths. No other middleman is involved. Distribution vehicles are yearly contracted on hire to transport the milk.

5.2 The milk products such as butter, ghee, yoghurt, cheese and ice creams are marketed through dealers, retailers and DDC's own sales centers. Cheese is produced in 11 cheese factories situated in Himalayan areas mainly from Yak and Cow milk. Most of the cheese plants have no road accessibility. The posters carry the cheese to near motorable roads and transport it to Kathmandu by trucks or bus for storage and marketing. The pasteurized milk and major milk products marketed by DDC for last 3 years have been reflected below:

Products	Units	1993	1994	1995
Milk	Million Ltr.	52	57	62
Cheese	Tonnes	185	168	134
Butter	Tonnes	956	1068	1041
Ghee	Tonnes	360	591	797

Since last year, DDC has also produced Skimmed Milk Powder (SMP) from a plant established at Biratnagar in Eastern Nepal. At present, SMP is not sold to market but only used for reconstitution to meet demand for liquid milk during the lean season particularly in Kathmandu Valley.

6. Packaging, Loading and Unloading

6.1 A few years back, the pasteurized milk was packed in milk bottles. But with the change in the consumer choice and in consideration of the high cost for loading, unloading and transportation, as well as difficulty in cleaning the bottles, DDC replaced the packing of milk from bottles to polythelyne pouches, filled and packed by automatic filling machines. The pouch packets of milk are distributed to milk selling booths and are kept in plastic satchet crates. Packaging of other products is almost completely manual. Ghee is packed in plastic as well as in tin containers. Butter is primarily packed in parchment vegetable butter paper. Ghee and butter have secondary packing in cardboard boxes for easy storage and distribution. The storage and loading of the milk in plants in facilitated through conveyor chain systems. However, loading in distribution vehicles and unloading at the market is handled manually.

7. Problems and Constraints

Nepal dairy industry has a peculiar situation. Dairy farmers are not able to market all their milk during peak period of production whereas sizeable quantity of milk powder and dairy products is imported in the country every year. This situation is mainly caused by:

— Lack of required milk chilling and coldstorage facilities.

— Clustering small private dairies around Kathmandu Valley.

— Inadequate processing and powder milk making plants in potential areas.

— Lack of knowledge about appropriate marketing management techniques.
— High cost incurred in marketing rural milk in comparison to imported products.
— Lack of finance to promote and develop the infrastructural facilities needed for physical distribution.

These problems are prominent and common, applicable to other product industries too.

QUESTIONS FOR DISCUSSION

1. What alternative methods of distribution should DDC consider for milk and mil products?
2. What are the alternative solutions of problems which are faced by the dairy industry in Nepal?

CASE STUDY 15.5

P&G'S NEW SALES AND DISTRIBUTION SYSTEM IN INDIA

It is a subject that is being discussed in hushed tones insides every fast moving consumer goods (FMCG) company today. Project Golden Eye—the code name for Procter and Gamble (P&G) latest initiative in rationalizing its sales and distribution system—isn't exactly eyewash.

On the contrary, it raises fundamental questions about channel design and network strategy issues which are agitating the minds of a great many FMCG companies.

For long, Hindustan Lever's famed distribution system was the only benchmark available. In other words, increased reach meant increased volumes. So the more outlets you could bring under your distribution coverage, the better chances you had of making a sales and hitting critical mass.

So almost every year, every FMCG company prided itself on setting itself ambitious targets to expand distribution cover, appoint new distributors and plumb for volume growth. For almost a decade, P&G too strained every sinew to match the Liver juggernaut. It pushed for growth not just in urban markets, but also tried very hard to established direct cove rage of rural markets.

But in its quest for reach, P&G like many other FMCG companies overlooked one critical factor: the cost of extending distribution cover. After failing to aggressively challenge Lever in soaps and detergents, P&G has rewritten its focus areas: laundry (Ariel), sanitary napkins (whisper), and Vicks, What's more, it has junked its local strategy of extending Ariel across the price spectrum, and instead gone back to its original strategy of promoting top end products.

While the process of redrawing the organisational boundaries was on, two things became apparent. One, 85 per cent of its sales came from the top 30 towns. Tow, its current volumes did not justify a large distributors network. Even in a market like Mumbai, there were close to six distributors.

A large distributor network meant that no single distributor had large enough volumes to achieve an attractive return on investment. This resulted in each distributor trying to extend its reach to push volumes. But with P&G's portfolio of high margin, low volume products, merely extending reach only increased the cost of servicing, not the off-take per outlet.

Today, P&G is busy slashing its number of distributors down to one tenth of its size and reworking the margin structure. And this has sparked off a debate among marketers whether it makes business sense.

In many ways, P&G's initiatives raise two clear issues. One, is a large direct distribution cover necessarily a strength for every marketer? Two, can an alternate model emerge in India which results in large cost savings and yet, is also effective in meeting marketing objectives?

More, Not Less

At the heart of the P&G's new system is the implicit assumption that lower reach does not lead to significantly lower off-take. "My marketing objectives tell me that our brands are over distributed," explains a P&G manager. If sales analysis shows 95 per cent of Ariel or Whisper sales comes from 70 per cent of the outlet, then it counts for very little of distribution cover that is actually reduced.

Given that the two prongs of FMCG distribution are cost and availability, P&G is likely to get a significant cost advantage, without losing out on availability by cutting down on reach.

Apart from reducing costs by knocking down direct coverage, how does P&G hope to achieve significant cost savings in its supply chain? That's where P&G has started rationalizing its distributor network. The intent: cut down its number of distributors to about one tenth of its current size. In Madhya Pradesh, for instance, P&G will now have just one distributor, who will operate like a super stockiest. "So if five distributors were handling Rs. 6 crore of business, now that entire business will be consolidated under one distributor," says a sales manager with Marico, who has been closely monitoring the new P&G system.

Earlier, since each distributor was working with small volumes, it wasn't economical for P&G to replenish them frequently. As a result, the average inventories lying with the distributor would be significantly high, forcing them to depend on the company's margins.

That is a dangerous loop for any distribution system. Typically, channel design in any FMCG system is driven by distributor's economics. The key issue is: How effectively can you leverage your distributor? "For most companies, managing distributor inventory is not seen as critical to channel design. Primary sales is where companies hand off", explains a senior consultant. "So long as the company has sold enough to the distributor, it is not interested," adds he.

Now, a distributor evaluates a company on how he is faring largely on return on investment (ROI). Simply put, ROI in a working capital-intensive business is the number of rotations (or the number of times that the distributor can turnover his investment in stocks) multiplied by the margin per rotation.

The consequences of ignoring distributor ROI can be disastrous. Take the recent example of a leading FMCG company which attempted to benchmark its distributor economics with Hindustan Lever. The findings were startling.

The distribution margin for the company was 6 per cent while it was 5 per cent for Levers. Distributors' stock levels for this company as an average of four weeks, while for Lever it is two weeks. Assuming that the distributors gave no credit to the market the company's distributor ended up rotating his stock 13 times (52 weeks over 4 weeks) as against a Lever distributor who rotated his stock 26 times.

Now, given that the distributor aimed to hit a return of 30 per cent (the risk-free rate of return was 30 per cent if the distributor invested in the money market), the margin that had to be kept aside to achieve the above ROI is 2.5 per cent. The corresponding figure for a Lever distributor was 1.2 per cent.

This effectively meant that the amount of money that the company distributor could spent on distribution (buying vans, investing in sales people, etc.) was 3.5 per cent, while the Lever distributor could spend 3.8 per cent on distribution.

The writing on the wall was clear: despite its lower distributor margins, Lever was successful in getting higher distribution. So even though the FMCG company in question spent Rs. 14 crore more by way of higher margins, it ended up poorer distribution. The reason: it fundamentally did not manage distributor's ROI.

The result can be disastrous. Even in healthy FMCG distribution systems, poor ROI usually results in distributor dropouts of around 10 per cent. The result? It leaves a vacuum in distribution, leading to obvious share losses.

Recently a leading FMCG company in the household insecticides business could not find any distributors to service its key wholesale market in Begum Bazar for nearly three months, leading to a significant share drop. The company simply couldn't get any distributors to buy into the economics of the business.

The other fall-out is that the distributor will stop extending credit in the market, resulting in retailers not picking up stocks. Gaps in distribution are then inevitable.

Competing on Size

Now, for P&G, by moving to a super-stockiest set up, it could now replenish its distributor more frequently and hence reduce their average stock level. No only, is its system complexity lower, it can also look at building stronger relationships with its super stockiest. By ensuring a better return on investment, P&G will now be in a position to make the distributor investment more in IT and distribution infrastructure. Sources in P&G say that they will now be able to replenish stocks every three days.

Moreover, P&G hopes to make significant cost savings through the increased number of stockiest. By offering him more volumes and reducing the distribution reach (hence his cost of operations), P&G is now trying to shave off distributor margins by a full two per cent. This saving will then be channeled into brand building advertising. A larger advertising kitty will undoubtedly help to fight competitors, particularly Levers, on mass media without being beaten on its share of voice in media.

Additionally, with a limited number of distributors, P&G will also not need to invest in C&F agents. The super stockiest will be expected to invest in storage and warehousing space, so that the stock transfer from the company can take place as soon as the stocks are shipped into the warehouse.

In the scheme of things, P&G has another reason for reducing the distributor's margins. That's because of peculiar distribution psychology at work. As in the earlier example, as soon as the company is able to reduce distributor stocks from four weeks to around two weeks, at 6 per cent margin, the distributor begin to earn almost 60 per cent rate of return. "That can be the starting point of the trouble," says a senior manager.

The key is to keep the distributor's ROI in a band between 30 per cent to 40 per cent. The moment it falls below 30 per cent, the distributor is inclined to undercut in a bid to recover his money. On the other hand, if ROI is as high as 60 per cent, the distribution is tempted to aim for a higher turnover by undercutting the distribution in the next territory.

Of course, the only brand that will continue to need distribution cover is Vicks cough drops. The reason is simple. Vicks' competitive set is other impulse-driven confectionary. But for P&G to extend direct distribution to cover for a single brand like Vicks is simply far too costly. So it has chosen to adopt wholesale distribution for the Vicks line. "If you don't have a portfolio to support a massive distribution thrust into the hinterland, there is very little point in aiming for direct distribution," avers a senior manager with a FMCG company.

However, for its future product launches, it is apparent that P&G has chosen to focus on key urban markets. "Reducing cover is in lying with future plans," affirms a sales manager at P&G. The year of jostling with Levers across the length and breadth of the country is over. Focus is P&G's new name of the game.

(*Source*: Business Standard, Tuesday, Dec.1, 1998)

QUESTIONS FOR DISCUSSION

1. Explains the reason for redesigning the re-distribution strategies with a focus on slashing the distributors and re-working margin structure.
2. Does this approach help in economizing company operations? Critically examine.

CASE STUDY 15.6

NESTLE INDIA LIMITED—DISTRIBUTION NETWORK ANALYSIS

Introduction

The marketing distribution channel decisions are among the most important decisions that a management faces. A company's channel decisions directly affect every other marketing decision. The company's pricing depends on whether it uses mass merchandisers or high quality speciality stores. The firm's sales force and advertising decisions depend on how much persuasion, training, and motivation the dealers need.

Distribution channel decisions often involve long term commitments to other firms. For example, a furniture manufacturer can easily change its advertising, pricing, or promotion programmes. It can scrap old product designs and introduce new ones as the market tastes demand. But when it sets up a distribution channel through contracts with independent dealers, it cannot readily replace this channel with company owned branches it conditions change. Therefore, the management must design its channels carefully with an eye on tomorrow's likely selling environment as well as today's.

The Nature of Distribution Channels

Most producers use middlemen to bring their products to market. They try to forge a distribution channel a set of interdependent organisations involved in the process of making a product or service available for use or consumption by the consumer or industrial user.

From the economic system's point of view, the role of distributors or dealers is to transform the assortments of products made by procedures into the assortments wanted by consumers. Producers make narrow assortments of products in large quantities, but consumers want broad assortments of products in small quantities. In the distribution channels, the agencies buy the large quantities, but consumers want broad assortments of products in small quantities. In the distribution channels, the agencies buy the large quantities of many producers and break them down into the smaller quantities and broader assortments wanted to consumers. Thus, the distribution channel plays a major role in matching supply and demand.

Distribution Channel Functions

A distribution channel moves goods from producers to consumers. It overcomes the major times, place and possession gaps that separate goods and services from those who would use them. Members of the marketing channel and distribution channel perform many key functions.

- **Information:** gathering and distribution, marketing research and intelligent information about factors and forces in the marketing environment are needed for planning and aiding exchange.
- **Promotion:** developing and spreading persuasive communications about an offer.
- **Contact:** finding and communicating with prospective buyers.
- **Matching:** shaping and fitting the offer to buyer's needs, including such activities as manufacturing, grading, assembling, and packaging.
- **Negotiation:** reaching on agreement on price and other terms of the offer so that ownership or possession can be transferred.
- **Financing:** acquiring and using funds to cover the costs of the channel work.
- **Risk Taking:** assuming the risks of carrying out the channel work.

Channel Organization

A conventional distribution channel consists of one or more independent producers, wholesalers, and retailers. Each is a separate business seeking to maximize its own profits, even at the expense of profits for the system as a whole. No channel member has much control over the members, and no formal means exists for assigning roles and resolving channel conflict.

A Vertical Management System (VMS) consists of producers, wholesalers and retailers acting as a unified system. One channel member owns the others, has contracts with them, or wields so much power that they all cooperate. The VMS can be dominated by the producer, wholesaler, or retailer. Vertical marketing systems have become dominant in consumer marketing, serving as much as 64 per cent of the total market.

Physical Distribution by Channels

Producers must decide on the best way to store, handle, and move their goods and services so that they are available to customers at the right time and place. Producers typically need to employ the services of physical distribution firms—warehouses and transportation companies—to assist in this task. Physical distribution effectiveness will have a major impact on customer satisfaction and company costs. Physical flow of materials and final goods, from points of origin to points of use, to meet customer requirements. The aim of physical distribution is to manage supply chains, and value added flows from suppliers to final users.

Distribution Network of Nestle India Limited

Nestle India Limited is the primary company in India involved in the production of food products. It is a very prestigious company and its food products are regarded as quality products.

Nestle India Limited has a wide distribution network operating on a national basis. The main factory of Nestle, situated at Moga in Punjab, is linked up with the mother godowns which are located in the different regions of the country. The mother godowns in turn are linked up with Clearing and Sales (C&S) Agents. The mother godown is responsible for holding of the stock.

The various channels of physical distribution for Nestle are Mother Godown, Clearing and Sales Agents, Cash Distributors and Retailers (outlets).

Mother Godowns

This is the first line agent in the distribution network or channel. Stocks are moved on consignment basis from the main factory to the different mother godowns at different regions. These mother godowns are responsible for taking care of the stocks. The mother godowns are the trans-shipment points. Nestle enters into a contract with the mother godown. These agents in the form of mother godowns are given flat fees by the principal company i.e. Nestle.

Clearing and Sales Agents (C&S)

These are the second line agents in the distribution channel. Clearing & sales agents generate invoices on the basis of the requirements of the cash distributors.

DISTRIBUTION NETWORK OF NESTLE INDIA LIMITED

At a Glance

Nestle Main Factory at MOGA, Punjab

Mother Godowns in various regions

Clearing and Sales (C&S) in respective regions

Distributors

Retailers

Customers

Once the invoice is generated by C&S agents and communicated to the mother godown then stocks are released by the mother godown to the C&S. These invoices are generated for the purpose of consigning the goods to the cash distributors which are in turn linked up with the C&S. The C&S persons are also paid flat fees by Nestle.

It may be mentioned here that mother godowns and C&S agents are directly under the control of Nestle. Mother godowns execute the function of storing the stock, whereas, C&S agents are involved in supplying the goods to the distributors.

Distributors

These are the third line agents in the distribution network. They are regarded as business partners by the company. The distributors send orders to C&S agents on a weekly basis. The C&S agents then generate invoices, get the stock from mother godown, and supply them to the distributors. Nestle never provides goods to cash distributors on credits. Distributors have to pay the company directly by demand draft or cheques. The demand draft is made in favour of the nearest company office. This payment is done in advance. When the order is raised by the distributors they are supposed to pay to the principal company by demand draft or cheques in advance. Once the payment is made, the goods start to move within 2 to 3 days time. A distributor once having paid the company for the purchase of goods becomes fully responsible for distribution of the goods. He becomes almost an independent entity and the company has no direct dealing with him. But the distributor has to work within the overall guidelines provided by the company. A distributor should cover 35 to 40 outlets a day. So the distributor has to cover approximately 240 outlets in 6 days. Each route or 40 outlets is called a beat. Each beat is covered once a week.

A distributor has to invest in a vehicle—either an auto or van. He also invests on a person called merchandiser. A merchandiser's job is to decorate the retail outlets by POS (Point of Sale) like banners, backing sheets, posters, etc. A distributor also performs the billing activity *vis-à-vis* retail outlets. Cash collection from retailers is the distributor's responsibility.

To train the distributors in the technique of the selling is the job of the sales officers who are employees of the company itself. The sales officers also perform the accounting work related to the company only. The main objective of sales officers is to make the right goods available at the right place.

Retailer (Outlets)

These are the fourth and final line agents in the distribution network. Categories of retailers are the following:

(i) Wholesalers
(ii) Grocery shops (also called Kirana Shop)
(iii) Medical shops
(iv) Non-conventional outlets like panwallahs, etc.

The distributors are responsible for the collection of money from the retailers. The retailers are not in direct linkage with the principal company, i.e. Nestle. Retailers are linked up with the distributors.

Selection and Appointment of Organs of Distribution Network by Nestle India Ltd.

- Overall distribution channel/network agents of Nestle India Limited are classified into the following categories:

  (i) Mother godowns
  (ii) Clearing and Sales Agents (C&S)
  (iii) Distributors
  (iv) Retailers

- Nestle enters into contract with mother godowns, C&S agents.
- Nestle enters into a well-documented agreement with distributors. Prospective distributors are to place a request letter to the company expressing their willingness to become distributors. Nestle selects from such requests. Sales officers of the company may also identify prospective distributors from the market channel.
- Criteria for selection of distributors are the following:
  - (i) **Financial Strength:** Any amount from Rs. 1 lakh onwards. In varies from party to party.
  - (ii) **Basic Infrastructure**: An office with telephone, fax, other essential office equipment.
  - (iii) **Manpower**: Approximately 10 staff. However, this varies from time to time on need basis.
  - (iv) **Experience:** At least 3 years with similar category of products.
  - (v) **Transport:** There should be a van to deliver stocks.
  - (vi) **Place to Operate**: Prime location with a godown for storing food products.
- The process of appointment of possible distributors involves the following steps:
  - (i) Establishment of need by company sales officers.
  - (ii) Details of the distributors are filled in the Cash Distributors Information form by Branch Manager of the Company.
  - (iii) The filled up forms are sent to the Area Sales Manager.
  - (iv) Area Sales Manager recommends to the Branch Office of the company on the basis of the CD information form.
  - (v) Branch Manager finally appoints a new cash distributor.
  - (vi) Mother Godowns should have an area of 25,000 to 50,000 sq.ft.
- Cash Distributor Information Form takes the following points into account.
- Name of the proposed distributor
- Place of operation
- Name of proprietors or partners
- Sales tax registration number
- Corporation food license
- Facilities for van
- Whether the distributor can provide its own salesmen or not
- Assets and liabilities of the party
- Market reputation

STANDARD OPERATING PROCEDURE

For distributors and their sales force, there are operating instructions and sometimes training as part of the main agreement by the principal company.

Commission

- Nestle collects money from cash distributors directly.
- New distributors make advance payments by demand draft as required by the company.
- Other distributors who are in the good books of the company may make their payments by issuing local cheques.
- A commission at the rate of 6 per cent is given for all types of products (except ghee) to the distributors.
- The company pays flat fees to the mother godowns and clearing and sales agents.
- No securities/deposits are accepted from the distributors.
- Retailers get 7.5% to 10%, and also to 12.5% at a time as margin.
- Transactions in volume and value are as follows:

A	Class City	-	average of Rs. 25 lakh
B	Class City	-	average of Rs. 10 lakh
C	Class City	-	average of Rs. 1 to 5 lakh

- Distribution channels have to maintain their tax liabilities as per conditions of agreement with Nestle India Limited.
- Another condition of agreement is that all labour law, work rules, insurance schemes, superannuation schemes, etc. are to be properly maintained by the agents. In case of default on these obligations, there is a breach of agreement.
- Nestle specifically oversees the following aspects for its distribution channels:
  - (i) Fire and safety measures
  - (ii) Good maintenance
  - (iii) Ventilation
  - (iv) Labour laws
  - (v) Child labour issues
  - (vi) Provident fund obligations
  - (vii) Cleanliness aspects
- The agreements with distributors are mutually binding.
- The distributors cannot supply specific food products without the permission of Nestle.
- Spoiled food products should be kept in a separate space by the distributor. Later these products are destroyed in the presence of company sales officers.

Performance Review and Audit

- Internal audit of stock and accounts takes place for mother godowns and C&S agents by the company representatives at least once a year. But the frequency may vary depending on the need. This audit also helps in reviewing the performance.
- Area sales manager and sales officers of the company have to check the stocks kept in the godown by the distributors. This checking is done every month on an average of three times.
- The company representatives in this type of review mainly deal with the operational performance related to the agents and the financial implication's for the company.

Financial Process

- Distributors make payments to the company through demand draft and cheques.
- There is an agreement with Citibank and this arrangement is called City Clearance. Distributors give local cheques to Citibank. Such cheques are cleared by Citibank within 24 hours and credited to the account of Nestle.
- If dues incur from any distributor due to any reasons, then further invoice from such a distributor is immediately stopped. No further trans-shipment of products to this distributor is done until the previous amount outstanding is cleared.
- Warning is given to such distributors to avoid recurrence of dues.
- Such defaulted distributors lose the facility of making payments by cheques. And consequently such distributors have to make advance payments by demand draft for getting products from Nestle.
- Stock and invoice monitoring take place on a weekly basis by the company personnel. This helps in monitoring the dues of the distributors.

SYNOPSIS

Nestle products are basically food items and there is regular and frequent demand for such products. The territory size for a normal distributor is not very big. But it again depends on the potentiality of the particular distributor as to how capable he is in expanding his sales territory size without decreasing sales volume.

Normally, the commodities produced by Nestle India Limited are such that they are sold more in metropolitan cities and other urban areas where transport facilities are stated to be good. Hence in such areas there is always a possibility that the distributors can cover a large territory depending on a case to case basis. But in the hilly areas of Himachal Pradesh, North Eastern States, Nilgiris in the South, etc., the territory size for a distributor is small because of poor transportation facilities.

Food product items generally fall in a tough competitive market environment. In fact, Nestle has competition with Britannia, Cadbury's, etc. Since there is tremendous competition among these companies, the territory size for an urban and those too big cities like Delhi, Bombay, Calcutta, Madras, Bangalore, etc. is comparatively smaller so as to tap greater number of customers.

At the same time population density is also given high weight-age by Nestle in determining the territory size of its distributors. Where population density is very high, the sales territory is smaller in size.

Nestle India Limited also gives primary importance to a skilled sales force of its own as well as that of its distributors. Hence from time to time Nestle organises training programs to upgrade the skills with a view to improving sales performance. For qualified and experienced sales personnel of the company, large territory areas are given in order to facilitate maximum possible sales volume. Again with a view to upgrading the quality of the sales force of the distributors, Nestle organises and imparts specialized training for the sales staff of the distributors. This in turn improves the skill, expertise of sales force of the distributors and also gives adequate motivation to achieve higher sales target.

Distributor—M/S Choudhary Pyarelal & Brothers

M/s Choudhary Pyarelal & Brothers is a distributor of Nestle India Limited. This distributor works in an area covering from Khan Market to Mehrauli in New Delhi. This distributor covers about 700 retailers in its territory. The distributor is selected and appointed on the basis of the provisions already discussed earlier. This distributor is an old one and it makes payment to Nestle by cheques. This distributor has a monthly transaction of Rs. 40 lakh with the retailers. Nestle has given this distributor a target of sale. The distributor has been successful in achieving this target. The company sales officers visit this distributor regularly to assess whether the distributor is working according to norms or not. This distributor makes all payments to Nestle India Limited by company cheques. It also takes cash from the retailers to whom it delivers products.

Retailer-beauty Palace

This is a retail shop in South Extension, New Delhi. This retail shop gets Nestle products from M/s Choudhary Pyarelal & Brothers. The retailer gets a commission of about 10% from the principal company. For example, if the maximum retail price of a product is Rs. 100, then the retailer gets the product at Rs. 90. This retailer has to make cash payment to the distributor for getting products. The retailer is itself responsible for income tax liabilities. There is no target of sale given to the retailer. If the product is sold, then he gets more amounts of such products from the distributor. The distributor visits retailers once a week. There is no performance review of this retailer by anyone.

QUESTIONS FOR DISCUSSION

1. Discuss the physical distribution channels used by Nestle.
2. What criteria are being used by Nestle in selection and appointment of organs of distribution network?

STRATEGIC SALES PROMOTION AND ADVERTISING DECISIONS

16

INTRODUCTION

The two wings of promotion are personal selling and advertising. The major function of sales promotion is to serve as a connecting link between advertising and personal selling.

According to the American Marketing Association, sales promotion is "those marketing activities other than personal selling, advertising and publicity, that stimulate consumer purchase and dealer effectiveness such as display shows, expositions, demonstrations and various non-recurrent selling efforts not in the ordinary routine".

Objectives of Sales Promotion

1. It is to increase buying response at the customer's level.
2. Secondly, it is aimed at increasing sales effort of dealers and sales personnel.
3. Sales promotion is to attract new customers.
4. Sales promotion is also aimed at capturing major share of the market.
5. Sales promotion is aimed at simplifying the job of middlemen.
6. To create a favourable attitude towards the product.

Advantages of Sales Promotion

1. Sales promotion is a demand creator.
2. Sales promotion is flexible. It can be used at any stage of a new product introduction.
3. Sales promotion is an effective supporter of sales. It helps the sales men and makes his effort more productive.
4. The promotional tools are the most effective to be used in increasing the sales volume.

Staple Salesmen

Sales salesmen are those who specialise in selling goods for common use like food, clothing, stationery, etc. The sale of such goods is easy for the salesmen as the goods are already in demand and calls for no special creation of demand. Staple salesmen sell goods in hulk and their area of operation is limited. He might find difficulty in their job if there is competition.

Control of Salesmen

Control is the process measuring the performance of the salesmen and interpreting it. Control also involves corrective action if found necessary.

Advantages of Control

(a) Increase in sales volume due to increased efficiency of sales force.

(b) Unnecessary sales operations can be avoided.

(c) There will be economy in sales expenses.

AIDA Formula

AIDA formula is one which is employed by trainers as to how a sale is to be made, The letter A stands for attention, I for interest, D for desire and A for action. This means that salesmen are to be taught as to how to get attention and how to arouse interest. Then how a desire is to be developed in a prospective customer and what should be done to make him to act, i.e. to by the product.

Sale Process

The general sale process which must be taught to the salesmen are six and they are:

1. Prospecting
2. Pre-approach
3. Approach
4. Presentation
5. Meeting of prospective customers – objections
6. Clearing the sale.

The first step the salesmen should do is to find out the people who need his products and the second task he has to perform is to get all the necessary information with a view to approach the salesmen in the most fruitful manner and is known as pre-approach. Then he has to express his view of the products which make the approach stage in the sales of the product. Sometimes some questions or objections may be raised by the prospective customer which must be answered fairly well and then the last stage of sale occurs and is known as closing the sale.

Factors influencing the Remuneration Plan

In order to make an effective sales performance, the salesmen are to be kept happy. If salesmen are to be induced to put in their maximum effort to make sales, they are to be rewarded adequately. While forming a policy to reward the salesmen adequately, the following points must be kept in mind.

1. **The financial position of the firm.** Basically all compensation plan must represent the financial capacity of the firm. A firm with sound financial backing is in a position to offer an attractive remuneration plan. On the other hand, a firm with unstable earnings is unable to offer a fixed attractive compensation plan.
2. **Nature of the work done.** The compensation paid to workers must directly correspond to the effort put in by the salesmen. The benefits to counter salesmen and that of a travelling salesmen can never be one and the same.
3. **The type of the product handled.** The type of the products in which the salesmen deal also must be given due weightage before making out a financial plan. Handling of fast moving items do not call in for a high remuneration compared to the handling of items

of luxury or comforts. Such articles which need a high push to be marketed requires ample remuneration of the salesmen.

4. **The conditions in the market.** The type of demand enjoyed by the product is termed as conditions in the market. If the product enjoys a wide demand, the task of selling the product is relatively easy and the remuneration plan can also be an easy one. As against this, if there is no wide patronage of the products and the product faces keen competition, then there must be an attractive remuneration plan.
5. **Economic condition prevailing.** Depending on the conditions faced by the economy also the plan must be made. In order to meet the rising cost of living during rising prices, higher remuneration has to be paid.
6. **The distribution policy of the manufacturer.** If the firm's policy is to sell to three or four big wholesales, the salesmen of such a concern will get a higher commission due to large orders. On the other hand if the firm's policy is to sell to a large number of retailers, the remuneration of the salesmen will be less due to the small orders placed by the retailers.
7. **Nature of the advertisement campaign of the firm.** The advertisement policy carried on by the firm also influences the remuneration of the salesmen. The salesmen of the products of the widely advertised company need not put in much effort to sell the product and could be given a low amount of remuneration. On the other hand, if the company does not have a regular advertisement campaign, the work of the salesmen is increased and correspondingly a high remuneration has to be paid.
8. **Need for control of salesmen.** Controlling the salesmen is the process of directing, guiding and checking with a view to ensure that all the activities of the salesmen are strictly is its accordance with the sales plan already chalked out. This act of controlling the salesmen is of dire necessity for the attainment of maximum result in sales. Even if salesmen are selected scientifically and the best training is imparted to them, control is necessary for securing efficient performance from the salesmen. The need to control salesmen assumes added significance when an organisation has got a number of salesmen scattered in different places. The need for controlling salesmen could be summarised as follows.

Salesmen are also human beings, some devoted to hardwork and others mediocre or indifferent. Though the devout ones work hard to get better results, the others will not put their maximum effort if a proper control is absent. Therefore, in order to extract the best out of every salesmen control is necessary.

Salesmen working in different places will not put their maximum effort without a proper control of salesmen.

The question of efficiency is also related to the control of the salesmen. Better controlled salesmen are found bringing out better results.

Importance of Performance Evaluations

Salesmen are considered to be the main instruments through which management tries to maximize the net profit contribution of the personal selling efforts. The performance of the salesmen individually and collectively affects the success of personal selling *effort*. All these facts point out the need for evaluating the performance of the salesmen. The evaluation of the work of the salesmen will help the management to know which salesmen are to be discharged. Who are to be given additional training, etc.

There must be good yardsticks to measure the performance, the salesmen. The measurement must also distinguish a good performance from a bad one. Standards of sales must be established against which the performance of individual salesmen are approved. Though quantitative standards are used qualitative ones are also needed by most companies.

The usual methods of evaluating sales performance are job description and fixing quotas. Job description is considered to be a good measure as it not only details the salesmen's duties and responsibilities but also the performance level considered satisfactory by management. The weakness of this method is that many of the duties and responsibilities do not lend themselves to quantitative measurement. Quotas are probably the yardstick which is used by the management to a great extent.

Different Types of Salesmen

Sales are the life blood of any business. Sales are necessary for any business to earn profit or survive. But for the manufacturer it is impossible to meet all the consumers and sell the products. Therefore somebody has to be there to act as a link between the manufacturers and final consumers. Thus the salesmen come into the picture. If sales are the life blood of any business, salesmen are the backbone.

Salesmen are grouped into the following categories:

1. Manufactures salesmen,
2. Wholesalers salesmen,
3. Retailers salesmen,
4. Sales engineers, and
5. Intangible salesmen.

1. **Manufacturers Salesmen.** Manufacturers salesmen are employed by the manufacturers. They are paid and controlled by the manufacturers. Manufacturers salesmen deal either with wholesalers and retailers or directly with consumers. Manufacturers salesmen can be classified into the following classes:
   a. Promotional salesmen,
   b. Dealer servicing salesmen,
   c. Merchandising salesmen, and
   d. Speciality salesmen.

   (a) ***Promotional Salesmen.*** Some writer use the name pioneering salesmen or missionary salesmen to mean promotional salesmen. Their duty is to promote new products or creation of demand for the new product. They are engaged in increasing markets for the new products of their employer. It is the duty of promotional salesmen to visit the dealers, convince them of the merits of the products. The job requires imagination and qualified and competent persons are necessary to handle the products.

(b) ***Dealer servicing Salesmen.*** Compared to the work of pioneering salesmen, the duty of dealer servicing salesmen is easy. Their duty is to sell the produce to the dealers and to secure repeat business. Their main function is to retain and expand the markets already existing. Sometimes they will be entrusted with the task of securing new outlets for company's products and expanding its business.

(c) ***Merchandising Salesmen.*** Such salesmen are employed not to secure any direct business for the organisation. They are entrusted with the task of advising dealers on vital matters like stores, display, advertising, credit policies, etc. Actually they are doing sales promotion activity and contribute indirectly in increasing the sale of company's products.

(d) ***Speciality Salesmen.*** Manufacturers of speciality goods bring in the service of speciality salesmen. Goods which have high unit value like refrigerators, washing machines, etc. are turned as speciality goods. Speciality salesmen are usually travelling salesmen. They travel extensively, interview a large number of potential customers, convince the potential buyers about the usefulness of the product. They also clear the doubts of the prospective customers and secure orders.

2. **Wholesalers Salesmen.** Wholesalers salesmen, as the name suggests, are the representatives of the wholesaler. He is the link between the wholesalers and the retailers or industrial users. They visit the stores of tie customers regularly, inspect the stores and take orders from them. The services rendered by the wholesalers salesmen are of a routine nature. They guide the wholesalers with regard to credit facility to be offered to the retailers. They also keep the manufacturers informed about the development in the market, competition, etc. They also help the retailers to arrange displays and demonstrations.

3. **Retailers Salesmen.** The duty of the retailers salesmen is to sell the products, to the final consumers who visit the shop. Retailers salesmen are of two types:

(a) ***Indoor Salesmen.*** Indoor salesmen's or usually known as counter salesmen's job is limited within the four walls of the shop. He is employed to serve the customer who visits the shop. Elaborate training need not be given to such salesmen as the person who visits the shop need no persuasion to purchase the product. But salesmen if they are dealing in high unit value consumer durable goods like refrigerators must have skill and knowledge of the product. Here the work of the salesmen is bit difficult as they have got to convince the customers about the better quality of the product and the prices.

(b) ***Outdoor Salesmen.*** Outdoor salesmen travel extensively, visit the houses of the customers and collect the orders. Usually only large-scale retailers employ outdoor salesmen. Such people show the samples to the customers, secure the orders to the retailers. Outdoor salesmen like any other salesmen must be polite, tactful and has to be intelligent while dealing with customers.

4. **Sales Engineers.** With advancement in science and technology, another class of salesmen emerged. Products like aircrafts, computers, automobiles, etc. require engineering skill in their installation and use. Manufactures of such products employ engineers or sales engineers as salesmen. They are becoming a must as science and technology advance.
5. **Intangible Salesmen.** Institutions like banks and insurance companies also employ salesmen to sell their products. But the products of such institutions cannot be seen or touched. The task of convasing customers for banks and insurance companies is bit difficult as intangible products offer advantages only in a very distant future.

Steps in the Selection of Salesmen

Selection of the right salesmen is necessary for the success of any enterprise. Even if there is a good training programme, it will be of no avail if the right people are not recruited. Similarly if the salesmen of a company is inferior to its competitor, the own company may suffer. All these facts point out the need for the selection of right men. Good people in the right place will reduce the expenditure on training and supervision and the image of the company with best salesmen shoots up.

Recruitment of the right type of salesmen includes the following steps:

(a) Analysis of the job to be performed by the incumbent.
(b) Finding out the number and type of people required.
(c) Finding out the source of recruitment.
(d) Selecting proper people.
(e) Finalising employment.

(a) ***Job analysis.*** Job analysis helps a great deal in the selection of the right type of salesmen. Job analysis is to bring out the duties and responsibilities to be assigned to the salesmen proposed to be appointed. Job analysis is necessary for the scientific selection of workers, since duties and responsibilities of salesmen differ form company to company and product to product. Various examples could be cited to substantiate this. The duties and responsibilities of retailers salesmen are different from that of wholesalers or manufacturers salesmen. The method of operation and responsibility of a promotional salesman and that of a manufacturing salesman is totally different. All these point out the need to have a clear idea about the duties and responsibilities to select the right personnel.

(b) ***Determining the number of sales force and manpower specifications.*** The determination of the number of salesmen is not that difficult. We can know in advance the number of people needed by a proper manpower planning programme.

Main specifications relate to the specific characteristic and qualities which should be possessed by salesmen proposed to be appointed so that the required job will be performed efficiently. The qualities which should be possessed by the salesmen is divided into three:

(1) General qualities,
(2) Particular qualities, and
(3) Technical knowledge.

General qualities consists of good appearance, health, honesty, intelligence and power of observation. Particular qualities comprise educational qualification, experience, knowledge of the producer, product, customer and the market. The knowledge of chemical or mathematical aspects comes under particular qualities. Technical qualities also include the legal implications in the sale of the product.

(c) ***Finding out the source of recruitment.*** When the job analysis and man specifications are over the next problem is to make an analysis of the source from which right man could be selected. Possible sources of recruitment are:

1. **Own staff.** Many companies follow the method of selecting the salesmen from its own employees. Persons working in other departments like advertising, correspondence, etc. should be considered if they fulfil the requirements of the job.
2. **Salesmen from competing firms.** Though ethically inadvisable, there is a practice to attract successful salesmen from competing firms. This source of recruitment has certain advantages:
   (a) No training is requires as he is already an experienced salesman.
   (b) He knows the selling technique and might have sold similar products.
   (c) They bring in their own customers to the new company as they possess the knowledge of the customers.
3. **Employment exchanges.** Employment exchanges provide a major source of recruitment. The employment exchanges may be public employment exchanges or private employment exchanges.
4. **Educational institutions.** Students fresh from the colleges who have a real aptitude could be selected to perform the job.
5. **Advertisements.** This is the most commonly employed method for selecting salesmen. Advertisements are inserted in the leading newspapers calling for applicants. Applications could be had from a large number of candidates and the best one could be selected.
6. **Employment seekers.** Salesmen who have resigned from their jobs or qualified and experienced salesmen who are not satisfied with the existing conditions of work may offer to serve other firms through advertisements. These people have the required experience and they can turn out to be better salesmen and a real asset to the company.
7. **Recommended candidates.** Sometimes persons in higher positions or business (wholesalers or retailers) may recommend candidates for appointment as salesmen. It is possible that exceptionally good persons may be working with the wholesalers or retailers. If such persons are selected, they will prove quite useful with little training.
8. **Casual applications.** Even if the firm does not advertise for a post, a company may be receiving applications from people seeking for job. The firms can keep such application forms and if a vacancy arises in the firm one could be selected among the applications.

(d) ***Selecting the proper man.*** Once the sources of selection is finalised the next step is to frame a programme for the selection of the right candidate. There are many well-tried selection programmes of which one could be used to select the right man. The first step usually is to ask the applicant to fill up an application blank. The information so received can constitute a history sheet which will enable the company to know about the person's background. A careful scrutiny of the applications will enable the firm to reject some applications which do not conform to the specifications.

After selecting some of the candidates who have a good chance of selection, the next step is to contact the referees to know about the real worth of the candidates.

The next step involved in the selection procedure is to ask the eligible hands to appear for a personal interview. Personal interview is an important milestone in, the process of selection. It will help the firm to find out whether the information given by the applicant is correct or not. In addition to personal interview many firms conduct psychological tests to discover their attitudes, aptitudes and abilities. Then a medical examination of the candidate is to be made to verify the physical fitness of the candidate for the job. Usually a final interview is also made with the selected candidate. Here a discussion is made with him about the duties and the terms of service will be made.

(e) ***Finalising the Employment.*** The last step in the selection procedure is to enter into an appointment agreement with the selected candidate. The agreement is to be signed by both the employer and employee. When the agreement is signed it constitutes a legal contract binding both the parties. The agreement safeguards the interest of the firm as well as the employee.

SALES TRAINING

Sales training is the process of informing the salesmen as to what they should do. It also involves in showing the salesmen what they should do. Sales training could be given to the salesmen either on an individual basis or if there are a large number of people training could be given on a group basis.

Objectives of Sales Training

The salesmen are educated with an idea to improve the productivity of the salesmen. The main objectives of educating the salesmen are the following:

(a) One of the objectives is to teach the salesmen about the principles and techniques of selling.

(b) If the training is imparted to an old salesman, the aim is to teach the salesman about the new techniques of selling.

(c) The training programme will give sufficient information to the salesmen about the history of the company, its products, the policies of distribution, prices, credits, etc. It also enables salesmen to have a full knowledge of the products they sell, their manufacturing process, characteristics, uses, etc.

(d) Another objective of training the salesmen is to improve the productivity of sales force. By proper training the general thinking of salesmen can be developed and the general selling cost can also be controlled.

(e) If by chance any unsuitable persons are selected they could be found out during training period and thrown out.

(f) A good training programme can also reduce the time necessary for a salesman to learn the job. If they have to learn everything from experience too much delay will be there to learn the techniques. This delay can be reduced by training.

(g) Another objective of training salesmen is to reduce the turnover rates of salesmen or to reduce the number of dropouts. Experienced and trained personnel stick on with the company. But inexperienced ones lose heart and leave the company or the slightest difficulty.

(h) Training will make the salesmen well informed about the laws and government regulations affecting the sale of goods.

(i) Education of salesmen can also help the salesmen to know about the techniques of competition and how to tackle it when faced with one such.

Advantages of Training Salesmen

A good training programme will bring about the following advantages:

(a) It will increase the volume of sales.

(b) When the volume of sale increases, the cost of production is reduced.

(c) The salesmen attain early maturity. By early maturity we mean that the normal level of efficiency will be reached early.

(d) There will be an improvement in the image of the firm since the better trained salesmen are cordial and have pleasant relations with the customers.

(e) The relationship between the employer and employee also strengthens on account of a good training programme.

(f) Yet another advantage of having proper training programme is that the firm can manage the selling work with a small number of trained salesmen.

ADVERTISING

Advertising essentially means spreading of information. From the earliest days men have proclaimed by word of mouth or in writing virtue of goods which they have produced.

The word originated from a Latin word *advertise* which means to turn to. The dictionary meaning of the term is to give public notice or to announce publicly.

The AMA has defined advertising as "any paid form of non-personal presentation and promotion of goods, services or ideas by an identified sponsor".

This definition requires some elaboration. *First*, advertising is paid for and hence it is a commercial transaction. This distinguishes publicity from advertising. Publicity is defined as any form of commercially significant news about a product, an institution, a service, or a person published in a space or radio that is not paid for by the sponsor. Publicity is not a commercial feature.

Advertising is non-personal. Whatever be the form of advertisements (visual, spoken or written) they are directed at a mass audience and not directly at the individual as the case in personal selling.

Finally, advertisements are identifiable with their sponsor or originator, which is not always the case with publicity or propaganda.

Though the terms advertising and publicity are different in the fields of marketing both are used interchangeably.

Objectives of Advertising

To make an immediate sale.

To build primary demand.

To inform about a product availability.

To build brand recognition or brand insistence.

To help salesmen by building an awareness of a product among retailers.

To create a reputation for service reliability or research strength.

To increase market share.

To modify existing product appeals and buying motives.

To inform about new products availability or features of price.

To increase the frequency of the use of a product.

To increase the number of retail outlets.

To build overall company image.

To effect immediate buying.

To reach new areas or new segments of population within existing areas.

To develop overseas market.

Kinds of Advertising

1. **Product advertising.** Normal characteristic of advertising is to create primary demand for a product category rather than for a specific brand. It is wrongly believed that product advertising must stress on brand name. This is based on the feeling that a good image often enhances the effectiveness of product advertising. Naturally the stress is made on the brand. However in practice, most companies were successful in making the product image by using the brand names (e.g. Dalda, Dettol, etc.) In short, where the company tries to sell its prcducts or services through advertising, it may be referred to as product advertising.
2. **Institutional advertising.** Where the objective of advertising is to project the image of a company or its services, it takes the form of an institutional advertising. These advertisements are not always directed only to consumers instead it may be aimed at various sets of public shareholders, creditors, etc. It may not at all product oriented, but is designed to enhance the image of the Company.
3. **Primary demand advertising.** It is intended to stimulate primary demand for a new product or product category. It is heavily utilized during the introduction stage of the product life cycle and when competition begins, advertising becomes competitive or selective. Here the goal of advertising is to influence demand for a specific product or service. Often promotion becomes less informative and more emotional during this

phase. Advertising may begin to stress subtle differences in brands, with heavy enphasis on brand name recall. Pricing will be used as a key promotional weapon as products become very similar.

4. **Comparative advertising.** Such types of advertisement stress on comparative features of two or more specific brands in terms of product service attributes. This method is adopted in the maturity stage when similar products fast appearing in the market constitute a stiff competition. Comparative advertising delivers information not previously available to consumers.
5. **Shortage advertising.** When shortage in the supply of product occurs advertising often disappears into the background, e.g. in the case of petroleum products since the oil crisis in 1974, virtually advertising for these products cased. But the intelligent marketers have found that advertising is still available marketing tool during times of shortage. This is what is termed as shortage advertising. Such kinds of advertising can be used for:
   (a) To reduce customer pressure,
   (b) Improve goodwill, and
   (c) Making appeal to save resources.
6. **Cooperative advertising.** When manufacturers, wholesalers and/or retailers jointly sponsor and share the expenditure on advertising, it takes the form of cooperative advertising, such advertising would carry the names of all parties involved. From the point of view of customers this is beneficial, as they get the articles directly from the authorised outlets. For example, the manufacturers of cars can undertake this type of advertising.
7. **Commercial advertising.** It is also termed as business advertising. As the name suggests such advertising is meant for effecting increase in sales.
8. **Non-commercial advertising.** These are usually published by charitable institutions preferably to solicit general and financial help, e.g. collection of donation or sale of tickets.
9. **Direct action advertising.** Advertising that stresses and persuades immediate buying of the product is known as direct action advertising. Direct mail advertising is capable of achieving immediate action to a large extent.

Benefits of Advertising

Advertising boardens the knowledge of the consumer. With the aid of advertising consumers can find and buy necessary products without waste of time. This speeds up the sales of commodities, the efficiency of labour in distribution increases, and the cost of selling diminishes. It is an accepted fact that without market stimulus of heavy advertising consumers might have waited another sixty years for the product evolution that took place in less than ten years.

Benefits to manufacturers

1. It increases sales volume on the one hand, it reduces cost of production on the other, and increases profits.

2. It helps easy introduction of products into the markets.
3. It helps to create an image and reputation not only of the product but also of the advertiser.
4. Retail price maintenance is possible.
5. It helps to establish a direct contact between manufactures and consumers.

Benefits to wholesalers and retailers

1. Easy sale of the products is possible since consumers are aware of the product and its quality.
2. It increases the rate of turnover of the stock.
3. It supplements the selling activities.
4. The reputation created is shared by the wholesalers and retailers alike.
5. It enables them to have product information.
6. If ensures more economical selling.

Benefits to consumers

1. Advertising stresses quality and very often prices. This forms an indirect guarantee to the consumers. Further more large-scale production assured by advertising enables the seller to sell the product at a lower cost.
2. It helps to them to know where and when the products are available. This reduces their shopping time.
3. It provides an opportunity to the customers to compare the merits and demerits of various substitutes/products.
4. This is perhaps the only medium through which consumers could know the varied and new uses of a product.
5. Modern advertisements are highly informative.

Benefits to salesmen

Salesmanship is incomplete without advertising. Advertising serves as the forerunner of a salesman in the distribution of the goods.

1. Introducing the product is made easy.
2. Advertising prepares necessary ground for a salesman to begin his work. Hence sales efforts are reduced.
3. The contact established with the consumer by a salesman is made permanent through advertising.
4. The salesman can weigh the effectiveness of advertising when he makes a direct contact with the customer.

Benefits to the community

1. Advertising in general is educative in nature. In the words of the late President Roosevelt of the USA, "Advertising brings to the greatest number of people actual

knowledge concerning useful things, it is essentially a form of education and the progress of civilization depends on education."

2. Advertising leads to large-scale production creating more employment opportunities
3. It initiates a process of creating more wants and their satisfaction resulting in a higher standard of living. To quote Winston Churchil, "Advertising nourishes the consuming power of man. It creates wants for a better standard of living.... It spurs individual exertion and greater production."
4. Newspapers would not lave become so popular and so cheap if there had been no advertisements. The cheap production of newspaper is possible only through the publication of advertisements. In other words, it is the advertising revenue that makes the newspapers live.
5. It assures employment opportunities for the professional artistes.

Is Advertising Necessary?

There is an old saying that "Good wine needs no bush". This saying originated from the fact that some liquor shops used to grow wine bush at the gate to show that wine was available inside. This may be needed on certain occasions and for certain products but need not be done universally. For instance, in the case of products that have come to stay as near necessaries advertising may be dispensed with or at least reduced. Perhaps this may be one of the reasons for subjecting advertising to severe criticisms. Various objections against it may be listed as follows:

Economic objections

1. **Advertising is not productive.** It is true that advertising does not produce any tangible goods. But all productive work need not necessarily result in tangible goods. On the other hand, it renders a very valuable service. Services are always intangible. The service rendered by advertising is highly necessary especially when one has to choose, from among the thousands of products which are similar in most respects. Advertising facilitates choosing, which in turn, leads to satisfaction.
2. **Advertising forces people to desire and buy things which, in fact, are not within their means.** It is true that advertising arouses interest for buying. But there is no physical force exerted on customers to buy things. Moreover cautious people do not fall into 'cheap trap', a term very often used to condemn advertising.
3. **Advertising simply, multiplies the needs.** It just takes business from one concern and gives it to another, e.g. people today are acquainted with the uses of soap, talcum powder, etc. When a new kind of talcum powder is introduced, advertising will help only to shift the demand from one product in favour of another. But this is not entirely true. Advertising also helps in the extension of demand.
4. **Advertising increases the cost of goods.** In a sense, it is true because expenses on it form a part of the cost. But here one forgets the benefits, derived from it. Moreover, advertising effects savings on the side of distribution cost.

5. **The monopoly argument.** Advertising usually lays emphasis on brands. This emphasis makes the consumer to become a slave of a particular brand. The best, answer to this argument is that it is the age of the survival of the fittest.
6. **Advertising encourages waste.** People are forced to use the product as fast as possible since new products with improvements are introduced. The production of any product requires the use of exhausting natural resources which are to be preserved by planned use. This is not considered in competitive advertising.

Social objections

1. **Misrepresentation of facts.** Most of the advertisements contain tall claims and the benefits advertised are not enjoyed in full. They are short lived only.
2. **Influence on the Press.** The press is influenced by advertisers because they provide the major source of revenue for the existence of newspapers.

Ethical objections

1. Advertising appeals make people to use such articles as might affect their health, e.g. liquors and cigarettes.
2. People with less purchasing power cannot afford to buy many articles though the advertisements create a strong need in them for the product. This makes a section of the society remain discontented.

On going through this criticism, one may naturally be led to conclude that advertising is a waste. Some criticisms are partly true, but not absolutely true. Most of it is now redundant since advertising has proved its effectiveness and efficacy in enhancing production and consumption. It is stated that attacks in advertising, on the grounds of deliberate deceit, have largely evaporated because of the efforts of the industry itself in setting standards and regulating its own product.

Advertisement Copy

The basic function of advertising, i.e. influencing and motivating people, is achieved through advertisement copy. The words used to convey the advertising idea or theme are called the copy. An analysis of the failures of advertisements would reveal that most of them fail for want of a good copy of advertisement. The aim of advertising copy is that it shall be seen and read, messages conveyed and then acted upon.

Qualities of a Good Advertisement Copy

An advertisement copy should bridge the gap between the advertiser and the readers, if it is to be effective. A great deal has been written and spoken about the science or the art of copy writing and the qualities necessary for an effective copy. The following are considered to be the attributes that should be present in an advertising copy:

1. Advertising is the business or the art of providing a substitute for talking to some one about something.
2. What must be clear must also be important.
3. It must have a personal appeal.
4. It should bring out the personality of the advertiser in terms of quality.

5. It must be reasonable but never dull.
6. It should be imaginative but never misleading.

The physical nature of an advertisement copy should have four factors:

1. Description
2. Narration
3. Exposition
4. Argumentation

Besides the advertisements must have the following values acceptable to the consumers and capable of attracting them:

(1) Attention value
(2) Suggestive value
(3) Memorising value
(4) Conviction value
(5) Sentimental value
(6) Educational value
(7) Instinctive value
(8) Action value

1. **Attention value.** People are generally busy and they go through the advertisements only very seldom. It should also be remembered that the customers are under no obligation to read the advertisements. Further, the advertisements are large in numbers and the readers are puzzled as to what should be read and what it should not be read? It is seen that the advertisements that do not catch the eye becomes fruitless. Thus it becomes inevitable for the advertiser to make the advertisement attractive. The methods usually adopted for making the advertisement copy attractive and capable of maintaining attention are:
   (a) Using pictures and drawings, e.g. Parke Davis (a leading drug manufacturing company) reproduces some classical paintings elaborating the need for modern medicines. The advertisements of cloth manufacturers also offer good example.
   (b) Using attractive headlines and slogans, e.g. "Neighbours envy owners Pride".
   (c) Using artistic borders and plenty of blank space. This would distinguish a particular—advertisement from the others. The same method is adopted in newspaper editing, e.g. some important pews is given in a box.
   (d) By introducing contests and reply coupons. Camelin pencil manufacturers invariably use this method. They award prizes on paintings made by using their colours.
2. **Suggestive value.** The advertisement should suggest the advantages of buying a particular make, e.g. Gleen Shampoo-beautifies your hair, controls dandruff.
3. **Memorising value.** The advertisement should leave a lasting impression upon the readers mind. It is for this purpose that advertisements are prepared. But even the

advertisement should be capable of making the reader remember the product image, e.g. Horlicks gives extra energy, Glaxo builds bonnie babies.

Memorising value could be easily created by using symbols, brand names, etc. In fact, most of the articles that we use today have become common things only because their advertisements contain a memorising value.

4. **Conviction value.** The advertisement should never be misleading. It should be true and that could be readily believed, e.g. Forhans—the paste created by a dentist.
5. **Sentimental value.** The advertisement should respect the sentiments and feelings of the people for whom it is meant. This aspect is extremely necessary in the case of products that are meant for the educated and people belonging to the higher strata of society. It is they who are more, sentimental. Tata used to stress the element in their advertisements when Swadeshi Movement was on. They advertised: Indian Co. Indian made.
6. **Educational value.** The advertisements should be in the nature of enlightenment concerning the use and values of a product. Fundamentally people keep certain habits which cannot be easily changed. The creation of demand is possible only if such habits are changed. Advertisements should be capable of introducing new habits and attracting the people towards new products.

   For example, Have you taken these four steps to protect your baby?

   Small Pox Vaccination,

   Triple Vaccination,

   Polio Vaccination, and

   Life Insurance.
7. **Instinct value.** This is largely a psychological problem. The human behaviour is fundamentally related to instincts. It is these instincts which make a person behave differently at different times. In order to create the desired instinct, the advertiser should plan well before the preparation of an advertisement copy. These instincts are pride, beauty, health, economy, fear, etc. and the advertisement should be capable of tickling these instincts and directing the people towards a particular product.
8. **Action value.** Action is often induced because of the goodwill which the advertiser has built up through advertising. When the purchaser sees the well-known symbol of a manufacturer, that itself satisfies him and the sales resistance, if any, reduced. 'Sealed units gain this value very easily'.

Kinds of Copy Forms

1. The announcement form

It is used when a new product is being introduced in the market. The purpose is not to persuade but to inform the public.

2. The descriptive form

Most of the advertising copies belong to this form. Detailed description of the product is given in order to create a desire in the minds of the people to possess it. Where mush selling efforts are required and where the decision of the buyers is based on 'style', descriptive form of advertisement is essential.

3. The dramatization form

This is meant to attract the attention of the readers to a particular advertisement. The advertisement copies in which the attention value is artificially created are said to have the dramatisation form. The headlines, colours, attractive questions, etc. are used to create this form in advertisements.

4. The reminder form

Various methods are adopted to make the advertisements remain deeply entrenched in the minds of the readers. Slogans and words, which are quite familiar, are used to create this element in the advertisement.

5. Inducement form

The essential characteristic feature of such a form is found in the stress on personal appeal. This aspect is generally considered by companies that are rendering services such as insurance, banking, etc.

Selection of Media

Having prepared an advertisement copy, the next step is to find out a proper medium though which it could be brought out. An advertising medium is any object or device that carries the advertising message. In general, an advertising medium should be capable of accomplishing three objectives:

1. It must reach the largest number of people.
2. It must gain their attention.
3. It must be less expensive.

But this is not enough. From the management point of view, an advertising medium requires consideration of the following major factors:

1. The character of the medium.
2. The atmosphere of the medium.
3. The coverage of the medium.
4. The cost of the medium.
5. The size of the advertisement.
6. The position of the advertisement.
7. The nature of the product.
8. The types of buyers.

Kinds of Media

There is no breath of media today. The media are broadly classified into Direct and Indirect. Direct method of advertising refers to such methods used by the advertiser with which he could establish a direct contact with the prospects. Direct mail is an example of this. Indirect method, on the other hand, involves the use of a hired agency for spreading information, Most of the media are indirect in nature. The various media that are commonly used are:

1. Press publicity
2. Direct mail
3. Outdoor advertising
4. Audiovisual methods
5. Point of purchase advertising
6. Speciality advertising

1. Press Publicity

This remains the most popular method of publicity today. Newspapers and magazines have become a part of the cultural and political life of people now. Press publicity takes two forms, Newspapers and Magazines.

a. **Newspapers.** Newspapers are bought largely for their news value. As such they are appropriate for announcing new products and new developments of existing products. Because of their frequency of publication, they are also well suited to opportunity markets. The various ***advantages*** may be summed up as follows:

   1. They reach every nook and corner, so their coverage is high.
   2. High frequency enables speedy preparation and publication of advertisement.
   3. Newspapers offer a lot of flexibility. According to the convenience and necessity of the advertiser, the size and shape of advertisements could be changed.
   4. Advertising in newspapers is a cheap method of advertising from the cost point of view.
   5. By inserting local advertisements (in local papers) the effectiveness of advertising copy could be tested.
   6. Visual appeals could be created.
   7. The reputation of the newspaper is available to the advertisers and to their products also.

Limitations

1. Visual effects may not be created in practice as the papers are usually printed on cheap newsprint.
2. The life of the newspaper is extremely short, so frequent advertisement is required.
3. There is waste of circulation. The advertisement is carried to places where there is no market existing nor the possibility of creating a new market. This effect is avoided in local newspaper advertising, since they have a concentrated coverage of a limited area.

Kinds of Newspaper Advertising

1. **Classified Advertisements.** They are grouped and published on the basis of the contents and nature of advertising. Advertisements having common themes such as

matrimonial, for sale, situations vacant are given under group headings. From the cost point of view, they are cheap.

2. **General Advertisements.** Usual advertisements which are published in different places creating some kind of identity.
3. **Teaser Advertisements.** A series of advertisements without any sales message are published consecutively over a number of days in the same place in a newspaper. This creates an interest among readers to follow the series until the last advertisement appears. This method is highly effective.
4. **News Type Advertisements.** From the outward appearance it would simply look like a news item. At the end of the news ADVT is added to denote the purpose. Most of the speeches of the chairmen of companies are given on this basis.

b. **Magazines.** Another medium under press publicity is magazines and journals. They also offer good facility, because magazines are read leisurely when the reader is mentally prepared to receive advertisements.

Magazines are periodicals but different from newspapers in two respects. One is that it pre-selects its readership through the nature of its content. Secondly, as mentioned above they are read leisurely. Magazines as a group may be further subdivided from the point of view of advertisers as follows:

1. **General Magazines**

   The content is meant for general appeal—Blitz, The Week.

2. **Specialist Magazines**

   They cater to a readership with clearly defined and specific interest—Commerce, Femina.

3. **Special issues such as Annuals, Directories**

Merits

1. Better reproduction of advertisements than newspapers.
2. Larger duration of interest.
3. Magazines are highly selective in nature and waste of circulation is avoided.
4. Trade magazines reach specialised groups.
5. Magazine advertising creates prestige, reputation and an image of quality.
6. There is no crowded atmosphere of advertisements as in the case of newspapers. Because of the small size of magazines, the number of advertisements in a page would be one or at the most two. This increases appearance and makes the advertisements attractive.

Limitations

1. Low flexibility is the chief demerit.
2. Preparation cost of magazine is high and hence advertising cost also would be high.
3. Inelasticity.

The coverage of the magazine and the coverage of the distribution of goods may not synchronise.

4. The advertisements cannot be brought out in time as needed by the advertiser. Usually the preparation of a magazine takes time and urgent advertising cannot be undertaken.

Newer Forms of Printed Publicity

Along with the increased use of certain articles, the printed publicity has come to occupy new horizons, e.g. Postage articles such as covers, inland letters, offer good place for advertisement.

2. Direct Mail

This method is direct in its approach and hence often referred to as 'Direct Advertising'. But it retains some of the characteristics of press advertising. For instance, here also printed materials are used to spread information.

Direct mail advertising involves two decisions. First, to determine the persons to whom advertising messages are to be sent. Secondly, to decide the manner in which the messages are to be communicated. Because of this controlling aspect, Direct Mail is also known as controlled advertising.

Direct mail may take various forms according to the method in which the advertisement is prepared.

1. Leaflets: A single sheet printed on one or both sides.
2. Folders: A single sheet folded to make an attractive form.
3. Booklet: It consists of a number of sheets bound in the form of a book.
4. Catalogue: It is an exhaustive list of the products of a manufacturer indicating the price also.

Characteristic features of Direct mMail

1. **Directness.** The message is directly addressed to the prospective customers.
2. **Flexibility.** The message could be changed or altered to suit different conditions.
3. **Timeliness.** Advertising could be timed according to the wishes of the advertiser.
4. **Economical.** Cheap compared to other form of advertising.
5. **Personal Appeal.** The greatest attraction of this method is its capacity to create and maintain personal contact.

Method of Direct mailing

The foremost job in such a kind of advertising is the preparation of a mailing list. It is a list containing the names and addresses of the prospective customers to whom messages are to be sent. Obviously, such a list should include only those who are able and likely to respond to the advertisement. This list can be prepared from the following sources:

(a) List of present and past customers.
(b) List prepared by salesmen.
(c) List compiled from directories such as telephone directory, voters list, etc.

(d) Govt. records—such as income tax list, birth registration, municipal records, etc.

(e) Records of membership kept by civil and social organisations.

The second step is to classify the list into groups of individuals where interests are similar.

This step is followed by the preparation of the message in a most attractive and suitable form. The advertiser has got some freedom compared to press advertising because they could be given detailed information. The final step is the distribution of the printed message for which the following ways are adopted:

(a) By Mail

(b) Through retail stores or through salesmen

(c) Inside packages.

Merits

1. Selectivity is the greatest advantage. Because of the widest network of postal services the advertiser could reach any part of the country and have his message conveyed.
2. Ability in creating personal contact. Press advertising is meant for large masses, whereas direct mail is intended for the addresses only.
3. The message that cannot be given through advertisements could be managed by direct mail.

Limitations

1. It is not cheap, especially when the printing and postal charges are high.
2. The preparation of a proper mailing list is not an easy job.
3. Even the list prepared with utmost care would become obsolete in a short span.

It has not proved its supremacy in all fields. Moreover, it has proved to be ineffective in case of products which need personal examination.

3. Outdoor Advertising

Historically, it is the oldest form of advertising and remains the most common medium even today. Press publicity is basically indoor advertising as papers are generally read indoors. Outdoor advertising projects the message to a large number of people of heterogeneous interests. As such the products that need a wide appeal use this method. Outdoor advertisements are meant for the moving population and provide the advantage of reminding the people frequently of the product. Thus it successfully incorporates the advantage of repetition found in good advertisement.

Merits

1. Outdoor advertising is capable of gaining more attention.
2. It offers great selectivity. It could be used locally, regionally or even nationally.
3. Flexibility is present.
4. It is semi-permanent. Once the hoard is exhibited, it could be kept there for a long time.
5. It is a very good medium to stress brand names and package identity.

6. Coverage is greater.
7. Low cost.

Limitations

1. It has to be brief. Therefore detailed explanation is not possible.
2. The exact effect created on prospects is difficult to measure. It could be used only as a supplementary form to other kinds of advertising, e.g. it cannot be used for introducing a new product but is effective for reminding of an existing product:

Kinds of outdoor publicity

(a) **Mural Advertising.** It refers to posters which are often pasted on wills. The size of such posters would be big and might contain pictures, etc. It is often found in cinema advertising.

(b) **Advertising Boards.** These are also posters but are kept at certain fixed places especially at points where people frequently assemble. Bus stops, railway stations, etc. offer good places for this kind of advertising.

(c) **Vehicular Advertising.** This refers to moving advertisement. The advertisements on moving vehicles such as buses and trains offer examples of this. This type of advertising has a very large circulation and is considered to be very effective.

(d) **Electric Displays, Neon Signs.** This is an attractive form of outdoor display. It attracts attention easily and acts as a memoriser, even when it is dark all around.

(e) **Sky Advertising (Sky Writing).** Notices and other advertisement materials such as printed balloons, etc. are distributed from aeroplanes. Usually near the circus tents a huge balloon is floated from which a board hangs down depicting the name of the circus.

(f) **Sandwitch Men.** They are hired persons who move in a procession with boards and notices and also playing musical instruments to attract the attention of the public. The cinema theatres usually arrange this kind of advertising, when a new picture is released.

4. Audio-Visual Methods

(a) Film advertising

Advertising could be effectively carried out through the use of motion pictures or cinema. It is one of the most popular medium of advertisement. There are three kinds of motion pictures used as the medium of advertisement.

Documentary Film

It is preferably used for publicity aspect and in most cases educative in nature. It has a broad aim and is used to show various aspects of as industry as a whole rather than to highlight the achievements of an individual firm.

Straight Advertising Films

These are common today. They concentrate on advertising message relating to only one product. Usually, they do not contain any entertainment elements.

Sponsored Advertising Films

It is a combination of advertisement and entertainment. Straight advertising becomes monotonous because of concentrated advertising materials. Cartoon films fall under this category.

Merits

1. Coverage is quiet wide.
2. Appeal is simultaneously made to all sections of the people.
3. It is able to explain and demonstrate the use of a product.
4. It is never wasted as no advertisement can escape the attention. It is stated that unless a movie, goer deliberately talks to his neighbour or walks out of the theatre he cannot escape the advertising message.

Limitation

1. Production cost of a film is high.
2. Restrictions are imposed against screening films, e.g. there is censoring.
3. A film can only be shown to the people who come to the theatre. Thus a large section of people are outside the scope of such advertising.
4. For screening films, the cooperation of theatre is inevitable.
5. Crowding of such advertisement films makes the audience feel bored.

(b) Radio advertising

AIR provides two programmes for commercial use.

Spot Programme

This is a short duration advertisement of less than one minute. The matter is read out simply by announcer.

Sponsored Programme

It is a lengthy programme prepared by the advertiser and contains some entertainment value.

Merits

1. Coverage is very wide even illiterate people are covered.
2. Psychology experts are of the opinion that what is learnt through ears is not easily forgotten. Thus radio advertising claims the advantage of memorising value.
3. Flexible—It may be used on a national or local level according to the need.
4. It easily catches the attention of the people.

Limitations

1. All the people do not own a radio set. Even if they own one a large number of people do not care to listen to all the programmes.
2. Advertising of products unknown to the average listener often becomes a waste. Soaps, powders, etc. are known to them but not various industrial products.

3. The more attractive programme alone creates interest among listeners.
4. There is a probability that the listener may immediately forget the product after the announcement is over as there is a multiplicity of advertisements in a short-time.
5. Radio advertisements are very brief and details cannot be elaborated.
6. There is no possibility of demonstration.

(c) Television

The main feature of TV is that it combines the advantage of both radio and cinema. Hence it is a powerful audio-visual medium.

(d) Exhibitions

This is a method in which the demonstration aspect is given importance. Further, exhibitions range from a small local level to national or even international levels. Seasonal trade fairs were common even in the past.

The basic aim of advertising through exhibition is to keep the name of the product before the public. One great advantage of this kind of advertising is that products can be demonstrated to the people and their doubts cleared. This method plays an important role in international marketing. An exhibition has come to be accepted as an extension of 'market place'. On government level, exhibitions are conducted officially by the Directorate of exhibitions, Ministry of Foreign Trade and the Indian Council of Trade Fairs and Exhibitions.

5. Point of Purchase Advertising (P.O.P.)

This a direct method because, the advertising process is either undertaken by the manufacturer or through the dealer. There are various forms commonly known as 'store display'. It is also a powerful medium. It is observed that point of purchase is the exact point where the prospects are remained finally about of a product.

(a) **Window Display.** Products are displayed in front of the shop at a place where they would be prominent so that passers by cannot escape the display. They are arranged most attractively. This method is often used not only to sell an article but as a means of creative selling. The dormant desires of people to own certain products are brought to surface. A window display is a combination of a poster, newspaper advertisement, a stage act, a speech and scarf dance.

The articles are displayed inside a glass window which is decorated attractively. The price of the product is also attached to the product. Window display is also named as window dressing. "Come and get it we have it, is the maxim behind this method of advertising."

(b) **Counter display.** Here also the products are displayed but inside the shop. Thus, the attention of rear buyers, who step into the shop, is directed towards the articles displayed. *Secondly*, the manufacturers arrange for such a show through a selected network of retailers who are awarded a prize for the best display. Manufacturers of cosmetic items usually arrange for such shows. This method is good for introducing a new product, as its peculiar advantages can be highlighted and questions from consumers can be answered by the salesman incharge.

(c) **Special Displays and Shows.** Most of the manufacturers have found that putting special displays of several products in selected store, is a good promotional device. This is extremely suitable when the manufacturer wants to advertise all his products and shows how they are related to each other. This kind of shows are capable of impressing a company's name generally on the public. Electrical appliances manufacturing companies usually arrange such shows with the help of a dealer in a selected locality.

(d) **Showrooms.** In case of certain products, personal inspection is an important prerequisite. Usually customers are not satisfied by reading or listening to an advertisement. Mixers, washing machines, etc. are always purchased only after a close took at the products. This is the reason why manufacturers keep showrooms at huge expenditure. Besides such showrooms could be used for exhibiting other products also. In fact, the curiosity raised by advertisement is satisfied by showing the real product. This is exactly the function of a showroom.

6. Specialty Advertising

It is a usual practice now with the manufacturers to provide free of cost various articles of low value to the existing and prospective customers. These articles constitute diaries, calendars, ball pens, etc. Needless to say, all these articles would bear some advertisements or would at least mention the name of the product or the manufacturer.

Advertising Agency

Advertising agency is defined as an organisation whose business consists in the acquisition as a principal of the right to use space or time in advertising media and the administration on behalf of advertisers, of advertising appropriations made by them It is organised to render advice and creative service for its client.

Selection of an Advertising Agency

The selection of an advertising agency is by no means an easy task. It requires careful consideration as is required in the case of selecting a proper medium. The following points are generally kept in mind while choosing an advertising agency:

1. Financial soundness
2. General reputation
3. Facilities and abilities available
4. Size and adequacy of staff
5. Basis of remuneration
6. Relationship they maintain with advertisers.

Advertising Budget

One of the objections leveled against advertising is based on its high cost. But no manufacturer would spend unscrupulously because of the simple reason that high expenditure cannot be accommodated in the margin of profits. How much a manufacturer can spend on advertising. This is a financial problem to be tackled by financial manager. Fundamentally advertising expenditure relates to two aspects. One is the cost involve and the effect created by advertising. Second is the volume of advertising and its relation to overall profitability. It is, thus a complex problem which is often solved by predetermining the amount that could be spent on advertising. This is done on the basis of the analysis of markets, consumers, nature of products, etc. In other words, an advertising budget will show how much, where and what purpose to for spent. Simply stated every manufacturer sets apart a sum to be spent for advertising which is referred to as advertising appropriation. As mentioned above the amount is not arbitrarily fixed but is determined on a scientific basis. The following methods are used in deciding scientific appropriation:

1. Market share approach

As market share analysis is common in most firms for their demand analysis and for evaluating market efficiency, the same method is adopted in allocating funds for advertising. Accordingly, advertising budgets are prepared so that money spent would retain a given market share or obtain a certain target share. If a firm is satisfied with its market it may decide to spend the same amount or percentage that it spent previously. But this method has the following drawbacks:

(a) It completely ignores quality and creativity.

(b) When a new product is introduced a heavier advertising budget may become necessary initially. It is impossible to create product awareness without high initial investment.

(c) Similarly the element of competition is not considered under this approach. As pointed out above, when competition is severe larger sums are to be spent to retain even the existing share.

2. Arbitrary allocation

This is a most unscientific method and some amount is spent on pry motion. Mostly, retailers with local status adopt this method, as and when they feel some advertisements would be given.

3. Percentage of sales method

Under this method, a certain amount is allocated for advertising as a percentage of sales, past or anticipated. It can also be used on sales by product/territory/customer group, and so forth. But in the absence of clear figurers it is doubtful whether this method would justify the efficiency expected. However, the credit of this method lies in its simplicity.

The defect is that past is not always a correct indicator for the future. This method would suggest that advertising expenditure is to be reduced when sales are declining and *vice versa*.

The inherent weakness of this approach is that the budget becomes a consequence of sales rather than a determinant of sales.

In spite of the above defects, many firms followed this practice on the argument that advertising expenditure tends to rise and fall with the business cycle.

4. Task and objective method

This is a most popular approach and offers management a sound technique for setting up a promotion budget. Under this Method, first of all advertising objectives are established. Then communication tools required to achieve these objectives are designed. The third step is to determine the cost required to executes promotional activities and prograrnmes. In short advertising expenditure is directly related to the objectives to be achieved.

In a survey conducted on 557 firms on the sales forecasting methods followed by them, it was revealed as follows.

Objective and task method	—	35.6%
Percentage of sales method	—	24.8%
Arbitrary	—	27.7%
Others	—	11.9%

5. Competitive comparison method

It is a method whereby the advertising expenditure of one firm is decided on the basis of expenditure incurred by a competing firm. This is called "we too approach". It is purely arbitrary, because due to various reasons the competitor may spend less or more than what can be accepted as the right expenditure.

6. Funds available method

This method implies that the amount available after meeting operating costs, dividend payments, etc. would be completely spent on advertising. As seen in the first case, under this method, when sales come down, there may not be funds available for advertising appropriation. Conversely, when sales rise, the appropriation would be greater, which tends to create careful expenditure on advertising.

7. Incremental method

This is also referred as 'rate on investment' method. This approach emphasises the relationship between advertising and contribution to profits. This method may be used to measure sales with advertising and sales without advertising.

QUESTIONS FOR DISCUSSION

1. "Money spent on advertisement is not wasteful." Critically examine this statement.
2. What are the objectives of advertising? Discuss the major ones.
3. What are the uses of advertising to various parties? Discuss.
4. Write a short note on scientific advertising.
5. How are the advertising functions organised in an organisation?
6. Differentiate between the following:
   (a) Advertising and Publicity.
   (b) Advertising and Salesmanship.
7. Why is advertising considered to have a place of pride in the framework of marketing? Discuss the statement.
8. Discuss any three methods of determining annual advertising appropriation of a company.
9. Describe the services rendered by an advertising agency to its clients and explain how an advertising agency gets remunerated for its services.

10. "Three major tools of mass-market promotion are advertising, publicity and sales promotion." Discuss the specific promotion functions of each of these tools.
11. "The only one and the basic objective of advertising in a company is to increase its sales and profits." Do you agree? Describe the advertising objectives which a company may possibly set out to achieve.
12. "A marketing communicator must start with a clear target audience in mind." Elaborate.
13. (a) What is the role of communication in market-buyer scenario in the case of cigarettes?
    (b) How do the elements of the promotional mix act on the consumer for selling a refrigerator?
14. Why do companies need advertising agencies? What does an advertising agency do? What are the different departments in an advertising agency and how relevant they are to each other?
15. "Advertisement pays when business is bad and it also pays when business is good." Justify this statement with examples.

CASE STUDY 16.1

IT'S NOT A JAM—IT'S NISHAN

In 1993, marketing executives at Green-Food Ltd. were concerned about the performance of their NISHAN brand of jams. They were debating whether or not to adopt a new strategy for advertising. The advertising campaign would involve an unusual and prospectively controversial direct comparison of the vitamin-nutritional value of NISHAN vis-a-vis the fresh natural fruits. The approach would be controversial in the sense that most Indians associated nourishment either to fresh fruits/vegetables or to medical preparations.

During 1992-93, the Green Food's executives were worried by the decline in NISHAN's market share. Upon gathering and analysing information from consumer panels, it was discovered that substantial portion of NISHAN's volume losses represented shifts to more 'exotic' tastes like 'mango-orange', '3-in-ones', etc. The other categories that appeared to be cutting into sales of NISHAN more than its competitors were the new introductions like cheese-spread and margarine.

The executives felt that NISHAN was failing to communicate its vitamin nutrition value which was a definite product attribute. They felt that the best way to improve NISHAN's sales performance was by developing a more compelling advertising approach.

Focus group interviews were conducted with consumers to evaluate the relative effectiveness of several alternative copy approaches making direct or implied comparisons between NISHAN and the other jams. These seven alternatives are presented below:

Alternative Copy Proposition—1993

1. NISHAN is the only jam which has the vitamins and minerals so essential as a part of diet.

2. Unlike other brands, only NISHAN has the vitamins and minerals of fresh fruits intact.
3. NISHAN jam spread over a toast is as good as a portion of fresh fruit eaten at breakfast.
4. Children may hate fresh fruits at breakfast. Relieve your anxiety by giving them NISHAN.
5. Fruits picked up from the orchard are packed into the jam bottle without delay keeping the nourishment intact.
6. NISHAN is more acceptable to children than any other rival brand.
7. No fuss on the breakfast table when you serve NISHAN.

Next, three different advertising executions were developed by NISHAN's advertising agency. These in turn were to be copy-tested to determine which seemed to most effectively fulfil the strategic objective set for the brand. The summary of the three alternative copy executions is as follows:

Conversation: Setting is the processed foods section of a large retail store. A mother picking up a bottle of a leading brand of jams, begins a dialogue with an off camera announcer. After she indicates her belief that all jams have natural fruits and freshments, the announcer asks her to look more closely at the label on the bottle. He then hands her a bottle of NISHAN jam and shows her the label where the vitamins and the mineral contents are listed. He then says, "All jams are made from fruits but only NISHAN preserves the natural vitamins and minerals in its jams."

Dining Table: Setting is a large dining table with breakfast laid out. Mother is serving while the husband has sat down with a young boy and girl for breakfast. The mother serves a fruit which the children refuse to take. She says, "Alright. I will give you only what you want." She puts the fruit on top of a toast and children watch. The fruit dissolves into a thin layer of jam. The children lap up the toast in delight. A proud mother speaks, "I served them fresh fruit but my children thought it was just the jam."

Laboratory. A large chemical/analytical laboratory in the background with a doctor in his overalls is on the desk. He speaks, "I recommend fresh fruit at breakfast because they provide essential vitamins and minerals to keep you going for the day." In the meanwhile he puts a fruit in a masticator, converts it to a paste, puts the paste in an auto-analyser and the computer screen reads the vitamins and mineral contents.

The doctor speaks again, "Mothers come to me asking for some prescriptions for their children who would not eat fruits at breakfast." He scoops a spoonful of jam from the NISHAN bottle and puts it in the auto-analyser. The computer screen lights up showing the vitamin and mineral contents.

These executions were prepared in the form of rough production advertisement costing about Rs. 60,000 to develop and test, rather than in the form of finished commercials which would have cost about 20 times this amount.

QUESTIONS FOR DISCUSSION

1. Appraise the alternative copy propositions in details.
2. Which of the three alternative executions would you choose to run? Why?
3. If you were the Brand Manager [or the leading competing brand to NISHAN], how would you respond to the advertising approach of NISHAN?

(A.I.M.A., Dec. 1997)

CASE STUDY 16.2

GOOD BROTHERS INDIA

Good Brothers India was an international organisation started in 1973 to prevent the proposeless massacre of the animal kingdom for superficial human pleasures. The advertising agency was approached by the Indian representative requesting them to do a communication programme, whereby public awareness of the company would be increased. The agency worked out the first advertisement, 'Pretty isn't it' and used it as a launching pad for contacting various organisations.

The campaign conceived by the agency was a self-generating programme. Several organisations were contacted and donations were requested from them. The organisations were informed that all the donations will be pooled and the desired form of communication programme will be worked out depending on the amount of collections received. The communication programme idea was well received by the organisations and collections approximating to Rs. 1,80,000 were received. Additionally, known publications like India Today, Readers' Digest and Business India offered free pages in their magazines.

The campaign attempted to bring out the cruelties animals are subjected to for superficial human pleasures. By informing the public and making them aware of the atrocities committed on these animals and by suggesting to them that man-made alternatives are available, a degree of success in changing public opinion was achieved. It will be interesting to note that after release of the first advertisement, membership increased by nearly 20 per cent and donations were received to the tune of Rs. 1,20,000. One organisation, which prefers to remain anonymous, offered to release a series of six advertisements once in *The Times of India*, equivalent to a donation of Rs. 1,40,000.

QUESTIONS FOR DISCUSSION

1. Evolve a plan for effective advertising for the above mentioned campaign through other media vehicles.
2. Do you think the above mentioned campaign will be satisfactory in poor countries which are conditioned to resource constraints, and if so how would you develop another campaign under conditions of shortcomings in resources and communications.

CASE STUDY 16.3

PEARS TOILET SOAP

Marketing executives of Hindustan Lever were debating with their advertising agency, Lintas, on the creative strategy to be adopted for the Pears Toilet Soap campaign.

The Market

Toilet soap has a very large market in India. In total tonnage (about 1,00,000 tonnes in 1969), it is one of the largest in the world. In 1969 the market comprised of numeroxis brands, some of which had national distribution and reputation. Five brands-Lifebuoy, Lux, Hamam, Rexona, and Jai—constituted over 85 per cent of the market. Each of these was then priced under a rupee and was in fact the common man's toilet soap. Then there were more expensive brands different from these general-purpose soaps, which offered a specialised reason for use. Each had a unique proposition for which it could afford to charge a higher price—even double that of the regular soaps. For example, Cinthol was advertised as the deodorant soap, Mysore Sandal for its exclusive perfume, Margo as a Ayurvedic soap, and there were medicated soaps like Neko which could be bought from a chemist Pears was such a speciality brand.

Pears had been in existence in India for many years, and like the other special soaps, it offered a unique reason of its purchase. It had an unusual shape, was transparent, and accounted for two per cent of the total market and about 10 per cent of the specialised soap market.

Pears Image

Gerson da Cunha, General Manager of Lintas, commented that the Pears image was "the result of years and years of advertising". It was in fact a "bundle" of elements; the "transparent" soap; it was "mild and pure" and "mild and pure because you can actually see through it". In fact, anything anyone said about Pears seemed to reflect an advertising statement made for over 30 years.

People felt that because it contained glycerine and was mild, Pears was good for the skin; it was used when the skin became dry in winter in North and East India. And so, Pears had attached to it a large bundle of "properties" which were thought to make the brand not just good, but special. It was a product that was difficult to manufacture. In fact, till 1967, Hindustan Lever could not really make enough to meet demand. All that was produced was eagerly snapped up. And all throughout, there was this background of advertising which made people perceive it as a special soap.

In 1968, Hindustan Lever faced a different problem. The company was able to produce more of Pears, and it wished to expand the market for the brand.

Here was Pears, very well regarded, clearly seen as a special soap, with a history of past advertising which talked about its purity, its mildness, its transparency, its glycerine, and its properties in looking after the skin. It had developed very special connotations: "The soap you used when you were a baby", "the soap that your great grandmother used when she was in London in 1887". A lot of people thought that it was imported. All these positive connotations had developed round the soap over many years. Now, because of these connotations and because it had not been freely available for sometime, people thought that it was far too specialised, "only use it on little babies", and, "only use it in winter", This implied: "This soap is not for me."

The marketing manager of the soaps group bid that the task now was to persuade more consumers to buy this soap and, not only that, but pay a lot more for it. At the same time they had to be very careful that, in doing so, they did not say anything which went against the well-entrenched image of the product.

With this analysis of the situation and of the Pears image, Hindustan Lever asked Lintas to present a campaign for Pears. As it happens, there was at that time little research background for the product.

The Consumer

The definition of the target consumer did not pose any particular problem. This was an expensive soap. Hence, first and foremost, it requires the consumer to have enough disposable income to pay about Rs. 1.50 for Pears (in 1969): 100 per cent more than for popular toilet soaps. Clearly the consumer would have to be in the upper or upper-middle income groups. By and large, the target consumer lived in towns of over 1,00,000 population; was sophisticated, but not necessarily very modem; clearly believed in good things for the whole family though they might be somewhat expensive; and had a professional background and more than average facility in English. The appeal would be to the housewife who did the bulk of the family purchasing. This was the approximate definition of the target consumer that Hindustan Lever gave to Lintas.

Distribution was believed to be adequate Pears was sold in about 45,000 outlets all over India. This was as much, if not more than, what was covered by the other expensive toilet soaps (approximately 40,000 shops). Obviously, this was much less than the number of outlets covered by the five popular brands (1,80,000 outlets).

The Advertising Brief

The company felt that brand loyalty in toilet soaps was not very high, not for instance, comparable to toothpaste. However, brand loyalty amongst the more expensive brands, which offered a more specialised benefit was significantly higher than in the popular general purpose toilet soap market. This statement was made on the basis of the company's understanding of consumer behaviour rather than from research. When the housewife did her monthly shopping, she would ask for one or two brands among the popular soaps, perhaps varying the proportion of the different brands each month. But in addition, she would buy one specialised brand, which she would not vary from month to month because it would be used in the home by a particular person, or at a particular time of the day or year, or for a particular reason. Whatever, the reason, it would be related to a specialised benefit that the soap promised.

The volume of Pears could be increased by persuading either the present consumer to buy more of it or more people to buy it. There were many dangers in using the first approach. The existing consumers of Pears were using it for a specific reason, for instance, in the winter months. One could recommend their using it all through the year and so expand usage. Now, if they felt that it was a soap they could use right round the year, might they not be inclined to think that it was not such a specialised soap after all? And would they still be willing to pay twice the money for it?

If the base was to be expanded by bringing in new consumers, where would the increase come from? Should one try to convert people who were buying similar priced brands, i.e. other specialised soaps? If a consumer bought Mysore Sandal, it was because he particularly liked the perfume. Would he respond to a Pears message?

On the other hand, the people who were buying special soaps obviously had the capacity to pay a higher price. They would be paying a higher price because they were getting some particular satisfaction.

The brief that the client gave to the agency was to create an increase in the demand for Pears by offering a reason for purchase, which was in line with the Pears image. This brief would appeal to the kind of consumer that had been described in socio-economic terms, and so would lead to an increase in the width of consumption, i.e. more people should be using the product.

Hindustan Lever wanted the agency to build its new campaign on the past strength of Pears. At the same time, it had to say something that would cover those who had not responded to the previous message.

Past Advertising

The first thing that the agency did was to look at the advertising over the years. Pears ads, for a long time, had shown little girls: sweet, prettily clad, and cute little girls with a line that said, "Waiting to be a beautiful lady." Hindustan Lever did away with this approach because Pears would become a purely children's soap.

Then came a campaign that emphasised a product attribute: the translucency of the soap. There was a shot of a girl holding it up and looking through it and a line saying, "A soap so pure you can see through it.... Only Pears lets you see how pure it is." This advertising stressed the glycerine content of a soap. After a while, Hindustan Lever felt that this advertising was merely telling people about a product feature and not creating a memorable brand image.

Then came a third phase which showed Pears as a sort of teenage soap. It was not promoted actively as a teenage soap but rather shown in this context. The idea was to make some use of its history and yet build a more youthful atmosphere round it.

The next phase in the creative strategy for Pears came in 1969 when Hindustan Lever asked Lintas to develop a new campaign based on the existing knowledge of the market.

The agency developed a series of advertisement appeals. Mr. Da Cunha opened the presentation to the marketing manager by recapitulating the content of the earlier campaigns:

"The consumer purchase proposition for the brand is 'Pears Soap Helps Keep Your Complexion/Skin Young.' We feel that this message is sufficiently meaningful to the target to whom we shall advertise. Now, we are going to show you the visuals of alternative approaches that we have attempted."

"This is the first idea we have tried. It shows a photograph of a pretty young lady in her mid-twenties and a line that says: 'This is innocent skin.' The idea is that your skin becomes 'wicked' that is, the opposite of innocent—when it is allowed to age; and lot of things make it at age. Pears is something that keeps your skin clear; keeps it pure because Pears itself is pure. We think we have a good idea here—the idea of making people feel that they can keep their skin 'innocent'. It is something that goes very deep into peoples desires for themselves.

"There is, of course, an important drawback. It might become a campaign that is just another beautiful woman's face campaign; and there is so much of that going around these days, so there is a chance of its getting lost."

"Here is another one. This one is not unlike the first except that here we show Pears as kind of jewel, as something that a woman wears on her neck, and a line says, 'Meet the soap with nothing to hide-except your age.' The advantage of this line is that it makes use of the physical attribute of the soap. It is transparent. It has nothing to hide. You can see through it. What it hides, in fact, is your age, if you use it. Hence, both these are concerned with youthfulness. They are both direct offsprings of the basic proposition."

Marketing Manager (MM): Yes, Gerson, but do you think that either of the ads is sufficiently distinctive? You have a good line there, but the total presentation is not really distinctive; and perhaps it is a bit too 'cosmetic'.

Agency General Manager (AGM): Possibly. Now look at this one. Here is a lady King on a reclining chair, and she is surrounded by all kinds of people attending on her, looking after her skin, looking after her toenails, looking after her eyes, somebody brushing make up on to her face, somebody is concerned—with her wig, and so forth. The line says: "There Must Be A Simpler Way to Keep Your Skin Young"; and a line at the bottom says, "Pears Keeps Your Skin Looking Years Younger." In other words, the suggestion is that, instead of going for complicated cosmetics and so forth, here is a simpler way of doing it by using this soap; or alternatively, even if you are using cosmetics you must start with the right kind of soap. The soap that contains glycerine and makes your skin look young. So that is the third approach.

Now here is the next one. The idea is to show six or seven girls all of whom could appear to be about the same age, about seventeen to eighteen years old; and the suggestion in the headline is, "Amongst them there is somebody as old as twenty-five-which one." It says, "Pick the twenty-five-year-old Pretender." Perhaps the lady in the upper right hand corner is in fact twenty-five? But can you tell? No, your can't. Because here is someone who has taken the trouble to keep her skin looking young with Pears. A very interesting idea certainly this ad has the advantage of involving the reader in an activity, something like an I.Q. test, involving the reader in the advertisement rather than just delivering a message. That is very much an advantage of this idea.

MM: You know, the "con" that can be applied to the previous ad applies to this one too. People might say, 'It is not really a sincere *ad,* it is?" There is an undercurrent of "addiness" about it.

AGM: Well, let's go to the next one, the "Kiss of Youth". This advertisement we hope will fit in with current fashion, and it has a style of illustration that would go well with the times; it is somewhat "mod-looking". It is that sort of advertising, we feel that zeros in directly on what we want to say. In other words, the headline and the picture are not too far away from the basic context of the story. The base line here says, "Young Skin can be yours for as long as you care-with Pears (You can see how pure it is)". So, "Kiss of Youth". You know, there is an element of being slightly wicked, but nicely wicked-using words like "Kiss" and so forth.

Now this next one follows from the previous ad, where you carry the idea forward and you talk about the bath with Pears being a "Youth Bath"—an association with the fountain of youth and all these things everybody likes deep down inside. "Introducing...the Youth Bath—Just you and Pears form the bare essentials...Pears keeps your skin young, delicious." There is a new element in this ad—that is, the element of offering Pears as more than just a complexion soap—a suggestion that it is to be used for the whole body and for the bath. You will notice that this is the first time this element has entered. This is introductory ad, and this is the follow-up ad, where we show a picture of a lady in the process of having a bath, but without displaying nudity. We make Pears a kind of slightly magical thing that would continue to keep you and your skin looking young.

MM: Is it wise to offer a soap that we intended to be a complexion soap, for the bath?

AGM*:* No, I think on the whole, not. Although, there are soaps making a claim for a young complexion, nobody had brought youth or young skin into such a hot focus as this. Now see a rather different idea.

Instead of having a boy and girl, we thought, why not use the mother and child? Pears has always been associated with the child, so why not use the mother/child situation for Pears advertising? And so we have a line which says, "Mrs. Dubey has inherited her daughter's good looks-Come again?" and the picture shows Mrs. Dubey and her daughter. We get the reader's attention by this unusual twist of the mother "inheriting" from the daughter. We then go on with our story in the body copy.

Here is another one: "Copy Cat-when you're out to copy a young complexion-cheat a little." And another very similar one: "Mrs. Dubey has an 18 years old daughter, and a skin just as young."

Now the advantage of this type of advertising, shown, in the last three ads, is that we are truly capitalising on everything that was gone before, on the Pears image, children, and so forth; and all we are doing is extending the goodness of Pears, so far associated with children, to mothers. We feel a large part of the audience for our advertising would be mothers with children.

Right, that's the lot. Let's hear what you have to say and then we will tell you which one we recommend.

MM: Out of all those you've shown, I think the last set is distinctly better than the rest. Specially the one that says, "Mrs. Dubey has inherited her daughter's good looks." It perpetuates the previous image. With the mother and child, you get the benefit of the previous advertising.

AGM: After having looked at all the ads together and considering all the pros and cons, the agency strongly recommends the "Youth Bath." We feel that, in the long run, it is the one thing that will become a brand "property". We feel that good advertising is something that happens over a length of time; that, being distinctive in its presentation, it will end up like "Waiting to be a beautiful lady" which, over a length of time, instead of decaying in effectiveness, will grow in effectiveness. All in all, we feel that the "Youth Bath" is an investment in the brand that will pay off.

MM: Honestly speaking, Gerson, I'm not in agreement with your recommendation. You say that this is a style of advertising that would become part of Pears, make it distinctive and give it the image of keeping your skin young. But the proposition "Pears helps keep your complexion/skin young" has to come through in a fashion that is memorable and understandable. The content of this particular campaign does not stand up against the original brief. Advertising is the sending of a message and the message being converted into a consumer response. Has this ad got the context that will make our consumers go out and buy the product? What, in the end, is the "Youth Bath"? And what will it mean to our target audience?

In the advertising brief, we stressed that it was the housewife who did the purchasing. Therefore, the advertising should be aimed at the housewife, towards women who have families. We cannot aim Pears advertising at teenagers. It is going to the wrong target group....

The debate continued for sometime without reaching a firm conclusion.

A deadline had to be met and the agency went back to the creative backrooms and drawing boards to work on a new presentation.

(AIMA, May 1993)

QUESTIONS FOR DISCUSSION

1. What is your view of the different creative approaches presented by the agency?
2. Do you think that the "Youth Bath" creative approach should be adopted for Pears?
3. Over a period of time what image would it create for the brand? Would this help to strengthen and expand its franchise?

CASE STUDY 16.4

SUCCESS LIMITED

Rajan, a Product Manager at the Success Ltd., is concerned about falling sales in recent months. His inventory is high. He is contemplating a sales promotion to reverse the sales trend and reduce the inventories. He is thinking of offering a case (off-take) allowance to the traders. He expects sales to be 40,000 cases (cartons) in the absence of promotion. One case is priced at Rs. 100 and the gross profit contribution is 40 per cent. He is currently thinking of offering Rs. 10 per case allowance and expects increased (additional) sales of 20,000 cases during the promotion period. The estimated cost of this promotion is Rs. 1,20,000.

QUESTIONS FOR DISCUSSION

1. Will he make a profit on this promotion?
2. What is the break-even sales increase that will justify this case allowance?
3. If he offers only Rs. 5 case allowance, he expects additional sales of 12,000 cases. Should he offer Rs. 10 or Rs. 5 per case allowance.

Interpret your results.

CASE STUDY 16.5

AIR CONDITIONING MARKET—SALES PROMOTION STRATEGIES

Sales Promotion

In consists of a diverse collection of incentive tools, mostly short-term, designed to stimulate quicker and/or greater purchase of particular products/services by consumers or the trade.

It includes tools for:

Consumer Promotion

Samples, coupons, cash refund offers, price off, premium prizes, patronage rewards, free trials, warranties, point of purchase displays and demonstration.

Trade Promotion

Prices off, advertising and display allowances and free goods.

Business and Sales Force Promotion

Trade shows and connections, contests of sales reps and special advertising.

- They are used by most organisations, including manufacturers, distributors, retailers, trade associations and non-profit organisations.

Rapid Growth of Sales Promotion

A decade ago the advertising to sales promotion ratio was about 60:40. Today, in many consumer-packaged-goods companies, sales promotion accounts for 65% to 75% of the combined budget.

Purpose of Sales Promotion

Sales promotion often attracts the brand switchers, because users of others brands and categories do not always notice or act upon a promotion. Sales promotion used in the market of high brand similarity produces a high sales response in the short run but little permanent gain in market share.

Major Decisions in Sales Promotion

- Establishing sales promotion objectives.
- Selecting the sales promotion tools:
  (a) Consumer promotion tools
  (b) Trade promotion tools
  (c) Business and sales forces promotion tools.
- Developing the sales promotion programmes.
- Presenting the sales promotion programmes.
- Implementing and controlling the sales programme.
- Evaluation of sales promotion results.

With respect to the air conditioning market brands taken into consideration are:

Bluestar
Carrier
Voltas
Amtrex
Videocon.

Consumer Promotion

In the air conditioning industry, Carrier and Voltas are giving a cutting edge to other members by giving something in the form of rebates, e.g.

Bluestar—provides with 1 tonne and above free installation worth Rs. 750.

Carrier—provides with 1 tonne and above free CVT and 1 year AMC.

Voltas—provides both installation and CVT free.

Trade Promotion

This is something the air conditioning market is relying on. It mainly includes:

- Target discounts
- Gift on target achievement
- Sales contests.

CARRIER

(a) Target Discount

Recently Carrier came up with a scheme of giving one tonne free with updated monthly target of 30 one tonne AC's in a month.

(b) Gift on Target Achievement

Offer a 7 day tour to Goa if you sell 24 one tonne ACs in the month of July.

(c) Sales Contest

News shows that Kelvin Point, a dealer at Rajindra Nagar won the contest by selling 300 Tonage/Annum.

VOLTAS

(a) Target Discount

Recently Voltas had a scheme of giving 1.5 tonne split (single) on a target selling of 12 TP Split (i.e. 1.5 tonne AC).

(b) Gift on Target Achievement

Offer a trip to Singapore on selling 30 split ACs a month in the month of June 1998.

(c) Sales Contest

Gem Refrigeration at Faiz Road won 1997 yearly maximum selling AC's and got a Bajaj Scooter as a reward.

BLUESTAR

As per my dealer "Air Excel" and my RSM Mr. K. Suderajan.

(a) Target Discount

They came up with a scheme of providing 2 tonne multi-split ACs with selling 20 1.5 Tonne multi split ACs and was won by Air Excel itself.

(b) Gift on Target Discount

Get a free 21 inch colour TV of Akai in the month of August 1998 if you sell 15 tonnes of AC in a month.

(c) Sales Contest

1997 sales contest of selling 200 Tonage of AC/annum was won by Air Excel, H-41, Lajpat Nagar (National Park).

QUESTION FOR DISCUSSION

1. Examine and compare the sales promotion schemes offered by airconditioner manufactures.

STRATEGIC MARKETING OF SERVICES

17

INTRODUCTION

We start consuming the product when we wake up in the morning. This consumption of goods is going on till the night. We bring milk, bread, vegetables, etc. which we can touch and see. These goods are visible to us and, have tangible attributes. Think about those products which are either combination of tangible or intangible attributes. For example, when you go to a restaurant, the product has combination of tangible and intangible attributes, food as a tangible and service of the waiter as intangible one. What about the barber or a hair-dresser? When a hair-dresser cuts your hair, at that time you are consuming an intangible attribute of the product provided by the hair-dresser. Here what the hair-dresser provides you is an example of pure service. Therefore, we can say for a moment, service is more intangible than tangible. We will define service in detail later. Before, defining service, we should focus on the different kinds of a company's offer to the marketplace. The offer can be divided into five categories:

(i) Offer as a pure tangible good: for example, bread, milk, toothpaste, etc.

(ii) Offer of a tangible good with accompanying services. For example, a car manufacturer like Maruti sells the car with customer service.

(iii) Offer of a hybrid containing equal parts of goods and services, for example, a restaurant provides food as well as service equally.

(iv) Offer of a major service with minor goods. For example, service provided by airlines consists of a major part of transportation service (intangible) with a minor part of goods such as food and drinks and an airline magazine (tangible).

(v) Offer of a pure service. For example, service provided by a consultant professional, like a Chartered Accountant, Doctor, Psychiatrist, etc.

We have explained enough about market offering. With the above classification we can say services are different from physical goods. This will become more clear by understanding Table 17.1.

Table 17.1: Difference between Physical Goods and Services

S. No.	Physical Goods	Services
1.	Tangible	Intangible
2.	Homogeneous	Heterogeneous
3.	Product and distribution are separated from consumption	Production, distribution and consumption are simultaneous processes
4.	A thing	An activity or process

Contd...

5.	Core value produced in a factory	Core value produced in buyer-seller interactions
6.	Customers do not participate in the production process	Customers participate in the production process
7.	Can be kept in stock	Cannot be kept in stock
8.	Transfer of ownership	No transfer of ownership

The Concept of Service: Definition

The term service is very general in concept and includes a wide variety of services. The list of selected services is contained in Table 17.2.

Table 17.2: List of Selected Services

Utilities: Electricity, Water Supply
Law Enforcing: Civil, Administrative, Police and Judiciary
Defence: Army, Air Force, Navy
Municipal Services: Sewage, disposal of corpses, maintenance of roads, parks and public buildings
Transport and Communication: Railways (Passenger and Freight), Air Transport (Passenger and Freight), Post and Telegraph, Telephone and Telecommunication
Broadcasting (All India Radio) and Telecasting (Doordarshan)
Distributive Trades: Wholesale Distribution, Retail Distribution, Dealers and Agents
Insurance, Banking, Finance
Share and Stock Brokers
Business, Professional and Scientific Activities
Advertising
Marketing Research
Consultancy Services
Accountancy
Legal
Medical
Educational
Research
Maintenance and Repairs (of plants, machinery and equipment)
Leasing
Computer Programming
Employment Agencies
Leisure, Recreation: Video Game Parlours, Casinos, Cinema, Theatre, etc.
Clubs, Gymnasiums
Restaurants, Hotels
Self-improvement Courses
Miscellaneous: Beauty Parlours, Health Clubs, Domestic Help, Dry-cleaning, etc.
Matrimonial Services

Source: Adopted from Donald Cowell, *The Marketing of Services,* Computer Programming, Heinemann, London.

We will define the concept of service from the marketing viewpoint so that everybody can understand what actually service is. For our clear understanding, it is desirable to go through the definition of various researchers who have defined 'service' over the last three decades.

It was the American Marketing Association which defined services first in 1960 as "activities, benefits, or satisfactions which are offered for sale or provided in connection with the sale of goods". This definition ultimately revolves round 'goods' and it proposed that services are offered when the sale of goods takes place. In this definition, services are not identified as separate intangibles.

In 1963, another definition was given by Regan that "services represent either intangibles yielding satisfactions directly (transportation, housing) or intangibles yielding satisfactions jointly when purchased either with commodities or other services (credit, delivery)". It is the first definition of service which recognised services as a pure intangible which can provide satisfaction to the consumer. The separate existence of services from the product reveals that services can alone satisfy the consumer like tangible products.

In 1973, another definition of services was given by Bessom stating that "for the consumer, services are activities offered for sale that provide valuable benefits or satisfactions; activities that he cannot perform for himself or that he chooses not to perform for himself.

In 1974, Blois gave an almost similar definition of services which is stated as "a service is an activity offered for sale which yields benefits and satisfactions without leading to a physical change in the form of a good".

In 1983, Lehtinen defined services as "an activity or a series of activities which take place in interactions with a contact person or a physical machine and which provides consumer satisfaction".

In 1984, Philip Kotler and Paul N. Bloom defined services as "any activity or benefit that one party can offer to another that is essentially intangible and does not result in the ownership of anything". Its production may or may not be tied to a physical product.

The last definition is the most suitable definition of services of this cadre. However, in 1990, Christian Gronross in his book *Service Management and Marketing* gave the definition of service, which is based on the Lehtinen, Kotler and Bloom's definitions. According to Gronross, "A service is an activity or series of activities of more or less intangible nature that normally, not necessarily, take place in interactions between the customer and service employees and/or physical resources or goods and/or systems of the service provider, which are provided as solution to customer problems."

Characteristics of Services

In Table 17.1, we have discussed the differences between physical goods and services. All those eight differences may be summarised in the form of characteristics of services. Some of the most common characteristics are:

1. Intangibility,
2. Inseparability,
3. Perishability,

4. Heterogeneity or Lack of Standardisation,
5. Customer Participation, and
6. Ownership.

1. Intangibility

Recollect the example of hair-dresser. The service provided by the hairdresser is totally intangible. You can't touch or see that service but you can feel that the hair-dresser has done something with your head, i.e. you can experience the result after consuming the service. In this case, service is essentially intangible or impalpable in nature. You are not getting anything tangible in pure service.

It is not necessary for all services to be intangible in nature. Not all the service products have similar intangibility. In other words, some services are high in intangibility, while others are low. For example, the airlines in which the core or the main service (i.e. the flight) is intangible in nature while auxiliary services (i.e. food and drinks, etc.) are the tangible aspect on a goods-service continuum. These services are in reality a combination of product and services which have both tangible and intangible components.

J. Bateson has mentioned the intangible characteristics distinct from that of the product. According to Bateson the intangible features are:

- Service cannot be touched.
- Production and consumption are inseparable.
- The consumer is a part of the production process.
- There are no inventories of service.
- Precise standardization is not possible.
- There is no transfer of ownership.
- Service cannot be patented.
- Roles of middlemen are different from those in products.

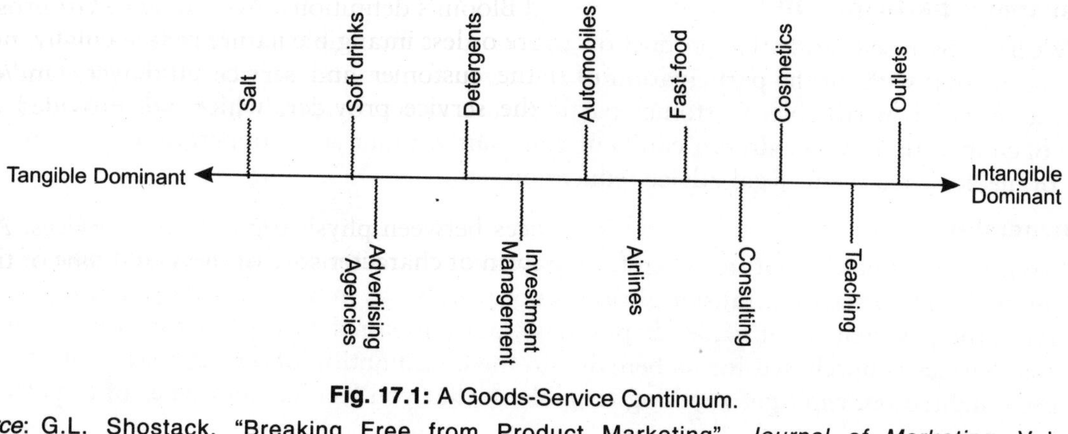

Fig. 17.1: A Goods-Service Continuum.

Source: G.L. Shostack, "Breaking Free from Product Marketing", *Journal of Marketing*, Vol. 41, No. 2, 1977.

2. Inseparability

Services are produced and consumed simultaneously. The production of services cannot be done separately from their consumption. For example, services provided by a hair-dresser are immediately consumed by you. Generally, goods are produced, stored and then sold while services are first sold, then produced and consumed simultaneously. In the example of an airline, the passenger buys the ticket first; after that airline generates the service (flight) and then, finally, the customer consumes it.

3. Perishability

Services cannot be stored because they are consumed when they are produced. Generally the utility of services is short lived; hence they cannot be produced ahead of time and stored for use at a time when their demand is high. For example, seats in a movie theatre, hotel rooms, etc., if unutilized during the course of service production, cannot be reclaimed later on. Christopher H. Lovelock describes in his book *Service Marketing* that capacity in a service business is rather like having a running tap in a sink with no plug and the consequent wastage of water. In the peak period, a marketer is unable to maintain the quality of services and, on the other hand, services remain unused in lean periods.

4. Heterogeneity or lack of standardisation

A physical product has great consistency when it is produced. This is so because the process is machinery intensive. On the other hand, the production of service is labour-intensive in which producer and customer both participate in the production process. The behaviour of persons varies from person to person because this is subject to emotion, stress and feelings of every individual. Persons show different behaviour in different situations.

Therefore, it is impossible to bring consistency in service. Variability is inherent in service. Every visit to the hair-dresser's shop gives you different experience, because your behaviour and that of the hair-dresser is not the same in every visit. It is possible to reduce variability up to a certain extent by training the service personnel and by using automatic vending machines (AVMs). This variability causes great difficulties for the service marketer or producer.

5. Customer participation

We have discussed earlier that production and consumption of service happens simultaneously. This means that without the participation of the customer service can't be produced. This is so because service is perishable. Customer participation in service production takes place in the form of cooperation. A hair-dresser can't cut your hair without your cooperation. Same thing in case of medical treatment, legal advice, education, etc.

6. Ownership

Service is intangible in nature. Therefore, physical possession of a service is not possible and without physical possession, transfer of title is not possible as in the case of a physical product. In service, the payment is not made for purchase, but only for the use of or for hire of items or facilities. Service is purchased for its benefits. In the consumption of hair-dresser's service, you will get benefited but can't get anything tangible so that you feel like an owner of the physical goods.

THE SERVICE MARKETING MIX

In an earlier chapter, you have studied that for marketing of products, the 4 Ps are used in a specific combination to arrive at the marketing strategy. You have also learnt that the concept of 4 Ps was given by McCarthy. In the case of services, three additional variables are used. These elements are people, physical evidence and process. The additional Ps in this framework refer to activities that are essential to meet the challenge posed by intangibility and customer involvement. We shall now discuss the seven Ps of service marketing mix.

1. Product

A service product refers to an activity or activities that a marketer offers to perform, which results in satisfaction of a need or want of a predetermined target customer. The most important issue in the service product is understanding what benefits and satisfaction the customer is seeking from the service. Service is the offering of a firm in the form of activities that satisfy needs such as hair styling done by a hair-dresser. The success of a service marketer depends upon the level of service. A product has four levels, viz.,

(i) **The General Product.** This is the rudimentary substantive thing. It is the basic benefit level.

(ii) **The Expected Product.** This is the customer's minimum set of expectations from a service.

(iii) **The Augmented Product.** This involves offerings in addition to what the customer expects.

(iv) **The Potential Product.** This is doing everything potentially feasible to hold and attract the customer.

The concept of different product levels can be illustrated in the context of a restaurant and a bank.

Most organisations start with the generic level. At this level; the customer is not satisfied enough to be a hard core loyalist. Hence, any competitor who opts to operate at a higher product level will be able to break into the service company's market share. When a service product exceeds the expected benefits, it comes as a pleasant surprise to the customer leading to his loyalty. Those service marketers are winners who add that 'little extra' of surprise to the service they sell.

Most often it is seen that service is in the form of a package. Actually a service package is the combination of intangible and tangible or physical component. Services like hospitals, restaurants, airlines, retailing a fast food, etc. have the product package in the form of the combination of intangibles and tangibles. However, pure service like consultation and teaching, generally do not carry any physical output. To create a well-balanced service package, the marketer must resort to an analysis of the benefits that customers seek and how they can be brought home. Marketing of services primarily involves balancing the mix of tangible and intangible components in a service package.

Table 17.3: Service Product Level

	Product Level	Benefit	Restaurant	Bank
1.	Generic	'The basic benefit'	Serving space, food, kitchen, staff.	Bank space, loanable funds, safety of deposits.
2.	Expected	'The expected benefit'	Cleanliness, timely service, polite and courteous behaviour, menu availability, pleasant atmosphere.	Correct transaction recording, timely service, hours, minimum courtesy.
3.	Augmented	'In addition to the expected benefit'	Sparkling floors, ambience, smiling employees, courtesy, welcome note, music of choice.	Congenial waiting room, friendly employees, relationship orientation, quicker service than the normal, admission of faults in the event of a mistake.
4.	Potential	'Beyond the usual; pleasant surprise'	Welcome flowers, manager's word of thanks, readiness to go out of the way.	Occasional greeting at home, surprise gifts, readiness to go out of the way to satisfy the individual customer.

Another important line in service marketing is to maintain consistency. Providing an intangible or service package at a level of consistency, is a complex issue. A person on visit to a bank on two occasions may have different experiences. This variability of experience is due to the inability of the bank to maintain intangible uniformity. Therefore, a service firm should learn to manage intangibles. Service level should be set in accordance with the desired customer satisfaction.

2. Pricing

Services have intangible nature. Due to this nature a marketer faces greater difficulty in fixing his price in service marketing. In the case of services, different terms are used for different services. Table 17.4 represents the terms used for some selected services.

Table 17.4: Terms used in Service Pricing

Service	Price
Education	Fee
Legal service	Fee
Consultancy	Fee
Health care	Fee
Property use	Rent
Advertising	Commission
Transportation	Fare
Employee services	Salary
Insurance	Premium
Roaduse	Toll
Utilities	Tariff
Financial services	Interest/Charge/Commission

Many service providers offer a range of services at various price levels to meet the needs of different target segments who may have different levels of pending power. There are many factors which influence the price ultimately charged. These factors are:

1. Structure of the market,
2. Type of the organisation,
3. Price charged by competitors,
4. The life-cycle stage of the service,
5. Organisational objective, and
6. Regulations of Government or trade associations.

In determining the prices of services, the characteristics of service also play a significant role. The first characteristic, intangibility, creates a problem in price determination. The higher the intangibility, the more difficult it is to calculate the cost because services do not have a tangible component. The customer views price as a surrogate for service quality. Due to this reason, low-priced services are often taken to be of inferior quality, and high-priced services are often taken to be of superior quality. For example, health consultants (doctors), educational institutions, management consultants, lawyers, etc. follow high-price strategy to rank their service in the higher quality position.

Another characteristic of services which has great impact on pricing is perishability. The fluctuations in demand can't be met through inventory build-up. Hotels and airlines offering lower rates in off-season are examples of how pricing strategy can be used to offset the perishable characteristic of services.

Other characteristics also influence the pricing strategy. In determining the price of services, a marketer must consider the characteristics of services. There are various pricing strategies in service marketing, the main ones among them are the following:

1. Skimming pricing,
2. Penetration pricing,
3. Mixed pricing,
4. Cost plus pricing,
5. Marginal cost pricing,
6. Promotional pricing,
7. Differential or flexible pricing, and
8. Market-oriented pricing.

3. Promotion

We have discussed in detail about promotion in the marketing mix chapter. In that chapter, we have dealt with strategic marketing mix in respect of physical goods. Here, we are discussing promotion of services.

Promotion is used to communicate information about services to the target audience thereby facilitating the exchange process. Promotion plays an important role in informing, educating, persuading and reminding the customer. The role of promotion in services becomes more important where there is a high degree of intangibility as there is no physical product or backing to attract the potential customer's attention. Effective communication is needed to inform customers about their role in the service delivery process. In services, customers rely more on subjective impression rather than concrete evidence. This is so because of three reasons:

(a) The inherent intangible nature of services;

(b) Quality of service based on the performance rather than actual service; and

(c) Difficulty in evaluating the quality and value of services before consuming and paying for it.

Therefore, we can say that excellent services are of no use at all if potential customers know nothing about them. A marketing manager of services must design a promotion strategy which helps the customer to overcome the above-mentioned three limitations. There are four element of promotional mix:

I. Advertising,

II. Personal selling,

III. Sales promotion, and

IV. Publicity/public relations.

I. Advertising. Advertising is paid for publicity transmitted through a wide variety of media. It is non-personal and involves mass media communication of messages to a large number of people at the same time. There are six basic guidelines given by George and Bery for the effective advertisement of services:

(i) Advertising should have positive effect on contact personnel.

(ii) Advertising should provide tangible clues to the customers.

(iii) Advertising should capitalise on the word of mouth publicity.

(iv) Advertising should make the service offering easily understood.

(v) Advertising should contribute to the continuity of message.

In India, advertising is frequently used for the promotion of services. But professional service firms like lawyers, consultants, doctors, C.A., etc. are not interested in advertisement of their service due to the following two reasons:

(a) Professionals think that good professionals do not advertise because advertisement is not accepted. This may lead to an impression that the quality of services is inferior.

(b) Some professional bodies and associations sometimes place constraints on members about the use of certain promotional tools like advertisement. However, the situation is changing now. Some professionals lave started using advertisement in a veiled manner. For example, one can occasionally see an advertisement in daily newspapers giving information about the location and timings when a particular doctor is available for consultation.

II. Personal Selling. Personal selling takes many forms but consists of the seller engaging in some kind of personal contact with the customers in order to persuade them to make a purchase. Five guidelines given by Johnson for personal selling services are:

(i) The person selling services should develop a personal relationship with the client.

(ii) He must adopt a professional orientation so that he makes a strong impression of competency, honesty and sincerity on the customers.

(iii) He should use indirect selling techniques as he is promoting an intangible.

(iv) He has to build and maintain a favourable image by managing word of mouth publicity.

(v) He must customise the service offering by showing that he is selling a service package (services) not just a service.

III. Sales Promotion. In service, sales promotion techniques are used to offset their perishability characteristic and to overcome the problem faced by customers in evaluating and judging the quality before making the purchase. Sales promotion techniques reduce the risk associated with the purchase. Sales promotion tools include:

— Free samples

— Money off coupons and special offers

— Competitors' price promotion

— Point of sale display

— Free gift and other incentives

IV. Publicity/Public Relations. Publicity refers to communication about the services, which is not paid for by the organisation. This publicity is unpaid for exposure which is desired by getting coverage as a news or editorial item. Service organisations should maintain good public relations using following public relations tools:

- Publicity through media.
- Involvement in social and community initiatives.
- Sponsorship of events.
- Public announcements and special publications.
- Corporate brochures and other publicity material.

It is possible to get publicity when the service is unique and, therefore, newsworthy, by holding a press conference in which you can associate your service with some issues of greater social relevance or by involving the interest of the newspaper or its staff in covering your service. Of course, a wrong choice of media vehicle will result in adverse publicity.

4. Place

Traditionally, it was assumed that distribution channels cannot be used for marketing services because services are intangible and cannot be stored and transported. But now distribution plays an important role in service marketing as services are inseparable and perishable. The inseparable nature of services means that services must be accessible to the customers and potential customers. Accessibility must be a component of the actual service offering for it to have value. The perishable nature of service means it is essential for the service to be available to consumers in the right place at the right time.

Therefore, we can say that *place*, a distribution element of service marketing mix, is concerned chiefly with two main issues: accessibility and availability. Accessibility refers to the ease and convenience with which service can be purchased and/or used. Availability refers to the extent to which a service is obtainable or capable of being purchased and/or used. The criteria must be met in order to achieve successful service marketing.

A key decision with regard to distribution is location. There are several key factors to be considered in decisions about service location:

- Service inseparability.
- Perishability.
- The role of the consumer as co-producer of the service.
- Customer's needs and wants.
- Importance of geographical location as part of the service.
- Target market.

Many service organisations choose a direct distribution method which does not use outside agents or intermediaries. The practical issues influencing the decision to undertake direct distribution include the following factors:

- Type of service.
- Customer preferences.
- Company objectives/resources.
- Legal and political restrictions on foreign operations.
- Geographic spread of the market.
- Level of technical expertise or skill required to deliver the service satisfactorily.

The role and functions of channel intermediaries in the marketing of services differ from those in the marketing of physical goods. Inseparable and perishable, these two characteristics of services, make the service channel very short and direct. Short-service channel means that the service marketer uses one or two intermediaries who act like an agent or a broker. The main role of an agent or a broker is to bring the producer of service and the consumer together. In this regard, Rathmell has given the dominant channel model in service sector where the agent and the broker play the key role in distribution of services, which is illustrated in Fig. 17.2.

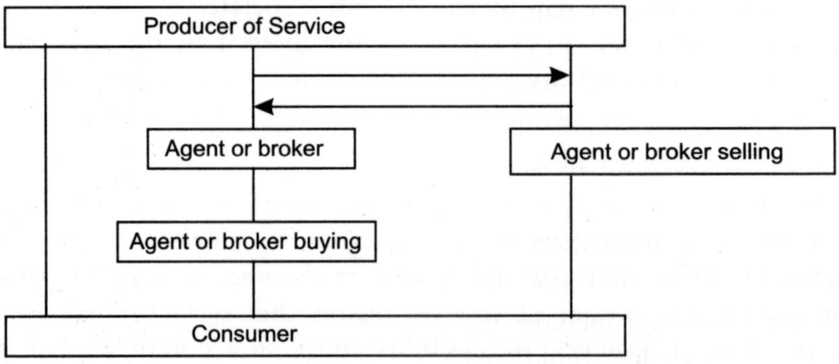

Fig. 17.2: Role of Agent and Broker in Service Sector

Source: John M. Rathmell, *Marketing in Service Sector* (Cambridge, Mass: Winthrop Publishers), 1974, p. 110.

In the case of hotels, airlines, property dealers, LIC, they may operate through middlemen. Table 17.5 provides an illustrative list of the intermediaries who sell services.

Table 17.5

Service	Middlemen
Airlines	Travel agent, Hotel agent
LIC	Agent
Hotel	Travel agents, Tour operators. Airlines
Shares	Stock brokers
Employment	Placement agency
Financial Service	Banks, Financial Institutions

5. People

People as the fifth element in the service marketing mix applies not only to service personnel, but also recognises the role that other people, the customers, play in service delivery. People constitute an important dimension in the management of services in their role both as performers of services and as customers. The inseparable nature of services means that the human element forms an intrinsic part of the service package. The role of employees in service organisations is critical in maintaining quality standards. Sometimes the role of the customer is an important part of the service itself. Management of people within the organisation is a key task. The organisation's staff is its prime resources, and human resource management is the professional approach to finding and developing the right people. Employees need to understand their role in the service exchange, and human resource management provides the programmes and strategies to ensure the highest standards of customer care. In 1983, a report was published by Christian Gronross on "The Internal Marketing Function." According to the report, "The internal marketing concept states that the internal market of employees is best motivated for service-mindedness and customer-oriented performance by an active marketing like approach where a variety of activities are used internally in marketing in a coordinated way." The initial point of internal marketing is that the employees are the first internal market for the organisation.

The level of contact within a particular service depends upon the type of service. In some services, people play a far greater part than in others. The staffs are the most important asset within the organisation, however, and recruitment and staff development are crucial aspects in the marketing of services. Internal marketing recognises that employees in the internal market are equally important as external customers and their needs and wants should also be examined.

The basic steps in recruitment can be broken down into several key stages as briefly illustrated below:

Preliminary Stage. (1) Identification of vacancies and requirements, (2) Processing applications, (3) Selection stage-arranging interviews offer/acceptance, formal appointment.

Follow-up Stage. This stage includes induction, training and ongoing development. Training is needed to impart knowledge, build expertise and also to give focus and direction for the future development of the organisation and its employees. Staff development incorporates training but goes a step further in designing strategies for a holistic approach to getting the most of people and helping them to maximise their potential.

Human resource managers working with managers in other functional areas (including marketing) should look after the people in an organisation. Their responsibilities cover a wide area with regard to selection, training, industrial relations and other related issues. They also play a central role in the organisation in terms of enabling organisational objectives to be me successfully through the efforts and understanding of all the people in the organisation.

6. Physical Evidence

The intangible nature of service means that they are not bought and owned by consumers in the same way that the physical goods are. A service is performed rather than handed over. Therefore, physical evidence has great importance in the service marketing mix because it gives satisfaction to the customers. As we have discussed, some services are more intangible than others. Some services are product-based and service providers will focus on ensuring that any facilitating goods which form a part of the service are of an appropriate quality and standard.

Physical evidence provides customers with a means of evaluating the service and includes facilitating goods, decor and comfort, for example, corporate image plays an important role in terms of physical evidence and this can be developed through corporate public relation programmes. The benefits which can arise out of a well-planned corporate relation programme elude an enhanced market reputation and greater employee satisfaction. Corporate identity takes corporate image a stage further by building a distinctive and recognisable physical identity for the organisation. Branding, house style and decor, logos and staff uniforms are typical example of the physical means which can be used as physical evidence. Physical evidence can be broken into two main categories:

Peripheral evidence. This type of evidence can actually change hands uring the service transaction, for example, a hotel room key, and railway ticket. The purchaser may become the owner of the item but it is, in itself, worthless unless hotel room is clean, reasonably furnished, and so on. Peripheral evidence includes those items which conform with the service, as mentioned in the above example but also includes items which are complementary to the service itself. This means that service can be performed without these items but they enhance the organisation's identity and can help make the customers' experience more enjoyable or positive, for example, free house wine with a meal and newspapers and magazines for airlines passengers.

Essential evidence. This type of evidence is integral to the service offering and includes, for example, the facilities offered by a leisure centre or the items on display in an exhibition which make a visit worthwhile. Essential evidence will not normally be owned by or passed on to the customer, except on a temporary basis as in the case of car hire or linen rental in catering. In all cases, the quality and standard of essential evidence will be a major influence in the customer's purchase decision. Both these types of evidence combine with the organisation's other marketing mix elements to create an impression on customers/potential customers and help in enhancing perceived service quality. They also help to make the service more tangible in that it can be associated with clear mental images, colour, names, and so on, in the mind of the consumer, as the following example illustrates:

The Automobile Association's handbook and membership card are permanent, physical reminders of the organisation's services, as is their distinctive delivery of petrol and allied products. The technical standard of the mechanics and the quality of spare parts carried are examples of the essential physical evidence which forms part of the service.

7. Process

While process has only recently been given much attention in the services sector, it has for many years been the subject of study in manufacturing sector (hence developments such as 'just-in-time'). The principles by which service delivery processes can be designed, implemented and monitored are influenced by the following specific characteristics of services:

— Customer participation in the process
— Location of service delivery
— The service itself
— High-contact or low-contact service
— Degree of standardisation
— Complexity of the service

Processes are often designed around how charts or blueprints setting a standard sequence of actions, must take place in order for service to be implemented.

The purpose of setting down clear-cut guidelines or blueprints for service delivery processes and transactions are as follows:

- To ensure that the service is carried out in the fastest, most efficient and cost effective manner possible.
- To enable service quality to be monitored and bench marks to be put in place thus allowing accurate measurement of both quality and productivity.
- To facilitate staff training and enable individuals to carry responsibility for individual stages of the service transaction and delivery.
- To reduce the amount of divergence thus enabling accurate budgeting and manpower planning, etc. to take place.

Sometimes, however, complete standardisation of the service is not the most desirable option either for the service provider or the consumer. Flexibility in both customer choice and staff actions can provide added benefits and help differentiate the service offering.

Perhaps the greatest impact on the process element of the service marketing mix has been due to technological developments, enabling automated service, for example, and using computerised systems to provide 'instant' service as with ticket reservations, and so on. Some new services have arisen directly out of developments in technology, such as mobile communications and advanced medical techniques.

As competition in the service sector is getting intense and the customer has many choices, the differentiating factor will be the quality of service in mic form or the other.

QUESTIONS FOR DISCUSSION

1. Describe the marketing mix for service industries. Also give reasons for its departure from the marketing mix of products.

2. What are the major differences between products and services?
3. What are the problems encountered by a sales manager in marketing of services?
4. Explain in brief the various kinds of services.
5. Why is the distribution method particularly important in services marketing?
6. What are the main steps in designing and implementing effective customer care programmes?
7. Outline the role of after-sales service and perceived quality in customer buying-decision processes.
8. Why is relationship marketing particularly appropriate in professional services marketing?
9. "For marketing purposes, services like products provide benefits and satisfaction. What is significant about services is the relative domination of intangible attributes in the make up of the service product." Do you agree with this statement? Explain giving suitable examples. What difficulties arise in attempting to define a service from marketing point of view in these circumstances?
10. What are the levels at which the services product should be analysed? How would you conceptualise your service product at these levels if you were offering:
    (i) Maintenance service for photocopies, and
    (ii) Security services for institutions.
11. How do characteristics of services render service promotion different from product promotion? What are the key considerations that you would need to examine while designing promotional efforts for any two of the following:
    (i) A diagnostic centre,
    (ii) A mobile creche for construction workers, and
    (iii) A new insurance policy.

CASE STUDY 17.1

WILL THEY TURN AGAIN

Sushil booked a table in a restaurant for 12 people at the beginning of the Diwali period to celebrate the festive season with his family and friends. He had been a regular visitor to Moti Restaurant and had developed loyalty for this place famous for South Indian food. Most of his friends were from the South so he preferred to treat them at Moti.

Another reason for his selection was that the patron of Moti, Raj Kumar know him well. Since he was regular visitor, he was quite confident that this dinner would be a success.

Three days before the scheduled get-together dinner Sushil spoke to Raj Kumar and asked him to increase the booking to 16. He looked busy but informed Sushil it would be quite in order and he looked forward to seeing Sushil and party later that week.

As per programme, all Sushil's friends met at his residence at 7 p.m. on the appointed day and after having a cup of coffee left for Moti to be there at the scheduled time of 8.30 p.m. They were all relaxed and exchanged jokes on their way and reached the restaurant at 8.20 p.m. With slight difficulty, they located parking place at three different locations for the four cars in which they were travelling.

The guests arrived at the restaurant on time and Sushil was taken aback to find that the table has been set only for 12 persons. Raj Kumar came over seeing a large group gathered around the small table laid in one comer of the dining room. Sushil reminded Raj Kumar of his earlier conversation, which he had with him three day ago. He asked him to recollect that the booking had been increased from 12 to 16, and suggested that it may be an oversight that he had forgotten to set the table for 16 people. Sushil then asked him to reset the table immediately for 16 people to avoid any embarrassment to him and his guests.

To Sushil's great amazement and embarrassment Raj Kumar denied that Sushil had asked for a booking for 16 people. He, rather, told Sushil that he had not phoned him at all this week to make amendments in the booking. "You must have been mistaken" said Raj Kumar.

Sushil tried to make him admit his mistake but Raj Kumar was too rigid and continued to take a stand that he had not received any such call and that the booking was for 12 people only. The restaurant was full and Sushil asked Raj Kumar to resolve the matter as his guests had been standing for more than ten minute? Raj Kumar expressed his helplessness and said there was nothing he could do at the moment.

At such time, Sushil knew that there was no where else they could go at this time. Sushil and his wife along with another couple opted to wait and let 12 members of the group seat themselves. It was after a long wait that they could be accommodated with the group. This could happen only when the guests sitting next to them left after their meal.

All of them settled for the dinner but discussions mostly centered around the service provided by the restaurant. At the end of the dinner Sushil checked the bill and did not leave any tip for the waiters. Before leaving the restaurant, Sushil met Raj Kumar in private and explained him that he would not be visiting him again. Raj Kumar admitted that he may have been hasty but thought Sushil was being unreasonable as it was his busiest evening and he should make allowances.

Sushil never visited the restaurant again and his friends too stayed away. They narrated this incident to many people.

QUESTIONS FOR DISCUSSION

1. What were the pitfalls in the service delivery?
2. How would you react to the behaviour of Raj Kumar?
3. Had you been Raj Kumar, what could you have done to turn this problem into a situation which would have won him customers for ever?
4. What are the problems and issues which cause such situations and such behaviour of service providers?

CASE STUDY 17.2

VILLAGE VOLVO

Village Volvo is the 'new kid in town'. It represents an effort by two former authorized Volvo dealer mechanics to provide quality repair service on out-of-warranty Volvos at a resoanable cost. On the basis of their 22 combined years of training and experience with local Volvo dealers, they have earned a respected reputed and a following of satisfied customers that make an independent service operations feasible. Village Volvo occupies a new building (prefabricated metal structure) that has four work bays in addition to the office, waiting room area and storage room. The owner feels that they have designed their operation to provide clients with 'custom care care' service that is unavailable at the dealers. They have set aside specific time each week when clients may drive in for quick, routine services such as tune-ups and oil changes. But they encourage clients to schedule appointments for diagnosis and repair of specific problems.

At the time of appointments, the mechanic working on the vehicle and the client discuss the problem the client has noticed. On occasion, the mechanic may take a short test drive with the client to be certain that both understand the area of concern. Another source of information available to the mechanic is the custom care vehicle dossier (CCVD). Village Volvo maintains a 'continuing file' on each vehiclist services. This history can help the mechanic diagnose problems and also provide a convenient record if a vehicle should be returned for warranty service on an earlier. The owners are considering the use of the CCVD as a way of 'reminding' customers that routine maintenance procedures may be due.

After the mechanic has made a preliminary diagnosis, the service manager gives the vehicle owner an estimate of the cost and the appropriate time the repair will be completed, if no unexpected problems arise. Company policy states that the owner will be consulted before any work other than the agreed upon job is done. Although the customer may speak with the mechanic during the repair process, the service manager is the main point of contact. It is the service manager's responsibility to be sure that the customer understands the preliminary diagnosis, to advice the customer of any unexpected problems, costs and to notify the customer when the vehicle is ready for pick up. Village Volvo has no provision for 'alternate transportation' for the customer at present. A 'shuttle service' 2 or 3 times a day is being considered, because the owner think that their suburban location may deter some clients. A waiting room equipped with a television set, comfortable chairs, coffee, a soft drink vending machine, magazines and the local newspaper is available. This facility is used almost exclusively by clients who come during the 'drop-in' hours—3-5 p.m. on Wednesdays and 8-10 a.m. on Thursdays—for quick, routine jobs such as tune-ups and buyers check of used cars.

The owner-mechanics do no repair between 7 and 8 a.m. and 5 and 6 p.m. because these are 'heavy customer contact' hours. They believe it is just as important to discuss with the client the repairs that have been done as it is to discuss what problems exist before work is started. As repairs are done, the owner-mechanic make note of any other problem that might need attention in the future (e.g. fan and alternator belts show some wear and may need to be replaced in about 600 miles). These notes are brought to the customer's attention at pick up time and are also recorded in the CCVD for future use, perhaps in the form of a 'reminder' post card to the owner.

All small worn out parts, that have replaced, are placed in a clean box in the car. More cumbersome replaced parts are identified and set aside for the client's inspection. Care is takes throughout the repair process to keep the car clean and the inside is vacuumed as a courtesy before pick up. After repairs are finished, the vehicle is taken for a short test drive, then it is parked, ready for pick up.

The Village Volvo owners see their responsibilities as extending beyond immediate service to their clients. The owners have developed a network of other providers, who assist in recycling used parts and waste products and to whom they can refer clients for work that is not part of Village Volvo's services, such as body work, alignments, reuphoistering. The owners are also considering the possibility of offering a mini-course on a Saturday morning each month to teach clients what they can do to attain their 2,00,000 miles Valvo medal.

QUESTIONS FOR DISCUSSION

1. Describe Village Volvo's service package.
2. How are the distinctive characteristics of service firm illustrated by Village Volvo?
3. How important are the extended marketing mix elements (people, process and physical evidence) to Village Volvo?

CASE STUDY 17.3

SERVICES MARKETING IS DIFFERENT

Arvind is a graduate mechanical engineer from one of the ten best engineering institutes of the country. He is young, energetic and a gold medalist. During the campus interviews he was selected by an industrial house to work in the industrial products division as sales executive. Though he found this job satisfactory he felt his qualifications were inadequate—as all the people superior to him in the organisation were management graduates in addition to their basic qualifications. This inadequacy made him insecure and he soon left this job to acquire an MBA.

He joined the MBA course as a regular student and completed it with distinction. As a part of the MBA curriculum he took up a project work to develop a marketing plan for Autocrop, a small organisation which was producing autoelectric parts for the replacement market. Though Autocorp had established itself as a quality product in the replacement market the lack of professional competence was a major drawback in establishing its roots in the market. The organisation did not have a professionally qualified marketing manager to energise its sales team members.

The plan submitted by Arvind was based on market analysis, competitor strengths and weaknesses, promotional marketing strategies and strategies of various players in the market. After making a systematic analysis he focused on issues related to demand projections, competitive analysis, marketing mix elements i.e., product offering, promotional, pricing and distribution strategies. Autocorp found the report quite useful and could implement some of Arvind's recommendations to its benefit. But being too small an organisation it could not absorb him.

MK Associates are consultants in the field of management consultancy and training and provide advice and training to various companies in the area of facilities planning, re-engineering and productivity improvement.

- The re-engineering department of MK Associates provides services of psychological testing, total quality management, employee training, efficiency studies, process planning, layout studies and application of information technology in business decisions.
- The facilities planning department of MK Associates have experts in the field of mechanical, electrical and civil engineering.

They have been provided with the full support of a computer lab, CAD/CAM facilities to optimise the use of facilities. They are fully equipped to provide services related to fulfillment of regulatory obligations, like building bylaws, pollution control, environmental issues and land use, etc.

- The productivity improvement department is competent to establish PIPS (Productivity Improvement Programmes) establishing and implementing Productivity Measurement System, selecting and advising productivity improvement approaches, suggesting productivity improvement methods through work redesign, through incentives, through job enrichment, through individual and group participation, etc.

Promoter directors and staff of MK Associates are qualified personnel in the area of mechanical, civil, electrical engineering, industrial engineering, computer assisted designing and have long industrial experience. In fact most of them were employed with reputed companies before promoting MK Associates.

Their client base is very broad and industries served by them include engineering and merallurgical industries and the mining and allied industries. The clients are from the private and public sector. Advisory and training services are also provided to some government departments.

Rajesh, Managing Director of Autocorp talked to Rakesh, Chief Executive Officer of MK Associates about Arvind and appraised him of the good work done by him for his organisation. He requested Rakesh to interview Arvind and see if he could be absorbed into MK Associates.

Arvind was called for an interview with the directors of MK Associates and was appraised of the business interests of the organisation. No one at MK Associates had ever worked in the field of marketing and their total business was based on their contacts. They were facing great difficulty in expanding the business base.

Since Arvind had a marketing background and experience in industrial products/he was a suitable candidate for marketing consulting services. As marketing consulting services is customer-oriented, they felt that hiring Arvind will result in winning more customers even in the competitive market place.

MK Associates had a competitive edge because of their technical superiority. Their company was doing exceedingly well for the past five years. During these five years of operations, three more consulting organisations in the same field had emerged and were establishing their base in the segment where MK had a stronghold. The impact of this was being felt as they were losing clients every now and them. They were not able to win the tenders they used to do in the past. The technical competency of the staff was no more a competitive edge. They were not even able to diagnose the cause of declining sales of the organisation.

To deal with the above situation, MK Associates offered the position of Marketing Manager to Arvind. Arvind realised that the combination of basic marketing knowledge (as he has worked as sales executive for three years with Autocrop), his technical background and newly acquired MBA degree will enable him to take on the challenges of marketing consulting services. His marketing knowledge blended with technical expertise of MK Associates will make the organisation proactive in the present competitive environment.

Arvind joins MK Associates to take up this challenge. He is assigned the task of making the marketing plan for the organisation.

QUESTIONS FOR DISCUSSION

If you were Arvind—

1. Explain where you will start?
2. What would you like to know about the service business?
3. What difference is there between marketing autoproducts and the consulting services?
4. How would you use the technical expertise of the staff to market consulting services?
5. What marketing strategy will you suggest to promote consulting services?
6. How will your offerings differ from those your competitors are offering?

CASE STUDY 17.4

GUPTA RENTALS—EQUIPMENT HIRE

Since 1990 Gupta Rentals suffered from cash constraints. The analysis of the performance of the company carried out by Rajesh Jain and Associates highlighted the reasons as under:

1. Addition of small petrol engine repair line to the existing business.
2. Increase in manpower to handle engine repair division.
3. Finances required for the purchase of parts and inventory maintenance. Presently this is also managed through existing cashflows and accounts payable.

To overcome the financial constraints a plan has been made which specifically addresses several methods that will be used to correct the cash flow, profitability and equity deficiencies. Several changes have been initiated which have started showing positive results. The next phase of plan requires changes in two categories: Management and Financial. It is felt that when these changes are introduced the company will return to industry norm within two years.

In 1985, the family of Guptas thought of starting a family business. Since they had their most of the relations at Chandigarh, they started thinking in terms of settling close to their relations. They started exploring the possibilities of potential business opportunities. Gupta was a Senior Executive of a public limited company, which manufactured equipment like generator sets, pumps, etc. He studied the market in and around Chandigarh and found that there were five equipment rental companies. Their equipment was obsolete, sub-standard and the people who hired equipment from them were not satisfied.

Before starting the business venture, the Guptas considered the following points:

- Providing long-term financial opportunity and to provide adequate standards of living.

- To go into business where competition could be and would be limited.
- To be in business with long-term growth.
- To be in business which could ultimately be taken over by the next generation.

After a careful analysis the Guptas decided to go in for the equipment rentals business.

PRODUCT AND SERVICE OFFERING/PRIMARY SERVICE MIX

- The Rental of Tools and Equipment. If your have a job to do, we have a tool to make it easier and quicker. Service to our customers, both professional and "Do-it-yourselves" is a primary part of our daily operation.

The philosophy of the Guptas was:

- Provide equipment in good working condition
- Provide equipment when it is needed
- Provide "How To" instructions verbally and in writing
- Provide pick and delivery
- Must be with the customer when he is in problem.

In addition to this the Guptas provide:

- Sale or rent of accessories needed with the equipment at a payment of an extra 100%.
- A damage waiver facility.
- Gupta are agents of Raj Equipments Movers, a premier transport company specialising in equipment movement. They could move the complete range of equipment in various dimensions and sizes.
- Guptas are dealers of Kirlosker Cummins, HMT, Eicher, Escorts and have inventory of vast tractor and engine lines. Because of this they have a supply contact division catering to the Agricultural and Mining Industry.

MARKET POTENTIAL AND COMPETITION

The Guptas have been in business for the past 13 years and have maintained detailed financial information. The company is making its projections and devising the marketing plan based on historical data augmented with the latest charges that are outlined in the plan. In addition they have maintained complete information on the requests they have not been able to meet and reasons thereof. This gave them knowledge about the market demand forecasts.

Before starting the business, Gupta made an extensive market analysis with the help of a local agency who was conversant with regional needs and locations. This helped them to make up their minds.

Today the Guptas know the demand is going to be up as many new construction avenues have opened and industrial growth is moving at a fast pace. They see a better future.

Bankers had been considerate to Guptas as their past records have been flawless and they helped them by giving attractive refinancing schemes. They accepted these schemes, now finance was no problem to enhance business.

Market Analysis

Gupta Rentals has several areas where they maintain a competitive advantage as they are the only service providers in the area for the equipments sought by the customers. They face competition only in one area where Satish Rentals are providing similar services but are not expanding their territory.

Marketing Strategy

The goal of Gupta Rentals are:

- Best service and equipment to our customers.
- Competitive prices to prevent competition at the present business location and surrounding areas.

Target Marketing

Guptas have been concentrating on supplying the equipment on rent to small contractors, the industrial sector and also house owners. The major share of the market being small contractors who account for fifty-five per cent of business followed by industrial sectors accounting for thirty per cent.

Since most of the business at present is coming from small contractors and the industrial sector, homeowners are not being paid sufficient attention. In the coming year plan, services to homeowners are gaining attention.

Sixty-five per cent and twenty-five per cent of this business is accounted for people moving out of the town, people moving in the town and commercial moves respectively. They have acquired the leaders position in this segment.

The sales parts division earns a revenue of fifty per cent, fifteen per cent and thirty-five per cent from industrial, institutional and homeowner markets.

Sales Plan

The Guptas have made the following plans to enhance sales:

- Identifying and targeting the homeowner market to gain ten per cent sale.
- over the previous years.
- Enhance the sales of 'moving needs' by creating more moves.
- Parts division will continue selling parts.

Promotional

To achieve the targeted sales as per market plan for the year 1998, radio and TV advertising shall be dropped and door-to-door flyers and direct mail will be used for homeowners. This decision was taken by Gupta as they had sufficient database about their customers and also about themselves. They propose to direct the mailing to the neighbourhood areas as discount offers to study the effectiveness. They propose to "start a thanks giving scheme" to all the equipment users in the past and with this they will offer a discount of 10% on the next rental. The technical expertise possessed by the Guptas shall be highlighted to create trust about technical capability and back up services. Door-to-door campaigning shall be introduced as a trial.

- Where we are?
- What we have?
- How they can use us to their advertising?

Another scheme, which will be introduced in 1999 shall be to make the equipment available for rent on the rental outlets of the respective companies, e.g. Kirloskar engine will be available for rent on Kirloskar outlets. For meeting the moving needs a cash incentive shall be offered to the person bringing the customer to them.

Since the year closing for the company is March 1999, the campaign for the year 1999 shall be completed by middle of May 1999. The campaign shall be budgeted by the type of media used and itemized by the type of equipment and service used for the promotional period. The complete information technology cell, website internet and answering machine facilities shall be made available for access of information any time, any where.

QUESTIONS FOR DISCUSSION

1. What market offerings have the Guptas planned and why?
2. Explain the service mix elements used?
3. What was the competition and how it was outsmarted?
4. Carry out the market analysis for the following:
   (i) Market niche selected.
   (ii) Marketing strategies used.
   (iii) Target market and market share.
5. What sales plan was devised to stay competitive?
6. What promotional strategies were used? In your opinion what will bring positive results?

CASE STUDY 17.5

TASTY BITE TURNED UNTASTY

Subhash, after going through an article about the good South Indian food at South—end was tempted to try it out with his family last Saturday. The contents of the coverage was too tempting and he would almost taste the food while going through the article. They all were looking forward to having dinner there.

Subhash tried to contact the manager on phone but couldn't reach him as the telephone was busy. So he could not book the table for his family.

He opted to drive out without any reservation and reached the area in which this restaurant was located. After great difficulty and enquiring from many people he reached the building in which the restaurant was located. He looked around for directions or signboards but could not find anything that could lead him to the restaurant. He looked for parking space but could not locate any. He found about 25 to 30 cars pailved outside residential apartments. There was no authorised parking and no one from the restaurant was able to guide the cars.

After parking the car, they entered the building, which was poorly lit. No signs were up to direct customers.

On enquiring from one of the visitors, they found out the entrance gate. It was difficult to enter the gate as many two wheelers were parked in front of this gate and they had to practically jump over a few to reach the steps leading to the restaurant.

The passage to the restaurant was through a stairway and more than 50 people were standing shoulder to shoulder and there was lot of push and pull on account of the to and fro movement of the people. Some young boys were in a hurry to get out and some young couples were standing in the middle of the corridor.

It looked like a scene from a movie interval. With great hesistance, Subhash asked about the restaurant from one of the persons in the crowd and he was told to proceed straight and turn left.

He was relieved to see the board carrying the sign "Dining Hall" on a 12″ × 6″ wooden plate. He was quite relieved and proceeded to the dining hall. Another surprise was in store for him when he was stopped by a restaurant boy Sundram who was compiling the waiting list.

Sundram was assigned the job of registering the guests, locating empty tables and directing people to the dining table. The restaurant did not accept advance reservations. Even the serial number of the waiting list was not adhered to. If a table for four was vacated, four guests were seated ignoring the groups who had been waiting for longer. The principle of first come first served basis was not followed. It was already 8 p.m. At this time it was too late to go somewhere else. So he registered himself and got the waiting slip. After getting the waiting slip Subhash asked Sundram, how long they would be required to wait. If it is too long they would prefer to try another South Indian restaurant a kilometer away. Sundram replied that compared to other restaurants in the vicinity, it should not take that long and they may have to wait not more than fifteen minutes.

During the waiting period Subhash started talking to another guest, Ramesh standing next to him. Ramesh was a regular customer of this restaurant and told Subhash that south-end is a South Indian restaurant most popular for South Indian Food. Being moderately priced it is very popular with people of middle income groups. In spite of long waits good food and its affordability is the factor arging the people to wait around standing in the open. Still no waiting area is available for the customers. An open space and staircase near the restaurant serves as the waiting area. In the rainy season there is no shelter and people take shelter under the stairways. In the summer people use their own umbrellas or trees in the courtyard of the building in which this restaurant is located.

Parking is a problem here. If you are first timer, it will take ten minutes from the parking to the restaurant gate. There is no authorised parking. You have to create parking space for yourself and then ask at least twice or thrice about the location and direction to reach the place.

This place is poorly lit and occassionally people are found slipping on the stairs. The toilets are located about fifty yards from the restaurant and to find them you must enquire from the waiter inside or a person assigned at the gate who register your name for the waiting slips. He enquiries about the number of people accompanying the guest. As soon as a table gets vacated, he announces the guest's by shouting at the top of his voice and gestures them with his hand. He always looks in a hurry. People, who are waiting for the turn, make repeat enquiries from him. He is always answering the enquiries of many customers simultaneously. His poor knowledge of the local language and English creates confusion among the customers. Half of them do not understand and some of them misunderstand.

South-end has good public relations. Many times, favourable articles have appeared in the supplements of national dailies of repute having very large circulations.

Subhash and his family was eagerly waiting for their call but even after half an hour their name was not announced. They were getting anxious and restless and felt they have made a wrong decision. It was only after one hour that they were seated inside the dining hall. By this time everybody had lost their patience, and tempers were high.

Subhash ordered the food. It was undoubtedly tasty. They had their fill. To express their anger of a long wait and unorganised customer handling they paid the bill but did not leave any tip. Tips from the customer was the yardstick for measuring the restaurant's performance and this matter was reported by the waiter to the restaurant manager. The manager called Sundram to find out the details about this transaction.

QUESTIONS FOR DISCUSSION

1. Critically examine the service delivery system?
2. What is the relevance of physical evidence, process and people in the service offering? Comment on the above three elements in the context of the above episode.
3. How do customer relate to waiting in the service offerings? Discuss strategies adopted in this case and how can you improve them if desired.
4. Examine the following communication model and identify what went wrong?

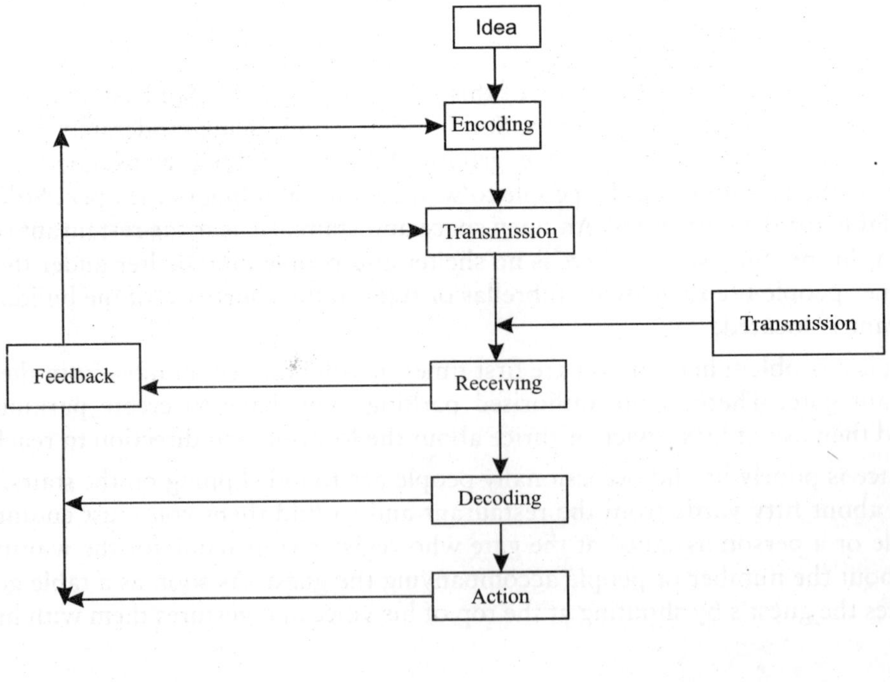

5. What communication mistakes were made in creating the problem?
6. What should Subhash have done to prevent the situation?
7. What should Sundram have done to prevent the situation?
8. If you are the owner of the restaurant what steps would you initiate to improve service delivery?

CASE STUDY 17.6

HOME BANKING

Call it room service or home delivery. Just make a call, place an order and cash is delivered at your doorstep. Launched almost four years ago, home banking is jumping to a higher orbit as more foreign and private banks embrace customer convenience as a retail banking proposition.

Silence is not golden anymore. Banks are no longer ashamed of creating a noise through aggressive marketing of their home alone schemes to a larger customer base. "Cash delivery has arrived," says in Anil Bhatia, head-direct sales, retail banking (Western region), Times Bank. "It has now become a must-feature of retail banking."

Lack of branch strength has compelled Citibank, ABN-Amro, Standard Chartered Bank, HSBC (Hongkong and Shanghai Banking Corporation) and Times Bank to go directly to the customer's door. Ironically, Bank of America, which is in the process of dismantling its retail business, pioneered the concept in India.

Citibank started cash delivery/pick-up in 1996, ABN-Amro followed in 1997. Standard Chartered Bank, HSBC and Times Bank have been late entrants—StanChart launched delivery service six months back, HSBC in December 1998 and Times Bank in February 1999.

The logistics of home banking are simple. With a large branch network, public banks can give foreign and private banks a run for their money. State Bank of India, for instance, has 8,909 branches across the country. The associate banks would take the figure to 13,229. Against this, ABN-Amro with six, Citibank with eight, StanChart with 18, HSBC with 25 and Times Bank with 35 branches paint a very feeble picture. The only answer, therefore, is to reach business with value differentiators—in this case, banking from home.

Sutapa Banerjee, head—consumer banking, India, ABN-Amro, claims the bank was first in 'unique' doorstep banking, in October 1997. "Others copied it. We didn't start is as a marketing too. It gives the customer an option, staying at home and not actually going to the bank," she says. "Home banking is all about convenience. The idea is to be close to the customer. Anyway, foreign and private banks cannot dream of becoming neighbourhood banks (like SBI). Instead, our USP is clockwork efficiency."

Citibank, of course, refutes her claim. Raj Kapoor, vice president, branch banking head India, Citibank, says: "We go back to 1996, when we started Citibanking. Our branding for this was not so much a feature branding, but just a whole different way of banking, which we called 'Citibanking'. This service is, however, fraught with risks. It requires a robust platform along with a solid infrastructure support system."

StanChart, on its part, claims that it started its home banking services (opening accounts, demand draft services, *et al.*) in 1995 itself, though it started cash-at-home six months ago.

"We are the pioneers", says Ajay Kanwal, head—product support, consumer banking, Standard Chartered Bank.

As for Times Bank, "we have got the term 'home banking' patented", says Bhatia.

Well, never mind who started it, the fact is that private banks consider this an important service for their retail business. HSBC's home banking services, when launched in December 1998, offered cash delivery up to Rs. 25,000. Says Sumit Dutta, manager (domestic liabilities), HSBC: "Delivery channel in retail banking is a function of options. Different banks will have different strategies. We are not offering cash pick-up at the moment."

HSBC's service is initially being offered in Mumbai to customers of the bank's Asset Vantage facility and current accountholders with balances of over Rs. 5,00,000. The Asset Vantage facility is offered to about 20,000 customers with a minimum balance of Rs. 1 lakh across the country. The bank charges Rs. 25 for a non-cash transaction and Rs. 50 for a cash transaction.

On the other hand, Times Bank services close to 50 per cent of its customers at their homes within four hours. The service also come free of cost but is limited to only priority customers with deposits worth Rs. 3 lakh and above. The cash limit is pegged at Rs. 15,000 and service is still restricted to Mumbai at present. Bhatia pegs the monthly growth in retail banking at Rs. 30 crore, out of which Rs. 15 crore, comes from home banking. He feels that bigger banks cannot handle such a service due to the volume of customers involved and the need to continuously innovate products for them.

ABN-Amro, StanChart and Citibank service all their accountholders, with varying limits. ABN-Amro has fixed a limit of Rs. 25,000 per transaction for individuals and Rs. 50,000 for non individuals. Around 60 to 70 per cent of all StanChart's business comes from home banking. Cheques totaling Rs. 1,000 or more are also picked up and requests accepted 24 hours a day. The bank charges Rs. 25 per pick-up and Rs. 50 for every cash delivery. At present, it operates this service in the four prime metres.

With Citibank, cash pick-up is done selectively for Citigold card customers (up to Rs. 4 lakh a day), while cash delivery (up to Rs. 1 lakh) is offered across the base. Kapoor calls the other players 'me-toos'. Citigold customers are not charged anything. Other customers are charged Rs. 100 for pick-up and delivery.

In all these banks, customers need to pass through the TIN' gateway for any transaction to be afrected. All to them also operate home banking courtesy courier services.

Kanwal says on a practical note: "The next logical step after account opening was cash delivery and pick-up. With this, we have completed the home banking cycle." Other banks, of course, do not think so. They prefer terming it 'convenience to customers'.

With Internet banking becoming a reality worldwide and retail transactions happening at the press of buttons, even home banking seems to be an outdated concept. But in India, it is a step ahead of the conventional branch banking that customers are used to. That is why the excitement among foreign and private banks is for real. And the competitiveness is borne out by the fact that everyone claims they have introduced home banking in India, in some manner or the other. Obviously, they're all in love with the idea. And obviously too, so are their customers.

(*The Economic Times,* Varsha Gupta, Mumbai)

QUESTION FOR DISCUSSION

1. Critically examine the advantages and disadvantages of electronic distribution system in home banking.

CASE STUDY 17.7

NEVER AGAIN

Manmohan was a Professor of Science and his son Adhish was a student of the eighth standard. Manmohan and Adhish had never traveled by air and were accustomed to local train and bus journeys. Only once had they experienced a long train journey between Delhi and Calcutta when they had opportunity to visit one of their relatives.

For the past three years Adhish's mother Mrs. Tirath was doing her doctorate in Philosophy in South India and she was being conferred this honour on December 20, 1998. On December 18, Mrs. Tirath talked to her husband and expressed her desire that both he and Adhish should be present on this occasion. To make it, Manmohan and Adhish had no alternative but to travel by air. They had never traveled by air before. Both were enthusiastic as they had heard the wonderful experiences of friends and were anxious to feel the experience themselves.

They contacted Western Express, an air ticketing agency to book two tickets for them for the destination airport and through a direct flight as they were new to flying and did not want to face any hassles enroute. The Western Express promised to deliver the tickets at their house four hours before the scheduled departure time and took all the fare money in advance. Both father and son were delighted. The flight was scheduled to depart for destination Airport at 2 p.m. on December 18, 1998.

At 10 a.m. the doorbell rang and Manmohan looked at his watch and was all praise for Western Express and asked Adhish to open the door for the boy and collect the tickets. To a great surprise of both of them it was Courier boy carrying some books ordered by Mrs. Tirath. Till 12 noon there was no positive response from Western Express and at about 1.15 p.m. it was informed that no confirmed tickets were available for December 18, and they had been booked for the 19th instead for a flight leaving at 12 noon. They were also asked to collect the tickets from the office as no delivery boy was available to deliver the tickets.

The office of Western Express is not enroute to airport but in opposite direction. So both Manmohan and Adhish had to travel to Western Express office located 15 km in opposite direction and then another 20 km to the airport. In order to reach one hour before the departure time both of them had to leave home at 8.30 a.m. to catch a flight at 12 noon to avoid traffic congestion.

They arrived at 'Originating Airport' at 11 a.m., one hour before the scheduled departure. They tried to contact the reception counter to find out the details of the flight, check in window number but preferred to stay away as there was a heavy rush. There were no queues, windows were crowded, and people were shouting to gain the attention of the enquiry attendant who was smoking and talking in an unbusiness like fashion to some acquaintance for a longtime on the telephone. They moved to the passenger information board on which the flight number, time of departure and window number for check in was clearly displayed. For 'Destination Airport' passengers, it was clearly stated to check in at window No. 19.

They started looking for window number 19. They went from window to window and could not locate window 19 and there were no directions or guide maps available near the passenger information board giving the location of check-in counters. They approached a uniformed employee working at window number 6 and enquired about window 21. He asked them to contact the assistance counter for this. When they were moving towards the assistance counter they chanced upon a security officer who was not an airline employee but a private security services employee. This agency provided security personnel in the departure lounge. He was very polite and personally escorted them to window 19 and also asked them if he could provide any more assistance to them.

To reach window 19 they had to make their way through many trolleys of luggage haphazardly parked and luggage unsystematically piled up. They could see long queues of passengers on each check-in window. As they reached window 19 they felt the first relief. There were hardly four passengers at this counter. This relief was short-lived as the counter boy informed them to move to window 20. The window 19 was meant for first class passengers only. They had to shift to window 20 and they had to join a queue where already more than 50 passengers were ahead of them.

Both Manmohan and Adhish were non-smokers. With great persuation they managed two seats in the non-smoking area. This was very crucial for Manmohan because he was non-smoker and also allergic to cigarette smoke. Despite all these hassles both of them were still pleased to travel by air which symbolised exotic travel but Adhish was quite upset at the treatment for the price of the travel.

Half an hour before the scheduled departure the security check was announced and passengers were asked to move to the security check area. The voice of the announcer was inaudible as if she was speaking with food in her mouth.

Interestingly the police officers on duty were discussing the passengers in their respective rows and the area looked quite ruly. As soon as they reached the security area they were asked several embarrassing questions. Anyway they were doing their job. After security check they proceeded towards the western lounge and anxiously awaited for the announcement for the flight departure. It was still half an hour for the flight to take off and they preferred to seat themselves at a position where they could see the TV screen on which flight information is displayed. The seating plan of this longue was such that only twenty to twenty five per cent passengers could have a look at single TV screen provided in the lounge. Passengers were frequently craning their necks to look at the TV screen and no announcements were made along with the information on the TV screen. The information on screen was displayed only in English. The system of displaying information made the area quite congested as passengers seated in front of the screen often raised their head obstructing the visibility of people seated in back-rows. As announcements were being made along with information displayed in TV, some passengers left their seats to see the information on the monitor. Some of the passenger were quite uncomfortable as the monitor displayed information in English only. Manmohan was quite perturbed over all this but Adhish looked unconcerned as he glued himself to his walkman listening to Hindi songs.

At 12.15 that was an announcement that their plane has developed some technical snag and the new flight departure schedule would be intimated shortly. There was no news about the rescheduling of this aircraft for about one hour and passengers started getting impatient. It was already lunchtime and no one was there to look after the passengers.

At 14.15 p.m. the announcement for the flight departure was announced and all passengers bound for "Destination Airport" stood up to form a queue for the bus to take them to the aircraft. After about five minutes wait the passengers were told to walk up to the aircraft which was about 400 meters away from the main building. The plane could be seen from a distance. As soon as they entered the plane, they started looking for their seats. No assistance came from the cabin crew and this created considerable confusion and crowd in the corridors. Adhish soon occupied his seat and started looking around at the fellow passengers who were mix of young boys and girls, old people, businessmen and some film stars.

Adhish settled himself in the flight by putting on the headphones and running through the music provided on the plane. He never bothered to go through the demonstration emergency procedures. Refreshments were served on board.

At 16.00 hours came an announcement to tighten the seatbelts as the plane has started for the "Airport enroute." It came as a shock for both of them as they had instructed the travel agent to book by the direct flight, On seeing the air ticket they realised that Western Express had booked them a flight having a stopover. They had also informed Mrs. Tirath to receive them at 'Destination Airport' as they were coming by a direct flight. She had rescheduled all her engagements for the day to receive them. She was quite tense for all the confusion going on.

At 16.30 hours the flight took off for 'Destination Airport' with a new crew landed at destination at 15.15 hours. The landing was very smooth. The cabin crew lined up at the gates to give parting smiles. They were all elegantly dressed, polite and helpful. They even helped an old couple in disembarking the plane. The bus was parked just near the plane. The passengers were directed by a smart, uniformed young man to the bus and driver of the bus helped the people in getting seated. The driver drove the bus smoothly and stopped it in front of the gate. The passengers were greeted by the airport staff and guided towards the luggage area. The airport was well lit. The passenger information provided on the screen accompanied by related announcements in a pleasing voice. Important information regarding flight schedules, instructions for proceeding to various gates, check in counter details were being flashed through electronic display media. Pleasing Indian music was being played. All-important locations had TV monitors displaying the current information, changes if any and distances and taxi fares to different places from the airport.

Manmohan and Adhish finally made it to the destination to be with Mrs. Tirath and share in her ceremony. All of them preferred to return home by train.

QUESTIONS FOR DISCUSSION

1. What is the service which a customer pays for?
2. When does a service start and when does it finish?
3. How do Manmohan and family contribute to service experience?
4. Are the provisions of service different for Manmohan and Adhish?
5. How do employees affect the service experience?

6. How does physical evidence affect the service experience?
7. How do other customers affect the service experience?

CASE STUDY 17.8

WILL IT BE WISE

Hotel Snowview is located at peak point and the rooms are so located as to present a panoramic view of valleys and peaks. During winter season the vicinity of this hotel experiences snow two or three feet deep and guests can really enjoy their stay. This hotel was the favourite of snowlovers and till 1993 it was famous for its services. The snowlovers had to plan three to four months in advance for getting reservations at this hotel.

In 1993 two more hotels—Hotel Landmark and Hotel Snowcamp came up in this area but the going was tough for them due to the established business of Hotel Snowview. The proactive policies of the new hotels started penetrating into the market share of Hotel Snowview and by 1994, Snowview started feeling the competition.

Due to more employment opportunities available, quite a few employees of Snowview joined Landmark and Snowcamp at higher salaries. The management of Snowview was not concerned about the employee turnover as they felt that the positioning of Snowview is enough to keep the customer share intact and it was only a temporary phenomenon.

By 1998 business had declined heavily and it was reported that the occupancy level has gone down to an average of 60 per cent as against 100 per cent of 1993.

In 1998 the management of Snowview changed at the board level and the new board was intent on reviving the performance of this hotel and bring it back to the level of 1993 when the occupancy rate was 100 per cent.

The first task taken up by Snowview was to identify a Director Marketing who would be solely responsible for formulating new strategies to bring the business back on stream.

Rakesh was appointed Director Marketing and he was given the task of creating business for the unfilled capacity at the top priorities. The hotel was able to retain a capacity level of 60 per cent as previously mentioned.

Snowview has a total of 400 rooms and all the rooms have the amenities required by tourists arid guests who love to spend holidays in the hills. Each room costs Rs. 1700 to the management and it includes a variable cost of Rs. 1000 and fixed cost of Rs. 700 per room.

Rakesh, Director Marketing started exploring the various options to bring the occupancy level to 100%. He talked to various tour and travel operators, event managers, winter sports organisers and many business organisations for block bookings. The going was tough as there was a severe competition and also availability of rooms had improved due to presence of Landmark and Snowcamp.

It was only after three months of continuous follow-up that Hill Express, a reputed tour and travel house which has its network throughout the world and is famous for attracting domestic as well as international tourists to hills, offered to book the entire 40 per cent capacity for the next three years but at a price of Rs. 1500 per room and also offered to pay one year advance rentals to confirm the deal. Rakesh sent this proposal to the Managing Director.

QUESTIONS FOR DISCUSSION

1. As Managing Director of Hotel Snowview will you accept the offer of Hill Express and why?
2. If you accept this offer what will be the impact on the economic health of the hotel? Explain?

CASE STUDY 17.9

MARKETING CONSULTANCY SERVICES

P.K. Mehta, Ph.D., is an economist who set u a consulting firm in New Delhi in 1992, right after completing four years as a high-level official in the government. P.K. Mehta went into this venture with the hope of providing economic advice, analysis and testimony for law firms and months after opening his firm, Mehta decided he needed to take marketing more seriously. His somewhat random approach to contacting and courting prospective clients had not allowed him to obtain the volume and mix of clients he had hoped to have by that time. He, therefore retained a marketing consultant who had been recommended by a friend to give him some direction for his marketing efforts.

The consultant and Mehta immediately agreed that a marketing plan should be developed. Mehta needed a carefully designed marketing programme to help him build his practice. But both agreed that before such a plan could be written a more careful examination of Mehta's external environment and his past marketing actions should be made. Hence, it was agreed that the consultant would first perform a marketing audit of Mehta's firm.

The marketing audit mainly involved a lengthy interview in which Mehta was probed by the consultant for information about potential markets, competitors, legal trends, distinctive competencies, fees, promotional efforts, and so on. Documents and data that Mehta had available in his office were also reviewed. The consultant offered much advice during the course of the interview and also wrote a follow-up audit report containing additional comments and suggestions.

The consultant's report acknowledged that Mehta did indeed have valuable services to offer to law firms and other prospective clients. His government background, his eight years as an economics professor at a major university, and his academic credentials clearly differentiated him as someone uniquely qualified to provide economic advice, analysis, and testimony in government regulatory matters. But the report pointed out that prospective clients might not immediately recognise what someone with Mehta's unique skills could do for them. The report, therefore emphasised how important it was for Mehta to try to educate prospective clients about how he could help them win cases.

The consultant recommended that Mehta should aim his educational effort at only a limited number of narrowly defined target markets. The report urged. Mehta to do some exploratory research immediately in order to identify some initial target markets. Additionally, more formal research on the potential of various markets was recommended for the near future. Mehta was advised to consider a variety of approaches for carrying out the educational effort, including the use of seminars, a newsletter, the direct mailing of an article he wrote, and cold-calling, followed up (where mutually agreed to) by a written proposal.

Mehta found the audit report to be very provocative and set out to implement some of its suggestions. He immediately began talking to various experts he knew about the potential of working on different types of cases. He also began to gather statistics on how frequently different types of cases were arising. After several weeks of implementing audit recommendations, he felt ready to write his marketing plan for 1993. In the plan he established marketing goals for different target markets. Strategies for educating and appealing to those markets time schedules for conducting seminars and implementing mailing, and a marketing budget.

QUESTIONS FOR DISCUSSION

1. What exactly is the service product being offered by Mehta? Can such a product be defined in terms of core, tangible and augmented product components? What suggestions do you have for Mehta, to augment his service product?
2. Do you think the marketing approach of 'educating' the prospective clients would succeed in the above case? Give reasons for your answer.
3. What constitutes the target market for Mehta? What are likely to be the consumer expectations of such customers?

(IGNOU, Dec. 1998)

CASE STUDY 17.10

NOT DELIVERED AS PROMISED: DON'T PAY FOR IT

Sunny and his wife Rekha both had degrees in Hotel Management with specialisation in catering and hospitality respectively. Both were working at Host, a restaurant located in the midst of the busy business locality. Just hundred metres away was the stock exchange where hundreds of people gathered everyday to exchange business transactions. The one kilometre of market had offices of many prestigious companies of India, reputed business houses, consultants, multinational companies and industrial houses. The area was known as the financial district of the city.

Because of the educational and work experience, Sunny worked in the restaurant kitchen and Rekha supervised the dinning area and handled the billing and cash register. The restaurant having space limitations had no scope of expanding its operations. So, for the past ten years they were doing same routine work.

Sunny and Rekha were keen on starting a enterprise of their own and were looking for the right type of business and opportunity. Rekha being in the dining area was always observing the guests coming to the Host. She observed that most of the guests coming for lunch were people belonging to the financial trade like investors, stockbrokers, bankers and their business operations were concentrated at the stock exchange. Since the lunch break was only for half an hour they could not afford to be out of their business premises for more than half an hour. Half of the break time went in the to and fro movement to the eating place. They were always found to be intent on finishing their lunch rather than enjoying it. Many of the guests were seen talking on their cellular phones even while eating.

Sunny and Rekha once visited the stock exchange to know the work place of their guests and realised how hard-pressed for time they were. They were convinced that if they could offer these customers an appealing lunch at their workplace, they can certainly develop a clientele. Moreover, the customers will be able to relish the lunch as they will be able to utilise the to and fro movement to the restaurant profitably.

They started talking to a select list of potential customers about the service they wanted to introduce. They found that their concept was acceptable to most of them. A demand for onsite food service was established. Sunny and Rekha worked on the economies of this service and established that they could build a very profitable business.

They decided to quit their jobs and open a small kitchen at their home exclusively to cater to customers requiring onsite food delivered as per their requirements. The focus of the service was 'quality food delivered on time'.

The operational strategy was very simple. They had met the potential clients and asked them to giving their requirements by 10 a.m. and also the time at which they would like the food to be delivered in their office. Normally 1.00 to 1.30 p.m. being lunch time gave them enough time to prepare food and deliver the packets.

The procedure followed by Sunny and Rekha was this:

(a) The service delivery start time fixed at 11 a.m. So all food must be filled, packed, labeled and sorted by this time.

(b) The delivery boys must report at 11 a.m. to pick up their packs. The delivery boys were selected on the basis of their location in the customer area, their knowledge about topography and distribution skills.

(c) The client base of 70 people located at seven different places was served by seven delivery boys each handling 10 customers whose offices were located either in the same building or in the immediate vicinity. The distribution strategy and mode was designed on the basis of client dispersion in the segment. On average, one delivery boy was supposed to handle 8 to 10 clients.

(d) The work study had indicated that each delivery boy can deliver the food and drop back the empty cases within one and half hour from the start of service. The kitchen was located five kilometres from the business offices.

In the same area there are four more organisations providing similar food delivery service and Sunny and Rekha had to compete with them in the same area. To have a proactive approach they started providing a service guarantee stating "Not delivered as promised—don't pay for it." Their main focus was speed of service (SOS).

As a consequence of this service guarantee their service started getting recognition and gained the reputation of reliability, accessibility and responsiveness. More and more customers were willing to enroll themselves as regular members for this service. The other suppliers in the same area are not willing to match me service and guarantee offers of Sunny and Rekha. Their customers started defecting thereby causing economic strain on their business. "How long can they offer this guarantee," commented one supplier as he felt it would be very difficult to continue this. In fact, this was also the concern of Rekha as she was incharge of customer management and Sunny was looking after the kitchen management.

The increased flow of customers was alluring them to expand the business but the type of guarantee was forcing them not to expand. But the experience of both convinced them to go ahead for expansion and cater to the segments they had identified and they were sure of winning without problems.

QUESTIONS FOR DISCUSSION

1. How could Sunny and Rekha create a market niche for their service offerings? What are the characteristics of the niche? What is the customer base?
2. What value-added services did they start offering the clients? Explain at least three of them.
3. What distribution strategies were adopted by them to deliver the food within the promised schedule? Did this build up customer satisfaction? Explain how customers and service providers benefited?

RURAL MARKETING

18

INTRODUCTION

The rural market is an area of darkness to Indian entrepreneurs. An area which is vast in size but amorphous in detail. An area where communications are poor and the population poorer because their operations are small scale and inadequate, therefore inefficient. An area which cuts itself off from the nation's economy because its own is not fully monetised.

And yet, the rural market represents the largest potential market in the country. It encompasses over 70 per cent of population. Its primary activities—agriculture, animal husbandry, fisheries, forestry—account for half of the national income. Rural assets also amount to more than 50 per cent of the country's tangible wealth. However, compared to the urban sector with 20 per cent of the population and 50 per cent of the income, money must be spread thinly. Yet there are pockets of wealth which an urban entrepreneur can tap.

Population. About 70 per cent of the Indian people reside in rural areas. In other words, for every consumer in urban area, there are three of them in rural areas. Though, the proportion of rural population to total population is showing a slight decrease over the years, but in absolute numbers the rural population is increasing at a higher rate than the urban population.

Table 18.1: Rural Population in India

Year	Rural Population in million	Ratio %	Urban Population in million	Ratio %	Total in million
1951	295	82.2	62	17.4	357.0
1961	360	82.0	79	18.0	439.0
1971	439	80.1	109	19.9	548.0
1981	508	76.0	160	24.0	668.0
1991	621	74.3	215	25.7	836.0
2001	736	70.2	285	27.2	1021.0

Source: Census of India, 2001.

When the rural market potential is determined, the marketer has to cover the vastness of the rural market in terms of areas covered and the location of the rural population. Table 18.2 shows the location and concentration of rural population.

Table 18.2: Location and Concentration of Rural Population

S.No.	Population range (No. of persons)	Number of villages	Proportion to total %	Population in millions	Proportion to total %
1.	Less than 200	1,20,073	21.55	12.19	2.4
2.	200 to 499	1,50,722	27.05	51.31	10.1
3.	500 to 999	1,35,928	24.40	97.03	19.1
4.	1,000 to 1,999	94,486	16.96	131.57	25.9
5.	2,000 to 4,999	46,892	8.42	137.67	27.1
6.	5,000 to 9,999	7,202	1.29	47.24	9.3
7.	10,000 and above	1,838	0.33	30.99	6.1
	Total	5,57,137	100.00	508.00	100

Source: Census of India, 2001.

EXPENDITURE PATTERNS

The expenditure patterns of the rural and urban areas are not the same. The National Sample Survey Organisation conducts consumer expenditure surveys in the country. The latest information available from the 47th Round conducted during July 2000 to June 2001 is presented in Table 18.3.

Table 18.3: Value of Consumption per Person per Month

S.No.	Items	Rural (in Rs.)	Urban (in Rs.)
1.	Cereals	45.38	42.34
2.	Gram	0.40	0.59
3.	Cereal Substitutes	0.20	0.22
4.	Pulses	8.31	10.04
5.	Milk and Milk products	18.35	29.53
6.	Edible oils	9.10	14.60
7.	Meat, Eggs and Fish	6.84	11.42
8.	Vegetables	0.25	14.65
9.	Fruits and Nuts	3.23	6.87
10.	Sugar	6.34	7.78
11.	Salt	0.33	0.38
12.	Spices	4.88	6.00
13.	Beverage and Others	8.13	21.04
14.	Total Food Items	121.78	165.46
15.	Pan, Tobacco and Intoxicants	6.69	7.57
16.	Fuel and Light	14.44	19.26
17.	Clothing	12.15	19.86
18.	Footwear	1.63	2.61
19.	Miscellaneous Goods and Services	27.80	55.89
20.	Durable Goods	4.33	15.38
21.	Rents	0.57	11.40
22.	Taxes and Cess	0.03	0.57
23.	Total Non-food Items	63.68	132.54
24.	Total Consumer Expenditure	189.46	298.00

Literacy Level

Literacy level helps the marketer in determining the promotional mix. Must be designed keeping in view the literacy level. The following table shows the literacy level in urban and rural areas:

Table 18.4: Literacy Level

Literacy level in percentage

S.No.	Sex	1971		1981		1991		2001	
		Rural	Urban	Rural	Urban	Rural	Urban	Rural	Urban
1.	Males	34	61	41	66	58	81	61	82
2.	Females	13	42	18	48	31	64	32	67
3.	All	24	52	30	57	45	73	50	75

DEMAND OF PRODUCTS AND SERVICES IN RURAL AREAS

Regional disparities heavily influence the income levels as also their level of awareness of the availability of various consumer goods. The increase in profitability in agriculture in fertile areas like the Punjab, Haryana, Maharashtra and Gujarat has generated increased purchasing power. Prosperity has also come by way of shifts from agriculture to horticulture and floriculture culminating in exports, leading to still higher purchasing power.

The potential of rural markets is immense. Research studies by organisations like NCAER and ORG-Marg have shown that rural markets are growing at five times the rate of the urban markets.

The relative importance of rural market *vs.* urban market can be seen from the following figures:

This portion is based on a write-up by Meena Galliara in Business Standard—the Strategist, November 3, 1998.

		Rural Markets	Urban Markets
Nail polish	Units	270 million	81 million
Lipstick	Units	250 million	131 million
Shampoo	Tonnes	2257	718
Mosquito repellents	Units	173 million	79 million

The type of product which a rural consumer intends to buy or has potential to buy, depends upon his needs, purchasing capacity and his attitude towards the product involving the cost-benefit analysis done by him before purchasing the product. For example, villagers very often feel that an investment of around Rs. 20,000 in a washing machine could fetch a monthly income of Rs. 200 which was more than enough to employ a maid to wash the clothes. Besides, there was no other recurring charge such as electricity or repairs. Again, a washing machine requires assured electric supply and piped water supply. Similarly, the rural folk would not purchase TVs or VCRs because they expect them as dowry coming along with the bride. At the same time, products like sewing machines, motor cycles and motorbikes, bicycles and three-wheelers would do well in the rural areas as these products aid in generating employment and wealth. Pressure cookers save fuel and time; radios and tape recorders provide pleasure in the otherwise routine life. Wrist watches are usually used as gift items. Practically ach and every item bought is based on a cost-benefit analysis.

In value term, the NCAER estimates that the rural market for FMCG durables and vehicles alone is worth Rs. 11,500 crore. Add a substantial market for agricultural inputs and the total market size is close to Rs. 31,000 crore. Sixty-eight per cent of the rural market lies untapped due to various reasons ranging from inaccessibility to lack of awareness.

The various types of goods and services demanded in rural areas may be classified as follows:

THE IMPORTANCE OF THE RURAL MARKET

The rural market is made of two broad areas:

(a) The market for consumption goods both consumer convenience and shopping and durable goods.

(b) The market for agriculture inputs and other investment goods such as tractors, etc.

Not surprisingly the entire demand potential for manufactured goods that exists in the rural areas has been largely untapped. Not even a fraction of the rural market has been serviced by the industries in the organised sector. But that does not in any way lessen the importance of rural market as the following factors will indicate:

1. Size of the Rural Market

An analysis of National Sample Survey—data shows that of the total expenditure on manufactured consumer goods, 75 per cent is spent in rural India. The percentage has remained almost unchanged since 1960-61. Thought per capita consumption and expenditure on manufactured consumer items is low in rural areas, the market is approximately three times larger. On the assumption that all persons or families above the poverty line form the market for some branded consumer goods, this market has a size of 62 million households. If we take Punjab, Rajasthan, Gujarat and Andhra Pradesh the target market of 72 million people is larger numerically than France, U.K. or West Germany.

2. Rural Market in Value Terms

For non-food consumption items the size of the market (estimated by applying NSS proportions to central statistical organisation data) in current prices was Rs. 5,500 crore in 1970-71, Rs. 9,500 crore in 1974-75, 13,500 crore in 1979-80 and Rs. 27,000 crore in 1999-2000. Assuming these items are mainly consumed by the rural population above the poverty line it represents an annual expense of Rs. 15.6 per head per annum. In real terms, however, the growth has been very modest at 3.5 per cent per annum due to a number of factors such as:

(a) Lack of concerted effort by the organised sector to penetrated the rural market.

(b) Averages are misleading in this type of analysis as peak opportunities which occur in certain pockets may not be fully realised.

(c) If the market for consumer products is considered as a whole it overshadows the opportunities that exist for selected products which may be growing at a much faster rate.

3. Rural Target Population

Wealth distribution in rural India is uneven and the top 13 per cent of the farmers land holdings account for 37 per cent of cultivated area. Further, NSS data show that the top 10 per cent of the rural population accounts for about 37 per cent of the expenditure on consumer goods. Not surprisingly the potential market is at the top of the spectrum. However with the increasing spread of the rural income, consumer goods are expected to make substantial penetration into the lower income strata by the normal percolation effect.

Then there is an increasing cross flow of population between urban and project town centres which act as conduits for cross flow of products and ideas thus supplementing the demand for such products and ideas thus supplementing the demand for such products.

4. The Market for Agricultural Inputs

There is a very rapidly expanding demand for agricultural inputs in rural market. This is borne out by the compound rate of growth in the off-take of agricultural inputs between 1990-91 and 1998-99:

Fertilizers	10 per cent
Pesticides	12 per cent
Area under high-yielding variety	11 per cent
Tractors	15 per cent
Pumps and Tubewells	11 per cent

A recent survey in Andhra Pradesh, Punjab and Haryana revealed that over 90 per cent of the farmers interviewed felt that they should use more and more new farm practices. The study established that in these areas the farmers are eager to use newer agricultural technology for improving profits and are prepared to take calculated risks.

5. Sources of Rural Purchasing Capacity

Following are the factors which contribute to purchasing capacity in rural areas:

(a) *Marketable agricultural surplus and rural/urban terms of trade.* So far as manufacture consumer goods are concerned, regression analysis indicates that there is a 0.7 per cent rise in consumption for every 1 per cent increase in marketable surplus of foodgrains. As the surplus is increasing every year, there will be increasing purchasing capacity with farmers.

(b) *Remittances.* The traditional remittances from within the country are now being supplemented in several states by remittances from overseas. In 1988 total inward remittances in the State of Kerala were estimated at Rs. 400 crore. This creates new consumption and purchasing patterns.

(c) *Government expenditure.* Investments in flood control and irrigation facilities will be around Rs. 22,000 crore in 1997-98 and central sector outlay for rural development and associated programmes will be Rs. 3,300 crore. These will generate income, and increased purchasing power of rural areas can be expected to support consumption of manufactured items. Further, these investments are expected to augment the income generation process from land in future years, which, in turn, will accelerate the growth of rural markets. The investment proposed during the Eighth Plan for developing village and khadi industries is of the order of Rs. 3,000 crore. This too will encourage the income generation process.

(d) *Dispersal of industry*. The investment in the development of backward areas will greatly speed up the income generation process in rural areas.

PROBLEMS AND CONSTRAINTS IN RURAL MARKETING

While developing rural markets, it is essential to keep the following points in view:

1. The Need for a Selective Approach

There are wide regional variations in the prosperity levels of various areas and hence in their market potential. These need to be analysed and understood sectorally in order to determine the methods for approaching them. A socio-economic survey undertaken in four progressive districts of Tanjore, Ludhiana and Kolhapur revealed a healthy per capita income growth of 5 per cent per annum among big and small farmers against a national average of 15 per cent. This has come about through improved use of land, Coupled with a reduction in family size. But there is wide variation in the various areas. The growth was mainly in:

(a) Areas which are agriculturally prosperous,

(b) Areas which get large amount of remittance, therefore a uniform approach to all rural areas is not possible.

2. Problems in Reaching the Rural Consumer

The population is thinly spread, 79 per cent of our half a million villages have a population less than 1,000. Almost 80 per cent of the villages do not have all weather roads. Rural consumers are also far less homogeneous than their urban counterparts and differ from region to region. Therefore, it is not possible to merely extend urban products to rural markets.

The low density of population and inaccessibility makes the problem servicing these villages individually and economically costly. Direct delivery of goods to even the top 1 per cent of villages cost twice as much as serving urban markets. Therefore in the initial stage, it may be better to concentrate only on the larger villages, mandi towns, and towns with large agriculture hinter lands that act as foci for distribution. The semi-wholesalers and retailers servicing smaller villages can obtain stores from these places or villages themselves can buy the necessary items.

About 90 per cent of the farmers visit the nearest towns at least once a month to sell their produce and purchase their requirements. In other words towns with large agriculture hinterlands can become the gateways for entry into the rural market.

3. Literacy and Medial Habits

Literacy and medial habits have changed significantly in the last 10 years. Five crore more people have become literate in the course of the last decade, a figure almost equal to the entire population of France and this growth in literacy shall continue in years to come. Radio and TV have reached all areas through transistors and community TV sets. A sizeable population of villages see cinemas regularly. And in States such as Punjab and Haryana 30 per cent of population read newspapers regularly. This change has led to greater awareness of products.

4. Constraints in Developing the Rural Market

There are several daunting problems in developing rural markets. The marketing effort for manufactured consumer goods as well as agricultural inputs in rural areas is constrained by

(a) High distribution costs.
(b) High initial market development expenditure.
(c) Inability of the small retailer to carry stocks without adequate credit facility.
(d) Inadequate infrastructural facilities (like connecting roads, warehouses, media availability, etc.).

5. Requirements for Success in Rural Marketing

Rural marketing should not be considered as an expense but as an investment. Of course, the initial costs for distribution and communication are high and returns come after a long period of gestation, yet it is an investment worth making. For success the following points must be kept in view:

(a) An efficient countrywide distribution network must be created so that company's products are available to the farmers near their door step.
(b) Advertising communications and servicing must be evolved in tune with rural needs and in ways different from what is effective in larger towns and cities.
(c) There should be a strong research and development team to produce products specifically for rural areas.
(d) Role of trade in distribution and communication must be strengthened.
(e) Pricing of products should be in line with the economic competence of villagers.
(f) Packaging should be simpler and more functional than ornamental.

6. Apart from high distribution costs as mentioned earlier there is high initial market development expenditure both in terms of promotion and personal selling. This cost of market development will have to be built into the pricing policy for specific brands. But government policies as they are penalise legitimate marketing activities such as advertising and promotion. This can be the single greatest impediment to the further rate of growth.
7. In rural marketing institutional promotion is more important than brand advertising. To a marketing man this is another hurdle because he may promote the institution and some other brand may be bought.
8. Inability of the small retailer to carry stocks without adequate credit facilities.
9. Inadequate warehousing. This leads to delay in replenishments of stocks which are urgently needed or which need quick replacement.

STRATEGY IN DEVELOPING RURAL MARKETS

Following are the basic functions in marketing. If rural markets have to be developed, each must be performed in a different manner than in urban market:

1. Marketing Research

This function mainly performs two things:

(a) *Opportunity Research*. This means what type of products at what price, what type of packaging where and when and in what quantities will be required.

(b) *Effort Research*. This means what type of efforts will be needed in advertising, promotion and distribution to realise the existing opportunity.

As rural markets are not homogeneous a general type of field survey will be impropriety. The survey has to be in a limited areas. Also as there is hardly any secondary information available, the marketing research approach has to be through:

1. Panel of upper 10 per cent population.
2. Household audits.
3. Semi-wholesalers and retailers in nearby mandi-towns.

The sources will provide the required information.

2. Product Development

This normally includes new product development, products innovations, marketing innovation, product life cycle, product mix and product diversification. But in the content of rural marketing it mainly means either new product development or modification of existing product to suit rural areas.

Following points must be kept in view when performing this operation:

(a) Product must be simple in design, simple to understand, operate, maintain and repair if need be.

(b) Functional aspect matter than sophisticated looks.

(c) Price should be well within the economic competence of the rural consumer.

(d) Packaging should be simple, should make the product easy-to-use and should be economical. If the package can lead to economy in use it will be better still.

(e) The brand name should suit rural background.

Considerations of the above points will help the marketing man to meet the requirements of villagers and thereby increase sales.

3. Distribution Management

Following are some of the channels that may be exploited to service rural markets:

(a) Ration shops.

(b) Retailers dealing in agricultural inputs.

(c) Semi-wholesalers in mandi-towns.

(d) Retailers in a village may be given some incentive to bring it from the wholesalers in a nearby town.

(e) National consumer cooperative society in the towns or through their Apex body.

(f) State consumer cooperative societies.

(g) Individual consumer cooperative society.

The better type of transport is road, or rail-cum-road agency or company-owned delivery vans.

4. Marketing Communication

(a) Advertising
(b) Radio
(c) TV where possible
(d) Painted walls
(e) Stalls in Rural Fairs
(f) Hoarding
(g) Vernacular newspapers where they are popular
(h) Personal selling:
   (i) Salesmen with vans from village to village. Vans may be fitted with projecting equipment or music system to collect people. Salesman can than talk about his product and do spot selling. Wherever, possible on the basis of these sales, a local dealer may be motivated to keep stock.
   (ii) Demonstration teams at trade fairs.
   (iii) Spot selling by offering premier.
   (iv) Bus stands.
   (v) Distributors salesman.

PRODUCT DEVELOPMENT IN RURAL MARKETING

Product development is as important in rural marketing as in marketing products in towns and metropolitan cities. The major reasons are also the same as listed below:

1. Development of new products through invention
2. New raw materials as polyster
3. Unmet need
4. Change in tastes
5. Change in economic conditions
6. Competition
7. To use waste products for higher use
8. Increasing literacy in villages.

But consumers in rural areas have different culture, habits, tastes and preferences. They belong to the various religious groups, castes and sub-castes. The multiplicity of this aspect from place to place. In Haryana, the population is largely homogeneous and the demands of consumers in rural area are also more or less similar.

When viewing the country as a whole, there are 15 major languages and about 40 dialects spoken and six major religious communities. Besides, the tastes and preferences for various goods vary from one geographical region to another and from one religious group to the other.

A marketer must know his target market very well. He must understand the expectations of rural consumers, their socio-economic background, tastes and preferences, etc., while marketing goods or providing services area-wise.

To get this information a general type of field survey will be inappropriate, as rural markets are not homogeneous. Also there is no secondary information available, as rural markets have not been researched so far. The best way to get this type of information is through:

(a) Panel of upper 19 per cent of rural population.

(b) Household audits in rural areas.

(c) Semi-wholesales and retailers in nearby mandi-towns.

These sources will provide information regarding the types of products that will be needed and in what quantities and at what prices.

Guidelines for Product Development

Product specifications like design, price and durability should be in accordance with the needs of the rural masses. There need not too much sophistication, but the product must be simple in its function and, of course, reasonably priced. The packing should be simple, rural culture.

Specifically the following points must be kept in views when developing products for rural markets:

(a) Product must be simple in design—simple to understand and repair, if need be.

(b) Functional aspects rather than sophisticated looks should be stressed.

(c) Price should be within the economic competence of rural consumers.

(d) Packaging should be simple, facilitate product use, should not add to cost and lead to economy in use of the product.

(e) The brand name should suit rural background.

Considerations of above points will help the marketing man to meet requirements of villagers and thereby increase sales.

DISTRIBUTION MANAGEMENT IN RURAL MARKETING

The most difficult hurdle in developing rural markets is for the products to reach these markets is distribution management.

As in all other types of marketing, distribution management comprise of

(a) Management of channels, and

(b) Management of physical distribution.

Management of Channels

Channels are pathways through which products flow from the end of production line to the end consumer. But unlike in town and cities there are not clear-cut channel network in rural areas. However following are some of the channels that may be exploited to serve rural markets:

(a) Ration shops selling sugar, kerosene and other items in short supplies are quire useful.

As people gravitate to these shops for their requirements of rationed items, they are likely to buy other goods stocked by these shops.

(b) Retailers dealing in agricultural inputs. As villagers visit these shops for seeds, insecticides and fertilizers, they will be exposed to the consumer goods and this may lead to purchasing those goods.

(c) Semi-wholesales in mandi-towns. It has been experienced that almost 90 per cent of villagers visit mandi-towns to sell their produce, buy agricultural inputs and other consumer goods.

(d) Retailers in a village can be used as an outlet for consumer goods by giving some incentives so that they may buy things from wholesales in nearby towns.

(e) National consumer cooperative societies in major towns or through their Apex body.

(f) State consumer cooperative societies.

Wholesales in mandi-towns can act as warehouses and from that point of view, the products can be distributed to village retailers by the wholesalers.

QUESTIONS FOR DISCUSSION

1. (a) Define niche Rural Marketing strategies.
   (b) "Marketing information benefits a firm in a variety of ways." Explain.
2. How will you segment the rural markets in the case of the following products:
   (a) Fair and Lovely Cream,
   (b) Hajmola,
   (c) Taj Mahal tea,
   (d) Nirma Detergent powder.
3. Your company has recently launched a range of technically superior television sets in rural market. The constraint that you face is the advertising budget. Your M.D. is not in favour of incurring huge advertising expenditure. Suggest the route you will take in your advertising planning.
4. With suitable examples, distinguish between "Distribution Channels" and "Distribution Logistics" for rural market. Briefly describe the role of warehousing in this context.
5. "Because of heterogeneity, analysis of behaviour is too difficult and may not be conclusive as well." If you agree to it how would you justify the consumer behaviour analysis and interpretation?
6. (a) What role do influencers play in the consumer decision-making?
   (b) "Indian rural culture is entirely different from west but still we accept Western products and we appreciate their culture also." Discuss.
7. (a) Explain the role of personal selling in rural marketing.
   (b) Sales promotion is an important too for increasing sales. Explain the relevant tools which can be used in rural marketing.

8. Explain any three rural problems with examples:
   (a) Problems of agricultural marketing;
   (b) Problems of rural banking;
   (c) Problems of changing rural environment;
   (d) Problems of package size.
9. Distinguish between rural markets and urban markets.
10. Enumerate the different types of rural buyer characteristics. Elucidate them with examples from real life situations.
11. "On account of consumer illiteracy, the audio-visual media provide an immense opportunity to communicate with consumers." Is it true? Outline the relative strengths and weaknesses of these media and describe their role in rural marketing.
12. What are the different ways of segmenting a rural market? What bases would you choose for marketing TV sets in rural India?
13. What are the advantages and disadvantages of branding in rural market?

CASE STUDY 18.1

IDENTIFYING RURAL MARKETING STRATEGIES

COMPANY PROFILE

(A) LG ELECTRONICS INDIA PVT. LTD.

LG Electronics (formally known as Lucky Goldstar), a US $73 billion (Rs. 2,84,700 crore) South Korean giant hit the Indian market with a spectrum comprising 10 models of CTV's 8 models of refrigerators and 3 models of washing machines during May 1997 through its wholly owned subsidiary LG Electronics India Pvt. Ltd. (LGEIL). Since then, LGEIL has created new landmarks in the history of consumer electronics and appliances industry. LGEIL is:

1. The first company to go nationwide in 4 months.
2. The first company to achieve a turnover of Rs. 100 crore in a time span of 200 days.
3. It has the largest product model portfolio-21 models of CTV's (Namely Golden Eye, Soundmax, Joymax, Mach-4, Sampooran), 8 models of refrigerator (preserve nutrition system), 3 models of washing machines (with the Chaos punch system), 2 models of VCD's and 3 models of airconditioners (with chaos logic).

In continuance to its innovative launches, LG Electronics India Pvt. Ltd. has launched 3 models of mircowave ovens in the month of February, 3 models of direct cool refrigerators in the month of April and 2 models of semi-automatic washing machine in the month of June.

To provide the best and prompt after sale services, LGEIL has a nationwide network of customer care centres equipped with the latest communication system and service vans. In customer service, the "Happy Call" system of LG Electronics keeps track of customers in case they need assistance.

LG is the first multinational to focus on rural marketing in a big way. It has launched a new CTV range by the name Sampooran. To reach the rural markets, LGEIL has started video-on-wheels mobile vans, which travel to far off destinations to create awareness. It is organising road shows, exhibitions, and participating in small local melas.

Within a span of six months LGEIL is a clear market leader in the 300 litre frost free refrigerator segment as well as in the fuzzy, logic washing machines and occupies the 6th position in terms of CTV sales. These achievements are solely because of the corporate philosophy of LGEIL,"We put people first".

LG Group of Korea will invest $ 600 million in Indian by 2005. Out of this, $ 289 million would be invested in the electronic sector, its thrust area in the years to come according to Kwang-Ko-Kim, Managing Director of LGEIL, a subsidiary of LG Electronics, Korea.

LG has a market share of 8.5 per cent in colour television, 37 per cent in refrigerators and 35 per cent in washing machines.

In a bid to expand market share, the company is planning to introduce a cheaper range of refrigerators, washing machines and colour televisions with simple and easy to use features.

"In fact, we fare going to bring down prices in this range practically every six months. This is not an attempt to strip down features but to cater to the rural markets, whose primary need in electronic goods is easy-to-use menus." Said Rajeev Karwal, vice president marketing and sales.

According to Kwang-Ko-Kim (MD) "We expect 20-30 per cent of our turnover to be contributed by rural markets".

Today, market share of LGEIL in CTV is 8.5 per cent.

LG Electronics launched many state-of-art products such as the Golden Eye TV, Punch +3 washing machines and refrigerators. LG felt that it was not enough to achieve a 10 per cent market share and turnover of Rs. 375 to Rs. 400 crore that it has targeted for 1998. The idea behind LG's rural foray was to support and create new markets rather than to try and stretch the existing market.

The company is looking at converting the existing six million B&W TV owners to colour TV owners hopefully at the rate of 10 per cent per year. The new products for the rural buyer to be launched in April 1998 include an economy TV with basic functions, priced at Rs. 12,000, a 165 litre direct cool refrigerator, a semi-automatic washing machine at Rs. 9000.

Last year LG struck a deal with Voltas Ltd. for original equipment manufacturing (OEM) facilities to manufacture and supply direct cool refrigerators. The conglomerate proposes to purchase one lakh refrigerators in a year.

LG will produce its own direct cool refrigerators by end-98, at its plant in Greater Noida (installed capacity of two lakh units/annum). CTV production (installed capacity of four lakh units/annum) will start in May 1998. Washing machines (installed capacity of one lakh units per month) will be in production by July 1998.

With the rural thrust all worked out, Kwang-Ko-Kim (MD) is confident that LG will meet its year's target, "We expect 25-30 per cent of sales from the rural market. Within three years, we hope to take this to 50 per cent."

MARKETING MIX VARIABLE OR THE FOUR P'S OF MARKETING USED BY LG ELECTRONICS FOR PENETRATION IN THE INDIA RURAL MARKETS

Products: In the first place, it chooses the product that will meet the identified needs of the chosen consumer/consumer group of the rural areas. The firm must find out what kind of product is required by the rural consumer and then make and supply the required product.

LG Electronics launched many state-of-the-art products such as Golden Eye TV. LG has also manufactured a special, easy-to-use television model branded Sampoorna, and it seems that LG, which launched itself in the country with Golden eye; seems to be making a transition.

Sampoorna is specially designed for rural areas, offers extra durability and can adapt itself to the high voltage fluctuations in Indian rural areas. The colour, size and packaging too have been specially designed for the rural target group.

Place (Distribution): For that, the company has a two-pronged strategy: a perfect customer service network developing along with its sales network and financing option countrywide. On customer service, LG's "Happy Call's" system keeps track of customers in case they need assistance.

LG Electronics too plans to enter 20,000 plus towns this year. LG will open 60 service franchises this year adding to the existing 28 and has similar ambitious plans for distribution too. From 874 dealers currently, it will have 2,000 by the year-end. And it will depend on the geography of the state.

Making products available in rural areas will be crucial. LG had used C&F agents for distribution in Goa. The company's logic in doing away with the distributors was that in the long-term, with more products it would be cheaper to go directly to the dealer. To cut the lead-time in ramping up distribution, LG choose to hire branch heads from the existing companies, who had both a good understanding of the market as well as a good rapport with the trade.

Price: LG has now reduced the price range for the rural markets. Rural Indian needs products at affordable prices. The new product for rural buyers is an economy TV with basic functions at Rs. 12,000. Its flagship brand of Golden Eye is available for Rs. 16,500 (20″ CTV) and the price of 14″ Soundmax all is only Rs. 10,500.

LGEIL proposes to bring down prices of its products practically every six months. LG have a new punch line: LG Electronics "Great Products – Honest Prices."

LG provides financing options through out the through countrywide. As in villages, the biggest customer is the farmer who is dependent on the harvesting season for extra liquidity countrywide will do away with the problem.

The corners of the trade marketing strategy was to ensure a higher rate to return to the dealer. The route, says Karwal, "We delinked the incentive from the volumes achieved and replaced it with a hidden incentive. From time-to-time, we will reinforce dealer margins with incentives on a per unit basis." This system forced the dealer to focus on volume sales, which would then form his regular source of income (finance available through AVCO Financial services).

Promotion: For promotion and advertising, LG is planning a big splurge. LG involved itself in local (providing free water, medical aid) and go in for wall paintings (at water tanks or even on tractors), and has already launched two vans in Maharashtra and Eastern Uttar Pradesh. These will promote the brand through jingles and gifts distribution in between movie shows. The vans will later be complemented by road shows, wherein a dealer will set up a promotion and sales outlet for three to four days. LG will also advertise on Vividh Bharti and regional TV networks in two to three months time. The company's advertising budget for rural markets, minus television spend is a substantial Rs. 3 crore (**LG Electronics**: "The face of the future") New Punch line "Greater Products – Honest Prices."

QUESTIONS FOR DISCUSSION

1. Is LG focus on the rural markets justified?
2. What can be the attribute based on which a company can hope to excel in this scenario of cut-throat competition?
3. Who will be LG's most susceptible target now that the price was has been declared in the CTV segment?

(B) SAMSUNG INDIA ELECTRONICS LTD.

Samsung the other Korean biggie also plans its thrust into the non-urban market with colour TV's followed by a host of other products. Over and above the US $20 million already invested in India so far, it plans to put in another $20 million in 1998 alone. The total investment by 2003 claims the company will be $200 million.

Says Samsung India Electronics Ltd.'s managing director B.M. Park, India was considered a major emerging market by SEC and is being accorded top priority amongst Samsung's other South-East Asian subsidiaries. We wish to take our 1997 turnover of Rs. 400 crore to about Rs. 600 to 700 crore.

Samsung, which sold 1.75 lakh CTV's last year. From being present in towns with population of 70,000 the company is now branching out into 25,000 plus towns, for which it is developing low-end television models at its Noida factory. Having launched two economy models in the 20″ model range with price tags of Rs. 13,500 and Rs. 14,900, it will soon be introducing 14″ models priced below Rs. 10,000. Samsung is hoping to convert the B&W (a 20″ model costs anywhere between Rs. 3,500 to Rs. 6,500) buying segment to CTV's especially with it's a below Rs. 10,000 range.

The company is targeting sales of 3 lakh CTV's this year. The TV's will be followed by the launch of direct cool (*vis-a-vis* frost free), small size refrigerators and semi-automatic washing machines.

MARKETING MIX VARIABLE OR 4P'S OF MARKETING USED BY SAMSUNG ELECTRONICS FOR PENETRATING THE RURAL AREAS

Product: Samsung will introduce a low lend, basic CTV developed especially for the rural market which will be manufactured at its Noida factory. Samsung introduced its 14″ CTV for the rural and semi-urban areas. It has products such as 38 series 14″ and 20″ (3338 and 5038) 39 and 85 series 14″, 20″, 21″, 25″ (3339, 5039, 5334, 15385) which are introduced in rural areas and semi-urban areas.

Place (Distribution): Samsung plans to fortify its distribution, often held up by rivals as being its weak point.

The rural areas with be serviced by distributors based in district headquarters with support from company appointed sales staff. Distributors will use multi-brand retailers to increase product penetration. This is a change from LG's earlier policy of using direct dealers. Samsung feels that was the urban policy Samsung's M.D. Park believes, "More distributors does not mean you are selling more. Fewer dealers with more support can sell more."

Samsung says the number of dealers will depend on the geography of the states.

Samsung Electronics has penetrated class II towns (population size between 50,000-99,999) and will reach class III towns (20,000-49,999) next year.

Price: The economy models have been launched to enhance Samsung's penetration levels in the country. Economy does not, however, mean any compromise in quality only the features may be reduced.

Samsung launched two economy models in the 20″ models range with price tags of Rs. 13,500 and Rs. 14,900. It will soon be introducing 14″ models priced below Rs. 10,000 Samsung also decided to join the exchange schemes.

Promotion: Samsung plans to go in for regional language wall paintings, participate in local fairs and in a little while start mobile vans. It will also do a minimal amount of local newspaper advertising.

Samsung has also used bus-shelter, glosings and on stop translities for advertising purpose.

QUESTIONS FOR DISCUSSION

1. What other promotional activities should Samsung undertake to attract people in the rural areas?
2. What other products apart from the CTV's can be introduced by Samsung in the rural market?
3. Draw up a profile of the target segment of the CTV's in the rural market. Do you think these people have the purchasing power to buy an expensive CTV set?

(C) BARON INTERNATIONAL LTD. (AKAI)

Akai Electronic Co. Ltd. of Japan set up in 1926 to make radio parts, was taken over in 1995 by a Hong Kong based conglomerate, Semi Tech Global Co. Ltd. (STG 1996-97 turnover: H.K. $112 billion or Rs. 5,667 crore today), which also markets Singer Sansui and Pfaff. The holding company has a 65 per cent stake in Akai. Since 1992, Akai has been closing plants in Japan and using cheaper bases elsewhere in Asia. In 1995 it acquired Kong Wah Holdings Ltd., claimed to be the largest TV manufactured in South-East Asia, outside of Japan. STG own five TV plants: in Finland, Malaysia, England and China. It also controls over 18 component plants in Southern China. Together the group companies may be over six million TV's two million VCR's and one million audio systems apart from telecom products. The group gets most of its sales from Russia and other south-east countries, the Indian subcontinent and China but the brand sells in 47 countries.

The group success formula has been its judicious eye for cheap inputs even from non-group manufacturing units. The potential it sees in selling recognised name such as Akai and Sansui in emerging markets. STG plans to emerge as a big player in newer product categories such as digital video players at a later stage. A TV with an internet browser is also coming up. Baron has a licence agreement with Akai Electronic Co. to make and sell its products in India.

Baron International set up its Akai operations with an investment of just Rs. 25 crore, in 1994. It got off the ground quickly, doing sales of Rs. 1518 crore in 1995-96. In the 15 months period from April 1996 to June 1997, that rose to Rs. 444 crore (annualised Rs. 396 crore). Now in the 12 months leading up to July 1998, Akai wants to place its TV in 4.5 lakh homes in a market estimated at 2.2 million units for this period. The aim is Rs. 1000 crore in sales.

In pursuit of volumes, Akai has given the colour TV (CTV) market a series of wooshes that have shaken the competition. The Akai has virtually destroyed the old perceived price line for the standard 21″ CTV and confounded the general equilibrium of the market. Listening to the consumer's needs and wants is a better way to put it.

"For Indian consumers, the primary driver of purchase is value for money." Hence Akai's base line: redefining the value of the rupee.

Because of the wide-income disparities, Baron believed that the replacement market will be active for years. So, in case you were waiting for an all time attractive replacement scheme, visit your nearest Akai dealer today to avail the mind bogging offer.

In the premium segment Akai is launching 28″ and 32″ wide colour TV's to enhance the pleasure of viewing and also 21″ CTV. Besides Akai is very conscious of providing prompt and effective service to its consumers. With this view in mind Akai have mobile service vans equipped with cellular phones for the easy accessibility of the component. The impact of Akai has taken the country by storm.

Baron International plans to enter rural markets. A progress has already been set in motion to replace B&W with CTV sets. Mulchandani of Akai says, Akai sold the bulk of its 3.7 lakh TV's in metros and mini metros last year. It has about 2,500 direct dealers in 2 lakh plus population towns and its products are otherwise available in 50,000 plus towns through 800 distributors.

Today due to its effective strategies it has become a dominant player in the Indian rural market. One of the most important strategies adopted by it is its pricing strategy. Today, Akai has a 50% market share in urban markets and 35% markets share in rural markets in India.

QUESTIONS FOR DISCUSSION

1. Do you agree that Akai has become a market leader as a result of its pricing strategy? Explain.
2. What should Akai do in order to further succeed in the rural market considering the fact that global giants LG and Samsung also have their eyes set on the rural markets of India?
3. Is Akai responsible for creating a buyers market in the CTV market in India?

STRATEGIC INDUSTRIAL MARKETING—AN INTRODUCTION

19

INTRODUCTION

Marketing delivers a standard of living. In the case industrial marketing, this standard is delivered to industrial organisations, public agencies, and not-for-profit institutions of all kinds, large and small. What is this standard and how is it delivered? The standard is what clients or customers expect information and quality products and services, priced right, and distributed at appropriate locations. Delivery may be around the corner or across the ocean. A small service station repairs and maintains the truck fleet of another enterprise just down the street. A crucial aerospace component is sent via air express, on short notice, from North to South America. Financial or health care advice is flashed instantly by telephone, fax, or satellite from England to Hungary or from Australia to Indonesia.

Figure 19.1 is a simplified view of the buying and selling activities of the three major participants in industrial markets private, profit-making organisations of all kinds and sizes; public institutions (government agencies) at all levels from local to international; and not-for-profit institutions, ranging from clinics to churches and trade associations to science museums. Although the table shows the arrows going one way, any enterprise can be both a seller and a buyer. Thus, a computer service organisation purchases parts and other items from its suppliers and sells sophisticated custom software packages to clients in both the public and private sectors.

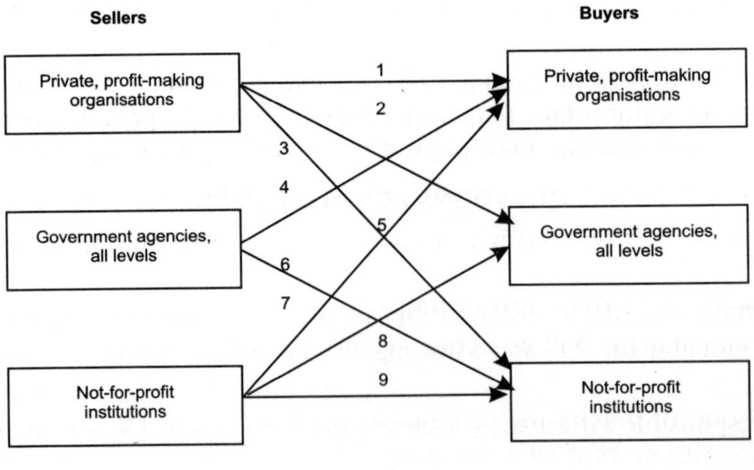

Fig. 19.1: A Simplified View of Buyers and Sellers in Strategic Industrial Marketing

Line 1: A foundry or plastic moulder sells parts to a truck manufacturer.

Line 2: A computer service company bids on a federal government contract.

Line 3: A furniture manufacturer ships beds to hospitals and pews to churches.

Line 4: A federal government agency offers geological maps to explorers.

Line 5: A state sewage authority connects a local public agency to its line.

Line 6: A space agency supplies satellite photographs to high schools line.

Line 7: A health care firm bids for the contract of a large chemical firm.

Line 8: An orchestra performs for a major government conference.

Line 9: A chamber of commerce gives export advice to a trade association.

Do strategic industrial marketing organisations cater to household consumers (families and individuals)? Yes, indeed. For example, an office equipment firm might expand its markets by selling modular furniture and small computers to families with teenagers who will use these items for homework. A company that makes industrial adhesives and cleaning compounds may offer its products to household users. Or, an industrial security firm may decide to begin protecting luxury homes.

What about the reverse? Do companies that offer consumer goods and services attempt to penetrate industrial markets? Yes, indeed. A producer of soaps and detergents for the home may decide to bid on a contract to supply a hospital or museum. A florist delivering to homes may want to broaden its client base by trying to place green plants in both downtown and suburban office buildings.

Consumer and industrial markets can overlap. In this text, however, we will focus on businesses that sell to or buy from other businesses. We will study organisational buying behaviour and the methods of measuring the size and characteristics of a potential industrial market.

The term strategic industrial marketing suggests that organisations deal with other organisations in a sort of faceless fashion. But keep in mind, each and every organisation is made up of many individuals with diverse backgrounds and characteristics. Industry-to-industry transactions involve people-to-people relations. Yes there are teams of sellers; yes, there are many groups in the buying firm who influence the purchase. Ultimately, however, it is individuals who deal with other individuals. It is essential to consider the perceptions, expectations, and motivation of these individuals if we are to achieve an understanding of strategic industrial marketing.

Here is an interesting dialogue that illustrates this point, and reveals a major gap between buyers and sellers:

Purchasing Agent: We require just-in-time delivery.

Salesperson: My company will do better than that. We'll deliver your parts before you need them.

About 90 per cent of purchasing professionals understand immediately the humor in that dialogue, but only 50 per cent of sales professionals recognise that it is a joke. Although humorous, the anecdote indicates that there is a serious problem. In the 1990s, sales managers must address this problem if they hope to achieve rapport with individual purchasing agents.

As we enter the field of strategic industrial marketing, we should note two phenomena. *First*, there is an incredible richness and variety to the field. Products and services can be simple or complex. Goods can range from small items such as pencils or nails to assembly lines, printing presses, and aerospace missiles. Services can be as elementary as tightening a screw to refurbishing a nuclear reactor. They can range from filling out forms to complex medical, financial, or technical consultancy. Prices can range from a fraction of a cent for processing a payroll check to millions of dollars for building a jumbo jet aircraft. Distribution can be near or distant, and invariably involves numerous decisions about dealers, agents, warehouses, trucks, and trains. Promotion decisions can range from placing a simple advertisement in the yellow pages to participating in a large trade show. Planning marketing strategy and coordinating the marketing mix are truly challenging tasks that are performed in a continuously changing environment.

Second, there is a jargon or special vocabulary in strategic industrial marketing, just as there is in any other functional area of business, sports, medicine, or any discipline. To communicate with other strategic industrial marketing marketers it is necessary to speak their language. We will highlight key words and concepts throughout this book to help you become familiar with the strategic industrial marketing marketer's vocabulary. You are now set to explore the exciting world of strategic industrial marketing—a field that is four times larger than consumer marketing.

STRATEGIC INDUSTRIAL MARKETING TERMINOLOGY

As the first step in your study of strategic industrial marketing, you will need to become familiar with some marketing terminology as it is used in this text.

Marketing is the creation and adaptation of products and services to provide greater utility or value to customers than do competing products and services. Marketing involves selection of potential customers (target markets) and management of the marketing mix (product, price, place, and promotion).

The **marketing concept** includes three key ideas: (1) the principal focus of the marketing manager is to provide customer satisfaction; (2) the entire organisation must be coordinated as an integrated system in which all employees and departments are aware of their roles in the organisation/customer relationship and work together to maintain that relationship; and (3) the long-range goals of the organisation (profit, stability of employment, service to society, a favourable public image, and so forth) must be fulfilled.

A **consumer** is an individual who purchases goods and services for self-gratification. Self-gratification may result from using the purchase (such as the enjoyment obtained from eating a chocolate candy bar or watching a rented videotape) or from giving the purchase to another person (such as the pleasure the buyer experiences in anticipating the appreciation that will be exhibited by the recipient of the gift).

An **strategic industrial marketer** is an individual or an organisation that sells goods and services to other business people, businesses, institutions, or organisations. The industrial marketer may also be called a business-to-business marketer or seller:

A **business buyer** is an industrial or business purchaser who buys for reasons other than self-gratification. Typically, the purchase or rental is made for one of three reasons: (1) to incorporate the product or service into the products or services that the organisation produces (for example, General Motors purchases laminated safety glass for auto windshields); (2) to facilitate the operation of the organisation (for example, IBM purchases automobiles for its salespeople); or (3) to resell the product or service (for example, a retail store purchases packaged food products to resell immediately, without any modifications, to consumers). The terms business buyer, industrial buyer, organisational buyer, buying organisation, client, purchasing agent, purchaser, buying centre, acquisitions officer, and customer are all roughly equivalent.

Strategic industrial marketing is the marketing of products and services to organisations rather than to households or ultimate consumers. The purchase is made, not for self-gratification, but rather to achieve organisational objectives. Strategic industrial marketing is also called business-to-business marketing industrial marketing, commercial marketing, institutional marketing government marketing or organisational marketing.

Strategic Industrial Marketing Defined

In past years, texts dealing with business marketing were titled "strategic industrial marketing", and many courses in business schools today are still called "strategic industrial marketing". However, the term strategic industrial marketing offers a more realistic and comprehensive image of the non-consumer marketing world. It avoids the confusion that may arise when, for example, a firm manufactures hair shampoo and then sells it to distributors and retailers. Although the product in such a case clearly is a consumer product, the decision-making and purchasing behaviour of the distributor or retailer is very different from that of a consumer.

Strategic Industrial Products Defined

Some products can be identified clearly as industrial products: forklift trucks, bulldozers, pallets, injection molding machines, cream separators, and jet engines are a few. Others, which appear to be industrial or business products, may find customers among groups of consumers. Vans, originally intended for commercial deliveries, have become popular family vehicles. Cellular telephones are finding their way into private vehicles for personal use. When consumers become attracted to business products, responsive marketers may adapt those products to suit the new found market's needs more closely. A good example of this is the huge consumer market that now exists for video cameras, which in past years were the domain of commercial television broadcasters.

Still other products with little or no adaptation may be considered either business or consumer products, depending on the circumstances in which they are purchased and used. For example, identical computers may be found in word processing applications in the office and in the home. And what about flowers and plants? In the home we know they are consumer goods. But in the office, they play the business goods.

More prosaically, consider toilet paper. A consumer product? Definitely. Or is it? Not so when purchased by a university or an industrial plant. In those settings, it is facilitating the operation of the organisation. And as a business product, it must be marketed in a different manner than it is to consumers. Business buyers are concerned less with its squeezable softness, pastel colours, or fresh forest scent and more with its timely delivery, quantity discounts, and dollars and cents.

STRATEGIC INDUSTRIAL PRODUCT CLASSIFICATION

Consumer goods are classified as convenience goods, shopping goods, speciality goods, and unsought goods. The basis for this classification system is the variability in the buying behaviour of consumers. Thus consumer goods are classified according to *how people buy*.

With industrial goods, there is a remarkably low degree of variability in buying behaviour. Consequently, the consumer goods classification system does not help industrial marketers classify industrial goods. Since most industrial follow the same pattern of search, evacuation, approval, and purchase for goods and services, we must find a classification scheme that points out other types of differences in product groupings. The traditional method of classifying industrial products is based on how the goods are used.

Capital Equipment and Investments

Capital equipment and investments require significant financial expenditure. Thus, marketers may have to extend credit to the buyer, assist the buyer in securing funds or loans, or offer the buyer leasing agreements. The high cost of capital expenditures also means that the buying organisation's top executives will be involved in the purchase decision. Capital equipment and investments can be subcategorized into land, buildings, and other companies; single-purpose equipment; and multi-purpose equipment. Capital equipment items are always installed in a fixed location.

Land, Buildings, and Other Companies. Land, buildings, and other companies (takeovers) typically involve lengthy negotiations and are the largest investments a firm will make. Associated professional business services—such as environmental impact studies, architectural design, and financial intermediation—may be purchased prior to and during the capital project acquisition decision.

Table 19.1: The Industrial Buying Decision Process

1. Recognition of needs
2. Definition of characteristics and quantity of item needed
3. Development of specifications to guide procurement
4. Search for and qualification of potential sources
5. Acquisition and analysis of proposals
6. Evaluation of proposals and selection of suppliers
7. Selection of order routine
8. Performance feedback and evaluation

Single-purpose Equipment. Typically, single-purpose equipment is custom-made for only one company or industry. For example, a conveyor system is custom-designed to traverse a certain factory configuration at a specific speed and carrying a stated maximum load. Alternatively, a certain leather-stitching machine might only be useful to plants in the shoe manufacturing industry. Customised equipment requires much interaction and negotiation between the technical sales and service people of the seller and the engineering staff of the client.

Older custom-made equipment can pose problems. Because of its specialised nature, it is extremely difficult to find buyers for used single-purpose equipment. Thus, if the buyer's products change rapidly (requiring different production equipment) or if the single-purpose machine is easily made obsolete by technological innovation in the machine-producing industry, the buyer faces high risk levels. Consequently, buyers of single-purpose equipment plan for shorter replacement periods and have to put more money aside annually for equipment replacement. All of these factors suggest that the astute business marketer may have to extend credit terms or help the client secure a loan if a sale of new equipment is to be consummated. Mainframe computer manufacturers have addressed this problem by providing trade—in schemes and offering leasing terms to their customers.

Multi-purpose Equipment. Multi-purpose equipment, such as boilers, compressors and hoists, is used by most manufacturing industries. Such equipment has a horizontal market—that is, a market extending across many industries. The product life cycle tends to be quite long, resulting in lower risk of obsolescence and longer replacement periods. The broad market for these products guarantees relatively easy sale of used equipment, and indeed, used equipment brokers play a role in bringing together buyers and sellers of older machines. The standardisation of multi-purpose equipment means that business marketers do not have to be involved in as much detailed selling, service, or negotiation with customers as in the case of single-purpose equipment.

Accessory Equipment

Accessory equipment includes such readily movable items as spot-welders, hand-held drills, and forklift trucks in industrial settings, and personal computers and furniture in office settings.

Accessory equipment and machines are standardised, and their marketing involves routine selling and negotiation. Their relatively lower cost permits most to be considered current-expense items—that is, their cost can be charged as an expense in the purchase period rather than having to be deducted in portions over several years of operation, as is the case for capital equipment purchases. Thus accessory equipment does not require high-level executive approval prior to purchase. High demand and extensive horizontal markets for accessory equipment permit the use of distributors.

Component Parts

Component parts are manufactured items, sub-assemblies, or completely assembled units that are incorporated into the buyer's final product. There are two types of components: standardised and custom. **Standardised components** conform to industry—accepted dimensions and performance specifications. Batteries, tires, and headlights are examples of standardised components in the vehicle market. In other industries, items such as fractional horsepower motors, integrated circuits, ballbearings, and LED (light-emitting diode) displays exhibit the standardisation inherent in this class of component parts. Such products can be held in inventor by distributors and sold "off-the-shelf". **Custom components**, on the other hand, can involve elaborate specifications. Forgings, castings, automotive windshields, and timing motors are examples of custom components designed to the exact specifications of the buyer.

Table 19.2: Industrial Goods Classification

	Standardisation of Grading	Used Across Various industries	Risk of Obsolescence	Required High-Level Approval	Credit Necessary OEM	Emphasis on Specifications	Delivery is important
Capital equipment and investments							
Land, buildings, other companies		M	M	P	M		
Singlepurpose equipment			P	P	P	P	
Multi-purpose equipment	P	P		P	P		
Accessory equipment	P	P					
Component parts							
Standardised	P	P				P	P
Custom			P			P	P
Process materials	P	P				P	P
Maintenance, repair and operating (MRO) supplies	P	P				M	M
Raw materials	P	P				P	P
Services							
Technical				P			
Non-technical		P					p

P = present M = may be present

Because many components wear out with use and need replacement, they have the potential for significant replacement sales. Also, the manufacturer using the components to build a product may buy substantial volumes of components and be a very important customer for the component supplier.

Original Equipment Manufacturer (OEM): The purchaser that uses component parts in some larger, final product is called an original equipment manufacturer (OEM). Thus, in the automotive business, Chrysler is an OEM, and the component parts purchased by Chrysler (windshields, tyres, door handles, and so forth) are referred to as OEM parts. The manufacturers that sell components to Chrysler are called OEM parts suppliers. Component parts suppliers must not only rigorously meet OEM specifications, but also ensure that the quality of the components is consistent and that their delivery is reliable so that the OEM can hold inventories at a low level. Japanese OEMs, such as Toyota, have achieved extremely low inventory costs by demanding that their suppliers provide just-in-time (JIT) deliveries. This indicates that business marketers must use short, direct channels of distribution to capture OEM business.

After-Market: Some components—such as treads in crawler tractors, vehicle batteries, tyres, headlights, fan belts, and air and oil filters—are subject to degradation or wear and present a sizable market, called the after-market or replacement market. Where such components do not lose their identity in the final product, it is possible to establish brands, such as Fram filters, Firestone tyres, and GE headlights. Many component manufacturers vie for a share of the after-market. For any component-say, auto tyres—one of these competitors is the OEM parts supplier. The rest are called **will-fit component suppliers**.

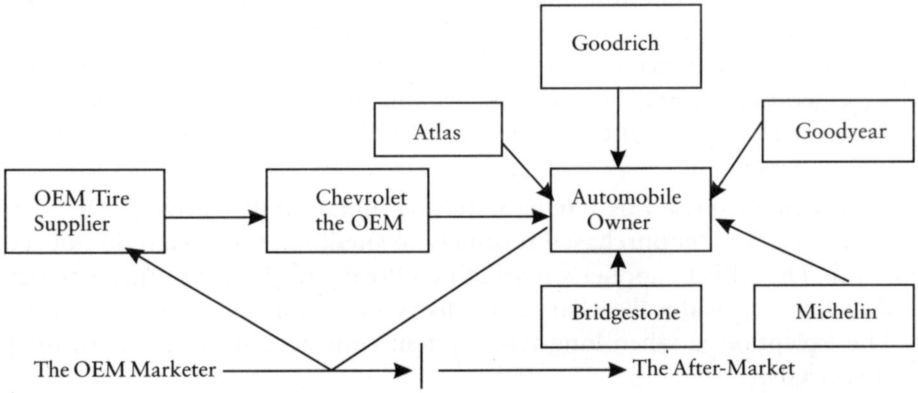

Fig. 19.2: The Component Business for Automobile Tyres

The implications of the after-market can be important to the industrial marketer. *First*, the user of a $20,000 product that requires a replacement component will be relatively insensitive to price. The after-market, therefore, can be quite lucrative. *Second*, when it comes time to replace a degraded component, a significant proportion of OEM product owners feel more confident when they purchase the OEM part rather than a will-fit part. *Third*, the existence of several competitors hotly contesting after-market business suggests that the part manufacturing firm that is the designated OEM supplier will have a distinctive competitive advantage over all of the will-fit part suppliers. *Fourth*, potential component suppliers will be willing to yield price concessions to the OEM, not only to obtain the substantial production-run order of the OEM, but also to win the follow-on business of the more profitable (per unit) after-market. *Fifth,* industrial marketers in the after-market all use a pull strategy in advertising their components—that is, they promote their products to final OEM product owners, who in turn place a demand for these products on the suppliers, thus 'pulling' the product down through the marketing channel. For example, the tyre manufacturers in Table 19.4 all advertise directly to consumers. *Finally*, such advertising also may help influence the OEM in the choice of which component manufacturer to select as the OEM parts supplier.

Process Materials

Process materials are manufacturing materials that tend to lose their identity and may even be indistinguishable in the final product. Examples of process materials are sheet metals, textiles, cement, chemicals, and electrical and electronic circuit wiring. Process materials that are indistinguishable in the final product include the additives used in lubricants, fuels, and antifreezes; the filler and other ingredients in pharmaceutical pills; and the ingredients in cake mixes. Process materials usually are standardised or graded and are sold by specification. The replacement market for process materials is not substantial. The business marketer may have to provide some technical assistance to customers, finds price competition keen because competing suppliers are readily available, and must provide reliable delivery because the customer's production is dependent on availability of materials.

Maintenance, Repair and Operating (MRO) Supplies

Maintenance, repair and operating (MRO) supplies are used to facilitate operation of the organisation but do not become part of the final product in the way that component parts and process materials do. Maintenance and repair items include cleaning agents and tools, paints, and light bulbs. Operating supplies include such items as lubricants and coolants for factory machinery, heating fuels, gasoline for company vehicles, and office supplies, such as envelopes and reproduction papers.

These items are characterised as having extensive horizontal relatively low cost, current-expense items. They are usually purchased routinely in small quantities and do not require high executive approval. The MRO supplier's marketing efforts are similar to those associated with consumer products and typically the channel of distribution for MRO goods is relatively long and indirect. The exception is when long-term system contracts are negotiated, for perhaps a year's anticipated needs.

Raw Materials

Raw materials are the products of the fishing, lumber, hunting, aqua-cultural, agricultural (farming, livestock), and extractive (petroleum, gas, and mining) industries. Sources of raw materials tend to be geographically concentrated—for example, industrial diamonds are found chiefly in South Africa; oil in Texas, Alberta, and the Arab States; bauxite in Guiana; nickel in Northern Ontario; and cotton in the Southern United States. Sixty per cent of the world's rhodium comes from South Africa, 20 per cent from the former Soviet Union (now the Commonwealth of Independent States), and 10 per cent from Canada.

In contrast, less geographic concentration is exhibited by meat rendering. This industry recycles a wide variety of livestock, poultry, and fish by-products into commercial products, such as tallow and meal. Tallow is used in the production of soaps, cosmetics and paints. Meal is used primarily in animal feed, pet foods, and fertilizer.

Swings in raw materials supplies can have a severe influence on their prices. For example, rhodium is used extensively in automotive catalytic converters to reduce the nitrous oxide in exhaust fumes, and to a lesser extent in chemicals, electronics, and glass. In a period of six months, the price of rhodium climbed from $1,746 an ounce in December 1989 to $3,425 an ounce on June 27, 1990. One week later, it had skyrocketed to $7,000 an ounce. Industrial users scrambled to seek substitutes for rhodium, ran their inventories down to critical low levels, and announced increases in the prices of products using rhodium.

Because of volatility of supply and sometimes extreme price fluctuations, raw materials markets may exhibit vertical integration. That is, companies buy the firms that supply raw materials, thus providing an assured source of supply and a more predictable acquisition price. The large Canadian steel manufacturer Stelco owns iron ore mines, operates pelleting plants at the mine sites, and ships the concentrated iron pellets to its Hamilton, Ontario steel-making furnaces in unit trains. This vertical integration not only assures stability in raw materials supplies and prices, but also provides economies in transportation.

In non-integrated industries (industries with little vertical integration, such as beef production and apple growing), raw materials are graded or otherwise specified by government or the supplying industry. Many raw materials can then be marketed through brokers.

Business Services

Business services are the fastest-growing segment in industrialized nations. In 1985 the share of services in the gross domestic product (GDP) of developed market economies averaged 61 per cent, compared with 55 per cent in 1965. Business services may be *technical*, such as computer repair contracts, or *non-technical*, such as janitorial service. Non-technical services usually can be sold across horizontal markets. Typically, the reliability of delivery of the service is important.

Business services are often purchased from sources outside of the organisation because they can be performed more quickly, more reliably, or more inexpensively by specialists who make the service their full-time activity. The buying organisation also may avoid investment in equipment and supplies that are necessary to perform the service. For example, non-destructive testing of metal parts can be accomplished with nuclear bombardment from the port of a nuclear reactor, but no industrial manufacturer would acquire a nuclear reactor to test a few hundred (or even a few thousand) pieces a year.

If the service rendered is highly technical in nature, the buying organisation can "rent" expertise, rather than hiring and underutilising its own full-time expert. Thus an organisation may purchase the services of a patent attorney, a marketing research consultant, or an advertising agency from time to time, or even a litigation lawyer when circumstances so warrant.

Even a non-technical service, such as janitorial work, can involve higher levels of technology than one would expect. Fifteen thousand employees of Service Master Co. of

Downers Grove, Illinois, provide contract housekeeping and plant maintenance to industrial plants, healthcare facilities, and educational institutions. The firm achieves high efficiency through extensive employee training and research and development on cleaning chemicals and equipment. For example, Service Master devised a battery-operated, cordless vacuum cleaner that permits the company's housekeepers to vacuum twice as fast as they could with conventional equipment.

As a business "product," services are treated as a current-expense item. Nevertheless, their purchase may be negotiated at fairly high executive levels in the buying organisation, particularly if union jobs may be replaced by the externally purchased service.

Because services are intangible, it is important to focus the marketing effort on managing the personal relationships between service personnel and contact people within customer organisations. Research indicates that although business customers have few problems conceptualising the benefits of a new service, they do have difficulty in evaluating the quality of service. Providing the customer with evidence relating to the intangible (and often invisible) services can be helpful in this regard. Thus, whenever possible, the business marketer should create tangible reminders that the service has been performed. For example, after applying fertilizer or insecticide, a landscaping service might stick a small notice in the lawn indicating the type of treatment and the date before leaving the work site. The key point is that business marketers should strive to communicate to customers the quality of the service they provide.

DIFFERENCES BETWEEN STRATEGIC INDUSTRIAL MARKETING AND CONSUMER MARKETING

Some marketers contend that 'marketing is marketing', no matter where or by whom products and services are bought and sold. To the extent that the marketing concept is incorporated into the strategy and tactics of the organisation, this is true. However, many others, including the authors of this text, contend that business marketing differs so substantively that it deserves special attention. In some cases the differences are a matter of degree or emphasis. Yet other aspects of business marketing are unique.

This section examines differences between business marketing and consumer marketing with respect to market structure, marketing philosophy, buyer behaviour, purchasing decisions, marketing research, product/service mix, promotion, distribution mix, and price mix.

Market Structure

Market structure refers to the characteristics used to describe the group of organisations that buy the products and services of an industrial marketer. These factors include competition, demand, price elasticity of demand, market and buyer size, and location of the market.

Competition. Industrial markets have fewer sellers and decidedly fewer buyers in any market segment than do consumer markets. Competition in industrial markets tends to be more oligopolistic (fewer sellers and many buyers), whereas consumer markets are more monopolistic (many buyers and sellers, and differentiation among competing products).

Demand. Whereas, consumers initiate a direct demand with their purchases, tile demand for industrial products or services depends on the level of activity that the buying organisation (the business marketer's customer) can generate in its own markets. Thus business demand is *derived* (second or third hand, or more). This derived demand would not exist if the customer organisation, in turn, could not find customers or clients for its own products or services.

Demand Levels. The organisational buyer may use a piece of production equipment to produce 10,000 units per year. Thus, a second machine is required only if sales are expected to exceed 10,000 units. As a result, there is no direct one-to-one relationship between the customer's (for example, a retailer's) sales fluctuations and the business marketer's sales. This accentuates the swings in derived demand, making sales to business buyers far more volatile than changes of demand experienced in consumer markets by a retailer.

Reverse Elasticity. When organisational buyers see prices start to decline, they may postpone buying in the expectation of obtaining an even lower price later. The opposite holds if the organisational buyer anticipates continuing price increases. In this case, when prices begin to rise, more volume than is immediately needed is purchased to avoid paying even higher prices later. Such **reverse price elasticity of demand** is infrequent in consumer markets.

Table 19.3: Differences between Strategic Industrial Marketing and Consumer Marketing

	Characteristic	Industrial Marketing	Consumer Marketing
Market	Competition	Oligopolistic	Monopolistic
Structure	Demand	Derived	Direct
	Demand levels	More volatile	Less volatile
	Reverse elasticity	Frequent	Infrequent
	Total market size	Larger	Smaller
	Size of buying unit	Group	Individual
	Market geography	Concentrated	Diffuse
Marketing	Market segmentation	Emporographics	Demographics
Philosophy	Investment requirements	Strategic	Tactical
	Market perspective	Global	Regional/national
	Tactical marketing emphasis	Profit performance	Market share
	Innovation	Technology-push	Demand-pull
	Buyer/seller interaction	Relationship	Transactional
	Reciprocity	Frequent	Rare
	Key accounts	Important	Non-existent
	Customer education	Strong	Weak
Buyer	Customer/prospect mix	Small	Large
Behaviour	Order size and frequency	Large, infrequent	Small, frequent
	Purchasing motives and skills	Rational, professional	Emotional, self-gratifying
	Contractual penalties	Common	Never
	Buying power	Strong	Weak
	Vendor loyalty	Strong	Weak
	Purchase involvement	Greater	Smaller
Purchasing Decision	Decisions-making process	Complex, lengthy	Simple, short
	Accounting/tax considerations	important	Unimportant
	Purchase risk	Very high	Low

(Contd.)

Marketing Research	Orientation	Strategic	Tactical
	Research approach	Empirical	Inferential
	Questionnaire terminology	Technical	Non-technical
	Precision of data	Rough estimates	Statistical precision
	Costs of projects	Low	High
Product/ Service Mix	Product life cycle	Shorter	Longer
	Product specification	Customised	Standardised
	Branding	Corporate family	Individual product
	Purchase timing	Requirement planning	Immediate use
	Degree of fabrication	Value-adding stages required	Mostly finished goods
	Type of packaging	Protective	Promotional
	Services	Much more, pre- and post-transactional	Less, point-of-purchase
	Equipment compatibility	Good	Poor
	Consistency of quality	Critical	Not Vital
	Industrial design	Less frequent	More frequent
	Systems selling	More frequent	Less frequent
Promotion	Promotional emphasis	Personal selling	Mass advertising
	Promotional objectives	Preparing for sales call	Positioning product and firm
	Promotional themes	Rational, factual	Fanciful, imaginative
	Role of salesperson	Problem solving	Persuasion
	Sales promotion tools	Specification sheets, catalogs, direct mail, trade shows	Coupons, samples, point-of-purchase displays
Distribution Mix	Channel length	Short, direct	Long, indirect
	Channel complexity	Complex	Simple
	Product knowledge	Strong	Weak
	Channel coverage	Direct, exclusive	Intensive, selective
	Delivery reliability	Crucial	Not critical
Price	Competitive bidding	Common	Rare
	Price negotiation	Common	Rare
	Leasing	Common	Rare
	Product life cycle costs and benefits	Important	Usually ignored
	Discount structures	Complex	Straightforward
	Promotional pricing	Seldom used	Frequently used

Total Market Size. Industrial markets include not only the various early, value adding stages of manufacturing and distributing consumer goods, but also the sales of business goods and services to manufacturing, processing, commercial, institutional, and government organisations. As a result, the business market is significantly larger—indeed, four times larger—than the consumer market.

Size of Buying Unit. The organisational buying unit—often called central buying unit (CBU), decision-making unit (DMU), multiple buying influence (MBI), or buying centre—usually involves several individuals. One reason is that various departments of an organisation are affected by the purchase. For example, in the factory, the purchase of certain machinery may affect output quality (quality control department), the plant manager's budget, machinist productivity (the union), the acquisition of funds (finance department), the engineering department, and a purchasing agent. Another reason is that many minds often can make a better decision. A third point of view is that group membership removes the decision-making responsibility from any single individual. This can be quite useful if the decision turns out to be a poor one. For the business marketer, the group of people involved in the purchasing decision represent a veritable "who's who" in the buying organisation. Each individual imposes different perspectives, expectations, and requirements on the purchase. In contrast, the consumer purchase usually involves an individual or, at most, one or two family members.

Market Geography. Think of oil, and Texas, Alberta, and Iran come to mind. Similarly, cutlery manufacturing suggests Sheffield, England, and Toledo, Spain. Pittsburgh, Pennsylvania, and Hamilton, Ontario, are associated with steel production. The Detroit/Windsor and Oakville, Ontario, areas are North American automobile manufacturing centres. Birmingham and Coventry are centers of British motor vehicle production. Semi-conductors and integrated circuit manufacturers have congregated in "Silicon Valley" near San Francisco, around Route 128 near Boston, and in "Silicon Valley North", near Ottawa. In industry after industry, business marketers tend to concentrate geographically because of the availability of natural resources or of a skilled work force, the distribution advantages, or the desire to be close to customers. Thus, business markets tend to be geographically concentrated, and business marketers travel significant distances from one cluster of customers to another. Consumer markets are more diffuse, generally spread out according to population location.

Marketing Philosophy

The concepts or philosophies of strategic industrial marketing differ substantially from those of consumer marketing. One basic difference we have already mentioned is that consumer goods are usually classified according to how they are purchased (convenience, shopping, speciality, unsought), and industrial goods are categorised according to their use or buying situation (task) or degree of customisation. Other significant differences occur in the areas of market segmentation, investment requirements, market perspective, tactical marketing emphasis, innovation, buyer/seller interaction, reciprocity, key accounts, and customer education.

Market Segmentation. Consumer marketers use demographics (age, income, location) and socio-psychological dimensions (attitudes, preferences, personality, lifestyle) to segment their markets. Industrial marketers, on the other hand, use **emporographics** (industry, end market served, level of technology, ownership), SIC (Standard Industrial Classification) codes, and characteristics of the buying units (number of influences, ad hoc *versus* standing committees, centralised *versus* decentralised, annual volume of purchase) to segment their markets.

Investment Requirements. Business marketers tend to have higher strategic investments—that is, investments in capital equipment and research and development (R&D). For example, it takes $100 million to build a silicon fabrication line, and a computer chip manufacturer must have several of them to be competitive. Consumer marketer's investments are more tactical—

that is, directed more toward marketing activities (researching their huge customer base and promoting to mass markets).

Market Perspective. Consumer marketers typically seek regional or national markets because their products are created to appeal to local tastes and they can find sufficient sales volumes at home. Business goods and services are less dependent on regional tastes and preferences. Furthermore, their specialized technologies and limited applications often require that customers be sought abroad to achieve economic production volumes and to justify high R&D costs and capital investments. Even a country with a large production in, for example, electronic equipment, may import as much as it exports. Strategic industrial marketing must, therefore, have a more global perspective of markets, in terms of both customers and competitors.

Tactical Marketing Emphasis. Most consumer marketers are concerned with seeking market share and sales volumes (frequently hoping for future profit as a result). Business marketers are more likely to have a sizable share of highly segmented, smaller, specialised markets, resulting in more restricted sales volumes. Thus, business marketers tend to focus on profit performance and profit improvement in the short run.

Innovation. In consumer markets, innovation involves greater emphasis on style and incremental changes to products that can justify model changes. Innovation tends to be more of a demand-pull type (new products are developed as a result of assessment of consumer needs and wants). In contrast, innovation in business markets is characterised by R&D technological-push and radical-breakthrough developments that may revolutionise entire industries. An example is the creation of the transistor, which came from Bell Labs' research efforts and quickly replaced vacuum tubes in the electronics industry. No amount of identifying unsatisfied consumer needs could have led to the development of the transistor.

Buyer/Seller Interaction. Because industrial marketers deal with a smaller number of customers, frequently on a face-to-face basis, they are more sensitive and responsive to their customers' requirements. In that sense, industrial marketers are far more customer oriented than are consumer marketers. Consumer marketers' relations with customers usually are distanced by long, indirect channels of distribution and are reduced to a mass of transactions made at 'arm's length'. Organisational buyers and sellers usually enter stable, long-term relationships in which each depends on the other for continuing business success. Thus, strong loyalty is developed between buyer and seller in organisational markets.

Reciprocity. Frequently in business markets, two organisations could be buyers of each other's products or services. For example, an automobile manufacturer requires computer word processors, and a computer manufacturer requires automobiles for its sales force. In such a situation, reciprocity may be practised: "I'll buy from you if you buy from me." Business marketers frequently use reciprocity as a tactic to win sales in the business market. This situation rarely is possible in the consumer market.

Key Accounts. Within the customer base of a industrial marketer there usually are from a dozen to as many as a hundred customer firms that the marketer designates as key accounts. These are firms whose business is so important that its loss could significantly impair the marketer's sales volume, profitability, or corporate image. Clearly, the marketer must maintain close contact with these important customers to maintain its supplier status. No similar situation exists in consumer markets.

Customer Education. For many industrial marketers, customer education is an important part of the marketing strategy. IBM gained a successful **niche** in the mainframe computer market by sending its representatives to spend periods of months, even years, in the customer's company, working side by side with the customer's staff to write and run programmes and help them learn how to use IBM equipment. Typically, business and industrial equipment has more complete instruction manuals, specification sheets, and repair and maintenance books than does consumer equipment.

QUESTIONS FOR DISCUSSION

1. Why is it important to avoid the term consumer when referring to organisational buyers?
2. Can a product be both a consumer and a industrial product simultaneously? If it is physically the identical' product, why would it be important to classify it as either a 'business' or a 'consumer' product?
3. Why is the consumer goods classification system of little use to business marketers?
4. Why are products such as icecream, nylon stockings, and fishing rods considered 'industrial' products when they are marketed to retail stores? What are the implications of classifying them in this manner?
5. Name three examples of systems contracts in the consumer market. How do they differ from systems contracts in industrial markets?
6. Organisational buyers are typified as being more rational than consumers. Describe three situations in which industrial buyers may appear to be behaving in a more emotional way.
7. Why is the term strategic industrial marketing falling from favour and being replaced by the term *strategic industrial marketing*?
8. Why do you think 2 per cent of college marketing students have studied strategic industrial marketing?

STRATEGIC MARKETING ORGANISATION

20

INTRODUCTION

Marketing organisation is a group of people working together to achieve the objective of sales—which is to capture a certain share of market while satisfying the customer. It undertakes the effective marketing of products produced by the undertaking or even products purchased for resale. It ensures timely distribution of products to the customers in an economical and efficient manner. It establishes restructuring between the customers and the organisation on terms that are both acceptable to the buyer and the seller.

A marketing organisation is both an orienting point for cooperative endeavour and a structure of human relationships. It is a group of individuals striving jointly to reach qualitative and quantitative objectives and bearing formal and informal relations to one another. Implicit in the concept of a marketing organisation is the notion that individual members cooperate to attain ends. The marketing organisation is not an end in itself but rather the vehicle by which individuals achieve given ends. Existence of a marketing organisation implies the existence of patterns of relationships among subgroups and individuals established for purposes of facilitating accomplishment of the group's aim.

Objectives

- A higher market share
- High growth opportunities
- Increased ability to compete in global markets
- Product innovation
- Recognition as a leader in technology
- Better customer services
- Good reputation with customers
- Low cost compared with competitors
- High quality goods and services
- Brand image and loyalty
- Wider profit margins

Goals

1. Sales volume goals,
2. Financial goals,
3. Activities goals, and
4. Combination of the above goals.

Long Term Planning

1. Assessing what has been done in the past.
2. Sizing up of the critically evaluated strengths.
3. Organisational objective fixation.
4. Forecasting.
5. Evaluating the performance of strategic activities.
6. Implementing strategies in the long-range plan, and bridging the gap.
7. Developing the time span for the long-range plan.

The Marketing Planning Appraisal Process

— External appraisal
— Internal appraisal
— SWOT analysis
— Gap analysis
— Forecasting
(a) Organisation-related factors:
— Organisation's structure
— Organisation's size
— Organisation's age
— Organisation's complexity
— Nature of business
— Nature of product and services
(b) Strategy-related factors:
— Experience in the formulation of strategies
— Education level
— Motivation level
— Styles of working
— Ability to work hard
— Team spirit
— Power equations.

Gap Analysis

1. Creative solution for closing the gap must be developed.
2. The desired future must be redefined with focus on those aspects of business objectives likely to be accomplished and those will have the most significant impact.
3. Conversion of long-range plans into short-range functional plans.
4. Budgetary control.
5. Updating and reconsideration of the plan as required.
6. Assignment of tasks of individuals.

SWOT Analysis

Strengths	Weaknesses	Opportunities	Threats
– Resources	– Deficiencies in resources, skills and capabilities	– Favourable situation	– Unfavourable situation
– Relative competitive advantages	– Financial resources	– Identification of a new market segment	– Entry of new competitors
– Image	– Sources of outfit	– Changes in competitive or regulatory circumstances	– Slow market growth
– Infrastructure	– Inadequate measures viewed against changes in product/market scope	– Technological changes	– Major technological changes
– Market leadership			– Appearances of substitute products

Resources

- Information
- Infrastructure (Road Development, Airlines, Telecoms, etc.)
- H.R. (Gallop)
- Financial resources
- Technology
- Experiences/Skills Sets
- Management system
- Organisation structure and culture.

Opportunities

- New Product
- New Market
- New Technology
- Competition/Competitors
- Business Growth.

Knowledge/Skills

- Quality Standards
- Educational Background
- Marketing Experiences
- R&D
- Product Innovations
- Demand Forecasting.

PRINCIPLES OF DESIGNING AN ORGANISATION

Organisation refers to any system, body or group of people, comprising various subsystems or parts which are interrelated and or interdependent on each other. An organisation may be informal or formal. An informal organisation has no specific objective to achieve. A formal organisation has a specific objectives to achieve and this is the very reason for the organisation's existence. Objectives may relate to making profit or there may be no consideration of profit whatsoever. Thus, when we refer to an organisation it can mean a firm or company involved in business, a non-business organisation such as university, hospital, a social organisation such as club, charitable trust, or a government agency.

Irrespective of the nature of an organisation, the principles involved in its design are the same. These are:

Specialisation: The division of labour on the basis of which a particular type (or set) of activity is differentiated from another. Jobs are assigned to individual on the basis of their specialization.

Departmentalisation: The integration of differentiated (or specialized) activities and grouping of individuals into departments, divisions, etc.

Standardisation: The existence of procedures and systems, which helps integrate the entire organisation.

Formalisation: The extent to which all procedures, systems and policies are written, so that the organisation becomes independent of the person(s) who founded it and acquires a life-span substantially longer than any one individual.

Centralisation: The level at which authority for decision-making is concentrated. It involves designing formal reporting relationships and information systems, leading to hierarchical levels and spans of control.

Evaluation: Providing systems for appraisal and compensation.

Structure: The total configuration or arrangement of individuals, department, reporting relationships, information flows, span of control, all of which give the organisation its specific 'shape'.

Given these basic principles, you have many kinds of organisation structures to choose from. In making the choice, you must evaluate the alternative structures on the basis of:

- Facilitating achieving of objectives and accomplishment of tasks.
- Managerial control, and
- Cost.

WHAT IS A MARKETING ORGANISATION?

A marketing organisation bridges the gap between the market and the productive capacity of the firm. If market changes by size, also trends, competition or other environmental factors, sales functions have to be adjusted. The role of an organisation can be compared to the skeleton of the human body. It provides a framework within which functions take place. Whereas, the skeletal function is the same for all human beings it varies between firms. This is because all enterprises have their own objectives, resources and corporate plans to achieve those objectives.

The Changing Role of Marketing Organisation

Role of the marketing function and its place in the overall organisation has been changing overtime. From a situation where marketing was treated as a selling arm of the factory, it has come a full circle where marketing 'dictates' what is to be produced. With the passage of time, not only has the organisation of the marketing activity undergone many changes but its growing importance has influenced the entire concept of viewing a business. More and more firms are now adopting the 'marketing orientation', i.e. the customer and his needs form the nucleus of all the activities of the firm. All the activities and tasks are organised around the customer.

The firm with marketing orientation has come into being after passing through many distinct phases. These are described below:

Simple sales department: The three most basic functions needed for every business are those of production, finance and marketing. Towards the end of the nineteenth century and during the early twentieth, production was considered to be of prime importance and was given all attention. Most firms had only a sales staff headed by a sales manager and no marketing activity. The sales function was treated as an adjunct to the production whose responsibility was only to sell, whatever the factory produced.

Sales department with some marketing function: As the firm expanded its operations it found that merely selling what the factory produced was not enough to sustain the growth momentum. A firm aspiring for growth and leadership must match its production to customer needs. Hence the need for some marketing research and new product development. At this stage, the selling department began to take on some semblance of a marketing department, and apart from marketing research and new product development, it also undertook some promotional and advertising activity.

Separate marketing department: This is a stage when the need for the complete range of marketing functions is felt and a full-fledged marketing department is established. The sales activity will continues to dominate but as compared to other activities, its importance is reduced. Sales and marketing may continue to be organised as two separate departments and there may be frequent clashes between the two. The sales department may feel that its existence is being threatened by the marketing department which has grand designs for its takeover. The marketing department, in its place may feel that the sales people are unnecessarily putting obstacles in the way of integrating all the marketing activities, including sales. The root cause of all such conflicts is the lack of understanding that sales is a part and parcel of marketing and needs the support of other departments to be truly effective.

Integrated marketing department: This is the stage where the sales and marketing are integrated and organised into a single department. The department is headed by a marketing director with the sales manager reporting to him. The other activities such as marketing research, promotion and advertising, marketing information, customer service and new product development are also organised in this department under the marketing director. Figure 20.1 depicts an integrated marketing organisation.

Marketing Oriented Organisation: A marketing oriented organisation is one which is guided by customer needs. Such an organisation obviously needs to be flexible to accommodate customers changing tastes and habits and accordingly modify its products or develop new products.

The distinctive characteristic of a marketing oriented organisation is that marketing is the front ranking department showing the direction for future growth. The organisation starts by

Figure 20.1: Integrated Marketing Department

identifying customer needs and products goods that satisfy these needs. Marketing research is conducted on a continuous basis to monitor technological innovation regarding the product, customers' changing preferences and giving feedback to the research and development cell and production department to work on new ideas. Marketing shows the way and production department follows.

This general pattern of evolution of a marketing-oriented organisation usually accompanies the process of economic development. In industrially developed economies, as compared to less developed and developing economies, customers are relatively more knowledgeable and sophisticated, the pace of technological change is very fast and the market is characterized by a high mortality rate of products and product ideas. All these factors work to exert great pressure on the firms to be marketing-oriented, since what sells like hot cakes today may be a total flop tomorrow.

As compared to the less developed economies, you would find more marketing-oriented firms in the developed economies. But there are always exceptions to this general pattern and even in developed economies you can find firms in which the marketing organisation is at an early stage of evolution. Or you may find that some divisions have fully integrated marketing organisation, but the firm as a whole is not marketing-oriented.

The objective of tracing the evolution of the marketing organisation is to highlight the importance of marketing to every firm. As we have seen with increased economic development the importance of marketing has also been growing. No firm can afford to be without a marketing orientation. No matter what the nature of the product, the ultimate success of every business firm is determined not in the laboratory, but in the market place. And to succeed in the market place, it is most critical that you have a marketing organisation which facilitates the process of marketing and supports the achievement of objectives.

Considerations Involved in Designing the Marketing Organisation

1. Statement of Objective and Goals of the Firm

The first consideration in designing the marketing organisation is the firm's marketing objectives and goals. These objectives may pertain to desired market share, desired sales and/or profit levels, desired position in the industry and/or market, desired customer image and competitive posture. Depending upon the stated objectives, a suitable organisation would have to be designed which would facilitate achievement of the objectives. For instances, a firm which strives to have the largest market share would need a different type of organisation than one whose objective is to have the highest quality products.

2. Nature of the Product/Line of Activity

The nature of product with which the firm is dealing would be the second consideration in organising the marketing set up. To sell soap, toothpaste, textile, tea, etc. no special skill or training pertaining to the nature of the products is required. These are products which are well understood and comprehended by everyone. The firm dealing in such products need not look for sales people with specialized knowledge when organising its marketing set-up. On the other hand, products such as air conditioners, refrigerators, industrial machines, cooling the other hand, products such as air conditioners, refrigerators, industrial machines cooling towers, anti-pollution plants and computers require that the marketing people have at least a functional knowledge about the equipment before attempting to market them. You require not only trained people but also need to organise a supporting set up wherein you can train your customers about the proper usage of the equipment and also an after sales service department to take care of product complaints. In case of products such as computer, you may need to provide technical guidance to the customer about which software packages to purchase and how to constantly upgrade the computer by compatible accessories.

Finally, there is the category of specially products such as ethical drugs and medicines, medical and scientific equipment. In case of such products you need thorough knowledge about the product and sometimes even a formal educational degree before you can market them. Drug stores and chemists cannot be licensed to sell before they have at least one qualified chemist in their employment. Ethical drugs (those which can be bought only on a doctors prescription) are directly promoted to doctors through salesmen who are known as medical representatives. Reputed pharmaceutical firms usually employ only science graduates for this job, since it requires a basic understanding of the composition of the medicine, its possible reactions and side effects and an ability to tackle queries on the product from knowledgeable doctors.

Thus, depending on the kind of product, which you are marketing, you need to induct suitably educated and trained salesman. If finding the right people is difficult, you can provide in-house training to help people acquire the knowledge and skill necessary for marketing your product. This kind of in-house training is provided by most airlines and hotels to their people before they actually go on to the job. Besides training facilities, the marketing organisation may need a separate cell for customer servicing, customer education and handling customer complaints.

The type of marketing organisation that you choose would also be influenced by the number of products that you are marketing. A firm marketing readymade children's garments may choose to segregate its range of exclusive premium price wear from the medium-priced range and organise two separate marketing teams as the two ranges are marketed to different sets of retail outlets. But since the basic products in both the price-ranges is the same, the firm can as well have a common marketing organisation catering to both categories of retail outlets.

Generally speaking, firms with highly diversified range of products need separate marketing organisations to effectively market each of them. In deciding whether you need separate marketing organisations or a common one, you would consider not only the similarities in the nature of product, but also similarities in the type of customer need and customer served, and similarity in the marketing channel.

3. Areas of Operation

The number of markets that a firm caters to, and the location of these markets is another factor which influences the decision regarding the type of marketing organisation that a firm should adopt. If there are many markets which are located at great distance from one another, a firm may have no choice but to have separate marketing organisations for different geographical markets. The greater the difference in individual markets in terms of customer tastes and habits, the greater is the need for a separate, flexible, autonomous marketing organisation at the local market level. This kind of autonomy in marketing organisation can be observed in the local operation of multinational companies which have subsidiaries in many countries of the world. The corporate headquarter may provide only the basic operating guidelines and specify the expected results, allowing the remaining operations to be organised according to the requirements of each market. These requirements may include modifying the products to suit local climate and taste, designing relevant promotional strategy, employing local people and adopting local personal selling techniques.

4. Nature of the Industry

The design and structure of a marketing organisation would vary depending on the nature of industry to which a firm belongs. A firm characterized by fast changing customer preferences (hi-fashion garments) or rapid technological improvements (electronics) needs a marketing organisation which is flexible to adapt to the changing situation. Moreover, the marketing organisation must be so designed that it facilitates active interaction within the related sub-functions which are critical to the marketing success such as sales and marketing research in case of hi-fashion garments, and sales and Research and Development in electronics. The more the interface required with other functions in the firm and sub-functions within the marketing itself, the more the need for a structure which is flexible, loosely organised and permits easy flow of information.

5. Computerisation and Upgradation of Information System

The marketing organisation is also affected by the type of information processing and communication technology used. The advent of computers has led to (a) replacement of humans by machines for information processing; (b) replacement of supervisory managerial cadres which were performing the roles of supervising and controlling, but which can now be done more efficiently by computers; and (c) greater decentralization of decision-making. The result is the progressive removal of many intermediate levels of managements and the evolution towards a flatter structure as shown in Figure 20.2.

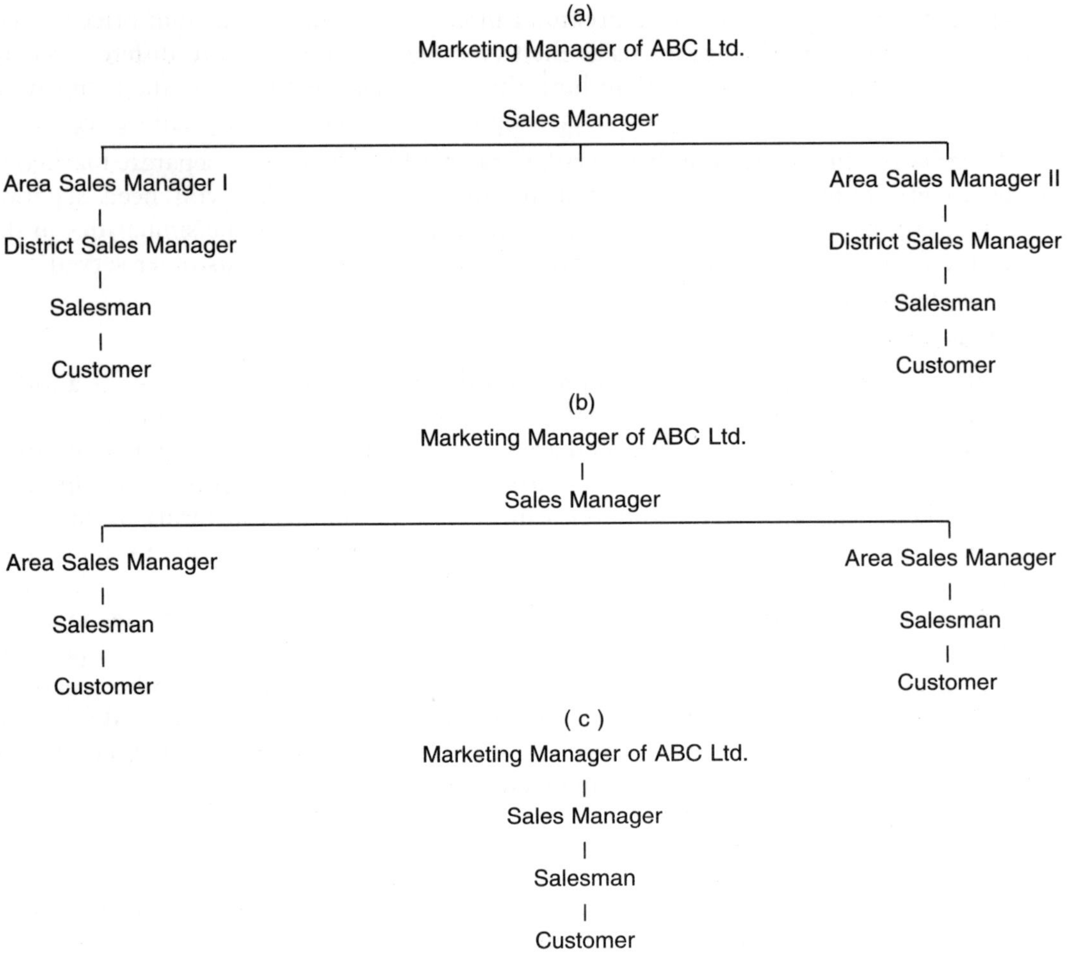

Fig. 20.2: Impact of New Information Technology on Marketing Organisation

6. External Environment and Government Intervention

The composition and character of the marketing organisation is influenced by the environment in which it operates. At the level of the firm, the environment is consisting of social, economic, political, legal and cultural factors. These factors impinge on all operations of the firm, including marketing. In addition specific rules and regulations governing the product category and its marketing affect the marketing organisation. Explicit media advertising, (describing the product and its contents) for alcohol and alcohol based drinks is not permitted in our country, given this restriction, liquor companies necessarily need strong sales organisation which can develop and retain dealers and command prominent shelf display at these dealer outlets. Drugs, cement, fertilizers and certain categories of steel are subject to price control. In such a situation, some firms are able to afford a marketing organisation, while other which are not so efficient and can barely cover their production costs cannot afford it.

Check your Progress

1. Name any three principles of designing an organisation?
2. Name any two considerations involved in designing the marketing organisation.

METHOD OF DESIGNING THE MARKETING ORGANISATION

There are many ways of organising the marketing department. We shall discuss in detail the four basic methods: functional organisation, product management organisation; market centred organisation and matrix organisation. Methods other than these four are either their derivatives or combinations.

Functional Organisation

In the functional organisation, various functions performed as part of the overall marketing function are the basis for organising the marketing set up. Each function is assigned to a specialist who reports to the marketing manager. The most common functions in marketing are:

Sales

Distribution

Advertising and Sales Promotion

Marketing Research

Marketing Information System

Dealer Development

Customer Service

New Product Development

Marketing Planning.

It is possible that in your firm you may be using terms different from these to describe various functions. You will be able to identify the functions according to the terms used here once you have gone through the description of each function. Moreover depending on the nature of product, service or industry to which you belong you may have some functions not described here. For instance, in a bank, public relation would be an important marketing function.

In a small firm, all these functions may not be individually identified and differentiated, even though they are actually performed. All the functions may be handled by just one or two individuals, who are 'jack-of all trades' rather than specialists in any particular function. But as the firm grows in size, it becomes imperative to differentiate and delegate the functions to separate individuals. One man can no longer perform all the functions, and even if he can, he would not have the necessary skill or knowledge for it.

All the functional specialists report to the marketing manager who has overall responsibility for marketing. Depending on the relative importance of each marketing function to the overall effectiveness of the marketing organisation, a function may either be organised separately or clubbed with another function. Further, the organisation of each marketing function within the overall marketing organisations may vary from firm to firm. Figure 20.3 depicts a typical functional marketing organisation. We shall now discuss the various options available for organising each of the marketing functions within the functional marketing organisation.

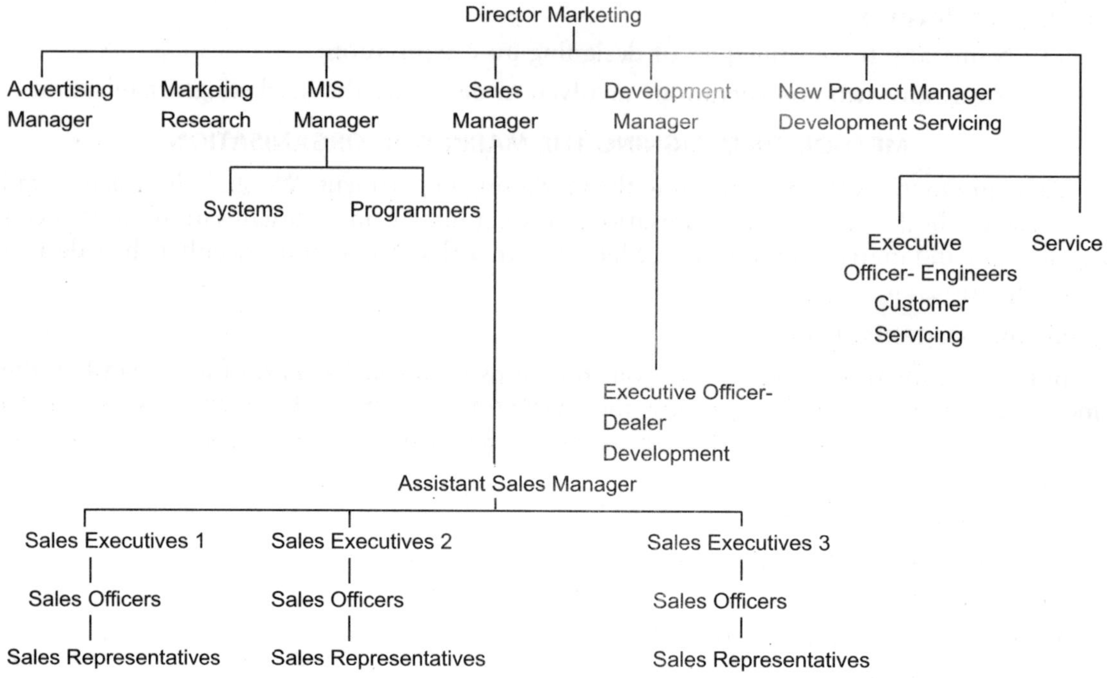

Fig. 20.3: Functional Marketing Organisation

Sales: The sales function is performed by a team of sales people who are responsible for actually selling the product or service. The product may be sold directly to the actual customers and this is known as direct sales. Or else the product may be sold to distributors, wholesalers, retailers or other middlemen, who in turn sell to the actual customers. This is known as indirect selling. A firm may sell either directly or indirectly or use a combination. We shall discuss indirect selling in the following section while here we shall confine ourselves to direct selling through company sale force. There are three basic methods in which the sales force may be organised: geographic division, product division and customer or marketing channel division.

It is wise to have the sales force organised on a geographical basis when the area of sales coverage is very large and there are marked difference in the market and buyer characteristic in each area. The entire market is divided into regions or zones and each region has its own sales force. Figure 20.4 depicts a functional marketing organisation in which the sales force is organised on a geographic basis. Such an organisation implies geographic division of authority and decision-making. This type of sales force organisation is very widely used and is effective when there is a single product or a range of similar products to be marked to many scattered markets.

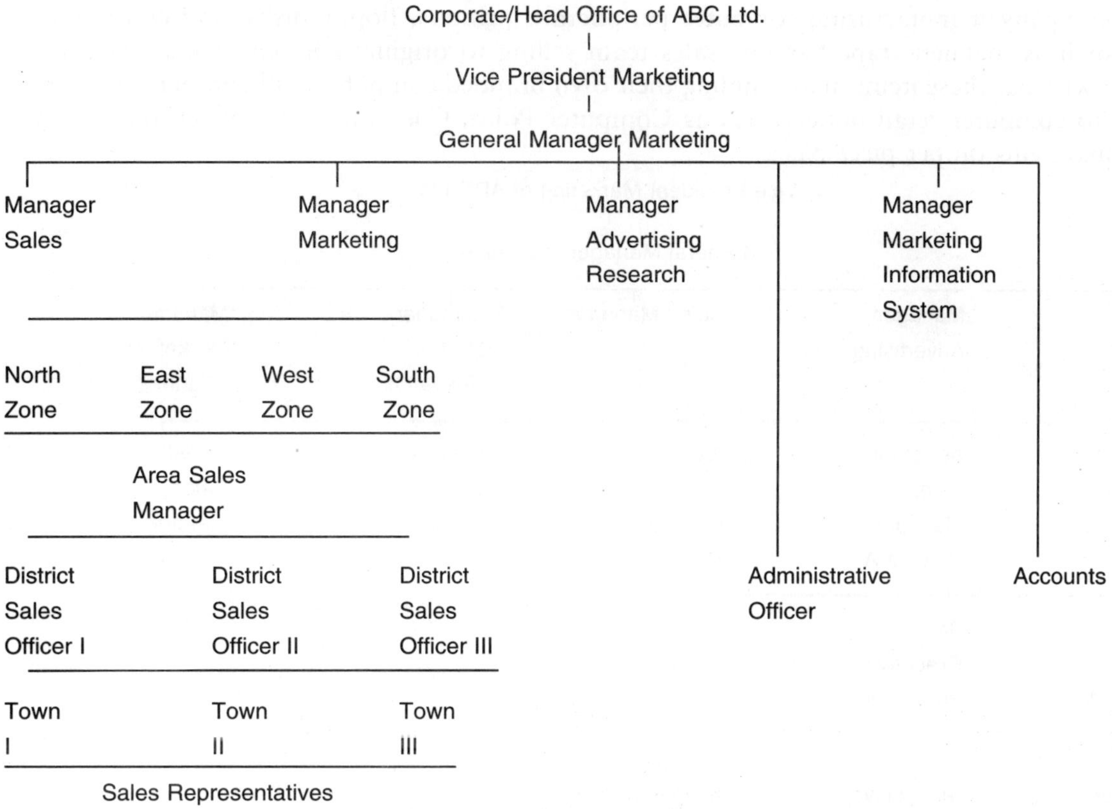

Fig. 20.4: Organisation of Sales Force on Geographic Basis

When a firm has a wide range of products, each significantly different from the other in terms of its physical and/or technical characteristics, the sales force is usually organised around each distinct product or product group. The basis for differentiating the products may be technical process involved or the customer characteristics so that the salesman's specialized knowledge of technology or the customers can be efficient used. Thus, there is a separate sales force for each product (Figure 20.5). Johnson and Johnson Ltd. in India markets a range of baby care products (soap, cream, oil, lotion) and a range of surgical sutures and meshes, the latter marketed by the Ethic division. The two product ranges are marketed by two separate divisions each having its own sales force.

Another basis for organising the sales force is the different customer groups served or the marketing channel used to reach the customers. A company marketing television sets has two distinct sales teams. One team serves the distributors and wholesalers (who in turn sell to the individual customers) while the other team is engaged in selling to institutions such as hotels, schools and universities which buy in large numbers. The company finds it useful to have this distinction because the methods and channels used for selling to these two customer groups are totally different. Many companies also find it useful to have separate sales team to sell to the private sector and to the public sector and government bodies.

A company manufacturing computer peripherals, printers, floppy disks, and consumable items such as magnetic tape has one sales team selling to original equipment manufacturers (OEM) who use these items in assembling their own branded computer, and another sales team selling to computer retail outlets such as Computer Point, Computer City, which retail these individual items on per piece basis.

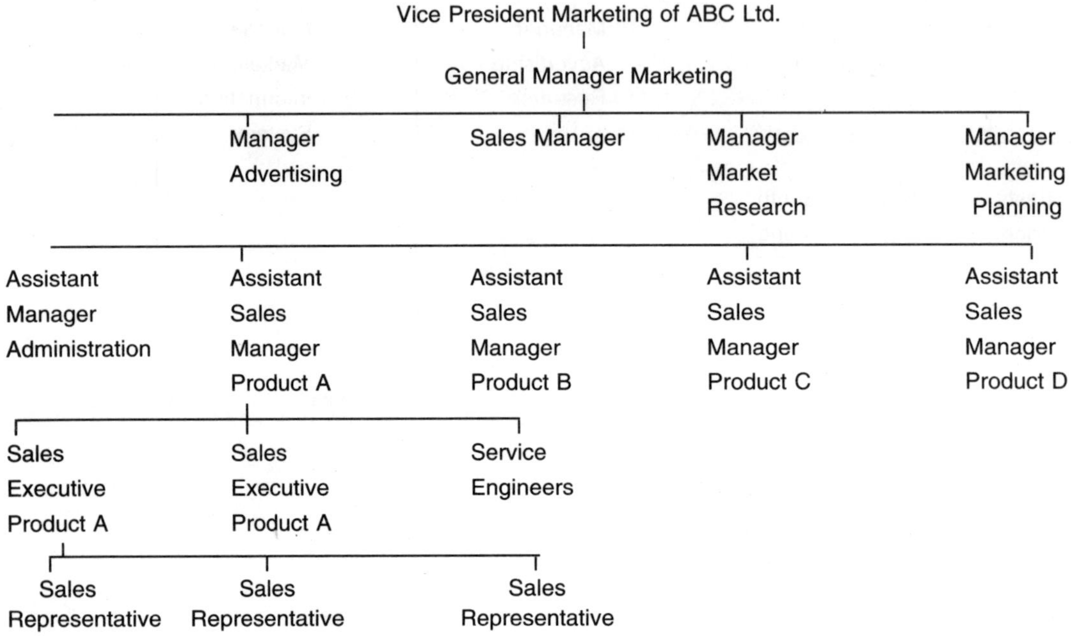

Fig. 20.5: Organisation of Sales Force on Product Basis

Many companies use a combination of above basis for organising the sales force. At the head office level, the sales team may be divided on a product basis, but if the market is very large, the team may be further subdivided on a geographic basis. Thus, there is sales specialization at the product level as well as the market level. Figure 20.6 depicts one such organisational structure.

Distribution: Distribution refers to the physical movement of goods from the factory to the customers. In organising the distribution function, the objective must be to find the least-cost physical distribution method which allows you to service your customers in the most efficient manner.

There are three most common types of physical distribution organisations. The first is where the company has one plant and delivers to a single market. In this case the plant is usually located close to the market, the godown/warehouse is next to the plant and the cost of distribution is relatively low. Examples of this kind can be found in case of perishable foods and confectionaries, such as bread. The company may use its own sales force or distributors who in turn use wholesalers and retailers to reach the actual customers or a combination of both distributors and own sales forces.

In the second type, there are many geographically far-flung markets which are served from one plant. The manufacturer can choose to ship directly to customers in each market, appoint regional or town level distributors, set up own godowns and branches in each important centre or use a combination of any these.

The third case is where there are multiple plants catering to multiple markets. The two problems in this situation are (i) those of minimizing the transportation and the stock carrying costs at the current level of facilities and (ii) the long-term problem of deciding whether the combination of existing godowns and distribution centres is the most cost-effective one.

At your end, you have to take decisions regarding the number and location of godowns, type of transportation to be used, strength and role of sales force. The decision regarding sales force has to be taken in relation to the type of intermediaries available. There are wholesalers, stockists, distributors, commission and freight (C&F) agents, who can act as middlemen for moving your product from your godown to the final customer. The combination of intermediaries varies from company to company, and may also vary within the same company, for each product and each market.

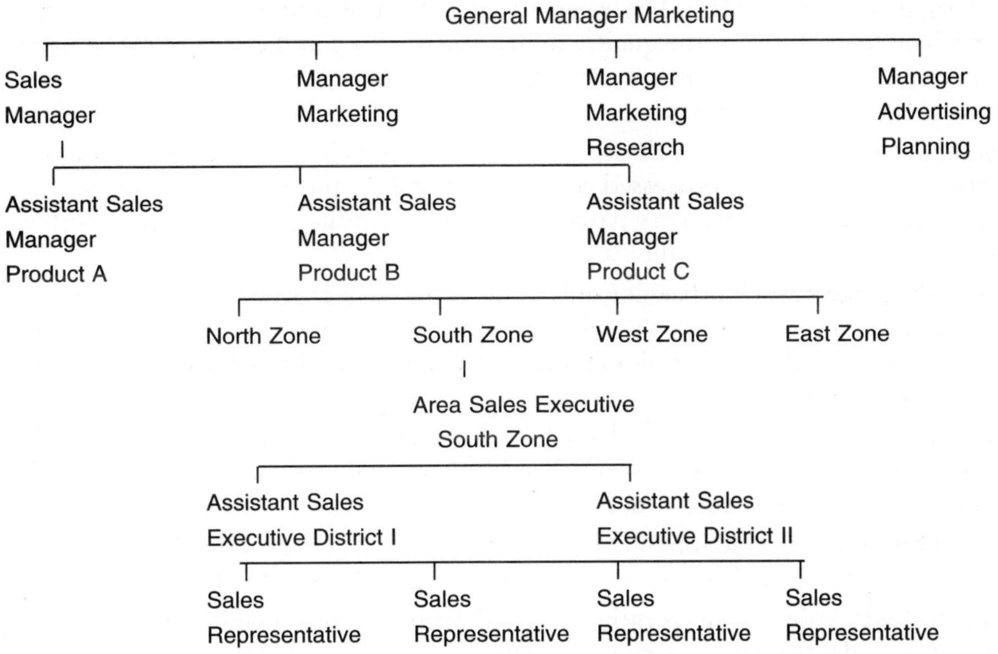

Fig. 20.6: Organisation of Sales Force on Product and Geographical Basis

Advertising and Promotion: There are many objectives for which advertising may be used. Some objectives are long-term and their scope is wide enough to include the entire operations of the firm. Other objectives are short-term and have a limited scope and coverage. Most firms divide their advertising budget into two parts, one part (and often the larger part) is reserved to be used by the head office for achieving long-term or corporate objectives. This part of the budget is used for advertising in national media such as television and magazines such as India Today. Some of the corporate objectives may be building corporate image, creating brand image at the national level, capturing a specified share of the national market. Thus, a large part of the advertising is planned, controlled and executed by the corporate office. The branch offices may be given a certain budget and authority which they can use for advertising in local newspapers, local radio, local hoardings, etc. The branch offices may also have freedom to undertake some local level sales promotion such as providing signboards to selected retail outlets, and holding display contests. This is the most commonly observed pattern of organising the advertising function, but there can be many variations.

Marketing Research: In many companies, marketing research is organised along the same lines as advertising. The major chunk of research activity is centralized at the corporate offices and the branch offices have the freedom to undertake only some local level research. In a country like ours, where most market research organisations are located in the major metropolitan cities, allowing the branch offices located in small towns to initiate local research is rather irrelevant simply because there exist no reputed research organisations in these towns. Thus for all practical purposes, the entire marketing research function is usually organised at the corporate office.

Marketing Information System (MIS): MIS refers to the system of collecting, processing and using information which helps improve the quality of decision-making in the area of marketing. The basic processes are collecting, processing, maintaining and using information. There are three ways in which MIS can be organised.

In the first method, the role of the branch office is restricted to collecting and passing on the required information, which is then processed and maintained at the corporate office. The relevant information, reports and analysis are passed on to the individual branch offices and the rest are maintained in a master file for future use.

In the second method, the branch office not only collects but also processes the information which it has collected. After processing, all the relevant and critical reports are passed on to the corporate office. However, all information files and records, collectively known as the data base are maintained at the head office.

In the third method, all the three tasks of collecting, processing and maintaining information, are decentralised at the branch level. The head office receives regular reports and can requisition any additional information that it requires.

The use of computers and introduction of real time information systems and networking has greatly increased the efficiency of MIS, irrespective of the manner in which it (MIS) is organised.

Customer and Dealer Relations: This is rather a broad-term and may include activities such as after sales service, and development of new customers, markets, and dealers. The specific activities included under this head would vary according to the nature of product and type of distribution channel which the firm has. In terms of organising this function, it is usually decentralized since efficient servicing of the relationship requires proximity to the customer and dealer. But the manner of servicing the customer/dealer may be strictly defined by company policies, guidelines and procedures.

New Product Development: This is probably the most critical function for a company which wants to be in business five, ten and fifteen years from today, and yet it is often the most neglected function. The reason for this is that most companies are organised for today and not for the future. New product development requires vision and foresight and the ability to take risks. It requires an organisation in which new product development is recognised and organised as a separate activity and allocated resources but the expectation of results is not specified.

It is not enough to merely create a research and development cell. At the most it may produce some technical improvements or modifications in the product. But unless there is a marketing person involved with the R&D, you cannot expect a new product which would satisfy customer wants. Ideally the organisation for new product development must include marketing people who have thorough knowledge of market and buyer characteristics.

One way of organising for new product development is to totally segregate the organisation for existing and new products as shown in Figure 20.7. Richardson Hindustan Limited (engaged in manufacturing and marketing the Vicks range of products and Clearasil Cream and soap) is organised on the basis of product teams. Of the total of 20 product teams, only 8 work on the existing products, while the remaining 12 work on new products.

Marketing Planning: This includes activities such as forecasting, target setting, budgeting, establishing control and review procedures, and strategy formulation.

Sales targets are usually set on the basis of market knowledge of the sales staff combined with the top management's vision for the future. Each area salesman provides feedback on the potential in his area and the competitor's strength. All this data are compiled into area-wise target plan which is discussed across the table between the marketing people and the top management.

Budgeting and establishing control and review systems have traditionally been the exclusive preserves of top management. The budget for the coming year is based upon last year's budget with a certain percentage increase to account for inflation and genuine increase in expenditures. The middle and lower levels of management have not much to contribute in this kind of budgeting exercise. But the introduction of zero-based budgeting has changed this. In zero-based budget there is no historical precedent to base the budget upon. Each expenditure head has to be justified afresh for inclusion in the budget, since the last year's expenditure on this head is assumed to be zero. The entire onus is on the operating managers for preparing and justifying expenditure heads.

In strategy formulation, top management requires the active participation of the marketing people in term of their feedback on success of present strategy, competitors activities, and consumer tastes.

Thus, the functional marketing organisation is based on the different sub-functions performed as part of the overall marketing function. The manner in which each sub-function is organised varies from one company to another, depending on the unique combination of internal company attributes and external environmental factors.

The role of a product manager in relation to his specific product is to:

- design strategies,
- makes plans,
- monitor progress,
- provide information relating to the product, and
- interface with other departments within the organisation and outside with customers, distributors and advertising agencies.

Table 20.1: Responsibilities of a Product Manager

Responsibility	Area Task/Role
Advertising	Major responsibilities for advertising strategy, getting advertising campaigns prepared, media selection.
Sales promotion	Major responsibility for budget determination, setting strategy measuring/ evaluating results.
Sales	Product Manager acts as information centre and coordinator.
Market Research	Major responsibility
New product R&D	Major responsibilities for product modifications launches and test marketing
Distribution	Little responsibility
Production	Role of coordinating and communicating
Accounting and Finance	Limited involvement

The first three roles are self-explanatory but the last two need some elaboration. In today's competitive world, a manager's power is based on information or the access to the information he has. This is especially true in case of product manager who is a man placed in a conceptual and informational hub of the organisation. To maintain competitive position and profit of his products, with his performance starkly exposed to higher management, he must strive to be the best informed man about any aspect substantially affecting their future. He must arrange and nurture a number of information interfaces attention or they serve similar customer needs, so that clubbing them together is meaningful and can help serve the customers better.

If you wish to adopt the product management concept, you must define the role in precise terms clearly specifying the limits of his authority. Moreover, you must bear in mind that the contribution of the product to the company's total turnover justifies the expenses of a full-time product manager.

Market-centred Organisation

We have seen that some companies with a product manager organisation have started to group together products which serve similar needs. Thus, the basis for differentiation is shifting from products to customers. A group of customers with similar needs and a common link between them constitute a market. When different markets, rather than functions or products from the basis for differentiating marketing roles, the organisation is known as market-centred.

A company marketing building hardware such as door and window handles, window frames and locks has two distinct customers. One hardware retailers who sell to individual household customer and second, construction companies. These two distinct customer segments represent separate markets each requiring a different marketing mix of advertising, distribution channel, and pricing. Airlines, railways, and road transportation companies have two major distinct markets to serve. They provide transportation for people (Passengers) and goods (cargo). Each market (passenger *vs.* cargo) has its distinct characteristics and needs a suitable marketing strategy and a matching marketing organisation with relevant skill to formulate and implement the strategy.

A market-centred firm seeks its growth by serving new needs in markets where it is already well established. Since knowledge and access to the market is the basis for organising the market setup, the question to be asked is "what other needs of the markets that we know well can be we serve profitably?" For instance, an airlines company, within the passenger markets can further identify markets such as group travel, and charter flights. This constitutes an instance of growth through intensively serving a well establish need (transportation) in a well established market (people). However, a market-centred organisation also has the flexibility to grow extensively by searching out closely related needs and entering new businesses around these. The airlines may enter a new business by providing a courier service. The need is still that of transportation, but the market is not people, or cargo but important documents and parcels. Through the extensive and intensive approach, a market-centred firm seeks to grow by the meeting the greatest number of interrelated needs of every market it serves.

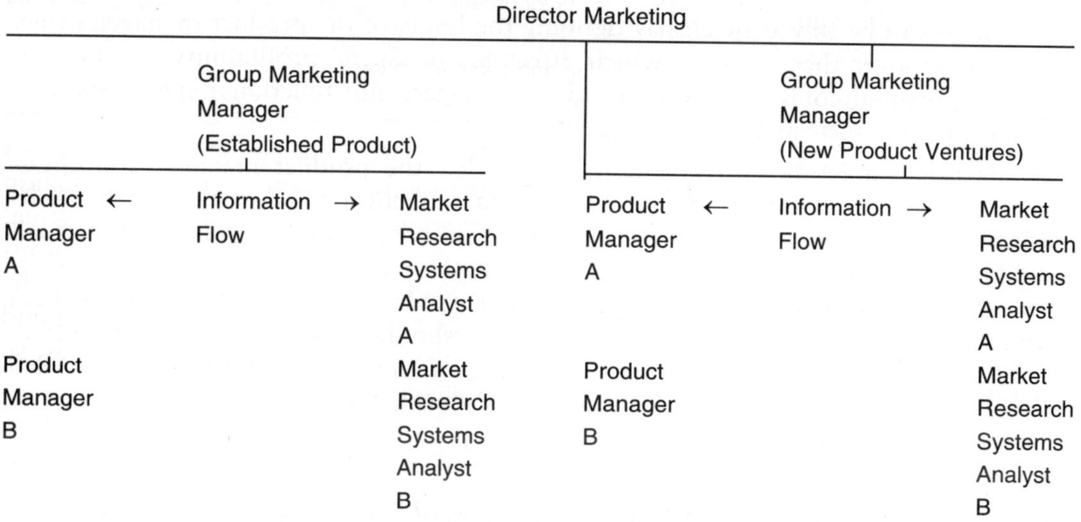

Fig. 20.7

Product Management Organisation

The functional organisation works well when there is a single product. But when there are multiple products and/or the products are very different from one another, the functional marketing organisation is no longer effective. The functional specialized cannot possibly coordinate all aspects of the marketing mix of each of the diverse products, with the result that some products are neglected and eventually become money losers.

Such a situation given rise to the concept of product manager. In a product management organisation, the marketing organisation is differentiated on the basis of different products. Each product or product group is assigned to a manager who is known as the product manager. The product manager is responsible for managing all aspects of the marketing mix pertaining to a specific product. Thus in a multi-product firm you would have as many product managers as the number of products. If there are many brands within the same product, as in the case of soaps, each brand may be assigned to an individual manager who is known as brand manager. Table 20.1 describes the typical responsibilities of a product manager.

As given in Table 20.1, the product manager has a number of diverse responsibilities. To discharge the responsibilities he has to interact with other departments in the firm. Though on paper the product manager is assigned all the responsibilities, but in practical terms he is rarely given the requisite authority to effectively discharge them. At best, he may be given direct authority over one or two areas, say advertising and may be marketing research. For getting co-operation from the other departments he has to use all his persuasive charms and skills, which may not work all the time, resulting in conflicts and tensions.

It is this interfacing aspect of the product manager's role which has potential for all types of conflicts and leads to erosion of his power. Responsibility without authority over resources, could reduce the role of product manager from that of a product 'mini-president' to a bureaucratic clerk. Instead of being a decision-maker responsible for profits the product manager is reduced to a low level coordinator.

These problems can be solved by clearly defining the limits of the product manager's role, giving him authority over the resources which affect his products' profitability, taking into account areas of potential conflict between product managers and functional specialists, and establishing a system for their amicable settlement.

Despite this role ambiguity and potential for conflict the product manager concept is gaining acceptance. In Richardson Hindustan Limited (manufacturing and marketing the Vicks and Clearasil range of products) the marketing organisation comprises 20 product teams. Each product team includes junior and middle level managers representing marketing, manufacturing, R&D, and purchase. In the words of the company president, Mr. Gurcharan Das, "We tell them it is they who are responsible, and that the senior people should be looked upon as resources only. With delegation of power they are more creative, more innovative and ideas come from the lowest level". The organisation on product team basis has led to greater decentralization of responsibility and decision-making within the company and the result is vastly improved performance.

The product manager concept introduces a number of advantages into the marketing organisation. Firstly, given the increased complexity of the marketing mix and diversity of products and brand, the product manager offers a way of coping with these complex marketing inputs in a balanced way. It ensures that all products and brands get proper attention and no product is allowed to languish. Secondly, it introduces flexibility into the system as the product manager can react quickly to a changed market condition since he has the overall responsibility for managing the product's profitability and does not have to waste time over long consultations. Quick reaction and timely action sometimes prove to be the winning factors in a fast changing market situation.

Third, the product manager concept provides a focal point for integrating and coordinating all efforts and resources for planning and implementing the marketing strategy.

Fourth, the product manager role provides excellent training for future managers, as they are exposed to all the operational aspects of management, viz., marketing, finance and production.

However, there are some disadvantage of the product management organisation as follows.

The anomaly of responsibility without control over resources, and lack of a direct line of authority lead to a situation in which conflict is always simmering under the surface, ready to explode at the slightest provocation.

A product manager is in a situation which can be aptly described as 'jack of all trades but master of none'. A product manager has a general and cursory knowledge of all functions but no specialized skill in any one function. This lack of expertise often puts him at a disadvantage when dealing with functional specialist, who are able to browbeat him on technical points (Often to the detriment of the product success).

The product manager has usually too many interfaces to manage, which consume a great deal of his time, with the result that important strategic decisions may be delayed or even ignored.

The product manager concept may turn out to be costly, as even minor products with a small sales turnover are assigned to full-time managers.

In recent times the product manager organisation has been undergoing a number changes. In many firms the product manager has given way to product team. The product team may be arranged vertically or in a triangular for (Figure 20.8). Some other companies have introduced the concept of horizontal product teams. Each team is headed by a leader who is supported by functional specialists. This horizontal product team organisation considerably reduces the potential for conflict with other departments, since now the product manager has his own independent resource pool of functional specialists. Finally, some companies are combining two or three brands/products under one product manager. This done when the products are individually not important enough to require full-time.

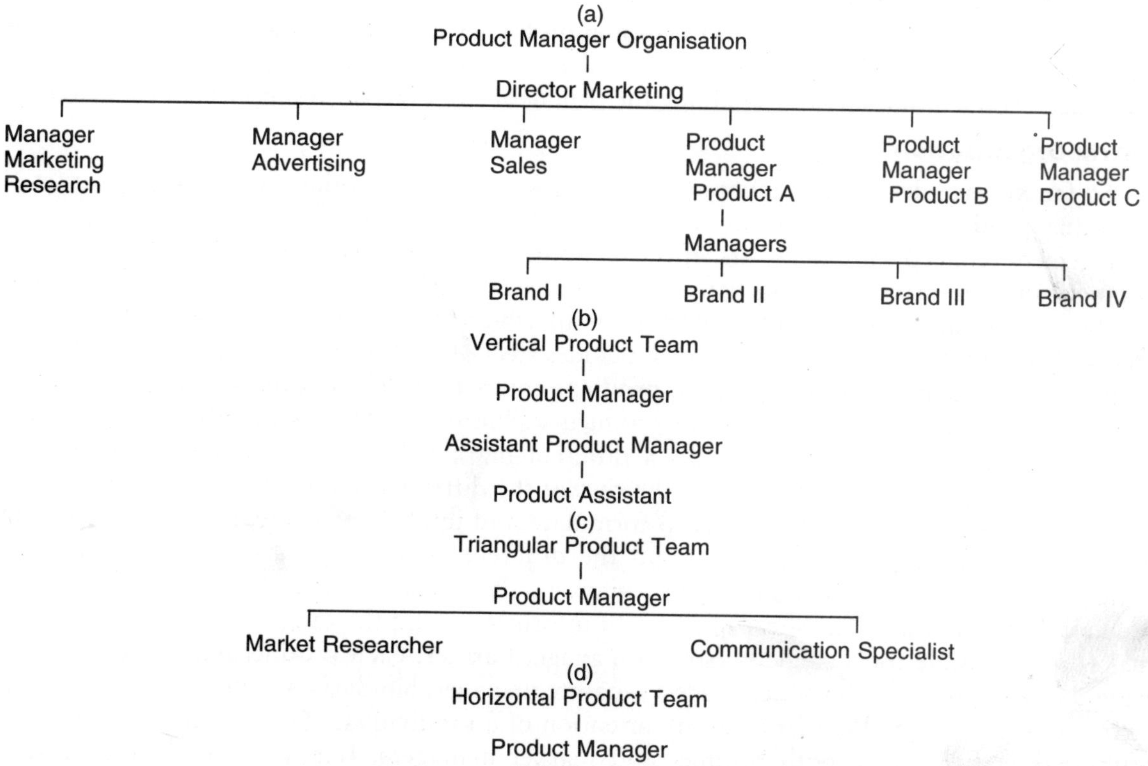

Fig. 20.8: Types of Product Management Organisation

In terms of organisation structure, a market-centred organisation can be organised in the same way as a product management organisation. Instead of product managers, with detailed knowledge of the product you would have market managers each having thorough knowledge about his market. However, we have seen that there are problems of control and authority associated with the product manager organisation. To overcome these, a market-centre should be treated as a profit centre and its manager be assigned the role of a business manager with full accountability for generating profits. The business manager is the chief 'line' officer, with full authority overall the other functions supporting and reporting to him.

At this stage, you may like to ask the question "why should I reorganise my marketing organisation to being a market-centred organisation?" There are two specific situations in which a market-centred organisation can be more effective than any other kind of organisation if you happen to be facing any one of them, a change to a market-centred marketing organisation is advisable.

1. When competitors have developed the same level of product sophistication and quality as the market leader and the leader's supremacy based on price advantage is seriously threatened. In such a situation, market-centring can help the leader revive its competitive advantages, detailed knowledge of customer and retailers helps frame creative marketing strategies.
2. When a firm wants to diversify either to expand the profit base, or gain a total hold on existing customers.

The first objective can be served by adding on higher margin products and services to the existing product line. The second objective is served by marketing a package or system of correlated products and services, enabling the firm to act as a one-stop supplier for each market.

Matrix Organisation

So far we have discussed companies which market different products to the same market or the same product to different markets. In the first case, organising around the product management concept provides an effective solution. In the second case, the marketing organisation can effectively be organised around each market. But what if a company has a number of products and a number of markets to which these products are sold? A company such as Godrej has a product range which includes steel office furniture, refrigerators, almirahs, soaps and detergents, and each of these products caters to a different market. Similarly, Food Specialities Limited has a wide range of products including infant milk powder, instant coffee, ketchup, noodles each of which fulfills a different market need. How should the marketing department be organised to effectively take care of the different characteristic of the product as well as the market? The manager has to formulate and implement strategies suitable for each individual market and also keep in mind the different characteristics of each product. For managing so many products and so many markets, the manager has to cope with an immense amount of information. The sheer quantity of information and the range of its diversity usually makes it impossible for a single person to manage. Further, each product may be so different from the others that each product needs a separate manager. Similarly, the unique buyer and the characteristics of a market merit the full attention of an individual. Thus, a multi-product and multi-market firm needs both product and market managers. But how should the product managers and market managers be integrated to form a workable organisation structure.

The solution lies in matrix organisation where tasks may be differentiated on the basis of functions and products; functions and market; or functions, products and market; and integrated by means of coordinating functions (such as finance, R&D, information system, etc.). In the functional, product and market-centred organisation discussed earlier, each manager has only one point of focus: function, or product or market. However, in the matrix organisation the points of focus are more than one. These focal points may be either functions and products; or functions and markets; or functions, markets and products. As is obvious from these figures, the matrix may have two or more bases for differentiating the functions.

The origin of the formal matrix organisation can be traced to the aerospace industry in USA. The different manufacturers in the aerospace industry were organised functionally; but the US Government wanted each project to have specialized attention and imposed a project management type of organisation on the industry. The horizontal project groups were superimposed over the vertical functional organisations and the result was a matrix organisation. But informally, the matrix organisation has been in existence much before its introduction in USA. In an advertising agency, each client is assigned to a specific accounts executive who is responsible for understanding the client's objectives and needs and getting them translated into advertising campaigns. For translating client objectives into specific advertisements or campaigns, the accounts executive draws on the agency's functional specialists, artists, copywriter, photographers, visualisers, etc. Thus on the one side you have the functional specialists while on the other you have the accounts executive who can be thought of as a market manager (each client represents a separate market) and only a few clients are assigned to each accounts executive.

The distinguishing characteristics of a matrix organisation are:

(i) members are allotted to two, or three groups with each group having its own boss,

(ii) the groups are work-related, though each on different base (e.g. functional, product or market related),

(iii) the groups are formally arranged rather than evolving informally or on an ad hoc basis,

(iv) information management is central to the concept and management of matrix organisation.

Thus, the matrix organisation is a blend of grouping by functions and/or markets and/or products, with the objective of retaining the advantages of specialization and gaining the advantage of a sharper focus on a task or project. The specific advantages and disadvantages associated with the matrix organisation are described in Tables 20.2 and 20.3.

Table 20.2: Advantages of a Matrix Organisation

1. Permits task/project focus without losing benefits of specialization.
2. Provides for increased information-processing capability, catering to information needs of each group.
3. Permits greater decentralization of decision-making since there are specialists in each area equipped with the necessary knowledge.
4. Provides a flexible structure, capable of adapting to new situations while retaining the basic framework of the structure.
5. Provides a means of coping with increased information processing needs and coordinating when the tasks are highly uncertain, complex and interdependent.

Table 20.3 : Disadvantages of a Matrix Organisation

1. Tendency to conflict exists because the different groups are organised on different bases and each group may try to superimpose its own objectives rather than the organisational objectives.
2. There is ambiguity in roles because each person reports to two bosses and this undermine the effectiveness of organisation.
3. Proves costly because of larger volume of information processing and the additional need of coordinating and supporting roles.
4. May be prone to power struggles and politics as each group tries to dominate.
5. Problems of designing a suitable information system, which now needs to cater to different requirements.

QUESTIONS FOR DISCUSSION

1. What is the meaning and purpose of a sales organisation?
2. What are the steps involved in developing a sales organisation?
3. What are the basic types of organisation structures?
4. Distinguish between line-staff and functional organisation with respect to sales.

STRATEGIC RETAILING MANAGEMENT

21

INTRODUCTION

Definition

Retailer is a person or agent or company or organisation who is instrumental in reaching the goods or merchandise or services to the end user or ultimate consumer.

Traditional Retail Scene in India

India is the country having the most unorganised retail market. Traditionally, the retail business is run by mom and pop having shop in the front and house at the back. More than 99% retailers function in less than 500 sq. ft. of area. All the merchandise was purchased as per the test and fancies of the proprietor also the pricing was done on ad hoc basis or by seeing at the face of customer. Generally the accounts of trading and home are not maintained separately. Profits were accumulated in slow moving and non-moving stocks which were to become redundant or consumed in-house. Thus, profits were vanished without their knowledge.

The manufacturers were to distribute goods through C&F agents to distributors and wholesalers. Retailers happen to source the merchandise from wholesalers and reach to end users.

The merchandise price used to get inflated to a great extent till it reaches from manufacturer to end user. Selling prices were largely not controlled by manufacturers.

Branding was not an issue for majority of customers. More than 99% customers are price sensitive and not quality or brand sensitive at the same time they are brand conscious also.

Weekly bazaar in many small towns was held and almost all the commodities were on the scene including livestock. Bargaining was the unwritten law of market.

Educational qualification level of these retailers was always low. Hence, market was controlled by handful of distributors and/or wholesalers.

Virtually there was only one format of retailing and that was mass retail.

Retailer to consumer ratio was very low, for all the categories without exception.

Variety in terms of quality, styles were on regional basis, community based and truly very low range was available at any given single place.

Almost all the purchases/buying by mass population was need oriented and next turn may be on festivals, marriages, birthdays and some specific occasions. Impulsive buying or consumption is restricted to food or vegetables, etc.

Having extra pair of trousers or shirts or casuals and formal and leisure wear and sports wear and different pair of shoes for occasions till date is a luxury for majority population except for those living in metros.

Purchasing power of Indian urban consumer is very low and that of branded merchandise in categories like apparels, are cosmetic, shoes, watches, beverages, food, jewelry are slowly seeping into the lifeline of Indian city folks. However, electronic and electrical home appliances do hold appropriate image into the mind of consumers. Brand name does matter in these white goods categories.

In the coming times also majority of organised retailers will find it difficult to keep balance with rest of the unbranded retail market which is very huge.

Retailing undertakes business activities or perform functions that increase the value of the products and services they sell to consumers. These functions are:

(a) **Providing Assortments:** Offering an assortment enables customers to choose from a wide selection of brand design, sizes, colours, and prizes in one location manufacturers specialize in producing specific types of products. For example, Kellogg's makes breakfast cereals, campbell makes soup. If each of these manufacturers had its own stores that only sold its own products, consumers would have to go to many different stores to buy groceries to prepare a single meal. These retailers often assortment of products.

(b) **Breaking Bulk:** Retailers offer the products in smaller quantities tailored to individual consumers and households' consumption patterns. This reduces transportation costs, warehouses cost and inventory cost. This is called breaking bulk.

(c) **Rendering Services:** Retailers render services that make it easier for customers to buy and use products. They provide credit facilities to the customers. They display products which attract the customers. Retailers keep ready information on hand to answer queries of the customers.

(d) **Risk Bearing:** The retailers bear a different kind of risk to the manufacturers and wholesalers.

(e) **Holding Inventory:** A major function of retailers is to keep inventory so that product will be available when consumers went there. Thus, consumers can keep a much smaller inventory of products at home because they can easily access from the nearby retailers.

RETAILING

Retailing is the set of business activities that adds value to the products and services sold to consumers for their personal family use. Many institutions—manufacturers, wholesalers and retailers do retailing. Although most retailing is done in retail stores, in recent years non-store retailing has been growing much faster than has store retailing. Non-store retailing includes selling to final consumers through direct mail, catalogues, telephone, the Internet, TV home shopping sows, home and office parties, door-to-door contact, vending machines and other direct-selling approaches. In some distribution channels, the manufacturing, wholesaling and retailing activities are performed by independent firming. But most distribution channels have some vertical integration. Vertical integration means that a fun performs more than one level of activity in the channel. In USA, such at Kmart, Walmart, Safeways—they do both wholesaling and retailing. They buy directly from manufacturers and to the warehouses for storage and distribute the merchandise to their stages.

Retailing differs from marketing in the sense that it refers to only those activities, which are related to marketing goods and/or services to final consumers for personal, family or household use.

Whereas, marketing, according to American Marketing Association, refers to "the process of planning and executing the conception, pricing, preservation and distribution of ideas, goods and sources to create exchanges that satisfy individual and organisation objectives".

Importance of Retailing

Retailing is the last stage in a channel of distribution, which comprises all the business and people involved in the physical movement and transfer of ownership of goods and services from producer to customer.

The retailers play a key role as the contact between manufacturers, wholesalers, and other suppliers and the final consumer. Here is now: Many manufacturers would like to make one basic type of item and sell their entire inventory to as few buyers as possible. Yet, final consumers usually want to choose from a variety of goods and services and purchase a limited quantity. So, retailers collect an assortment of goods and services from various sources, buy them in large quantities, and offer to sell them in small quantities to consumers. This is the sorting process.

As a result each manufacturer become more efficient, and final consumers are pleased with the available selection. Wide retail assortments let consumers do one-stop shopping, and they can choose and buy the product version and amount desired. The word retailing is actually based on this breaking-bulk function. It is derived from the old French word retailer, which means to "cut up".

Retailers communicate both with customers and with manufacturers and wholesalers. From ads, sales people and displays, shoppers learn about the availability and characteristics of goods and services, store hours, sales and so on. Manufacturers, wholesalers, and others are informed about sales forecast delivery delays, customer complaint, defective items, inventory turnover (by style, colours, and size), and more. Many goods and services have been modified due to feedback received by suppliers.

For small manufacturers and wholesalers, retailers can provide assistance by transporting, storing, marking, advertising, and pre-payment for merchandise.

Retailers also complete transactions with customers. This means striving to fill orders promptly and accurately and often involves processing customer credit via the retailers' or another charge plan. In addition, retailers may provide customer services such as gift-wrapping, delivery, and installation. How the retailer meets the expectations of both manufactures and customers?

Manufactures Expectations	Customers Expectations
Retailer will:	Retailer will:
1. Promote the product	1. Offer high quality/low prices
2. Make product visible	2. Hire knowledgeable sales force
3. Be knowledge about its use	3. Provide prompt services
4. Provide necessary service	4. Provide service after sales
5. Offer easy return policy	

Hence, this lets the manufactures reach more customers, reduce costs, improve cash flow increase sales more rapidly, and focus on its area of expertise.

Three Basic Tasks of Retailing

1. Get consumers into your store
2. Convert them into customers
3. Operate as efficiently as possible

To successfully complete these three basic tasks is not an easy task. After all inducing a person to part with his/her hard earned cash is not easy. Hence, retailing is not only the last step but also a decisive one that determines whether the efforts made were fruitful or wasted.

Therefore, retailing is carefully planned after segmentation and identifying the target market.

Segmentation is a method retailers use to examine ways to segment, or break down, heterogeneous consumers populations into smaller, more homogeneous groups based on their characteristics. Because any single retailer cannot serve all potential customers, it is important that it segments the market and selects a target market(s).

A target market is that segment of the market that the retailer decides to pursue through its marketing efforts. Retailers in the same line of retail trade pursue different target markets. When the target market is clearly identified then the retail can plan factors like location, assortment of merchandise, pricing and ambiance.

Targeting enables the retailer to efficiently utilize his/her scarce financial resources and efforts to position their products in a favourable light in the minds of customers.

Through positioning, a retailer devises its strategy in a way that projects an image relative to its retail category and its competitors, and elicits consumer response to that image. The image perceived in the mind of customer induces them to go for transaction and repeat the behaviour.

These concepts—segmentation, marketing and positioning help in finally devising a retailing strategy.

A retail strategy is the overall plan for framework of action that guides a retailer. It outlines the mission, goals, consumer market, overall and specific activities and control mechanisms of retailers. A retail strategy combines both controllable and uncontrollable variables.

Controllable Variables	Uncontrollable Variables
Store location	Consumers
Managing a business	Competition
Merchandise management and pricing	Technology
Communicating with customer	Economic conditions
	Seasonality
	Legal restrictions

The retail mix from the part of such mechanism that is deployed to reach its target markets and achieve the firm's objective. The retailing mix brings the firm objective in final and practical form.

Retail mix describes how major factors like price and merchandise are traded off against other retail factors—service, location, marketing communication, quality and store's ambiance—to form an overall store image, create value for customers, and produce profit for the retailer.

RETAILING MIX

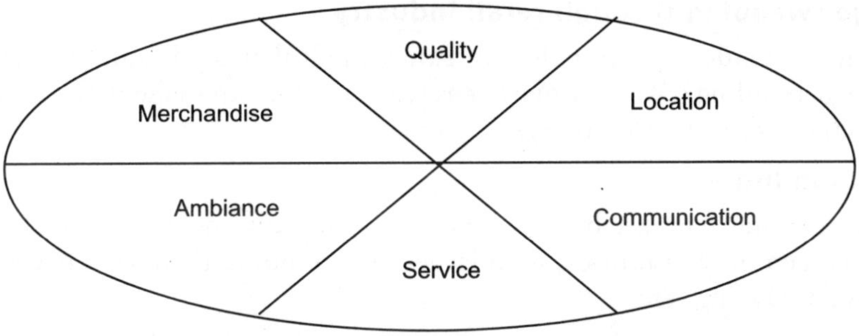

Service: In retailing the word service describes the personal attention and amenities a store provides to its customers. Most store offer at least some services. The help of a trained sales staff for example adds value for customers other types of retail services are credit, gift-wrapping, installation, and tailoring.

Location: Even though today's consumer is highly mobile, the convenience of location is still one of the top criteria people use in choosing where to shop. This is especially true for FMCG's and durables.

Ambience: Most successful stores have distinct images-store personalities—that is a result of many factors besides price and quality. Retailers often talk about atmosphere or ambience, when describing their image. Atmosphere reflects the environment both outside and inside the store; it includes window display, signage, decor, furniture, store layout, lighting, sounds such as music, and even scents. Contrast the image of ITC WILLS Lifestyle showrooms and any local MBO. The differences are tangible—the arrangement of merchandise, the signs and banners, the material and texture of counters and displays. Some differences however are intangible—the feeling of warmth and friendliness, excitement—all these are as much part of the store's personality as its physical ambiance.

Marketing Communication: A store's image as well as other information about the merchandise for sale is communicated largely through advertising and in-store promotional materials. The store front and display windows, store layouts, and merchandise display help gain consumer enthusiasm present a fresh look, introduce new products categories, and reflect changing seasons and themes.

Pricing: Pricing refers to a retailer's comparative strategy: prestige pricing (creating a quality image by high prices), competitive pricing (setting prices at level of competitors) or penetration pricing (under pricing other retailers to attract value conscious consumer).

Quality: Service, location, marketing communication, merchandise selection, and price all come together when consumers make a decision about quality and what to buy. Consumers generally try to get the best quality he can afford. In other words, quality is relative—it is evaluated in relation to price, and the best value in maximum quality for minimum price. Quality may be low, medium or high depending on the target market the fun has chosen.

Globalisation of Retailing

Today retailing both in India and abroad, are venturing beyond their borders on every type of product.

Winds of change sweeping through retail industry

What is it that has made the Piramals, the Tatas, the Rahejas, ITC and scores of others take a plunge into mega retailing? Why is market research, space management, ERP, promotions, etc. now a necessary tool in this industry?

Retail Economics in India

Traditionally retailing has not been a structurally organised industry in India. Organised retail network was seen only in fabrics, with large mills building their own exclusive stores, e.g. Raymond's, Bombay Dyeing, etc.

Currently there are about 5130000 retail outlets selling about Rs. 4790 billion worth of products. Retail universe in India comprises large, medium general stores, chemists and pan-bidi (apart from accessories stores). Of these—thanks to unemployment, the number of pan-bidi outlets are steadily rising. On account of the fragmented nature of Indian retail industry the inhabitants to stores ratio in India is about 150:1, i.e. there is a store catering to every 150 people. This ratio varies from country to country. In China the ratio is similar to that of India, whereas in case of more developed countries the ratio would be higher. For instance, in Europe the inhabitant to stores ratios is 2000:1.

As markets mature, consumer expectations rise it would be necessity for small retailers to come together and form innovative and strong supply chain that will cut through distribution and increase margins.

Turnaround times

In last couple of years this industry has made agile move from its nascent stages. Organised retailing started picking up in Southern India. Availability of land at price locations coupled with cheaper real estate prices (compared to Mumbai and Delhi) made it possible to have multi-stored shopping complexes here. It took two years of recession to get this concept of shopping to major cities like Mumbai and Delhi. Recession brought property prices down in these cities. It was during this period of industry slump that big business houses took notice of the potential in retailing.

A classical example being Lakme Ltd. The company after selling off its cosmetic division of HLL, made an aggressive foray into retailing. Its retail chain branded "Westside" already comprises 4 stores—one each in Bangalore, Hyderabad, Chennai and Mumbai. A cash hoard of Rs. 107 billion will enable Lakme to roll out stores aggressively. The company plans to open 10 stores by December 2000.

Consumerism cycle

Consumer cycle starts with industry dictating the market. Eventually with time the distributor gains control over the market. At this stage distributor becomes an important link between manufacturer and customer. When markets start developing further expanding its horizons, suddenly retailers turn out to be vital point in this supply chain.

In India we are entering into this third stage where retailers control the market. With shopping attitudes of people changing, Indian markets today desires for value added products and services with good ambience and brands, which only a retailer can provide.

Whereas, developed countries have reached the final stage where customer dictates. US, UK and other developed markets have now reached a stage wherein consumers are willing to save on price by going to discount stores where ambience and services are low and goods are unbranded.

It's a vicious cycle, but for the new aspect—omnipresent net. Though it would be sometime before e-commerce gears up in India. But all the same a merger of Internet, catalogues, telephone and television is inevitable.

Yet what makes it attractive

Today the number of smaller retailers ($500 pa) has shot up from 40% in 1990 to 54% in 1996, whereas the number of large stores (turnover of $3000 pa) increased from 2.8% to 6.5%. Thus, though large retailers are growing the smaller outlets are growing even faster. However, changing shopping attitudes of an average customer will make future growth increasingly difficult for unorganised retail sector.

Currently in India, organised retailing accounts for 5% of the industry turnover, comprising value-added foods (Rs. 770 bn), music and entertainment (Rs. 40 bn), colour cosmetics (Rs. 12 bn), etc. By 2005 organised retailing will account for 20% the total retailing industry turnover (Rs. 23000 bn).

Big business houses today are in a position to provide Indian masses with shopping satisfaction, entertainment, quality product, polite salesperson, product information and discounts. Though margins currently are low due to high property cost and poor infrastructure. This is the only business where one buys in credit and sells for cash.

Further the number of households earning more than Rs. 150000 per annum amounts to 30 mn today and is expected to grow to 80 mn by 2007.

Additionally financial institutions are encouraging such ventures. ICICI has recently sanctioned term loans to Vivek & Co., a mega-regailer in Chennai to meet their expansion plans. Very shortly the market will also witness IPOs for some these *retail ventures.*

Proven success

In early 90's, K. Raheja Group started a mega apparels stores in Mumbai *Shoppers Stop.* Initially, the group was averse to start outlets at South Mumbai for various reasons like low walkins, space constraints, narrowed. Presently the company is focusing on apparels under Westside brand and cosmetics, etc. under other brands but had plans to foray into other products too.

Retailing view—Agmarknet

Agmarknet's goals are ambitious and need all the support it can gather. It aims to create a 'nationwide network for speedy collection and dissemination of market information'. This itself is a vital step forward, for it reduces the scope of the prices paid for intermediaries since now the end prices could be known. It also intends to computerise data regarding market fees and charges, arrivals, dispatches, sales transport, losses and wastages and various issues like APMC infrastructure and faxes. If envisages connecting 670 mandis and 40 agricultural boards across India. At 75, Maharashtra has the number of wholesale markets or nodes connected followed by Andhra Pradesh (65) and Uttar Pradesh (64). For such an ambitious and very urgently needed network to function, connectivity all the times is an absolute must. When an attempt was made to link to the Mumbai APMC at the site called falbazar.com, online access was unavailable for three consecutive days. Such glitches could render these efforts futile.

All this large scale project work has to be supported by break-end system and training. The National Information Centre of the government states that it will procure maintain and install the hardware and software, train the operators to upload and uplink. From wholesale market or node that is connected to agmarknet will pay Rs. 2,750 per year as Internet access charges. Software like Windows 98, Lotus Suite for office productivity. Lotus Notes for e-mail and a relational database RDBMS of MS SQL is part of the set up. Details of vendors and requirements have also been put up on the site.

At a glance agmarknet fulfils exactly what is needed to give the extra edge to Indian agriculture—the access to information at reasonable cost. But once the first difficult steps have been taken, the battle will be to continuously upgrade and develop this network deep into rural India. It must at the end of the day, benefit the farmer and improve his lot.

Source: *Rural Market Economic Times*, May 29, 2002.

Fee for nothing

A visit to APMC, Vashi.

APMC, Vashi, Navi Mumbai is one of the largest markets in Western India. Spread over 122 areas, 67 of which have been developed for trading and marketing and receiving agricultural produce from Maharashtra and surrounding states. 3,500 trucks roll in daily, and it feeds Mumbai city and its suburbs. APMC Vashi controls not just the flow of food products but the price at which it goes into retail.

An important player in the APMC set up is the sub-broker. The sub-brokers deal with the traders and no traders will deal directly with buyers. On going to the sub-broker, prospective buyers will take you to the trader. If there's a problem with price or delivered quality, the trader won't bargain with the broker who does. You cannot bypass the broker and go to the traders directly in the APMC. The sub-broker makes payments to the traders. This market works on.

Open market

Under this system, arhatia or broker invites bids for the produce and the highest bidder is sold the produce. It is better than any other system as sale is by an open auction. The buyers and sellers clearly know the price quoted and there is no scope for cheating. The system ensure fair dealing to the parties and secures a premium for superior quality.

Phar system

Here, one bid is given for all the lots in a particular shop and all the lots are sold at that price.

Random bid system

In this method agent invites a few buyers when the produce is brought to his stop for sale. All the prospective buyers are not informed. As a result, the competition is poor.

Roster bid system

Bidding starts from a point in the market at a notified time about which the prospective buyers are given information in advance. The bidding party after the auction of the produce at one shop moves to the next in a clock-wise or anti-clock wise direction till the auction of the produce at all shops is over, or the scheduled auction time expires. On the following day, the auction starts from the next point, and so on. The auction clerk supervises the auction or the person nominated by the market committee.

Check Your Progress—1

1. What are retail functions? Mention any three.
2. What are three basic tasks of retailing?
3. What do you mean by Retail Mix?

Environmental Analysis

In order to understand the industry we undertook two different environmental analysis. The first is the PEST Analysis where the political, environmental, social, and technological aspects are looked into. In the Porter's Five Forces the competitive environment of the industry is analysed.

1. **PEST Analysis:** Now, in a particular geographic region, the environment there affects the retailers in the region in various ways. We have studied the effects under the following heads:
   - Political Environment
   - Economic Environment
   - Social Environment
   - Technological Environment

(a) **Political Environment:** With the opening up of the economy, more and more MNC's have pervaded the Indian business arena, through joint ventures, franchisees or even self-owned stores. The very first MNC getting into the business was Spender's, a tie up between the RPG Group and Dairy Farm International, a $10 billion Hong Kong based company, and a part of the Jardine Methenson Group.

Government uses regulation to prevent development of monopolies, which results in restricted competition and fixed prices (MRTC). Government also propounds price competition laws and unfair trade practice laws. Retailers must understand what rights they have in pricing merchandise, what provision they should make for customer relations, what rights and responsibilities they possess when making sales, what rights their employees have and what liabilities they may face while selling products to the consumers.

(b) **Economic Environment:** The type of economic system (capitalism or socialism, etc.) existing in a country has a direct bearing on the potential for and the development of the retailing industry in that country. A retailer cannot escape the effects of the factors the macroeconomic environment, be it domestic or global that influences the local market.

Inflation, unemployment, interest rates, tax levels, the GDP and the rate of real growth in GDP (inflation adjusted) are some aspects of the economy which a retailer must cope with.

Real growth makes more income available to people who then tend to spend more, leading to higher sales and more profits for the retailers. However, growth also leads to higher competition in the long run. As the economy expands, higher demand levels lead more firms in the market, trying to fulfill the consumer needs. The inflation (i.e. increase in price) leads to less goods being bought at higher prices. As the retailers' cost of goods increases, they attempt to pass on this increase to the consumers.

However, it is often not possible to pass on the entire amount to the consumer, hence resulting in cuts in the retailers' profits. With the increase in Purchasing Power Parity (PPP) and the disposable income of the Indian consumer, retailing is catching up at a very fast pace in the country.

(c) **Social Environment:** As discussed under the title "demographic and lifestyle trends" above, the demographic trend and lifestyle patterns, of the society that a retailer intends to serve, decide the retailer's strategy.

Traditionally, children seldom accompanied their parents while grocery good shopping. Shopping for children was confined to that during festivals when dresses were brought for them. But, in the present day, due to scarcity of time, working parents prefer to spend as much time as possible with their children and this includes their shopping hours also. As the organisation retail sector offers the option of entertainment along with shopping, the younger couples opt for these retail outlets for shopping.

Speaking at KSA Retail Summit, 2000, Peter Lau, Chairman of Glordans International, Hong Kong, said, "It is the format of consumer expectation that changes, not the goods or services they want." This is depicted in the following diagram:

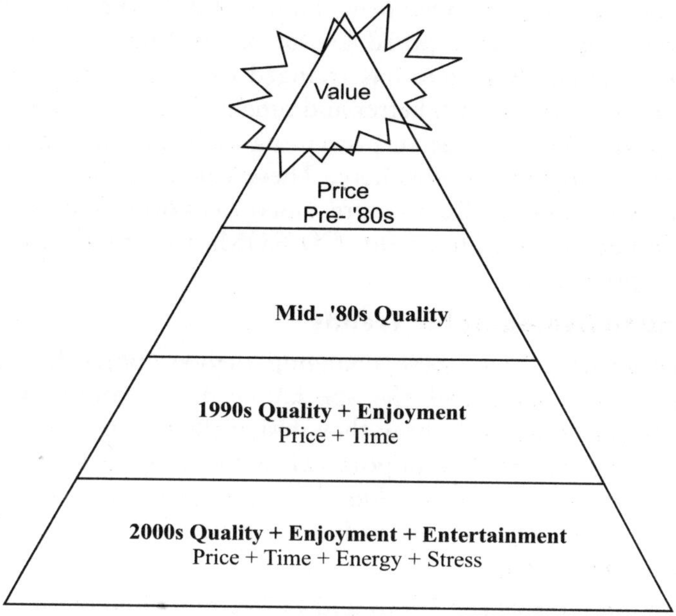

Fig. 21.1: Changing Customer Expectations in India

KSA Technopark conducted a study on consumer attitude towards shopping in association with the market research from ORG-MARG in January and February 1999. The study was spread over the four zones of India, viz. North, South, West and East and covered a random samples of 7300 respondents in twelve cities. Findings of the study are given in Annexure.

The results of this study clearly reflect that the buying patterns do vary according to the customs and lifestyle of a region. In the south approximately seven hours are spent on shopping per week. This figure is the highest amongst the four zones, which probably explains the more spurt of new malls and supermarkets in the south than in the other zones.

Further, the study was attempted to find out what a customer expects out of a store. Here, the six attributes desired by most number of people (65% and above) are polite and courteous salespeople, quality of products, non-intrusive sales persons, value for money, attractive displays and range of products.

Although desired by a very low percentage of people (only 10%) of the attribute of an entertainment center for children has also figured in. That is to say, apart from quality and range of products, value for money and attractive displays, the human touch has a vital role to play. Smart, polite and courteous sales people might make all the difference for a store, which is like any other in terms of its product offerings. There is also emphasis on schemes and promotions, which, as the study ratifies, do pull customers. Further the trend is towards more convenience and flexibility in terms of exchange/return policies, which play a vital role in encouraging the purchasing.

(d) **Technological Environment:** Technology is probably the most dynamic change agent for the retailing industry. The computerisation of the various operation sin a retail store, including inventory management, billing and payments as well as database (of customers) management, widespread use of bar coding, point-of-sale terminals and Management Information System has changed the face of retailing drastically. Apart from providing the retailers with better and timelier information about their operations, the technology also does the job of preventing theft, promoting the store's goods and creating a better shopping atmosphere. These can be done with the help of closed circuit televisions, video walls, in-store video networks, kiosks and other forms of interactive applications ranging from CD-ROMs to virtual reality to let customers select and buy products.

Retailing Responding to Demographic Trends

Retailing must understand how these changing demographics features influencing the retailers. All retailers must understand the special needs of young population and older consumers in the merchandise they sell, how they design their stores, and the way they attract the consumers. Recognising the growing importance and special needs of certain ethnic groups is also imperative in many markets. Like America, people in India have dual incomes, less leisure time, more tastes towards quick and readymade products which has changed the demand for retailers merchandise and services.

Due to falling birth rates during the 1960s and 1970s, more longer life, retailers consider the customers purchasing power more strong. Today in America, children have baby boomer parents. They are members of families with a smaller number of children then in the past, and probably live in a low-income or single-parent household. In fact, the opportunity for marketing to these children is threshold. First, they have their own money to spend. Second, children spend through their requests to parents, thirdly, children are a future market for all goods and services. Baby boomers the term used for Americans who were born between 1946-64, today this group is relatively large, economically comfortable, and well-educated. These aging baby boomers pose significant challenges to retailers. The term is derived from a historically significant rise in the birth rate following the Second World War. At the time this spike in the birth rate was name 'Baby bum'. Whereas 'baby busters' (the next oldest group, also known as flyers), they are the children of baby boomer parents. They have different values. Shopping habits and income levels then their parents they have less college education than baby boomers but with the same education they earn much more salaries but from different types of employed.

Silver Streakers

The older populations are referred as empty nesting, the 50 and over age group. Earlier the Silver Streakers were very conservative with their savings. They wanted something to pass on to their children. But that attitude is changing. Older people seem to be buying goods and services at the same pace as their boomers children. They spend that money on travel, second homes, luxury and electronic equipment, investments, home furnishings, clothing and gifts are frequent purchases. Retailers can offer senior citizen discount days which can make shopping easy for older people.

THEORIES OF RETAIL EVOLUTION

Cyclical Theories

Retail institutions go through cycles over-time:

- Wheel of Retailing Theory
- Accordion Theory

Evolution Theory

Retail institutions change similar to patterns observed in biological evolution:

- Dialectic Process Theory
- Natural Selection

CYCLICAL THEORIES

Wheel of Retailing Theory

One of the original theories addressing the issues of retail institutional changes is the wheel of retailing (Nair, 1931, 1958).

WHEEL OF RETAILING (CYCLICAL)

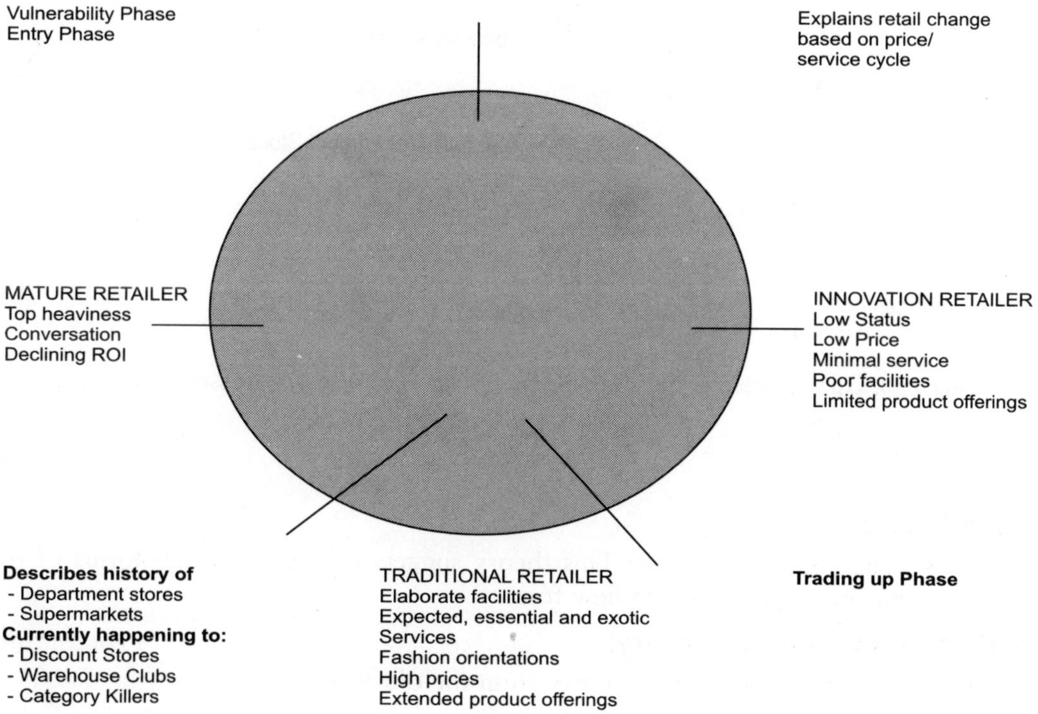

Fig. 21.2

The concept proposes 'a more or less definite cycle'. If exploring retail change is based on price/service cycle. When retailers enter a market they compete by offering goods at the lowest possible price or 'the bold new concept, the innovation', in order to attract customers. As retailers develop their price, the opportunity for new to enter the market starts and these new retailers attract the customers and old retailers become mature retailers and enter into up market position. This is called wheel of retailing. This is explained in Figure 21.2.

Accordion Theory

The retail accordion theory suggests that retailers initially enter a market as a general retailer, with experience they focus down on particular groups. Over-time they begin to diversify their offer in order to grow, but again well revert to specialization. Thus, retail accordion is based on cyclical functioning in variety and adjustment. This is shown in Figure 21.3.

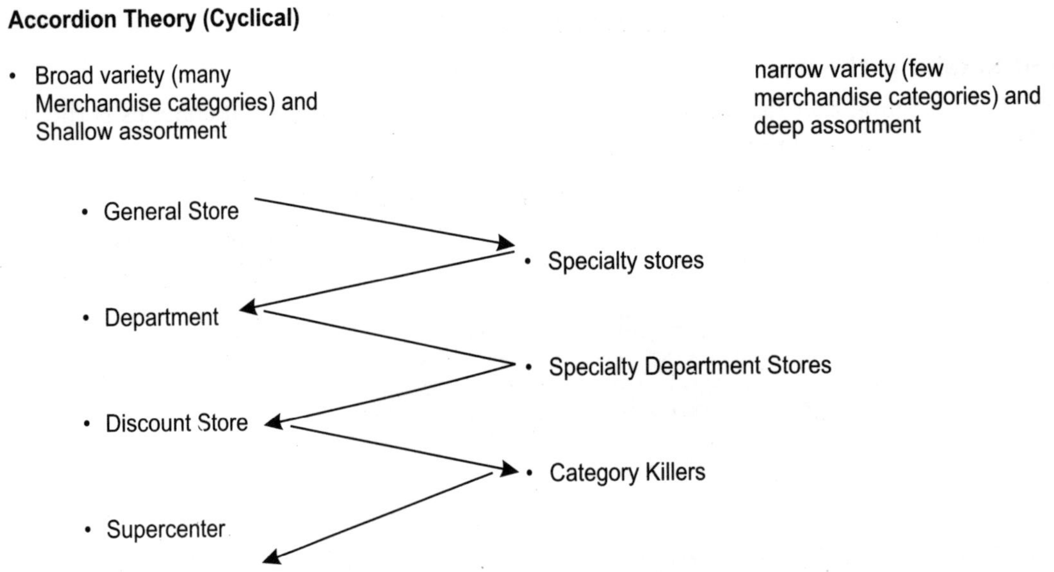

Fig. 21.3: Explains retail change based on cyclica fluctuations in variety and assortment

Evolution Theory

- The Dialectic Process: This theory suggets how the original forms of retailers has been changed into new form.

The Dialectic Process (Evolutionary)

1. New form (antithesis) differentiates from the old (thesis)
2. Newest (synthesis) borrows from both
3. Distinction between formats blur

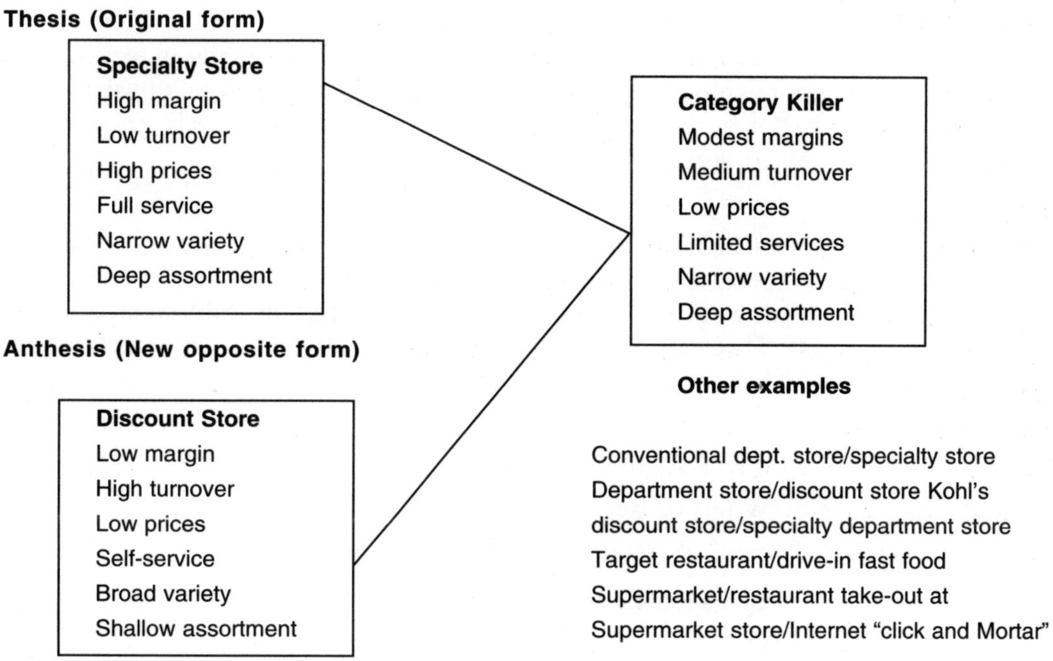

- Based on Charles Darwin's view that organisms change and evolve on the basis of survival of the fittest.
- Formats best able to adapt are most likely to survive.
- Current supermarket trends and department store trends are attempts to adapt and survive.
- Stores originally resisted Internet channel, but now are benefiting from it.
- Must adapt in response to environmental changes.
- Customer needs (e.g. longer store hours, ability to shop online).
- Technology (e.g. logistics efficiencies).
- Competition (maintain competitiveness in the face of new and more sophisticated competitors, more inter-type competition, etc.

CHANGES IN CONSUMER VALUES

So far, we have discussed the retail customers' changing demographic make up. As a result of these changes and other environmental factors, consumer values are also changing. Dual-income families and older families appear to be searching for convenience and value.

Social Consciousness

Retailers have made their citi zone social conscious by offering them branded products and better product assortment. Retailers have created a mutually beneficial relationship between itself and socially at large.

Value-oriented Customers

Offering better value has been an important tactic for a variety of companies in recessionary times. In 1980s J.C. Penny become more fashion—forward and higher priced as it pushed more national brand like Levis, etc. But in the early 1990s it returned with moderately priced roots. The shift in strategy appears to be working.

Cocooning

It is a behavioural pattern of consumers who increasingly turn to the nice, safe, familiar environment of their homes to spend their precious leisure time. The cocooning phenomenon is due to number of reasons—a rather to traditional values, families having children later in life, individual's time consciousness. This leads to strong demand for VCRs, home computers, stereo systems, security systems and other products used in the home.

Check Your Progress—II

1. What do you mean by 'PEST Analysis'?
2. What do you mean by Wheel of Retailing?
3. What is 'Accordion Theory' of Retailing?

QUESTIONS FOR DISCUSSION

1. What is a retailer and what is his functions?
2. What is the importance retailing in our society?
3. What career and entrepreneural opportunities does retailing offer?
4. How are retailers responding to demographic trends like the natural baby boomers and changing baby busters?
5. How retailers responding to demographic trends like the natural baby boomers and changing baby busters?
6. The retailers have to create the right environment, additional advantages, and values, or loyalty scheme in order to ensure the customers is offered a complete package of benefits. Comment.
7. Discuss the different theories of Retail Institutional Change.
8. How the heel of retailing is different form retail accordion?

MARKETING PLANNING

22

INTRODUCTION

The importance of planning can best be understood with reference to the oft-quoted poem:

For want of a nail, the shoe was lost
For want of a shoe, the horse was lost
For want of a horse, the rider was lost
For want of a rider, the battle was lost
For want of a battle, the kingdom was lost
And all for want of a horse shoe nail

The importance of planning lies in the fact that it is like a navigator operating under varied business circumstances. A marketer has to work in an environment, which is uncertain and ever changing. It is proper planning only that enables a manager to carve out the future course of action. Peter Drucker has rightly defined business planning "as a continuous process of making present entrepreneurial decision systematically and with best possible knowledge of their futurity, organizing systematically the effort needed to carry out these decisions against expectations through organised feedback".

Marketing planning of an organisation is planning for that organisation's revenue-earning activities. It must begin with setting down the corporate objectives and should be followed through with strategies and plans for each separate function.

The *first* step in marketing planning process is setting down marketing objectives and policies. The objectives here must be only the long-term objectives, which can be fixed in terms of turnover.

The *second* step is designing the marketing system. In the marketing system, a company has to design/define each function with its contribution.

The *third* step is to develop separate objective, programmes and strategies of each function, so that they can be assessed for the target purpose and the broad objectives. If any function cannot meet its objectives, those have to be modified for that functional area.

The *fourth* step is drawing of detailed plans for each function for a shorter period, i.e. a quarter, half a year or a year. It will be helpful in defining responsibilities, timing and costs needed to achieve the short-term objectives.

The *fifth* step is merging the marketing plans into organisational plans.

MARKETING PLANNING SYSTEM IN A FLOW CHART

We may now summarize the importance of marketing planning:

1. It helps in avoiding future uncertainties.
2. It helps in management by objectives.
3. It helps in achieving objectives.
4. It helps in coordination and communication among the departments.
5. It helps in control.
6. It helps the customers in getting complete satisfaction.

Marketing provides inputs for strategic planning. Strategic planning starts with business mission, and end with goals by achieving business objectives. Marketing planning plays a vital role in formulating marketing strategies, objectives and goals. Richard F. Vancil and Peter Lorange defined strategic planning process cycle as is given following:

Steps in Marketing Strategic Plan

- Determine the mission objectives and goals.
- Develop a company profile that reflects internal conditions and capabilities.
- Analysis of company's external environment in terms of both competitive and general factors.
- Match the company's profile with external environment.
- Prepare annual plans for short-term objectives.
- Implementing the strategies based on resources allocation.
- Review and evaluation of the success of the strategic process to serve as a basis.
- For control and as an input for future decision-making.

STRATEGIC PLANNING PROCESS CYCLE

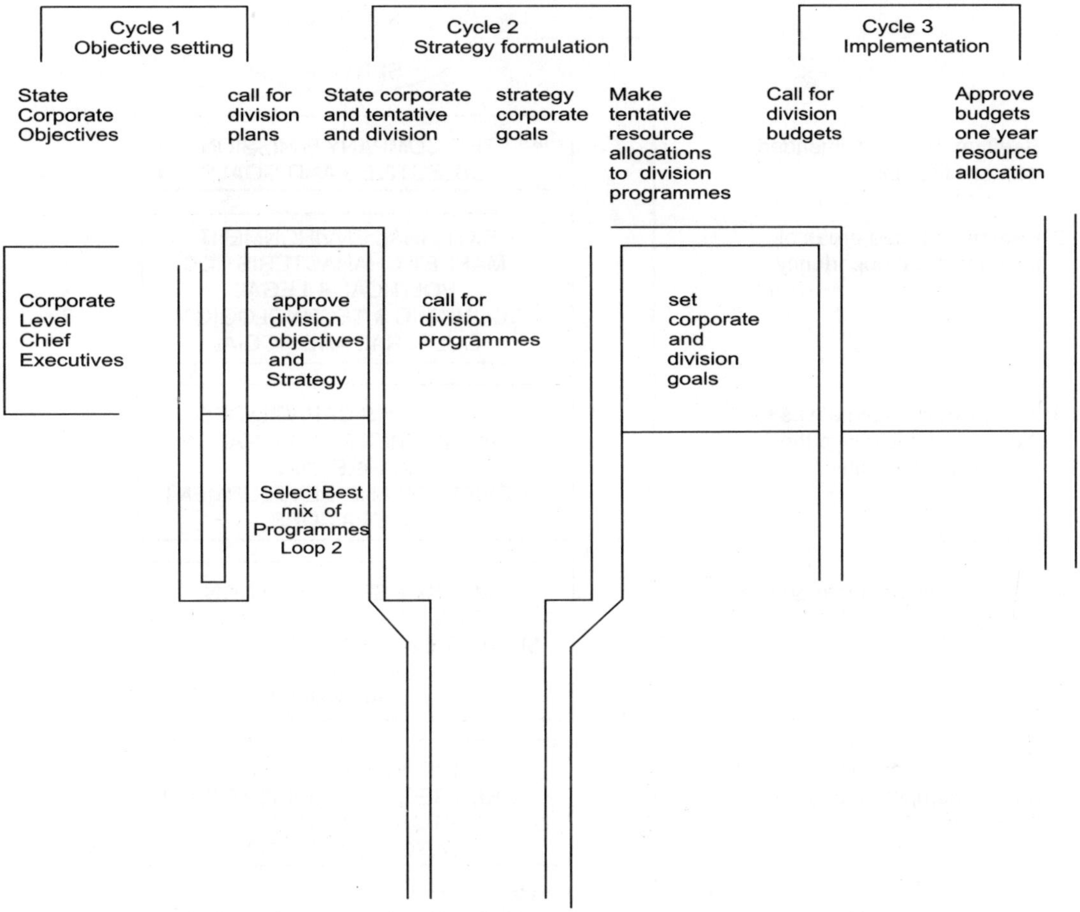

Strategic Marketing Decision Process: The diagram given on the next page provides an outline of the decision-making steps to follow for successful marketing planning.

NATURE OF MARKETING PLANNING

Marketing planning is a systemic and disciplined exercise to formulate marketing strategies. Marketing planning can be related to the organisation as a whole or strategic business units (S.B.U.). Marketing planning is a forward-looking exercise, which determines the future strategies of an organisation with special reference to its product development, market development, channel design, sales promotion, profitability, etc.

STEPS IN STRATEGIC PLANNING

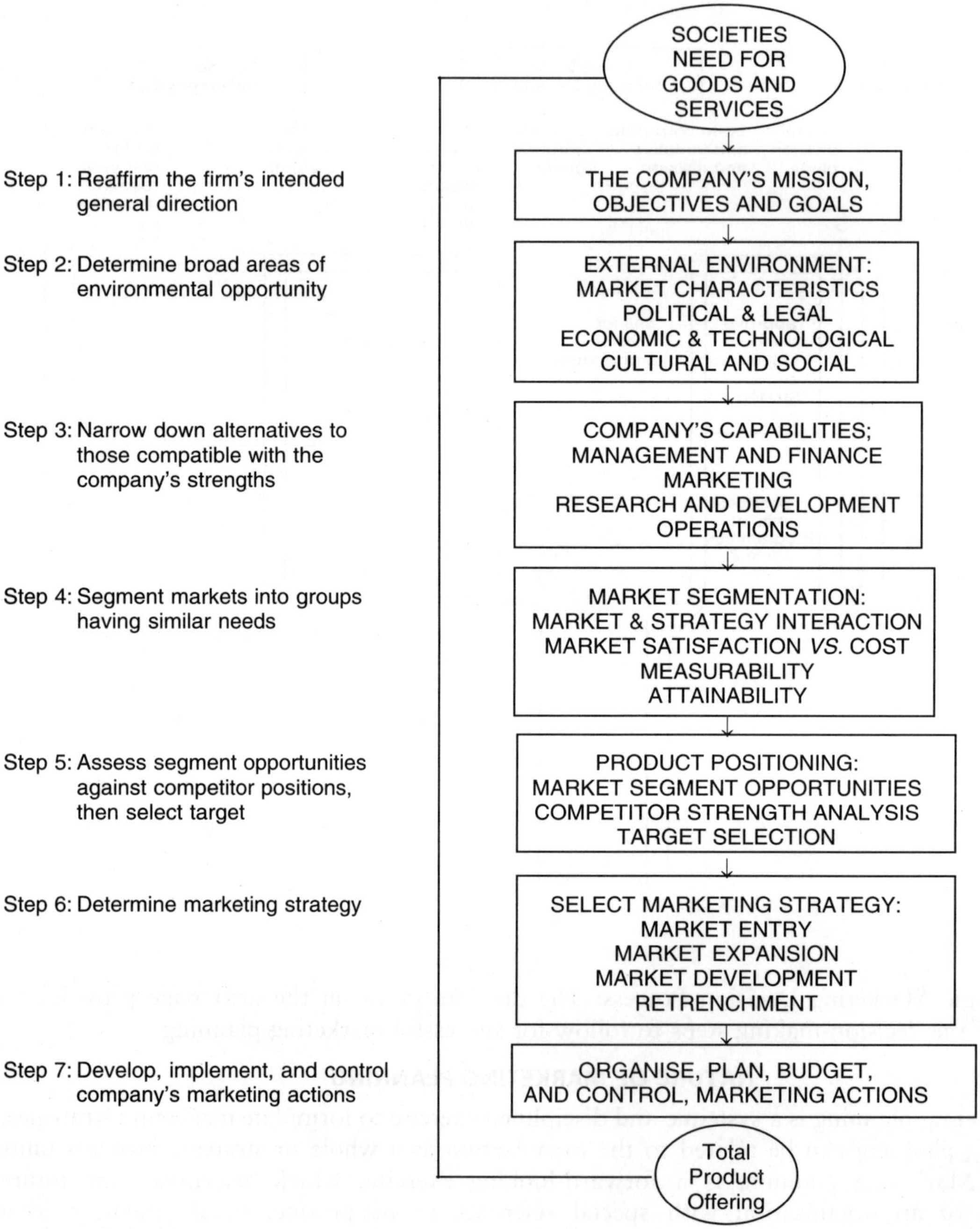

There are three broad areas of marketing planning within the corporate planning:

MARKETING PLANNING

Corporate Planning	→	includes mission, objectives and goals
A Long-term Planning	→	includes long-term forecasting, budgets, etc.
B Short-term Planning	→	includes short-term forecasting, budgets, etc.
C Strategic Marketing Planning	→	includes marketing strategies

CORPORATE PLANNING

Corporate planning is a term used to denote a formal, comprehensive and systematic appraisal and internal environment to achieve organisational objectives. It helps in the formulation of plans, strategies and policies on the basis of allocated resources. It is systematic as it covers the whole planning process in a logical and sequential manner. Corporate planning plays a vital role in defining mission, objectives and goals.

(A) Mission

Peter F. Drucker raised important philosophical questions related to business: what is our business? What will it be? And what should it be? These questions determine the purpose of the mission. Thus, a mission statement addresses the organisation's fundamental reason for existing and specifies the functional role that the organisation is going to adopt in its market place. The mission statement should possess the following seven characteristics:

- It should not be an impossible statement.
- It should be short.
- It should be motivating.
- It should be enough to define the functions, the clientele and the method of operation.
- It should be clear.
- It should be distinctive.
- It should indicate how objectives are to be accomplished.

Examples of Mission Statement

1. DUPONT: "Better things for better living through Chemistry."
2. O.N.G.C.: "To stimulate, continue and accelerate efforts to develop and maximize the contribution of the energy sector to the economy of the country."

(B) Objectives

Objectives help in identifying and achieving the desired future positions or destinations. Every company has a potential set of objectives. It has to exercise a choice from among these objectives. A possible list of objectives could be as follows:

- A higher market share.
- High growth opportunities.
- Increased ability to compete in global markets.
- Product innovation.
- Recognition as a leader in technology.

- Better customer services.
- Good reputation with customers.
- Low cost compared with competitors.
- High quality goods and services.
- Brand image and loyalty.
- Wider profit margin.

An example of long-term objectives will be Dow Chemical Company, USA.

"To seek maximum long-term profit growth as the primary means to ensure the prosperity and well-being of our employees, stockholders and our customers by making products that the people of the world need, and to do so better than anyone else."

(C) Goals

Setting goals is the first step in the marketing planning process. Essentially, the goals are quantitative assignment to a marketing unit relating to a particular time period. A marketing unit may be a sales person, a territory, a branch office, a region or a distributor.

Goals are used to plan, control and evaluate marketing activities of a company. They provide a source of motivation, a basis for incentive compensation, standards of performance evaluation of the marketing personnel and uncover the strengths and weaknesses in the marketing structure of the firm. There are four types of goals.

1. Sales volume goals,
2. Financial goals,
3. Activities goals, and
4. Combination of the above goals.

Goals should have the following qualities:

- Motivating
- Measurability
- Flexibility
- Acceptability
- Suitability
- Understandability
- Achievability

Long-term Planning

In the words of Peter Drucker, "Long-range planning is the process of making current risk-taking decision with the best possible knowledge of the future consequences." Indeed, a good critique would be "driving a car by looking at the side mirror". Long-term plan formulation involves the following steps:

1. Assessing what has been done in the past.
2. Sizing up of the critically evaluated strengths.
3. Organisational objective fixation.

4. Forecasting.
5. Evaluating the performance of strategic activities.
6. Implementing strategies in the long-range plan, and bridging the gap.
7. Developing the time span for the long-range plan.

The following methods may be adopted for checking the appropriateness of the long-range plan:

1. Are the environmental factors considered or not?
2. Is the S.W.O.T. analysis carried out or not?
3. Is the strategy appropriate to the resources available?
4. Is the risk in the strategy an appropriate one?
5. Does the strategy have an appropriate time horizon?
6. Is the strategy workable?

Short-term Planning

Short-term planning is also known as annual planning. Short-term plans are specific, measurable statements of what an organisation is expected to achieve in contributing to the accomplishment of the business's grand strategy. Short-term planning must be clearly linked to long-term planning of the business's grand strategy. There are a few basic differences between long-term and short-term planning:

1. **Time factor:** Long-term planning focused on five years or more into the future. Short-term planning is more immediate, usually involving one year.
2. **Focus:** Long-term planning focuses on the future position of the firm in its competitive environment. Short-term planning focuses on functional plans.
3. **Specifically:** Long-term plans are broadly stated. Short-term plans are very specific with company's operational plans.
4. **Measurement:** Long-term plans are measured in broad relative terms, whereas short-term plans are in absolute terms.

Strategic Marketing Planning

Strategic marketing planning is based on these two questions, "what business are we in and what business should we be in?" These two questions are based on three elements.

1. The customer groups that will be served;
2. The customer needs that will be satisfied; and
3. The technology that will be used to meet these needs.

Strategic marketing planning formulates the strategies based on the strategic business unit (S.B.U.) or strategy center. The S.B.U. has the following characteristics: (a) separate responsibility for strategic planning and profit performance, and profit influencing factors; (b) separate set of competitors; and (c) single business or a collection of related businesses, which offer scope for independent strategic planning from remaining organisation. The understanding of S.B.U. is therefore a convenient starting point for planning since the company's strategic business units have been identified. In practice, big companies in India (Reliance Industries Ltd.) work on the basis that strategic planning at S.B.U. level has to be agreed to by corporate management.

S.B.U. helps in developing a marketing portfolio analysis. The following portfolios are based on S.B.U. alongwith strategic marketing planning: (1) Boston Consulting Group Matrix (B.C.G.), (2) General Electric Matrix (G.E. Model), and (3) Arthur D. Little Model (A.D.L.).

MARKETING PLANNING APPRAISAL PROCESS

The marketing planning appraisal process consists of the following major element:

- External appraisal
- Internal appraisal
- SWOT analysis
- Gap analysis
- Forecasting

External Appraisal

External appraisal includes all the factors outside the organisation, which provide opportunities or pose threats to the organisation. The external appraisal involves scanning of external environment. (External environment has already been discussed in chapter 2.) The following factors affect external environment appraisal:

(a) Organisation related factors

- Organisation's structure
- Organisation's size
- Organisation's age
- Organisation's complexity
- Nature of business
- Nature of product and services

(b) Strategy-related factors

- Experience in the formulation of strategies
- Evaluation level
- Motivation level
- Styles of working
- Ability to work hard
- Team spirit
- Power equations

Internal Appraisal

Internal appraisal can be understood in terms of the organisational resources, behaviour, strengths, weaknesses, synergistic effects, and distinctive competencies. Resources as a basis of internal superiority are explained in the following diagram.

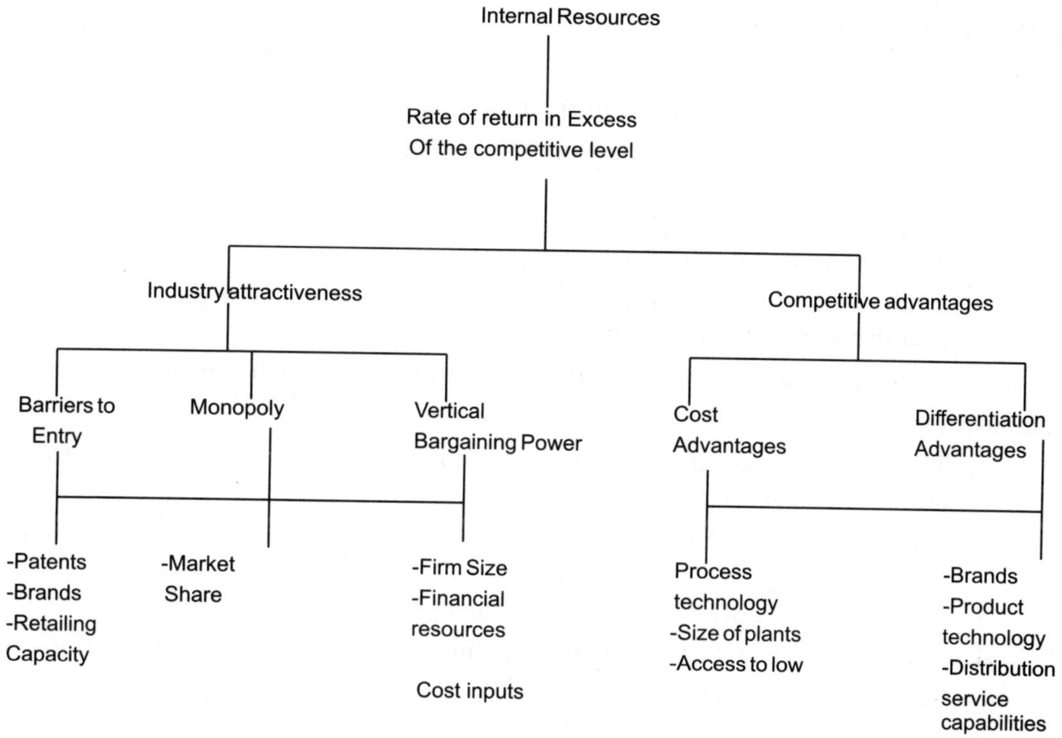

S.W.O.T. Analysis

S.W.O.T. are best appreciated in the context of marketing analysis and strategy formulation. Together, a consideration of the environment, the resources, values, expectations and objectives provide the basis for marketing analysis, so as to arrive at a view of the organisation's strategic situation. It helps to form a basis for deciding on the extent to which a change in strategy is necessary. The components of S.W.O.T. analysis are as follows with a few examples.

Strengths	Weaknesses	Opportunities	Threats
Resources	Deficiencies in resources, skills and capabilities	Favourable situation	Unfavourable situation
Relative competitive advantages	Financial resources	Identification of a new market segment	Entry of new competitors
Image	Sources of outfit	Changes in competitive or regulatory circumstances	Slow market growth
Infrastructure	Technological changes	Major technological changes	Inadequate measures viewed against changes in product/market scope
Market leadership	Appearance of substitute products		

S.W.O.T. Analysis: Pepsi

Strengths

1. It is the most famous drink in the Indian and foreign markets.
2. It has target customers of the young generation who spend a lot of money on food and drinks.
3. It has the maximum sales of its product called Fountain Pepsi, which is becoming increasingly popular and most acceptable in all forms.
4. It has large resources to take care of advertising and sales promotion required for a cold drink industry from time to time.
5. It does aggressive advertising and sales promotion, which is making the drink popular.

Weaknesses

1. The price of Pepsi cans is too high, the quantity being only 30 ml more than the bottle due to which sales are not picking up.
2. No sales promotion has been undertaken for Pepsi cans. This may be a reason for its falling sales.
3. Pepsi dispensers are not doing well due to the high cost of Pepsi cans.
4. Retailers are not motivated to keep huge dispensers outside their shops due to the discomfort in its operation.
5. Pepsi has been concentrating on only one aspect of sales promotion that is sponsoring events, other methods, which can also prove fruitful are being completely ignore in the recent past.
6. No sales promotion or advertising of Fountain Pepsi has been done since a long time.
7. Pepsi has been concentrating on promotional schemes in short run. It has not come up with aggressive advertising and sales promotion for a long time.

Opportunities

1. Some of the customers are brand loyal to Pepsi.
2. The concept of Fountain Pepsi has gained acceptance and popularity due to taste, price and easy use.
3. The cost of Fountain Pepsi is much less as compared to other forms because the company has to supply mainly the concentrate. Hence, the cost of transportation is also reduced. Pepsi should try and build customers for Fountain Pepsi to a large extent.

Threats

1. Coco-Cola is the main threat to the company as it is also a multinational with large resources to spend on attainment of customer satisfaction and understanding their preferences.
2. Coke is perceived as a 'known brand' by most customers with a known taste due to its re-launch in India.

3. Thums-Up and Coca-Cola have come up with aggressive sales promotion, which is likely to cut Pepsi sales in both short-run and long-run.

   Short-run: Because some of Pepsi's customers may shift to Thums-Up due to its lucrative free gifts/offers/contests.

   Long-run: Because some of Pepsi's customers may develop a taste for Thums-Up and switch their brand.
4. Recently, sales promotion scheme introduced for Fountain Pepsi flopped due to unattractive offers.
5. Coke has also come up with fountain concept with a wide range to offer for Colas like Cherry Coke, Diet Coke and Regular Coke.

S.W.O.T. Analysis: Coca-Cola

Strengths

1. Coke after its re-launch in India has gained wider consumer acceptance.
2. It is not as sweet in taste as Pepsi as perceived by most customers.
3. It is popular in both Indian and foreign market.
4. It has resources to undertake aggressive advertising and sales promotion.
5. It does heavy sales promotion, which has enhanced its sales to a considerable extent.
6. Its ads are different and sales promotional schemes interesting and exciting too.

Weaknesses

1. Consumers, as a whole, are still brand loyal to Pepsi.
2. The taste of coke is bitter as perceived by most customers.
3. Concept of Fountain Coke is still not popular.

Opportunities

1. Coke has brand loyalty of consumers due to its taste.
2. Concept of "Cherry Coke" (fountain) is likely to get accepted due to a different taste.
3. Pepsi is not doing aggressive sales promotion other than sponsoring events.
4. Coke has gained several customers due to its recent sales promotion scheme of giving a cassette of latest songs.

Threats

1. Most of the target groups are still brand loyal to Pepsi.
2. Concept of Fountain Pepsi is more popular than Fountain Coke.
3. Similar promotion as that of Pepsi for bottles (300 ml) is likely to result in confusion amongst customers.

The example of the festival offer of Coke and Pepsi at the time of Holi will make the point clear. Coke offered a packet of Gulal with every 1 litre bottle. Pepsi offered a packet of Gulal with every 300 ml bottle. This kind of rival advertising on part of Pepsi is likely to cancel out the effect of Coke's sales promotion. Hence, Coke should keep a track of competitor's strategy and anticipate competitor's reaction. Otherwise, Pepsi is likely to pose a threat in the future.

Gap Analysis

It helps in understanding the gap between the current situation and the desired situation. The objective of gap analysis is to understand the reasons for the gap and how can the gap be bridged when it is too large. Broadly there are three types of gap analysis: (1) Profit gap, (2) Sales gap, and (3) Risk gap.

The following actions are necessary to avoid too large a gap in an organisation.

1. Creative solution for closing the gap must be developed.
2. The desired future must be redefined with focus on those aspects of business objectives likely to be accomplished and those will have the most significant impact.
3. Conversion of long-range plans into short-range functional plans.
4. Budgetary control.
5. Updating and reconsideration of the plan as required.
6. Assignment of tasks to individuals.

Forecasting

Forecasting is based on certain assumptions about the future course of events. In a world of uncertainty future conditions can never be predicted perfectly. Forecasting is used in all management areas and depends upon certain assumptions made. The assumptions and methods employed in forecasting depend upon the nature of the planning needed. There are two major types of planning, which always require forecasting, short-term planning and long-term planning.

(a) Short-term planning requires short-term forecasting. In this type of forecasting, the forecasts are prepared for short-term normally not exceeding one year. The importance of short-term forecasting can be discussed as follows:

1. It helps in understanding of near future prospects, regarding rapid fluctuations, which occur in production scheduling and sales planning.
2. Price forecasting may help the firm in reducing the costs of operation and determining the price policy.
3. It helps in the fixation of sales targets and for establishing controls and incentives.
4. It helps in short-term financial forecasting also. Cash requirements will depend upon the level of sales and production operations.

(b) Long-term forecasting. Forecasts are important for several aspects of long-term planning.

- It helps in analyzing long-term demand potential of the products and services. It helps in allocation of resources.
- It considers growth of the organisation, its market share and market position in the long-run.
- It helps in demand estimation of various products and their broad categories for purpose of demand analysis:

(i) Consumer non-durable goods,
(ii) Consumer durable goods, and
(iii) Capital goods.

STRATEGIC MARKETING PLANNING MODELS

(I) The Bostan Consulting Group's Growth-Share Matrix (B.C.G. Model)

B.C.G. involves S.B.U. being positioned in a matrix on the basis of market growth rate and their market share relative to that of the largest competitor, or competitive position is measured on a logarithmic scale against the share of the firm's largest competitor. Market growth rate provides an indicator of the relative attractiveness of the market sewed by each of the businesses in the company's portfolio. Relative market share is calculated as an S.B.U.'s market share divided by the market share of the largest competitors in the same S.B.U. S.B.U. can also be positioned in the circle in the matrix. The size of the circle represents the proposition of company's sales generated by S.B.U. Market growth rate plotted on vertical axis indicates the annual growth rate of the market in which the business operates. It ranges from 0 to 20 per cent, it can be separated into 'high' and 'low' areas. Relative market share is plotted on horizontal axis. It ranges from 0.1 to 10. For example, a relative market share of 0.15 means that the company's sales volume is only 15 per cent of leader's sales volume.

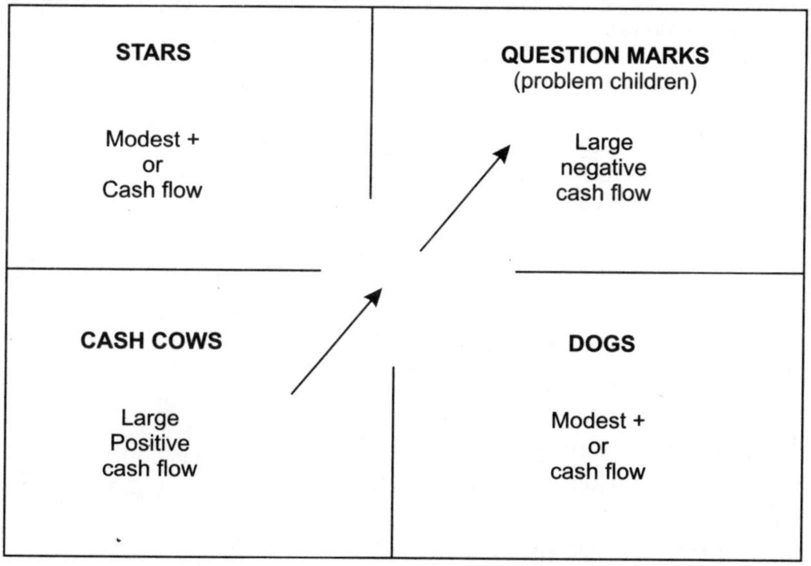

The Boston Consulting Group's Growth-Share Matrix

Further, a relative share '5' means that the company's S.B.U. is the leader and has 5 times the sales of the next strongest competitor in that market.

The B.C.G.'s S.B.U. Classification and Suggested Strategies

S.B.U. Classification	S.B.U. Characteristics	Strategy	Strategy Characteristics
1. Dogs (Low share, low growth)	Generate low profits or losses Consume more management time	Divest	Sell or liquidate the business because resources can be better used elsewhere.
2. Question Marks (Low share, high growth)	Requires a lot of cash for fast growth Continue investing in the SBU or withdrawing from the market	Build/Harvest	Increase the SBU's market share/increase the SBU's short-term cash flow and eliminate R&D expenditure
3. Stars (High share, high growth)	Generate large amount Competitors attack on SBU of cash	Build	Increase the SBU's market share
4. Cash flows	Generate considerable sums of cash enjoy economies of scales and higher profit margins	Hold/Harvest	Reserve the SBU's market share/increase the SBU's short-term cash flow and involve eliminating R&D expenditure

Example: The following information is available for M/s Max Ltd. regarding their SBUs. Suggest appropriate SBU classification and strategies.

S.B.U.	Sales (in crores)	Sales of the top 3 (in crores)	Market Growth Rate (per cent)
P	1.0	1.4, 1.4, 1.0	15
Q	3.2	3.2, 3.2, 2.0	17
R	3.6	3.6, 2.4, 2.0	7
S	6.4	6.4, 1.6, 1.4	5
T	1.0	5.0, 3.6, 3.4	5

Solution:

SBU P's relative market share (per cent):

$$= \frac{1}{1.4} = 0.71 \text{ Market growth} = 15$$

SBU Q's relative market share (per cent):

$$= \frac{3.2}{2} = 1.6 \text{ Market growth} = 17$$

SBU R's relative market share (per cent):

$$= \frac{3.6}{2.4} = 1.5 \text{ Market growth} = 7$$

SBU S's relative market share (per cent):

$$= \frac{6.4}{1.6} = 4 \text{ Market growth} = 5$$

SBU T's relative market share (per cent):

$$= \frac{1.0}{5.0} = 0.2 \text{ Market growth} = 5$$

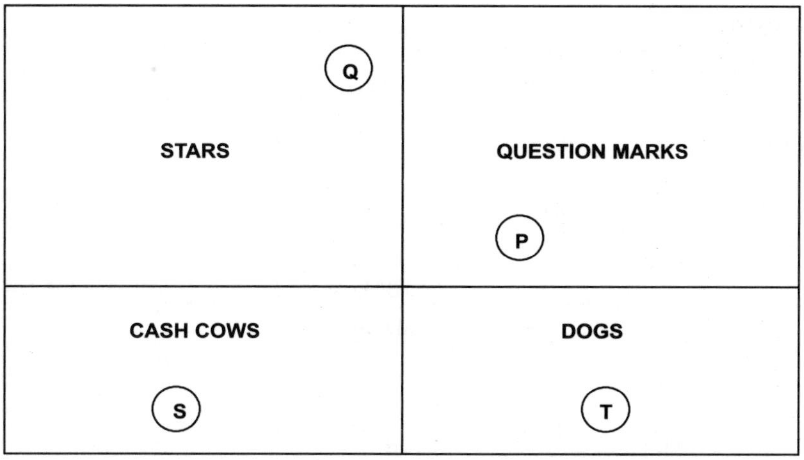

P	Question mark	The management should try to increase the SBU's market share in order to strengthen its position, and efforts to be made for increasing cash flows as far as possible.
Q	Star	The management must lay emphasis on long-term returns.
R	Cash cow	The management should ensure to continue to generate the maximum amounts of cash and preserve the market share.
S	Cash cow	The management should ensure to continue to generate the maximum amounts of cash and preserve the market share.
T	Dog	The management should try to sell or liquidate the business.

(II) General Electric Matrix (G.E. Model)

G.E. involves S.B.U. being positioned on a matrix on the basis of market attractiveness and business strength. These two factors make excellent marketing sense for rating an S.B.U. Market attractiveness and business strength depend on a number of factors. The procedure involves assigning each of the factors a weight depending on its perceived importance, followed by assessing how each S.B.U. compares on each factor on a 1 to 7 rating scale, and then computing a weighed composite rating.

Example: M/s B.T. Ltd. considered the following factors for market attractiveness and business strengths for S.B.U. 'K':

(A) Market Attractiveness

	Weight	Rating	Value
Market size	0.30	5	1.5
Market growth	0.20	4	0.8
Substitutes	0.10	4	0.4
Competition	0.20	2	0.4
Market quality	0.20	1	0.2
	1.00		3.3

(B) Business Strength

	Weight	Rating	Value
Production	0.1	3	0.3
Research & Development	0.1	3	0.3
Suppliers	0.1	3	0.3
Relative Market share	0.4	5	2.0
Distribution Network	0.3	4	1.2
	1.0		4.1

Business Strength

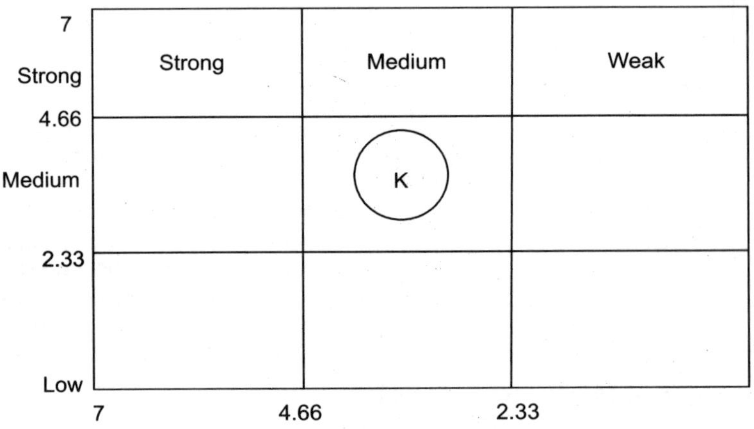

S.B.U. K's Position in G.E. Model

S.B.U. 'K' is in medium market attractiveness and medium business strength cell. Therefore, management should use selectivity strategy for S.B.U. 'K'

G.E. Model and Strategies

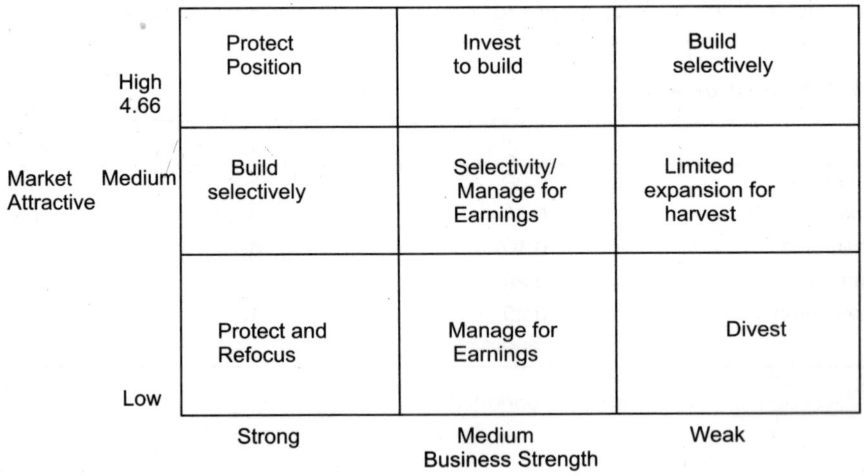

(III) The Arthur D. Little Model

This model is based on competitive position and stage of industry maturity. The competitive position is recognised in five main categories: (a) dominant, (b) strong, (c) favourable, (d) tenable, and (e) weak. The second dimension of the model—the stage of industry maturity ranges from embroyonic to ageing. The combination of competitive position and industry maturity provides the basis for determining the S.B.U.'s strategic conditions and subsequently the identification and evaluation of the strategic options open to the company. The ADL model is as follows:

	Embryonic	Growth	Mature	Ageing
Dominant	Grow fast Build barriers Act offensively	Grow fast Aim for cost Leadership Defend position Act offensively	Defend position Increase the importance of cost Act offensively	Defend position Focus Consider Withdrawal
Strong	Grow fast Differentiate	Lower cost Differentiate Attack small firms Focus	Lower costs Differentiate	Harvest
Favourable	Grow fast Differentiate	Focus Differentiate Defend	Focus Differentiate Hit smaller firms	Harvest
Tenable	Grow with the Focus	Hold on or withdraw industry Niche Aim for growth	Niche. Hold on or withdraw	Withdraw
Weak	Search for a niche Attempt to catch others		Withdraw	Withdraw

Source: Adapted from ADL.

STAGE OF INDUSTRY MATURITY

Marketing Elements: Functional Planning

The marketing strategy is to be developed on the basis of functional plans and programmes. Further, detailed plans will act as a guide for marketing objectives and marketing strategies. Functional plans are instruments, which translate grand strategy to market place reality. If the functional plans are not drawn properly, the marketing strategy may turn into failure at the market place.

Marketing Organisation Plan	Sales Forecast	Sales Plan	Product Plan
Organisation structure	Setting sales objectives	Market analysis	Product policies
Size of organisation	Internal appraisals	Sales programmes	Product life cycle
Communication and coordination	External appraisals	Allocation of sales territories	Portfolio analysis
Direction and controlling	Spotting opportunities	Sales reports	Branding
		Sales budgets	New product development Packaging

Marketing Functional Plans

Distribution Plan	Sales Force Plan	Advertising and Sales Promotion Plan
Challen stock levels	Selection	Media Planning
Ordering system	Training	Sales promotion tools and techniques
Challen relationship	Controlling	Personal selling
Channel motivation	Motivating	Public relations
Channel negotiations	Retaining	Direct marketing
Distribution strategy	Performance Rating	
Physical distribution		
Transportation		
warehousing		
inventory handling		

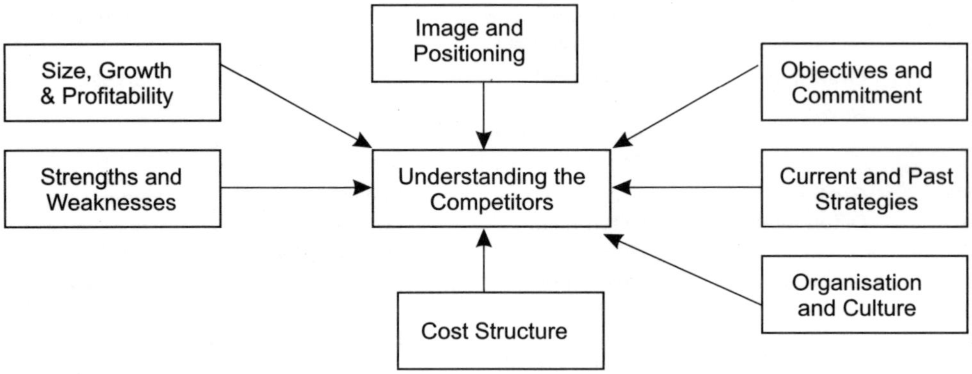

The Value Chain

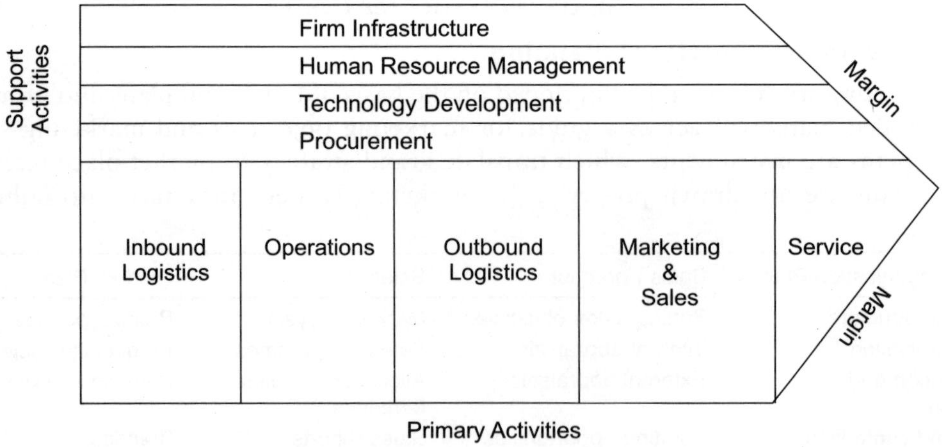

Competitor Analysis

Potential Competitors

- — Market expansion
- — Product expansion
- — Backward integration
- — Forward integration

Strategic Competitors

Basics of Competitors Analysis

- Competitors can be identified by customer choice (the set from which customers select) or by clustering them into strategic groups (firms that pursue similar strategies and have similar assets, competencies, and other characteristics).
- Competitors should be analyzed along several dimensions, including their size, growth and profitability, image, objectives, business strategies, organisational culture, cost structure, exit barriers, and strengths and weaknesses.
- Potential strengths and weaknesses can be identified by considering the characteristics of successful and unsuccessful businesses, key customer motivations, and value-added components.

QUESTIONS FOR DISCUSSION

1. What is meant by marketing planning? What steps are involved in marketing planning? Discuss.
2. "Marketing planning involves the development of forecasts, objectives, policies, programmes, procedures, schedules and budgets." Discuss with reference to the significance of planning in marketing.
3. Marketing plans to achieve coordinated and well-thought objectives through planning. Comment.
4. What is meant by strategic marketing planning? How can marketing objectives be preset?
5. A multinational company manufacturing sports shoes and entering Indian market for the first time has appointed you as its marketing manager. Prepare a marketing plan keeping in view the influence of internal and external factors.
6. Prepare a marketing plan for a company producing a premium car.

DIRECT MARKETING

23

INTRODUCTION

Peter F. Drucker has rightly observed that there is only one valid definition of business purpose to create and keep a customer. "Companies are not into business to make things", he said, "but to make customer". The essence of keeping a customer is to stay in touch. This is also fundamental to Direct Marketing.

What is Direct Marketing?

On a simplistic note we can say that Direct Marketing is nothing but getting the message through, directly. However, the Direct Marketing Association (U.S.A.) defined it as an "interactive system of marketing which uses one or more advertising media to effect a measurable response and/or transaction at any location".

In the above definition we identify some key words, which differentiate Direct Marketing (DM) from other marketing communications disciplines.

These key words are:

Interactive: One to one communication or interaction between the marketer and the prospect/customer.

One or more advertising media: A combination of media used to synergize, often more effective than any single medium.

Measurable Response: Possible to measure response, quite accurately.

Transaction at any location: May take place by phone, at a kiosk, by mail or by personal visit.

Direct Marketing (Direct Mail, Mail Order, Direct Response Advertising): Many relate Direct Marketing to a medium (Direct Mail) or a technique (Direct Response Advertising) or a channel of distribution (Mail Order). In fact DM is all the three, and much more.

Direct Mail is a medium through which a pre-defined and pre-determined number of selected consumers are addressed through the form of mail. Using computers, letters are easily personalised to make the maximum impact on the person receiving it. This medium becomes very effective in respect to selectivity of consumers, timings and the ability for the customer to respond using coupons or pre-paid reply envelopes.

It is one of the media, the others being newspapers, magazines, television, radio, telephone and such others used for Direct Marketing.

Mail Order is a method of selling that relies on direct Response Advertising to effect a measurable response and/or transaction by mail, telephone or other interactive media. Mail order usually means the sale of products or services to a customer or to industrial users by means of catalog or Direct Response Advertising. In many cases, the medium used in Direct Mail and the fulfillment is also by mail. As distinguished from Direct Mail, which remains one of the several advertising media used by Direct Marketers, Mail Order is a selling method.

The buyer personally visits the sellers' location to effect a transaction. The seller calls at the buyer's location in person or by telephone to effect a transaction.

Direct Mail

Even though Direct Mail is only one of a number of Direct Response Techniques, yet it is the category most associated with Direct Response Advertising in terms of both format and execution. It is rare that major advertising campaigns do not at least consider Direct Mail is media vehicle.

According to the American Association of Advertising Agencies, Direct Mail offers five primary advantages. They are:

1. **Selectivity**: The market that the marketer wants to tap can be identified and covered in the way he wants it to be. Elimination by region, by state, by market, and by individuals is possible. The medium offers the benefit of minimum waste and maximum efficiency. The entire market can be hit with a single mailing or the market can be segmented and some prospects can be mailed six times as often as the others. Through a continuous process of selecting mailing lists, testing them and segmenting them, targeting can be made more effective.
2. **Ideal for Response**: A ready to use, pre-addressed, postage paid reply card or envelope can be included to promote maximum response. Hence, it is an action-oriented medium.
3. **Personal Impact**: The Personal "One-at-a-time" quality of Direct Marketing implies that the prospect reads the communication without competing intervening messages.

When mailing is done by name, copy and offers can also be adjusted to fit things known about the recipient. The computer letter has made a number of creative possibilities available to copywriters who want to individualise the letters they write. Addressing the person by name instead of addressing him as "Dear Friend" can make a significant difference in bridging the gap between the sender and the receiver of the message, leaving an enormous impact.

4. **Flexibility of Format and Timing**: Minimum standardisation of format is required and each Direct Mail package can be made interesting through the use of various devices.
5. **Measurability**: Direct Mail lends itself to precise calibration of results. In a lead getting effort, the number of prospects converted into sales can be found out. An analysis of responses by variables such as list, copy approach, offers can be made.

The four primary objectives of an effective Direct Mail campaign are:

1. **Building Sales**: It can be used to introduce sales people, promote other forms of advertising or announce a product introduction. It can also be used to make a sale.
2. **Cultivating Customers**: It should be effectively used to build customer relationships in the long-run.

3. **Supporting Dealers:** Direct Mail can alert dealers to future customer promotions, educate them on service problems and survey them concerning their needs.
4. **Providing Internal Benefits:** It can also be used to build company morale. Internal newsletters and other employee communication are often used to personalise large corporations.

To depict two Direct Mail packages, we would like to take examples of the Reader's Digest.

The key to successful Direct Mail is reaching the right person. The best product, the most creative message and even the lowest price are all wasted on a non-prospect.

Information about who the prospective buyers are, what they buy, how often they buy, whether they buy by phone or by mail, how much they spend and by what methods they pay, becomes crucial to any Direct Marketer. These databases are the secret weapons of most Direct Marketers.

In the 90's, the key work in Direct Marketing will be 'Database Marketing'. The process is one of feedback between the sellers and their customers to more precisely define the letter's interest and purchase intentions and its constant updation. In its simplest form, database larger pool of prospects. Outfits like Reader's Digest and Bull Worker have built up exhaustive databases which are very closely guarded. The Kamat's Club has built it's database by asking the consumers to staple their business cards to the Coupon Response advertisements which are to be mailed back. This technique has also been applied by the Travel Corporation of India.

The major sources of input for databases are the mailing lists. They are simply a way to organise otherwise random material into market segments.

There are basically four types of lists:

1. **Compiled lists:** This is a list of names, addresses and information about the prospects combined usually by some common interests. Examples of such lists include telephone directory listings, the newly born, public records such as voters' lists. There are other extensive complications in the business, professional, educational, technical and agricultural markets. These lists are generally less valuable and less expensive than response lists as they do not offer a previous record of direct response purchase. Many see them as a supplement to response lists. They represent a source of external data.
2. **Response lists:** Mailing list houses may rent lists of people who have ordered something by direct mail or who have responded to an advertisement for further information. The people on response lists are those who are prone to order by mail and therefore these lists are more productive than compiled lists. A mail-derived list can either be a house list (Internal data or a list of customers/inquiry rented from other companies).
3. **House lists:** These are the finest asset of any Direct Marketer. The customers on these lists are those who may have bought by mail, have dealings with the company, have confidence in its integrity and merchandise. Such house lists active customers, inactive customers, inquiries and referrals represent additional value at no extra cost.

   House lists can be made more productive if these are looked at as specific segments in terms of geographic, demographic and pychographic.

4. **Rental lists:** In effect, these are house lists of other business houses. Magazine publishers like the Reader's Digest can be a valuable source of information for such lists since they lend to reach certain demographic groups.

Within the Response lists, there are certain factors which determine the likelihood of getting a response. Catalog giants, Sears and Wards have suggested the RFM-Recency, Frequency, Monetary-formula as a criterion to effectively and cost efficiently promote such an effort. It is based on the premise that recent responders are better prospects than prospect from long ago. Again, frequent responders are better than less frequent responders and, last but not the least, high volume purchasers are better than low volume purchasers are better than low volume purchasers.

The RFM formula forms a basis for manipulating the databases to extract the more profitable segments.

Another important factor affecting responses is seasonality for most products. The same Direct Mail package sent to the same list may have widely varying responses depending upon the time of the year it is mailed.

Reader's Digest are pioneers in running Direct Mail campaigns during Diwali and New Year seasons.

Regardless of the nature of the lists, they should be clean and up-to-date. The contents of the list must be 'as described' or wasted mailing will occur. Names and addresses that are undeliverable clearly result in wasted expenditure.

Such a file maintenance procedure will involve continuous updation with regard to addition of names, change of addresses, recording new orders and requests, etc.

A serious problem faced by Direct Marketers in compiling and maintaining list is the potential for duplicating the same individual or organisation not only within the house list but also without and between the response lists and even between the house lists and response lists.

Such a problem is removed by the data-processing operation of MERGE-PURGE wherein the computerised lists are merged together and duplicate names are purged so that what is obtained finally is only a list of net names and addresses along with a unique source key that will enable responses from each list to be tracked. This also avoids damage to the goodwill of the public.

Other Direct Mail Techniques

1. **Package Inserts:** These are used to promote additional purchases of products sent to customers or to promote other items in their product line. They do not involve additional postage costs and are directed at proven customers who have just made a direct mail purchase since they are sent along with the packages of the recently ordered goods. Ride along are inserts which are sent along with packages of other companies after careful negotiations with them at a fraction of the original costs.
2. **Co-operative Mail Advertising:** This may be pursued in an attempt to share expenses keeping in view the high cost of mailing. However, such a mailing may be highly impersonal since each advertiser's message will have to be very short. Secondly, it is

difficult to reach specific customers through joint mailing and hence this also decreases the value of mailing.

3. **Syndicated Mailing:** Here, the marketer may though prepare the price himself but may make financial arrangements with other mail order companies to mail the offer under their letterhead.

Direct mail can be used appropriately under any of the following circumstances:

1. When sampling would be both practical and desirable.
2. When the advertising message is too complicated or too detailed to be conveyed efficiently in other media.
3. When a specific, selected market is desired and other media can provide it only at the cost of waste circulation.
4. When personal, personalized, or confidential communication is desired.
5. When the format or colour that an advertiser's marketing strategy requires can't be carried in other media.
6. When a specific market area needs to be covered with a minimum of slop-over into adjacent areas.
7. When specific timing or frequency of contact is desired.
8. When couponing is desirable.
9. When controlled research is called for (for example, measuring of effectiveness within certain markets; ascertaining prospect profiles; or testing price, packaging or logical users for new products).
10. When controlled mailing is desirable (mailings will go only to certain income groups, owners of certain makes of cars, boat owners, etc.).
11. When Mail Order (sale of the product directly to the prospect, without retailers, dealers or other media) is desirable.

As suggested above the variety of forms or devices that can be mailed is limited only by one's imagination. Among the more popular forms are the following:

Letters	Programmes
Folders	Sales, research and informative
Broadsides	Bulletins
Booklets	Charts
Brochures	Posters
Self-mailers	Blow-ups
Postcards	Coupons
Mailing cards	Calendars
Catalogues	Reprints
House magazines	Memorandums
Blotters	Printed novelties

Price lists
Sale and informative
Invitations
Telemarketing
Business cards
Order forms
Reply cards and envelopes

Effective communication is vital to corporate survival and success and the telephone is becoming the most important part of the communications strategy. In many areas, it is replacing post and personal contact as the most efficient way to send, receive and process information. The combination of database information and effective telemarketing techniques can help to develop a powerful competitive edge. Many companies now recognize that telemarketing can help them make the most effective use of the telephone-increasing revenue, reducing costs and improving customer service.

Although telephone technology is advancing rapidly and sophisticated telemarketing systems are available for small, medium and large businesses, companies are still reluctant to take advantage of the marketing opportunities.

BT's Business News quotes research that shows people are increasingly keen on buying by phone. 67%-80% of those interviewed, claimed they found telephone ordering easy and convenient. Telephone ordering is used successfully in a wide variety of industries, including computer hardware and software, car insurance, office stationery components and catalogue-based products.

The telephone is probably the most important interface between your organisation and your customers. It is vital for increasing sales, taking orders, handling enquiries, delivering customer service or collecting payments. Here is how two leading companies are using telemarketing.

The Importance of the Telemarketing Database

Telemarketing offers considerable business benefits but the database is crucial to success. It has three main roles:

1. To provide customer information to operators so that they can improve customer handling.
2. To provide a basis for proactive selling to the customer.
3. To help gather and use additional customer information via the telephone.

At minimum, a telemarketing database should contain the following information:

- Name
- Address
- Account number
- Purchase history
- Preferences/special requirements
- Products and services bought
- Frequency of purchase
- Contact history

The operator has all the information to hand whether it is an outbound sales call or an inbound call handling orders or enquiries. By linking telephones and computers, for example, staff can handle calls quickly and efficiently and provide a highly personalized service. With Computer Technology Integral (CTI), calls can be coordinated with computer-based business applications. Information screens can be transferred simultaneously. That improves both productivity and customer service.

CTI can also be used to generate outgoing calls automatically and intelligently, again with screen information. This can increase the productivity and efficiency of telemarketing staff, particularly in intensive outbound applications.

Three Basic Properties of Direct Marketing

(i) A definite offer to the consumer;

(ii) All the necessary information provided to make a decision; and

(iii) A mechanism to respond to the offer. Within this framework fall all direct marketing options—sales letters, catalogues, telemarketing, direct response, TV advertisements and the Internet.

Direct marketing is an effective tool for both consumer and business-to-business marketing. Business that rely heavily on direct marketing include magazine and newsletter publishers, mail-order merchandisers, fund raisers and book clubs. Marketers often find that employing a combination of various direct marketing options in a given campaign works best.

Customers are getting used to the concept of personalised delivery. Direct marketers customise their products and services to satisfy their clients. With the increase in travel time and pollution, more and more customers are being attracted to the facility of direct marketing.

Entrepreneurs and businessmen also find direct marketing attractive for several reasons:

(i) Investment required is low;

(ii) It does not require any specialised skills either;

(iii) All that is required is a database with consumer profiles;

(iv) Returns are quick and its effectiveness can be measured to the last rupee; and

(v) Customer reaction can be known immediately.

If one is a little more enterprising, he could start something on his own with just a telephone.

An interesting example of direct marketing is the case of a person who started his business in a locality of Delhi with 1500 apartments. He got leaflets printed announcing free home delivery of any product required with his residential address and phone number. That cost him Rs. 2,000. He also paid Rs. 150 each to the newspaper vendors for inserting this leaflet in every newspaper they delivered. Once a week he went to Sadar Bazar to stock goods at home. He not only earned enough money to quit his job but also substantial goodwill in the locality.

Of course, everything depends upon trust. If one misuses the trust bestowed upon and overprices his product he will soon find his business collapse.

Also the Internet has made direct marketing more exciting. Some of the world's biggest retail shops are offering millions of products on the Internet. Customers can browse through the product list and order from the comfort of their homes. Businessmen can also build their business on the net.

According to the Direct Marketing Association (DMA), "Direct marketing is an interactive marketing system that uses one or more advertising media to effect a measurable response and/or transaction at any location".

Mass Marketing versus Direct Marketing (One-to-One Marketing)

Mass marketing	DIRECT MARKETING (One-to-one marketing)
Average customer	Individual customer
Customer anonymity	Customer profile
Standard product	Customised market offering
Mass production	Customised production
Mass distribution	Individualised distribution
Mass promotion	Individualised messages
Share of market	Share of customer
All customers	Profitable customers
Customer attraction	Customer retention

Source: Adapted from Don Peppers and Martha Rogers, the one-to-one future (New York: Double day/currency, 1993).

Don Peppers and Martha Roggers have also listed the main differences between mass marketing and direct marketing (one-to-one marketing techniques). Organisations know their individual customers, can customise their product offer, message, shipment and payment methods to maximise the customer appeal. Today's companies are building customer database. These database help in maintaining and using other database and information (products, suppliers, resellers) for the purpose of contracting and transacting. Database marketing is exhaustively used by business marketers and service retailers (hotels, banks and airlines). A well-developed customer database is a proprietary asset that can give the company a competitive edge.

METHODS OF DIRECT SELLING

Telemarketing: Selling over the Phone

What would you do to market your banking products, home shopping services or anything else you would like to sell? Easy. You advertise. Where? On television, radio, in the print media, hoardings and in exhibits. But how do you know if your advertisements are catching the attention of specific potential customers and not spilling over into unrelated areas? Moreover, how do you know that the customer will come back for a repeat purchase? The traditional way of benching and promoting products with a huge splash is still around. But now the economic slowdown is being overcome and company budgets are increasingly providing for alternative direct marketing tools to sell their products. Tools are becoming more specific and comparably tools to sell their products. Tools are becoming more specific and comparably cheaper. Enter telemarketing (TM), that is marketing products and services over the telephone, a direct marketing tool, which has touched a high in the last three years. The rising demand for telemarketing services has spanned off a host of outfits like Direct Telephone Information Services Performance International (a joint venture of UK-based Tele-performance and the Indusland Media and Communications run Phone-in and several other TM companies.

These companies count only multinational banks, finance companies, electronic and computer companies, also media and publishing houses, hotels or holiday resorts, airlines, telecom firms, relation firms and so on among their clients.

Apart from professional TM services outfits, many companies including MNCs have set up their in-house TM cells. Young energetic and self-driven people with excellent communication and persuasive skills are recruited and trained to hunt out prospective clients. Typically, a TM outfit works through a well-networked team of trained telemarketers who make calls to potential clients and customers and establish direct contact with them. The key lies in convincing the customer about the value of the product or service and fixing up an appointment. The major challenge for the telemarketer is to talk to the customer on a one-to-one basis by telling him about the organisation, explaining the product so as to catch the interest of the customer and build a long lasting relationship for mutual profit. The back up team of field personnel then approaches the client and finalises the deal. Say, for instance, a team of tele-callers of the in-house TM cell of a bank or its TM associate are put on the task of providing banking products like car finance, hire and purchase schemes and so on. They are given a ready list of the company's client base, which comprises roughly 25 per cent of the target list. The remaining 75 per cent are cold calls in which potential customers are picked up at random from telephone directories. Suppose the target customer is not available, then the tele-caller has to interact equally effectively with the person who answers the phone so that he message is passed on to the actual person.

More than the salary, it is the added incentives that make the pay packets of tele-callers lucrative. Salary usually hovers around Rs. 2,500, the added incentive of about 35 per cent for every clinched deal can help one ear a cool Rs. 5,000 and above every month. In some cases, tele-marketers are also allowed to go and meet the client personally and close the deal, which gets the executive a handsome incentive of around 65 per cent. As a field marketer, one can earn an additional Rs. 6,000 every month as incentives, taking the pay package to Rs. 9,000. Some holiday resort chains even pay Rs. 8,000 to Rs. 12,000 a month, since the job involves concept selling and promotion of time-share holiday schemes.

This also involves educating the customer about a new idea and convince him to put in his money. Clearly, it is a profession where the go-getters walk away with the rewards. The marketing leads from the client base are equally distributed among the tele-callers but it really depends upon how enterprising and motivated one is to seek out new buyers and expand the company's customer base. Telemarketing can prove to be a real test of one's patience and perseverance because customers sometimes can prove to be difficult, rude and argumentative. Tele-callers must also process customer files and cross-check their credentials. Computer knowledge is an added advantage while the profession demands a minimum educational qualification of 10+2, it is one's fluency and confidence over the phone and selling abilities that count more than anything else.

Concept selling through TM is also a favourite tool of the mushrooming plantation companies. Tele-callers are also in demand for space selling, whether it is for newspapers and magazines, database information directories or any other publications. Some media houses and advertising agencies have their own space selling teams. Training for TM is usually provided on the job. The teams are handled by project managers who are responsible for setting up and managing a TM operation, including manpower administration and training. TM also offers a wide entrepreneurial scope where you can set up your own outfit and provide service to the growing number of companies opting for the direct marketing route to sell their products and services.

Sales on the Internet

If your wife happens to be out of town and you do not have a clue about household management, Intercorp's new multidimensional distribution network could offer a solution.

An access to your wife's web page listing the previous month's purchases would supply all the information and an order placed through the Internet, would instantly have the goods delivered at your doorstep.

After a market survey into the lifestyles of 250 people, Intercorp has identified a range of intermediate fast-moving consumer goods (FMCGs) which have been defined as products which a consumer would rater not dress up to buy. These include toothpastes, cosmetics, detergents and contraceptives. Convenience, price and assurance of quality are the prime considerations in buying these products.

"Our direct customer marketing system allows customers complete flexibility to purchase our products. Orders can be placed via Internet, over the phone, by mail, through our catalogue or the company personnel", says Anand Shrivastav, CEO of Intercorp, "Intercorp's marketing network seeks to eliminate the glitches that make existing distribution systems suspect. Network marketing is popular but we have observed that customers face problems as there is no guarantee that the salesperson is always going to be there. We are offering may avenues through which the customer can approach us by incorporating the latest that technology has to offer. Tele-shopping is limited to consumer durables, minimum purchase values are high, the telephone is the only means to place an order and the customer has to be watching TV", he says. However, Anand fears stiff competition from the unorganised sector.

"Home delivery by retailers and grocers is popular among housewives. We will try to wean them away by offering an assurance of quality as well as corporate backing in case of any complaints. Intercorp has devised an uncomplicated system of hiring business directors. Tenure based benefits would include home furnishing grants, child education, scholarships, interest subsidy, life/medical contributions, superannuating contributions benefits, etc. We are going to tap housewives and single women initially on a part-time basis. The sales commission earnings are attractive and there is the added attraction of invitations to exclusive events and paid holidays, gifts and cash rewards. Currently there are 5,000 localities in Delhi where Intercorp business directors are operating.

Mail Order Sales

Mail order houses are retail trading organisations engaged in main order business. This is also known as carrying on business through post or mail. In this method, customers do not visit the seller's business premises, nor do they make a personal examination of the goods before they are purchased. In this system, orders are received from customers by post and the goods are dispatched usually by V.P.P. (Value Payable Parcel) or Registered Post. In case of the mail order business the selling function is performed without the intervention of personal salesmen. Therefore, it is obvious that not all types of goods are suitable for retail selling by mail. The goods should be known for their utility so that there is no need of convincing prospective buyers about their usefulness. They must fetch sufficient price to have a wide profit margin. They must command wide demand. They must not be easily perishable. They should be available in large quantities throughout the year.

Goods of well-known brands are the most suitable articles for mail order business. Usually chemicals, patent medicines, footwear, jewellery, leather goods, watches, readymade clothes, fountain pens, toilet goods, books, etc. are sold by mail orders.

Direct Selling

Direct selling identifies the unfulfilled needs of ordinary customers. It is true that many companies believe that direct selling would work in this country. Amway, Avon, Medicare, Modi Telstra, Eureka Forbes, Indal are a few companies using direct selling and adding values for customer satisfaction. In this method, it only takes a minute to clinch a sale buy choosing the right minute to contact the customer involves a day's of work for a direct marketer. For example, 80 per cent of Eureka Forbes sales turnover came from the direct sale of vacuum cleaners, air purifiers and water purifiers. Direct marketing companies have an advantage over conventional marketers in that the relationship between the company and the customers starts building even before a sale is made. At Eureka Forbes too, the value addition continues at the follow-up stage. For example Eureka Forbes does not make a sale beyond a radius of 60 kilometers from a service center.

Lessons Learnt by Direct Marketers

The Strategy. Eureka Forbes structures its demos according to the time at the customer's disposal.

The Lesson: Keep the process flexible enough to accommodate individual needs.

The Strategy: Modi Telstra uses a clearly structured sales call process to market its cellphone services.

The Lesson: Simplify the process of negotiation to save the customers time.

The Strategy: Oriflame uses multilevel marketing to enlist direct sales agents from its customer base.

The Lesson: Use your customer to sell your product to other customers.

The Strategy: Indal empowers its salesforce to take pricing decisions on the spot when closing sales.

The Lesson: Ensure that your direct seller can conclude a deal immediately.

The following figure shows how to add value through direct selling.

Fig. 23.1: How to Add Value through Direct Selling

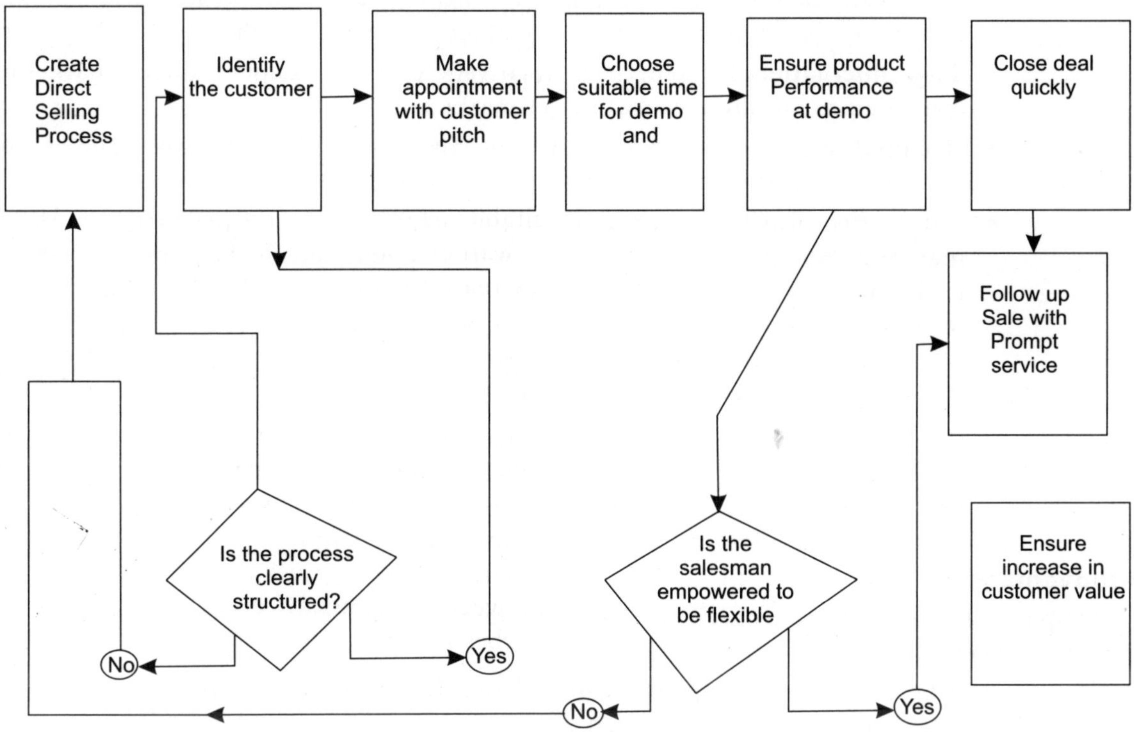

Advantages and Disadvantages of Direct Marketing

Advantages

- **Focussed approach:** It is possible to identify a very specific target market using direct marketing techniques. This makes it a very useful promotional tool for niche products because it is possible to target only those who are likely to respond to the promotion—there is less wastage.
- **Cost effective:** Although cost per thousand people reached may be high as compared to other mass marketing promotional techniques, direct marketing can be very cost effective for niche products.
- **Measurable and attributable:** It is possible to link a particular sale as being a response to a particular direct marketing activity. This is very useful information since over a period of time it is possible for an organisation to build up a picture of the kind of marketing messages to which a particular group of customers is more likely to respond.
- **Immediate and flexible:** Some promotional activities can take a great deal of time to develop from first idea to final execution—TV ads for example. Direct marketing is flexible and there are short lead times associated with its use. Direct marketing often has an immediate impact on customer responses.

- **Ability to test, retest and measure the impact of single variables:** Its flexibility also means that a number of pilot versions of a direct marketing campaign can be run before the final version is rolled out on a large scale.
- **Easy international reach:** It is relatively easy to adapt a direct marketing campaign to an international target market.
- **Tailored messages:** Direct marketing also offers greater opportunities for developing tailor-made messages for particular groups of consumers.
- **Alternative distribution channel:** Many organisations are realizing that direct marketing not only offers the opportunity to communicate with customers but it is also a means of getting their products to the customer as well. In other words, it is a mechanism for distribution as well as promotion. For example, shoe retailers such as the Bata Group see direct marketing as a way of making their merchandise available to customers who, for some reason, are unable to get to its retail outlets.
- **Opportunity to build a database:** Over-time, the details on customers—what they bought, when and so on can be used to build up a detailed picture of purchasing patters.

Disadvantages

Despite all these advantages there are a number of problems associated with direct marketing. They are:

- **May be seen as competing with existing intermediaries.** May upset marketing intermediaries as sales through direct marketing may be taking sales away from them. In effect, you may end up competing with your customers, that is, the intermediaries.
- **May be seen as intrusive by consumers.** Especially a problem for door to door and tele-marketing direct marketing techniques.
- **Costs.** Initial customer acquisition costs are high—high cost per thousand reached; and database development can be expensive.

QUESTIONS FOR DISCUSSION

1. Direct mail can be used for direct-response advertising, but all direct-response advertising do not use direct-mail. Explain.
2. Direct-response advertising is an effective device for a two-step marketing strategy. Explain.
3. The keystone in the arch of direct-mail advertising is the mailing list. Explain.
4. Interactive systems of direct marketing are the wave of the future. Do you agree or disagree? Explain.
5. Enumerate in brief the various forms of Direct Marketing.
6. What do you understand by Database Management?
7. It is said that Telemarketing will revolutionise the marketing communication process. Do you agree?

INTEGRATED STRATEGIC MARKETING

24

INTRODUCTION

Planning and communication processes within a firm run parallel to each other. This enables the firm to continuously update itself with the growth in knowledge and use this knowledge to devise its own competitive strategy. In the last few decades growth of knowledge has had a tremendous impact on the efficacy of communication methods. Technology is continuously making communication simpler.

Growth of knowledge has enabled the fast exchange and flow of ideas. It has shaped and reshaped product and service offerings, changed channels of distribution of customer access and enabled customer to get the same or added values at lower cost. Information about the growth of knowledge is, therefore, critical to firms responses.

Today, video conferencing allows people from all the world to "meet" without stepping in an airplane. This enables quick transmission of information and exchange of ideas. Therefore, new possibilities of adding values can emerge faster. Similarly growth of knowledge has improved delivery of information and services. Internet is revolutionizing the delivery of banking services. Personal banking and investing can now be done from personal computers. Growth of knowledge has also made execution of tasks simpler. Mini computers strapped to inventory clerks wrists greatly increase warehousing and distribution efficiency. Wearable computers guided by voice navigation can now be used for inventory and maintenance of industrial machines. Computers can transmit to the firm, data of movement of stocks as soon as they are lifted from store shelves. This data can be immediately transferred to suppliers enabling minimising of inventory costs and keeping track changes in customer tastes. The availability and transmission of information has a direct impact on a firm's planning process. These processes may need to be re-engineered to meet the quick supply of information inputs. The key question the firms face is what can facilitate the growth of knowledge within a firm, how to do it and how to process and deliver this addition to knowledge in a way that the customer perceives as value added.

Growth of knowledge depends on the availability of information. Information needs to be sourced. This requires co-operation with those who posses it and building channels for its inward flow. The firms planning processes increasingly depends on the ability to process this information with discrimination. The firms' output or response to this inflow and its processing can be called as the firm's competitive response.

The planning process and communication tasks have a parallel flow. The planning process, shown below, highlights this through the depiction of three sub-processes:

(i) **Inflow:** Information from many sources is available to a firm. How to choose the right sources that can help the value addition process of the firm is the first task. These sources generally be suppliers, related industries, scientific community, new customers, present customers, trade association, etc.

(ii) **Processing:** The firm needs to evolve a discrimination process that first sifts the clutter from the information flow. Next it needs to build with its human capital the systems, processes, skills, etc. that can process this information inflow in a manner that can identify where value addition can be done by the firm. The nature of internal processes of the firm is important here.

(iii) **Value Added Outflow:** Finally the firm needs to deliver value added to both customers and society. If the firms outflow also helps build value added for its suppliers or related industries, or even its competitors it can start a mutually supportive process of value addition helping create competitive advantage for the nation.

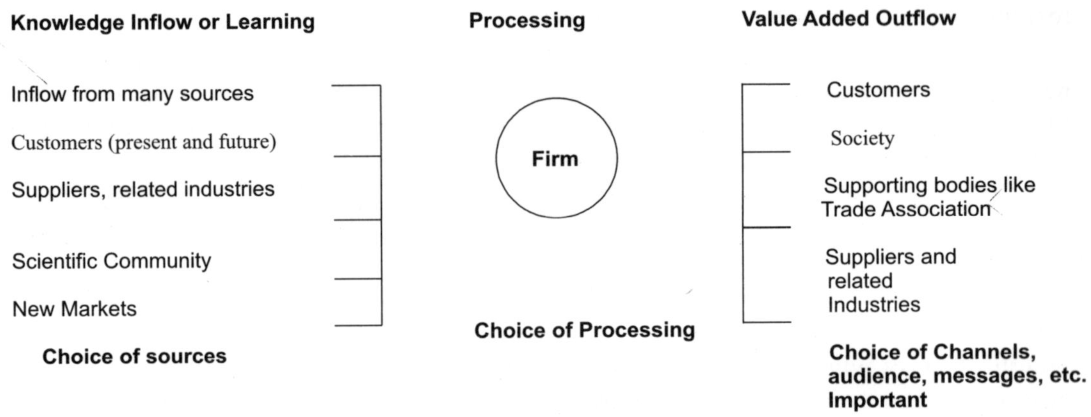

MARKETING COMMUNICATION

Marketing Communication: Beyond Traditional Definitions

While 'planning communication strategy' the word communication holds the centre linking both planning and strategy. Communication has enabled homo sapiens to progress both by transmitting knowledge. It encompasses within itself the potential for generating change as well as development of behaviour and response systems.

What holds true for mankind equally to both organizations and marketing strategy. Our study of communication, however, is often limited by the definition we give it. Marketing communication, as we define it, remains always a subset of the company's communication, it does not result from formal planning but is something that is informally achieved. Competitive success if achieved due to this overall communication that may be a result of accident rather than design. The effort here is to give a formal structure to this overall or integrated communication of the firm.

Purpose of Marketing Communication Revisited

Before we attempt an understanding of marketing communication, it is essential to start with the purpose that it seeks to achieve.

We know that the purpose of marketing effort is to increase value delivered to the customer. This is to be done at the minimum cost to the customer. The following equation sums it up

Customer Delivered Value = Total Customer Value – Total Customer Cost

The purpose of marketing communication can be no different from the purpose of marketing, i.e. to maximize customer delivered value. This can be increased by increasing the total customer value or lowering customer cost. Offering to customers which involve delivering more value or lowering cost can not be successful by effort of only the marketing department but has to involve all departments of the firm. A need, therefore, exists to recognise all communication that is innovation—driven (or driven by a desire to add value to customers) as part of marketing communication. Cross-functional cooperation is essential to design and implement a superior customer value delivering system. Hence, efforts of marketing department alone in building a communication strategy may not be able to ensure greater delivered value. The formal recognition of this mutual interdependence within the firm to deliver value, will make its focussed concern build a superior competitive strategy.

Today's age has been revolutionised by communication. Scientific technology that aids it has enabled this process. The world today is a world of innovation and open competition. Every firm, therefore, in the words of Porter, "has to attempt to put itself in a position where it is likely to perceive and best address the imperatives of competitive advantage". To achieve this competitive advantage firms must focus their concern on improvement and innovation. This has to result form a willingness to compete and realistic understanding of the environment and how to improve it. Information and communication play a very important role in the ability and capacity of a firm to innovate and successfully deliver competitive response through value added offerings to their customers.

Where communication has so significantly affected the ability of a firm to influence itself, its customers, suppliers and related industries, it is time for communication to update its own theory and upgrade the level comprehension of its enhanced abilities.

Value Addition for Customers and Society

Communication, again, is not just with present and prospective customers but also with employees, vendors, related industries, other advanced factors like human resources including skilled and scientific resources and external environments. This appreciation of the role of communication is especially critical in "knowledge intensive" industries. The primary task of all firm's efforts is to devise a competitive strategy and communication can contribute effectively to it. In-company training is one of the most important tools of communication. A good in-company communication strategy about what the customer needs and the need for ensuring cost control or increasing customer satisfaction could help increase productivity, profitability as well as offer value and satisfaction to the customer. This will especially be the case as the service element attached to the product keeps increasing.

STRATEGY

Strategy: Build it with Integrated Communication

Corporate strategy depends on understanding the business and marketing environments. Only after a correct understanding of the environment has resulted can the marketing or marketing communication planning be determined. Hence, strategy should be one that flows thematically across the corporate and marketing plans to the promotion planning process of the firm.

In today's competitive scenario communication strategy cannot ignore the imperative of competitive advantage. In fact, strategy of a firm should germinate from its ability to (a) perceive and (b) create this advantage through value added offerings. Communicating the competitive advantage of this value added is the third or final task to which all discussion of communication strategy are usually restricted. IT is suggested that a full appreciation of communication strategy is not possible unless all the three roles are understood. A firms strategy, thus, has to be built with communication. Before exploring the inter-relationship of communication and strategy building, it may be useful to begin with the parameters of strategy first.

Three Generic Strategies and Their Three Strategic Fits

To counter the competitive forces, Porter shows how the firm's Strategy can be built in three ways:

1. **Overall cost leadership:** Developing a focussed concern for and investing in cost-saving processes enables this. So does a high market share, economies of scale in production or favourable access to raw material.
2. **Differentiation:** This is the ability to create something that is perceived as unique. This could be in product design, brand image, technology, product features, customer service, and dealer network of other dimensions.

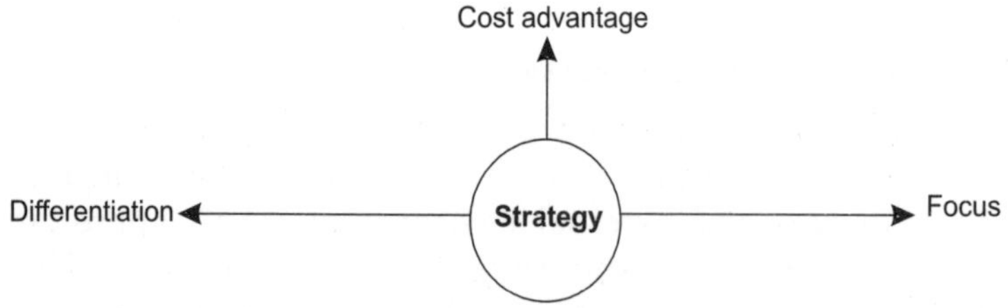

Fig. 24.1: Porter's Strategic Alternative

3. **Focus:** Instead of targeting the complete market, the firm focuses on a particular buyer group or geographic market to serve it more effectively and efficiently.

Each of the three generic strategies can be fulfilled if the three fits, listed by Porter, occur in all the activities undertaken by the firm.

A successful strategy should ensure that these three things are occurring in the activities as well as their interactive process within the firm.

(i) **Simple-consistency**: There should be a consistency between each activity (function) and overall strategy. Identifying these three C's of communication strategy of a firm in the manner described here enables this simple consistency to occur. Co-operation between the functions of the firm followed by a focussed concern for ensuring consistency leads to delivery of the firm's competitive response.

(ii) **Reinforcement**: The various activities of the firm should reinforce each other. This is exactly what identification of the three C processes seeks to do.

(iii) **Optimisation effort**: The configuration of the individual activities of the firm and the way they relate to each other should be an optimisation effort. This is the objective of identification of the three C processes.

The task of communication within a firm is, therefore, to ensure that its activities are consistent, reinforcing and optimising in nature. The ability of communication to ensure this will enable the firms competitive advantage as well as competitive success. Communication strategy and firm's strategy building processes, therefore, flow with each other. The communication processes help build the strategic processes of the firm. This appreciation requires having a re-look at the role of communication, as it has been popularly understood, till date.

From Integrated Marketing Communication to Integrated Communication Concept

The focus of integrated marketing communication is to integrate all sources that deliver the outflow of communication from the firm to ensure the delivery of a clear and consistent message to target markets. The integrated communication concept, on the other hand, stresses on the dynamic integration between both inward and outward channels of communication. This enables a consistent, mutually reinforcing and optimisation effort to make the firms plan and build its strategy. Finally, the integrated marketing communication of the firm is developed. This enlarges the appreciation of the role of communication to: (a) highlight its contribution to the value addition process of the firm and (b) enable the delivery of the value added with the help of a clear consistent message.

The integrated communication concept starts with the customer as a focus and recognises that his needs and wants are evolving and not static. It recognises that firms need to build their communication processes keeping in mind the three forces that are acting on consumer needs at all times. These forces of primary influences on consumer needs and wants are:

(i) **Seeking better value delivery for current wants through current products:** This is met by the firms ability to satisfy current consumer wants through current products in a better way. This often requires modification strategies only. The modification could be in production or distribution processes, product attributes or in carrying products uses.

(ii) **Seeking better value delivery for current wants through alternate products:** Alternate strategies are required when there are alternate ways of satisfying current wants which are developing or have developed. Technology usually builds up such threats. Kodak for example is worrying about the long-run threat from the recent invention of filmless camera. This is one of the biggest threats to the film business.

(iii) **Seeking better value delivery for new wants through new products:** New strategies are required for new emerging want opportunities in the market emerging from new innovations that the firm can offer. Such innovations could be the result of working closely with the customer or they could emerge from related or supporting industries, firm's own R&D or by new people joining the firm or its competitors. The role of supporting industries and links between scientific people across firms in spurring innovations has been widely acknowledged.

(i) The national environment and available international resources.

(ii) Forces within the firm to spur innovation, deliver three fits and manage the dynamics of competition and co-operation.

(iii) With customers.

This can ensure that it is able to devise a competitive strategy that delivers customers additional value and gives the firm a long-term competitive advantage.

To build these linkages:

(a) It needs to appreciate the determinants of competitive advantage especially in the national context the firm operates in.

(b) It needs to learn from internal practices of firms seeking excellence.

(c) It use tools of strategy building in a manner that is competitive strategy is delivered by activities that are consistent, reinforcing and optimum.

A good communication strategy builds channels that help the firm absorb information from the environment especially the national environment, enable it to 'process' the absorbed information within the organisation in such a way it can offer a unique delivered value to customers and finally communicate this value added to them in a manner that they can perceive it.

THEIR INTERRELATION

Planning and Strategy Depend on Communication

All three tasks of planning, communication and strategy formulation are interdependent. Communication, however, is the key tool they use. The role of communication within the firm nurtures and fosters the process of bottom-up planning. One of the advantages of such a process could be what Ries and Trout call "Bottom-up" marketing where one marketing tactic generates the necessary value to build a strategy around it. When the same bottom-up communication happens in non-marketing departments along with an upgradation of skills, knowledge of techniques of production and understanding of customer needs it could lead to cost advantage, productivity increase or even innovation as in new product and process ideas. The advantages that "good communicator" organisations have are the ones crucial to attaining strategic positions and competitive advantage. Hence, both strategy and planning depend upon communication.

Communication, too, should Germinate from Planning and Strategy

Communication that germinates from needs of planning and subsequent development of strategy enables the creation and delivery of additional value lower cost of both. The answer, then, to the 5W's of communication (listed below) cannot be found without inputs from firms planning and strategy development process. These 5W's are **Who** (source), **What** (message), **Whom** (Audience), **Which** (channels) medium and with **What** effect.

The Role of Communication in Value Creation and Delivery

Communication has critical role to play in the new competitive scenario where global players have easy access to local markets and can deliver better value to the customer if the local firm has not kept itself abreast of developments in technologies, processes, marketing and changing nature of consumer demand. To safeguard its position the firm has to develop and nurture its channels of communication to enable it to anticipate and adequate meet these challenges.

Primary Influences on Consumer: The Basis of Communication Strategy

This study of communication strategy begins by taking a dynamic view of the customer. The customer and his wants are not taken to be static which respond to give cues. Instead it is an exercise that recognises the involving nature of the customer and seeks to understand the influences working on him. Instead of using predetermined cues, it is itself in the process of seeking those cues that can help to comprehend the influences on the customer in better way.

To understand the primary influences on the customer we have appreciate the factors which are the main influencers. These influencers are both internal and external to the customer. The internal influencer is the 'inner drive'. For simplicity it is being shown as being expressed in two ways, i.e. seeking better value and individuality and creativity. It is affected by the position of the customer in Maslow's need hierarchy. Customers at the lower level of need hierarchy may express their individuality and creativity in a different way while seeking better value. The inner influencers form part of the customers private 'self'.

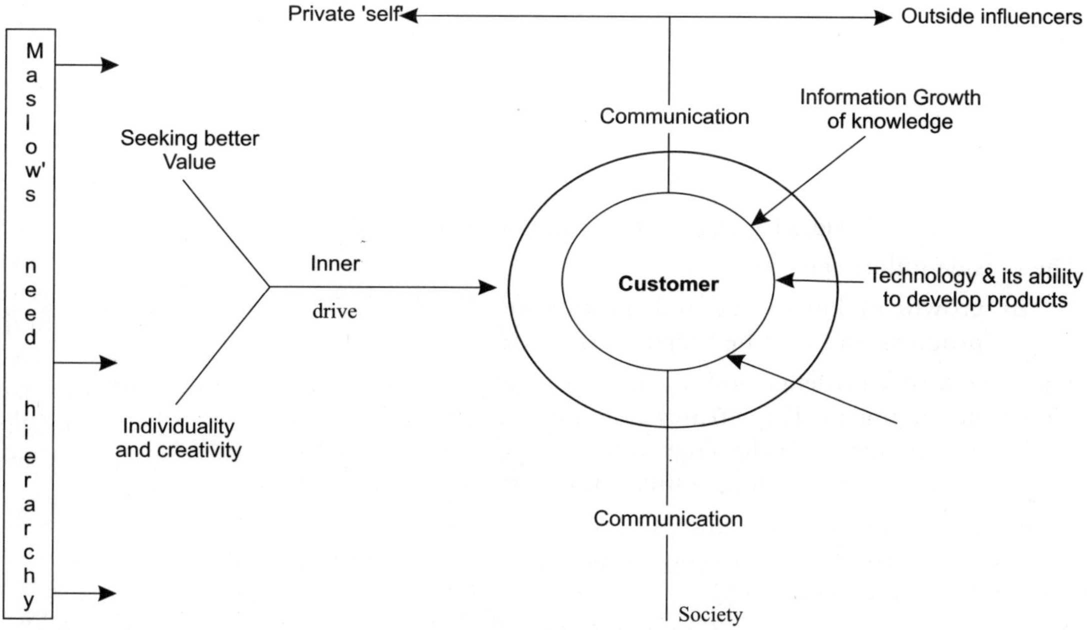

Fig. 24.3: The Shaping and Reshaping of Customers

Communication is the common thread that not only ties up the customer's private 'self with the outside influencers' but also has a role in linking the outside influencers with each other too. The importance of communication can be understood in Fig. 24.2. Influencers play a very important role in shapping customer wants. The nature of this influence has been illustrated to this figure.

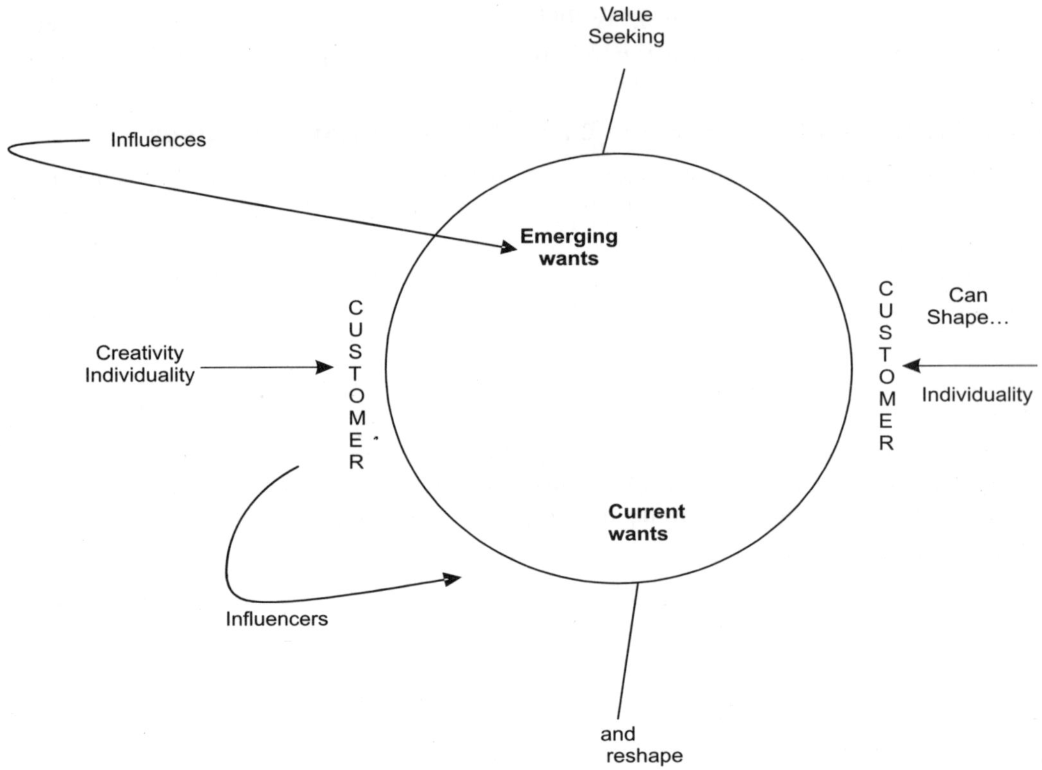

Fig. 24.2: The 'Influences' and Customers: Their Interplay

The outside influencers are:

(i) growth of knowledge and information, (ii) technology and its ability to deliver products and (iii) the socialisation process.

The growth of knowledge and availability of information has an impact on the process of technology development. This creates not only the present products but also new products through efforts of firms. Technology influences the way customers fulfill their needs. This sometimes has social implications. Often these may be hidden influences.

Figure 24.3 shows the influencers at work on the customer to both shape and reshape wants. They tend to shape emerging wants and re-shape current wants. This process is a dynamic and ongoing one.

While seeking better value is an inner desire of all customers, it is the individually of customer which enables segmentation. All customers do not seek greater value in exactly the same way. They have their individuality of needs. Creativity is another important variable which imparts the element of dynamism to customer wants. This aspect makes the study of marketing management interesting. Customers possess an ability that enables then to relate the ever-increasing knowledge and information in new and different ways. This creates the need for better products to satisfy current wants. This creative process can shape new wants as the customer is exposed to greater information, knowledge and technology possibilities in the socialisation process of course, some customers and firms may prefer *status quo* in varying degrees. Such firms may be less exposed to the growing information and knowledge or may not be able to develop access to it. Organisational inertia may be a cause of this. Similarly, some customers may not be inclined to assimilate the new learning curve that consumption of new products may require. Others may not feel the need for doing so. Their response to the influencers may be slower or non-existent.

The influencers' impact on the customer results in the emergence of the primary influencers for customer wants. These primary influences can be satisfied through present, new and alternate products.

A view of the emergence of primary influences on customer needs and wants is shown in figure below.

We have seen above that the value seeking customer has three primary influences working on him.

(a) Seeking better value delivery for current wants through current products, i.e. the desire to satisfy the present needs and wants through present products in a better way.

(b) Seeking better value delivery for current wants through alternate products, i.e. the alternate ways of satisfying present needs and wants.

(c) Seeking better value delivery of new wants through new products. Here products have to be designed for fulfilling new and emerging needs and wants.

The value seeking customer re-shapes his current wants which can be satisfied with present or modified present products. These could also be satisfied through alternate products that satisfy the same want in a different way. Emerging or new wants, being different from current ones, are unlikely to be satisfied with present products or even their alternates.

The nature of these three primary influences give a new dimension to the firm's dynamism. Firms which ignore the continuing nature of these influences are unlikely to hold loyalty of such customers who keep evolving their needs and wants based on new information and knowledge. To keep their loyalty the firm has to concentrate on the wants of the customer and develop and adapt its products to suit them. This may require different strategic choices.

For giving better value through present products, firms may need to rely upon modification strategies. The modification could be in product features and attributes or in production processes to give more efficiency and result in lower cost for customers. The quality of product could be improved and newer model designed to suit individual needs offered. The styling of the product could be improved to improve its functional use. Even repositioning could be done to highlight those features which can give additional value but were not perceived by the customer in that manner. New or alternate distribution channels may be opened to make it more convenient for customers to access the product.

Technology fuelled by growth of knowledge could create alternate ways of satisfying current wants. Such threats could be faced more by firms in the knowledge based industries. Development of new software could make many old processes redundant. The use of computers could change delivery of banking services. Internet has opened many new possibilities. In the area of impact of technology Kodak, for example, is worrying about the invention of the filmless camera and the bearing this could have on its future business.

The firm also needs to develop new products to meet the emerging wants of the customers. While the customer has many alternatives in terms of firms and countries offering products, the individual firm has to develop core strengths that can help built systems as well as structure that augments innovation. This process should form a part of the firm's strategy. Innovation often results from working close with the customer or from cooperation within the firm's departments with a concerned focus for delivering better value. It could also emerge from cooperating with related or supporting industries, firm's own R&D as well as new people joining the firm. Even if a firm keeps track of competitors who have inducted new people, a study of their responses and processes could give a firm many new ideas. Links with scientific community, laboratories, universities and other research institution also helps the firm prepare itself for the challenge of change thrown up by the new and emerging wants of customers.

The firm and the customer view the changing nature of time differently. Customers view the future based on the three primary influences working on them. Firms have to understand these primary influences but prepare for their future using core strengths.

While the customer can choose products that are being offered by firms all over the world, the firm that has to offer has to produce these products within its own national context. Of course, it can set up production facilities overseas but even at the new location it will be working within a national context.

The national context, then, emerges as a critical variable in determining how firms address their future and its tasks. However, firms may choose a national context to work in.

Firms, therefore, to succeed have to plan to achieve a competitive advantage through present and future product offerings in a given/chosen national context.

The Relevance of National 'Diamond' and Mckinsey's 7S Model in Communication Theory

Porter's theory of competitive advantage shows that there are four determinants of competitive advantage within a nation or a national context. These form the "diamond". The favourable factors (and therefore strategic choices before the firm) in producing the product are largely determined by the forces working along the 'diamond'. Therefore, the first task of communication strategy is to build its communication channels around the forces working within the diamond to enable it to formulate winning strategies that can make it offer enhanced value to its customers.

The four determinants are:

(a) Factor conditions

(b) Demand conditions

(c) Related and supporting industries

(d) Firm structure and nature of competition within an industry.

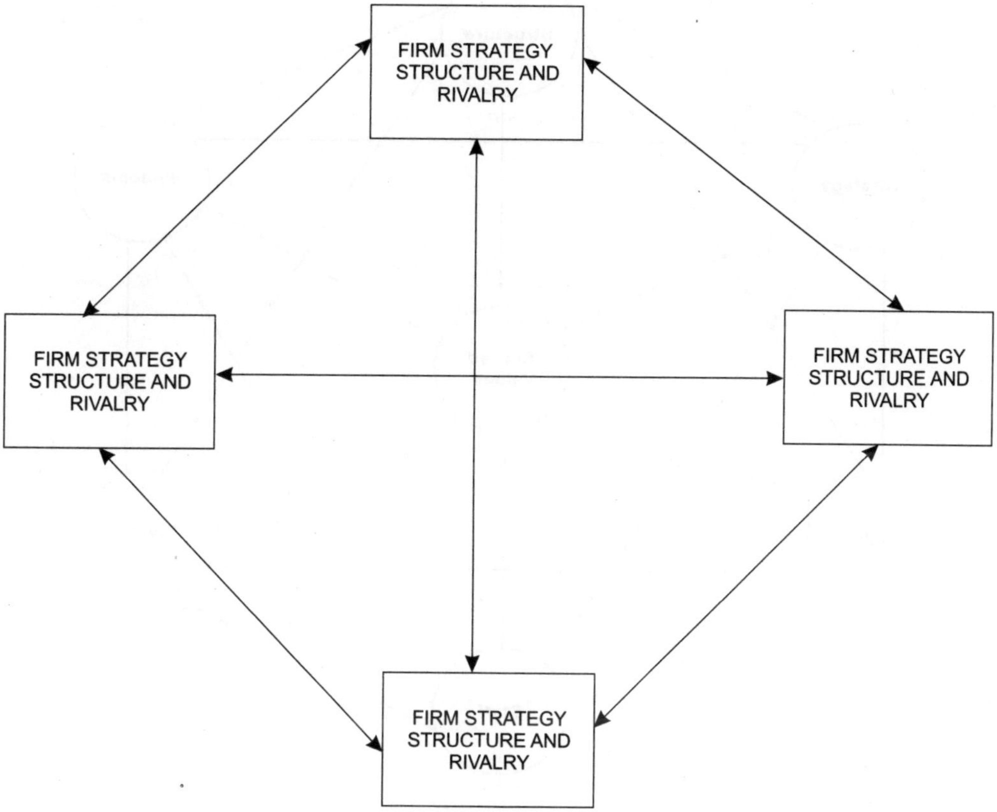

Fig. 24.4: The Determinants of National Competitive Advantage

Source: Michael Porter, *The Competitive Advantage of Nations*.

The ability of a firm to succeed within a national context depends on:

(a) How is it able to seek information and build communication channels with the determinants of competitive advantage.

(b) Process the 'information' received within the firm to formulate a value adding strategy. For doing this task it has to be understood how firms seeking excellence build their organisation strategy. The Mckinsey's 7S Model illustrated here is a good beginning along with a study of excellence-seeking processes of successful firms.

(c) Communicate the strategy with customer to enable them to perceive the value addition.

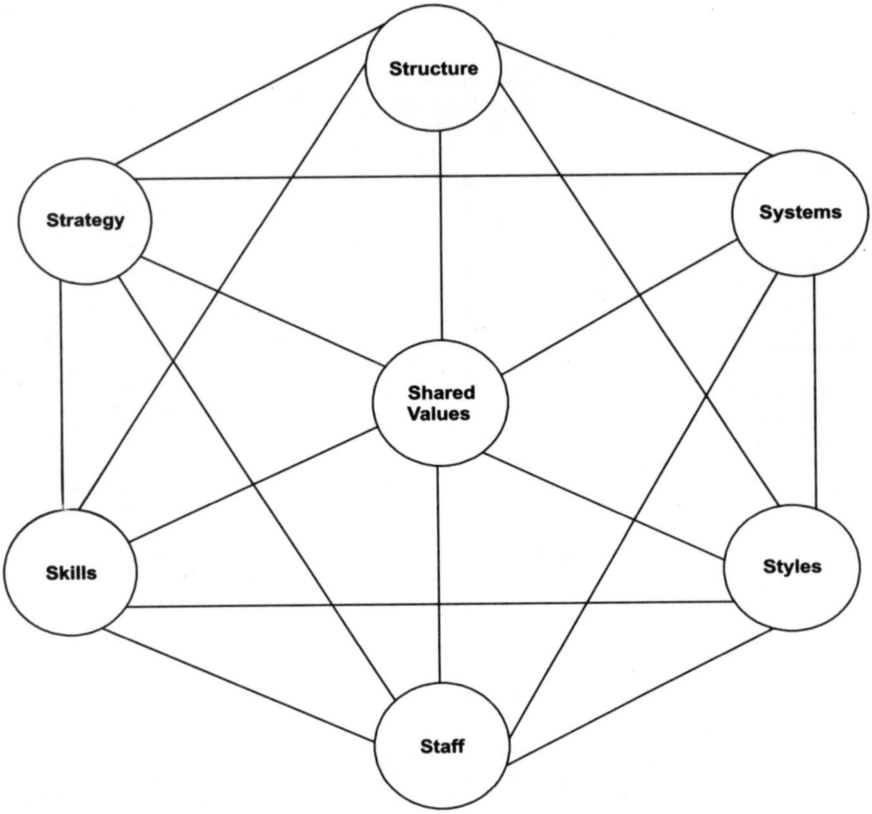

Fig. 24.5: McKinsey's 7S Model

The New Model of 'Communication and Strategy'

Keeping these tasks in mind the imperatives of the firm's strategy building efforts can be summed up in Fig. 24.5. Kotler, when discussing abut the development of management thought, has remarked: In the 60's "Theory Y" called on companies to treat their employees not as cogs in a machine but as individuals whose creativity can be released through enlightened marketing practice. In the 70's "Strategic Planning" offered way of thinking about building and managing company's portfolio of businesses in a turbulent environment. In 80's "Excellence and Quality" received major attention as new formulas of success. All of these are valued and inspire business thinking. In the 90's many firms have acknowledged the critical importance of being customer-driven in all their activities. It is not enough to be product-driven or technology-driven... Success in 1990's and beyond rests on a market and customer based view of business. "His analysis seeks to present such a view."

The two figures shown earlier presented a market and customer-oriented view of business. The first figure showed the forces of growth, the knowledge, information, technology and the socialisation processes as the predominant forces working in the market. The second figure showed how the needs of the following build a model of how the firm should respond within this market and customer orientation. Therefore, it seeks to create a 'fit' between the firm's activities and the customers emerging requirements. Firms that are able to generate this 'fit' or this match between product and market/customer are likely to build competitive advantage and achieve competitive success.

Figure given below presents a customer-centric view of the market, the opportunities it presents as well as how the individual firm can develop its strategic responses. Each of the lines representing the boundaries of the concentric circles could represent channels of two way communication. The first-two concentric circles represent the interactive nature of customer wants and market opportunities. The last three concentric circles represent the three C's, which are necessary ingredients of both communication and strategy building. These help develop the firm's competitive response to the customers need and the market opportunities that they create.

The area outside the concentric circle (firm's interaction with society) will be discussed in point four below.

These three represent processes of strategy and communication. These are:

1. **Co-operation** (the first and the area within the third concentric circle). The circle mainly represent external communication (communication with external world) to generate a 'net inflow' or information. This entails both working closely with sophisticated buyers (through understanding 'home demand composition' in the demand conditions) and developing communication channels around the determinants of national competitive advantage. In fact, working closely with sophisticated buyers and trade association is so important that it needs separate attention. A good framework of understanding this process is through appreciating Porter's National Diamond and the implication it has for both the firm's strategy development and communication strategy.
2. **Focussed concern:** (The second 'C' and the area within the fourth concentric circle) for successful strategy development two focal strength need to be developed by the firm in this concentric circle. These are:
   (i) ***Internal communication (processing):*** To internalise the interaction or "process" the inputs received. A good framework of understanding this process is through Mckinsey model and study of processes of firms seeking excellence.
   (ii) ***Discrimination:*** This implies the ability to sift the 'wheat' from the 'chaff', i.e. separate the relevant information from the irrelevant one. Then it should identify where the firm can add value. This needs a good understanding of the firm's current strengths as well as realistic assessment of the strengths it can or needs to develop. It also implies an ability to identify the key activities critical for the firm's competitive success and to focus on them.

The area of focussed concern contains within itself the forces of both cooperation and competition which have to be managed with discrimination.

3. **Competitive Response**: (The third 'C' and the area within the fifth concentric circle). This represents the area of execution of both strategy and communication with the customer (i.e. Net Outflow). The firm develops the delivery system for its competitive response. The firm has two tasks here, (a) delivery value added, and (b) making the customer correctly perceive the value addition. Such communication meaningful.

(Net outflow is the term used here because inflow of information through distribution channels, salesmen, Market Research (MR), etc. also exist in this circle.)

4. The above 3C's represent the present processes of communication and strategy (whether formally planned or informally achieved). However, some unfulfilled tasks remain in the depiction of the three C's. When the interaction between the firm and society generates competitive responses that are compatible with society's long-term interests, the 4th C emerges. This is shown in figure and involves anticipating the impact of firms value addition on society. Satisfying customer wants and serving long-run customer interests may not always be the same thing. Firms need to study the impact of their offerings on social processes, earths resources as well as look at other legal, ethical and moral issues. When a firm has anticipated these issues, it enables a competitive response that benefits from a compatibility advantage. This offers the customers, firms, cluster, industry, nations and society the advantage of compatibility in their value seeking, value delivery and value creation processes. It ensures that conflicts that are reflected today through concerns for environment, decay in cultural values through influences of new behaviour patterns and lifestyles associated with 'development', ethical and legal issues are resolved by informal processes of firms and society before they can arise. The emphasis here is on tempering the growth of knowledge with the realisation of wisdom. This has been elaborated upon in following section as the challenge facing communication.

The First 'C' Co-operation: Helping Firms, and Industry

The firm, in today's scenario of global competition is likely to have its fortunes interlinked with the cluster, industry and home nation. Global market shares depend on competitive strategies built on the strength of a home nation's competitive strategies built on the strength of a home nation's competitive advantage. This competitive advantage is usually the result of cooperation and communication.

Cooperation: The New Challenge for Communication

Porter's study of competitive advantage of nations has thrown up a new challenge to firms and nations that wish to achieve competitive success. The challenge is one of cooperation. Firms can no longer fight shy of cooperating if they need to build up their own competitive strategy and their nations competitive advantage. Governments, it has been demonstrated, have a marginal role to play. The dynamics of competition and cooperation has to be nurtured by domestic firms themselves in their quest for excellence and competitive strategy. In fact, Porter conclusively observes that the greater the degree of competition, the more conductive the environment for cooperation to generate innovative results.

Cooperation is essential to augment the firm capabilities. The consumer needs are not static but are empowered by the dynamism of the three primary influences. The firm has a national context, an internal structure and the option of building channels of communication that are backed by easy international flow of certain information and offerings. The firm has to adequately meet the challenge of change imposed by influences on consumer. For this it has to recognise the imperative of cooperation.

Often innovation that reshapes products and creates new products is the result of cooperation. Information plays a large role in innovation. Innovation is in both methods and technology. Innovation in methods involves, new production method, new ways of marketing, identification of new customer groups, etc. Organisational inertia is the biggest barrier to the possibilities of innovation. For sustaining advantages the firm has to continually move earlier than its rivals. The ability of the firm to innovate has much to do with information sources available and consulted by it. Information that will be useful is that which is not sought or available to competitors, or information available to others that is interpreted in new ways. Sometimes it results from sheer investments in R&D and Market Research. Seeking information that can help the firm respond to the primary influences working on the customer implies cooperation. The cooperation is the new challenge for communication.

The National Diamond Implies Cooperation and Communication

Porter states, "The mutually reinforcing activities of the diamond all conceal important channels of communication that add value, give competitive advantage and therefore, marketing strengths. All these channels, therefore, contribute to both firm as well as marketing strategy."

Further, he elaborates, "Underlying the operation of the national diamond and the phenomenon of clustering is the exchange and flow of information about needs, techniques and technology among buyers, suppliers and related industries."

Finally, he concludes that "Advantages throughout the diamond are necessary for sustaining competitive success in knowledge intensive industries. Advantage in every determinant is not a prerequisite but the interplay of advantage in many determinants yields self-reinforcing benefits that are hard to nullify and replicate." This interplay is the result of cooperation.

Role of Cooperation in Firms Strategy Building

The 'diamond' highlights the role of factor conditions, related and supporting industries and demand conditions. Among factor conditions, the advanced factors are critical in our analysis for they include modern digital data communication, educated personnel and university research institutes. The advanced factors are now the most significant factors to achieve higher order competitive advantages like differentiated products and proprietary production technology. They have to be built by human resources and capital factors and may be difficult to procure in the global market. The U.S. stock of human skills and scientific experience in both computer hardware and software interact and cooperate to yield advantage not only in these industries but also related ones like medical electronics and financial services. The advanced and specialised factors reflect the firms capacity to absorb information, process and add value through its products, process and design. Therefore, they reflect the cooperation, communication and innovation abilities of the firm.

Sometimes, the home base advantage itself can even be translated through a communication strategy to create an international competitive position.

Competitive advantage comes not only through using current factors but also through factor creation. It is firms (and not the governments) in most cases that indulge in factor creation that leads to factor advantage in industries. The Italians indulge in factor creation through cooperation by transfer of knowledge within extended families for there is strong family interlinkage between operating firms in most of the industries.

Cooperation of working with buyers, suppliers and channels involves not only helping them upgrade and extend their own competitive advantage. Open communication with suppliers can give early access to new equipment, supplies and ideas that are critical for creating competitive advantage. The Japanese case illustrates how working closely with suppliers with free information flow leads to superb service and rapid changes. The role of related industries in spurring innovation has been widely acknowledged and recorded. It is cooperation that builds channels of communication, which lead to sharing technology, channels and buyers.

Similarly demand conditions are important for a firms success. Understanding buyer needs requires access to buyers, seeking their cooperation through building open communication between them and a firm's top technical and managerial personnel. This interaction should help create an intuitive grasp of buyer circumstances. Again, firms that 'cooperate' and do not shy away from demanding buyers push a firm towards innovation. However, working with them alone may unnecessarily drain resources or may not produce commensurate results. Ries and Trout call it as "Bottom-up" marketing. This tactic can be the basis of a winning strategy. The inability to understand the changing market place, customers and the need to provide competitive values has created a situation where some powerful US companies of the 70s are struggling to remain profitable today.

The Second 'C': Focused Concern

The first task, while discussing concern, is to recognise that the area of focussed concern contains within itself pressures of both cooperation and competition. It is like the brain bank of the firm which not only processes the received information but perceives the information in a way that is capable of translating itself through value asses processes, techniques, product, etc. The "discrimination" ability is the key variable here. The same information may be available to more than one firm, yet the response to the information can be different. Therefore, the task of sifting the relevant information from the irrelevant is important. Viewing the relevant information in a different way is the next task. Moreover, the dividing line between cooperation and competition as well as managing its dynamics both within the firm and with the outside world needs discriminating ability. A firm needs to be clear about what information to share with competitors, cluster and industry and what secrets to keep. This is the role of discrimination. Finally the firm has to decide how to optimise and reinforce activities in a consistent way. Discrimination, again, plays a role (though a different one) here.

The Third 'C': Competitive Response

The firm's strategy, as has been pointed out earlier, is a flow. What is the nature of this flow? How do the marketing and communication tasks flow from strategy? How and where do the various tools of strategy contribute to this flow? The discussion below will explore answers to these questions.

Delivering the Three Strategic Fits Implies Using The 3 Cs

Strategy building by the firm is not an event but a process. Understanding the importance as well as dynamics of this process results in competitive success. Every firm irrespective of size, location or position in the market is indulging in this process formally or informally. The advantage for formally acknowledging the process is that due importance can be given to certain key activities which were related as "informal" in nature and therefore left to the judgement of say the top management. Lack of adequate feedback and data on these could lead to 'safe' or 'in-between' strategies which damage the ability of the firm to take a position in the market place.

The strategy building and communication tasks need to be understood together. For in a world based on communication, strategy building and execution both depend on (a) knowing where to build communication channels, (b) the ability to build them, and (c) their profitable use for inflow and outflow of desired information and response:

I. What the customer and target audience see (4P's. marketing communication, total purchase experience, etc.)	These include all activities of the firm visible to the outside world. It also includes the product, packaging, etc., and all non verbal cues the target audience are exposed to communication
II. What the firm explicity recognises: (the building of strategy, say: differentiation, cost advantage or focus)	The firm has a visible process for strategy building. While the target audience view the firm based on what it communicates verbally and meta verbally, the firm recognises those explicit strategy building activities which are traditionally accepted within the firm as the routine for taking strategic decisions. Perceptions about these activities may vary from detailed bureaucratic, informal, unstructural, etc.
III. The area of activities that communication theory needs to explicity recognise	These sets of activities are being informally or formally undertaken by every firm it is then important in strategy building that needs to be recognised not only by the firm, the industry but also by communication theory as critical for building competitive advantage.
(a) Cooperation with cluster, industry, trade association, competitor, scientific community, other source of community, other source of competitive advantage. information.	
(b) Needs to 'process' information received for possible value addition.	

The ability of a firm to deliver better value than its competitors is determined not only by which activities the firm will perform and how it will configure individual activities but also-how activities relate to each other. Porter states that formulating a strategy implies having three orders of fits among activities of the firm. These "fits" are not mutually exclusive. The first order fit is simple consistency. This implies a simple consistency between each activity and overall strategy. The second-order fit occurs when activities are reinforcing each other. The third order fits goes beyond reinforcement to an optimization effort.

It is not difficult to see that three fits cannot occur without the 3Cs. Cooperation among the 'skills' of the 'staff' is essential for simple consistency, reinforcement and optimisation. Focussed concern helps choose the activities which will be consistent, reinforcing and optimise results in terms of greatest value added at least possible cost. The strategy or competitive response is nothing but the three fits working in harmony with each other to create differentiation, focus or cost advantage.

Three competitive response alternatives in terms of positioning (identified by Porter) need to be considered here. The 3Cs are interlinked in the execution of these strategic potions: variety based, needs based and access based positioning. First, cooperation among the firm resources and focussed concern leads the firm to identify and bring together a distinctive set of activities that can best produce particular products or services. This implies that the firms product or services range need not be produced identically and there may be better ways of producing a subset of them through unique activities or activities done in a unique way. This is variety based positioning. Secondly, where groups of consumers express their individuality through different need, it is possible to focus concern on needs of a particular segment or group. Cooperation or bringing together of the firm activities can be done in such a way to serve the individuality of these needs best. This competitive response is called need-based positioning. The third alternative is a variant of need based positioning. This clarifies those instances where needs may be same but the customers need to be accessed or reached in different ways. This may be due to customer geography, customer scale or anything that requires a different set of activities. A focussed concern on ways of accessing them and a cooperation or bringing together of the firm activities to offer value added to them can give the competitive response called access-based positioning. Building the strategy of differentiation or focus or deciding on one of the three positioning alternatives involves a clear identification of the target audience, marketing objectives and subsequently the communication objectives. These two important tasks of marketing communication are thus done at the early stage of competitive response planning and delivery. The three fits are designed to deliver to the target audience the firms competitive response in a manner that meets the marketing objective. Executive of this process requires using the 3C's.

QUESTIONS FOR DISCUSSION

1. What is meant by advertising strategy?
2. How can we develop the Advertising Strategy for an organisation? Elaborate with examples?
3. What advertising strategies were adopted by H.L.L. for introducing their famous product "Fair and Lovely" which achieved a grand success?

STRATEGIC GLOBAL MARKETING

25

INTRODUCTION

Global marketing, even though it has certain distinct characteristics, is essentially similar to domestic marketing in terms of certain technical attributes. Marketing can be conceived as an integral part of two processes, viz., technical and social. So far as the technical process is concerned, domestic and global marketing are identical. The technical process includes non-human factors such as product, price, cost, brand, etc. The basic principles regarding these variables are of universal applicability. But the social aspect of marketing is unique in any given stratum, because it involves human elements, namely, the behaviour pattern of consumers and the given characteristics of a society, such as customers, attitudes, values, etc. It is obvious that marketing, to the extent it is visualized as a social process, will be different from domestic marketing.

Global marketing can be defined as 'marketing carried on across national boundaries'. According to Hess and Cateora, Global marketing is 'the performance of business activities that direct the flow of goods and services to consumers or users in more than one nation'. It is different from domestic marketing inasmuch as the exchange takes place beyond the frontiers, thereby involving different markets and consumers who might have different needs, wants and behavioural attributes.

The existence of more than one market necessarily complicates the marketing process. Since the countries are sovereign and independent, the respective governments enact legislations for the control of foreign trade. Global marketing will have to take care of such barriers to free trade which may be both visible and invisible. Even when there is complete free trade, logistics may create problems totally different from those experienced in domestic operations. Foreign exchange regulations, which do not affect domestic sales, have considerable impact on financing of overseas sales and operations.

Similarly, since human needs and wants will have different attributes in foreign markets, perception of these needs will require an overall appreciation of the environment, and the social and individual value systems.

It is necessary at this stage to introduce the concepts of 'controllable' and 'uncontrollable' factors in global marketing. Control will have to be defined with reference to a company's management. The company is in a position to control and design marketing mix elements, namely, product, price, place and promotion. But the total environment in which the marketing mix elements will operate is beyond the control of the company. Meidan has identified 13 uncontrollable factors which can be classified under the following heads: anthropological, economic, competitive, risk and distance factors. A slightly modified listing of the factors relevant to global marketing is given below:

1. Social Factors

- National legal regime
- Political situation
- Financial system
- Marketing infrastructure
- Culture
- Language
- Climate

2. Economic Factors

- Commercial policy variables, e.g. tariffs, quotas, licensing, non-tariff barriers
- Currency restrictions
- Internal demand management policies and instruments.

3. Competition

- Competition *vis-a-vis* producers in the importing country
- Competition *vis-a-vis* exporters from the competing country
- Competition *vis-a-vis* other exporters from one's own country.

4. Logistics

- Availability of required type of transport (sea, air freezer space, etc.)
- Costs of transportation.

5. Risks

- Political risks
- Commercial risks
- Acts of God
- Acts of enemies, pirates, thieves, etc.

Scope of Global Marketing

Though global marketing is in essence export marketing, it has a broader connotation in marketing literature. It also means entry into global markets by:

(a) Opening a branch/subsidiary abroad for processing, packaging, assembly or even complete manufacturing through direct investment;

(b) Negotiating licensing/franchising arrangements, whereby, foreign enterprises are granted the right to use the exporting company's know how, viz., patents, processes or trade marks, with or without financial investment;

(c) Establishing joint ventures in foreign countries for manufacturing and/or marketing;

(d) Offering consultancy services and undertaking turnkey projects abroad;

(e) Sub-contracting and counter-trade; and

(f) Importing for export production.

Depending upon the degree of a firm's involvement, there may be several variations of these arrangements.

GLOBAL MARKETING *vs.* DOMESTIC MARKETING

There are three basic points of similarities between domestic marketing and global marketing:

1. Both in domestic marketing as well as in global marketing, success depends upon satisfying the basic requirements of the consumers. This necessarily involves finding out what the buyers want and meeting their needs accordingly.
2. It is necessary to build goodwill both in the domestic market as well as in the global market. If a firm has been able to develop goodwill of the consumers, its task will be much simpler than that of one which has not been able to do so. The days of caveat emptor have gone and the basic principle now is caveat vendor. In fact, to win over customers, liberal guarantees have to be given and facilities of after-sales may have to be provided on an extensive scale.
3. Research and development for product improvement and adaptation is necessary both for global marketing and domestic marketing.

However, there are some salient features of difference between global marketing and domestic marketing.

Sovereign Political Entities

Each country is a sovereign political entity and goods and services have to move across national boundaries. As a result, they may have to face a number of restrictions. These may fall in any of the following categories:

(i) *Tariffs or Customs Duties.* These only make the goods expensive and are not intended to ban entry of foreign goods completely. In the post-war period, there has been a significant reduction in tariffs both globally, due to the efforts of General Agreement on Tariffs and Trade (GATT) and on a regional basis, due to the emergence of regional economic groupings.

(ii) *Quantitative Restrictions.* These are mainly intended to restrict trade in the specific commodities subject to restrictions, the major objective being protection of domestic industries.

(iii) *Exchange Controls.* In some cases, though the entry of goods is not banned, importers may not be allowed the necessary foreign exchange for payment of the goods due to the existence of exchange controls. But in many cases, quantitative controls have been coupled with exchange control and the grant of an import license automatically involves the grant of foreign exchange.

(iv) *Local Taxes.* One of the objectives is to make the foreign goods comparatively costlier than domestic goods.

Different Legal Systems

Each country has its own legal system and very often the legal systems operated by different countries differ from each other. However, a number of countries follow English Common Law while several important European countries follow the civil law. The East European countries have developed their own legal system. The existence of different legal systems makes the task of businessmen more difficult as they are not sure as to which particular system will apply to their transactions. However, attempts are being made to bring about uniformity in some specific areas. INCO Terms and Uniform Customs and Practice on Documentary Credits developed by the Global Chamber of Commerce are examples of these attempts. The United Nations Commission on International Trade Law (UNCITRAL) is also trying to bring about uniformity in global trade law.

Different Monetary Systems

Each country has its own monetary system and the exchange value of each country's currency is different from that of the other. For sometime under the rules framed by the Global Monetary Fund, exchange rates were more or less fixed. However, since 1973 the exchange rates are fluctuating and are being determined by forces of supply and demand. Some countries also operate what are known as multiple exchange rates, each exchange rate applying to a certain set of transactions.

Lower Mobility of Factors of Production

Factors of production are less mobile as between nations than in the country itself. However, due to the advent of air transport, mobility of labour is now increasing. Due to the development of global banking, capital is also becoming more mobile. However, in spite of these, the fact remains that mobility of labour and capital is much less between different countries than it is within the country itself.

Differences in Market Characteristics

Each country is a separate market having its own demand pattern, channels of distribution, methods of promotion, etc. These differences are accentuated due to the existence of government controls and regulations. However, this is a difference of degree only. Even in one single country there may be differences in demand characteristics in different parts of the country. This is especially so for bigger countries like India and the USA where the demand pattern differs from State to State.

Greater Degree of Risk

There is a greater degree of risk involved in global marketing than in domestic marketing due to:

(i) larger volume of transactions and higher value of these transactions.

(ii) longer time period involved in these transactions due to longer time in transit and the longer credit period involved;

(iii) comparatively less knowledge about the parties, reputation and credibility; and

(iv) exchange fluctuation risk.

Differences in Procedures and Documentation

Each country has its own procedures and documentary requirements and traders have to comply with these regulations if they want to export or import goods from foreign countries.

Cultural Dimensions of Global Marketing

Exporting means operating in a cross-cultural environment. This makes the task of marketing more complex because the marketer must appreciate how different is the foreign culture from his own and how this difference has to be reflected in shaping his behaviour pattern as well as his export marketing strategy.

Culture, though a very commonly used term, is not, however, easy to define. An accepted definition is by Edward Taylor: "Culture is that complex whole which includes knowledge, belief, art, morals, law, custom and any other capabilities and habits acquired by individuals (as members) of society."

There are three major characteristics of culture: (a) it is not inborn but learned and passed on to the next generation; (b) it is all pervasive and interrelated; and (c) it is shared by all the members of the group. Quite often, a culture is synonymous with the political boundary of a nation, e.g. Chinese culture, Japanese or British culture.

But even national cultures are not always totally homogeneous. Each culture may have different sub-cultures. For example, groups based on religion. Within the same country, people having different religions may display distinct behavioural patterns. Racial groups, such as blacks and Hispanics, have different attitudes and preferences compared to white Angle Saxon Protestants in the USA.

High and Low Context Culture

Since cultures vary quite drastically across nations, it is necessary to develop concepts which can help to understand cultural connotations. In a low context culture, verbal/written communications dominate interpersonal and business relationships. In a high context culture, on the other hand, it is the context which matters more than the verbal/written part of the communication. To illustrate, in a high-context culture, your word is enough proof of your commitment; written agreement is incidental. This is something quite easy to appreciate because in India too, a large amount of business has traditionally been carried simply on the basis of oral agreements. Some examples of how cultural contexts influence business behaviour are given in Table 25.1.

Table 25.1: High and Low Context Cultures

Factors/Dimensions	High Context	Low Context
1	2	3
Lawyers	Less important	Very important
A man's word	Is his bond	Is not to be relied upon—'get it in writing'
Responsibility for organisational error	Taken by the highest level	Pushed to the lowest level
Space	People breathe on each other	People carry a bubble of private space with them and resent intrusions

1	2	3
Time	Polychronic—everything in life must be dealt within terms of its own time	Monochronic—time is money. Linear one thing at a time
Negotiations	Are lengthy—a major purpose is to allow the parties to get to know each other	Proceed quickly
Competitive	Infrequent	Common
Country/Regional examples	Japan, Middle East	USA, Northern Europe

Inability to appreciate the cultural environment can result in marketing disasters. Some examples are given below:

Warner-Lambert Company used the ad copy it used successfully in the USA to promote 'Listerine' mouth wash in Thailand. The copy showed a boy and a girl being affectionate to each other. The ad did not click because in the conservative society of Thailand such proximity was frowned upon. When the copy was slightly modified to show two girls, sales picked up.

Few years later, Singer Company found that while marketing sewing machines in the Middle East, the husband and not the wife, has to be approached with the argument that a sewing machine would make his wife more efficient.

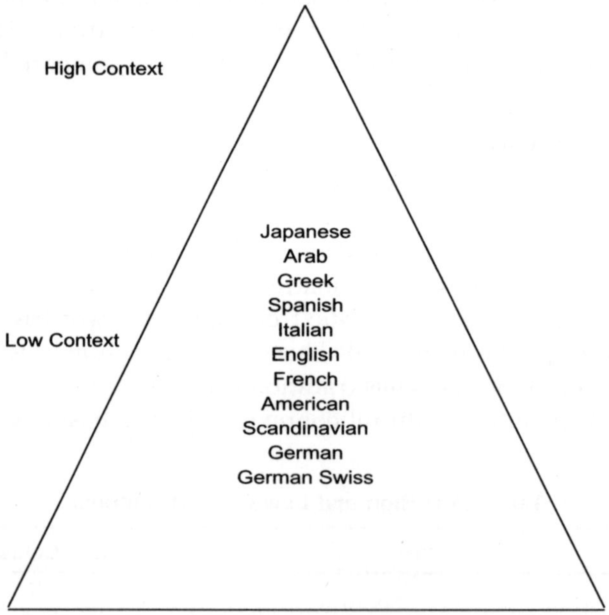

Figure 25.1: Classifies the major cultures according to their contextual level

Carlsberg, the world famous producer of beer, had to add a third elephant to its label of elephant beer in its ad in Africa. Two elephants are considered to signify bad luck there.

Flat level tones in English normally connote boredom or sarcasm. In Russia, on the other hand, the level tone is associated with matter of fact presentation. A Russian will, therefore, tend to speak English with a level tone which will sound intentionally natural to his own ears but to an English listener, he will sound uninterested and rude. Similarly, Americans speak louder than the Europeans and given the impression of assertiveness which may not be at all intended.

WHY GO GLOBAL?

In a country like India, at present going global means a decision to go in for exports. We would now discuss why would a firm find it useful to seek export markets. Some basic economic reasons which might influence a company's decision regarding export business are:

(a) Bulk Sales

The firm has the advantage of selling in bulk. Export orders are larger than those from the domestic market.

(b) Relative Profitability

The rate of profit to be earned from export business may be higher than the corresponding rate on the domestic sales. Further, experience shows that there has been a progressive improvement in the unit value realization of certain export products.

(c) Insufficiency of Domestic Demand

The level of domestic demand, either at a point of time or over-time, may be insufficient for utilizing the installing capacity in full. Export business offers a suitable mechanism for utilizing the unused capacity. This will reduce costs and improve the overall profitability of the firm. Recession in the domestic market often serves as a stimulus to export ventures. In fact, export of engineering goods from India picked up momentum at the time of recession in the Indian economy during 1967-69, when Indian manufacturing units faced with large inventories and weak order book position, turned to export markets. Developing diversified export markets thus provides a firm with a degree of protection against cyclical domestic economic slowdown. But it must be emphasized that there is an inherent danger in looking at exports to merely supplement the domestic business at the time of crisis. Penetrating foreign markets is a difficult job but sustaining them is even more onerous. Therefore, once a decision is taken to enter global markets, every *effort* will have to be made to retain them. And this can be done only when export marketing operations are recognised as an integral part of the total corporate activity. In fact, what is needed is full involvement in and commitment to exports.

(d) Reducing Business Risks

A diversified export business may help in mitigating sharp fluctuations in the overall activity of a company. When a firm is selling in a number of markets, the downward fluctuation in sales in one market, which may be the domestic market may be fully or partly counterbalanced by a rise in the sales in other markets. Secondly, geographic diversification also provides the momentum to growth inasmuch as a single or a few markets will have only limited absorptive capacity.

(e) Legal Restrictions

Governments may impose certain restrictions on further growth and capacity expansion of some firms within the domestic market in order to achieve certain social objectives. But there may not be any such restrictions on making investments overseas or the restrictions may be relaxed even in the domestic market, provided the additional capacity envisaged by the company is utilized for exports. In such situations, a firm may contemplate export operations, because it offers a way to achieve corporate growth, which may otherwise not be possible. This was the position in India before industrial licensing was virtually removed.

(f) Obtaining Imported Inputs

Nations have to export to pay for imports of materials, technology or processes not available within their national boundaries. Governments, therefore, may be compelled to impose export obligations on the firms, specially those in need of imported inputs.

(g) Social Responsibility

In many cases, businessmen themselves feel a sense of responsibility and contribute to country's foreign exchange reserves by increasing their exports. Incidentally, by exporting at a time when it is difficult to export they build up their image in the domestic market. They also look at exporting to attain status and prestige.

(h) Increased Productivity

Increased productivity is necessary for ultimate survival of a firm. This itself may lead a company to increase production and then seek export markets. Moreover, in these days of technological developments, bigger companies have to spend a lot on research and development. To meet the increased costs of research and development, larger markets become a necessity and exports become unavoidable.

(i) Technological Improvement

Entry into export markets enable a firm to (i) pick up new product ideas and to add to product line, (ii) improve its product, (iii) reduce costs, and (iv) discover new applications for its product. As was pointed out by Telco Chairman at its 1980 Annual General Meeting, "Export exposes us to the fiercely competitive glóbal market and compels us to update our products. This upgradation of our vehicles unmistakably benefits the Indian customer also."

(j) A product may be near the end of its cycle in the domestic market while beginning to generate growth abroad

HOW MUCH COMMITMENT

Once a decision to enter the export market or "go global" is taken, the next question relates to the degree of commitment to be made towards global operations. There are four distinct but overlapping categories:

(a) No Involvement

The firm does not involve itself in export marketing. Yet the manufactured by a firm may enter export markets due to (i) foreign buyers coming on their own accord and purchasing the requirement and intermediacies like export houses purchasing its goods and selling them in overseas customers.

(b) Temporary Involvement

The firm gets involved in foreign business to dispose of temporary surpluses or to utilize temporary excess capacity.

(c) Continued Involvement

Here the firm makes a serious commitment to export. It may demarcate a definite percentage of capacity for exports. Visits to foreign countries are more frequent and overseas agents are appointed to look after the firm's interest.

(d) Global Involvement

In such a case, a firm becomes a truly global company involving itself in global operations by establishment of branches in a number of countries.

However, before actually entering into the export markets, the firm should undertake a thorough analysis to find out whether or not it is ready to enter into global marketing. In fact, a very special and crucial job of resource audit is necessary to make this decision. The questions to be answered by the firm are:

(1) Do you have or can you acquire the management knowledge to operate in global markets?

(2) Do you have or can you acquire the productive capacity to service new markets?

(3) Do you have or can you acquire the financial resources necessary to service global markets?

(4) Do you want to make the commitment necessary to approach global markets properly?

TASKS OF GLOBAL MARKETERS

The basic tasks of an global marketer are: (1) choosing export markets, and location of buyers therein, (2) product planning for export markets, (3) pricing for exports, (4) methods of entry into foreign markets, and (5) promoting products abroad. We will discuss these tasks one by one.

1. Choosing Export Markets

In theory, a firm could have the whole world as its market. In practice, it is limited to a few markets. From this point of view, developed countries could prove to be good markets for developing countries like India. This is so for the following reasons:

(i) There is more information available about developed countries than about developing countries.

(ii) They have higher purchasing power and hence can afford to purchase many more products like home furnishings, decorative articles, gold and imitation jewellery, woodwork, cane furniture, leather goods, etc.

(iii) They have comparatively freer imports. Developing countries in general impose import controls to develop their own indigenous industries. Again, development countries are admitting goods imported from developing countries free of duty or at low rates of duty under Generalised System of Preferences.

(iv) Developed countries have vacated certain areas of production which could be filled up by developing countries like India. These are: (a) Labour intensive industries as labour is very expensive in developed countries; (b) As resources everywhere are limited; developed countries are devoting their resources to sophisticated areas of production and are interested in importing simple industries where the demand declined and they are not able to reap economies of scale; and (c) They are also leaving pollution-prone industries as also industries involving dirty work. Some examples of industries vacated by developed countries are motorcycles by the UK, black and white TVs by developed countries, 800 CC car by Suzuki, casting and forging industries, etc.

It may be of interest to know that five countries, viz., the United States, Germany, Japan, France and the U.K. account for 43 per cent of the world imports.

In order to encourage imports from developing countries, the developed countries have also established import promotion centers. An idea of the services offered by these centers would be obtained by the following:

1. Statistical information on the market concerned.
2. Information on sales opportunities in the market concerned.
3. Information on import regulations and procedures.
4. Information on marketing techniques and business practices in the country concerned.
5. List of importers, wholesalers, agents and distributors.
6. Arrangements for contacts for visiting businessmen.
7. Trade fair and exhibition assistance.
8. Publications on the market concerned.
9. Names of buyers seeking supplies of a specific product in specific quantities.
10. Free ads of product offers in weekly trade information bulletin; circulation of product offers to the importers.
11. Showrooms for product display.
12. Advice and planning for marketing in the country concerned.

In most cases, these services are provided without charge.

Again, India may have some particular advantages in some markets like (i) proximity, (ii) trade dominated by persons of Indian origin, (iii) ethnic population, (iv) existence of shipping facilities, and (v) good political relations.

Travel abroad

After having located some probable markets for his products, it might be useful for the exporter to visit the market and see at first hand what each market has to offer. However, before visiting markets a number of precautions have to be taken:

(a) It is necessary to have the fullest background information on the market and the conditions therein. For example, lot of preparations is necessary to find out suitable dates for the visit to different markets. A visit to Saudi Arabia in Ramzan month or a visit to European markets in Christmas may not be fruitful. So also, it might be useful to do the ticketing and hotel booking from India itself to save time. It is desirable to contact before hand the parties before meeting them. The Indian embassies and the Import Promotion Centres are to be informed well in advance so that they can help the exporters to plan visits and establish contacts.

(b) The man visiting the market must know his product well. He must have a detailed product knowledge and his product knowledge should be better than that of the customer. Only then he would be able to convince the buyer.

(c) Some adaptability in food habits is also necessary. Otherwise he might be put in awkward situations.

(d) It is better to visit the market when a trade fair is on. This will help the exporter to have an idea of what is available in the market concerned. Who would be his competitors? What is the extent of product adaptation necessary? It will also be possible to have an idea of the prevailing prices and to study the strengths and weaknesses of the competing products. In addition, he will be able to know the new developments and technological trends in his industry. Very often, the import promotion centers provide substantial financial aid to the exporters from developing countries to exhibit their products in trade fairs and exhibitions and it would be useful for an exporter to know what these facilities are. The German Government is prepared to assist developing countries in their efforts to participate in German fairs and exhibitions. Besides covering part of the expenditure, the German Government provides expert advice on all questions regarding trade fair participation.

Concluding remarks about choosing markets

Market testing is the best way of minimizing export marketing risks and it would be desirable to test the market carefully before mounting any major export offensive. Again, it would be useful to find out the market segment which offers the best potential. For example, it has been found that Indian sewing machines in the Middle East sell in the low price segments. In many cases, it is easier to attack a high price segment. For example, Japan is a major producer of watches yet Swiss timepieces and watches are imported in large numbers at far higher prices.

It might be stressed again that it would be better to concentrate on a few markets and avoid spreading too thinly. There are many good reasons why it is better to concentrate on a few markets: (i) Profitability can be maximized by putting the maximum efforts into areas of maximum potential. (ii) It is essential to utilize export salesmen to the best advantage. (iii) Experience shows that almost every company has a comparatively small number of markets that account for the bulk of its turnover. (iv) The firm may not have the capacity to cater to all markets.

Moreover, it would be necessary to review from time to time the export markets and to reassess their characteristics and potential. It might be desirable to more out of certain markets and concentrate on some others in order to maximize the overall profitability of the firm.

Location of individual buyers

The following sources could be utilized for locating of individual buyers:

1. Indian Embassies and High Commission in foreign countries.
2. Import Promotion centers in developed countries.
3. Newsletters issued by export promotion councils and the Federation of Indian Export Organisations.
4. Trade Intelligence Bulletin issued by the India Trade Promotion Organisation.
5. Importers' Association in foreign countries.
6. Chambers of Commerce and Trade Association's in foreign countries.
7. Directories of Importers and Manufacturers.
8. Commercial sections of Foreign Embassies and High Commissions in India.
9. Monographs on Trade Channels published by the International Trade Centre.
10. Visits to trade fairs.
11. Listings and advertisements in trade fair catalogues.
12. Business Opportunities issued by the Federation of Indian Chambers of Commerce and Industry.
13. Overseas Business Contacts issued by the Associated Chambers of Commerce and Industry.
14. Yellow pages issued in foreign countries.
15. Purchase of mailing lists from firms supplying commercial information.
16. Insert advertisements in specialized trade journals.

2. Product Planning for Export

Need for product planning

Consumers will buy only what suits them? This may not be what the company is presently manufacturing. What is acceptable in India may not be accepted in foreign markets? Again, what is acceptable in Germany may not be acceptable in the UK. Tastes may differ. This may be specially important in the case of manufactured food products. There are 100 varieties of Nescafe to suit the tastes of people in different countries. Thus, export markets need a different approach to product planning.

The scope of determining the product line is rather circumscribed in many cases because the company will already have a product line which it is marketing in the domestic market. The product planning exercise will, therefore tend to be restricted to the task of identifying a few items out of the existing line which will *offer* the maximum potential in the large markets.

Product adaptation

A product that is perfectly good for one market may have to be adapted for another. There can be many reasons for this. Physical conditions may be different. Functional requirements may vary from market to market. People in different places may use products differently or for different purposes. The outdoor garden furniture would require a different type of finish than furniture used indoors. Again, a manufacturer of men's suits would have to take into account that arms of Frenchmen tend to be longer in proportion to the rest of their bodies than those of Germans. In some cases cultural factors are very important. For example, Mattel Toys of USA wanted to sell their Barbie Doll in Japan. But the Japanese did not buy the American favourite doll. Later the firm introduced a modified Barbie—slightly oriental eyes and a more girlish figure. With the culturally modified Barbie, sales in Japan accounted for 12.7 per cent of the total international sales. Barbie Doll has also been adapted for sale in India. Finally, tastes, levels of skill and technical development may be different and may dictate changes in products.

There are certain items, generally ethnic products, which sell in foreign markets, precisely because these are foreign. Indian handicrafts or handloom fabrics are examples of such products. There are also speciality items which have become so famous that they are automatically demanded by the foreign consumers, for instance, Darjeeling tea, Scotch whisky or Danish cheese. For such items, no change in the product itself is required for marketing it overseas, though changes in packaging may often be called for.

Many items, however, may require some adaptation for making them suitable to the foreign markets. Some obvious examples of product adaptation are differences in voltages (110 to 220) and right hand drive or left-hand drive. Adaptation may pertain to size, functions, materials, design, style, colour, tastes and standards. Sometimes this could be done easily and at low cost but at times it may cost much.

To try to aid its sales, Westinghouse modified its washing machines. The company discovered that European housewives, long accustomed to boiling clothes, prefer hotter water in washing machines than their American counterparts do. So Westinghouse installed special heating elements in its machines being exported to Europe.

Product adaptation may also be used as a strategy to enter a market which is dominated by the existing manufacturers. A slightly modified product will have a better change of success in getting a total hold in the market than a product which is similar to the existing product in all essential aspects. The modifications in the product will serve as the 'selling points'. If the process of adaptation results in cost reduction, that will be an additional advantage.

Product standardisation

Even though product adaptation becomes inevitable in the case of certain products, it should be realized that there is sound economic logic behind a product policy which suggests uniformity in all markets. Terpstra has identified six factors which may favour international product standardization.

1. ***Economies of scale in production.*** When only one standard version is marketed in all the areas, it will be possible to have larger production runs, which will result in lower manufacturing costs.
2. ***Economies in product research and development.*** Similarly, product standardization will allow recovery of the costs incurred in product research and development from the entire sales. This will reduce the recovery period as also lower the break-even point. Moreover, additional expenditure on adapting product to each individual market can be avoided.

The above three factors which are economic might motivate a company to go for international product standardization. There are also three marketing factors which may reinforce the standardization level:

1. **Consumer Mobility**. Consumers are becoming increasingly more mobile and transcontinental travel is now fairly common. A consumer who is loyal to a particular brand in his home market, is more likely to remain loyal in a foreign country as well when the product in question is the same.
2. **Made-in-Image**. When the name of a country is associated with a high standard of quality in the minds of the consumers, a product manufactured in that country may enjoy a psychological premium in the foreign markets.
3. **Impact of Technology**. Industrial products generally tend to have standard specifications and do not require much adaptation for foreign markets, unless climatic and similar considerations call for it.

The basic argument in favour of uniform multinational product strategy is that it is least costly in terms of both manufacturing and marketing costs for the company. For example, Italian companies concentrated on manufacturing a limited range of standardized refrigerators and washing machines in great numbers. This strategy which reduced the cost of such manufacture and marketing helped them in capturing sizable shares in the UK and the continental markets at the cost of such industrial giants as Frigidaire, Seimens or AGE. Pepsi-Cola and Coca-Cola are the two outstanding examples which offer the same product and follow identical promotional themes in all the markets. Therefore, the question before the management would be to find out how far uniformity would be a feasible, and at the same time, a profitable strategy. There are certain factors, e.g. technological and legal, which will not allow an exporting company to have any option with respect to product adaptation. For example, if a company wants to export electrical goods to Japan, these will have to be of 110 volts and not 220 volts. Similarly, for export of food items, the health regulations, as imposed by the importing countries, must be adhered to. Where the company has the choice, it will be a matter of relative costs and benefits of the alternative strategies of uniformity *vs*. adaptation. The strategy of adaptation involves greater costs but promises more flexibility and more marketing success. The strategy of uniformity is least costly but is more rigid and consequently may be less successful in market penetration.

Cross Country segmentation

While there is some elements of truth in both the approaches—product adaptation and product standardization—a view is emerging that ideally a firm should attempt a combination of both. Basically it would involve standardizing across similar crossnational segments. The principle behind this approach is simple. It is found that within a country the market can be divided into segments which are highly dissimilar. But if several countries are segmented, it is found, while making cross-country comparison, that some segments are quite similar. For example, "the 6,40,000 up-market, educationally elite readers of those magazines (i.e. *Scientific American*, *Time*, *Newsweek*, *The Financial Times* and the *Economist*) in Western Europe, have more in common with each other than their fellow countrymen who are less well-off.... The growing awareness of shared 'life style' traits, transcending national boundaries will usher in a new era of Europe-wide marketing and advertising strategies".

By targeting to such culturally similar market segments across countries, a firm can reap the advantages of both product standardization and adaptation.

Before closing the discussion on product standardization, a reference is necessary to a very interesting and thought provoking article on The Globalization of Markets by Theodore Levitt. Levitt point out that the powerful force of technology is driving the world toward a converging commonality. "The result is a new commercial reality—the emergence of global markets for standardized consumer products on a previously unimagined scale of magnitude. Corporations geared to this new reality benefit from enormous economies of scale in production, distribution, marketing, and management." According to Levitt, the sweeping gale of globalization is not confined to raw materials of high-tech production and he cites the examples of McDonald's from the Champs Elysees to the Ginza, of Coca Cola in Bahrain and Pepsi Cola in Moscow, and of rock music, Greek salad, Hollywood movies, Revlon Cosmetics, Sony televisions, and Levi jeans everywhere. He asserts that if a company forces costs and prices down and pushes quality and reliability up—while maintaining reasonable concern for suitability—customers will prefers its world-standardized products. If the price is low enough, they will take highly standardized world products, even if these aren't exactly what mother said was suitable, what immemorial custom decreed was right, or what market research fabulists asserted was preferred.

To sum up, product adaptation may lead to greater market acceptance and greater market sales. But it would involve costs: shorter production runs leading to higher costs, additional expenditure on R&D and market research to find out what form adaptation should take and it may be fairly expensive.

It must also be noted that there is no guarantee that a product, once successfully developed, launched and introduced, will continue to be successful and profitable unless steps are taken to review periodically and upgrade the product itself and its presentation. Again, no product is completely immune to technical obsolescence, changes in demand, substitution or progressive competition.

3. Pricing for Foreign Markets

As stated before, for fixing export prices, the minimum to be charged for experts is provided by direct costs and the maximum is determined by 'what the traffic will bear'; The following sources may be utilized for finding out 'what the traffic would bear'; (i) previous files if the firm has exported in the past with suitable for the possible inflation in the target market; (ii) average unit price realized for exports made to different markets from the Monthly Bulletin of Foreign Trade Statistics—Exports; (iii) average unit price paid by importers in the target market to the various suppliers from its import statistics (with suitable adjustments being made for the fact that import prices are c.i.f. except in the U.S.A.); (iv) a visit to trade fairs; and (v) a reference to the departmental store catalogues which give the retail prices of the various goods sold by them—the Indian exporter may receive 25 to 33 per cent of the consumer prices.

Having found out the maximum and the minimum of the possible export prices, the exporter may be well prepared to negotiate with the importer. The process of negotiation should start on the following lines: (1) The exporter should first discuss the attributes of his product with the importer, the idea being to impress on the buyer that his product is much better than the products of his competititors with the ultimate objective of preparing him to pay more for his product. (2) The exporter should then discuss his dependability and reliability as a supplier again with a view to prepare him to pay him a little more on this ground. (3) The actual price quoted should be the last point to be discussed.

Another point to be noted while pricing for exports is that like domestic marketing, price is only one element of global marketing mix. Some non-price factors to be considered in global marketing are:

Very often, importer in developed countries do not have adequate confidence in the quality of goods produced in India and other developing countries. For example, Indians had to sell their storage batteries 10 per cent cheaper in Saudi Arabia than U.S. and European batteries even though the quality was comparable. Lower price may become inevitable to make our products acceptable in foreign markets. However, in some cases Indians have established themselves well, e.g. transmission line towers, sugar mill machinery, textile mill machinery, etc.

If products are well differentiated and they have built up a brand image for themselves, manufacturers are in a position to charge comparatively higher prices. Brand names like Dunlop, HMT, Bata, GKW, Lucas, L&T, Kirloskar, etc. have already built up a good image and these products are able to realize a much higher price. It may be pointed out here that 75 per cent of German imports and 75 per cent of U.S. exports are attributable to some degree of product differentiation.

The price a purchaser is willing to pay often depends upon the frequency of purchase. In the case of durable consumer goods, products having a snob value and gift items, price is not the material factor. People may be willing to pay a very high price if the particular goods and catch their fancy. This applies particularly to handicrafts manufactured by developing countries.

There appears to be a close association in the consumer's mind between price and quality; the higher priced goods carry a much greater conviction about quality than the low priced goods. In this respect, it may be useful to note that it is easier to sell in developed countries with a higher price tag but in developing countries, lower price may help increase sales. In general, price constitutes a barrier to demand when it is too low just as much as when it is too high. Above a particular price, the article is regarded as too expensive, and below another price as constituting a risk of not giving adequate value. What is stressed here is that lower prices do not necessarily lead to higher sales. And in periods of inflationary price rise, a reduction in price may have an adverse reaction on the consumers and may, in fact, lead to reduction in demand rather than an increase in demand.

In the case of industrial goods, price is not likely to be an indicator of quality. A buyer of industrial goods is more keen to check what he gets for the price he pays than an average consumer. His knowledge of products and their quality is more exact, if not perfect. A technically sound product, steady availability at a reasonable price and comprehensive after-sales service, are the more important factors in the case of industrial goods.

In the case of engineering products and equipment, both before and after-sales service are very significant factors, and assurance of after-sales service particularly is much more important than a lower price. Before sales service in the case of engineering goods includes (i) advising the purchaser about the relative suitability of competing products for his requirement, and (ii) demonstrating the use of the products. For example, TELCO sent their mechanics to Zambia for maintenance of buses and training of the Zambian personnel. After-sales service includes (i) rectification of genuine technical failures in the product, (ii) educating the users on the use of the product and providing for its maintenance, (iii) free service during the warranty period, and (iv) ensuring supply of spare parts and components after the expiry of the warranty period.

On the other hand, in the case of consumer goods, service before sales, as, for example, attractive packaging and good finish, tend to be more important. MTGROS, a department store of Switzerland, requires the suppliers to pack the products in such a manner that they can be put immediately on the shelf without further packaging.

Foreign markets are not available at will. They are to be wooed and when won, they have to be maintained by constant attention and continuous efforts. Continuity of supply thus assumes great importance. If supplies to export markets are not maintained, the country becomes an undependable supplier and, therefore, loses and export markets. This point is very important in the case of supply of ancillary products the original equipment manufacturers. Unless supplies of ancillaries are guaranteed, the original equipment manufacturers will find other dependable suppliers. The development of substitutes for a number of products exported by developing countries is also due to the failure of these countries to maintain regular supplies. Prompt deliveries are equally important and this is the point where most developing countries fail. Delayed deliveries affect India's exports to Sri Lanka, Burma and Arab countries as well. An example is provided by Indian exports of machine tools. While foreign importers would like to have deliveries within three months of placing their orders, Indian manufacturers are not in a position to deliver their goods before six months. Speed of delivery is also an important factor. Buyers are willing to pay higher prices for early shipment. In fact, the vendors are evaluated according to their performance. The higher the rank enjoyed by the exporter, the better the price realized by him. Studies made about the generalized system of preferences also confirm that reliability of product quality and delivery dates appear to be more important factors than price.

Prompt acceptance and settlement of claims are also important factors especially where the consumers and the manufacturers do not have a chance to come close to each other.

Very often the ability to supply complete range of products and in large quantities is also an important factor. This is an area where developing countries are unable to come up to expectations. For example, cycle manufacturers want cycle components in huge quantities which Indian manufacturers find unable to supply. Again, Indian manufacturers usually specialize in one or two items and are not in a position to supply a complete line of products. For example, foreign importers would like to have the entire range of kitchen equipment or electrical appliances or hand tools. But Indian manufacturers are very often unable to do so.

India's inability to supply sugar in poly-lined jute bags of 50 kg each resulted in lower price realization to the extent of 15 to 20 per cent.

For sale of machinery and equipment, availability of finance and terms of credits are very often the main determining factors. In this respect, too, developed countries score over developing countries by providing tied credits to the purchasers. In the U.S.A., importers and other buyers are very cautious about tying of their funds and therefore are very keen to buy on credit terms. Japan and South Korea are usually willing to supply them goods on credit.

Price also does not matter much if goods are promoted under aggressive marketing and sales promotion. Here again developing countries find themselves lagging far behind the developed countries.

The importance of these non-price factors varies from product to product and market to market. But they undoubtedly have substantially influenced on global competition. Moreover, taking advantage of these non-price factors would also involve costs. But if proper efforts are made, the returns are likely to be higher than costs.

4. Methods of Entry into Foreign Markets

Basically, there are two methods of entry into foreign markets: (1) Indirect exporting, and (2) Direct exporting. Under the first method, the manufacturer takes the help of merchant exporters to get his products exported to foreign markets. Under direct exporting, the manufacturer decides to export himself. Thus the manufacturer has to decide, whether he will go directly for exports or take the help of merchant exporters who are very often recognised as export houses, trading houses, etc. Some government trading organisations like State Trading Corporation, MMTC and National Small Industries Corporations also act as trading houses.

There are specific advantages of utilizing the services of export houses, etc.:

(i) They have extensive knowledge about exportable products and the markets therefore.

(ii) In many case they have dealer network in many important markets.

(iii) They can extend pre-shipment finance to supporting manufacturers.

(iv) They can provide samples of exportable products and guide them on product development.

(v) They have arrangements with shipping and insurance companies and get their services at favourable rates.

(vi) They handle all the work connected with shipping and documentation.

(vii) They generally pay the supplier as soon as the goods are received by them. Hence there is no credit risk.

Export houses, etc. are also interested in promoting exports of small and cottage industry products. For recognition as export houses, etc., they have to show a minimum export performance, and in calculating the export performance, double weightage is given for export of products manufactured by small industries, tiny sector/cottage sector. Products manufactured by the handlooms and handicrafts sectors, hand-knotted carpets, and carpets made of silk are given (i) double weightage on FOB value earned by exports of such products, or (ii) triple weightage on net foreign exchange earned by export of such products. Some export houses work as buying agents of foreign departmental stores.

Information about export house, trading houses, star trading houses, and superstar trading house can be obtained from the Federation of Indian Export Organisation.

However, there are some disadvantages of indirect exporting: (i) the name of the manufacturers is not associated with the products manufactured by them. There is no publicity about brand name and the seller does not enjoy any goodwill or brand image. (ii) The cost to the ultimate user is higher because of the addition of an intermediary. (iii) Export merchants may concentrate on products, which offer them higher profits. (iv) Export merchants may not be available for all markets.

A manufacturer may, therefore think of going in for direct exports. There are two specific reasons why a manufacturer may resort to direct exporting: (i) Success in foreign markets can boost the manufacturer's image in the domestic market. (ii) There are a number of benefits available to exporters as, for example, exemption from income tax for export profits.

In case it is decided to go in for direct exports, it may be desirable to proceed on the following lines:

A. For exporting consumer products, the manufacturer may contact:

(a) Big Department Stores: There are a limited number of department stores in every developed country. The number of persons to be contacted would be limited, not more than 10 or 15. If the marketer is a good salesman, and his product is good, he should be able to persuade through personal contact, at least one of these buyers to purchase his product. If he is successful, his entire production may be purchased by one department store, as their requirements are large. Of course, the department store may ask him to manufacture the product in the Department Store's brand name, as they would find it easier to sell the product under their brand names rather than unknown manufacturer's brand name. If the marketer is able to rope in one big department store and successfully meet its requirements word will spread and other buyers may also contact him, thus having snow-balling effect, and leading to more business.

(b) Institutionally buyers like educational institutions, hospitals, military, Government Departments, hotels, etc. In every country, the number of such institutions is limited and the number of persons to be contacted would be limited. If the marketer is good at personal selling and his product is good, he should be persuade some of them to try his product. They would also be able to provide him a large volume of business.

(c) Cooperative purchase unions of retailers in countries, where retail business still dominates. To purchase at economical rates the supplies required by them, these retailers have formed cooperatives to purchase their requirements. Here again, the number of buyers to be contacted would be small and the volume of business secured would be large. Of course, effective personal selling and a good product are must.

B. For exporting industrial products like components, the manufacturer may contact the original equipment manufacturers. The number of such manufacturers in any particular country would be limited. Their names could be obtained from directories of industrial manufacturers. If the product is accepted by these manufacturers, it would lead to large orders. Of course, the marketer would have to give the potential buyers an opportunity to try this product regarding quality and specifications. This may be done by providing free samples or, if the product is expensive, by quoting specifically low introductory price.

Promoting Products in Foreign Markets

In case a firm wants to export directly, it will have to bring its product to the notice of potential buyers. But this is a much more difficult task than the corresponding task in domestic marketing for three reasons: (i) The exporter does not have sufficient information as a basis for making promotional decisions, (ii) Customer abroad has no previous knowledge of the firm and its products, and (iii) Only limited effort is possible because of resource constraint.

The basic difference between domestic and global promotion is essentially a cross cultural communication and, therefore, global promotion will have to take into account the social customs, attitudes, beliefs and such other factors. Of the various means of promotion, such as advertising, direct mailing, point of purchase displays, trade fairs and exhibitions, advertising is most susceptible to such sociological differences.

Apart from cultural and social differences, there are some other points of difference between domestic and global advertising: (1) Media availability may differ from country to country. In many countries, Radio and TV are State-controlled and advertising may not be allowed, or they may be allowed only to a limited extent. Sweden, for example, has no advertising on Radio and only a fraction of TV time is allowed for advertising in other European countries. The use of newspapers is very often limited because of the level of literacy prevailing in the markets concerned. Again, newspaper availability ranges from 1 daily newspaper per 2 persons in Japan and 1 per 4 persons in the USA to a range of I to between 10 and 20 in Latin America and extreme cases such as 1 to 200 persons in such countries as Bangladesh, Nigeria and Sudan. Again, cost of advertising would be definitely higher than that in India. Effectiveness of media may also vary from country to country, especially so far as rural areas are concerned. (2) Laws and regulations of the country concerned will have to be respected and complied with specially in regard to (i) rules relating to the use of female models, (ii) comparison with competing products may not be allowed, and (iii) alcohol and cigarette advertisements may be banned. (3) Language may also create a problem. This is specially so in Middle Eastern countries where Arabic and Persian are in use. An advertisement about a detergent created a disastrous situation. What was sought to be conveyed was taken in an absolutely different light. A bucket containing clean clothes when mixed with the detergent came out dirty. Again motorcycle promoted with the brand name 'NOVA' completely failed as NOVA in Spanish means 'does not move'.

Advertising in foreign markets is a pretty expensive affair. Hence, advertising on a large scale and in a meaningful way can be resorted to only by large multinational operating through their own subsidiaries in several markets. For small enterprises, advertising in overseas markets in a big way is out of question for reasons of cost. They can, however, advertise in trade directories or in some specialized journals. It would be desirable for them to approach professional consultants regarding choice of media, message, etc. That done would ensure getting their money's worth.

MANAGEMENT RULES FOR GLOBAL ADVERTISING

There are some elements, which have to be followed in order to make advertising a success. These elements are:

1. Know Your Markets

The parent office must go on collecting all relevant market data in each export market. Data will include demographic details, buying behaviour, product uses, etc., i.e. the same type of information as is sought for an advertising campaign in the domestic market. The analysis of such data by each market will clearly indicate the appropriateness of a uniform localized advertising policy.

2. Travel in Your Foreign Markets

It is extremely important to have first-hand personal feel of the market. In the absence of this personalized knowledge, interpretation of market data becomes impersonal and strategy formulation becomes an abstract conceptual exercise.

3. Use A Network Agency

It is better to have the service of an global media agency, having its set up in the target market of the exporting company. If separate agencies are hired for each different market, generally poor co-ordination is the result. It is also desirable to know the personnel working in the media agency selected for the advertising campaign. Knowledge about their style, media biases and preferences help in evaluating the advertising proposals submitting by the agency.

4. Use Long Planning Lead Times

This helps in developing campaigns when localized approach to advertising is called for. For localized advertising a good deal of information is to be collected and processed alongwith the creative work which is the foundation of all advertising. A long lead-time is, therefore, essential. Even in the case of uniform advertising, long lead-time helps the parent office to develop and sell the campaign idea to other divisions.

Campaign Design

In this task, the advertiser will have to closely work with the advertising agency appointed to do the job. Three specific questions are to be answered in this connection, viz.,

(a) What to communicate?

(b) To whom to communicate?

(c) How to communicate?

Answer to these questions will depend on the basic objectives of the exporting company and its perception of the target market. While the ultimate objective of any product advertising campaign is to increase sales, the immediate objective may be the establishment of the brand name, indicate market presence, etc. What to communicate, therefore, depends on the corporate objective related to the advertising campaign. Market segment identification is what is meant by the question of target audience. Identification of the market segment involves finding out who are the buyers, how, when and where do they purchase, the strengths and weaknesses of the advertiser's products *vs.* competing products, etc. Segmentation base for consumer products may be age, sex, income and other relevant marketing variables.

When the theme of the campaign and the target audience have been identified, the advertising message has to be brought to the notice of the target audience in a way so as to make the greatest possible impact. There are various media available, especially in the developed countries, such as TV, Radio, specialized Journals and Cinemas.

Which particular medium should be selected for the campaign is to be decided on the basis of following criteria:

(a) Coverage. How may potential buyers are exposed to the medium?

(b) Selectivity. Is the medium heavily titled on a particular segment, viz., some journals may have a very large proportion of female readership, some others may be favoured by only professionals, etc.?

(c) Regional flexibility. Does it allow advertising to be concentrated on a specific area of flexible enough to have a wider geographic dispersion?

(d) Frequency. Does it allow the audience to see the advertisement often? Does it allow high concentration of advertising suitable for tactical advertising to seize a seasonal opportunity or to support a consumer promotion?

(e) Creative scope. Does it allow the message to be developed as fully as necessary? Does it allow visual inspection? Does it allow colours (some of these elements are especially important for fashion items)?

Another very important factor in deciding the medium is the relative costs of each medium. The objective is not only to have maximum impact but also at the least costs. The real cost calculation is rather difficult and will also involve some managerial judgement. For example, the cost of medium may be cheap but it may also be less effective. Therefore, the real cost per unit will be higher. On the other hand, the cost of TV commercials may be high, but in many developing countries, where the entire family may sit down for a TV show, the real cost per unit will be lower. Therefore, in deciding the relative cost effectiveness, such relevant information will have to be considered.

Because of the advent of foreign TV networks in India, it is now possible to get products advertised in South East Asia and Middle Eastern countries and the payment of the charges could be made in rupees in India.

Direct Mailing

One of the most cost effective methods of promotion is the direct mailing method. Two distinctive features of direct mailing method are that the system is selective and that it is personal. It is selective because the approaches are made directly to only those who have been identified as the target audience. It is personal because the letter and other publicity materials are mailed either by name or by designation of the identified receiver.

The crucial first step in direct mailing method is the preparation of the mailing list. The mailing list will have to be up-to-date and comprehensive and, therefore, its preparation is a laborious process. Mailing lists can be prepared either by the exporting companies or can be purchased from merchandising service companies.

Once the list is ready, the letter and other printed materials are to be designed in a way so as to give a personal touch. The receiver must feel that it is not merely a letter but something different and personal and, therefore, should be glanced. It should be made attractive to bring attention.

The cost involved in direct mailing is the lumpsum cost of producing he publicity material plus the cost of each letter, envelope and the postage. Considering that all letters will not be responded to, the real cost to be considered is the cost per response. Even taking into account the real cost per response, direct mailing is the most effective when the literature is aimed at identified readers. Sales literature can take the following forms, company brochure or leaflet, product leaflets, price lists and catalogues containing full listing and basic description of specific products.

Personal Selling

Though the oldest method, it continues to be the most widely used and effective means of reaching the buyers. This involves an alive, immediate and interactive relationship between two or more persons. The major advantages of personal selling are:

1. The strategy can be adjusted to meet the requirements of the buyers.
2. The seller gets to know the prospective buyer's reaction almost instantaneously.
3. He can collect information about the buyers, markets and environment.
4. He can provide technical and commercial information to the buyers.

Personal selling calls for very meticulous preparation on the part of salesmen in terms of acquiring all the necessary information about the product, pricing, etc., but also skills for personal communications. He should have ample supply of product literature should be well presented and accurately translated. Salesman should develop the necessary skills to be able to survive and grow in the competitive markets the world over. Personal selling can also cultivate long-term personal relationship with the customer. Personal selling can also be used mainly in industrial markets for selling technical goods such as machinery and equipment.

Sales Promotion

Another increasingly popular method is stores promotion where a country's merchandise is promoted by a chain or a department store. India had earlier arranged such promotion in association with Bloomingdales in the USA and Gallerie Laffaitte in Paris. The most important event in the category of stores promotion for Indian products, however, is the 'Expedition India' organised by one of the largest US Chain Stores, J.C. Penny, along with their Indian associate Banaras House, Air India and Government of India Tourist Office also collaborated with this venture.

Trade Fairs and Exhibitions

Fairs and exhibitions constitute the means of presenting goods and services in an attractive manner with the aid of colour, light and motion in order to catch the imagination of the visitor, attract his attention and get him interested in the objects displayed. They help reach the public which may not be reached in any other way or which by nature would disregard other media of publicity. Fairs are more useful for industrial products where demonstration is more effective.

Here are some of the reasons for going to global trade fairs:

1. To find a good agent to handle your products in one or more foreign countries. Agents and distributors usually come to these fairs looking for new agencies to take on or new products to buy and distribute.
2. To support an agent, if you already have one.

3. To test out the market. By showing your product, you can find out what agents and potential customers think about it. If you do some pre-fair publicity, the people interested in your product will come to your stand and you can exchange ideas with them. You may adapt your product if you think that it will give you a better chance.
4. To study the competition in your field. Looking at the products on display, talking to exhibitors, collecting and studying their sales literature, will give you a good idea of the competition you would face. You will get plenty of information on the range of prices, on acceptable quality and on the type of packaging used.
5. To makes sales. You may not make immediate sales but the contacts made at the fair, followed up, may lead to sales later on.
6. To learn about sales and promotion methods. You will know how competitors offer their products. The display cards used, the methods of attracting attention to a stand, what sales arguments are employed, all this data could be put to use in future. And it is more easily acquired at a fair than almost anywhere else.

When a firm participates in a fair, it should ensure that the persons at the stall should be knowledgeable about the company and its products. They should be empowered to conduct business negotiations. They should answer all questions as forthrightly and as factually as possible. The visitors at the stall should be requested to give their reactions to your products.

Samples may be distributed at the fair. They give the customer a chance to see and try the products. The cost should, however, be included in the fair budget. Gifts like calendars, pens, diaries and key-rings may also be distributed to remind the receiver about your company.

The India Trade promotion Organisation participates in nearly 40 global fairs and encourages participation by Indian parties.

DOS AND DON'TS FOR SUCCESS IN EXPORTS

A manufacturers willing to enter exports must remember that in most cases, there are many suppliers and he would have to fight his way into the market. He must be prepared to suffer some losses in the initial stages.

1. React promptly to enquiries received by you.
2. Give the buyer the information wanted by him. You may give any additional information if you so desire.
3. Deliver in time. If you fail to do so. The customer is demoralized. You will lose your goodwill, reputation and customer for good. In addition, it may have a snowballing effect for India.
4. Quality of product supplied should be consistent.
5. *Offer* what the target market wants/demands and not what you want to sell.
6. Set apart a part of your capacity for exports, so that you do not have to refuse export orders when the domestic market is good.
7. Always follow up with the buyer to find out his reactions to the supply made by you.
8. Always settle any claims promptly.

Some Don'ts

1. Don't go in for exports unless you are fully convinced about the desirability of exports for your firm.
2. Do not overbook yourself Avoid over-commitment. This is necessary to avoid delayed deliveries.
3. Do not fail to explain to the buyer the reasons if you expect delayed delivery well in time so that he could make alternative arrangements or take other corrective steps.

There are 3Ps for success in export marketing:

1. Patience: The will or ability to wait or endure without complaint.
2. Perseverance: Continuing to do something in spite of opposition or obstacles.
3. Persistence: Refusing to relent in the face of opposition and interference; tenacity or holding firmly.

Export markets can be compared to walnuts. Walnut's rich and nutritious contents are covered by a hard shell. Once the shell is broken, you can enjoy its tasty contents.

QUESTIONS FOR DISCUSSION

1. State and explain the high risks involved in entering and competing in foreign markets.
2. Explain the role of non-price factors in formulating export policy.
3. Define global marketing and discuss its scope.
4. Why should a firm think of entering into export markets?
5. Distinguish between marketing and global marketing
6. How would you analyse foreign markets to identify a few possible markets for your products?
7. Discuss in brief the various tasks of an global marketer.
8. How would you locate buyers for your products in foreign markets?
9. Discuss the various arguments for and against standardization of products.
10. Write notes on (i) Direct Mailing and (ii) Personal Selling.
11. Discuss the Do's and Don'ts for success in export marketing.